Windows XP Registry

Windows XP REGISTRY

Olga Kokoreva

A-LIST, LLC
295 East Swedesford Rd.
PMB #285
Wayne, PA 19087
702-977-5377 (FAX)
mail@alistpublishing.com
http://www.alistpublishing.com

This book is printed on acid-free paper.

Windows XP Registry
By Olga Kokoreva

ISBN: 1-931769-01-X

Printed in the United States of America
02 03 7 6 5 4 3 2

A-LIST, LLC titles are distributed by Independent Publishers Group and are available for site license or bulk purchase by institutions, user groups, corporations, etc.

Book Editors: Jessica Mroz, Rizwati Freeman

Contents

Introduction

Intended Audience

Surely, Windows XP is the most important release of Windows since the arrival of Windows 95. Despite the fact that it was the first OS from the Windows family that was delivered on quite a reasonable schedule, it was also one the user community waited impatiently for. It is no wonder; technically speaking, Windows XP is the next version of Windows 2000. However, it is also positioned as an upgrade for Windows 98, 98 SE, Millennium Edition (ME), 2000, and NT 4.0 users. What's more, it finally combines the traditional strong points of the two lines of Windows operating systems—the convenience, compatibility, and easy-to-use characteristics of Windows 9*x*/ME, and the security, reliability, and stability of Windows NT/2000. In addition, Windows XP also puts an end to the old DOS/Windows product line, since we are now dealing with a new OS, which is finally based on the new version of the Windows NT/2000 kernel. And this new approach is definitely a success, since when it comes to reliability issues, Windows XP practically outshines all its predecessors. If you don't want to see the Blue Screen of Death (BSOD), you never will (unless it's your intention—one of the tips provided in *Chapter 11* explains how to intentionally make the system fall into a BSOD just to see what it is).

Microsoft is releasing three editions of Windows XP: a Home Edition, a Professional, and a 64-bit Edition, the latter of which will run only on new workstations based on Intel's 64-bit Itanium processor. Windows XP Home Edition and Windows XP Professional are essentially the same 32-bit operating system, based on the same kernel. As most people expect, the Home Edition is intended for the vast majority of end users who previously worked with Windows 9*x*/ME. Windows XP Professional, on the contrary, is targeted at business users and power users. Because of this, it offers some business-oriented features and additional capabilities unavailable in Windows XP Home Edition, since they would be out of place in a home system. The most significant difference is, of course, multiprocessor support: Windows XP Home Edition supports only one processor, while Windows XP Professional supports two. Furthermore, users of Windows XP Professional can logon to Active Directory domains, work with roaming user profiles, use the encrypting file system, Offline Folders, and other features particularly important for mobile users.

I became a member of a small team of Windows XP beta testers when the system was an early beta. Even at that early stage of beta testing, we could see that there were differences between Windows 2000 and the two systems, codenamed "Whistler". It was an amazing experience to see how the system improved with the release of each new beta or Release Candidate. To generalize the common trend, the system became more and more powerful and reliable. However, despite all these improvements, and the fact that the system was renamed Windows XP (Windows for eXPerienced users, and one designed to provide for new user *experiences*), the new system didn't entirely eliminate the features that existed in Windows 2000; rather, it improved and extended this functionality while adding new tools and features. The new operating system implements all the best features of its predecessor. In this way, Windows XP continues the Windows 2000 tradition, emphasized by the "Built on NT Technology" slogan displayed at boot time. Windows 2000 had many features in common with the previous version of Windows NT, and so does Windows XP. If you examine it carefully, you'll see that it has many features in common with Windows 2000 as well.

Will thousands of users all over the world migrate to Windows XP immediately? Some probably will (especially those who get the system with the new hardware), but many others will continue using Windows 2000 while examining this new system and testing existing applications for compatibility. This book is addressed to such readers, including system administrators, technical support personnel, and experienced Windows NT/2000 users.

Aims of this Book

Like many other Windows XP system components, the Registry is very much like the Windows NT/2000 Registry. However, there are also many differences, some of which are obvious (such as removal of the registry size limitation), while others are hardly noticeable. Mostly, the changes in Windows XP registry are due to the kernel enhancements introduced with this new release of the operating system. Throughout the book, I'll emphasize these differences and draw your attention to them. Windows XP Registry also contains a large number of new records. This isn't surprising, since each new registry entry corresponds to a new feature introduced with the new release. The registry is a centralized storage area for all the information on the hardware and software system components. Because of this, all new features introduced with Windows XP have to be reflected in the registry.

Can this book be considered a reference describing all registry keys, or a handbook of practical solutions for everyday work? Unfortunately, no, it cannot. I dream about a book like that myself! I also know what a bulky book that would be (if it's possible to write at all). My aim isn't quite so ambitious. In this book, I'll describe the important components of Windows NT/2000 and Windows XP registries, and emphasize the similarities and differences that exist between them. I'll also discuss various techniques of backing up and recovering the registry, and provide essential technical information on other aspects of working with the registry as well. I hope that this book will be useful for system administrators and advanced users who want to improve their knowledge of the Windows NT/2000 registry and get acquainted with the Windows XP registry. However, Windows XP is also positioned as an upgrade for Windows 98, Windows 98 SE, and Windows Millennium Edition (ME). Users who migrate to Windows XP from Windows 9*x*/ME must not be deceived by apparent similarities between Windows XP registry and the registries they are accustomed to. On the contrary, Windows XP registry is quite different!

Quite often, one may hear users say "I hate Windows registry because it is rather cryptic, contains tons of redundant information, and makes the system vulnerable, since Windows can't run without it". If you hate the Windows registry too, I am not trying to convince you to love it. After all, most people tend to hate a thing that they can't properly understand. I can also agree that this opinion is partially valid, because the registry actually is cryptic, difficult to understand, and really is required for the system to run. However, from this point of view, a human being is also very far from perfect, since the human body doesn't live without a brain (and even if someone supports this life artificially, how miserable it would be!). What I am really after is helping you understand the registry. Therefore, I didn't try to describe all known registry tips and tricks. Rather, I tried to explain how these tricks work and why they work at all. I think that when you get a sound understanding of the registry architecture, structure, and data types, you'll soon be able to discover such tricks yourselves.

Obviously, my own experiences of working as a technical support specialist have influenced both my methods of work in general and this book in particular. When

I begin working with a new operating system, I'm mainly interested in providing a trouble-free environment—various aspects of backing up and recovering the more important system components (the registry, in our case), including non-traditional and rarely used ones. Various aspects of registry backup and recovery, together with methods of eliminating system failures, take priority in this book. I'm sure that before migrating to the new operating system and experimenting with it, the user will need to study these topics very carefully. Testing backup, restore, and troubleshooting procedures will also be helpful.

The book contains the following chapters:

- *Chapter 1* contains an overview of Windows NT/2000/XP registries. It provides a brief description of registry structure, valid data types, and methods of storing Windows NT/2000/XP registry data. At the same time, it considers some Windows XP kernel enhancements that resulted in registry changes—for example, the removal of registry size limitation.
- *Chapter 2* is dedicated to various methods of backing up and restoring the registry. Even the most experienced Windows NT/2000 user should read this chapter carefully, since these procedures have changed significantly in Windows XP.
- *Chapter 3* discusses the user interface of the registry editor (Regedit.exe). Most experienced Windows NT/2000 users should remember that Windows NT 4.0 and Windows 2000 actually included two registry-editing utilities—Regedt32.exe, the more powerful utility with extended capabilities but an old-fashioned interface, and Regedit.exe—the newer utility with an enhanced UI, which lacked, however, some powerful features of Regedt32. In Windows XP, the situation has changed, and there is now only one registry-editing tool—Regedit.exe, which combines the functionality of the two registry editors. Beginners can use this chapter as a brief reference on this tool (which, by the way, Microsoft is positioning as one of the reliability enhancements).
- *Chapter 4* looks at the simplest methods of configuring Windows XP. This chapter describes both the method of configuring the system using administrative utilities and the method that requires registry editing. Some of the tips provided here also apply to Windows NT and Windows 2000, while others are Windows XP-specific.
- *Chapter 5* discusses the problem of storing hardware information in the registry. It also provides basic information on Plug and Play architecture implementation in Windows 2000/XP, including two new kernel-mode subsystems—Plug and Play Manager and Power Manager. Also covered are the OnNow initiative and the ACPI specification. Special attention is given to Windows XP-specific enhancements.

- *Chapter 6* contains a detailed description of the boot process for both Windows NT/2000 and Windows XP. It describes the registry's role in the boot process and provides a brief overview of the methods of eliminating boot failures. Special attention is focused on Windows XP built-in reliability enhancements, including safe mode, Driver Rollback, Recovery Console, and code signing options such as Windows File Protection, System File Checker, and File Signature Verification.
- *Chapter 7* can be used as a brief reference to the registry keys.
- *Chapter 8* discusses network settings in the registry for both Windows 2000 and Windows XP.
- *Chapter 9* has a special place in this book, because it discusses one of the most important topics, namely, various aspects of protecting and securing the registry.
- *Chapter 10* discusses the problems of managing user working environments, including user profiles and group policies.
- *Chapter 11* contains recommendations and tips on eliminating the most common problems (including boot failures) by means of editing the registry. It is of special interest for system administrators and technical support personnel.
- *Chapter 12* is dedicated to advanced customization and troubleshooting topics.
- *Chapter 13* provides a brief overview of the handy third-party registry utilities.
- *Chapter 14* provides an overview of automating registry management using Windows Script Host (WSH). Of course, it can't be considered a reference on Windows automation and scripting languages (this topic deserves a special book). However, we will consider the registry-manipulation methods provided by WSH, then create a simple example illustrating their usage, and then produce a small but really useful script.
- *Appendix 1*—Internet resources. If I intended to create a reference on the Internet resources dedicated to Windows 2000/XP, it would be a large book indeed! Of course, not all of these resources are equally useful. Because of this, I included only the most informative and reliable ones in the appendix.
- *Appendix 2*—Bibliography. This appendix provides a list of sources where the reader can find supplementary information concerning the topics discussed in this book.
- *Appendix 3*—Glossary.

To conclude this brief introduction, I would like to thank all the members of the A-LIST Publishing team for offering me the opportunity to work on this book.

Chapter 1

Windows XP Registry Overview

Well, you know fairly well what I mean...

E. M. Blake
"SF story for telepathists"

This book is addressed to system administrators, technical support personnel, and advanced Windows XP users. Most of you already have at least some previous knowledge of the registry. The prototype of the modern registry existed even in Windows 3.1, and most programmers already knew what their interlocutors meant when they mentioned the registry. Registry topics became popular with the user community after the release of the Windows 95 operating system. This isn't surprising, since the registry is the most important component of any modern Windows operating system. This chapter provides a brief overview of the Windows NT/2000/XP registry, describes registry structure and data types, and also covers the methods of data storage used by the Windows XP registry. Unfortunately, the size of this book is quite limited, and doesn't allow me to provide a detailed description of the differences between Windows 95/98/ME and Windows NT/2000/XP registries. However, the main differences will be emphasized further in this book.

Introduction

Have you ever encountered a situation when urgent work had to be done, but strange and frightening messages appeared on screen, informing you that the operating system couldn't be loaded because of registry corruption? For example, among Windows NT 4.0 users, there are many persons who were shocked by the following message during the system boot:

```
OS Loader V 4.0
. . . .
Windows NT could not start because the following file is missing or
corrupt:
\WINNT\SYSTEM32\CONFIG\SYSTEM
You can attempt to repair this file by Starting Windows NT Setup using
the original Setup floppy disk or CD-ROM.
Select 'r' at the first screen to repair.
```

If you've already migrated to Windows 2000 or Windows XP, you might see almost the same message:

```
Windows 2000/XP could not start because the following file is missing
of corrupt:
\WINNT\SYSTEM32\CONFIG\SYSTEM
You can attempt to repair this file by starting Windows 2000/Whistler
Setup using the original Setup floppy disk of CD-ROM.
Select 'r' at the first screen to repair.
```

The examples provided above clearly show that a single error in the system registry (the *System* file mentioned in the messages shown above contains registry information) can influence the whole system configuration and even prevent the operating system from booting. Furthermore, there are some applications, which can run correctly only after editing the system registry. For this reason, the importance of understanding the registry and having practical skills to be able to work with it can't be underestimated.

The registry is difficult to decipher and understand. However, it's one of the most important components of any modern operating system belonging to the Windows family. Neither Windows 9*x*/ME nor Windows NT/2000/XP can run without it. So, what exactly is the registry? It's a centralized database that stores all the settings of the operating system and the applications running in it. This makes the registry similar to various INI files, and also to files like Autoexec.bat and Config.sys used in earlier Windows versions. The registry also stores information on all the hardware, including Plug and Play devices, OLE data, and file associations. The registry contains all the data concerning the applications that support Plug and Play and OLE, networking parameters, hardware profiles, and user profiles.

To summarize, if there's any hardware or software in the computer system that influences it in some way, you can be sure that the system registry stores information on that component.

History of the Registry

The registry concept itself isn't new to Windows. However, the modern registry is an impressive advance in improving system manageability from a single source—the *registry database*. This database was developed as a basis for all system-wide hardware and software parameters and custom user settings that exist in Windows.

The first successful operating system from the Windows family was Microsoft Windows 3.1. This system had three different types of configuration files:

- *System initialization files.* The standard Windows 3.1*x* installation had six system initialization files: Control.ini, Progman.ini, Protocol.ini, System.ini, Win.ini, and Winfile.ini.
    - The Win.ini file contained basic information concerning the software configuration, as well as some parameters that were added by applications as the user installed additional programs. In earlier Windows versions, each newly installed application introduced its settings to the Win.ini file. Thus, the file grew rapidly if the user installed a large number of applications. At the same time, the file was limited in size (no more than 64 K). This limitation began causing problems when the file size reached its upper limit. Windows 3.1*x* didn't warn the user when the Win.ini file grew above its limit and all modifications added to the last sections of the file (out of the initialization range) were ignored by the system. Because of this, Microsoft recommended that software developers store application-specific information in separate files—so-called *private initialization files* (private INI files).
    - The System.ini file served as the main storage for system information related to the hardware. In contrast to the Win.ini file that stored information mainly related to system behavior, System.ini contained hardware-related data and information about device drivers, shells to load, and so on.
    - The Progman.ini file contained initialization settings for Windows Program Manager, and the Winfile.ini file contained Windows File Manager settings. If one or both of these files were missing (in contrast to the Win.ini and System.ini files), Windows could still start. However, both Windows Program Manager and Windows File Manager would then start using the standard configuration and all custom settings would be lost. As for the Control.ini file, it contained the Control Panel settings.
    - The Protocol.ini file was added with the release of the Windows for Workgroups 3.1*x* operating system. This file stored initialization settings for Windows networks.
- *Private initialization files.* These were INI files added by applications that were installed in the system. The files were used for storing application-specific information, including the size and position of application windows and lists of recently used files (the `MRUList` parameter).
- Finally, there was the Reg.dat file, which was the direct predecessor of Windows 95/98/ME and Windows NT/2000/XP registries. This was a hierarchical

database that comprised a single root container structure named HKEY_CLASSES_ROOT. This root structure contained nested structures, which stored the system information needed to support OLE (Object Linking and Embedding) and file associations. This registry database allowed Windows 3.1*x* users to modify the behavior of linked or embedded objects and provided the ability to view the list of applications registered in the Windows environment.

In contrast to INI files, which were ASCII text files available for editing by any text editor or word processor, the Reg.dat file was a binary file. To edit this file, the user needed a special application called Registry Editor (Regedit.exe). When the user started the `REGEDIT.EXE /v` command, this application displayed the Reg.dat file as a hierarchical structure with nested parameters. However, the structure of Reg.dat was far simpler than the structures of the modern registry.

Drawbacks of INI Files

One of the most significant problems related to INI files was their manageability. The standard set of INI files, created during the installation of Windows 3.*x,* didn't present any difficulties. However, as the user installed and deleted applications, the number of INI files constantly grew. This approach had some serious drawbacks:

- Editing INI files manually and setting correct values for various application-specific parameters wasn't very difficult for advanced users. However, even experienced users sometimes had to make more than one attempt to obtain the desired result. As for beginners, these tasks were sometimes far beyond the scope of their skills and knowledge.
- Clear rules for storing INI files didn't exist. Private initialization files could be stored in any directory; they weren't write-protected, and there was always the chance of deletion. As a result, users frequently had to search for the INI files they needed, and sometimes these files were hard to find.
- INI files didn't provide any support for a multi-user environment. Consequently, the users couldn't customize the settings for computer systems and applications.
- INI files didn't support multiple hardware configurations. Because of this, there was no Plug and Play support in Windows 3.*x*.
- Each application stored its settings in its own private initialization file. This, of course, was an official recommendation issued by Microsoft and was intended to provide a workaround for the Win.ini size limitation mentioned earlier.

On the other hand, however, this recommendation was just producing another limitation, because it was restricting the capabilities of sharing information among applications.

NOTE

Any Windows-compatible application (this is true for both Windows 9*x*/ME and Windows NT/2000/XP) has to meet a set of requirements, one of the most important being the presence of uninstall capabilities. Automatic uninstall capabilities which allow the user to delete the application correctly aren't new. However, implementation of this concept in Windows 3.*x* was far from easy. Modern operating systems that belong to the Windows family store all configuration data in the registry, which makes implementation of uninstall capabilities an easy task.

The Purpose of the Registry

The registry is a successor to INI files, which had serious drawbacks and limitations and were so inconvenient to use. Windows NT 3.5 was the first operating system from the Windows family that had a registry more or less similar to the modern one (at that time, the registry had 4 root keys: `HKEY_LOCAL_MACHINE`, `HKEY_CURRENT_USER`, `HKEY_CLASSES_ROOT`, and `HKEY_USERS`). The new component of the operating system represented the centralized source of configuration information, which provided the capability of managing the system environment much more efficiently.

Windows NT/2000/XP system components that use the registry are briefly described below:

- *Setup programs.* Any time a setup program runs (including both Windows Setup program and other setup utilities that install software or device drivers), it adds new configuration data to the registry. If the Setup program is developed correctly, it reads the registry information to determine if all the components necessary to successfully complete the installation procedure are present in the system. Because the registry is a centralized storage of configuration information, all applications can share this information and get broader capabilities of interaction with each other. Any application program claiming to have the "Designed for Windows" status has to use the registry and provide a special uninstall utility allowing the user to delete this application correctly (Fig. 1.1). Application-specific information stored in the registry allows the user to perform this procedure correctly without deleting the shared components (DLL, OCX, and so on), which may be needed by other applications.

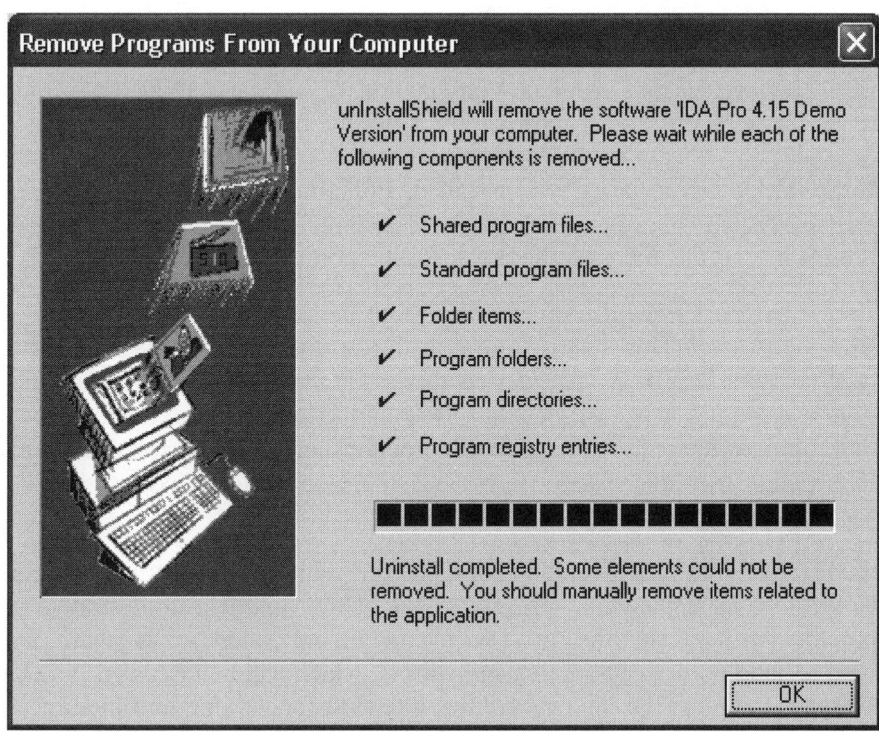

Fig. 1.1. The uninstall utility deletes registry settings that correspond to the application to be uninstalled

- *Hardware recognizer.* Each time Windows NT/2000/XP starts, the hardware recognizer creates a list of the devices it's detected and stores it in the registry. On Intel-based computers, hardware detection is performed by the hardware recognizer (Ntdetect.com) and the Windows NT/2000/XP kernel (Ntoskrnl.exe).
- *Windows NT/2000/XP kernel.* During the system boot process, Windows NT/2000/XP kernel reads the registry to retrieve information on the device drivers and the sequence in which they should be loaded. The Ntoskrnl.exe program also passes its own information to the registry (for example, data on the system version and build). Microsoft has made many enhancements to the Windows XP kernel, mainly intended to increase system performance and stability. As will be shown later in this chapter, these kernel enhancements also include registry enhancements (the removal of the registry size limit, for example).
- *PnP Manager.* This new kernel-mode component was first introduced in Windows 2000. PnP Manager detects and identifies hardware devices using two

identifiers: *vendor identifier* (Vendor ID or VID), and *device identifier* (device ID or DID). The combination of these two numbers uniquely identifies the device. Having detected a unique combination of VID and DID, PnP Manager requests the registry to get information about the bus where the device has been detected, and checks to see if the appropriate device driver has been installed. If the device driver hasn't been installed, PnP Manager informs the user-mode PnP subsystem. The user-mode PnP subsystem, in turn, has to detect the appropriate INF file and start the driver installation procedure.

- *Device drivers.* Device drivers exchange boot parameters and configuration data with the registry. This data is similar to the `DEVICE=` lines in the Config.sys file used to start MS-DOS. The device driver has to provide information on the system resources it needs, including IRQ and DMA. The system then includes this data into the registry. Application programs and device drivers can read this information from the registry to provide the users with the correct installation and configuration tools.

- *Administrative utilities.* Windows NT/2000/XP administrative utilities, including Control Panel applets and programs that belong to the Administrative Tools program group, are the most convenient and safest tools that can be used to modify the registry. Registry editors, which will be discussed in detail in *Chapter 3*, are special built-in utilities intended for viewing and modifying the registry. However, they should be used with care and caution.

- *User profiles.* Windows NT/2000/XP supports multiple user profiles. All information related to an individual user name and the user rights associated to it is stored in the registry. *Chapter 10* describes user profiles in more detail. At this point, let's note that the user profile defines custom display settings, networking parameters, printers, and so on. There are three types of user profiles: *local user profiles*, which are created automatically when the user logs in to the local computer for the first time; *roaming user profiles*, created by network administrator and stored on the server; and *mandatory user profiles*—these are roaming profiles, which are bound to be used. User profile information is also stored in the registry. To manage Windows 2000 user profiles, double-click **System** in the **Control Panel** window and go to the **User Profiles** tab. To manage user profiles in Windows XP Professional, start the System applet in Control Panel, go to the **Advanced** tab (Fig. 1.2), and click the **Settings** button in the **User Profiles** group to open the **User Profiles** window (Fig. 1.3). You can create new user profiles here by copying existing ones; you can also delete user profiles or change their types. Note that to perform this task, you need to log in to a local computer as the Administrator.

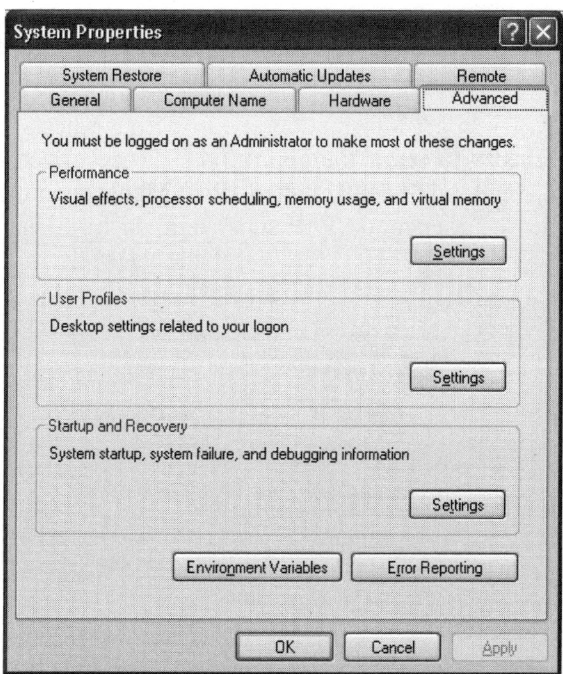

Fig. 1.2. The **Advanced** tab of the **System Properties** window

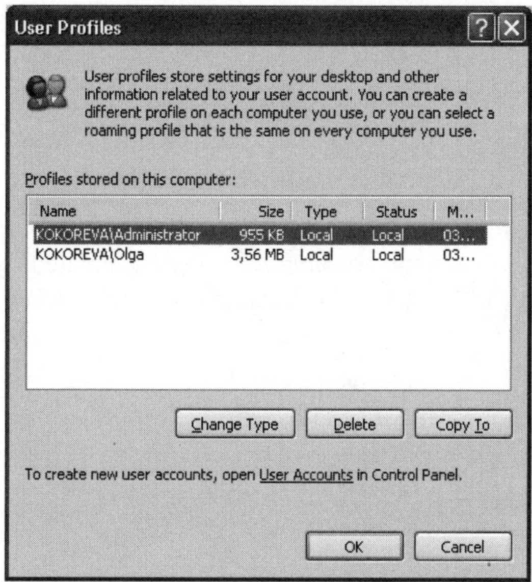

Fig. 1.3. The **User Profiles** window

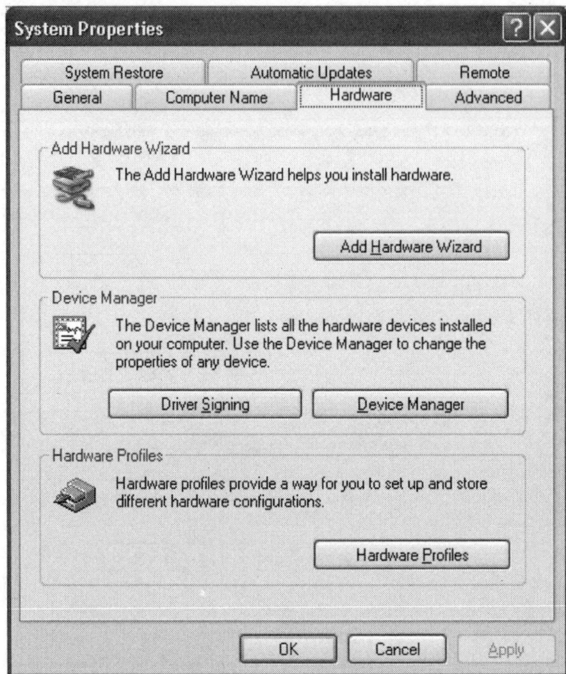

Fig. 1.4. The **Hardware** tab of the **System Properties** window

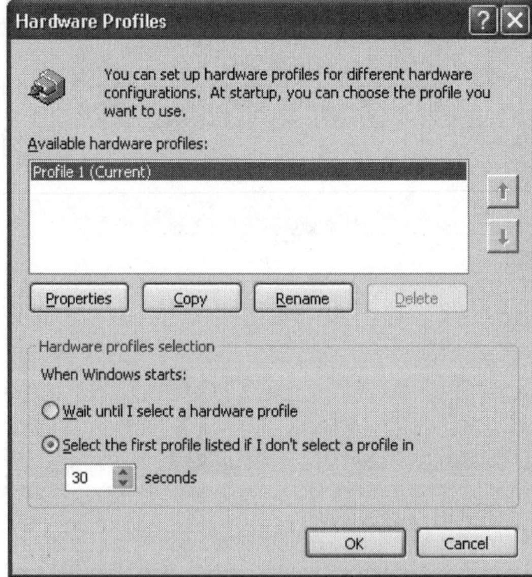

Fig. 1.5. The **Hardware Profiles** window

- *Hardware profiles.* Unlike INI files, the registry supports multiple hardware configurations. For example, you can create hardware profiles for dock stations (this is essential for laptop users) and removable devices. Each hardware profile is a set of instructions used to specify device drivers that have to be loaded when booting the system. To create new hardware profiles in Windows XP, double-click **System** in the **Control Panel** window, go to the **Hardware** tab (Fig. 1.4) and then click the **Hardware Profiles** button. This will open the **Hardware Profiles** window shown in Fig. 1.5. Like in Windows 2000, when you install Windows XP, the Setup program creates the standard hardware profile, which includes information on all hardware devices detected at the time of installation.

Registry Structure

For a better understanding of the registry logical structure, let's compare it to the file system that exists on the disk. The registry contains *keys*, which are similar to folders, and *values,* which can be compared to the files stored on the disk. Registry keys are container objects that can contain both *subkeys* and values. Registry values contain the data (like the files). The top-level keys of this hierarchical structure are called *root keys.*

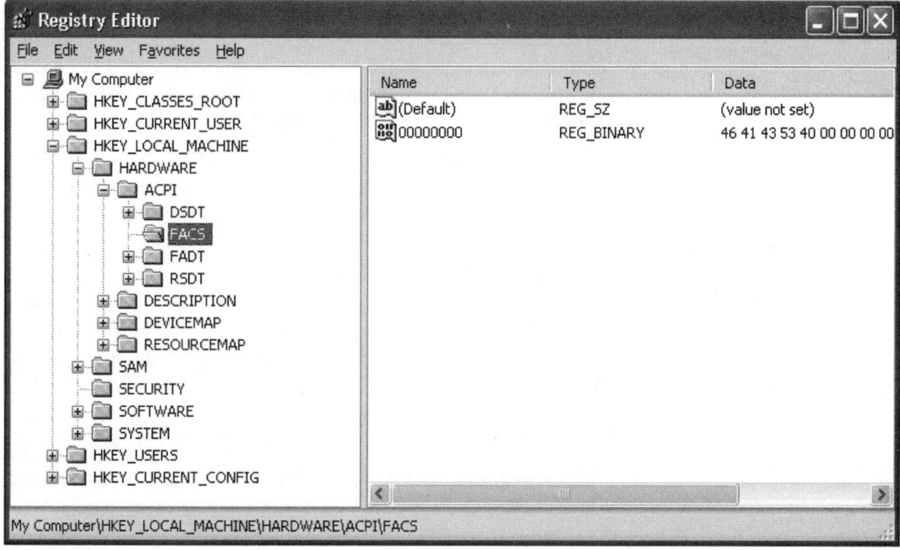

Fig. 1.6. Hierarchical structure of the registry

The naming convention used to name registry keys and values is also similar to the one used to name files and folders. For example, compare a typical folder path like D:\WORK\BHV and a typical registry path: HKEY_LOCAL_MACHINE\SYSTEM\CurrentControlSet.

Windows 2000/XP registry comprises the following five root keys: HKEY_CLASSES_ROOT, HKEY_CURRENT_USER, HKEY_LOCAL_MACHINE, HKEY_USERS, and HKEY_CURRENT_CONFIG. This hierarchical registry structure is illustrated in Fig. 1.6.

All the names of the root keys begin with the HKEY_ string, which indicates that this is a handle that can be used by a program. The handle represents the value used to uniquely identify the resource that can be accessed by a program. Table 1.1 lists the root keys that exist in Windows NT/2000/XP registries and provides a brief description.

Table 1.1. Registry Root Keys

Root key	Description
HKEY_LOCAL_MACHINE	Contains global hardware information and operating system data, including bus type, system memory, device drivers, and other information used during the system boot process. Information on this key is applicable to all users who log in to the local system. There are three top-level aliases for this registry key: HKEY_CLASSES_ROOT, HKEY_CURRENT_CONFIG and HKEY_DYN_DATA
HKEY_CLASSES_ROOT	This key contains information concerning filename associations, OLE (Object Linking and Embedding) information associated with COM objects, and file-class associations (this data is equivalent to the registry that existed in earlier Windows versions). Parameters contained in this key are equivalent to those stored under the HKEY_LOCAL_MACHINE\Software\Classes key. You can find more detailed information on the HKEY_CLASSES_ROOT key in the *"OLE Programmer's Reference"* manual included with the Windows Platform Software Development Kit (SDK)
HKEY_CURRENT_CONFIG	Contains configuration data of the current hardware profile. Hardware profiles are sets of modifications introduced into the standard configuration of services and devices set by the Software and System subkeys of the HKEY_LOCAL_MACHINE root key. The HKEY_CURRENT_CONFIG key contains only changed data. Moreover, the data contained in this key is also contained in the HKEY_LOCAL_MACHINE\System\CurrentControlSet\HardwareProfiles\Current key

continues

Table 1.1 Continued

Root key	Description
`HKEY_CURRENT_USER`	Contains the user profile of the user who's currently logged in to the system, including environment variables, desktop settings, network settings, and application settings. This key is a reference to the `HKEY_USERS\user_SID` key, where *`user_SID`* is the Security ID of the user who's currently logged in to the system
`HKEY_USERS`	Contains all active user profiles, including `HKEY_CURRENT_USER` and the default user profile. Users who can access the server through the network don't have profiles under this key because their profiles are loaded remotely on their workstations. Windows NT/2000/XP requires that each user who logs on to the system have his own user account. The `HKEY_USERS` key contains the `\.Default` subkey which is used to create a user profile for the user logging in to the system for the first time. It also contains other subkeys associated to the Security ID assigned to the appropriate user

NOTE

As noted earlier, the registry concept was originally introduced in the first Windows NT version—Windows NT 3.1. Windows 9x/ME registries were developed based on this first version. At present, however, there are significant differences between the registries that exist in Windows 9x/ME and Windows NT/2000/XP. The most important one is that the Windows 95/98/ME registry has one more top-level key—`HKEY_DYN_DATA`. This key contains system information that may need continuous updating. Windows 9x/ME stores this information without flashing it to the hard drive. The `HKEY_DYN_DATA` key was present in all the Windows 2000 beta versions, but any attempts to open the key resulted in error messages. At present, the Regedit.exe and Regedt32.exe utilities in Windows 2000 and Windows XP Registry Editor (Regedit.exe) don't display this key.

Registry data are parameters stored within registry keys. Each parameter has its name, data type, and value. The three parts of the registry entry are also stored in the following order:

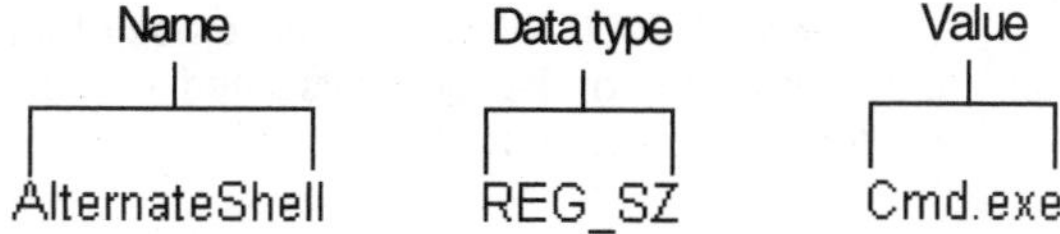

All registry data types defined and used in Windows NT/2000/XP are listed in Table 1.2.

Table 1.2. Registry Data Types

Data type	Description
REG_BINARY	Binary data. Most hardware components use binary information. Registry editors display this information in hex
REG_DWORD	This data is represented as a 4-byte binary value (double word). Most services and device drivers use this data type. Registry editors display this data using binary, hex, or decimal formats
REG_EXPAND_SZ	Expandable data string. This text string contains a variable name, which can be substituted by a variable value when called by an application
REG_MULTI_SZ	Multi-string field. Normally, all values that actually represent lists of text strings have this data type. A NULL character is used as a separator
REG_SZ	Text string in user-friendly format. Normally, this data type is used for component descriptions
REG_DWORD_LITTLE_ENDIAN	32-bit number in little-endian format. Equivalent of the REG_DWORD data type. When using the little-endian format, the lowest bit ("little end") appears first when representing the value. For example, the A02Bh hex value will be represented as 2BA0. The little-endian format is used in Intel processors
REG_DWORD_BIG_ENDIAN	32-bit number in big-endian format. In contrast to the little-endian format, the highest bit ("big end") appears first when representing the value
REG_LINK	Unicode symbolic link. This data type is intended for internal use only. The REG_LINK is especially interesting because it allows one registry entry to reference another registry key or registry value. For example, if a registry contains the entry \Root1\Link with the REG_LINK data type and its value is \Root2\RegKey, and the RegKey key contains the RegValue value, then this value can be identified using the following two paths: \Root1\Link\RegValue and \Root2\RegKey\RegValue. Windows NT/2000/XP makes active use of this method. For example, some of the root keys listed in Table 1.1 are links to the nested keys of other root keys

continues

Table 1.2 Continued

Data type	Description
REG_NONE	No defined data type
REG_QWORD	64-bit value
REG_QWORD_LITTLE_ENDIAN	64-bit value represented using little-endian notation. Equivalent of the REG_QWORD data type
REG_RESOURCE_LIST	List of hardware resources, which are only used in HKEY_LOCAL_MACHINE\HARDWARE
REG_FULL_RESOURCE_DESCRIPTOR	Hardware resource handle, which is only used in HKEY_LOCAL_MACHINE\HARDWARE
REG_RESOUECE_REQUIREMENTS_LIST	List of hardware resources, which is only used in HKEY_LOCAL_MACHINE\HARDWARE

Registry Data Storage

Windows NT/2000/XP stores registry entries as an atomic structure. The registry is subdivided into components, called *hives* for their resemblance to the cellular structure of a beehive. The Registry hive is a discrete body of keys, subkeys, and values rooted at the top level of the registry hierarchy. The main difference between registry hives and other groups of registry keys is that hives are constant registry components. Hives aren't created dynamically when the system boots, and aren't deleted when someone shuts the system down. Thus, the HKEY_LOCAL_MACHINE\Hardware key, which is created dynamically by the hardware recognizer when the system boots, can't be considered a hive.

NOTE

As with Windows 2000, Windows XP registry also resides on the disk as multiple files called hives, serving as a repository for system configuration data. The registry code is redesigned for Windows XP, providing enhanced performance while remaining transparent to applications by using existing registry programming interfaces. Windows XP registry enhancements are mainly intended to provide performance improvements, and will be covered in more detail later in this chapter.

Registry hive data is stored in disk files, which in turn is stored in *%SystemRoot%*\System32\Config and *%SystemRoot%*\Profiles*Username* folders (Windows NT 4.0). Windows 2000 stores registry hives in *%SystemRoot%*\System32\Config and *%SystemDrive%*\Documents and Settings*Username* folders.

Each registry hive is associated with a set of standard supporting files. Table 1.3 lists standard Windows NT/2000/XP registry hives together with supporting files.

Table 1.3. Windows NT/2000 Registry Hives

Registry hive	Supporting files
HKEY_LOCAL_MACHINE\SAM	Sam, Sam.log, Sam.sav
HKEY_LOCAL_MACHINE\Security	Security, Security.log, Security.sav
HKEY_LOCAL_MACHINE\Software	Software, Software.log, Software.sav
HKEY_LOCAL_MACHINE\System	System, System.alt*, System.log, System.sav
HKEY_CURRENT_CONFIG	System, System.alt*, System.log, System.sav
HKEY_USERS\.DEFAULT	Default, Default.log, Default.sav
(Files that aren't associated with keys)	Userdiff, Userdiff.log, Userdifr**, Userdifr.log**
HKEY_CURRENT_USER	Ntuser.dat, Ntuser.dat.log

* Files that were eliminated in Windows XP

** Files that were first introduced in Windows XP

NOTE

As you can see from this table, some registry files were eliminated in Windows XP, while other files were first introduced. This is due to the enhancements to the Windows XP registry, which will be covered in more detail later in this book.

All hive files, except for HKEY_CURRENT_USER, are stored in the *%SystemRoot%*\System32\Config folder.

The HKEY_CURRENT_USER hive is supported by Ntuser.dat and Ntuser.dat.log files. Ntuser.dat files contain user profiles, while Ntuser.dat.log files reflect all changes introduced to Ntuser.dat file. Windows NT 4.0 stores these files in subfolders of the *%SystemRoot%*\Profiles folder (except for the \All Users subfolder). Windows 2000 stores these files in *%SystemDrive%*\Documents and Settings*%Username%* folders.

The Ntuser and Userdiff files were first introduced in Windows NT 4.0:

- Ntuser.dat. This is the file where the user profile is stored. It replaced the username*xxx* and admin*xxx* files used in earlier versions of Windows NT.

- The Ntuser.dat file stored in the *%SystemRoot%*\Profiles\Default User folder replaced the Userdef file used in earlier versions of Windows NT. This user profile is used to create the `HKEY_CURRENT_USER` hive when the new user logs in to the system for the first time.
- Userdiff files stored in the *%SystemRoot%*\System32\Config folder aren't associated with any hive. They're used for updating user profiles that existed in previous Windows NT versions to make them compatible with Windows NT/2000 and Windows XP.

There are four types of files associated with registry hives. All of these file types, with the appropriate filename extensions, are listed in Table 1.4.

Table 1.4. Types of Files Associated to Windows NT 4.0/Windows 2000/ Windows XP Registry Hives

Filename extension	Description
None	Contains the registry hive copy
ALT*	In Windows NT/2000, the ALT files contain the backup copy of the `HKEY_LOCAL_MACHINE\System` hive. The `System` hive is the only hive that has this type of backup copy stored in the System.alt file. As was already mentioned, ALT files were eliminated in Windows XP because registry code was redesigned to provide improved algorithms for faster queries, improved reliability, and larger registries
LOG	Contains the transaction log; any changes introduced to the keys and values make up this hive
SAV	Contains copies of registry hive files from the time the text-mode part of installation process was accomplished. There are SAV files for the following registry hives: \Software, \System, \SAM, \Security, and \Default. Windows NT/2000/XP makes backup copies of the registry hives during the installation process. The installation procedure consists of two parts; namely, the text-mode and the GUI-mode part of the installation. When the text-mode part of installation procedure is complete, the Setup program backs up the registry hives to the SAV files. This is done to protect the hives from failures which may occur during the GUI-mode part of setup. If such a failure occurs, the GUI-mode setup will resume after reboot, and SAV files will be used for rebuilding the registry hives

* Files that were excluded from Windows XP

Hive Atomicity and Recovery

The registry ensures the atomicity of individual operations. This means that any modifications done to a registry value (resetting, deleting, or saving) either work or don't work. This mechanism eliminates corrupt combinations of old and new registry values, in case the system stops unexpectedly due to a power failure, a hardware malfunction, or problems with the software. Consider, for example, a case when an application sets a value, and the system shuts down unexpectedly while this change is being made. After rebooting the system, this registry entry will be either reset to its previous value or have a new value, but no meaningless combinations of both registry parameters will appear. Moreover, the size and time data for the key containing the affected value will be accurate, whether this value has been changed or not.

Flushing Data

Windows NT 4.0 and Windows 2000 save registry data only after a flush occurs. Data flush occurs only after the modified data ages past a few seconds. Furthermore, data flush can be initiated by a direct call from the application, which intentionally flushes its data to the hard disk.

The system performs the following flushing procedure for all registry hives (except for the \System hive):

1. All changed data is saved to the LOG file of the respective hive, together with information on the exact location of the changed data within a hive. When this is done, the system performs a flush, and all modified data is written to the LOG file.
2. The first sector of the hive file is marked, which means that this file is in a transitional state.
3. The modified data is written to the hive file.
4. Finally, this hive file is marked as completed.

NOTE

If the system shuts down unexpectedly when performing this procedure (between steps 2 and 4), it will recover the affected hive. When this hive is loaded during system startup (except for user profile hives, which are loaded when the user logs in to the system), the system will note the marker left in step 2, and it will continue recovering the hive using the changed data saved to the LOG file. Thus, if the hive isn't in transition, its LOG files aren't used. If the hive was in transition when the system stopped, it can't be loaded without a respective LOG file.

The \System hive is vitally important and is used at the earliest stages of the system boot. This hive includes the `HKEY_LOCAL_MACHINE\SYSTEM\CurrentControlSet\Control` key, which contains information necessary for initializing the registry during the boot process. For example, registry entries stored with the `HKEY_LOCAL_MACHINE\SYSTEM\CurrentControlSet\Control\hivelist` specify the location of all other registry hives. Thus, if the \System hive is missing or corrupt, it can't be recovered using the procedure described above. Because of this, the system uses a different flushing process for the hive.

The System.alt file contains a copy of the `System` hive data. During the flush process, all changes are marked, saved, and then marked as completed. After this process is completed, the same flush process is done for the System.alt file. If there's a power failure, hardware malfunction, or problems with the software that cause system shutdown at any stage of this process, the system will try to find the correct information either in the System file or in the System.alt file.

The System.alt file is similar to the LOG file, except that the system during the boot will switch to using the System.alt file rather than trying to reapply all the changes saved in the LOG file. If the System file isn't marked as being in transition, then System.alt won't be needed.

NOTE

Windows XP solves this problem by moving the registry out of paged pool and using the cache manager to do an in-house management of the registry. Therefore, there is no need to use the System.alt file in Windows XP.

NOTE

Methods of storing registry data used by Windows 9x/ME and Windows NT/2000/XP also have significant differences. Windows 95/98 uses only two registry files, namely, System.dat and User.dat (in Windows ME there is another registry file, Classes.dat, which was introduced to improve boot time). To simplify the editing process, the registry editor displays both DAT files using unified interface. The User.dat file stores user-related information (for example, custom settings for the desktop), while the System.dat file contains system-related information, for example, default settings for the desktop, hardware profiles, network settings, and so forth. Both files have Hidden attribute and are stored in the Windows folder (the folder where the Windows 95/98 operating system is installed). Note that when installing Windows 95, the Setup program automatically creates backup copies for each of these files (User.da0 and System.da0, respectively). These backup copies are also hidden files stored in the Windows 95 directory. In contrast to Windows 95, there are no such files in Windows 98, because this operating system uses a newer and more efficient method of ensuring registry integrity. If the User.dat or System.dat files become corrupt, Windows 95 will make an attempt to use the User.da0 or System.da0 files. During the boot process, Windows 95 automatically updates these backup copies by replacing them with the current registry files. Theoretically, this mechanism ensures that the most up-to date configuration (the last best boot configuration) is always present on the computer.

Registry Size Problem

When we discussed the drawbacks of INI files earlier in this chapter, we mentioned the problems caused by the Win.ini size limitation. The Windows NT/2000 registry seemed to solve this problem, but it still remained limited in size. At the same time, there was a steady trend among registry consumers to use the registry like a database, which was constantly increasing the demands on registry size. The original design of the registry kept all of the registry files in the paged pool, which, in the 32-bit kernel, is effectively limited to approximately 160 MB because of the layout of the kernel virtual address space. A problem arose because, as larger registry consumers such as Terminal Services and COM appeared, a considerable amount of paged-pool was used for the registry alone, potentially leaving too little memory for other kernel-mode components.

Registry Size Limit in Windows NT/2000

To solve the above described problem, Windows NT 4.0/Windows 2000 provides the capability of restricting the size to which the registry can grow. To set the registry size limitation in Windows 2000, use the following procedure:

1. Double-click **System** in the **Control Panel** window. The **System Properties** window will appear.

2. Go to the **Advanced** tab and click the **Performance Options** button to open the **Performance Options** window (Fig. 1.7). Click the **Change** button in the **Virtual Memory** group of options. The **Virtual Memory** window will appear (Fig. 1.8). At the bottom of this window is the **Registry size** group with the **Maximum registry size (MB)** field, allowing the user to manually set the maximum registry size.

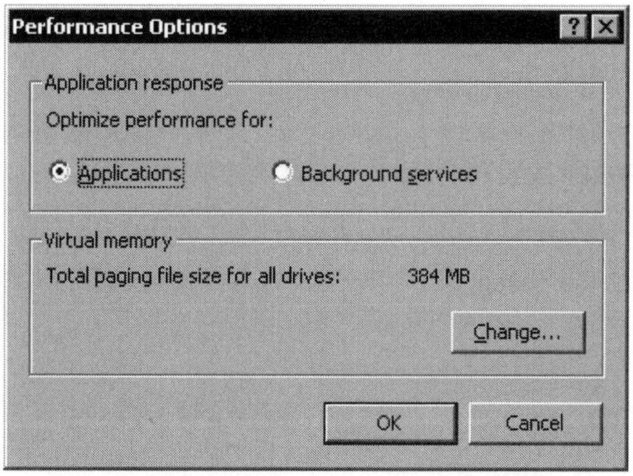

Fig. 1.7. The **Performance Options** window

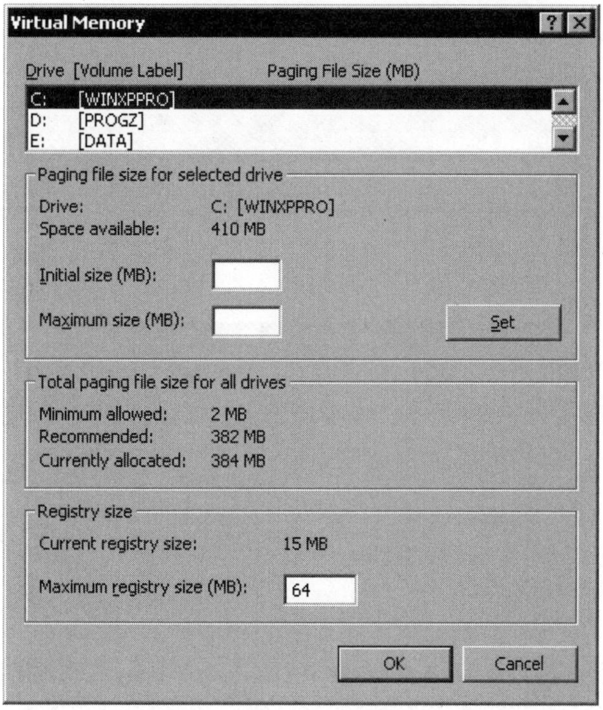

Fig. 1.8. Setting the registry size limitation for Windows 2000

Windows NT/2000 registry data loaded to the memory is stored in a paged pool, which is a region in the physical memory used for storing data that can be flushed to the hard disk if these are not used for a long time. The size limit on the registry is set to prevent this sort of situation when the registry consumes all the space needed by other processes.

Registry Enhancements in Windows XP

In contrast to Windows NT/2000, in Windows XP the registry size limitation has been removed. The registry code is now redesigned to provide enhanced performance while remaining transparent to applications by using existing registry programming interfaces.

The new registry implementation delivers two key benefits:

- Larger registries
- Faster queries

Therefore, in Windows XP you won't find an option allowing you to establish a registry size limit (Fig. 1.9).

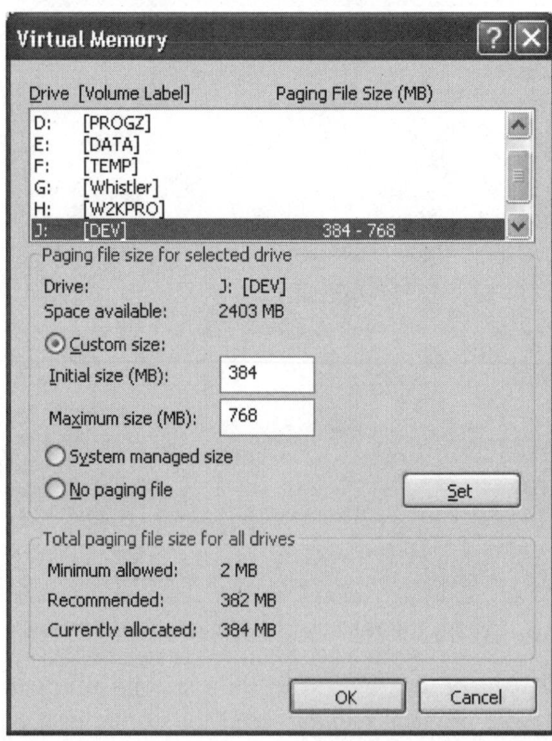

Fig. 1.9. In Windows XP, there is no option for setting the registry size limitation

Let us consider the above mentioned Windows XP registry enhancements in more detail.

- *Larger Registries.* Windows XP supports larger registries than previous versions of the kernel, which were effectively limited to about 80 percent of the total size of the paged pool. The new implementation is limited only by available system disk space. In Windows XP, this problem was solved by moving the registry out of the paged pool and using the cache manager to do the management of mapped views of the registry files. The mapped views are mapped in 256K chunks into system cache space instead of the paged pool.
- *Faster Queries.* Another issue that affected registry performance in earlier versions is the *locality problem.* Related cells are spread through all of the registry files. Accessing certain information, such as attributes of a key, could degenerate into page-faults, which lowers performance. The Windows XP registry uses an improved algorithm for allocating new cells that keeps related cells in closer proximity—such as keeping cells on the same page or nearby pages, which solves the locality problem and reduces the page faults incurred when accessing related cells. A new hive structure member tracks freed cells instead of relying on linked freed cells. When future cells are allocated, the freed cell list and a vicinity argument are used to ensure that they are put in the same bin as the hive.

Windows XP improves the way the registry handles big data. In versions before Windows XP, if an inefficient application steadily increased a value by a small increment, it created a sparse and wasteful registry file. Windows XP solves this problem with a big cell implementation, where cells larger than 16K are split into increments of 16K chunks. This reduces fragmentation when the data length of a value is increased within a certain threshold.

When Should You Edit the Registry

The best answer to this question is: "Only in an emergency". You certainly shouldn't get in the habit of editing the registry any time a problem arises. The Windows XP developers didn't develop this system in order to have users solve minor problems by editing the registry. Microsoft has made significant efforts to develop powerful and flexible graphical administrative tools to help users solve everyday tasks related to system configuration and troubleshooting. All users are recommended to try solving the problem using these tools, and proceed with editing the registry only when all other methods have failed.

However, there's always a chance that all the methods of configuring the system using Control Panel applets or resetting device settings using Device Manager will fail. If this is the case, you'll need to know how to work with the registry and how to edit it using the registry editor.

Some actions related to customizing applications can be performed only by editing the registry directly. For example, if you need to open Windows Explorer when the user double-clicks **My Computer**, or to enable Windows XP built-in leak detection, you'll need to edit the registry, because these tasks can't be achieved using other methods. If you need to edit the registry, do it very carefully and in accordance with the instructions.

The Internet contains many tips related to registry editing. Usually, these tips are related to setting some registry entries. If you decide to modify the registry, don't forget to backup the registry before proceeding with these changes.

Alternative Methods of Editing the Registry

Remember that even in cases when registry editing is necessary, an unskilled user can create even greater problems when performing this task. For example, errors that occur when editing the registry may lead to problems with loading device drivers or with logging in to the system. If you're not absolutely sure that the registry changes you're going to make are correct, or simply can't afford significant time for troubleshooting, don't experiment with the operating system registry (this relates both to Windows NT 4.0/Windows 2000 and Windows XP). A single error could mean reinstalling your operating system.

CAUTION!

Administrative tools always provide a method of configuring the system preferable to direct registry editing. Using administrative utilities is much safer, because these utilities don't allow you to save incorrect values in the system registry. If you make an error while using one of the registry editors, you won't get a warning, because registry editors don't recognize these errors and don't take any corrective actions.

After you get acquainted with the registry, you may feel tempted to edit it in order to install or configure hardware devices. Registry editor, discussed in *Chapter 3*, is a special tool used for viewing and modifying the registry. However, before proceeding with direct registry editing, try to perform the same task using the administrative utilities. Most hardware-related registry entries are very hard to understand unless you have a working knowledge of the hex format. These settings only affect the hardware devices that use them.

For example, you shouldn't manually edit the registry when installing new hardware because of the methods the system uses to configure Plug and Play devices. As you'll see in *Chapter 5*, Plug and Play devices now have default settings. If a device requests a resource that's already in use by another Plug and Play device, the system may change the Plug and Play device settings in such a way as to eliminate hardware conflicts with the new device. If you manually change the registry settings for Plug and Play devices, you'll get constant settings. These settings can't be changed by the operating system if another device requests the same resource.

Installing New Devices

Even if Windows XP encounters a new device not currently included in the registry, and the system has no information on this device, it first attempts to detect it. If the new device has been successfully detected and recognized, you'll see a small pop-up window in the lower right corner of the desktop, informing you that the system has found new hardware (Fig. 1.10). Notice that in this case the system will automatically install the device driver, configure the device settings and after a few seconds display another pop-up window, reporting that the newly installed device is ready to use (Fig. 1.11).

Fig. 1.10. Windows XP automatically detects new hardware

Fig. 1.11. The newly detected device is successfully installed and configured

In contrast to Plug and Play devices, legacy devices developed before the release of Windows 95 have fixed settings. The task of installing and configuring legacy devices is more complicated than installing Plug and Play devices. Always remember one thing though—before modifying the registry directly, try to achieve the same result using Hardware Wizard. In Windows XP, this program was significantly improved by extended functionality and a more intuitive user interface, even in comparison to Windows 2000. To install a legacy device in Windows XP, follow the instructions provided below:

1. Open the **Control Panel** window, then double-click the **Add Hardware** icon, or, alternately, start the System applet to open the **System Properties** window, go to the **Hardware** tab, and click the **Add Hardware Wizard** button. Any of these methods will open the **Add Hardware Wizard** window shown in Fig. 1.12. Click the **Next** button.

Fig. 1.12. The first window of the **Add Hardware Wizard** program

2. The wizard will try to detect the new device. If it fails, it will display another window prompting the user to specify if the new device is already connected (Fig. 1.13). The wizard will display a series of screens containing options available for selection and step-by-step instructions. To install and configure the

new device, just follow these instructions, select the required options, and click **Next** to continue. Besides new device installation, Hardware Wizard allows you to view the list of installed devices and troubleshoot the devices that are not working properly (Fig. 1.14). To install a new device that is not listed here, select the **Add a new hardware device** option and click **Next**.

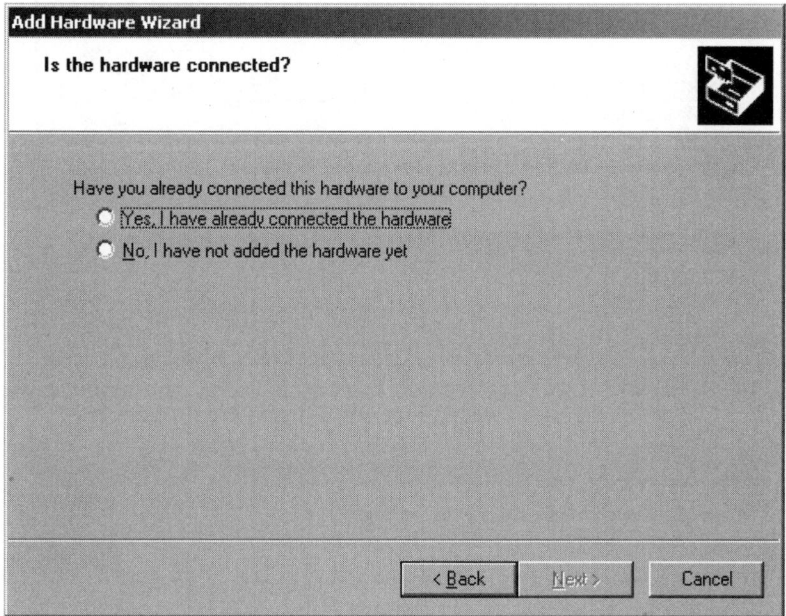

Fig. 1.13. The next screen of the Hardware Wizard

3. Next, the Hardware Wizard prompts you to select if you are going to search for the hardware automatically or select an appropriate device from the list (Fig. 1.15). Since Windows XP provides enhanced hardware support, even in comparison to Windows 2000, to say nothing about previous Windows NT versions, it is recommended that you select automatic search. As a general rule, the system successfully detects all the hardware correctly connected to your system, both Plug and Play and legacy. Therefore, you'll need to manually select the device from the list only in a worst case scenario (Fig. 1.16). If you don't find your device even in this list, set the **Show all devices** options and click **Next**. In this case, the next window will open (Fig. 1.17), containing a long Windows NT/2000-style list of all supported hardware.

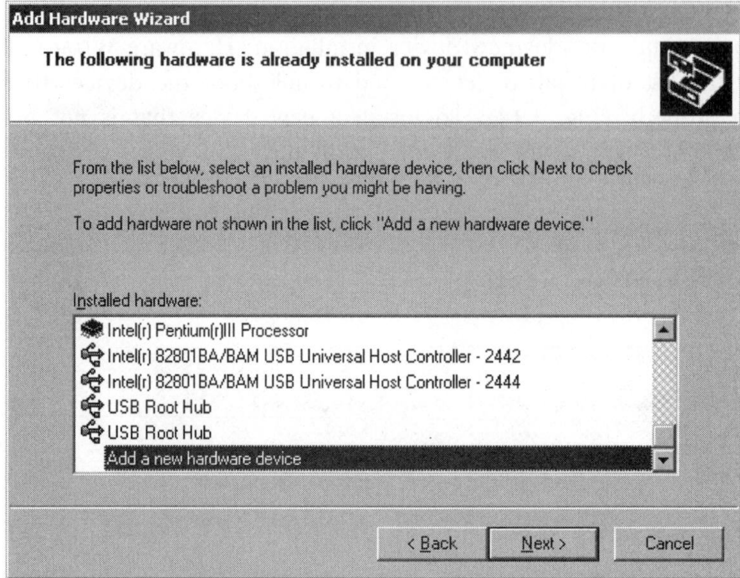

Fig. 1.14. Hardware Wizard enables you to view the list of installed devices and troubleshoot the devices that are not working properly

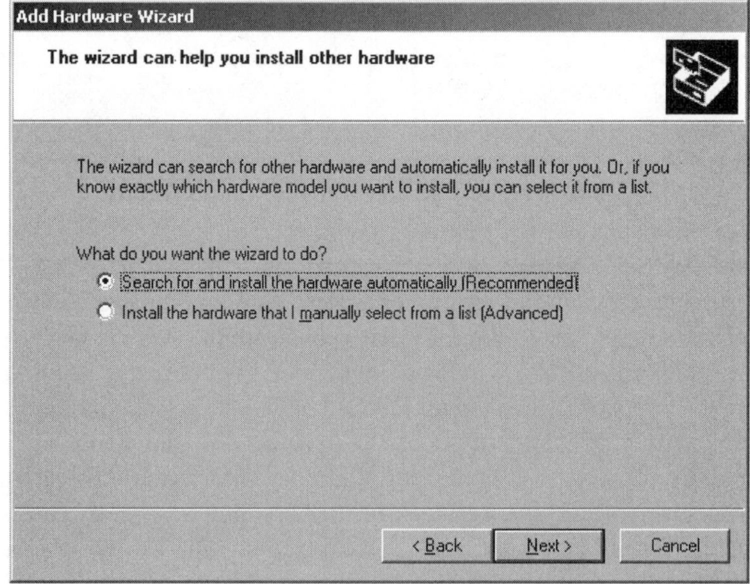

Fig. 1.15. When installing new hardware, the Hardware Wizard provides capabilities of searching the new hardware automatically or manually selecting an appropriate device from the list

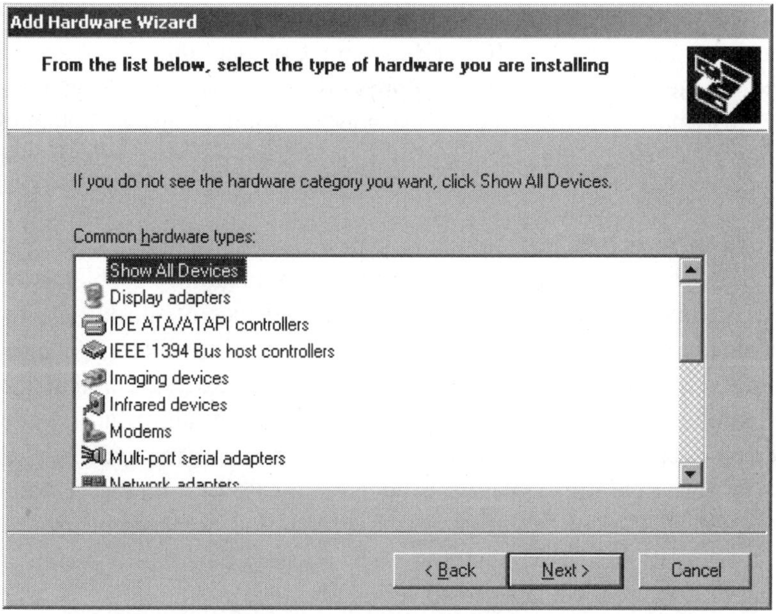

Fig. 1.16. Hardware Wizard provides a list of device classes. Select **Show All Devices** if you don't see the hardware category that you require

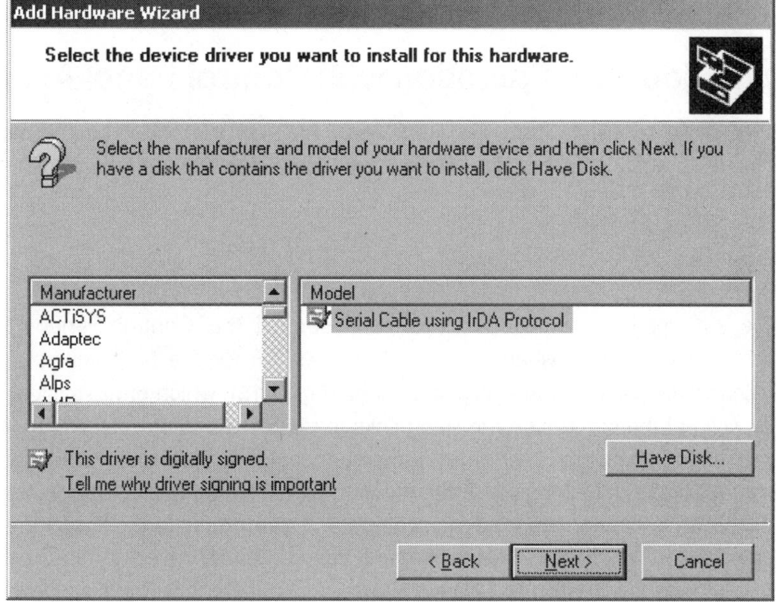

Fig. 1.17. The Windows NT/2000-style list of supported devices

As was stated above, Hardware Wizard will detect all compatible hardware devices that have been listed in the HCL (Hardware Compatibility List) and correctly connected to the system. This also applies to legacy devices. If you encounter problems, first make sure that the device you are going to install is included into the Windows XP HCL, then check that it is usable and correctly connected to your system.

This method of installing and configuring new devices is much safer than direct registry editing, because it eliminates the risk of compatibility problems. However, from time to time you may need to change the settings of the legacy devices by means of direct registry editing. Many advanced users are interested in changing the resource settings for the hardware devices. You already know that the device manager automatically controls these settings when installing a new device or booting Windows. Sometimes, though, you may need to manually set these parameters. For example, this situation is possible in case of a hardware conflict that can't be solved by the configuration manager. Suppose, for example, that there's a conflict between IRQ and DMA settings for two legacy devices. In such a case, you can also use the Device Manager to solve the problem.

Hardware-related registry keys are discussed in detail in *Chapters 5* and *6*, where you'll also find instructions on editing registry parameters and selecting appropriate values.

Changing Your Configuration with Control Panel Applets

Most of the truly useful system and hardware settings can be changed using the Control Panel applets. To complete these tasks, you don't need to edit the registry at all.

NOTE

Don't be surprised or confused if you can't see all the Control Panel options in Windows XP. By default, when you start Windows XP for the first time, the **Control Panel** window displays only the general options (Fig. 1.18), which group system settings logically while at the same time providing links to related areas and access to Help topics. Experienced Windows users may remember that a similar feature was first introduced with Windows Millennium Edition. This new Control Panel design, known as Category View, is mainly intended for beginners. If you prefer to work with the Control Panel interface to which you are accustomed, you can easily revert to the Classic View by simply clicking the **Switch to Classic View** link. Your Control Panel window will then display all available options (Fig. 1.19).

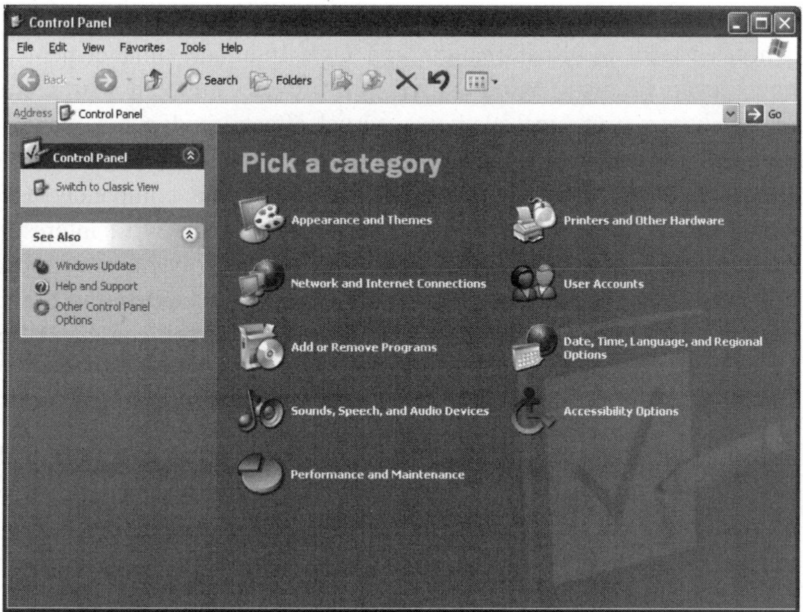

Fig. 1.18. The new Control Panel design provides a Category View, which displays only the most common options by default

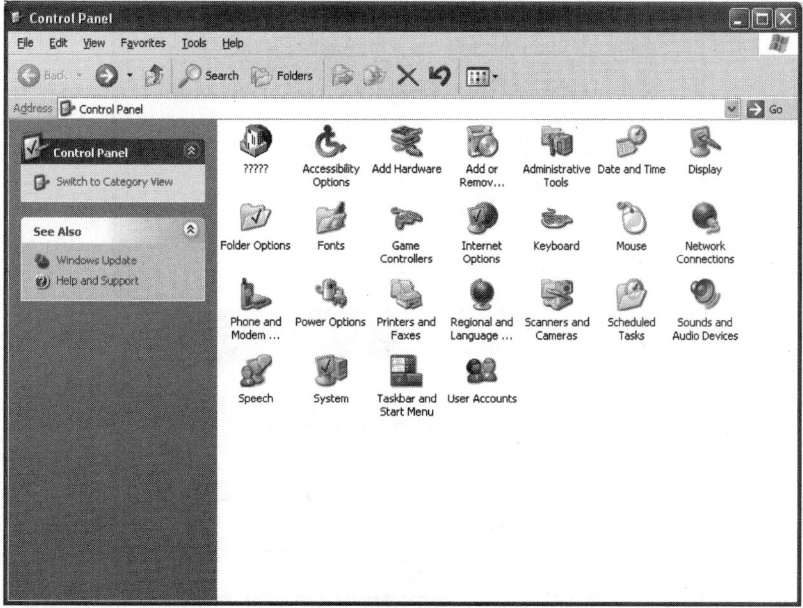

Fig. 1.19. Classic view of the Control Panel window displays all available options

Certainly, anyone who has installed Windows XP and worked with it for some time has noticed a lot of visual changes and User Interface enhancements, which mainly encompass two areas. Windows XP now provides quite an artistic choice of icons, color schemes, graphical elements, visual effects, and much more. At the same time, the user interface becomes less cluttered and more customizable. For example, the desktop is now by default nearly empty and completely devoid of icons and shortcuts other than the Recycle Bin. One of the most interesting enhancements relates to the taskbar and **Start** menu, which has a new appearance and lots of interesting customization options. To access the taskbar and **Start** menu settings, simply right-click the taskbar and select the **Properties** command from the context menu, or, alternately, start the **Taskbar and Start Menu** applet in Control Panel. The **Taskbar and Start Menu Properties** window will open (Fig. 1.20).

As you probably have noticed, Windows XP groups similar taskbar buttons by default (some users welcome this feature, while some get annoyed with it). If you are among those who are not great fans of this feature, simply disable it by clearing the **Group similar taskbar buttons** checkbox on the **Taskbar** tab in this window.

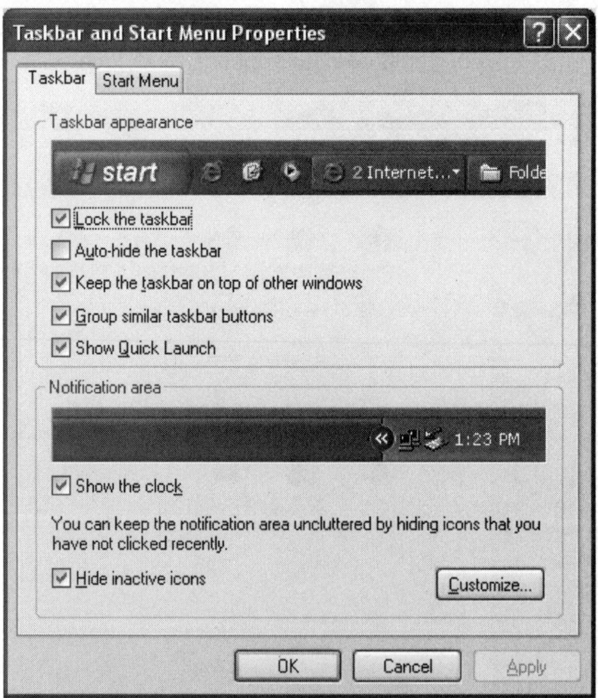

Fig. 1.20. The **Taskbar** tab of the **Taskbar and Start Menu Properties** window

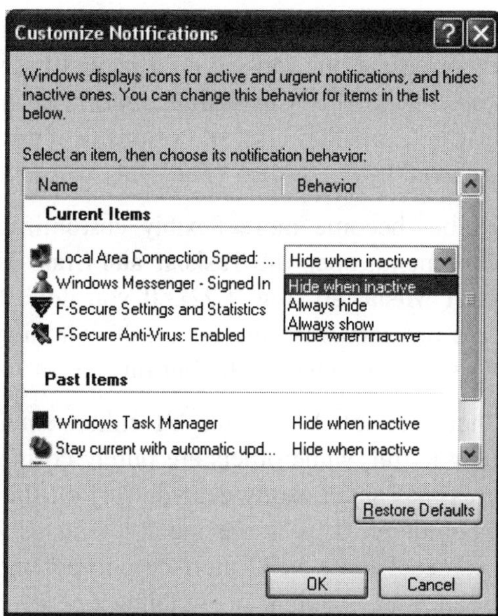

Fig. 1.21. The **Customize Notifications** window

Fig. 1.22. The **Start Menu** tab of the **Taskbar and Start Menu Properties** window

Also notice the **Notification area** option group at the bottom of this window. If you are annoyed by the notifications you see on a regular basis at the bottom-right corner of the desktop, click the **Customize** button to open the **Customize Notifications** window, which provides a set of options for customizing the behavior of the notifications displayed by the system (Fig. 1.21).

The **Start** menu itself has become more flexibly customizable. To specify your preferences for the **Start** menu, open the **Taskbar and Start Menu Properties** window and go to the **Start Menu** tab (Fig. 1.22). If you don't like the new look of the **Start** menu, you are provided with the option of switching to the classic **Start** menu by setting the **Classic Start menu** radio button.

Generally speaking, there are lots of various UI enhancements in Windows XP, some of which are really useful, while others are purely cosmetic. Enabling or disabling these components may significantly degrade (or, on the contrary, boost) the performance of your computer. This is the main reason why at some point you may want to disable some of these new interface components. To customize the Windows XP user interface by enabling or disabling one or more of the system's new features, proceed as follows.

1. Start the System applet in Control Panel. The **System Properties** window will open. Go to the **Advanced** tab (Fig. 1.23), then click the **Settings** button in the **Performance** option group.
2. The **Performance Options** window opened at the **Visual Effects** tab will appear (Fig. 1.24). To enable all visual effects, set the **Adjust for best appearance** radio button; to disable all effects, click **Adjust for best performance**. If you want to restore the defaults, set the **Let Windows choose what's best for my computer** option. Also notice that you can set a custom combination of options by selecting the **Custom** radio button and setting the required checkboxes in the list below.

Displaying Protected Operating System Files

Starting with Windows 2000, the developers began including into the UI some protective measures, which are intended to protect beginners from themselves. Among these novelties are "super-hidden" files. By default, Windows Explorer does not display files that have both Hidden and System attributes. These files are considered protected operating system files, which should not be modified or even seen by ordinary users. Obviously, the default list of such files includes all files required for starting the operating system. A similar feature was also included with Windows Millennium Edition, and, naturally, it is present in Windows XP.

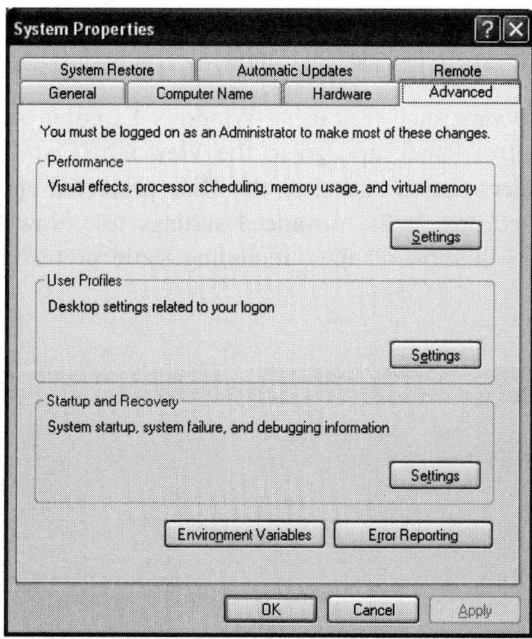

Fig. 1.23. The **Advanced** tab of the **System Properties** window

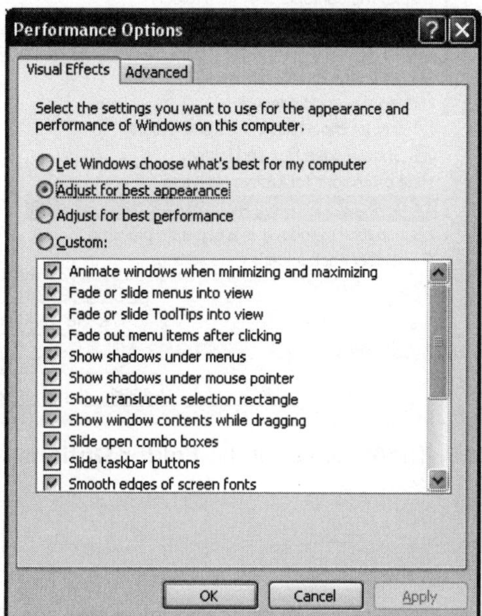

Fig. 1.24. The **Visual Effects** tab of the **Performance Options** window

Note, however, that you can always use the command line. To view all files independently from their attributes, use the following command: `dir /a`.

To get the ability to view such files using Windows Explorer, start the Folder Options applet in Control Panel, and go to the **View** tab (Fig. 1.25). Set the **Show hidden files and folders** option and clear the **Hide protected operating system files (Recommended)** checkbox in the **Advanced settings** list. Now Windows Explorer and My Computer will show all files, including those protected by the operating system.

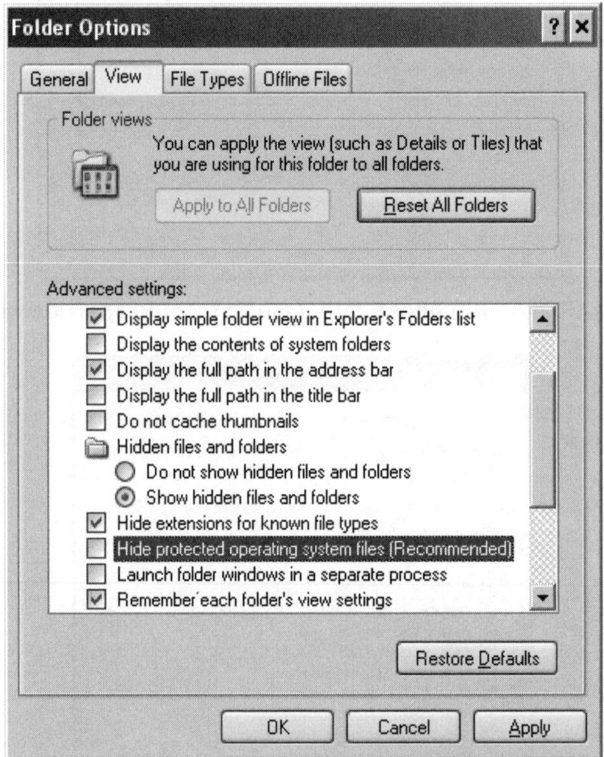

Fig. 1.25. The **View** tab of the **Folder Options** window

NOTE

In Windows 2000, you need to log in to the local system as Administrator or a user belonging to the Administrators group (otherwise you will not get the desired result).

Other Tools for Changing the Registry

Besides Control Panel applets and other GUI tools provided by Windows XP, there are other tools for changing the registry. These tools are listed below:

- You may use the **Options** dialogs present in Windows-compatible applications. As was already mentioned, any Windows-compliant application has to store its settings in the registry and provide the user with graphical tools enabling him or her to change these registry settings.
- The registry settings can also be changed using shareware or freeware applications (both Microsoft and third-party). More detailed information on the most popular registry utilities will be provided later in this book.
- REG and INF files.
- Installation programs.

Summary

This chapter provided a brief description of Windows NT/2000/XP registries, as well as an overview of the registry's history, its role, and its capabilities. We've also discussed the place of the registry in Windows NT/2000/XP architecture. Most registry aspects covered in this chapter will be discussed in greater detail later in this book.

Chapter 2

Registry Backup and Recovery

Solutions to problems are easy to find:
the problem's a great contribution.
What's truly an art is to wring from your mind
a problem to fit a solution.

Piet Hein
The Last Things First grook

What? A backup copy? What is a backup copy...

A sad, everyday experience

If you're a system administrator or technical support specialist, you're certainly able to provide many examples illustrating situations where users called for technical support when encountering registry problems. Sometimes (fortunately, this case isn't common) the user encounters registry corruption problems before he or she can start Windows for the first time. Registry corruption is especially probable when inexperienced users modify the registry, because they often set incorrect values or even delete necessary keys. All these actions result in registry corruption.

Before proceeding any further, I recommend that you study alternative methods of modifying the registry and various techniques of registry backup and recovery. There are several alternative methods of editing the Windows NT/2000/XP registry you can use to solve the problem or configure the system parameters. Some of these methods were described in *Chapter 1.* Some Internet resources provide various tips on solving problems using complicated registry editing procedures. Users with a sound knowledge of Windows XP functionality may find simpler and, at the same time, more elegant solutions, since most problems can be solved using Control Panel applets and other administrative utilities.

CAUTION!

If you make an error while modifying the registry (for example, by setting incorrect values or deleting vital registry entries), you may prevent Windows NT/2000/XP from booting. Whenever possible, modify the system configuration using Control Panel applets or other administrative utilities. Registry editor should be used only as a last resort. System administrators may wish to restrict user access to the registry in order to protect the system configuration. This topic will be discussed in detail in *Chapter 9.*

Preparing for Registry Editing

So, you need to open the registry and solve your problems by modifying it. This is a normal situation, and I suppose you'll edit the registry directly. Some methods of configuring and troubleshooting the system, discussed later in this book, do require direct editing of the registry.

However, before you go any further, you'll need to backup the registry. Registry backup is the first thing that should be done before you begin editing the registry. Never start editing the registry without backing it up. No one is insured against errors, and registry editor (which will be discussed in the next chapter) doesn't have the **Undo** command present in most programs. Don't create unnecessary problems for yourself (unless you're fond of this!). There's a ready solution, and this solution is registry backup.

Windows XP provides various methods of registry backup and recovery, along with reliability enhancements. Some of these features were inherited from Windows NT/2000, while other ones were first introduced with Windows XP. This chapter provides detailed instructions on performing these procedures, and I tried to cover nearly all existing methods of registry backup.

Microsoft documentation and Microsoft Knowledge Base articles always contain standard warnings, which inform the user about the potential danger of direct registry editing. Microsoft doesn't guarantee that the problems caused by registry editing can necessarily be solved. If the system registry becomes corrupt, and you have no backup copy, it's highly possible that you'll need to reinstall the operating system.

Using System Restore

New to Windows XP, the System Restore function recalls a similar functionality first introduced with Windows Millennium Edition. Using System Restore enables you to "rollback" the operating system to one of the restore points that fix the system state at the moment when the system was stable and worked correctly. A particular advantage of this tool is that it is user-friendly, and enables you to recover the damaged system quickly without performing tedious troubleshooting procedures or even reinstalling the operating system. System Restore doesn't overwrite user files, such as documents, spreadsheets, mail messages, archives, etc. Therefore, this function must become your first line of defense.

System Restore contains the following two components:

- *File monitoring tool.* File monitoring is performed by the kernel-level file system driver that tracks all the changes to the predefined set of system files and application files. The list of files to be monitored is stored in the Filelist.xml file located in the *%Systemroot%*\system32\restore directory. Notice that the following files and folders are excluded from the monitoring process:
    - Virtual memory paging file.
    - User data (the contents of the folders such as My Documents, Recycle Bin, Temporary Internet Files, History, and Temp).
    - Graphical files with filename extensions such as BMP, JPG, EPS and so on, and data files with filename extensions such as DOC, XLS, MDB, PST, PDF, etc.
- *Restore points.* Restore points are "snapshots" of the system state (including, of course, the registry), which are regularly saved to the hard drive. Restore points are created according to the specified schedule (for example, every day after successful logon) or based on system events (for example, installation of new applications or device drivers). Besides, the users can manually create restore points as necessary.

Creating a Restore Point

The process of creating restore points is straightforward. To create a new restore point manually, do the following:

1. Start the System Restore utility. You can do this using various methods:
    - From the **Start** menu, select **All Programs | Accessories | System Tools | System Restore**.
    - From the **Start** menu, select **Run** and enter the following command in the **Open** field: `%Systemroot%\system32\restore\rstrui.exe`.
    - From the **Start** menu, select **Help and Support**, then select the **System Restore** command from the **Tools** menu.
2. The first screen of the System Restore utility will appear (Fig. 2.1). Set the **Create a restore point** radio button, then click **Next**.
3. The next window will open (Fig. 2.2). Here you will be prompted to enter the restore point description. Enter the description string in the **Restore Point description** field and click **Create**.

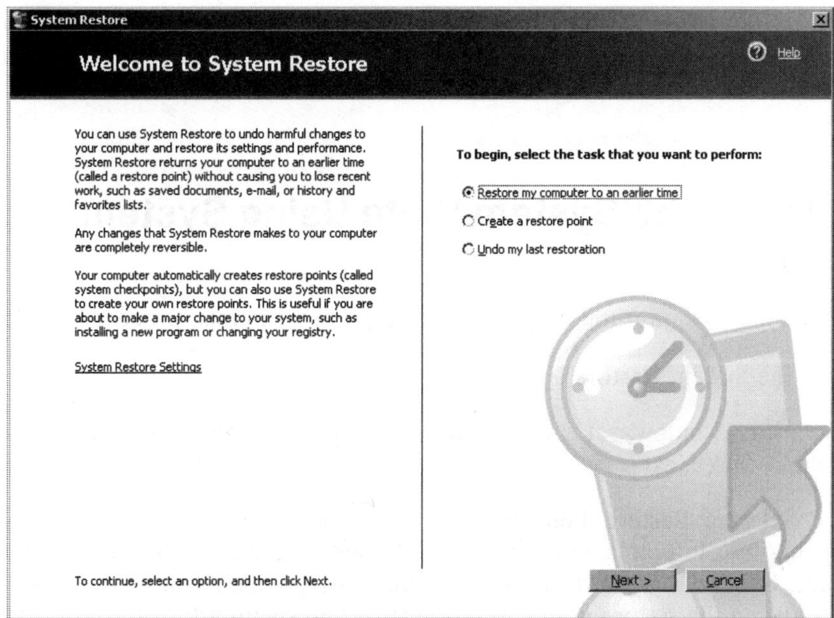

Fig. 2.1. The **System Restore Welcome** screen

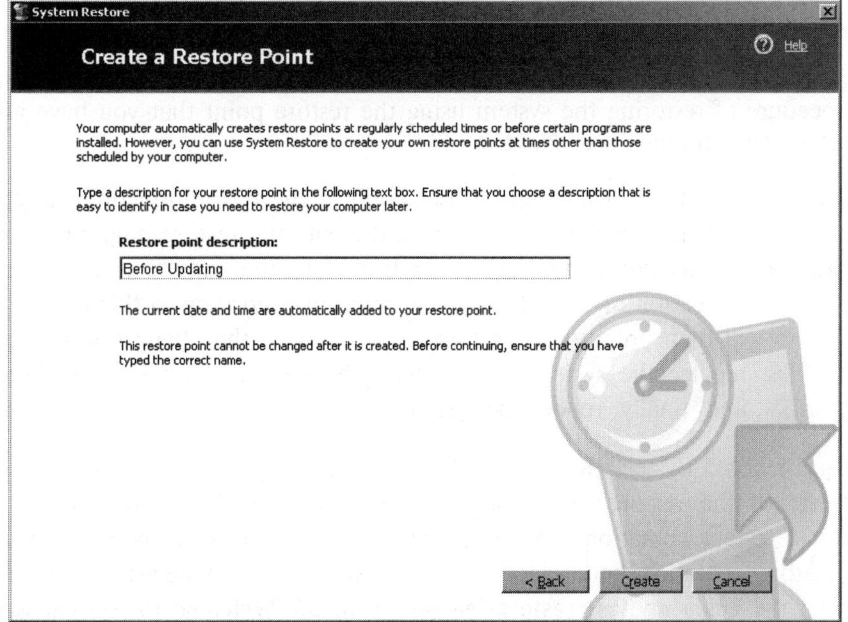

Fig. 2.2. Entering the restore point description

4. The restore point will then be created. The final window of System Restore will open, prompting you to either close the System Restore application or return to the first screen by clicking **Home**.

Restoring the System State Using System Restore

To restore the system using one of the existing restore points, proceed as follows:

1. Start the System Restore application.
2. In the first window, set the **Restore my computer to an earlier time** radio button and click **Next**.
3. The **Select a Restore Point** window will appear (Fig. 2.3). Select one of the existing restore points and click **Next**. To help the user with selecting a restore point, System Restore displays a calendar, using which you can determine the dates when the restore points were made. If you spend a lot of time working on the computer, then some dates will have two or more restore points, as shown in the example presented here. On the other hand, restore points will not be created for days when you did not use your computer.
4. In the final window, **Confirm Restore Point**, you'll be prompted to confirm the procedure of restoring the system using the restore point that you have just selected. To continue, click **Next**.
5. After you select the restore point and confirm the restoration procedure, System Restore will read the change logs and create the restore map based on the log information. The system will be returned to the state that existed at the moment of creation of the selected restore point according to this map. System Restore will then process the restore map, undo all the changes introduced to the files, replace the system registry with the backup copy included into the snapshot, and, finally, reboot the system.
6. After reboot, System Restore will display a window informing you of the results of the restore operation (Fig. 2.4). It should be noticed that successful restore operations are reversible; therefore, you can undo the results of a restore operation and select another restore point, if necessary. To do so, select the **Undo my last restoration** option in the **Welcome to System Restore** window.

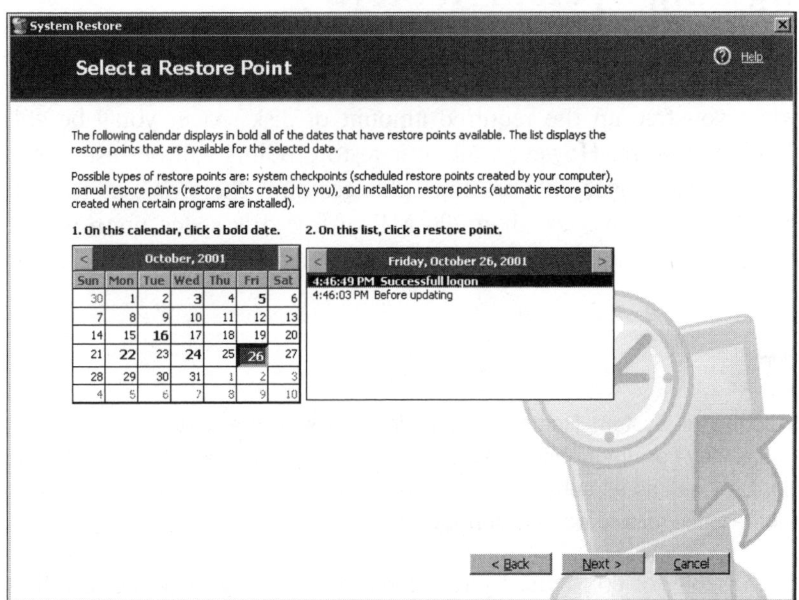

Fig. 2.3. Selecting the restore point in the **Select a Restore Point** window

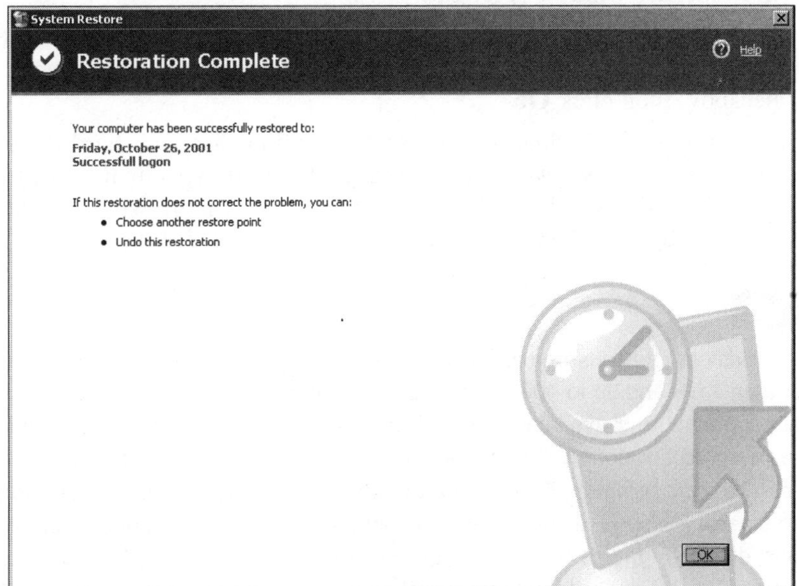

Fig. 2.4. The **Restoration Complete** window

Configuring System Restore

Notice that System Restore requires no less than 200 MB of free disk space. If you are short of disk space, the System Restore function will be automatically disabled. Later, when you free up the required amount of disk space, you'll be able to re-enable System Restore. However, all your restore points will be lost, because System Restore is no longer able to track changes and, therefore, can't undo them. Furthermore, if you have less than 200 MB of free disk space upon installation of Windows XP, you'll have to manually enable System Restore after freeing up the required disk space.

NOTE

Don't configure System Restore in parallel with software installation procedures, because this may corrupt the initial restore point that System Restore creates when you re-enable it, as well as all subsequent restore points. Notice that there is no way to determine if the initial restore point is corrupt.

To enable, disable, or configure System Restore manually, proceed as follows:

1. Start the System applet in Control Panel. Go to the **System Restore** tab of the **System Properties** window (Fig. 2.5).
2. To disable System Restore on all local hard drives, set the **Turn off System Restore on all drives** checkbox. If you need to re-enable System Restore, clear this checkbox, then click **OK**.
3. If you need to set individual System Restore options for each hard drive, select the drive or partition for which you need to configure System Restore from the **Available drives** list. Click the **Settings** button to open the window that allows for setting the System Restore parameters for the selected drive (Fig. 2.6).

NOTE

System Restore can consume up to 12 percent of the available free disk space on disks larger than 4 GB and up to 400 MB on disks less than 4 GB. Depending on your individual requirements and available free disk space, you can manage the amount of disk space reserved for storing System Restore archives on each of the local hard drives. This can be done using the **Disk space to use** slider. Notice that the system won't allow you to disable System Restore for the system partition without disabling it on all the remaining drives (Fig. 2.6). However, you can exclude any other drive from the list of those used for storing System Restore archives by setting the **Turn off System Restore on this drive** checkbox (Fig. 2.7).

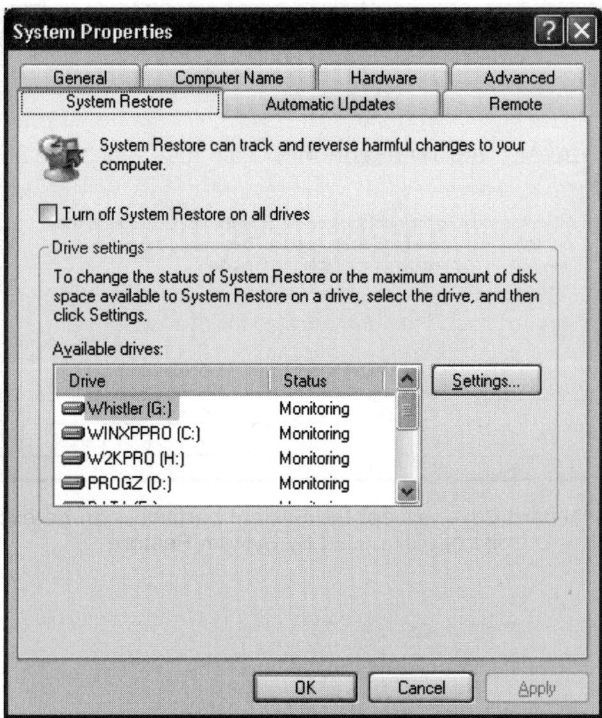

Fig. 2.5. The **System Restore** tab of the **System Properties** window

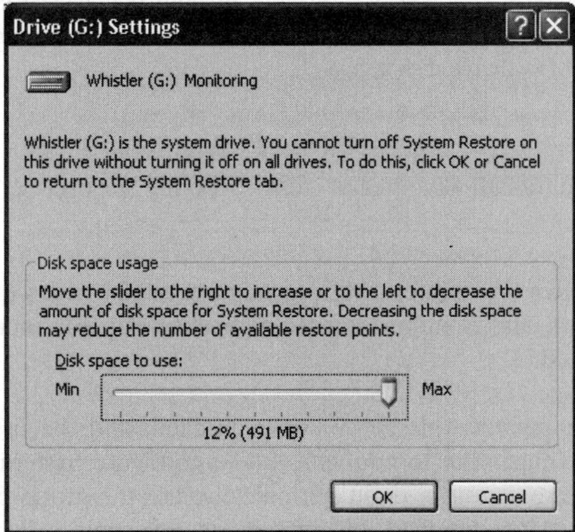

Fig. 2.6. System Restore settings for the system partition

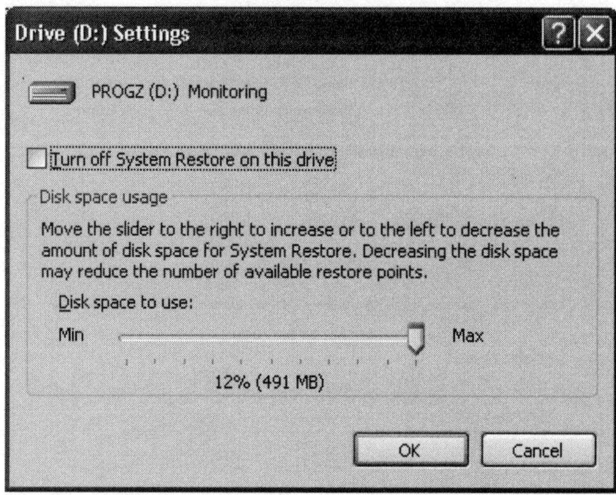

Fig. 2.7. Any local hard drive, except the System partition, can be excluded from the list of disks used by System Restore

NOTE

On NTFS drives, System Restore compresses archived data. This operation is done when the computer is idle. Besides, System Restore periodically clears the archives using the FIFO (First In First Out) algorithm based on the restore point creation dates and the amount of available disk space.

System Restore automatically creates restore points according to the following rules:

- *Daily*. System Restore creates a restore point every 24 hours (provided that the computer is on), and if more than 24 hours has elapsed since the last restore point was created.
- *Periodically*. By default, this capability is disabled, and the user interface does not provide the capability to configure it. To configure System Restore in such a way as to create a restore point periodically, use the group policy or edit the system registry. More detailed information on this topic will be provided later in this book.

Troubleshooting System Restore

This section provides step-by-step instructions on performing basic troubleshooting procedures when you have problems with System Restore:

1. Make sure that the System Restore service is up and running. This can be done using two methods. First, you can start the Administrative Tools applet in Control Panel, then select **Computer Management | Services and Applications** (Fig. 2.8). Check if the System Restore Service is started. There is a quick way of performing the same operation. Click **Start | Run**, type `Cmd`, and press the <Enter> key, then run the `Net start` command at the command prompt to view the list of running services and make sure that the System Restore service is included into this list.

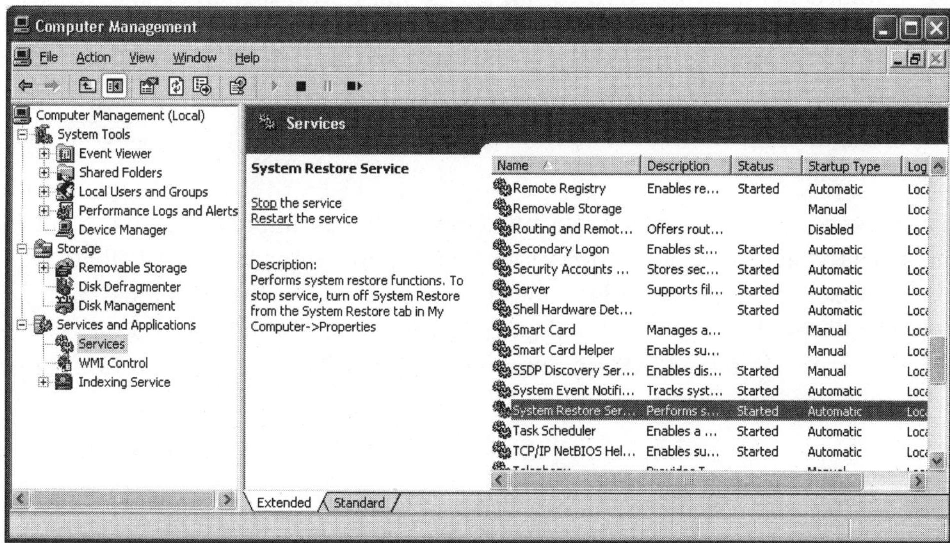

Fig. 2.8. When troubleshooting System Restore, first make sure that the System Restore service is started

2. Make sure that System Restore is enabled on all the drives that you want System Restore to be enabled on, then check if you have enough disk space on these drives.

3. If you suspect that you do not have as many restore points as you should have, make sure that the data store is the size that you want it to be.

4. View the System event log to find out if there are errors related to the System Restore service. To do so, start Administrative Tools in Control Panel, then

select **Computer Management** | **Event Viewer** | **System**. Click the **Source** column to sort events by name, and then look for the `srservice` string. Investigate the event description, since it may provide an indication of the cause of the problem. Most System Restore issues generate an error message that contains a description of the issue and suggestions on how to resolve the problem.

Using the Microsoft Backup Program

Using the built-in Backup program is the officially recommended method of backing up Windows NT/2000/XP registry. The Backup version supplied with Windows NT 4.0 required a Windows NT-compatible tape device to be installed in the local system, which represented one of the most serious shortcomings of this utility. Furthermore, the list of supported tape devices that could be used with Windows NT Backup in Windows NT 4.0 is quite limited as well. Moreover, this utility doesn't allow you to perform registry backup of remote systems, even if the user attempting to perform this operation has all the required access rights to the remote system.

The Backup version included with Windows 2000 has improved and extended functionality, including support for various types of backup media. This allows the user to backup information using any media supported by the operating system, including floppy disks, hard disks, floptical media, or other supported devices besides streamers. Windows XP, in turn, provides several new technological improvements and enhancements.

NOTE

Microsoft Windows XP introduces volume snapshots, a technology that provides a copy of the original volume at the instant a snapshot is made. A snapshot of the volume is made at the time a backup is initiated. Data are then backed up from the snapshot rather than from the original volume. The original volume continues to change as the process continues, but the snapshot of the volume remains constant. This is helpful if users need access to files while a backup is taking place, since it significantly reduces the time required to accomplish the backup job. Additionally, the backup application can back up files that are kept open. In previous versions of Backup, including the one supplied with Windows 2000, files open at the time of the backup were skipped.

To start the Backup utility in Windows XP, select the **All Programs** | **Accessories** | **System Tools** | **Backup** commands from the **Start** menu. If you use this utility often (and you're expected to do so), create a desktop shortcut for this program. Besides the traditional method of starting the Backup utility, you can also start it using the right-click menu. Open the **Windows Explorer** or **My Computer** window, right-click on the disk you need to backup, and select the **Properties** command from the context menu. A tabbed window will open. Navigate to the **Tools** tab (Fig. 2.9).

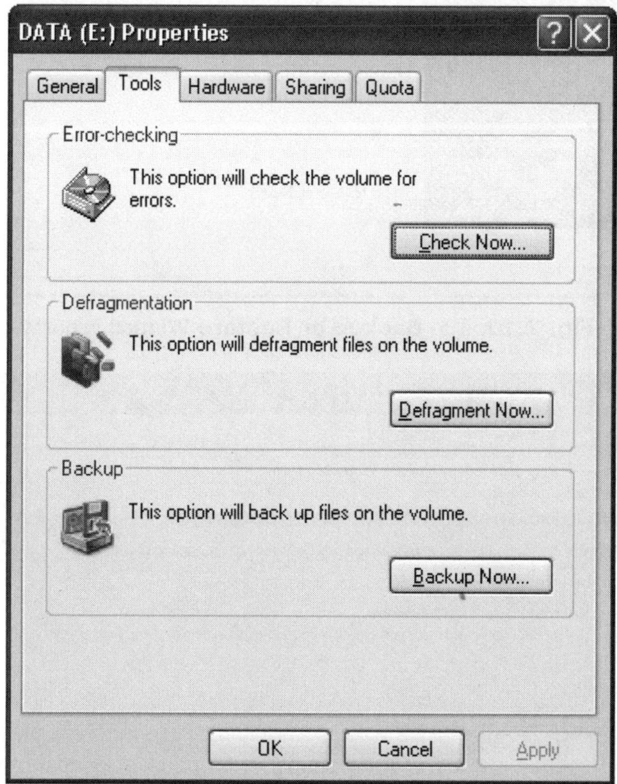

Fig. 2.9. The **Tools** tab of the disk properties window

Click the **Backup Now** button in the **Backup** group, and the **Backup or Restore Wizard** window will open (Fig. 2.10). The Backup utility can run in two modes: the wizard mode (in which it starts by default) and in advanced mode, recommended for power users. If you want to change the default settings, clear the **Always start in wizard mode** checkbox and select the **Advanced Mode** option. The **Backup Utility** window will appear, opened at the **Welcome** tab (Fig. 2.11).

Fig. 2.10. The **Backup or Restore Wizard** window

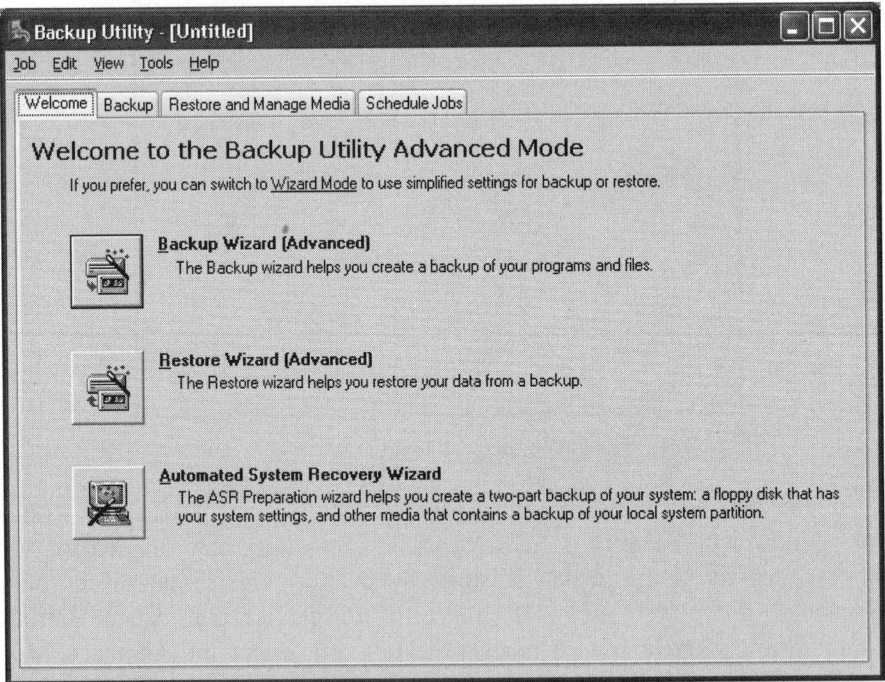

Fig. 2.11. The **Welcome** tab of the **Backup Utility** window

NOTE

Before proceeding with a backup operation, check the file system of the disk you need to backup. This is important, because you need to have a usable backup copy. Remember that the backup software (including the Backup tool supplied with Windows 2000/XP) can't recognize errors and inconsistencies in user data. Note that the method we just described provides a convenient way of performing this operation—you simply need to click the **Check Now** button on the same tab. You also need to consider the defragmentation software used to defragment your hard drives. Microsoft recommends that everyone use the built-in defragmentation software supplied with the operating system. If you're planning to use a third-party defragmentation utility, make sure that this software is compatible with Windows 2000 or Windows XP and has the "designed for Windows" status. Detailed information on the software tested for compatibility with Windows 2000/XP can be downloaded from **http://www.microsoft.com**.

One of the most important goals of Windows XP development was to create an operating system which would combine all the advantages of Windows 9*x*/ME with the traditional strong points of Windows NT/2000. Most of the attention was drawn to tasks such as making the new operating system easy to use even for beginners, simplification of administrative tasks, and making the system more reliable. Most tools and utilities were rewritten, and the Backup tool is no exception. Besides the traditional functionality of backing up and restoring the data, the Windows XP version of this utility includes the function of preparing the Automated System Recovery (ASR). Automated System Recovery is a two-part recovery system that allows you to restore Windows XP operating system states by using files saved to tape media, and hard disk configuration information saved to a floppy disk.

NOTE

Most experienced users remember the ERD functionality that existed in Windows NT/2000. In earlier versions of Windows NT, there was a special Rdisk.exe utility used to perform this task. Windows 2000 combines the functionality of the Backup and Rdisk utilities, and in Windows XP, as was already mentioned, ERD functionality was replaced by ASR.

Preparing for the Automated System Recovery

The easiest method of using the Backup program is with special wizards, similar to all other programs of this type. These wizards display dialogs prompting users to select options, and provide instructions on selecting the options. Normally, these windows contain the following three buttons: **Back**, **Next**, and **Cancel**. When the user clicks the **Back** button, a window appears allowing the user to correct the data entered after completing the previous step. To open the next window, the user needs to click the **Next** button. To cancel the whole operation, the user needs to click the **Cancel** button. This method is the easiest one for novice users, who have little or no experience of working with the system.

NOTE

Materials provided in this section can't be considered as a complete description of the Backup program functionality, and in no case should these materials be considered as a replacement for the user manual. This book is intended to describe the system registry. Because of this, this chapter provides only the most basic information related to using the Backup program for backing up and restoring the system registry. If you're interested in a detailed description of the Backup program or step-by-step instructions on performing the typical tasks, you can find this information in the Backup Help system. Any user who intends to edit the registry should read this information very carefully.

To prepare for the Automated System Recovery, proceed as follows:

1. If your computer is equipped with a tape device, prepare the backup media. If this is not so, you'll have to perform the backup operation to the hard disk, therefore, make sure that you have sufficient disk space. In any case, you'll also need a blank formatted diskette.

2. Click the **Automated System Recovery Wizard** button at the **Welcome** tab of the **Backup Utility** window or, alternately, select the **ASR wizard** command from the **Tools** menu. Click the **Next** button in the first window of the ASR wizard.

3. In the next window, you'll need to specify the backup media type and specify the backup destination. If your computer is equipped with a tape backup device, select this device from the **Backup media or file name** list. Notice that if there is no tape backup device in your system, the **File** option will be set by default in the **Backup media type** field. Enter the path to the backup media or file into the **Backup media or file name** field (backup files always have a default BKF filename extension) or click the **Browse** button to navigate the file system.

4. In the last window of the ASR preparation wizard, click the **Finish** button to start the backup process.

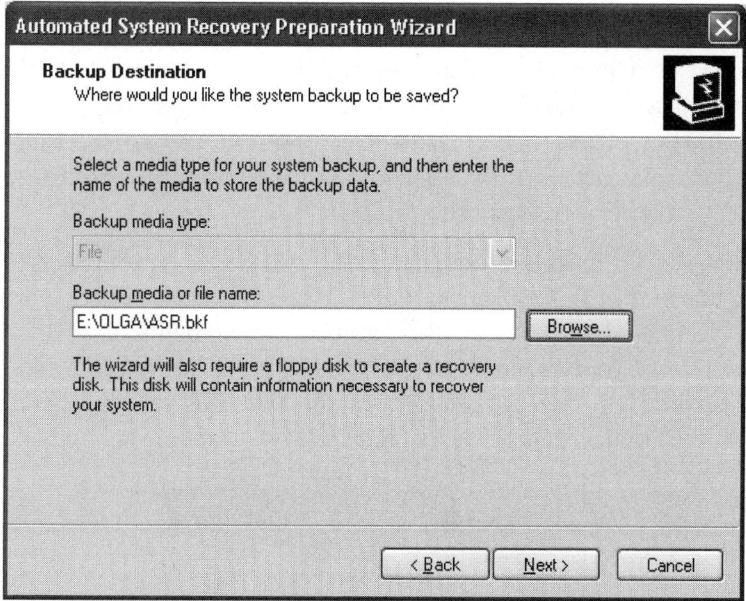

Fig. 2.12. The ASR preparation wizard prompts you to specify the backup media type and select the backup media or file name

Backup Progress

Cancel

Drive: G: Whistler

Label: ASR.bkf created 19.09.2001 at 13:20

Status: Backing up files from your computer...

Progress:

	Elapsed:	Estimated remaining:
Time:	18 sec.	13 min., 31 sec.

Processing: G:\...ments\My Music\Sample Music\doc2.nws

	Processed:	Estimated:
Files:	132	19 578
Bytes:	49 802 037	2 290 723 675

Fig. 2.13. The **Backup Progress** window

5. The Backup utility will scan your system and list files to save for an ASR backup. Next, it prompts you to provide backup media. Insert backup media when prompted by Backup and follow the directions on-screen. The wizard will display a series of messages such as `Mounting the media` and `Preparing to backup using a shadow copy`, then the **Backup Progress** window will appear (Fig. 2.13), reflecting ASR backup progress.

6. When the backup operation completes, the ASR wizard prompts you to insert a blank floppy disk (Fig. 2.14), to which it saves hard disk configuration information, such as disk signatures, the partition table, volume data, the hardware configuration of your system, and the list of files to be restored. No user data will be recorded to this diskette. If you run the ASR restore operation later, ASR Restore configures disks by using data saved to the ASR floppy disk.

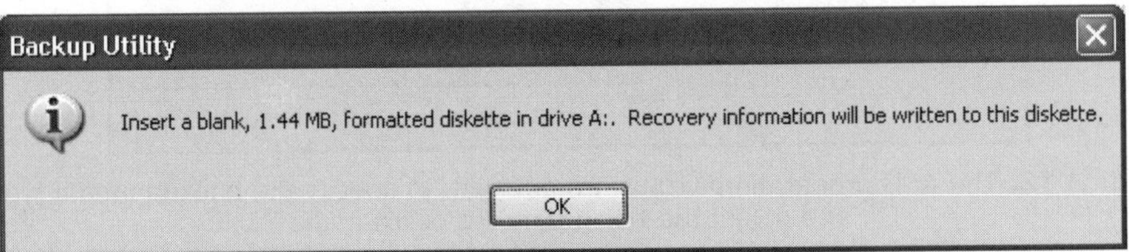

Fig. 2.14. As the final step of the ASR backup procedure, the wizard prompts you to provide a blank formatted diskette to store the recovery information

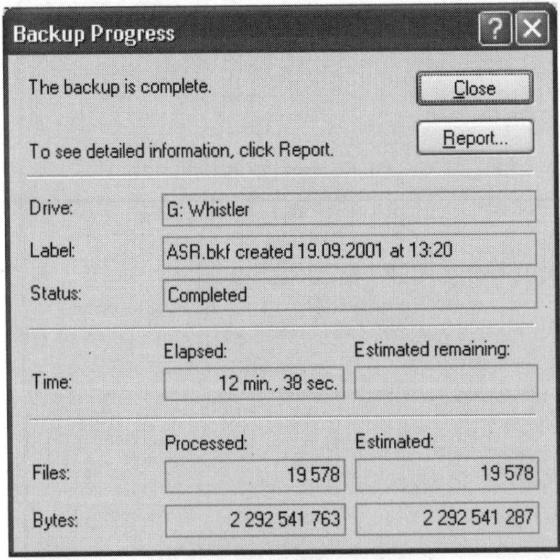

Fig. 2.15. The **Backup Progress** window informs you about completion of the backup operation and allows you to view the report

7. When ASR backup wizard finishes creating the ASR diskette, it displays a message box with a message recommending you to label the diskette as ASR recovery disk and store it in safe place. Click **OK** to close this message box. If you want to view a report on the results of the backup operation, click the **Report** button in the **Backup progress** window (Fig. 2.15).

Performing the Automated System Recovery

The process of restoring the damaged system using the ASR procedure relies on the Windows XP Setup program; therefore, besides your backup media and the most recent ASR floppy disk, you'll also need the Windows XP distribution CD. In fact, this process is very similar to unattended setup of the operating system, since ASR will restore your disk configuration using the data saved to the ASR floppy, reformat your *%Systemdrive%* partition (the one where the Windows XP copy to be recovered is installed), and then reinstall Windows XP on that partition and restore the system files using the backup media.

NOTE

ASR is not a replacement for regular backup procedures, since it doesn't eliminate the possibility of data loss. Always remember that ASR doesn't backup application files and user data. As was already mentioned, it formats the *%Systemdrive%* partition as part of the recovery process, and doesn't restore personal data or application files that may reside on that drive. Therefore, if you store user data files or install applications on the system partition, these data will be lost. Therefore, always consider other recovery options, such as System Restore or Recovery Console, before using ASR. More detailed information about Recovery Console will be provided later in this chapter.

To recover your system using ASR, proceed as follows:

1. Prepare everything that you'll need during the ASR restore process, including:
   - The most recent ASR floppy disk
   - The Windows XP distribution CD
   - The most recent ASR backup media set, typically removable media such as data tape cartridges
2. Start the Windows XP Setup program. Insert the Windows XP distribution CD into your CD-ROM drive and reboot the computer.

3. Press any key to answer the `Press any key to boot from the CD...` prompt.

4. The Windows XP Setup program will start. When you see the `Press F2 to run Automated System Recovery (ASR)` prompt, press the <F2> key to start the ASR restore process.

5. Insert an ASR floppy disk when prompted.

6. Windows XP Setup will display the following message:

   ```
   Preparing to ASR, press <ESC> to cancel
   ```

   Notice that at this stage you still have a chance to cancel the ASR by pressing the <ESC> key when prompted. This is important, since if you decide to continue, your *%Systemdrive%* partition will be formatted as a next step.

7. If you don't react to the message prompting you to cancel the ASR restore process, Windows XP Setup will display a series of messages:

   ```
   Setup is starting the ASR...
   Setup is loading files
   Setup is starting Windows
   ```

   After that, the ASR process will reformat your *%Systemdrive%* partition and check other partitions that it may determine as requiring repair.

NOTE

Besides formatting the *%Systemdrive%* partition, ASR might also initialize volumes that it determines require repair. As I already mentioned, it restores only operating system files. Therefore, there is a risk to user files stored on these volumes, too.

8. When formatting and disk checks are completed, ASR will build a list of files to be copied and prompt you to insert your ASR backup media (typically one or more removable media such as data tape cartridges). If you performed the ASR backup to a file, you will not be prompted to insert the media.

NOTE

You must use locally attached devices, because restoring from network shares is not an ASR option. Examples of locally attached devices include tape backup drives, removable disks, or other hard disks. Concerning other hard disks, bear in mind that ASR supports FAT16 volumes up to 2.1 GB (32K maximum cluster size) and does not support 4 GB FAT16 partitions (64K maximum cluster size). If you start the ASR using a 4 GB FAT16 partition, the process will stop at this point. If this is the case, first convert that partition from FAT16 to NTFS before using ASR.

ASR is different from the System Restore feature discussed earlier in this chapter. ASR is a recovery tool that backs up all operating system files on the system partition, and is used to bring a system back online if startup fails. System Restore saves only incremental changes, known as snapshots. Always try to use System Restore before resorting to ASR.

Backing up and Restoring the System State Data

Besides other extended capabilities, the built-in Backup utility supplied with Windows XP allows the user to complete the procedure of backing up the whole set of system configuration files, the so-called System State Data. As I already mentioned, the Windows NT/2000/XP registry is one of the most important system components, becoming necessary even at the early stages of the boot sequence. Because of this, the registry has to be included into this essential set of system files. However, there are some other files besides the registry that are included into the System State Data set. Let's take a look at these files.

The concept of System State Data was first introduced with Windows 2000. As you probably remember, in Windows NT 4.0 and earlier, Backup programs can selectively backup and restore operating system files as they do data files, allowing for incremental backup and restore operations of most operating system files. Windows 2000 and Windows XP, however, don't allow incremental backup and restoration of vitally important operating system files, which must be backed up and restored as a single entity. This is the first, and the most important thing that you should know about System State Data.

The second interesting thing relating to the System State Data is the fact that this set is slightly different for different operating systems. The System State Data set defined in Windows 2000 Professional includes the following files:

- The registry
- COM+ classes registration database
- Boot files, which are necessary to boot the system

The System State Data set for server platforms contains all the same components included in the System State Data set for Windows 2000/XP Professional, plus the following data:

- The Certificate Services database, if the server is a certificate server.

- The Active Directory database and the \SYSVOL directory, if the server is a domain controller.
- All information required to restore the cluster, if the server runs the cluster service. This information includes the registry checkpoints and quorum resource log, containing information on the cluster database.

The System State Data set in Windows XP Professional includes the following:

- Boot files, including the system files, and all files protected by Windows File Protection (WFP)
- The registry
- Performance counter configuration information
- The Component Services class registration database

Since the registry is included in the System State Data set, the procedures of backing up and restoring the system state data can be considered a method of backing up and restoring the system registry.

Backing up the System State Data

It's recommended that you perform the procedures of backing up the System State Data on a regular basis. The simplest method of performing this operation is using the Backup Wizard. There are two methods of starting the Backup Wizard: you can click the **Backup Wizard** button on the **Welcome** tab of the Backup program main window, or you can select the **Backup Wizard** command from the **Tools** menu. To backup the System State Data, set the **Only back up the System State data** option displayed in the second dialog (Fig. 2.16), then click **Next** and follow the instructions provided by the wizard.

The same procedure can also be done manually. To perform manual backup of the System State Data, start the Backup program, go to the **Backup** tab, and select the **System State** option (Fig. 2.17). When the user selects the **System State** option, the right pane of the **Backup** window will display the list of files to be included into the backup. As was previously mentioned, the System State Data set will be different for Windows 2000/XP Professional and Server. As I said earlier, the Backup utility doesn't allow the user to select options from this list to perform a selective backup—the checkboxes beside all the right pane options are grayed. Microsoft provides an explanation of this by declaring that all the components included in the System State Data set are interrelated.

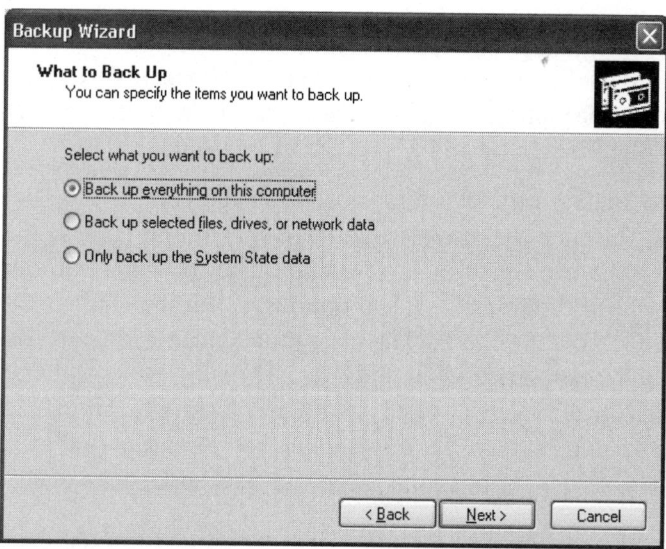

Fig. 2.16. To backup the System State Data, set the **Only back up the System State data** in the second dialog displayed by the **Backup Wizard**

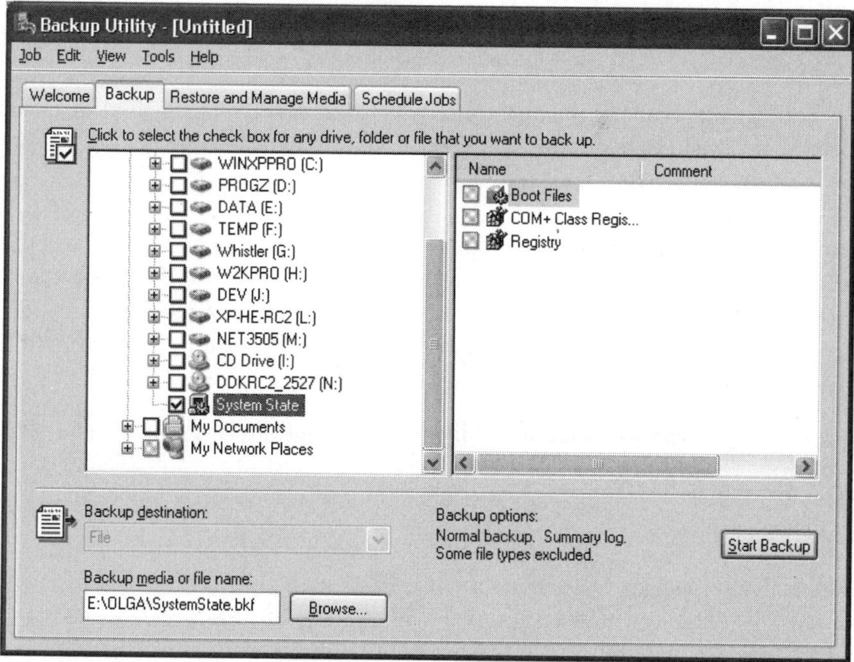

Fig. 2.17. Set the **System State** checkbox to include the System State data into the backup

If you need to perform a backup operation, and your computer is equipped with a tape backup device, select this device from the **Backup destination** list. Otherwise, select the **File** option from this list. If your computer isn't equipped with a tape device, the **File** option will always be set by default.

If you need to backup data to a file, specify the file path in the **Backup media or file name** field, or click the **Browse** button to specify the path to the backup file. If you perform the backup to tape, select the tape to which you need to backup your data. To specify additional backup options, select the **Options** command from the **Tools** menu. To start the backup procedure, click the **Start Backup** button. The **Backup Job Information** window (Fig. 2.18) will open. Although you cannot perform the selective backup of the System State Data, you are still able to specify the advanced backup options. To do so, click the **Advanced** button in the **Backup Job Information** window to open the **Advanced Backup Options** dialog (Fig. 2.19).

The advanced backup options along with their brief descriptions are listed below:

- **Back up migrated Remote Storage data.** If you set this option, the Backup utility will back up data that has been designated for Remote Storage.

NOTE

You can restore Remote Storage data only to an NTFS volume that is used with Windows 2000 and Windows XP. Also notice that Remote Storage is available only on Server-based computers.

- **Verify data after backup.** This option verifies that the backed up data is exactly the same as the original data. Notice that to ensure that you have a correct and usable backup copy, it is strongly recommended to set this checkbox, despite the fact that this can substantially increase the time required to complete the backup procedure.
- **Use hardware compression, if available.** This option is useful if you need to save more data on a tape. Hardware compression is only available for tape devices. Therefore, if it is grayed, you do not have a tape drive on your computer or your tape drive cannot compress data.
- **Automatically backup System Protected Files with the System State**. Although you cannot change which components of the System State are backed up, you can choose to include all system-protected files into the backup copy or exclude them from the backup operation. By default this option is enabled, but you can disable it by clearing this checkbox.

NOTE

The system-protected files only change if you install a service pack or application, or upgrade your operating system. Typically, system-protected files represent a very large portion of System State data—the default, including the protected files, is about 180 MB. Include these system-protected files only if new programs have been installed, otherwise a restore causes the new application to fail.

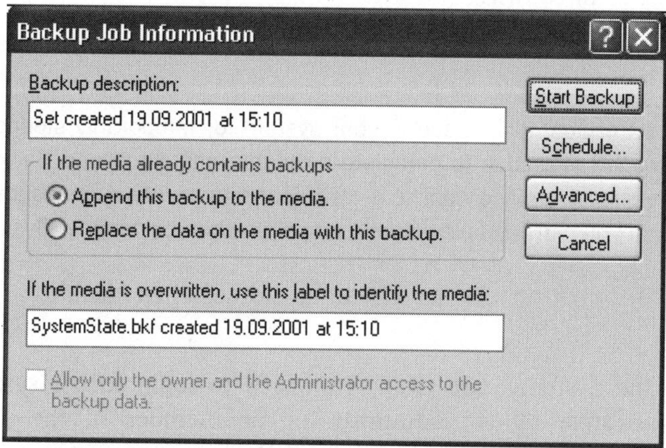

Fig. 2.18. The **Backup Job Information** window

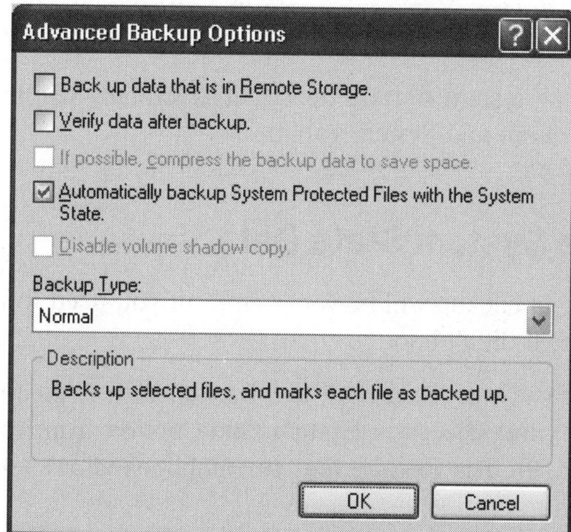

Fig. 2.19. The **Advanced Backup Options** window

- **Disable volume shadow copy.** Allows you to disable volume snapshot technology. As I mentioned earlier in this chapter, the volume snapshot technology introduced with Windows XP allows the Backup application to run together with other applications and services. By default, Windows XP uses free disk space on any NTFS volume to store the snapshot data until the backup is completed. The amount of disk space temporarily consumed depends on how much file data on the volume has changed during backup. Windows XP uses volume snapshot technology by default, but you can disable it, if you only want to back up a few files or directories.

NOTE

If there is not sufficient disk space in your system for temporarily storing the snapshot data, Windows XP is unable to complete a volume snapshot, and Backup skips open files. Thus you must provide sufficient disk space to create a snapshot of open files. Also notice that you can't disable volume snapshot when backing up System State Data.

The following information also needs to be noted when backing up the System State Data:

- To backup the System State Data, you need to login to the system as a user with administrative rights (Administrator or member of the Administrators group) or backup operator (member of the Backup operators user group).
- The Backup utility will allow you to perform the System State Data backup only for a local system. You can't perform System State Data backup for remote systems.
- To ensure that the system starts properly, it is strongly recommended that you also back up the Boot and System volumes.

Restoring the System State Data

The System State data backup will be very helpful if you need to reinstall the operating system because it didn't boot.

To restore the System State Data, call the Backup utility, go to the **Restore and Manage Media** tab, and select the **System State** option from the list of available media items (Fig. 2.20). The **Restore files to** combobox allows you to select one of the following options:

- **Original location**—the files will be restored to their original location.

- **Alternate location**—the files from the backup copy will be restored to a specified alternative folder. This option allows you to preserve the original folder structure.
- **Single folder**—the files from the backup copy will be restored to the specified alternative folder without preserving the original folder structure.

Click the **Start Restore** button, and the Backup utility will restore the System State Data using the options you've specified.

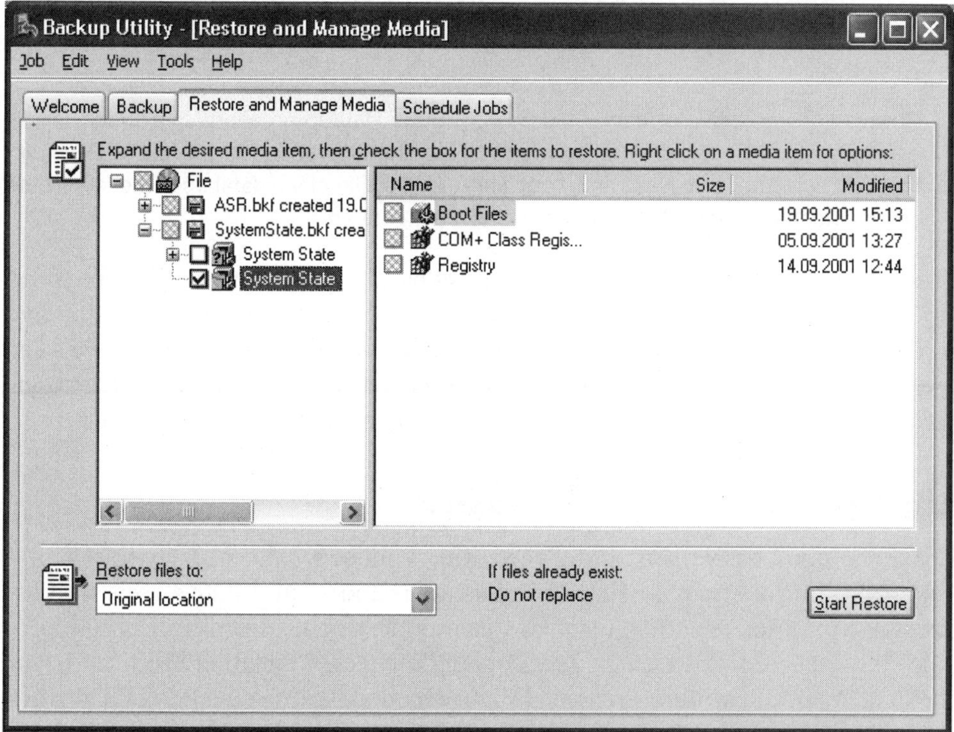

Fig. 2.20. The **Restore and Manage Media** tab of the **Backup** window

The Help system supplied with the Backup utility provides more detailed information on the System State Data, as well as step-by-step instructions on performing the backup and restore operations. All the limitations of the System State Data backup procedure are also applicable when performing the restore operation. These limitations are as follows:

- To perform this operation, you need to have administrator or backup operator permission for the local system

- Since all of the components of the System State Data set are interrelated, you can backup or restore this data only as a whole set
- You can restore the System State Data only in the local system

NOTE

If you don't specify an alternative folder when restoring the System State Data, the Backup utility will replace the current System State Data with the files restored from the backup copy. Note that because all the components included in the System State Data set are interdependent, the Backup utility only allows backing up and restoring this data as a whole set.

However, it's possible to restore the System State Data to an alternative folder. In this case, Backup will restore only the registry files, the files stored in the \SYSVOL directory, cluster database files, and boot files. Active Directory database, the certificate sever database, and COM+ information won't be restored.

The following fact is important from a registry backup point of view: when performing the System State Data backup, the system saves current copies of the registry files in the *%SystemRoot%*\Repair folder. If the registry hives become corrupt, you can use these copies to restore the system without performing the procedure of restoring the System State Data. However, only advanced users should use this method.

Using Recovery Console

The Recovery Console, first introduced with Windows 2000, is a console with a command-line interface, providing administrators and administrative users with the necessary tools for repairing a system that wouldn't boot. Recovery Console provides the capabilities of starting and stopping services, formatting disks, retrieving the data from and writing the data to local hard disks (including NTFS drives), repairing corrupt master boot records (MBR) and/or boot sectors, and performing other administrative tasks.

This tool is especially useful if you need to restore a damaged system by copying one or more system files from diskette or CD to the local hard drive; or reconfigure the offending service or driver preventing Windows 2000 or Windows XP from booting.

NOTE

The Recovery Console requires you to login to the selected operating system as the Administrator.

Methods of Starting Recovery Console

There are several methods of starting Recovery Console:

- Start Recovery Console from Windows XP Setup program
- As an alternative method, you can install Recovery Console on the local hard drive and include it as an option in the boot menu

Starting Recovery Console Using Windows XP Setup

As I already mentioned, you can start Recovery Console from the Windows 2000/XP Setup program. The easiest way of doing so is to boot your computer from Windows XP distribution CD (if your computer is equipped with a bootable CD-ROM device).

If you can't boot from the CD, but there is another operating system installed on your computer, you can use that operating system to start the Setup program. However, consider a situation where there is no other operating system on your computer that you could use to start Windows XP Setup (or the alternative operating system is also unbootable). In Windows 2000, you could start the Setup program using four setup diskettes. In Windows XP, unfortunately, there is no such option. However, to start the Setup program you can proceed as follows:

- Create a Windows 98/ME Emergency Boot Disk. In addition to the files automatically copied to this diskette when it is created, copy the Smartdrv.exe file to this diskette (this file is needed to make the Setup procedure to run faster).
- Reboot the system from this diskette and select the option of booting the system with CD-ROM support.
- Run SmartDrive from the command prompt, then start Winnt.exe program residing in the /I386 directory on the distribution CD. Windows XP Setup will then start.

In either case, you'll need to wait until the system completes initial file copying. After this is completed, Windows XP Setup prompts you to select one of the following options: you may install Windows XP, restore a damaged Windows XP installation, or exit Setup (Fig. 2.21). When this screen appears, press the <R> key.

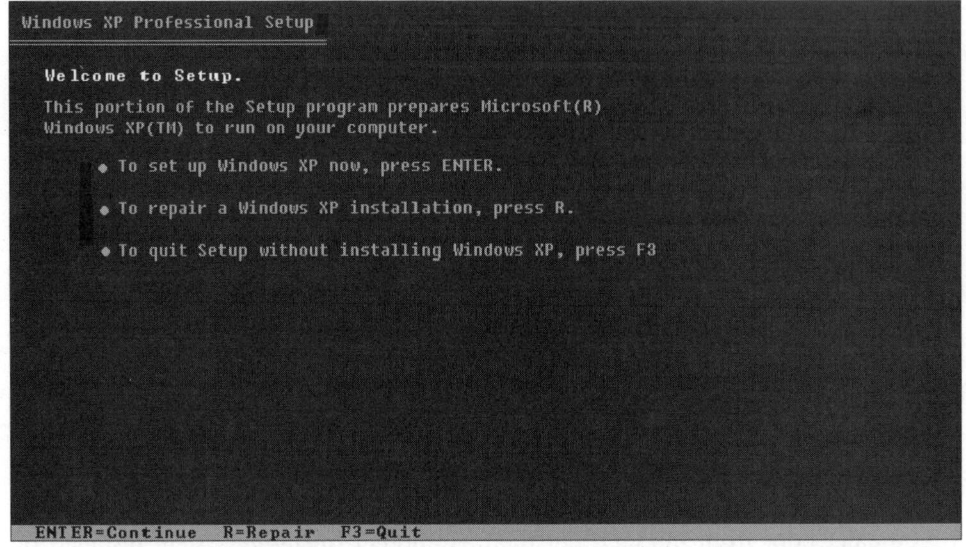

Fig. 2.21. The Welcome to Setup screen, prompting the user to select between installing Windows XP anew, repairing a damaged Windows 2000 installation, or exiting Setup

Setup will then search your hard drives for existing Windows XP installations and prompt you to select the one that needs to be restored. Recovery Console provides a powerful set of tools, including the following capabilities:

- Formatting partitions
- Starting and stopping services
- Reading and writing files
- Repairing damaged boot sectors and master boot records (MBR)

After you select the **Recovery Console** option, Setup will prompt you to select the Windows XP installation to be repaired (if you have installed multiple copies of Windows XP). Next, Setup will ask you to enter the Administrator's password for the Windows XP installation selected.

Including Recovery Console into the Boot Menu

If you need to include Recovery Console into the boot menu as an option, do the following:

1. Login to the local Windows 2000/XP system as the Administrator or a member of the Administrators group.

2. Insert the Windows 2000/XP distribution CD into the CD-ROM drive.
3. If you're prompted to upgrade your current operating system, click **No**.
4. Go to the Windows 2000/XP distribution CD, and from the command line execute the following command:

```
\i386\winnt32.exe /cmdcons
```

5. Follow the instructions that appear on the screen.

Deleting Recovery Console from the Boot Menu

If you need to delete Recovery Console from the boot menu, proceed as follows:

1. Go to the root directory of the system partition. Delete the \Cmdcons folder and Cmldr file.

NOTE

Both the \Cmdcons folder and Cmldr file have the Hidden and System attributes. This means that they're considered operating system protected files which, by default, aren't displayed by Windows Explorer. To delete these files using Windows Explorer or My Computer, configure the file and folder display options (**Folder Options** Control Panel applet) to display the operating system protected files. Step-by-step instructions related to this operation will be shown in *Chapter 4*.

2. Open the Boot.ini file for editing (notice that Windows XP allows you to do this from the System applet). Find the string corresponding to the Recovery Console option, and delete this command string. An example showing the syntax of this command is shown below:

```
C:\cmdcons\bootsect.dat="Microsoft Windows XP Recovery Console"
  /cmdcons
```

NOTE

If you are working with Windows 2000, the instructions provided above are also applicable, the only difference being that you'll need to clear the Read-Only attribute from the Boot.ini file, and then open the file for editing using any text editor (Notepad, for example). And don't forget to restore the Read-Only attribute after saving the Boot.ini file.

Using Recovery Console

The Recovery Console provides a full-screen command line interface similar to that existing in MS-DOS. You can easily get acquainted with the Recovery Console interface using the `help` command; this displays a complete list of all available Recovery Console commands. The Windows 2000 online help system also provides a list of Recovery Console commands (search using the keywords *Recovery Console*).

Backing up and Restoring Windows NT/2000/XP Registries Manually

If the boot partition of Windows NT/2000/XP is formatted using the FAT file system, you can easily backup the system registry manually by booting the computer under an alternative operating system (for example, MS-DOS or Windows 95/98) or even using the boot diskette. When this is done, you'll be able to copy registry hive files to the backup media using any method of copying (for example, you may use both Windows Explorer and the command line).

If the Windows NT 4.0/Windows 2000/Windows XP boot partition uses NTFS, you may have some difficulties using this method of backing up the registry (however, contrary to information provided by some sources, this isn't always the case). Sometimes you may need to format the Windows NT/2000 boot disk using NTFS (this may be required by the security rules adopted by your organization, or by certain software products which need to be installed on NTFS partitions). However, you may wish to continue using a manual method of backing up the registry. The simplest method of avoiding any possible problems is a parallel installation of Windows NT 4.0 or Windows 2000/XP. Microsoft officially recommends this method of improving system reliability. This tip can be found in both the Windows NT Resource Kit documentation and in Microsoft Knowledge Base articles. If you follow this recommendation, though, you'll need to consider the compatibility aspects of NTFS 4 and NTFS 5. You can also use shareware or freeware NTFS drivers, which can be downloaded from the Internet).

To backup Windows NT/2000/XP registry manually, copy the files contained in the *%SystemRoot%*\System32\Config folder to the backup media. Note that you need to use backup media of sufficient capacity since the contents of this folder probably won't fit on a 1.44 MB diskette.

The files that need to be copied from the *%SystemRoot%*\System32\Config folder are listed below:

Appevent.evt	Secevent.evt	Sysevent.evt
Default	Security	System
Default.log	Security.log	System.alt*
Default.sav	Software	System.log
Sam	Software.log	System.sav
Sam.log	Software.sav	Userdiff

*This file was eliminated in Windows XP. It is only present in earlier versions of Windows NT/2000.

Restoring the registry from a backup copy that was created using this method requires booting the computer under an alternative operating system. After rebooting, you simply need to copy the registry files from the backup media back to the *%SystemRoot%*\System32\Config folder.

Registry Export and Import

Registry editor (Regedit.exe), which will be discussed in detail in *Chapter 3*, allows you to export the whole registry or individual keys. You may export the registry to any device installed in the local system.

TIP

Export registry files to a folder specially created for this purpose. This folder may be located on the network drive and contain individual subfolders for each user. If you add this folder to the list of folders to be included in the regular backup procedure, both you and all the users will benefit from the improved reliability.

To export the registry, proceed as follows:

1. Start Regedit.exe and select **My Computer** (to export the whole registry) or any individual key (to export the key only).
2. Select the **Export Registry File** command from the **File** menu.
3. The **Export Registry File** dialog will open (Fig 2.22). Select the target folder and specify the file name for the file which will contain exported registry information.

The exported registry file has an ASCII text format. You may open this file for editing using any text editor.

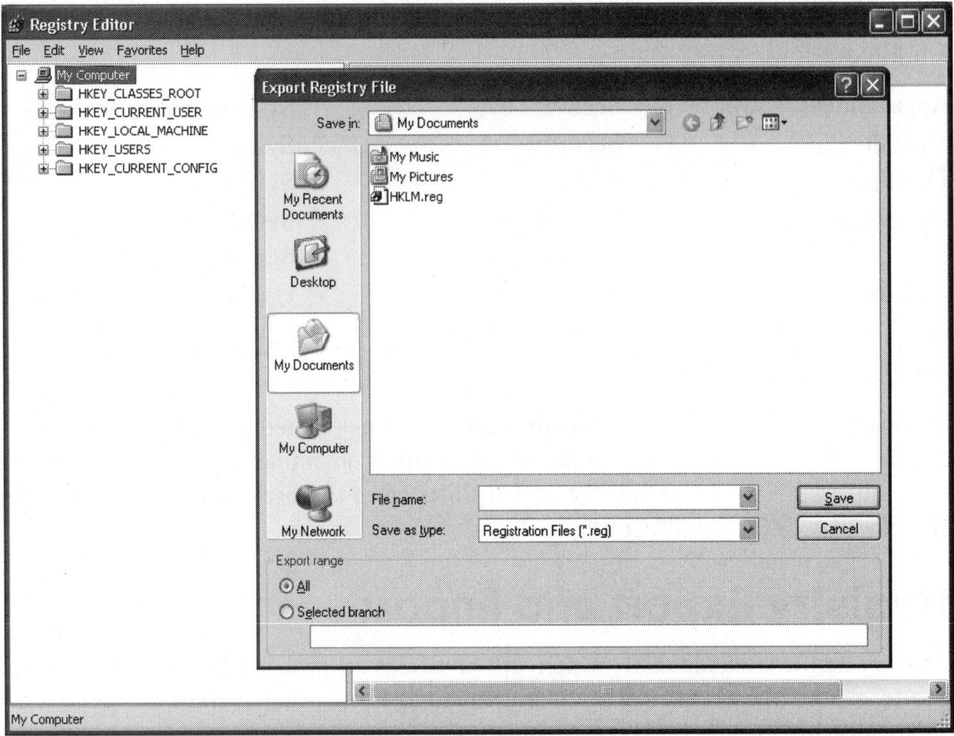

Fig. 2.22. The **Export Registry File** dialog. The whole process of exporting the registry file is very similar to the process of saving files

Exporting the whole registry or individual registry keys is the simplest method of backing up the registry before proceeding with any operations that can modify registry content. To discard an incorrect modification introduced into the registry, simply import the previously exported registry file.

To restore registry keys using Regedit, select the **Import Registry File** command from the **File** menu. The **Import Registry File** dialog will open (Fig. 2.23). You need to select the file to be imported.

NOTE

After getting acquainted with the registry, you'll be able to experiment with it or even solve problems by editing the exported registry file and importing it back to the system. However, before you proceed with editing the exported registry file, make a backup copy of this file to safeguard against possible errors.

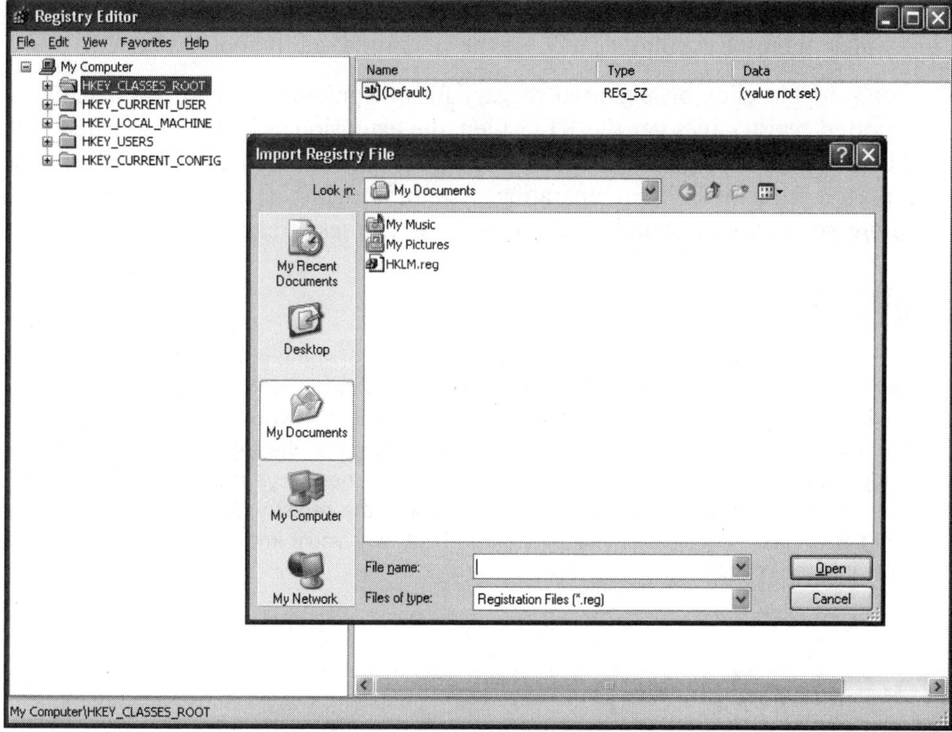

Fig. 2.23. Importing the registry file

Some tips concerning working with registry import and export functions are shown below.

- If you use the import/export function for backing up and restoring the registry, don't forget to copy the exported registry files to removable media or to the network drive.
- Before completing the export operation, make sure that the key range you're going to export is precisely the one that you need. If the **All** option is set, the operation will export the whole registry. If you set the **Selected branch** option, the export operation will export the key specified in the field below.
- Be very careful when working with exported registry files. Don't attempt to import incompatible registry files (for example, don't import registry files exported from Windows NT v. 4.0 or v. 3.51 into a Windows 2000 registry, and vice versa; never try to import Windows 95/98 registry files into a Windows NT registry). The import process will fail, but if it saves incorrect registry data before the error

occurs (which will probably happen), you'll have problems that can either manifest themselves immediately, or the next time you reboot the system.

- Don't double-click on exported registry files of unknown origin. By default, all exported registry files get the REG filename extension, which is associated with the REGEDIT program. If you double-click on an incompatible registry file exported from a different operating system, the import procedure will begin before you can understand what's happened. The result can be devastating.

NOTE

Be very careful with REG files! The Distribution disks of some applications include these files and use them when installing the application to set registry values needed by the applications. Don't neglect any precautionary measures! If you double-click on a REG file, Regedit.exe will read this file and insert its content into the registry. If the registry already contains the same keys, they'll be replaced by new keys retrieved from the REG file. Before entering the contents of these files into the registry, always open REG files using a text editor (Notepad, for example). That way you'll know what you're going to enter into the registry.

Registry Backup Using Resource Kit Utilities

Windows NT/2000/XP Resource Kit software products can simplify the process of administering and supporting Windows NT/2000/XP. Normally, any software product of this type includes a distribution CD and several volumes of supplementary documentation. Despite the fact that Microsoft doesn't officially support Resource Kit products and doesn't provide any warranties, Resource Kit utilities are valuable tools for the experienced system administrator. Furthermore, Microsoft warns customers that they should use these tools at their own risk. Resource Kit utilities aren't subject to localization; they were only tested with the U.S versions of Windows NT/2000/XP, and their usage with localized versions may lead to unpredictable results.

In spite of all the facts mentioned above, Resource Kit software is very popular among system administrators, support specialists, and programmers. Most Resource Kit utilities were developed for internal use, and they significantly extend existing Windows NT/2000/XP functionality. It's not surprising, then, that Resource Kits also contain registry tools.

CAUTION!

Resource Kit utilities intended for working with the system registry are command-line tools. Use these tools with caution. Note that registry editors, which at least have a graphical user interface, are much easier to use. When using the Resource Kit command-line utilities for modifying the registry, you need to have a proper understanding of the changes you're going to introduce into the local or remote registry.

The REG Utility from Windows 2000 Resource Kit

The REG utility included with the Windows 2000 Resource Kit allows you to add, modify, delete, and search registry keys and values, perform registry backup and restore, as well as other administrative operations. This command-line utility can also be used in the batch files. It can operate over both local and remote registries.

The REG utility implements the functionality of the following registry tools from the previous Resource Kit versions: Regchg.exe, Regdel.exe, Regdir.exe, Regread.exe, Regsec.exe, Restkey.exe, Rregchg.exe, and Savekey.exe. In Windows 2000, it replaces all of these utilities.

Reg.exe supports the following commands:

- `REG QUERY`

  Returns information on the keys and values contained within the specified registry key or hive.

- `REG ADD`

  Adds a new value into the specified key.

- `REG UPDATE`

  Modifies the current state of the registry element. If the registry doesn't contain a specified value, the command is ignored.

- `REG DELETE`

  Deletes a registry value, key, or several keys.

- `REG COPY`

  Copies a registry element into a new registry key on the local or remote computer.

- `REG SAVE` and `REG BACKUP`

  Saves the indicated registry values, keys, or hives to the specified file. This command is particularly useful for backing up the registry before introducing any changes. The `REG SAVE` and `REG BACKUP` commands are identical.

- `REG RESTORE`

  Restores the specified value, key, or hive from the file created using the `REG SAVE` or `REG BACKUP` commands.

- `REG LOAD`

  Temporarily loads the specified key or hive from the file created using `REG BACKUP` or `REG SAVE` into the root level of the registry. This command is useful for viewing information, editing registry data, or performing troubleshooting operations.

- `REG UNLOAD`

  Unloads the specified key or hive previously loaded using `REG LOAD`.

The `REG SAVE` and `REG BACKUP` commands support the following syntax:

```
REG SAVE RegistryPath FileName [\\Machine]
REG BACKUP RegistryPath FileName [\\Machine]
```

The *`RegistryPath`* argument specifies the registry path to the registry key or value in the following format: `[ROOTKEY\]Key`.

The `ROOTKEY` parameter specifies the registry root key containing the key to be backed up (the default value of this parameter is `HKEY_LOCAL_MACHINE`).

The root key may be specified using one of the following abbreviations listed below:

```
HKEY_LOCAL_MACHINE—HKLM
HKEY_CURRENT_USER—HKCU
HKEY_CLASSES_ROOT—HKCR
HKEY_CURRENT_CONFIGURATION—HKCC
```

`Key`—this parameter specifies the complete path to the registry key contained within the root key specified by the `ROOTKEY` parameter.

`FileName`—this parameter specifies the file name (without an extension), where the registry data will be saved. (On a local computer, this file will be stored in the

current directory. When working with remote systems, this file will be saved in the Windows installation directory.)

`Machine`—this parameter specifies the name of the remote computer (by default, the local system is used). Use a UNC notation when specifying computer names. For example: \\STATION1.

NOTE

Only `HKLM` and `HKU` keys are available when working with remote systems.

The `REG RESTORE` command supports the following syntax:

```
REG RESTORE FileName KeyName [\\Machine]
```

where:

`FileName`—the name of the file to be restored (without the filename extension). This parameter should specify a file previously created using `REG SAVE` or `REG BACKUP`.

`KeyName`—name of the registry key, in the following format: `[ROOTKEY\]Key`.

> *`Key`*—complete path to the registry key contained within the root key specified by the `ROOTKEY` parameter.

`Machine`—name of the remote system in UNC format (by default, the local computer will be used).

Summary

Any time you open the registry to modify it, a situation may occur where you won't be able to boot the system because of registry corruption. It is for just such a case that you should always have a usable backup copy of the registry. Always test the usability of the backup copies you create. The material provided in this chapter contains detailed instructions on backing up Windows 2000 and Windows XP registries. I also tried to provide tips on performing an emergency recovery of a damaged system.

Chapter 3

Using Registry Editor

> The user does have to take responsibility for the computer and what happens on it.
>
> *Lou Grinzo*
> *"Zen of Windows 95 Programming"*

If you call Microsoft for technical support and ask about editing the registry, they'll tell you that the end user shouldn't edit the registry. Microsoft documents are full of these notices, warning you that improper editing could make your system unbootable.

At the same time, registry tools are present in all Microsoft operating systems (what's more, they're installed by default). Why, then, does Microsoft provide these utilities to you? The answer is simple: these utilities are necessary because, in some cases, they're the only way to solve the problem. Try to imagine how the user community would react if the Windows operating systems didn't include these utilities. Of course, some users wouldn't even notice the lack of tools, but others... If you don't believe me, then you should read the following book by Lou Grinzo—"Zen of Windows 95 Programming". Besides an alternative point of view on the Windows registry, you'll find lots of other interesting facts and ideas presented in this book. The author also declares that he would be among those who would protest if Microsoft tried to force him to write the registry-editing applications himself. And you can be sure that he'd have many supporters of this point of view as well. All modern Windows operating systems, including Windows 95/98, Windows NT 4.0, Windows 2000, and Windows XP, contain special utilities for viewing and editing the registry called Registry Editors. Windows NT 4.0 and Windows 2000 actually contain two registry editors. Regedt32.exe is the traditional Windows NT registry editing program inherited from previous Windows NT versions. It allows you to edit the registry using methods that aren't supported in Windows 95/98. Regedit.exe is a newer application initially written for Windows 95. This application provides many of the capabilities of Regedt32.exe and has a Windows Explorer user interface (UI). The Windows 2000/XP version of Regedit.exe is similar to applications provided with Windows 95/98 and Windows NT 4.0.

As compared to Windows NT/2000, Windows XP provides an improvement also in this area. For the moment, all tasks related to registry administration and editing can be performed with a single utility—Regedit.exe, which now integrates its traditional strong points with the functionality that was earlier available only in Regedt32.exe. Besides, Regedit.exe now supports extended import and export capabilities. However, Regedit.exe lacks one of the most useful Regedt32.exe functions, namely, read-only mode.

All versions of registry editors supplied with all versions of the Windows operating system are automatically installed during the OS installation. However, neither of these registry tools are included in the **Start** menu, and Setup doesn't create desktop shortcuts for them. To start these programs, use the **Run** command from the **Start** menu. If you plan to use these utilitites on a regular basis, you may want to add them to the **Start** menu or create desktop shortcuts for them. (Of course, you'll need to consider various security aspects, particularly if someone you don't trust uses this computer.)

You can use registry editors for viewing, adding, deleting, and modifying registry elements. This chapter will probably seem boring to those of you with knowledge of earlier versions of Windows NT. However, you can hardly find any book on Windows NT in general, and Windows NT registry in particular, that goes without a chapter dedicated to this topic. Nor can you find any book on this topic that doesn't warn you that the Registry editor isn't a toy. Let's also note that neither of the registry editors can be considered a "program that simplifies your life" (despite the fact that Windows 2000/XP developers have actually made some steps in this direction). On the contrary, most users (especially beginners) can make their life much more complicated by creating lots of problems. Does this mean that I'm trying to scare beginners? No, since this entire chapter is intended especially for them.

Using Regedit

As I mentioned earlier, the Windows XP version version of the Regedit.exe utility is very much like the application included with Windows 95/98/ME and Windows NT/2000. However, the version included with Windows XP has many improvements and now integrates the functionality that earlier was available only in Regedt32.exe.

Like other utilities, this one is installed by default. However, the Setup program doesn't create a shortcut for this program and doesn't include it in the **Start** menu. The next section of this chapter contains a brief description of the Regedit.exe user interface, which can be used as a reference on all functions of this registry editor.

NOTE

Regedit.exe, especially the version supplied with Windows XP, is easy to use. The difficult task is making sure any registry modifications to the hardware configuration are correct. Because of this, I'd recommend that you don't make any registry modifications without first reading this chapter. It provides detailed instructions on registry editing, and also some useful tips. Incorrect modifications introduced into the registry can result in software failures or even make your system unbootable. I'd recommend that you make a backup copy of the system registry, using any of the techniques shown in *Chapter 2*, before you proceed any further. Specifically, prepare the Automated System Recovery (ASR) and make a backup copy of the System State data. The boot diskette created for Windows NT/2000/XP may also be helpful when eliminating possible problems.

Starting Regedit

By default, Regedit.exe is copied to the *%SystemRoot%* (for example, D:\WINNT) during installation of the operating system. To start Regedit.exe, find the file and double-click it or use the **Run** command from the **Start** menu.

Like most of the other viewing tools now available for Windows operating systems, Registry Editor has a user interface similar to that of Windows Explorer. Note that Regedit is simply a tool for registry visualization, and all the magic is hidden behind the scenes rather than in the UI.

In practice, the similarity between Regedit and Explorer goes somewhat further than simple analogy. For example, the same menu commands for keyboard shortcuts are used for creating new registry elements. Regedit.exe uses context (right-click) menus similar to Explorer. Despite interface improvements, however, Regedit.exe doesn't provide any warnings to the user, nor does it recognize errors. What's more, it doesn't have an **Undo** command, making most operations irreversible.

Examining the Regedit User Interface

This section can be used as a brief reference when working with Regedit. It provides a description of all the functions of the registry editor. The following sections contain instructions and tips on using Regedit, as well as directions on modifying the registry.

The Regedit window contains four main regions (Fig. 3.1):

- *The menu bar.* The menu bar contains the following menu items: **Registry**, **Edit**, **View**, **Favorites** (a new menu item introduced with Windows 2000), and **Help**.
- *Left pane.* The left pane displays the registry hierarchy organized in the keys and subkeys.
- *Right pane.* The right pane displays value entries contained within a selected registry key. Each value entry is identified by its name, displayed in the **Name** column; data type, displayed in the **Type** column (a small icon to the left of the name helps to identify the data type); and the value, which is displayed in the **Data** column.
- *Status bar.* The status bar indicates the path to the selected registry entry. It's helpful when you need to view the full path to the registry key containing the selected registry entry.

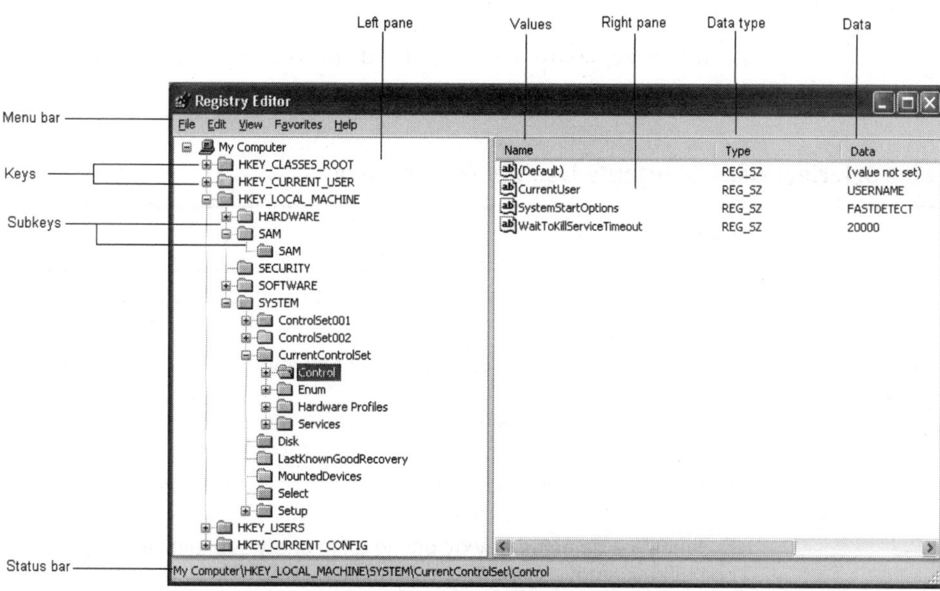

Fig. 3.1. Regedit window

When you start Regedit, the **Registry Editor** window displays only the top-level registry keys below the **My Computer** icon. These are the root keys described in *Chapter 1*.

If you click [+] to the left of the folder, this will expand the respective registry key displaying its subkey hierarchical structure. This operation expands the key tree to the next nesting level and resembles similar methods of opening folders in Explorer.

If the subkeys contain other nested keys, they'll also have the [+] sign to the left of the folder. The subkeys, in turn, can also be expanded to view the next level of registry hierarchy. This method of organizing the registry information is known as nesting. Any number of nesting levels is allowed. This hierarchical organization is the main difference between the registry and the initialization files. It provides a significant advantage over the methods of storing the initialization information used in Windows 3.*x*.

When you reach the lowest level of nesting, the [–] sign will appear to the left of the folder icon. This means that the key can't be expanded further, and you can only go up the hierarchical tree.

If neither the [+] nor [–] icons are present, this means that the key doesn't contain any subkeys.

Table 3.1 provides a list of keyboard shortcuts used for viewing and navigating the Registry using Regedit.

Table 3.1. Keyboard Shortcuts Used in Regedit.exe

Key	Description
<+>	Expands the selected registry key by one level to show its subkeys
<–>	Collapses the selected registry key by one level
<↑>	Moves you up to the next key
<↓>	Moves you down to the next key
<→>	Expands the selected key by one level to show subkeys; if there are no subkeys, moves you down to the next key
<←>	Collapses the selected key if it was open; otherwise, moves you up to the next key
<Tab>	Moves you to the next pane of the **Registry Editor** window

Registry value entries are displayed in the right pane of the **Registry Editor** window. Each value entry contains three parts: name, data type, and value data.

Like any parameter, each registry value entry has a name. Many value entries provided by Microsoft use a "Default" name (as you'll see later when you begin intense work with Regedit). All the names of the value entries are displayed in the **Name** column in the right pane of the **Registry Editor** window. These names are assigned to the value entries by the software and hardware developers.

Data types that describe the registry value entries are displayed in the **Type** column.

Definitions of all the registry data types defined and used in Windows NT/2000 are provided in *Chapter 1.*

For convenience sake, the Regedit.exe utility uses special icons displayed to the left of the value names. These icons allow the user to quickly distinguish between binary and text data. A brief description of the icons displayed in the Regedit window is provided in Table 3.2.

Table 3.2. Icons Used for Designating Registry Data Types in Regedit.exe

Data type	Description
	Designates binary data (including `REG_BINARY` and `REG_DWORD`)
	Designates text data and readable characters. For example: "On The Microsoft Network" (string data types, such as `REG_EXPAND_SZ`, `REG_MULTI_SZ`, and `REG_SZ`)

The **Data** column contains text or binary data that correspond to the value of the selected registry entry. You can edit, create, or delete this data to optimize software functionality or troubleshoot problems.

A brief description of the Regedit menu items is shown below.

The *File* Menu Commands

The **File** menu contains the following commands:

- **Import**
- **Export**
- **Load Hive**
- **Unload Hive**

- ❒ **Connect Network Registry**
- ❒ **Disconnect Network Registry**
- ❒ **Print**
- ❒ **Exit**

The **Import** command allows you to import previously exported registry files in ASCII or REG format.

The **Export** command exports either the whole registry, or only a part of it, as a REG file or an ASCII file.

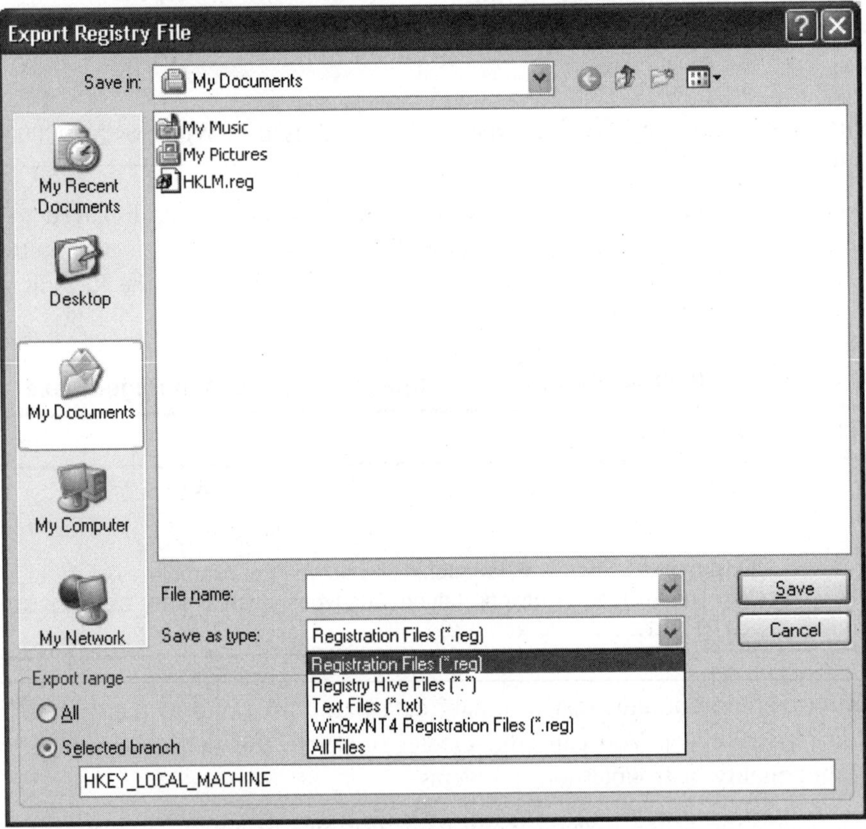

Fig. 3.2. The **Export** Registry **File** dialog

To export the registry branch, proceed as follows:

1. Select the registry branch you wish to export, then select the **Export** command from the **File** menu.
2. The **Export Registry File** window (Fig. 3.2) will open. Enter the file name into the **File name** field. By default, this file will get the REG filename extension.

If you need to save the exported file in another format, select the option you need from the **Save as type** list below the **File name** field. Despite all the apparent similarity of the Regedit versions supplied with Windows 9*x*, Windows NT 4.0/Windows 2000, and Windows XP, these are different versions of the same application. The Regedit version included with Windows XP allows you to save exported registry files in various formats, including both the Windows 2000/XP format (use the **Registration files (*.reg)** option for this purpose), and the registry file format used by Windows 9*x*/NT 4. (Use the **Win9x/NT 4 Registration files (*.reg)** option for this purpose). Furthermore, now you can save the exported registry file as a hive (select the **Registry Hive Files** option) and in text format (use the **Text Files (*.txt)** option)

3. If you need to export only the branch that you have previously selected, set the **Selected branch** radio button in the **Export** range option group. However, if you frequently modify the system registry, exporting the whole registry would be better. Exported registry files will provide you with additional options if you need to troubleshoot a damaged system.
4. Click the **Save** button.

You can view the saved file using any text editor to make sure that everything was saved correctly. Exported registry files contain unformatted ASCII text.

Be very careful when working with exported registry files, especially when you export registry files for experimental purposes. For example, experienced administrators can solve problems by editing the exported registry file, and then importing this file back into the system. However, before you start introducing changes, take all the necessary precautions:

1. Create a backup copy of the exported registry file that you need to edit. If you make an error during the editing session, you can correct the problem by importing the backup copy of the REG file.
2. If you're going to experiment with the various operating systems' registries (including Windows 95/98/ME, Windows NT 4.0/Windows 2000, and Windows XP), store the exported registry files for each operating system in folders dedicated specifically to this. This will help you avoid problems caused by importing incompatible registry files.
3. By default, REG files are associated with the Regedit application (Fig. 3.3). The Regedit application merges these files into the registry (**Merge** is the operation performed by default). In Windows XP, when you double-click such

files, Regedit.exe will start and prompt you to confirm if you really want to add the contents of an exported file into the registry (Fig. 3.4). Be very careful at this step, to avoid accidentally importing incompatible or incorrect registry settings.

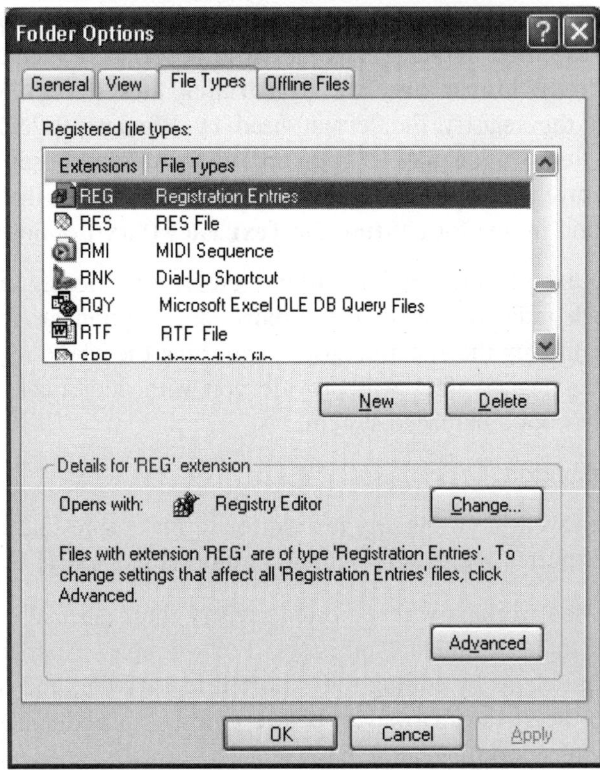

Fig. 3.3. By default, REG files are associated with the Regedit application

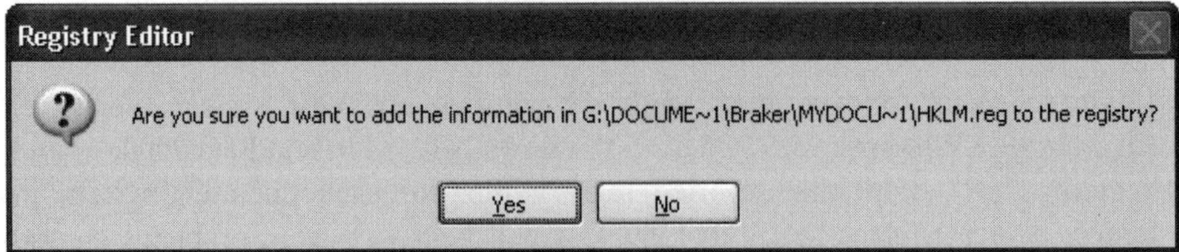

Fig. 3.4. Registry Editor prompts you to confirm if you really want to add the contents of the exported REG file into the registry

The **Load Hive** and **Unload Hive** commands are new to Regedit.exe. We saw above that they represent the same functionality that was provided by the similarly named command present in Regedt.32. These commands allow you to load registry files previously exported from the registry and saved in the registry hive format, or unload registry hives, respectively. Note that these commands are only applicable to the `HKEY_USERS` and `HKEY_LOCAL_MACHINE` keys. Therefore, these commands will be available only if one of these registry keys is selected. In all other cases the commands will be grayed and unavailable. The hive that you have loaded into the registry becomes one of the subkeys under the root keys mentioned above.

To load a registry hive, proceed as follows:

1. Select the `HKEY_USERS` or `HKEY_LOCAL_MACHINE` registry key to activate the appropriate menu command.
2. Select the **Load Hive** command from the **File** menu. The **Load Hive** window will open, allowing you to select the previously exported registry hive. Select the required hive file and click **Open**.
3. Enter the name that will be used for newly loaded hive (Fig. 3.5). This name will be used for the new subkey that will appear in the registry after you load the hive (Fig. 3.6). Now you will be able to edit the loaded registry hive to provide the required modifications.

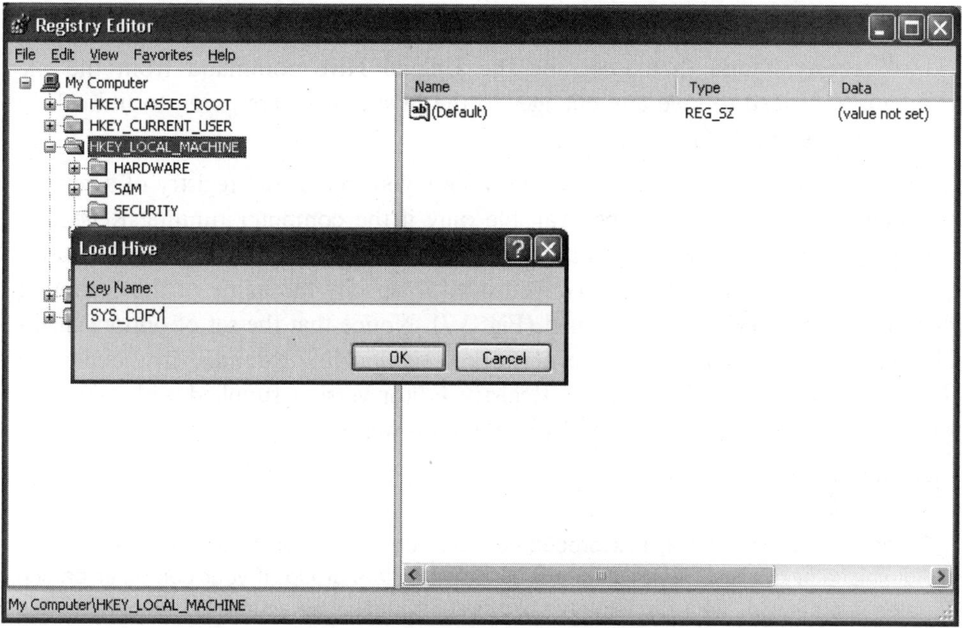

Fig. 3.5. Loading a registry hive

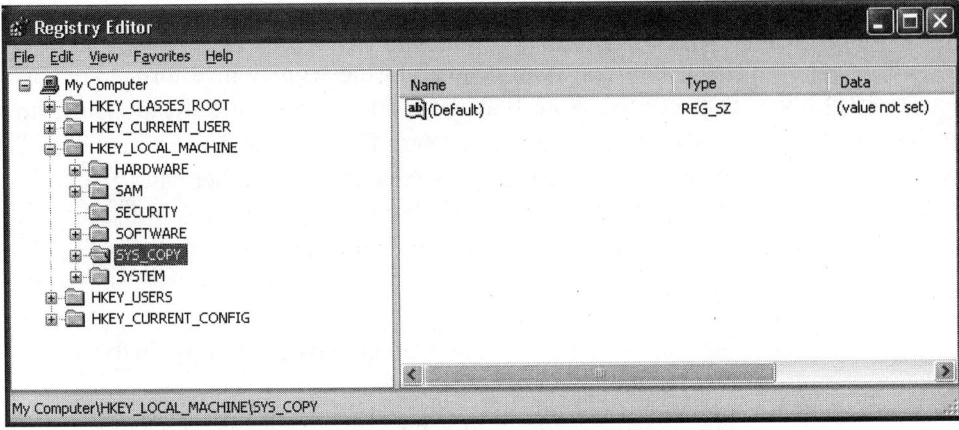

Fig. 3.6. The newly loaded copy of the `SYSTEM` hive now appears as a nested subkey under `HKEY_LOCAL_MACHINE` root key

NOTE

To be able to accomplish this procedure, you need to log on to the local system as Administrator or a user belonging to the Administrators group. If your computer participates in a network, network security policy will also influence your ability to perform this operation.

4. Having accomplished the editing of the loaded registry hive, you can unload it by selecting it and then choosing the **Unload Hive** command from the file menu. You need to save any changes to the hive that you're going to unload, in order to restore them later.

The **Connect Network Registry** command allows you to edit the registry of a remote computer. This command will be available only if the computer running Regedit is participating in a network that contains Windows NT/2000 or Novell NetWare servers. To connect to a remote registry, you need to specify the name of the computer where the remote registry is contained (Fig. 3.7). Notice that the set of options available for browsing and searching the network is significantly extended in comparison to the functionality provided by the Registry Editor version supplied with Windows NT/2000, where, actually, only the **Browse** option was available.

NOTE

To be able to accomplish this procedure, you need to log on to the local system as Administrator or a user belonging to the Administrators group. If your computer participates in a network, network security policy will also influence your ability to perform this operation.

To disconnect the remote registry, use the **Disconnect Network Registry** command. If you're not currently participating in a network, this command will be unavailable.

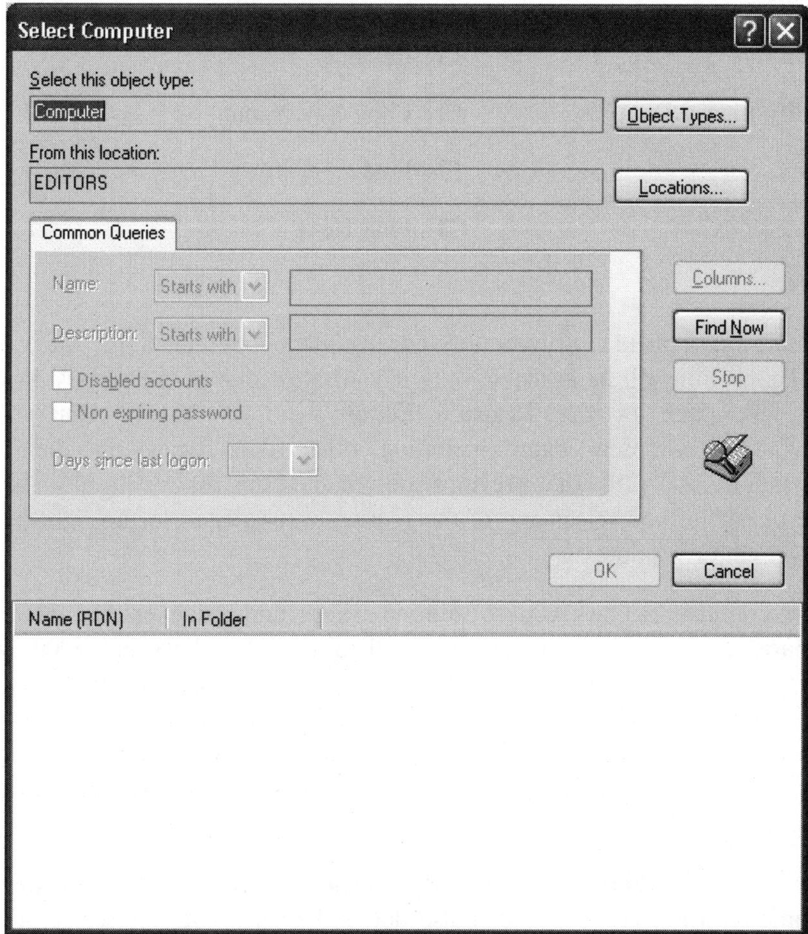

Fig. 3.7. The **Select Computer** window now provides extended browsing and searching functionality

You can use the **Print** command from the **File** menu to print the whole registry, or only a part it. The capability of printing a selected branch of the registry is a convenient alternative.

Use the **Exit** command to close the Regedit window and terminate the registry editing session.

The *Edit* Menu Commands

The **Edit** menu contains commands that allow you to find and modify registry entries:

- **Modify**
- **Modify Binary Data**
- **New**
- **Permissions**
- **Delete**
- **Rename**
- **Copy Key Name**
- **Find**
- **Find Next**

The **Modify** command is used for editing data contained in the registry entries. This option will be available only if you select one of the entries displayed in the right pane of the **Registry Editor** window. **Modify Binary Data** allows you to edit any data (including other data types) in the binary editor window. As with the previous command, this one will also become available only after you select one of the registry values listed in the right pane of the registry editor window.

The **New** command allows you to add new keys and value entries. Note that in comparison to the Regedit version supplied with Windows NT/2000, which allowed you to add only string data, binary data, and DWORD data, the Windows XP version of Regedit.exe provides an extended set of options. It allows you also to add multi-string and expandable string data (Fig. 3.8). These options become available after selecting the **New** option. The same options will be available in the right-click menu.

Other options of the **Edit** menu, such as **Rename** and **Delete,** allow you to delete and rename the value entry. You can also delete the value entry by selecting it and clicking the <Del> key. To rename the value entry, right-click it, select the **Rename** command, and enter the new name.

NOTE

Deletion of registry keys and value entries using the Regedit utility is irreversible. Regedit has no **Undo** command. Because of this, you should be very careful when deleting keys and value entries. Windows will display a warning message prompting you to confirm your intention to delete the registry entry. After you confirm it, it will be impossible to cancel the operation.

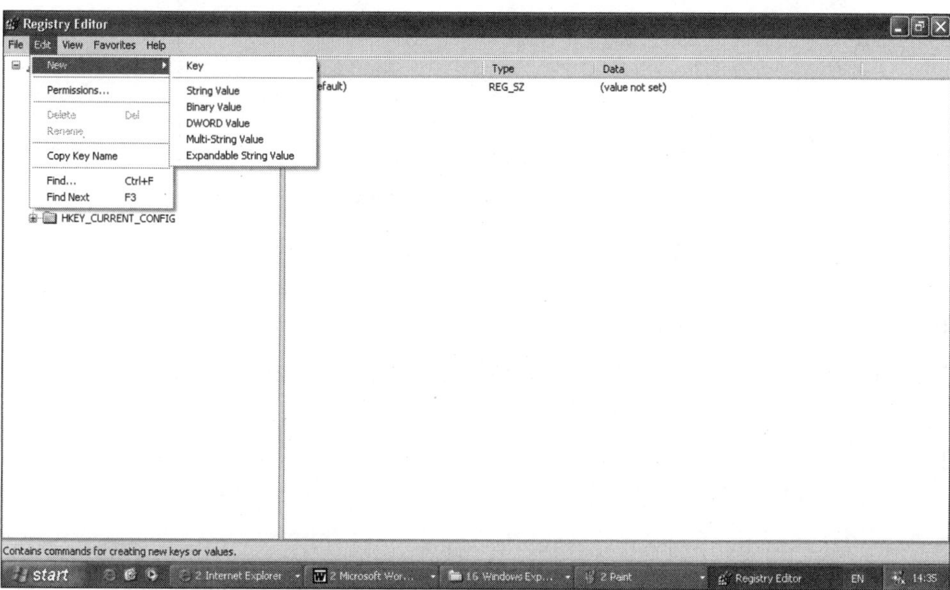

Fig. 3.8. The **New** command allows you to add new keys, string, binary, DWORD, multi-string, and expandable string values

The **Copy Key Name** command allows you to copy the selected key name to the clipboard. Later, you can paste the copied key name using the **Paste** command present in any text editor. If you remember, the registry is a hierarchical database, and the path to the registry entry you need may be very long and difficult to memorize. Because of this, many users appreciate this feature. The **Copy Key Name** command is easy to use in combination with other commands such as **Find** and **Find Next;** you may use it for various purposes, including registry editing and inserting key names into the text.

Commands such as **Find/Find Next** are used for searching registry keys and value entries. When you select the **Find** command from the **Edit** menu, the **Find** dialog opens, where you can describe the key, value entry, or its data (Fig. 3.9). You can search for keys, value entries or data in any combination. The values to search for can be both text and numeric.

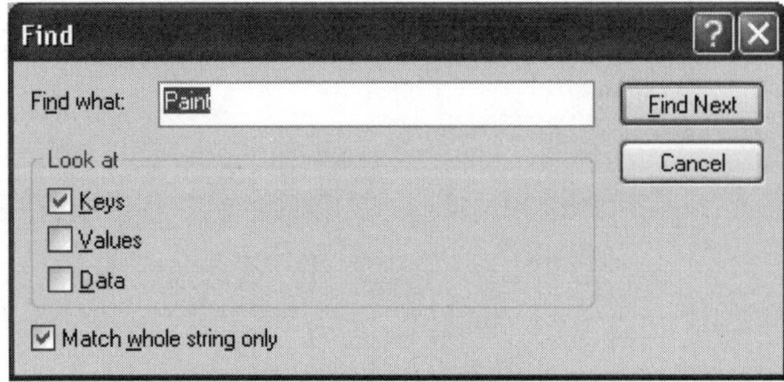

Fig. 3.9. The **Find** dialog

To find the registry entry you need, enter the value to be searched into the **Find what** field. You can also restrict the search range by selecting one of the following options listed in the **Look at** group:

- **Keys**. The function will only search for registry keys. Both root and nested keys will be found.
- **Values**. The function will only search for value names that are displayed in the right pane of the **Registry Editor** window (in the **Name** column).
- **Data**. The function will only search for data.

The **Find** dialog contains the **Match whole string only** option. When this option is set, Registry Editor will only find whole strings, excluding partial hits from the search range.

For example, if you've installed a number of applications with names including the "Paint" string (for example, Microsoft Paint, PaintShop Pro, etc.), Regedit will find them all. However, if you only need to find entries related to Microsoft Paint, then use the **Match whole string only** option. If you need to find all the entries that contain the "Paint" string, clear the checkbox if it's set. This feature is useful if you don't remember the exact spelling of the string you're searching for, and need to find all possible variations.

Using the **Match whole string only** option increases the time required to perform the search. This can be significant if the registry is large.

To start the search procedure, fill in all the required fields in the **Find** dialog and click the **Find Next** button.

When Regedit finds the matching item, it will highlight it, thus helping to determine the key or subkey where the matching item resides. If Regedit finds the data or value names, it will open the associated registry keys in the left pane and highlight the value name. However, it still may be difficult to determine the registry path to the item just found. Because of this, you should use the status bar, since it displays the path to the highlighted registry entry, including all parent keys and the name of the computer (as you know, the computer name won't necessarily be the name of the local system).

You've finally found the registry entry. But is it the entry you really need? If it is, you may edit this item and finish the search procedure; otherwise, ignore the result and continue searching. To find the next match, press <F3> or select the **Find Next** command from the **Edit** menu.

NOTE

When searching the registry, remember that the names of the keys and value entries may not be unique. The same name may be encountered many times. Because of this, the more information you provide for the search function, the more correct your result will be. For example, the "inbox" string is encountered about 10 times.

Finally, the **Permissions** command allowing you to manage registry key permissions and audit the actions related to the registry keys deserves special mention. Once again, it is necessary to emphasize the fact that in Windows NT/2000 this functionality was available only in Regedt32.exe, where there was the **Security** menu command. In Windows XP, this functionality was integrated into a single version of the registry editor—the Regedit.exe utility. Registry key permissions can be assigned independently from the file system type on the system partition.

Modifying Keys and Value Entries

Now, since we have provided a brief overview of the **Edit** menu commands, let us proceed with a more detailed discussion of their use for adding, modifying, or deleting registry keys and value entries, and setting registry key permissions.

Adding New Keys

To add a new key to any registry hive, select the **New | Key** commands from the **Edit** menu. The procedure is straightforward and very similar to that of creating new folders in Windows Explorer. The new key will be created without prompting the user to provide a name, but you'll be able to rename the new key after it has been created.

Adding New Value Entries

To add new registry value entries, select the **New** command from the **Edit** menu, then select the appropriate command, depending on the data type of the value entry to be created. Using Windows XP version of Regedit.exe, you can create string value types (`REG_SZ`, `REG_MULTI_SZ`, and `REG_EXPAND_SZ`) and binary values (`REG_DWORD` or `REG_BINARY`). The new value entry will be created without prompting the user to provide a name, but you'll be able to rename and edit the value after it has been created.

Using the Binary Editor

When you select the binary value (`REG_BINARY` data type) and then select the **Modify** command from the **Edit** menu, Regedit.exe starts the **Edit Binary Value** window (Fig. 3.10). Notice that you can use the binary editor to edit a value of any type by selecting the **Modify Binary Data** command. Enter the data into the **Value data** field of the **Edit Binary Value** window.

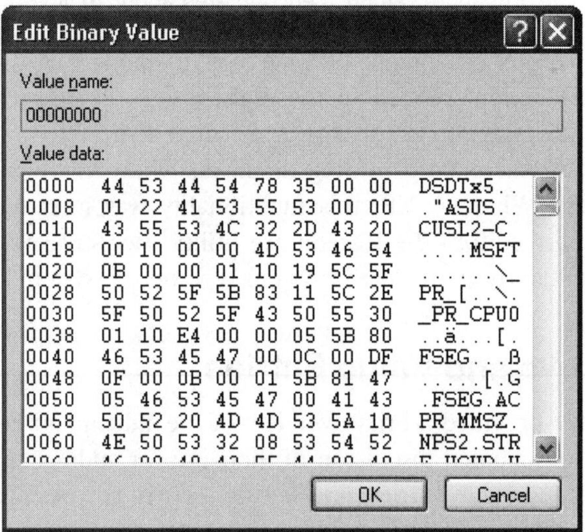

Fig. 3.10. The **Edit Binary Value** window

Editing String Values

Select the `REG_SZ` value in the right pane of the Registry Editor window, then select the **Modify** command from the **Edit** menu to start the String Editor. The **Edit String** window (Fig. 3.11) allows you to edit string values.

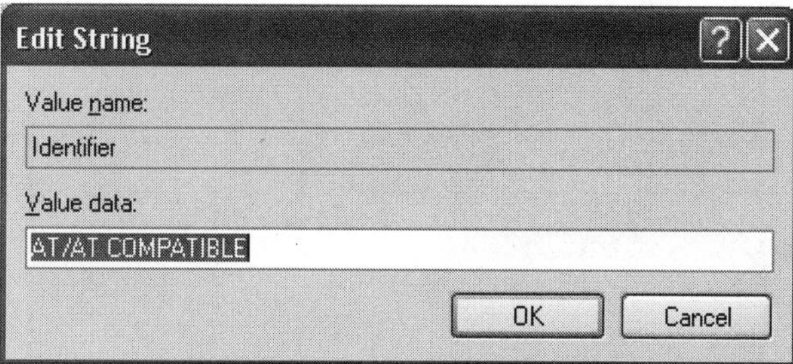

Fig. 3.11. The **Edit String** window

Editing DWORD Values

When you double-click a `REG_DWORD` registry value entry or highlight an entry of this type and select the **Modify** command from the **Edit** menu, the `DWORD` editor starts (Fig. 3.12). By default, all `REG_DWORD` data are displayed in hex format. However, you can also display data using decimal format by selecting the appropriate radio button from the **Base** group at the bottom of the window.

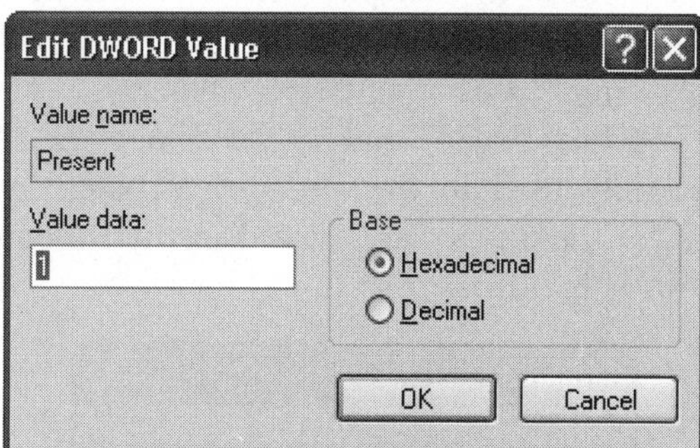

Fig. 3.12. The **Edit DWORD Value** window

Editing Multi-String Values

The **Edit Multi-String** window (Fig. 3.13) opens when you double-click the multi-string value or select a multi-string value and then choose the **Modify** command from the **Edit** menu. This window allows you to edit multi-string values.

Fig. 3.13. The **Edit Multi-String** window

Viewing Resource Lists

As was already mentioned in *Chapter 1*, the system registry stores all information on the hardware installed on the computer. The registry even has special data types for this purpose, namely, `REG_RESOURCE_LIST`, `REG_FULL_RESOURCE_DESCRIPTOR`, and `REG_RESOURCE_REQUIREMENTS_LIST`. These data types are only used in the `HKEY_LOCAL_MACHINE\HARDWARE` registry key. The value entries of these types are viewed in the **Resource Lists** (Fig. 3.14) and **Resources** windows (Fig 3.15).

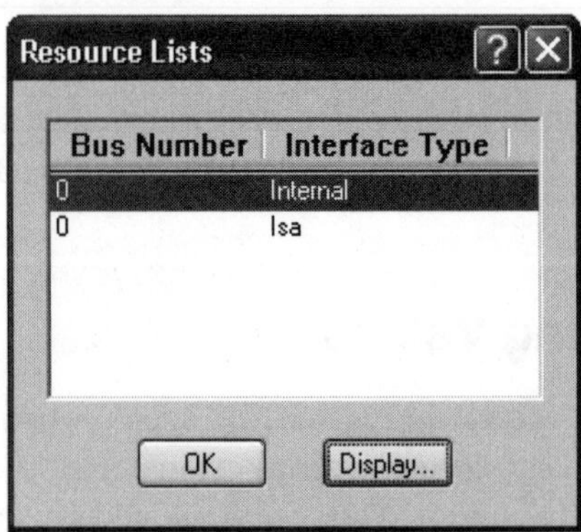

Fig. 3.14. The **Resource Lists** window

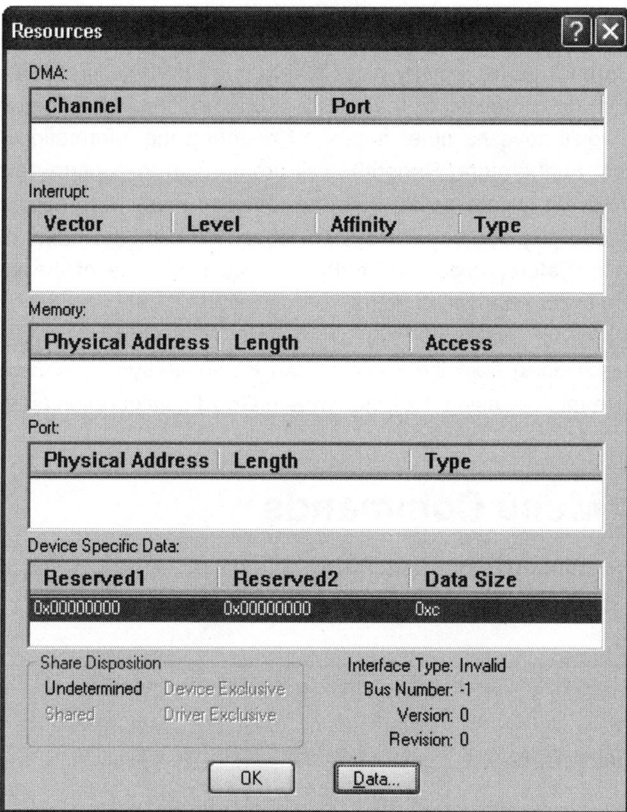

Fig. 3.15. The **Resources** window

Deleting Registry Keys and Value Entries

To delete a registry key or value entry, select the object you're going to delete and then select the **Delete** command from the **Edit** menu. The system will prompt you to confirm your intention to delete the selected key or value entry (Fig. 3.16).

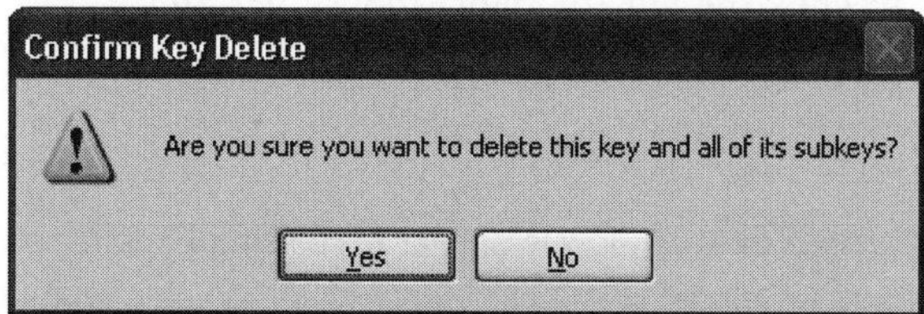

Fig. 3.16. The system prompts you to confirm your intention to delete a registry key or value entry

NOTE

Don't forget to backup the registry hives where you'll be deleting keys or value entries. Registry editors don't provide the capability of undoing this operation; after you confirm the deletion, you'll have no other means of restoring the information except by using backup copies. Furthermore, Regedt32 will prompt you to confirm deletion only if you set the **Confirm On Delete** option from the **Options** menu. As shown in Fig. 3.14, the warning message displayed by the system doesn't specify the name of the key you're going to delete. Before proceeding further, check the name of the selected key and make sure you know what you're doing.

If you delete something from the `HKEY_LOCAL_MACHINE\System\CurrentControlSet`, you can restore this key using the **Last Known Good** configuration (see *Chapter 6*).

The *View* Menu Commands

The **View** menu contains commands that allow you to select the method of displaying the registry. It contains the following commands:

- **Status Bar**
- **Split**
- **Display Binary Data**
- **Refresh**

The **Status Bar** command from the **View** menu allows the user to hide the status bar. The status bar is useful because it helps you navigate the registry. For this reason, I recommend that users (at least beginners) don't hide it.

The **Split** option moves the mouse cursor to the divider separating the left and right panes of the **Registry Editor** window. All you have to do is to move the mouse right or left to find a new position for the divider. After that, the only thing you need to do is to click the left (or right) mouse button.

TIP

Resizing the Registry Editor window is similar to resizing Explorer or My Computer windows. You just need to move the mouse cursor to the divider, wait until it changes to a double arrow, click the left mouse button and drag the divider left or right. When you're done, release the mouse button.

The **Display Binary Data** command from the **View** menu, which was introduced with Windows XP, becomes available only after you select one of the value entries listed in the right pane of the **Registry Editor** window. It allows you to view the selected data item using one of the three formats: **Byte**, **Word,** or **Dword**. Notice that it doesn't allow you to edit the data (if you need to, select the value entry and choose the **Modify Binary Data** from the **Edit** menu).

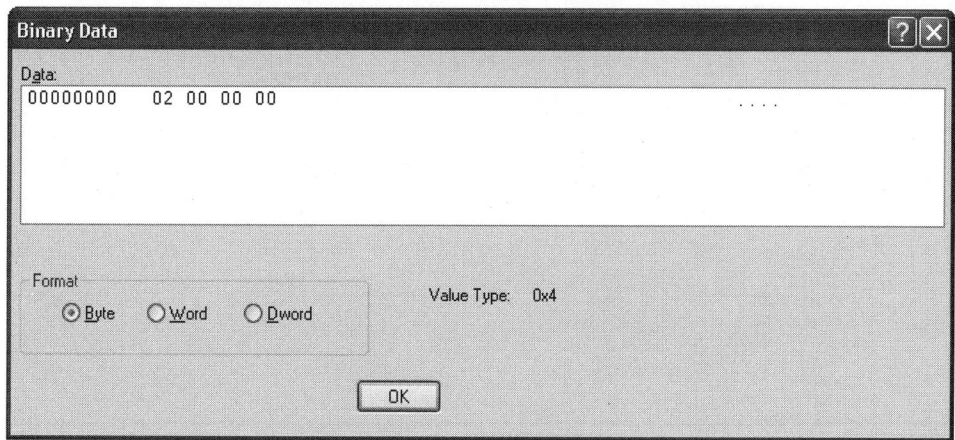

Fig. 3.17. The **Binary Data** window

Another option of the **View** menu is the **Refresh** command. Note that when you enter changes into the registry, not all of them will be immediately displayed in the **Registry Editor** window. To refresh the **Registry Editor** window, select the **Refresh** command or press <F5>.

NOTE

Normally, most configuration changes introduced into your Windows NT 4.0 system (including the changes to the system registry) come into force only after rebooting the system. Windows 2000 and Windows XP provide full-featured Plug and Play support. Windows 2000/XP requires fewer reboots than previous versions of Windows NT. However, there are certain modifications that can come into force only after rebooting the system.

The *Favorites* Menu

As was already mentioned, the version of Regedit included with Windows 2000/XP closely resembles a similar application supplied with Windows 95/98 and Windows NT 4.0. However, this version of the registry editor provides many new features. One of the most useful functions introduced in Windows 2000/XP is the **Favorites** menu, which is now present almost everywhere. The Regedit.exe utility is no exception (Fig. 3.18).

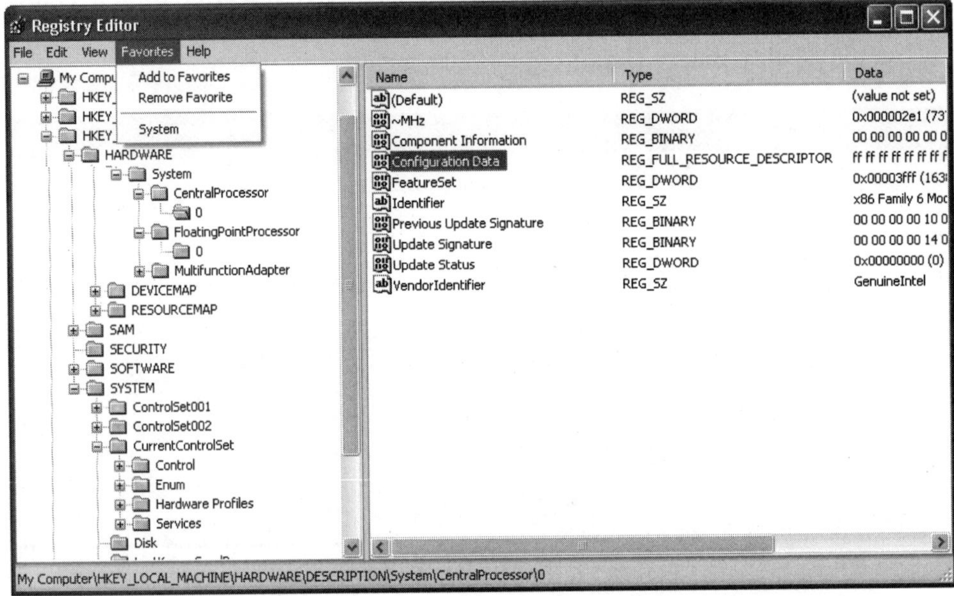

Fig. 3.18. The new version of Regedit utility contains a **Favorites** menu

Anyone who frequently searches and edits the registry will like this convenient feature. Using the **Favorites** menu, you can create a list of the registry keys you edit most frequently and thus avoid a time-consuming search procedure.

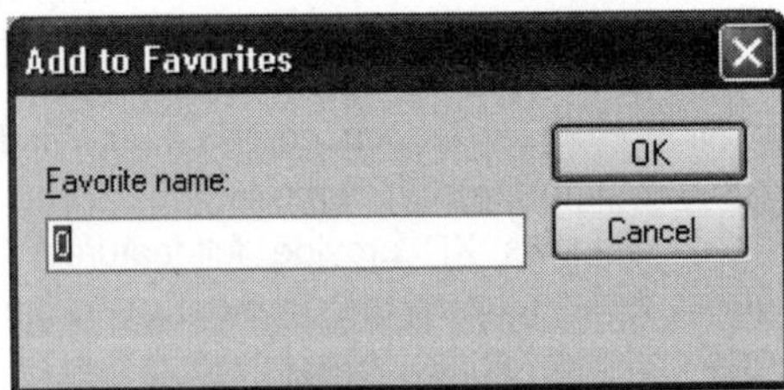

Fig. 3.19. The **Add to Favorites** dialog

To add a registry key to the **Favorites** list, proceed as follows:

1. Select the registry key you want to add to the **Favorites** list.
2. From the **Favorites** menu, select the **Add to Favorites** command.

3. The **Add to Favorites** window will open (Fig. 3.19). You can accept the key name proposed by default, or enter a new name into the **Favorite name** field. Click **OK** to add the key to the **Favorites** list.

Now you'll be able to navigate to this key by selecting its name from the **Favorites** list. If you need to delete the key from the **Favorites** list, select the **Remove Favorite** command from the **Favorites** menu. Select the key you need to delete from this list and click **OK**.

Managing Registry Security

To manage registry security, Windows XP Registry Editor provides the **Permissions** command. Using this command, you can edit registry key permissions and set the rules of auditing registry key access.

It should be noted that in Windows NT/2000 these capabilities were only available in Regedt32.exe. As you remember, Regedt32.exe had a special **Security** menu, which allowed you to specify registry key permissions and establish auditing rules. In Windows XP this functionality was delegated to Regedit.exe. Notice that registry key permissions can be set independently from the file system type on the disk partition containing Windows XP files.

This chapter provides only a brief overview of these functions and general instructions on performing operations needed to protect the registry.

More detailed information on these topics will be provided in *Chapter 9*, which is dedicated to registry protection.

As in previous Windows NT/2000 versions, Windows XP provides the following capabilities for protecting the system and managing security:

- All access to system resources can be controlled
- All operations that access system objects can be registered in the security log
- A password is required for accessing the system, and all access operations can be logged

Setting Registry Key Permissions

The **Permissions** command opens the **Permissions for the <*Keyname*>** window intended for viewing and setting registry key permissions. The capability of setting registry key permissions doesn't depend on the file system used to format the partition that contains Windows XP files.

NOTE

Changing registry key permissions can lead to serious consequences. For example, if you set the No Access permission for the key required for configuring network settings using the Control Panel applet, this applet won't work. Full Control permissions to the registry should be assigned to the members of the Administrators group and the operating system itself. This setting provides the system administrator with the capability of restoring the registry key after rebooting the system.

Since setting registry key permissions can lead to serious consequences, reserve this measure for the keys added in order to optimize software, or other types of customizing the system.

NOTE

If you change permissions for the registry key, I recommend that you also audit the key access (or at least audit the failed attempts of accessing this key). A brief overview of registry auditing will be provided later in this chapter.

The **Permissions** command follows the principles used by the Explorer commands to set file and folder permissions on NTFS partitions. To set registry key permissions, proceed as follows:

1. Before modifying registry key permissions, backup the registry keys you're going to modify.
2. Select the key for which you're going to set permissions, and then select the **Permissions** command.
3. The **Permissions for <*Keyname*>** window allowing you to specify registry key permissions (Fig. 3.20) will open. Windows XP provides lots of enhancements, including security enhancements. However, the main types of access permissions and basic principles of setting these permissions are similar to the ones found in previous versions of Windows NT/2000. Select the name of the user or group from the list at the top of this window, and then set the required access

level by selecting the option you need from the **Permissions for *<Username>*** list provided below. Brief descriptions of the available access types (**Read**, **Full Control**, and **Special Permissions**) are listed in Table 3.3. To set permissions for a selected registry key, proceed as follows:

- From the list at the top of this window, select the user or group for which you need to set registry key permissions. If the user or group needs the capability of reading, but not modifying, the key, set the **Allow** checkbox next to the **Read** option.
- If the user or group needs the capability of opening the selected registry key for editing ownership, set the **Allow** checkbox next to the **Full Control** option.
- To assign the user or group a special combination of permissions (special permissions), click the **Advanced** button.

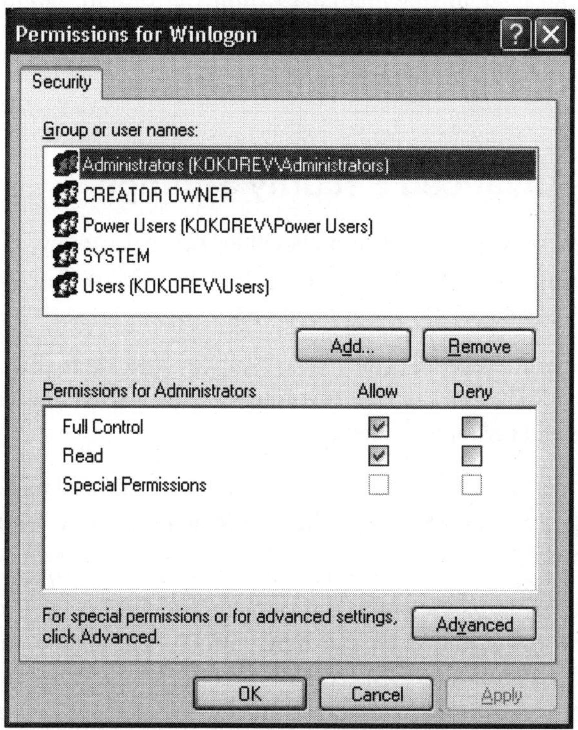

Fig. 3.20. The **Permissions for *<Keyname>*** window allows you to specify registry key permissions

Table 3.3. Registry Key Permission Types

Permission type	Description
Read	Users who have permission to access this key can view its contents, but can't save any changes
Full Control	Users who have permission to access this key can open the key to edit its contents, save the changes, and modify access levels for the key
Special Permissions	Users who have permission to access this key have individual combinations of access rights for the selected key. A detailed description of all these types and their combinations will be provided later in this chapter

4. Set the system audit for registry access (more detailed information on this topic will be provided later in this chapter). Audit the system carefully over a period of time to make sure that new access rights have no negative influence on the applications installed in your system.

Specifying Advanced Security Settings

To set special access types for a Windows 2000/XP registry key, click the **Advanced** button in the registry key permissions dialog (see Fig. 3.20). The **Advanced Security Settings for <*Keyname*>** window will open (Fig. 3.21).

If you're setting permissions for the registry subkey and want this subkey to inherit permissions from its parent key, set the **Inherit from parent the permission entries that apply to the child objects...** checkbox.

If you're setting permissions for the parent key and want all its subkeys to inherit permission to the selected key, set the **Replace permission entries on all child objects...** checkbox.

Double-click the name of the user or group for which you need to set special access (or select the name and click the **Edit** button). The dialog shown in Fig. 3.22 will appear. In the **Permissions** list, set **Allow** or **Deny** checkboxes next to the type of access that you need to allow or deny for the selected user or group. The list of special access options is provided in Table 3.4. Note that the list doesn't differ from the similar list in Windows NT 4.0 and Windows 2000.

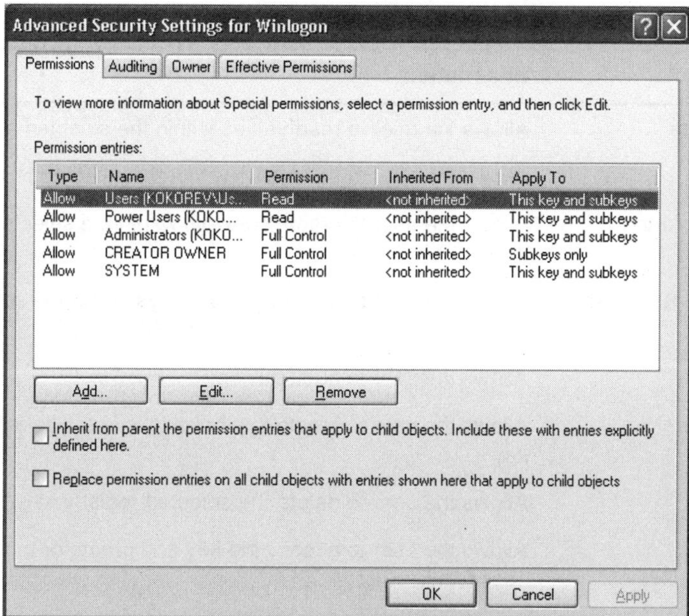

Fig. 3.21. The **Permissions** tab of the **Advanced Security Settings for *<Keyname>*** window

Fig. 3.22. The **Permission Entry** window

Table 3.4. The Special Access Options

Checkbox	Description
Query Value	Allows the user to read values within the selected registry key
Set Value	Allows the user to set values within the selected registry key
Create Subkey	Allows the user to create subkeys within the selected registry key
Enumerate Subkeys	Allows the user to identify the subkeys within the selected registry key
Notify	Allows the user to audit this key
Create Link	Allows the user to create symbolic links in the selected registry key
Delete	Allows the user to delete the selected registry key
Write DAC	Allows the user to access the key and create or modify its Access Control List (ACL)
Write Owner	Allows the user to take ownership of this registry key
Read Control	Allows the user to view the security parameters set for the selected registry key

Taking Registry Key Ownership

As a system administrator, you may take ownership for any registry key and restrict access to this key. Anyone who logged in to the local system as a member of the Administrators group may take ownership of any registry key. However, if you have owner rights without full control access type, you won't be able to return this key to its initial owner at a later time, and the appropriate message will appear in the security log.

To take ownership of the Windows XP registry key, proceed as follows:

1. Select the registry key for which you have to take ownership.
2. Select the **Permissions** command from the **Edit** menu.
3. Click the **Advanced** button. The **Advanced Security Settings for <*Keyname*>** window will open. Go to the **Owner** tab (Fig. 3.23).
4. Select the new owner from the **Change owner to** list and click **OK**.

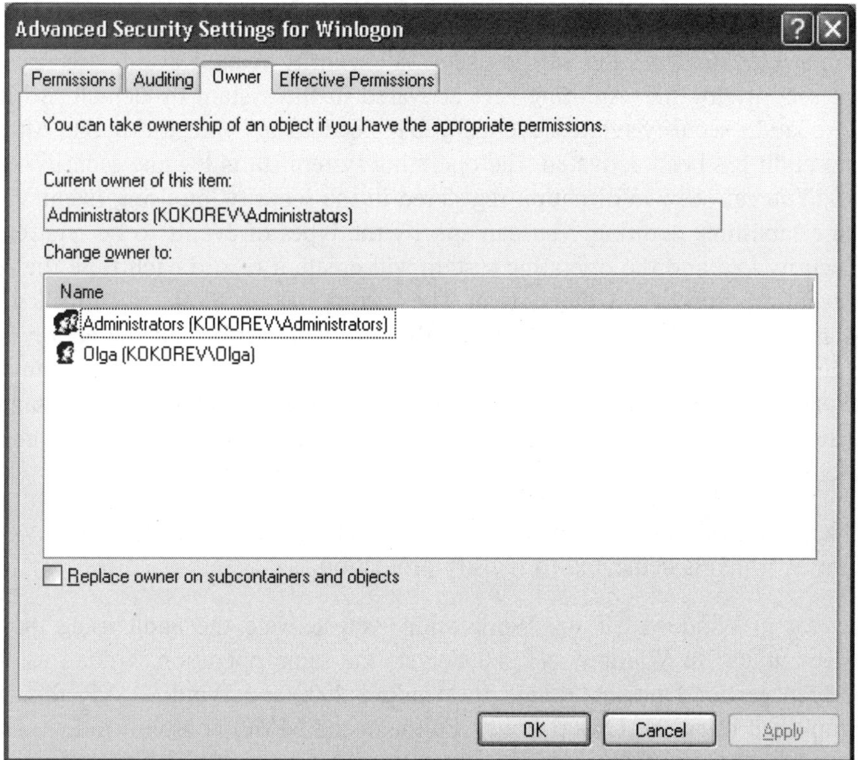

Fig. 3.23. The **Owner** tab of the **Advanced Security Settings for <*Keyname*>** window

NOTE

If you need to change the owner for all nested objects of this key as well, set the **Replace owner on subcontainers and objects** checkbox.

You can change the registry key owner only if you log in as an Administrator (or a member of the Administrators group) or if the previous owner has explicitly assigned you owner rights for this key.

Registry Auditing

Auditing is the process used by Windows NT/2000/XP for detecting and logging security-related events. For example, any attempt to create or delete system objects, or any attempt at accessing these objects are security-related events. Note that in object-oriented operating systems, anything is considered an object, including files, folders, and registry keys. All security-related events are registered in the security log file. Auditing isn't activated in the system by default. So if you need to audit security-related events, you'll need to activate the audit. After the system audit has been activated, the operating system starts logging security-related events. You can view information registered in the security log using Event Viewer. When establishing auditing, you can specify the types of events to be registered in the security log, and the operating system will create a record each time the specified event type occurs in the system. The record written to the security log contains an event description, the name of the user who performed the action corresponding to the event, and the event date/time information. You can audit successful and failed attempts, and the security log will display both the names of the users who performed successful attempts and the names of the users whose attempts failed.

Detailed information on this topic and tips on auditing registry access are provided in *Chapter 9*, which is dedicated to registry protection.

Note that in Windows NT 4.0 Workstation, you activate the audit using the User Manager utility. In Windows NT 4.0 Server, the same operation is done using the User Manager for Domains utility. In Windows 2000 and Windows XP, this task is accomplished using the Group Policy Editor in the MMC console window. Having activated the system audit, log in to the system several times as different users and administrators, and observe the various types of security-related events for a period of time.

To establish registry auditing, proceed as follows:

- Activate the audit and set the audit policy for each event that requires auditing
- Specify users and groups whose access to the specified registry keys should be audited
- Use the Event Viewer for viewing the audit results in the Security log

To perform any of the actions mentioned above, you need to log in to the local system as a member of the Administrators group. The audit policy is specified individually for each computer. Before you can set the registry auditing policy, you need to activate the audit in the system. Regedit.exe will display an error message (Fig. 3.24) if you attempt to set registry auditing without activating the audit in the system.

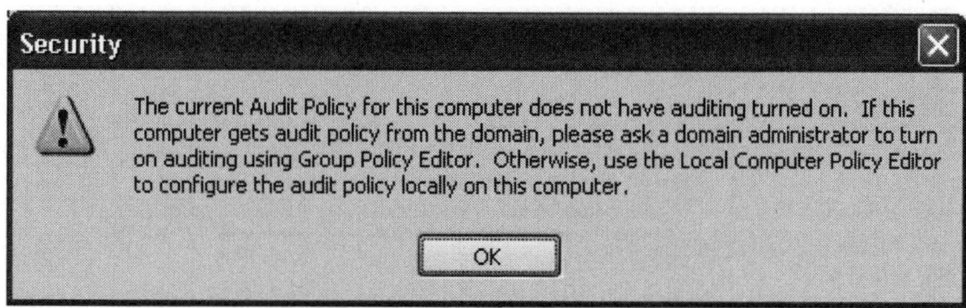

Security
The current Audit Policy for this computer does not have auditing turned on. If this computer gets audit policy from the domain, please ask a domain administrator to turn on auditing using Group Policy Editor. Otherwise, use the Local Computer Policy Editor to configure the audit policy locally on this computer.
OK

Fig. 3.24. Error message displayed if you attempt to set registry auditing without first activating the audit in the system

Activating System Auditing

To activate system auditing in Windows 2000 and Windows XP, proceed as follows:

1. From Control Panel, start the Administrative Tools applet and select **Local Security Policy**.
2. The MMC console window will open. Expand the console tree in the left pane and select the **Audit Policy** option (Fig. 3.25). The right pane of the window will display the list of event types that can be audited.
3. Double-click one of the list items in the right pane. A new window will open (Fig. 3.26) where you need to set the audit options. Notice that, similar to the previous versions of Windows NT/2000, Windows XP allows you to audit both successful and failed attempts. Set auditing options for the **Audit object access** event type.

Having activated the system audit, you now need to set the audit for the registry keys. I recommend that you audit the following registry keys:

- Registry keys accessed and modified by users and application programs
- Registry keys needed by the custom applications you have to test

Auditing the Registry

To set the auditing options for the Windows 2000/XP registry, proceed as follows:

1. Select the key that you need to audit.
2. Select the **Permissions** command from the **Edit** menu, and then click the **Advanced** button. The **Advanced Security Settings for <*Keyname*>** window will open. Go to the **Auditing** tab (Fig. 3.27).

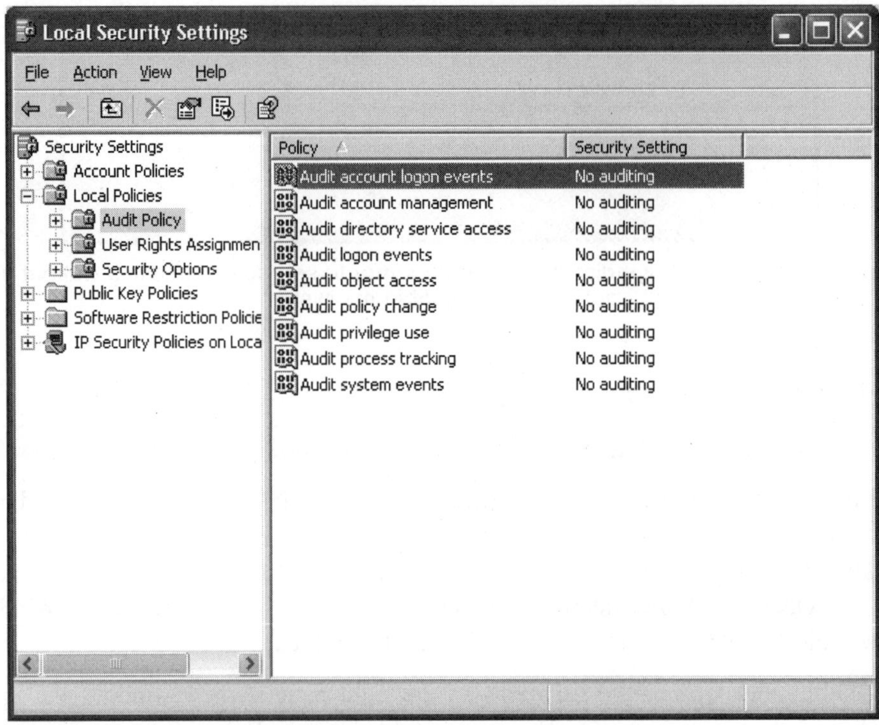

Fig. 3.25. System auditing in Windows 2000/XP is activated using the Local Security Policy MMC snap-in

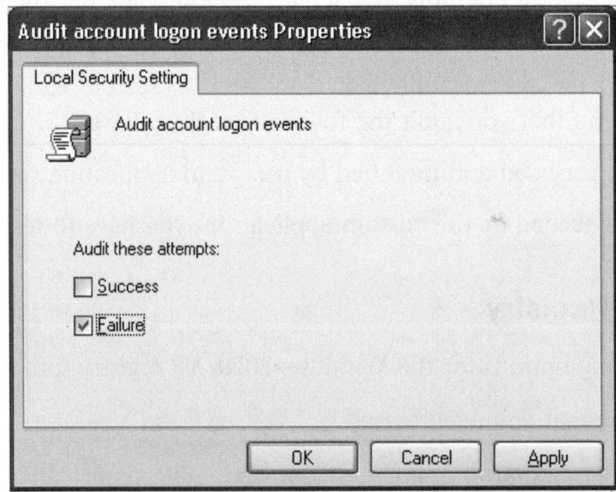

Fig. 3.26. Like Windows NT/2000, Windows XP allows you to audit both successful and failed attempts

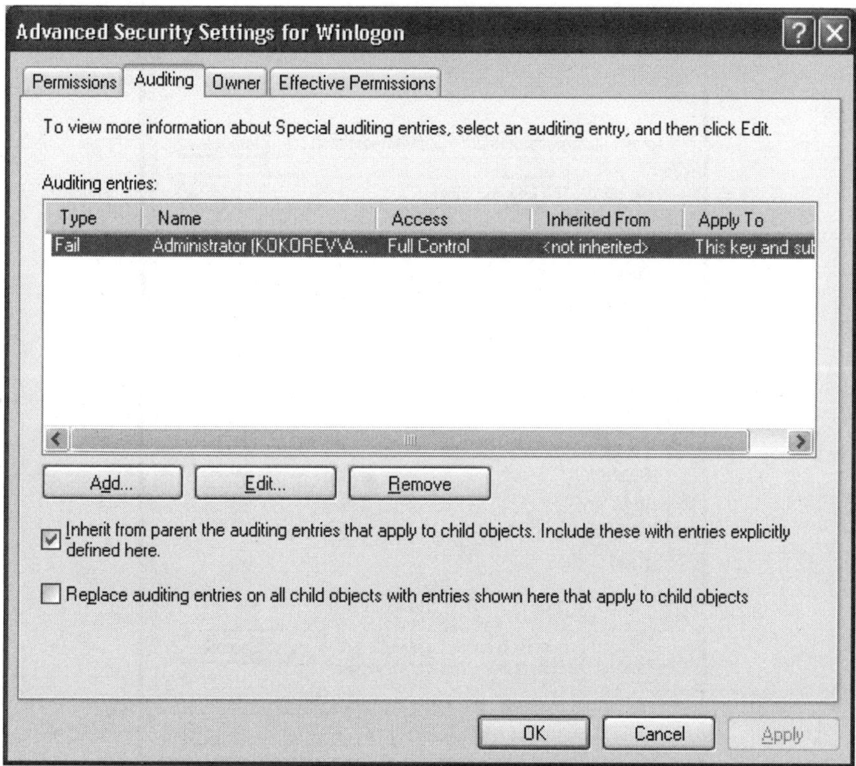

Fig. 3.27. The **Auditing** tab of the **Advanced Security Settings for *<Keyname>*** window

3. If you are setting the auditing options for this key for the first time, the **Auditing Entries** list will be blank. Click the **Add** button below this list, select the users and groups whose activity you need to audit, and add them to the list.

4. To audit the activity of a certain user or group, select the name of this user/group from the **Auditing Entries** list, and click the **Edit** button. The dialog shown in Fig. 3.28 will appear. In the **Access** list, set the **Successful** and/or **Failed** checkboxes for the access types that require auditing.

The auditing options available to you are described in Table 3.5. Note that the set of options hasn't changed from those in Windows NT/2000.

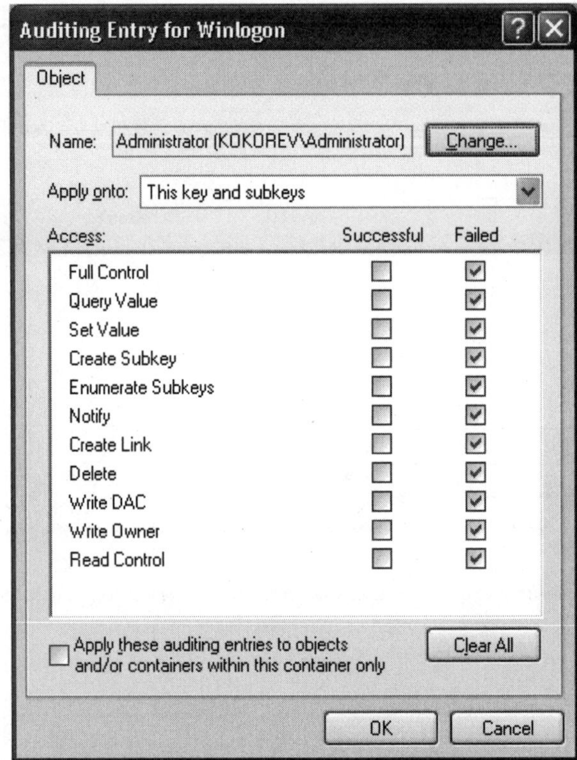

Fig. 3.28. The **Auditing Entry for *<Keyname>*** window

Table 3.5. Auditing Option Types for Registry Keys

Auditing option	Description
Query Value	Accessing the key with the right to query the value
Set Value	Opening the key with the right to set the value
Create Subkey	Opening the key with the right to create subkeys
Enumerate Subkeys	Opening the key with the right to enumerate its subkeys. This option controls events which open the keys and attempts to get a list of the subkeys contained within the key being opened
Notify	Accessing the key with the right to notify
Create Link	Opening the key with the right of creating symbolic links within this key

continues

Table 3.5 Continued

Auditing option	Description
Delete	Deleting the key
Write DAC	Attempts to modify the list of users who have access to this key
Read Control	Reading owner-related information on this key

NOTE

To set the registry key auditing, you need to log in to the local system as an Administrator or a member of the Administrators group. If the local computer is connected to the network, then network security policy may prevent you from auditing the registry keys.

To view the auditing results, select the **Programs | Administrative Tools | Computer Management** commands from the **Start** menu. Expand the console tree in the left pane of the MMC window by selecting the **System Tools | Event Viewer | Security Log** options. The right pane will display a list of security-related events. Viewing this list is similar to viewing the security log in Windows NT 4.0.

Options included in other menus, such as **Window** and **Help**, are standard for most Windows applications.

Summary

This chapter concentrates on the new Windows XP registry editor—Regedit.exe and its use in modifying, viewing, importing, exporting, and printing the registry. Basic knowledge of this material allows you to simplify the troubleshooting process. However, always remember that improper use of registry-editing tools can create situations when you introduce errors directly into the registry. Use these tools carefully and at your own risk. If you're going to introduce any changes, remember the initial values. This will save you time later on if you need to restore the damaged system.

Chapter 4

The Easiest Ways to Customize Windows

'Can the Ethiopian change his skin
or the Leopard his spots?'

R. Kipling
"How the Leopard Got His Spots"

Now and then, you'll hear people ask, "Can a Leopard change his spots?" This epigraph, taken from the story by Rudyard Kipling, describes how the Leopard and the Ethiopian once did that very thing. This is a fairy tale, of course, and all the events described there took place "In the beginning of years, when the world was so new". Many things didn't even have their proper names yet, so in order to point something out, you needed to put a finger on it.

Windows 95/98/ME and Windows NT/2000/XP are very new, especially when compared to our little story. Immediately after the final release of each of these operating systems, though, the whole user community began to discuss the problems of optimizing and customizing them. Some methods of customization are evident, but others aren't as obvious (this doesn't mean, of course, that these customizations are impossible). Both the Internet and many of the books on the market today now contain a large number of tips on customizing Windows by editing the registry. However, before doing any registry editing, try using the Control Panel applets and administrative tools first (in most cases, this approach is much safer and easier than registry editing). In any event, my goal is to point this out and even "put my finger on it".

As I mentioned earlier, most tasks related to configuring Windows NT/2000/XP can be done using Control Panel applets and administrative tools. However, some of these tasks can only be accomplished by directly editing the system registry. This chapter describes various methods of customizing, fine tuning, and troubleshooting Windows NT/2000/XP. At the same time, this chapter can't be considered a complete reference on Windows customization. Many other methods of modifying the registry will be discussed later in this book, in chapters dedicated to specific aspects of customization and troubleshooting the system.

Preparing to Edit the Registry

Even though this book is dedicated to registry editing, remember that an incorrect modification or accidental deletion of a registry element can result in making your system unbootable. Before you start editing the registry, take a close look at the following recommendations:

- Microsoft doesn't provide any official support for users who want to solve their problems by editing the registry. However, you can get additional information, and even some advice, by subscribing to Microsoft technical support services.
- Modify the registry only when you know that all the information related to the registry keys, values, and restrictions for devices and applications that you're going to troubleshoot is correct.
- Start editing the registry only when all attempts to set or modify a certain function using the Control Panel applets or administrative utilities have failed. Note that using the Device Manager is the best way to modify hardware settings, since this tool won't let you delete any of the required registry keys or make other critical mistakes. Registry editors don't safeguard you against mistakes like these.
- When you start the registry editors, remember that these tools are incapable of undoing or redoing your actions. Any changes that you make will be saved automatically (and almost immediately). If you make an error, the only method of quickly undoing your change is to import the previously created registry file before rebooting the system.

TIP

Never introduce a large number of changes at one time. Always try to introduce only one modification per registry editing session, and reboot the system when you're done. This will allow you to test the changes you've made. If you've made a lot of changes during a single registry editing session, and your system becomes unbootable, it will be hard to identify the modification that caused the problem. When you're sure that the modification to the registry is usable, you may proceed with any other changes. Don't forget to backup the registry on a regular basis. The frequency of the backup depends on the frequency of registry modifications (and on the tool used to edit the registry). Generally speaking, you should backup your registry at least once a week. If you edit the registry every day, create a backup copy at the end of the working day. I also recommend that you have the most recent files of the system policies, INF files, and system policy templates.

More detailed information on the Windows NT/2000/XP registry backup and recovery procedures is provided in *Chapter 2*.

Before going any further, read *Chapter 2* carefully and make sure that you haven't skipped anything.

TIP

Before you edit the registry to make any of the changes described in this chapter, read the appropriate section carefully. You'll have to make the decision as to whether or not you (or the user whose computer you're going to configure) really need this customization, and if so, just how much you need it. The customizations described in this chapter change the default settings of the operating system. Note that these default settings are satisfactory for most users. Before going any further, export the registry keys that you're going to modify. This will allow you restore the keys if you make an accidental change, or if you don't like the effect of the modifications.

Customizing the Boot Sequence

Most Windows operating systems automatically configure the default boot sequence. However, there are many users who may need to modify this. For example, if you have a multi-boot system, you may need to change the default operating system. Sometimes you may need to increase the default interval when the boot menu is displayed, add custom logo files, and so forth. We'll discuss all the methods of customizing the boot sequence. These methods aren't complicated, and any system administrator, support specialist, or advanced user should know them.

A detailed description of all the processes that take place when Windows NT/2000/XP is booting is provided in *Chapter 6*; you'll also find the role of the system registry in the boot process there.

To customize the boot sequence of Windows NT/2000/XP, you only need to edit a single INI file: Boot.ini. This file resides in the root directory of the system partition. This file is required for Windows NT/2000/XP to boot; because of this, it has the Hidden, System, and Read-only attributes set.

NOTE

Starting with Windows 2000, the developers included some protective measures that were meant to protect beginners from themselves. One of these new devices is known as "super-hidden" files. By default, Windows Explorer doesn't display files that have both Hidden and System attributes. These files are considered protected operating system files, and shouldn't be modified or even seen by ordinary users. The default list of these files includes all the files required for starting the operating system, including the Boot.ini file.

However, you can always use a command line. To view all the files independently from their attributes, use the following command: `dir /a`.

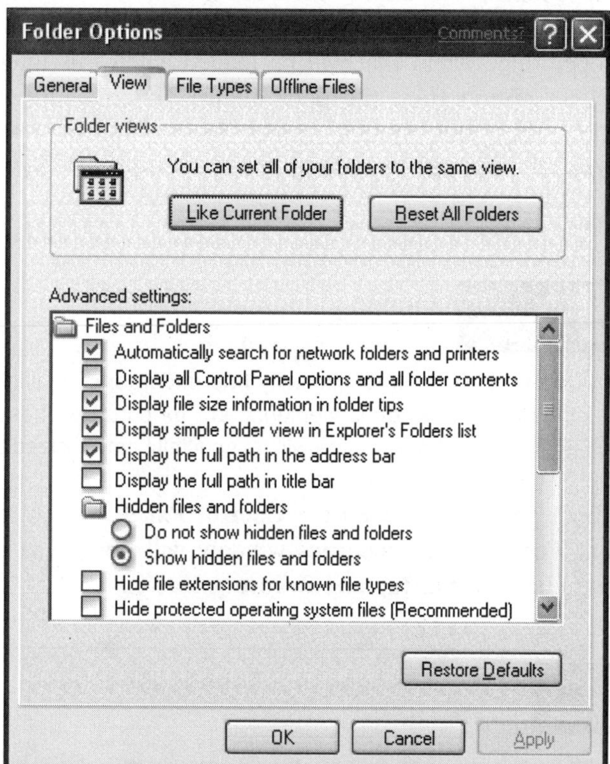

Fig. 4.1. The **View** tab of the **Folder Options** window

To be able to view these files using Windows Explorer, log in to the local system as an Administrator (otherwise you won't get the results you need). Start the Folder Options applet in Control Panel or select the **Folder Options** command from the **Tools** menu in Windows Explorer or My Computer. The dialog shown in Fig. 4.1 will open. Go to the **View** tab, and then go the **Advanced Settings** field. Set the **Show hidden files and folders** option and clear the **Hide protected operating system files (Recommended)** checkbox.

The Simplest Method of Editing the Boot.ini File

If you have enough experience using the Boot.ini file format, you can edit it manually using any text editor. For an advanced user, this won't be difficult. However, for a beginner, the easiest method of editing this file is to use the **System** applet from the **Control Panel**. This option allows you to specify the time interval for which the boot loader will display the boot menu, thus allowing you to select the operating system (for multi-boot systems). This option also allows you to specify the default operating system that will be loaded when this interval expires and you don't select an option from the boot menu. To configure these options in Windows NT 4.0, start the System applet from Control Panel, go to the **Startup/Shutdown** tab, and set the options you need using the **System Startup** option group.

Starting with Windows 2000, this functionality has undergone significant changes, and Windows XP introduces further enhancements. Let us consider these new features in more detail (Windows XP enhancements will be specially emphasized).

To specify the boot parameters, open the **Control Panel** window and double-click the **System** icon. The **System Properties** window will open. Go to the **Advanced** tab (Fig. 4.2) and click the **Startup and Recovery** button.

A careful look at the **Advanced** tab of the **System Properties** window reveals one of the Windows XP enhancements—the so-called *Error Reporting Options*, introduced by Microsoft in order to encourage users to help developers improve future versions of the operating system. Any time an error occurs, Windows XP displays a dialog prompting the user to produce an error report and send it to Microsoft. This option is enabled by default, but if you want to customize its settings or totally disable the feature, click the **Error Reporting** button in the **Advanced** tab of the **System Properties** window. The **Error Reporting** window will open (Fig. 4.3), where you can disable the reporting feature altogether or customize its options by choosing the programs that you want to include or exclude from error reporting. To customize the program list, select the **Programs** option (Fig. 4.3), and then click the **Choose Programs** button to open the

Choose Programs window (Fig. 4.4). In this window, you can change the default reporting mode by setting one of the radio buttons in the **Default reporting mode** option group. If you set the second option, **Do not report errors in any programs**, you'll be able to edit the lists of programs included or excluded from error reporting.

To set the boot and system behavior parameters, click the **Startup and Recovery** button at the **Advanced** tab of the **System Properties** window. The **Startup and Recovery** window will open (Fig. 4.5).

At the top of this window is the **System startup** option group that allows you to specify the default operating system and set the time interval when the system will display the boot menu.

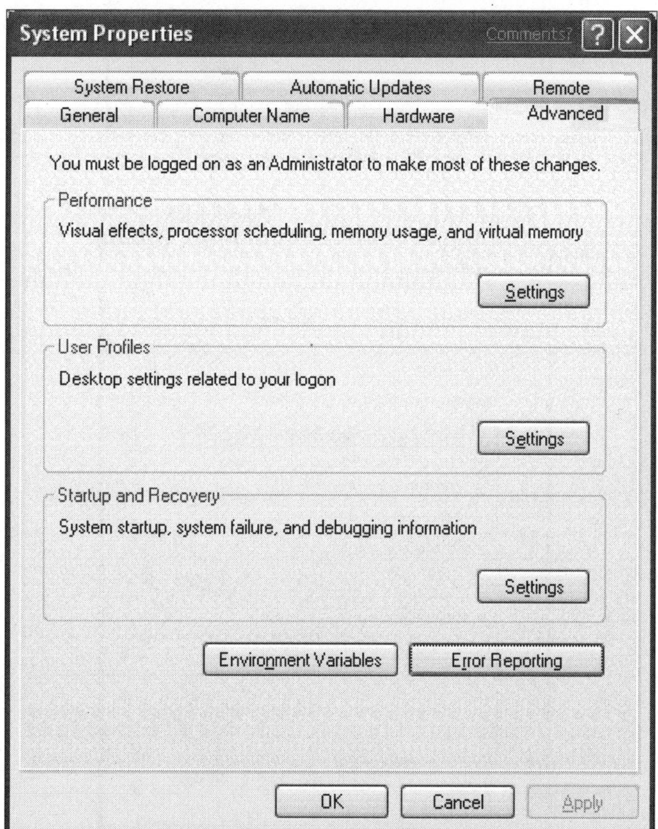

Fig. 4.2. The **Advanced** tab of the **System Properties** window (Windows XP)

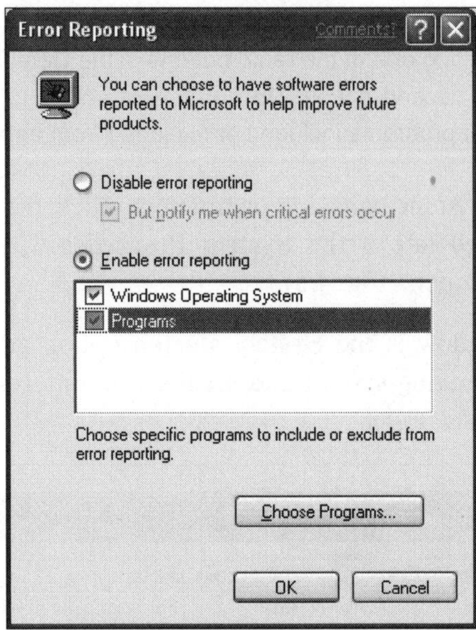

Fig. 4.3. Windows XP provides new error reporting options

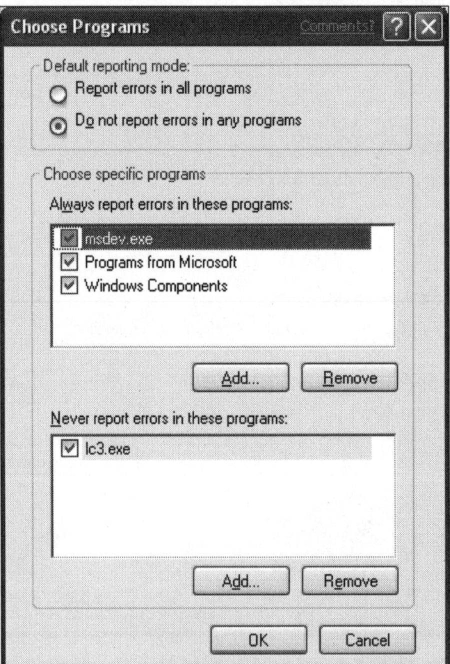

Fig. 4.4. The **Choose Programs** window

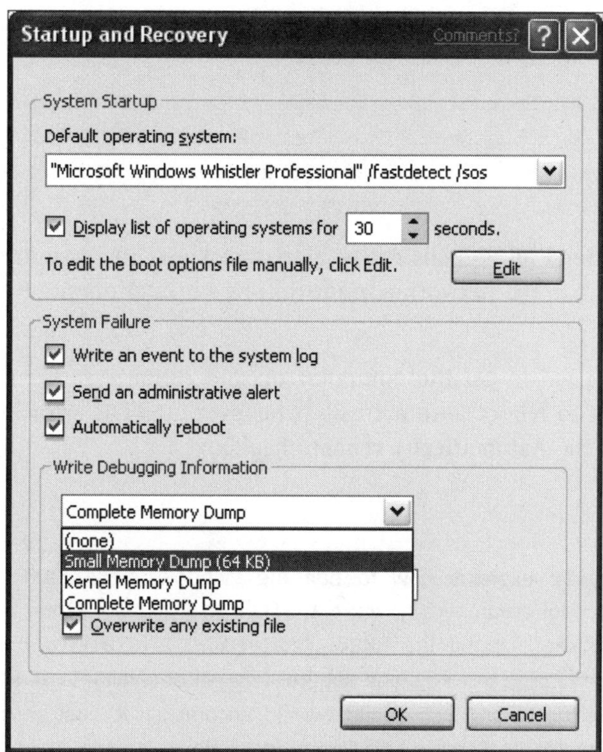

Fig. 4.5. The **Startup and Recovery** window

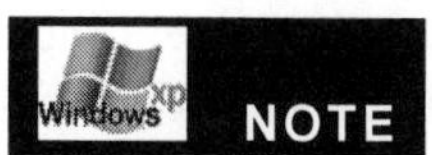

NOTE

In Windows 2000, the **System startup** options are the same as those in Windows NT 4.0, but Windows XP provides a very convenient enhancement—now the **System startup** group provides the option of manually editing the Boot.ini file. To do so, simply click the **Edit** button (Fig. 4.5).

The most interesting option group is **System Failure**, which allows you to specify system behavior in case a STOP error occurs (these errors are also known as kernel errors or "blue screens"). Let's look at these options in more detail.

If you need to identify a problem and find out what caused it, you shouldn't overlook the system log. Because of this, I recommend that you set the **Write an event to the system log** checkbox. If this option is enabled, the system will register an event in the system log any time a STOP error occurs. An example illustrating what this record looks like is shown below:

```
Event ID: 1001 Source: Save Dump Description: The computer has
rebooted from a bugcheck. The bugcheck was : 0xc000021a (0xe1270188,
0x00000001, 0x00000000, 0x00000000). Microsoft Windows NT (v15.1381).
A dump was saved in: C:\WINNT\MEMORY.DMP.
```

If you set the **Send an administrative alert** checkbox, the system will send an administrative alert to the network administrator's workstation any time a STOP error occurs.

Finally, if you need to get the computer up and running as soon as possible, you can configure it to reboot automatically whenever a STOP error occurs. To enable this option, set the **Automatically reboot** checkbox.

NOTE

The following tip explains how to edit the Windows NT/2000/XP registry to make the system reboot automatically when a STOP error occurs. Open the system registry using Regedit.exe, expand the `HKEY_LOCAL_MACHINE\SYSTEM\CurrentControlSet\Control\CrashControl\` key, and set the `Autoreboot` value to 1. Theoretically, this tip is correct, but there's a much easier way to accomplish it. Just set the **Automatically reboot** checkbox in the **Startup and Recovery** window.

If STOP errors persist, you need to find out what's causing them. The best way to do this is to analyze the memory dump. To instruct the system to create a memory dump when a STOP error occurs, use the **Write Debugging Information** option. To specify the name of a file in which to store the debugging information, fill in the **Dump File** field. If you need to overwrite the contents of this file when the memory dump is created, set the **Overwrite any existing file** checkbox. Note that these options haven't changed since the release of Windows NT 4.0.

Starting with Windows 2000, Microsoft included an extended function for saving the memory dump. If you're an experienced Windows NT user, you'll remember that Windows NT 4.0 dumps the entire contents of the physical memory. The size of the memory dump file generated by this system is slightly larger than the amount of physical memory that's present on the computer. Since STOP errors initiate in the system kernel, it's the kernel data (for example, the state of a system at the time of a crash, including what applications were active, what device drivers were loaded, and what code was being executed) that's of interest to the support specialists analyzing the dump. User-mode data isn't useful for determining the cause of a crash. It just contributes to the size of a crash dump file.

Because of this, starting with Windows 2000, the developers included a new option in the **Startup and Recovery** window. This option provides you with some control over the size of the crash dump. The first combobox from the **Write Debugging Information** option group allows you to select the mode used for saving the crash dump. Besides the capability of saving the complete dump (this option is similar to the one existing in Windows NT 4.0), Windows 2000 provides a **Kernel Memory Dump** option that allows you to exclude application (user-mode) data. Only kernel information will be stored in the crash dump. All Windows 2000-compatible crash analysis tools, including Dumpexam and WinDbg, will interpret this file correctly. This option allows you to save disk space (the amount will be different for each system; it also depends on the type of crash). For example, my own experience has shown that on computers having 128 MB RAM, a complete crash dump will consume about 128 MB (actually a little more); while a kernel dump will only consume about 40 MB.

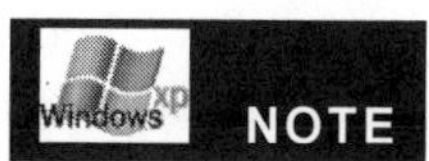

Windows XP enhances this functionality even further by providing an additional option—namely, the **Small Memory Dump**, which allows you to limit the dump to 64 KB (see Fig. 4.5).

Editing the Boot.ini File Manually

As was already mentioned, Windows XP provides a very convenient way of editing the Boot.ini file. However, if you are working with Windows NT/2000, and still want to use a text editor to open the Boot.ini file for editing, clear the Read-Only attribute. This is necessary to save your changes.

To do this, run the following command from the command line:

```
attrib -r boot.ini
```

Boot.ini File Format

The Boot.ini file is automatically created by the Setup program when installing the operating system. This file is located in the root directory of the system partition, and is needed by the boot loader to display the boot menu (the screen that allows the user to select the operating system).

A typical example of the Boot.ini file is shown below:

```
[Boot Loader]
Timeout=5
Default=multi(0)disk(0)rdisk(0)partition(2)\WINXP
[Operating Systems]
multi(0)disk(0)rdisk(0)partition(2)\WINXP="Microsoft Windows XP
Professional" /fastdetect
multi(0)disk(0)rdisk(0)partition(3)\WINNT="Microsoft Windows 2000
Professional" /fastdetect /noguiboot
multi(0)disk(0)rdisk(0)partition(7)\XPRC1="Microsoft Windows XP
Professional" /fastdetect
multi(0)disk(0)rdisk(0)partition(9)\WINDOWS="Microsoft Windows 2002
Server (Tchek)" /fastdetect
multi(0)disk(0)rdisk(0)partition(8)\WINDOWS="Microsoft Windows XP Home
Edition (RC2 Tchek)" /fastdetect
multi(0)disk(0)rdisk(0)partition(1)\WINDOWS="Microsoft Windows
Whistler Professional" /fastdetect /sos
C:\CMDCONS\BOOTSECT.DAT="Microsoft Windows Recovery Console" /cmdcons
C:\="Microsoft Windows" C:\="Microsoft Windows"
```

The Boot.ini file contains two sections: `[boot loader]` and `[operating systems]`. Both of these sections are described below.

The *[boot loader]* Section

The parameters contained in this section are described in Table 4.1.

Table 4.1. `[boot loader]` Section Parameters

Parameter	Description
`Timeout`	The number of seconds the boot loader provides for the user to select an operating system from the boot menu displayed on the screen. If the time interval expires and the user doesn't choose an operating system, NTLDR will start loading the default operating system. If this value is set to 0, the boot loader starts loading the default operating system immediately without displaying the boot loader screen, which prevents the user from making a choice. If this value is set to –1, the boot loader will wait until the user selects an operating system. Note that you must edit the Boot.ini file to set this value since the **System** option in the **Control Panel** interprets it as invalid
`Default`	The path to the default operating system

The startup menu does not appear if Windows XP is the only system installed on your computer. In this case, Ntldr ignores the time-out value and starts Windows XP immediately.

The *[operating systems]* Section

This section contains the list of available operating systems. Each record contained in this section specifies the path to the boot partition of the operating system, the string displayed in the boot loader screen, and optional parameters.

The Boot.ini file supports the capability of loading multiple Windows NT/2000/XP installations, as well as starting other operating systems, including Windows 9*x*, MS-DOS, OS/2, LINUX, and UNIX.

The entries contained in the `[operating systems]` section of the Boot.ini file support several optional switches described in Table 4.2. Note that these switches aren't case-sensitive. Switches that are introduced with Windows 2000 (Win2K) are marked with an asterisk (*).

Table 4.2. Boot.ini Switches

Switch	Description
`/BASEVIDEO`	This switch causes Windows NT/2000 to load using a standard VGA driver. If you've installed a new video driver that isn't working correctly, this switch will allow you to start the computer so you can change the video driver
`/BAUDRATE`	This switch enables kernel-mode debugging (it also sets the `/DEBUG` parameter) and specifies the baud rate to be used for this purpose. If you don't set the baud rate, a default value will be used. If a modem is attached, the default baud rate is 9,600 (for a null-modem cable, the default baud rate is 19,200)
`/BOOTLOG`*	If this switch is specified, Windows 2000 will write the boot process log into the *%SystemRoot%*\NTBTLOG.TXT file. This log will enable you to find out which drivers were loaded successfully, and which weren't

continues

Table 4.2 Continued

Switch	Description
/CRASHDEBUG	If you include this switch, the kernel debugger is loaded when the system boots, but remains inactive unless a crash occurs. This allows the specified COM port (or COM1 by default) to be available for other uses while the system is running. This switch is especially useful if your system is subject to random STOP errors
/DEBUG	Enables kernel-mode debugging. The debugger is loaded when the system boots, and can be activated at any time by a host debugger that's connected to the computer. This mode is recommended when STOP errors are persistent and reproducible
/DEBUGPORT=com*x*	Enables kernel-mode debugging and specifies an override for the default serial port (COM1) that the remote debugger's connected to. For example: /DEBUGPORT=COM2
/FASTDETECT*	This switch is new to Windows 2000. When you dual boot NT 4.0 and Windows 2000, the Windows 2000 version of NTDETECT.COM is used during the boot process. In Windows 2000, detection of parallel and serial devices is performed by plug-and-play device drivers. Windows NT 4.0, however, expects NTDETECT to perform the detection. Specifying FASTDETECT causes NTDETECT to skip parallel and serial device enumeration for a boot into Windows 2000; whereas omitting the switch has NTDETECT perform enumeration for a boot into Windows NT 4.0. Windows 2000 Setup program automatically recognizes dual-boot configurations and sets this switch for BOOT.INI lines that specify a Windows 2000 boot
/MAXMEM	This option will limit Windows NT/2000 to using only the amount of memory you specify. The number is interpreted as MB. For example: /MAXMEM=16 would limit NT to using 16MB of the system's memory. This option is useful if you suspect that a memory chip is bad
/NODEBUG	Prevents kernel-mode debugging from being initialized. Overrides the specification of any of the three debug-related switches, /DEBUG, /DEBUGPORT, and /BAUDRATE
/NOGUIBOOT*	This switch is new to Windows 2000. When this option is specified, the VGA video driver that's responsible for presenting bit-mapped graphics during Win2K's boot process isn't initialized. The driver is used to display boot progress information, as well as to print the Blue Screen crash screen. Disabling it will disable Win2K's ability to do those things as well

continues

Table 4.2 Continued

Switch	Description
/NOSERIALMICE=[COMx,y,z,...]	Disables serial mouse detection of the specified COM port(s). Use this switch if you have a component other than a mouse attached to a serial port during the startup sequence. If you use /NOSERIALMICE without specifying a COM port, serial mouse detection is disabled on all COM ports
/SAFEBOOT*	This option is new to Windows 2000. You should never have to specify this option manually, since NTLDR does it for you when you use the F8 menu to perform a safe boot. Following the colon in the option, you need to specify one of three additional switches: MINIMAL, NETWORK, or DSREPAIR. The MINIMAL and NETWORK flags correspond to a safe boot with no network and a safe boot with network support A safe boot is a boot where NT only loads drivers and services that are specified by name or group in the Minimal or Network registry keys under HKLM\System\CurrentControlSet\Control\SafeBoot. The DSREPAIR (Directory Services Repair) switch causes NT to boot into a mode where it restores the Active Directory from a backup medium you present. An additional option that you can use is "(ALTERNATESHELL)". This tells NT to use the program specified by HKLM\System\CurrentControlSet\SafeBoot\AlternateShell as the graphical shell, rather than the default, which is Explorer
/SOS	This switch causes Windows NT/2000/XP to print information about what drivers are being loaded as the system boots. It's useful when Windows NT/2000/XP won't start and you suspect that a device driver is missing

The list of Boot.ini switches shown above shouldn't be considered a complete list since it only includes the most frequently used switches. The most complete and up-to-date list of Boot.ini switches can be downloaded from **http://www.sysinternals.com/bootini.htm**.

Customizing the Login Process

The standard login process can be customized by editing the registry. The procedures described in this section are applicable for both Windows NT 4.0 and Windows 2000.

Specifying the Custom Logo Displayed at Login Time

This tip applies both to Windows NT/2000 and to Windows XP. You can change the screen logo used as a background for the login dialog. Any BMP file can be used for this purpose (for example, a custom logo or any graphical file). To introduce this modification, you need to do the following:

1. Start the registry editor and expand the `HKEY_USERS\.DEFAULT\Control Panel\Desktop` registry key.
2. Find the `Wallpaper` value entry, and specify the path to the BMP file that you want to use as a background for the login dialog (Fig. 4.6).

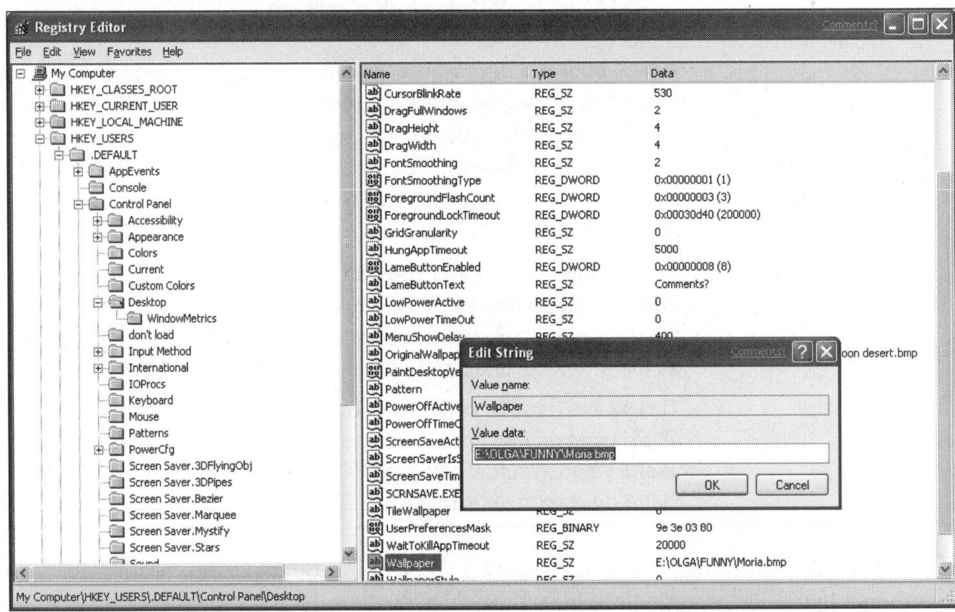

Fig. 4.6. To specify the custom logo displayed at login time, edit the `Wallpaper` value under `HKEY_USERS\.DEFAULT\Control Panel\Desktop`

NOTE

In Windows XP this tip will also work, but only if you disable the Welcome screen (Fig. 4.7), which by default is enabled. To disable the Windows XP Welcome screen, open the **Control Panel** window, start the User Accounts applet, click the **Change the way users log on or off** option, and clear the **Use Welcome screen** checkbox (Fig. 4.8).

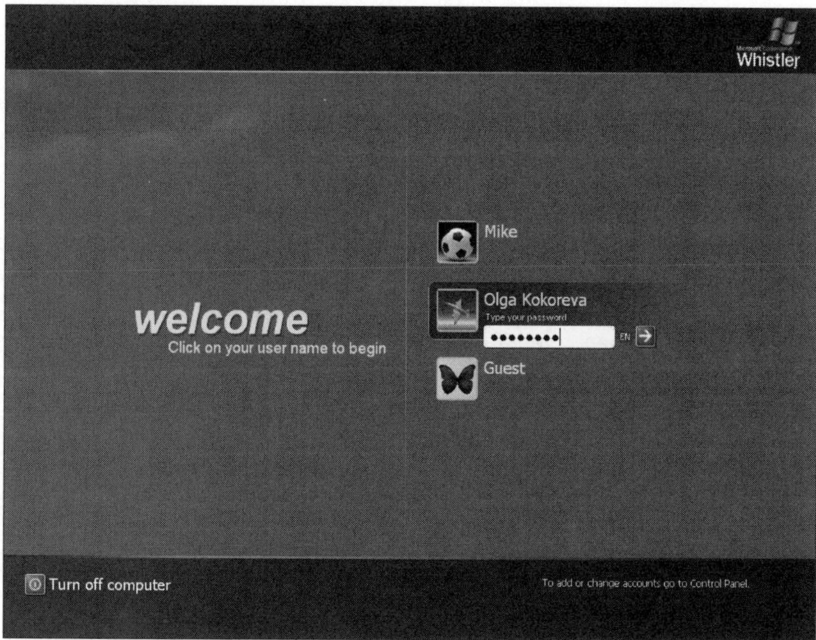

Fig. 4.7. Windows XP Welcome screen

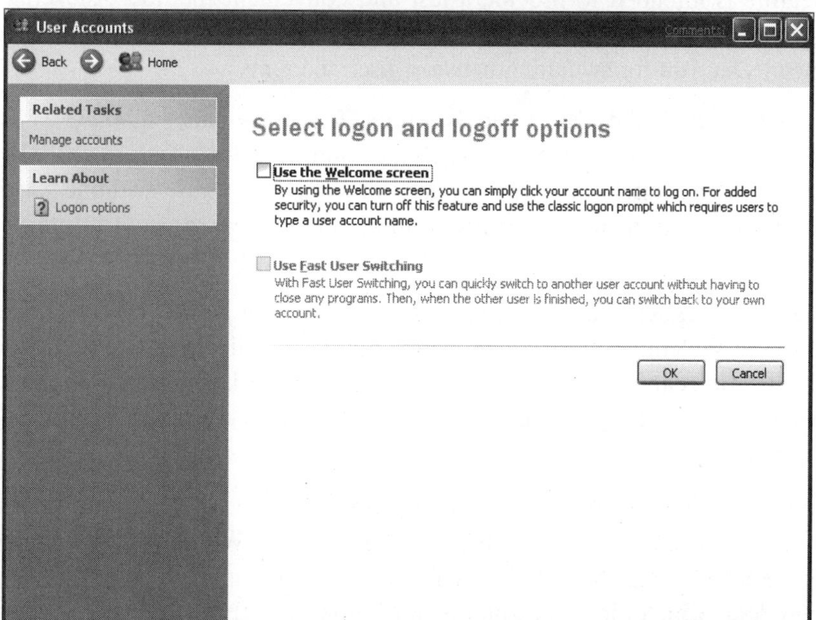

Fig. 4.8. Disabling the Welcome screen in Windows XP

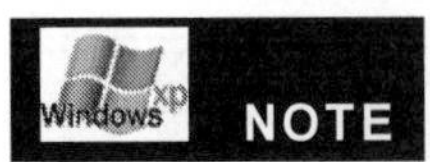

Notice, that you can customize the Welcome screen itself by adding or removing user accounts to it. To do so, simply expand the `HKEY_LOCAL_MACHINE\SOFTWARE\Microsoft\Windows NT\CurrentVersion\Windologon\SpecialAccounts\UserList` registry key. Add the value of REG_DWORD data type, name it as required, and set the value to 0. This account will be hidden from the Welcome screen. If you want to make the account visible again, set the value to 1, and it will appear at the Welcome screen. For example, if you want the Administrator account (which is hidden by default) to appear at the Welcome screen, create the `REG_DWORD` value, name it Administrator, and set it to 1.

Windows XP Fast User Switching

If you carefully look at the screen shown in Fig. 4.8, you'll immediately notice another interesting Windows XP enhancement—namely, the Fast User Switching option. Since Fast User Switching is new to Windows XP, let's consider it in more detail.

This feature is intended to provide a fast and convenient method of leveraging the data separation technology of Windows NT profiles and providing a fast and convenient mechanism for switching between user accounts.

In Windows XP, if the Fast User Switching feature is enabled, there is no need for the user to log off, since the user's account is always logged on. Therefore, it is possible to switch quickly between all open accounts, without logging off the previous user and preserving his running applications or active Internet connections.

When a Windows XP machine is left alone with a user logged on, the system will return to the Welcome screen while keeping all the applications running. Additionally, notifications appear on the Welcome screen providing information such as the number of users who are logged on, whether a user has unread e-mail, and how many programs are running.

Windows XP Professional also enables users to access data and applications from other machines. On business workstations, Windows XP Professional allows users to access their desktops from remote computers. Thus, for example, you may lock your office workstation, go home, and then connect to your office computer.

Both Fast User Switching and Remote Desktop use terminal services technology and work with most earlier Microsoft Win32® applications without requiring any changes. If your application is Windows 2000 Logo Certified, or has followed the Application Specification for Windows 2000, it should run fine in Windows XP.

Also notice that the Fast User Switching feature will be unavailable on Windows XP Professional workstations participating in the domain.

If you are using Windows XP Home Edition or Windows XP Professional on a standalone workstation or workstation belonging to a workgroup, you can enable or disable the Fast User Switching feature by setting or clearing the **Use Fast User Switching** checkbox. If this checkbox is grayed, as shown in Fig. 4.8, open the **Folder Options** window, go to the **Offline Files** tab (Fig. 4.9) and clear the **Enable Offline Files** checkbox. Confirm your changes, then re-open the **User Accounts** window. The **Use Fast User Switching** option will now be available (Fig. 4.10).

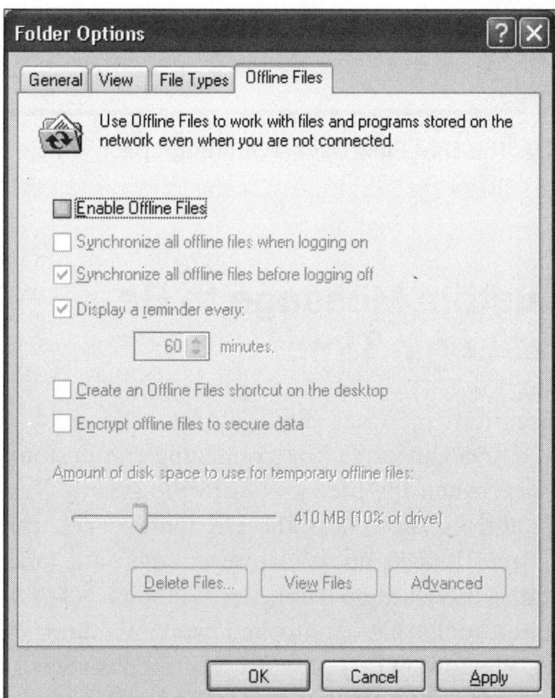

Fig. 4.9. The **Offline Folders** tab of the **Folder Options** window

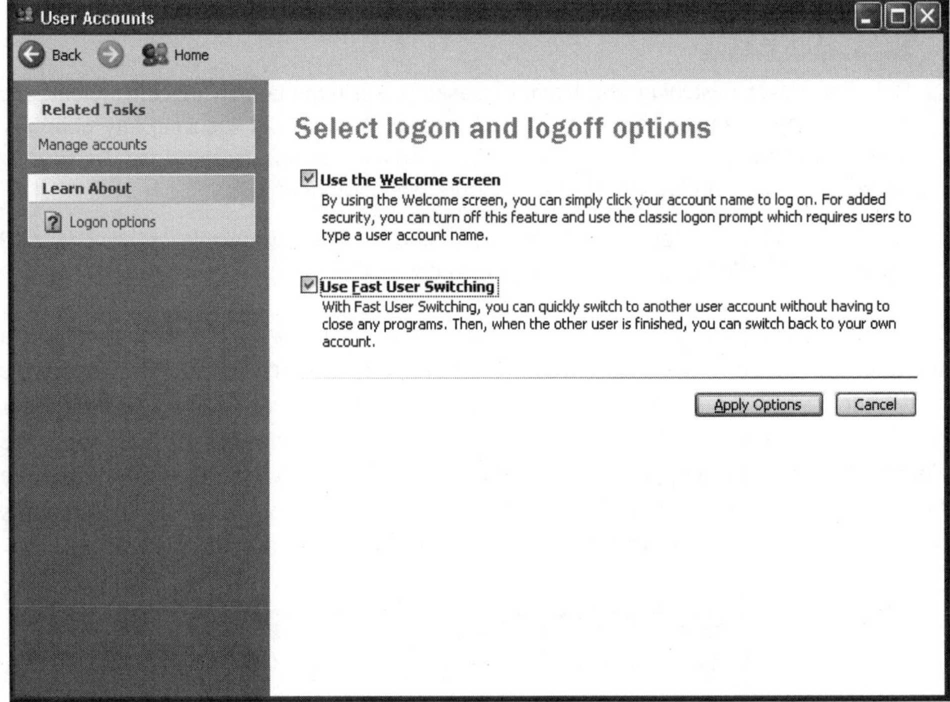

Fig. 4.10. The **Use Fast User Switching** option is now available

Adding a Custom Message to Be Displayed at Login Time

You can also add custom messages displayed for all users at login time. If you make this change, a small message box containing the custom message text and **OK** button will appear when the user logs in to the system. The boot process will continue as usual after the user clicks the **OK** button. You can find tips on this both in Internet forums and in books. However, there's a much easier and safer method of performing this customization. In Windows NT 4.0, you can use the System Policy Editor tool, that is supplied with Windows NT 4.0 Server. In Windows 2000 and Windows XP, you can use the Local Security Policy snap-in. In this section, we'll cover different ways of adding a custom message, using both administrative tools and by editing the system registry directly.

Adding a Custom Windows 2000/XP Login Message Using the Local Security Policy Snap-in

To create a custom login message, proceed as follows:

1. Start the Administrative Tools applet in Control Panel and select the **Local Security Policy** option. Expand the **Security Settings** hierarchical list by selecting the **Local Policies | Security Options**. The right pane of the MMC window will display the system policies that can be specified for the local system.
2. Double-click the **Interactive logon: Message text for users attempting to log on** option, or right-click this option and select the **Properties** command. The **Interactive logon: Message text for users attempting to log on** window will appear (Fig. 4.11).
3. Fill in the text field in this window with your custom message text and click **OK**. To specify the text for the title bar caption, select **the Interactive logon: Message title for users attempting to log on** option.

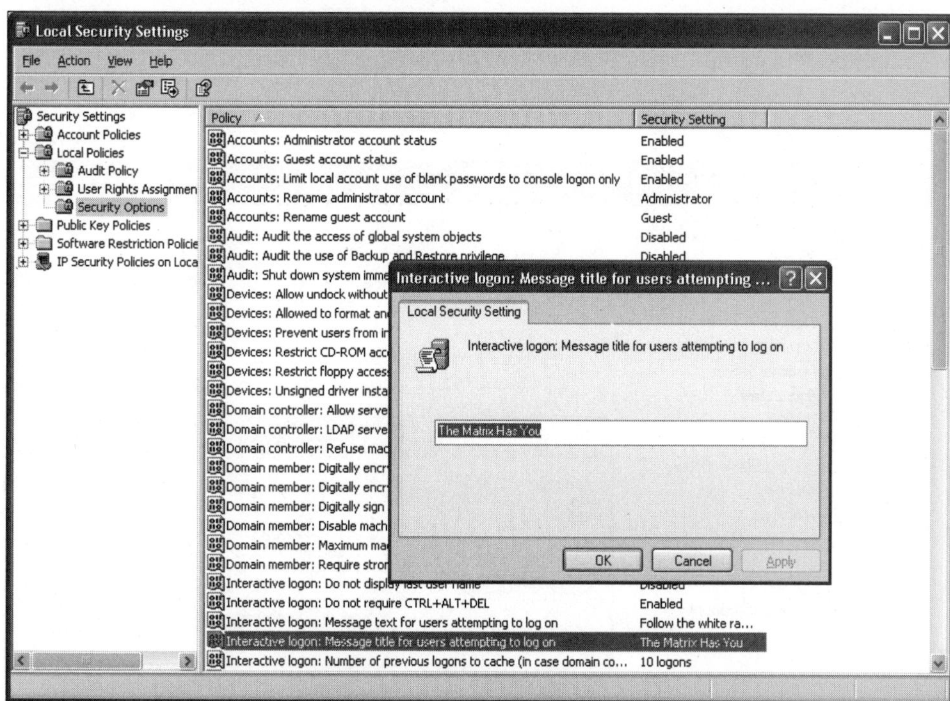

Fig. 4.11. Using MMC for specifying a custom login message (Windows 2000 and Windows XP)

Chapter 10 contains more detailed information on using system policies.

Adding a Custom Logon Banner by Editing the Registry Directly

Both the System Policy Editor (Windows NT 4.0 Server) and the Local Security Policy snap-in (Windows 2000) modify the `LegalNoticeCaption` and the `LegalNoticeText` registry values located under `HKEY_LOCAL_MACHINE\SOFTWARE\Microsoft\WindowsNT\CurrentVersion\WinLogon`. To specify a custom logon banner by direct registry editing, proceed as follows:

1. Open the `HKEY_LOCAL_MACHINE\SOFTWARE\Microsoft\WindowsNT\CurrentVersion\WinLogon` key (Fig. 4.12).

2. Find the `LegalNoticeCaption` value entry. Edit its value to specify the phrase that will be displayed as the caption of the custom message box.

3. Next, open the `LegalNoticeText` value entry and edit its value to specify the text of your custom message. The message shown in our example is only a joke, but experienced administrators will find this capability useful for more practical purposes.

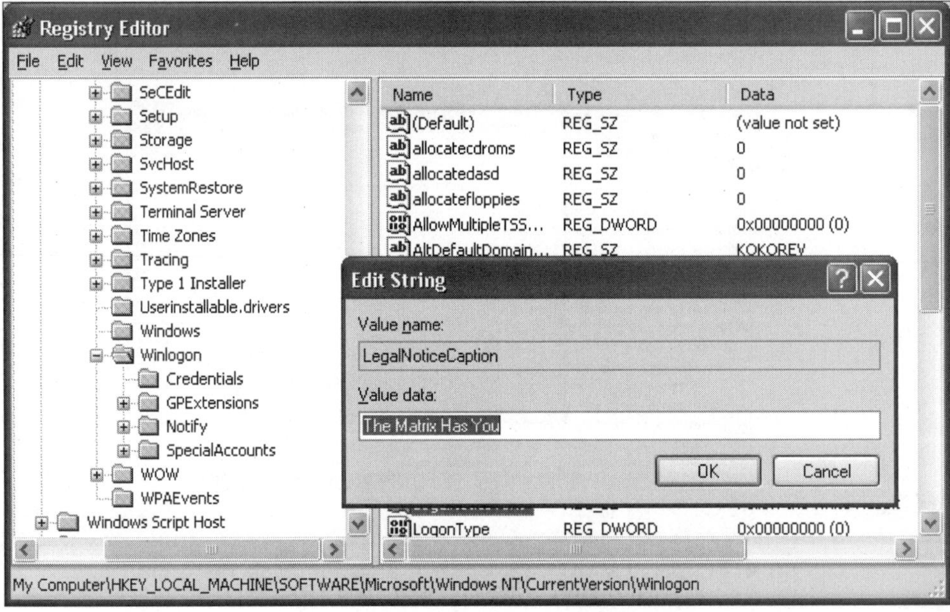

Fig. 4.12. The `Winlogon` registry key

In Windows XP, the `LegalNoticeCaption` and `LegalNoticeText` values were moved to the following registry key: `HKEY_LOCAL_MACHINE\SOFTWARE\Microsoft\Windows\CurrentVersion\policies\system` (Fig. 4.13). Values with the same names also exist under `HKEY_LOCAL_MACHINE\SOFTWARE\Microsoft\WindowsNT\CurrentVersion\WinLogon`. However, the `LegalNoticeCaption` and `LegalNoticeText` values under `HKEY_LOCAL_MACHINE\SOFTWARE\Microsoft\Windows\CurrentVersion\policies\system` have priority, and if they are set, the values under the `Winlogon` registry key will have no effect.

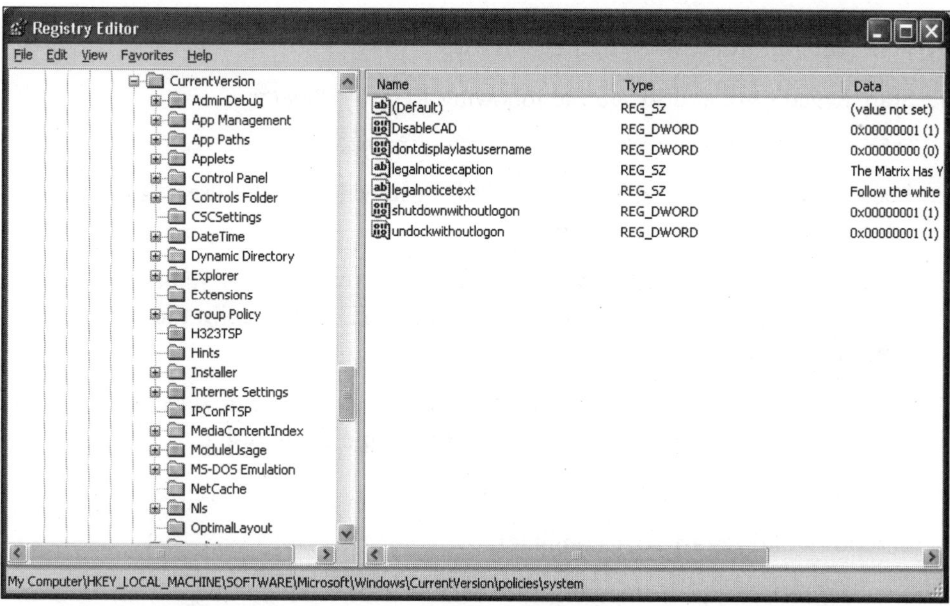

Fig. 4.13. The `HKEY_LOCAL_MACHINE\SOFTWARE\Microsoft\Windows\CurrentVersion\policies\system` registry key (Windows XP)

Automating the Logon Process

In contrast to Windows 95 and Windows 98, the logon procedure used in both Windows NT/2000 and Windows XP is an integral part of the security subsystem. However, there may be times when you want to automate this procedure, so that other users can start your computer and use the account you establish for automatic logon.

NOTE

Notice that enabling the Autologon feature, however convenient it may seem, also represents a security risk. Setting a computer for Autologon means that anyone who can physically obtain access to the computer can gain access to all of the computer's contents, potentially including any network or networks it is connected to, and any users who have logged on remotely can view and read it. Therefore, this option is not available for server platforms (for example, you can't configure Windows 2000 Server to use Autologon). The automatic logon feature is also unsupported when you log on to a domain, and therefore you must join a workgroup to use this feature. However, if your computer belongs to a Windows 2000 domain, you can still enable automatic logon by editing the registry (however, in this case doing so is highly risky and undesirable).

To add logon information using Regedit.exe

1. Start Regedit.exe and locate the following Registry subkey:

   `HKEY_LOCAL_MACHINE\SOFTWARE\Microsoft\WindowsNT\CurrentVersion\Winlogon`

2. Locate the `DefaultUserName` entry, and set its value to the user name that you want to be logged on automatically.
3. If the `DefaultPassword` value does not exist, create a new value entry of the `REG_SZ` data type, rename it to `DefaultPassword`, and specify the default password as its value.
4. If the `AutoAdminLogon` value entry doesn't exist, create a new value of the `REG_SZ` data type, rename it `AutoAdminLogon`, and set its value to 1.
5. Save your changes, and then exit Regedit.
6. Shutdown and restart your computer.

When you restart the computer, the default user will be logged on automatically.

NOTES

Note that the `AutoAdminLogon` is a type `REG_SZ` value entry, not a `REG_DWORD` registry value entry. Also notice that to enable automatic logon, you need to disable the **Interactive logon: Do not require CTRL+ALT+DEL** Local Security Setting (Fig. 4.14).

To configure the Windows 2000 system for automatic logon, open the **Control Panel** window and double-click **Users and Passwords**. In the **Users and Password** window, clear the **Users must enter a user name and password to use this computer** checkbox. After you've finished, don't forget to go to the **Advanced** tab in the same window to check if the **Require users to press Ctrl-Alt-Delete before logging on** checkbox is set. You'll need to clear this checkbox if you're going to configure the system for automatic logon.

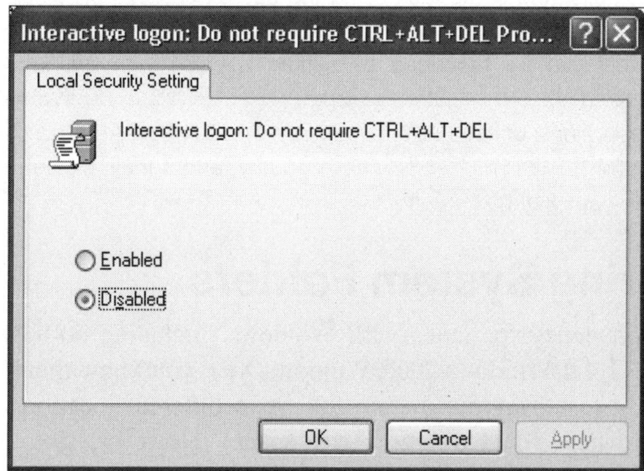

Fig. 4.14. To enable automatic logon, the **Interactive logon: Do not require CTRL+ALT+DEL** local security setting must be disabled

Hiding the Last User Name Logged On

In the previous section, we discussed a setting that weakens your Windows XP security system. Now we're going to discuss a method that will allow you to strengthen security. When the standard Windows NT/2000/XP configuration is used, the system displays the name of the user who successfully logged on last. If you hide this name, the security rules will become more restrictive since guessing both the user name and password is more difficult. This customization is one of the most frequently used. As you can guess, it also requires you to add a new value into the registry. To hide the last logged on user name, proceed as follows:

1. Run Regedit.exe and open the following key: `HKEY_LOCAL_MACHINE\SOFTWARE\Microsoft\Windows\CurrentVersion\Policies\System`.
2. Add the `DontDisplayLastUserName` value and specify the `REG_DWORD` data type for it.

3. Set this entry to 1. When you log on to the system next, the name of the user who logged on last won't be displayed. If you need to disable this feature later, set this value to 0.

NOTE

You can accomplish the same task using the Local Security Policy snap-in, which has the **Interactive Logon: Do not display last logged on user name** option. Notice that the same effect can be produced by setting a value with the same name under `HKEY_LOCAL_MACHINE\SOFTWARE\Microsoft\WindowsNT\CurrentVersion\WinLogon`. However, the settings under `HKEY_LOCAL_MACHINE\SOFTWARE\Microsoft\Windows\CurrentVersion\Policies\System` have priority, and if they are set, the same value under the `Winlogon` key has no effect.

Configuring System Folders

If you've had previous experience with Windows (including both Windows 95/98 and Windows NT 4.0/Windows 2000/Windows XP), you know there will be a time when you'll want to move your system folders to different locations (for example, to other drives where you have more free space). However, if you simply move these folders, what you'll get will be a new copy for each of these folders in the previous locations. Why is this so?

It's because both Windows 95/98 and Windows NT 4.0/Windows 2000/Windows XP store the system folders paths in the registry. So, if you want to correctly move the system folders, you need to modify the appropriate registry values that specify the location of the system folders. Microsoft Office applications behave the same way—all of the paths to the standard folders are also stored in the registry. That's why you can't get rid of the My Documents folder. Registry values that specify the locations of the system folders are stored under `HKEY_CURRENT_USER\SOFTWARE\Microsoft\Windows\CurrentVersion\Explorer\Shell Folders`. Windows XP parameters stored under `HKEY_CURRENT_USER\SOFTWARE\Microsoft\Windows\CurrentVersion\Explorer\Shell Folders` are shown in Fig. 4.15.

Notice that even in Windows 2000 the user interface provided you with the capability of moving the My Documents folder to where you wanted. In Windows XP this functionality was further enhanced. Right-click the My Documents folder to open the **My Documents Properties** window (Fig. 4.16) and click the **Move** button. In the next window you will be prompted to select a new location for the My Documents folder, either by selecting an existing folder or by creating a new folder. There is now therefore no need to edit the registry directly.

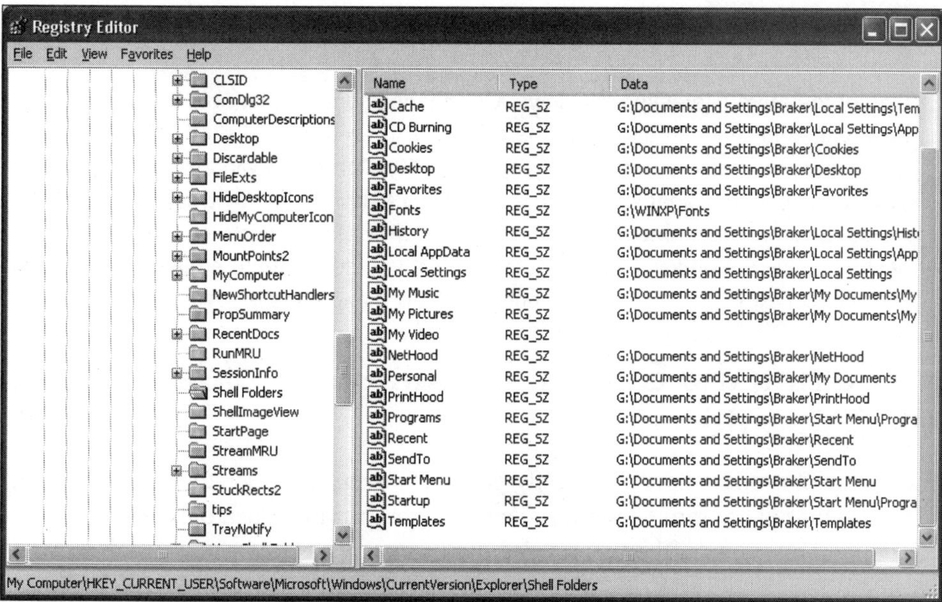

Fig. 4.15. Registry values that specify the default path values for Windows 2000 and Windows XP shell folders

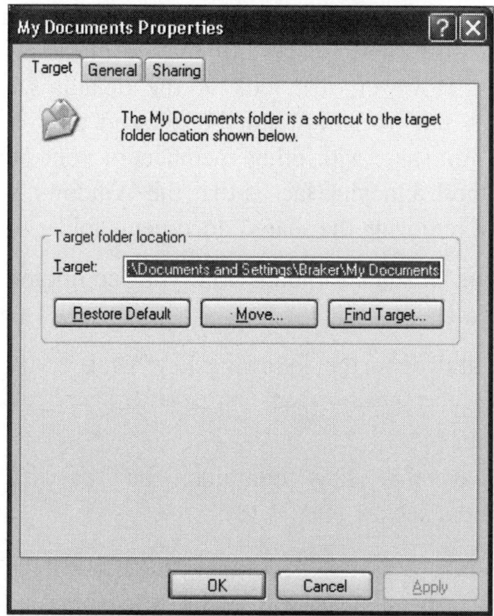

Fig. 4.16. Windows XP provides you with the capability of moving the My Documents folder

One of the more interesting Windows XP enhancements is that now the My Music and My Pictures folders can also have the same status as a special shell folder. To change the location of these folders, simply open the **My Computer** window, navigate the file system to open the folder where you want the My Music and/or My Documents folders to reside, and then open the My Documents folder in another window and drag them to the desired location. Windows XP will automatically update all the references to those folders to their new locations, including both the **Start** menu and the system registry.

Removing the Shared Documents Folders from My Computer

Though we no longer need to directly edit the registry in order to redirect the shell folders, there still are some customizations that you can introduce only by direct registry editing. For example, the tip provided in this section can't be performed otherwise.

If you have already worked for some time with Windows XP, you have probably noticed one of the UI "enhancements" that certainly need to be removed, if you care for your security. Yes, I mean preventing the UI from displaying the shared folders at the top of the **My Computer** window. Of course, shared folders provide a place where you can store files, images, videos, or music that everyone on your computer can access. However, just look at the default settings for that folder (Fig. 4.16). I dare say that this must not be allowed as a default, even on your home computer that you share with other members of your family, whom you certainly trust. And the most annoying fact is that the Windows XP user interface provides no capabilities of removing the shared documents folder from your computer.

However, you can remove shared folders from your computer by editing the registry. Here's how you do it:

1. Start Regedit.exe and open the following key: `HKEY_LOCAL_MACHINE\SOFTWARE\Microsoft\Windows\CurrentVersion\Explorer\MyComputer\NameSpace\DelegateFolders`.
2. You'll notice that this key contains the `{59031a47-3f72-44a7-89c5-5595fe6b30ee}` nested subkey (Fig. 4.18).
3. Delete this key, and all shared documents folders will be gone from the **My Computer** window. The change will come into force immediately, i.e., you don't need to reboot the system to see the change.

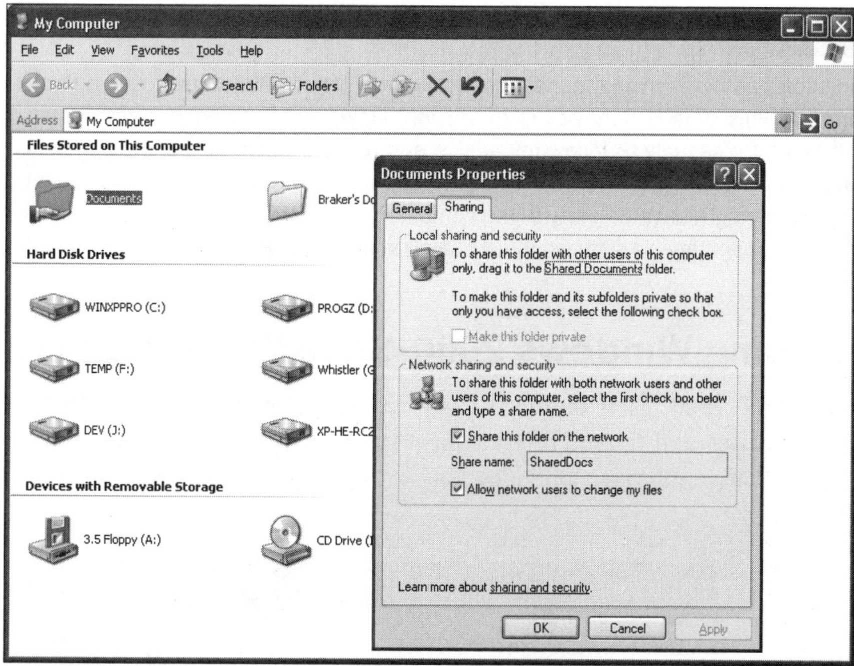

Fig. 4.17. The shared documents folder is always present at the top of the **My Computer** window

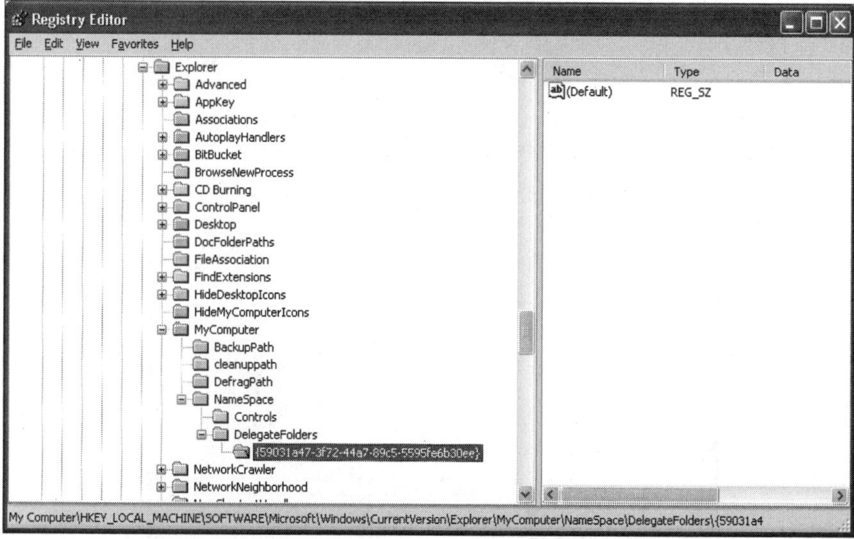

Fig. 4.18. The subkey that needs to be deleted in order to remove the shared documents folder

NOTE

Microsoft has made this UI enhancement to allow family members to share documents; therefore, this default behavior is by design. However, I strongly recommend anyone who cares for security to follow my advice and remove unneeded shares, especially on computers that are members of workgroups where there are Windows 9*x* clients. The reason is straightforward. If any of the computers on your LAN gets infected with a worm or virus propagating via a network, you'll almost certainly get infected too.

Displaying Windows 2000-Style Sharing Options

The Windows 2000 user interface provided quite a powerful set of sharing options for drives and folders in your local system. Compared to this, the default Windows XP user interface provides you with quite a limited set of capabilities (Fig. 4.19).

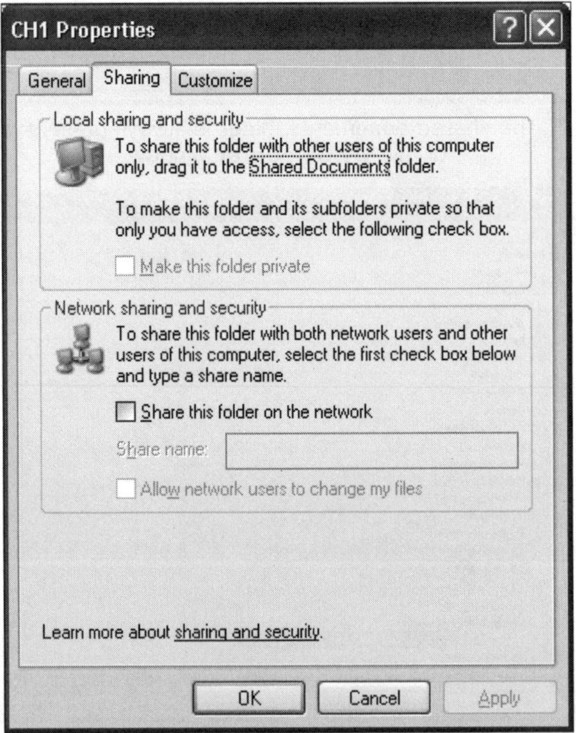

Fig. 4.19. The default settings of Windows XP UI provide a limited set of sharing options

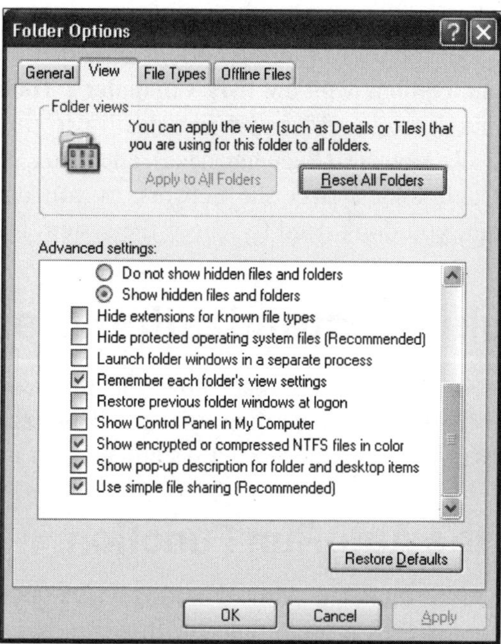

Fig. 4.20. The **View** tab of the **Folder Options** window

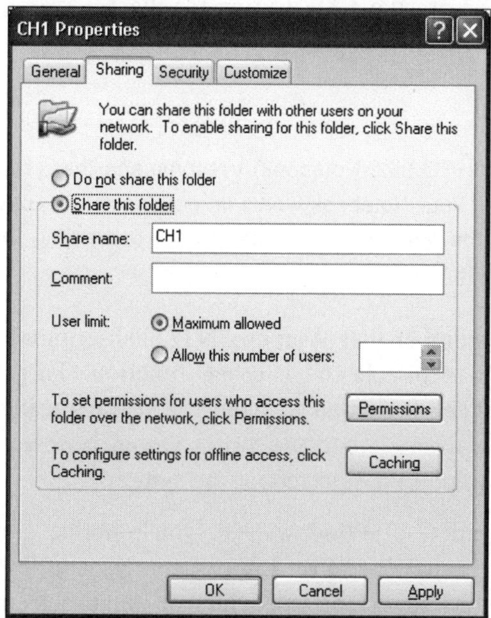

Fig. 4.21. Now you can use Windows 2000-style sharing options

However, these options have not been removed completely, and you can easily reset this behavior to the rich set of sharing options provided by Windows 2000. To do so, open the **Folder Options** window (**My Computer | Tools | Folder Options**), go to the **View** tab, and scroll the **Advanced Settings** list to the bottom (Fig. 4.20). Clear the **Use simple file sharing (Recommended)** checkbox, and you will be able to share your drives and folders over the network as you did in Windows 2000 (Fig. 4.21). Once again, you don't need to reboot the system to see the effect.

Other Popular Customization Methods

There are many other customizations that allow you to modify the standard behavior of Windows NT/2000/XP operating systems. This section describes some helpful customizations, which are safe from a system stability point of view.

Configuring the AutoRun Function

The `AutoRun` function is included with Windows 95/98 and Windows NT 4.0/ Windows 2000/Windows XP as a useful add-on. It really is useful, too, when you start programs from CDs or install new software. However, if you only need to copy one or two files from the CD, waiting for the `AutoRun` function to complete can leave you feeling less than happy.

NOTE

If you use a portable PC (like Notebook) I recommend that you disable the `AutoRun` function, especially if your Notebook works on batteries. The `AutoRun` function will significantly decrease the time you can work without recharging the batteries (it doesn't provide any advantages, either).

Experienced users remember that Windows NT/2000 required you to edit the registry directly in order to disable the `AutoRun` function. To get the desired result, users of Windows NT/2000 needed to open the registry using one of the registry editors, find the `HKEY_LOCAL_MACHINE\System\CurrentControlSet\Services\Cdrom` key, set the `AutoRun` value to 0, and reboot the system.

After a brief investigation of Windows XP, you'll notice a new enhancement—namely, the `AutoPlay` capability (Fig. 4.22). `AutoPlay` is a new feature that detects content such as pictures, music, or video files on removable media and removable devices, and then automatically starts applications required to display or reproduce an appropriate content. This simplifies the use of specialized peripheral devices such as MP3 players and digital photo readers. It also makes it easier for users who are unfamiliar with the software needed to access various content types. If you are an experienced Windows user, you may remember that Windows Millennium Edition (Windows ME) also implemented similar functionality for picture content on imaging devices, automatically running the Windows Image Acquisition user interface (Scanner and Camera Wizard) when a camera or scanner is plugged in. Windows XP has extended this functionality by making it universally available for all hot-plug removable storage devices that appear in **My Computer**. `AutoPlay` is extensible so that other devices and media can benefit from this architecture, even the legacy ones.

Fig. 4.22. Windows XP provides a rich set of options for configuring the `AutoPlay` function

NOTE

Notice, however, that `AutoPlay` should not be confused with `AutoRun`. The `AutoRun` functionality, introduced in Windows 95, enables a compact disc to automatically launch a function (such as an application installer or game play), when the user inserts the CD into the CD-ROM drive. This is accomplished through the use of an Autorun.inf file in the root directory of the compact disc. If you want to disable the AutoRun functionality in Windows XP, proceed the same way as you did in Windows NT/2000.

Resetting the Default Icons

Sometimes you may notice that the **Recycle Bin** icons reflect a situation incorrectly. For example, when your recycle bin contains something, but the icon indicates that it's blank, and vice versa.

To correct this situation, follow the instructions below:

1. Empty the recycle bin.
2. Start the registry editor and find the `DefaultIcon` key that resides under the `{645FF040-5081-101B-9F08-00AA002F954E}` key.
3. Make sure that this key contains the following values:

```
Default    "%SystemRoot%\System32\shell32.dll,31"
empty      "%SystemRoot%\System32\shell32.dll,31"
full       "%SystemRoot%\System32\shell32.dll,32"
```

Renaming the Recycle Bin

Perhaps renaming the recycle bin isn't "The Reason You Should Buy the Book". Nevertheless, if you've never renamed the recycle bin before, try doing it now. Start the registry editor and open each of the three keys listed below. The value for each key should be replaced by a new name ("Dumpster", for example).

```
HKEY_CLASSES_ROOT\CLSID\{645FF040-5081-101B-9F08-00AA002F954E}
HKEY_LOCAL_MACHINE\Software\Microsoft\Windows\CurrentVersion\
explorer\Desktop\NameSpace\{645FF040-5081-101B-9F08-00AA002F954E}
HKEY_CURRENT_USER\username\AppEvents\EventLabels\EventLabels\
EmptyRecycleBin
HKEY_CURRENT_USER\Default\AppEvents\EventLabels\EmptyRecycleBin.
```

Some users consider searching for "Recycle Bin" more convenient. You can also try searching for the following substring: "-5081-". This method will allow you to find the Class Identifier (CLSID). Replace the "Recycle Bin" string with any (new) name you like.

Changing the Recycle Bin Icon

To change the icon identifying the recycle bin, click [+] near the {645FF040-5081-101B-9F08-00AA002F954E} key. Open the DefaultIcon subkey residing under this key. The right pane will contain the following three value entries: **(Default)**, **Empty**, and **Full**. The data column will contain the appropriate DLL ("SHELL32.DLL, *no*") that contains the icon. The *no* parameter represents the icon number with the file.

The **Empty** and **Full** icons are numbered 31 and 32, respectively. The Shell32.dll file contains alternative versions of the **Full** icon (in positions ranging from 49 to 51). Select any icon and set the value according to your preferences.

Removing Shortcut Arrows from Windows Shortcuts

To get rid of the arrows that appear on the Windows shortcut icons, the following steps need to be taken:

1. Start the registry editor and find the following key: HKEY_CLASSES_ROOT\lnkfile.
2. Delete the IsShortcut value.
3. Find the HKEY_CLASSES_ROOT\piffile key.
4. Delete the IsShortcut value.

Restart Windows NT/2000. The shortcuts will now be displayed without the arrows.

Preventing Windows Messenger from Auto-Starting

If you are not a fan of Windows Messenger, you can prevent it from auto-starting by simply deleting the HKEY_CURRENT_USER\Software\Microsoft\Windows\CurrentVersion\Run\MSMSGS registry key.

Uninstalling Undesirable Windows Components

Most users who don't particularly care for specific Windows components, such as Internet Explorer, Windows Messenger, and Microsoft Games, often complain that these components are installed by default and Windows doesn't provide a way of uninstalling them. However, you can do it by trying the following tip.

1. Open the *%Systemroot%*\inf folder and locate the sysoc.inf file. Make a backup copy of the file, then open it for editing. The contents of this file might look as follows:

```
[Version]
Signature = "$Windows NT$"
DriverVer=07/01/2001,5.1.2600.0

[Components]
NtComponents=ntoc.dll,NtOcSetupProc,,4
WBEM=ocgen.dll,OcEntry,wbemoc.inf,hide,7
Display=desk.cpl,DisplayOcSetupProc,,7
Fax=fxsocm.dll,FaxOcmSetupProc,fxsocm.inf,,7
NetOC=netoc.dll,NetOcSetupProc,netoc.inf,,7
iis=iis.dll,OcEntry,iis.inf,,7
com=comsetup.dll,OcEntry,comnt5.inf,hide,7
dtc=msdtcstp.dll,OcEntry,dtcnt5.inf,hide,7
IndexSrv_System = setupqry.dll,IndexSrv,setupqry.inf,,7
TerminalServer=TsOc.dll, HydraOc, TsOc.inf,hide,2
msmq=msmqocm.dll,MsmqOcm,msmqocm.inf,,6
ims=imsinsnt.dll,OcEntry,ims.inf,,7
fp_extensions=fp40ext.dll,FrontPage4Extensions,fp40ext.inf,,7
AutoUpdate=ocgen.dll,OcEntry,au.inf,hide,7
msmsgs=msgrocm.dll,OcEntry,msmsgs.inf,hide,7
RootAutoUpdate=ocgen.dll,OcEntry,rootau.inf,,7
IEAccess=ocgen.dll,OcEntry,ieaccess.inf,,7

Games=ocgen.dll,OcEntry,games.inf,,7
AccessUtil=ocgen.dll,OcEntry,accessor.inf,,7
CommApps=ocgen.dll,OcEntry,communic.inf,HIDE,7
MultiM=ocgen.dll,OcEntry,multimed.inf,HIDE,7
AccessOpt=ocgen.dll,OcEntry,optional.inf,HIDE,7
Pinball=ocgen.dll,OcEntry,pinball.inf,HIDE,7
MSWordPad=ocgen.dll,OcEntry,wordpad.inf,HIDE,7
ZoneGames=zoneoc.dll,ZoneSetupProc,igames.inf,,7

[Global]
```

```
WindowTitle=%WindowTitle%
WindowTitle.StandAlone="*"

[Components]
msnexplr=ocmsn.dll,OcEntry,msnmsn.inf,,7

[Strings]
WindowTitle="Windows Professional Setup"
 WindowTitle_Standalone="Windows Components Wizard"
```

2. Delete the word `HIDE` for any component that you want to see in the Windows Components Wizard (but don't delete the commas). Notice that you can also edit the `[Strings]` section of this file to rename the windows (for example, let's make it "Wizard of OZ").

3. Save the Sysoc.inf file, close it, and reboot the system. Then start the Add/Remove Programs applet in Control Panel. Look at the screenshot presented in Fig. 4.23. Windows Components Wizard doesn't allow you to remove, for example, Internet Explorer, but the Wizard of OZ does.

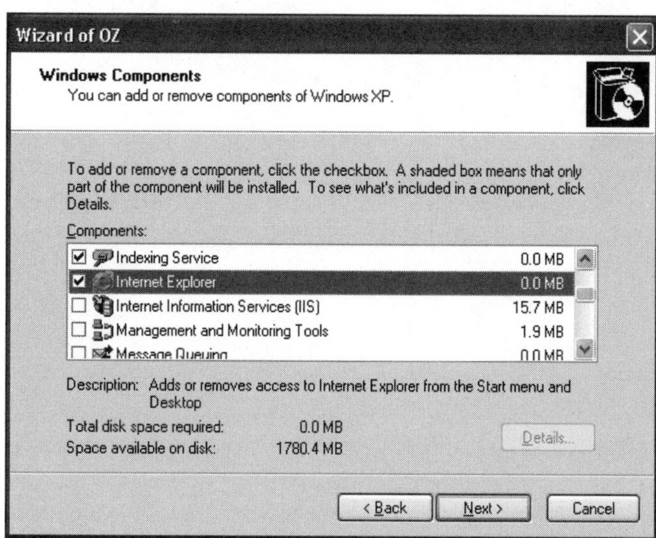

Fig. 4.23. Now you can uninstall Windows XP components that you no longer need

Summary

The tips shown in this chapter are the most common and frequently used, but I hope they'll still help you in customizing your Windows NT/2000 user interface.

Chapter 5

Plug and Play in Windows XP

We all are prisoners in the dungeon of our devices...
Plug and Pray!

Folklore

Many tasks related to configuring and fine-tuning the different operating systems from the Windows family (be it Windows 9*x*/ME, Windows NT/2000, or Windows XP) can be done using Control Panel applets. These applets are closely related to the registry. When you're viewing configuration information using Control Panel applets, this information is retrieved from the registry. On the other hand, all the configuration changes introduced using Control Panel applets are saved in the registry. This is the main reason why Windows NT 4.0 and all earlier Windows versions often required restarting after performing certain configuration changes. This is because the changes that you introduced wouldn't come into force until they were read from the registry during boot time.

NOTE

Thus, the whole boot process is interrelated with the registry. To identify the boot stage when the registry is initialized, it's necessary to understand the processes that take place when Windows starts loading. These topics will be covered in detail in the next chapter.

Limited hardware support and frequent reboots were the most serious drawbacks of Windows NT. In Windows 2000 and its successor, Windows XP, these disadvantages were eliminated due to implementation of Plug and Play support. In this chapter, we will consider Plug and Play (PnP) concepts in more detail and cover the following topics:

- How the registry stores hardware information.
- Plug and Play specification, its evolution, and PnP support implemented in Windows NT 4.0 and Windows 2000. We will pay special attention to PnP support enhancements that were introduced with Windows XP.

- Plug and Play specification and the registry, Plug and Play device detection, device installation and management.
- Advanced power management capabilities in Windows 2000 and Windows XP.

Registry and Plug and Play Subsystem

At the end of *Chapter 1*, I provided a simple example allowing you to gain a general understanding of the process used by the system to install new devices and resolve hardware conflicts. However, that example was too simplistic, and what's more important, it presented the process of hardware installation from the user point of view. But what actually happens when the system installs new hardware? What components are required to accomplish this task? How should we configure hardware and resolve hardware conflicts? These certainly are topics of great interest for anyone who's going to start full-scale support for Windows XP. With the release of Windows 95, Microsoft introduced a new concept simplifying PC usage: Plug and Play (or PnP). What is Plug and Play? A standard, or a specification of a concept? Actually, Plug and Play is a combination of the general approach to designing PCs, and a set of specifications describing the hardware architecture. Strictly speaking, it is a combination of the system BIOS hardware devices, system resources, device drivers, and the operating system software.

NOTE

In 64-bit computers, BIOS is known as Extensible Firmware Interface (EFI).

All Plug and Play components have the same purpose: to provide automatic functioning of the PC, peripheral devices, and their drivers, with minimum intervention from the user. Users working with systems that meet all Plug and Play requirements don't have to spend time wondering if a newly installed device will cause hardware conflicts with another device. The registry provides the basis for developing such a system.

The `HKEY_LOCAL_MACHINE\HARDWARE` registry key contains a description of the system hardware and the relationship between hardware devices and their drivers. Before we go any further, it should be noted that this key is volatile, and all information it contains is re-created every time the operating system boots.

The hardware recognizer (Ntdetect.com) collects information related to the system hardware, and Windows NT/2000/XP kernel stores the information under the

HKEY_LOCAL_MACHINE\HARDWARE\DESCRIPTION registry key. As the drivers are loading, they pass their information to the system so that it can associate the hardware devices and appropriate drivers. Windows NT/2000/XP saves this information under the HKLM\HARDWARE\DEVICEMAP registry key. Finally, all the necessary information related to the resources for the hardware devices (including ports, DMA addresses, IRQs) is stored under HKLM\HARDWARE\RESOURCEMAP.

With the arrival of Windows 2000, two new Executive subsystems were introduced: Plug and Play Manager and Power Manager. Plug and Play Manager is integrated with the I/O Manager, and doesn't participate in the initialization process. However, the drivers are initialized in such a way that Plug and Play drivers recognize some hardware devices. Windows NT 4.0, on the other hand, recognizes hardware devices using only Ntdetect, because of limited Plug and Play support.

Though Windows XP is based on the Windows NT/2000 kernel, the Plug and Play support provided by this operating system was further enhanced, improved, and optimized. The general idea of this design was to combine the respective advantages of the two lines of Windows products—Windows NT/2000 and Windows Millennium Edition (Windows ME). This approach was a success, since it achieved greater stability of the OS and better device compatibility.

For the moment, Windows XP includes Plug and Play support for hundreds of devices not covered by Windows 2000, such as scanners, cameras, audio devices, storage devices, and media (CDs and DVDs). At the same time, it provides better support for Universal Serial Buses (USB), IEEE 1394, Peripheral Component Interconnects (PCI), and other buses. Improvements introduced to the Plug and Play subsystem resulted in better stability and performance. This is especially true for the device installation process, which was streamlined and automated, as was illustrated by the example presented in *Chapter 1*. Besides, power management support was also improved, which certainly will be beneficial to both desktop and mobile computer users.

Plug and Play Historical Overview

Plug and Play represents a technology that supports automatic configuration of the PC and all the devices installed in the system. It allows you to start using newly installed hardware (for example, a sound card or modem) immediately after installation and without having to configure the device manually. Plug and Play is implemented at the hardware level, the operating system level, and in the device drivers and BIOS.

Plug and Play is the result of co-operation between software and hardware vendors who created an industrial committee in order to unify their efforts. This committee was founded in May of 1993, and initially included three corporations: Microsoft, Intel, and Compaq. By the end of 1995, several vendors were already producing hundreds of hardware devices complying with this standard.

Microsoft® Windows® 95 was the first operating system that implemented Plug and Play support. However, since that time, PnP standards have undergone a significant evolution, mainly due to the unified efforts of the members of the OnNow industrial initiative. OnNow aims to identify a universal approach for controlling both the operating system and hardware device configuration. Its main achievement is the *Advanced Configuration and Power Interface* (ACPI) *Version 1.0* specification, which defines the basic interface between the motherboard and the system BIOS. This interface expands Plug and Play capabilities, allowing the operating system to control power and provide other extended configuration capabilities.

Windows 2000 and Windows XP implement extended Plug and Play functionality. Windows 2000 was the first operating system from the Windows NT family that provided full-featured support for Plug and Play and power management. However, those of you who want all the advantages of Plug and Play and power management support need to ensure that both the system BIOS and the computer system as a whole meet ACPI specification requirements. More detailed information concerning this topic will be provided later in this chapter.

For the moment, Plug and Play technologies are defined for USB, IEEE 1394, PCI, ISA, SCSI, ATA, LPT, COM, and Card/CardBus. Each Plug and Play device must have the following capabilities:

- Be uniquely identified
- Provide a list of services it supports and resources it requests
- Identify the driver that supports this device
- Provide the software capabilities to configure this device

Plug and Play Support in Windows NT 4.0

One current opinion is that Windows NT 4.0 doesn't support Plug and Play. Actually, Windows NT 4.0 does support Plug and Play, but this support is very limited in comparison to Windows 9*x*/ME and Windows 2000/Windows XP. Except for PCI devices, the settings for all the other hardware must coincide with the settings specified in the registry. If this condition isn't satisfied, the device driver won't load, and the device won't function properly.

All PCI devices are configured automatically when Windows NT 4.0 starts booting. After the device has been configured, its settings normally won't change. Windows NT 4.0 changes device settings in the registry only if these settings aren't consistent with the number or type of PCI devices.

Windows NT 4.0 reads BIOS data and information obtained from physical devices only once—at the hardware detection stage at boot time. When the system is up and running, all device management operations are only performed by the device drivers and registry. After a successful boot, Windows NT 4.0 never reads BIOS data.

Plug and Play Implementation in Windows 2000 and Windows XP

Plug and Play systems require combined interaction between the PC BIOS, hardware components, device drivers, and operating system software. In contrast to all the previous versions of Windows NT, Windows 2000/XP provides improved reliability and decreased downtime. These improvements are due to an extended range of supported hardware and full-featured Plug and Play support. Implementation of all this new functionality is part of the Microsoft Zero Administration initiative, which is aimed at minimizing possible Windows downtime. For example, Plug and Play devices can often be plugged in or removed while Windows is running, and the system detects the action. Devices that can be removed while the system is running include, for example, all USB devices, some IEEE 1394 devices, etc.

Decreasing the frequency of required reboots is one of the most significant advantages, because it simplifies the procedure of installing both the operating system and hardware components. In most cases, new devices can be added dynamically; that is, without rebooting the system. The Hardware Compatibility List has also been significantly extended. Now HCL includes hundreds of new printers, modems, tape devices, floptical drives, and other devices. All this became possible thanks to full-featured Plug and Play support and Power Management features.

Removing a device from a computer without first notifying the operating system is known as a *surprise removal.* Typically, Windows XP can handle this situation correctly, because device drivers developed according to the *Windows XP Logo*

Requirements specification must notify the operating system when the device is removed. For such devices, the removal of the device does not affect the system. However, surprise removal is not recommended for some devices, particularly some storage devices, modems, and network adapters. Surprise removal of such devices causes the operating system to display an Unsafe Removal of Device screen, which tells the user to use the Safe Removal application when unplugging the device the next time. The user can manually disable the message for devices that can withstand surprise removal. The Safe Removal application is used to notify the operating system that a device is going to be unplugged, and can be found in the notification area, if such a device is installed on the system.

NOTE

However, some devices must be installed or removed only when the system is turned off. This is true if the device requires internal installation in the computer. Also, if data transfers are in progress when certain devices are removed, or if the operating system tries to access particular types of devices that have been removed, data loss, data corruption, or even a system failure might result. For example, surprise removal of a PC Card, a CardBus, or parallel or COM-port devices while the device driver is attempting to write to its ports can freeze the system or cause a STOP error, which requires that you reboot the system.

In contrast to Windows 95, Plug and Play implementation in Windows 2000 and Windows XP isn't based on Advanced Power Management (APM) BIOS or Plug and Play BIOS. These two BIOS implementations were developed for Windows 95. Windows 98 and Windows ME support both of these legacy Plug and Play implementations (this support is mainly provided for backward compatibility). Actual Plug and Play support both in Windows 2000 and Windows XP is based on the ACPI interface.

Some ACPI-compliant types of system BIOS may cause STOP errors in Windows 2000/XP. To minimize these situations, Microsoft developers have included a special functionality with a text-based Windows 2000/XP Setup phase. This functionality allows the disabling or activating of ACPI mode support based on the following lists:

- *Good BIOS list.* This list is used for activating ACPI mode for some types of BIOSes dated earlier than 01/01/1999. If the system BIOS ACPI tables match any entries in the Good BIOS List, ACPI mode will be enabled. Since the 01/01/1999 date is now past, Microsoft isn't adding any new entries to the Good BIOS List.

- *Incompatible BIOS list.* This list is used to disable ACPI mode for certain BIOSes dated 01/01/1999 or later. If the system BIOS ACPI tables match any entries in the Windows Non-compliant ACPI List, ACPI mode will be disabled. BIOSes are added to this list if they have been discovered to cause system stability problems by either Microsoft test teams or the BIOS developers. That is, if a system doesn't pass the ACPI Hardware Compatibility Test (HCT), fails to boot, or doesn't provide minimal functionality under Windows 2000, then Microsoft will place the machine's BIOS on the Windows Non-compliant ACPI list. The ACPI HCT is available on the Web at **http://www.microsoft.com/hwdev/acpihct.htm**.

If a system's BIOS isn't on either of these lists, the ACPI mode will be enabled if the BIOS presents itself as an ACPI BIOS that has a date later than 01/01/1999. The date that's used by the operating system is the standard PC-AT date, which is found at F000:FFF5.

NOTE

If the ACPI BIOS is detected as non-compliant in the Windows 2000 or Windows XP pre-setup system check, then the BIOS must be updated to ensure complete Plug and Play and power management functionality. Complete information on this topic is available at **http://www.Hardware-Update.com**.

For *x*86-based systems, there is a significant difference in the way the system BIOS interacts with the Plug and Play devices. For some systems, the BIOS Setup program has the **Enable Plug and Play operating system** option, which influences this interaction. Strictly speaking, this option specifies whether the system BIOS or the operating system controls the hardware. If you have a non-compliant ACPI system or a non-ACPI system, it is recommended that you set this option to **No/Disabled**. Microsoft also recommends that you disable this option if you dual-boot Windows XP and Windows 9*x*/ME, especially if the system check for Plug and Play on a Windows 98/ME ACPI system passes, but the system check for Plug and Play on Windows XP fails. If you have a fully compliant ACPI system (which means that ACPI BIOS is present and ACPI HAL installed), the device resources are assigned by Windows XP rather than by BIOS settings. BIOS settings are ignored, including the **Enable Plug and Play operating system** option. Because of this, this BIOS setting can be left as it is. However, Microsoft states that the **No/Disabled** setting for this option is still preferred.

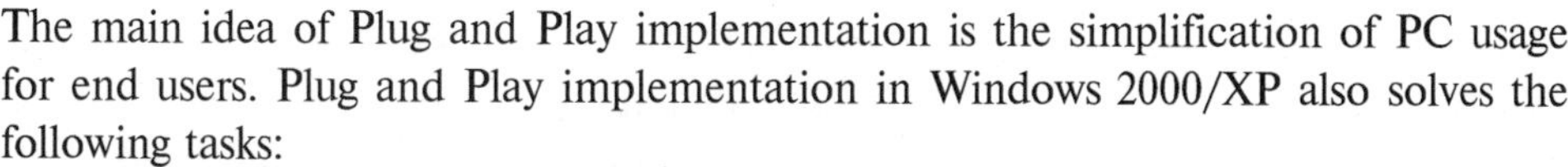

The main idea of Plug and Play implementation is the simplification of PC usage for end users. Plug and Play implementation in Windows 2000/XP also solves the following tasks:

- Extending the existing Windows NT I/O infrastructure in such a way as to support Plug and Play and power management while providing backward compatibility for existing Plug and Play hardware.
- Developing common driver interfaces that support Plug and Play and power management for multiple device classes under Windows 2000/XP and Windows 98/ME.
- Optimizing Plug and Play support for various types of computers, including portables, desktops, and servers equipped with ACPI-compliant motherboards. Additionally, support for Plug and Play drivers is provided by Microsoft Win32® Driver Model, WDM, which also supports power management and other new and extended functionalities that can be configured and managed by the operating system.

Plug and Play Support in Windows 2000 and Windows XP

To include Plug and Play support with Windows 2000, it was necessary to combine Plug and Play implementation with the basic Windows NT source code. The results of this integration are listed below.

- *Bus drivers are now separated from the Hardware Abstraction Layer (HAL).* Bus drivers manage the I/O bus, including slot functionality independent from specific devices. In the new architectural model, bus drivers are separated from the HAL in order to provide co-ordination with the changes and extensions introduced into the kernel-mode components, including Executive, device drivers, and the HAL. Usually, Microsoft supplies bus drivers.
- *New functionality is available for installing and configuring hardware devices.* The new architecture includes changes and extensions for existing user-mode components, including the spooler, class installers, Control Panel applets, and the Setup program. New user-mode and kernel-mode components have also been added. These new components are Plug and Play-aware.
- *New Plug and Play APIs were developed for reading and writing registry information.* The registry was modified in order to achieve this. Now it supports Plug and Play and allows further improvements and extensions of the registry structure while providing backward compatibility.

Windows 2000 supports legacy Windows NT drivers, but the drivers don't support power management or Plug and Play functionality. Software and hardware vendors need to provide complete Plug and Play support for the hardware devices and drivers they supply. New drivers should also be developed that integrate Plug and Play functionality with power management. If this were done, the same drivers could function in both Windows 2000/XP and Windows 98/ME.

You'll find a brief description of the Windows 2000/XP Plug and Play architecture later in the chapter. A complete description of all the modifications you need to introduce to provide full-featured Plug and Play for Windows 2000/XP is shown in the documentation supplied with Windows DDK.

ACPI Specification

The Plug and Play system requires combined interaction of the system BIOS, its hardware components, device drivers, and the operating system. The ACPI specification identifies all the necessary requirements to the motherboard and system BIOS for supporting Plug and Play in Windows 2000/XP. Both Windows 2000/XP and Windows 98/ME use this specification as a basis for Plug and Play architecture according to the requirements of the OnNow initiative.

The ACPI specification defines the new interface between the operating system and the hardware components that provide power management and Plug and Play support. Notice that all the methods defined in ACPI are independent both of the operating system and of the processor type. ACPI defines the interface on the registers level for basic Plug and Play and power management functions. It also defines a descriptive interface for additional hardware functionality. This allows the developers to implement a whole range of Plug and Play and power management functions for multiple hardware platforms while using the same driver. ACPI also provides a general mechanism for managing system events for Plug and Play and power management.

Besides ACPI, there are other industrial standards. For example, Universal Serial Bus, Version 1.0, PCI Local Bus Specification, Revision 2.1, and PCMCIA.

System Support for Plug and Play

Windows 2000/XP provides the following Plug and Play support:

- *Automatic and dynamic detection of installed hardware.* This includes initial installation of the operating system, detection of changes in Plug and Play hardware between reboots, and reaction at run-time hardware events, including installation and removal of devices and plugging/unplugging docking stations.

- *Assigning and reassigning hardware resources.* Plug and Play drivers don't set specific resources. All resources required by the device are identified when this device is enumerated by the operating system. Plug and Play Manager requests these resources when the system allocates resources to each device. Based on these requests, Plug and Play Manager allocates resources to each device, including I/O ports, IRQs, and DMA channels. When necessary, Plug and Play Manager may reconfigure the resource allocation. For example, this may be necessary when a new device is installed, and the device requests resources that are already in use by another device.
- *Loading appropriate drivers.* Plug and Play Manager determines which drivers are necessary to support a certain device, and then loads these drivers.
- *Interface for interaction between drivers and Plug and Play subsystem.* This interface includes input/output procedures, I/O Request Packets (IRP) and necessary entry points for the drivers, and registry information.
- *Interaction with power management system.* Dynamic handling of the events is the key feature of the Plug and Play implementation in Windows 2000/XP. Adding or removing a hardware device is an example of a dynamic event. Furthermore, the system can dynamically change to hibernation mode and vice versa. Both the Plug and Play system and power management system use WDM functions and implement similar methods of reacting to dynamic events.
- *Registration of device notification events.* Plug and Play provides user-mode code with the capability of registering events and getting notification on certain Plug and Play events. The `RegisterDeviceNotification` procedure allows the calling code to filter the class or device necessary to receive notifications. This filter may be specific, like the file system handle, or general, like the device class. Notification methods inherited from earlier Windows NT versions are also supported for backward compatibility.

Support Levels for Devices and Drivers

The Plug and Play support level that is provided by a device depends both on the hardware support for Plug and Play and on the Plug and Play support provided by the device driver. This concept is illustrated by the data presented in Table 5.1.

Table 5.1. Plug and Play Support Levels for Devices and Drivers

Device type	Plug and Play driver	Non-Plug and Play driver
Plug and Play device	Full-featured Plug and Play support	No Plug and Play support
Non-Plug and Play device	Partial support for Plug and Play	No Plug and Play support

As shown in this table, the appropriate driver is necessary for providing complete PnP support. A brief description of all possible configurations is shown below.

- *Full-featured support—both the device and its driver support Plug and Play.* To provide optimum Plug and Play support, the hardware component has to meet the OnNow initiative requirements, including ACPI specification. Plug and Play support implemented in Windows 2000/XP is oriented towards ACPI systems only.
- *Plug and Play device/legacy driver—no Plug and Play support.* If the device driver doesn't support Plug and Play, then the Plug and Play device will behave as a legacy device. Notice that this may limit Plug and Play functionality for the whole system.
- *Legacy device/Plug and Play driver—this combination may provide partial Plug and Play support.* If you have a legacy device that doesn't support Plug and Play at the hardware level, it may provide limited PnP support if the appropriate Plug and Play driver has been loaded. Although this system won't be able to automatically and dynamically detect the hardware and load the appropriate drivers, it will provide the capability of managing hardware resources. This system will also provide the interface for the driver to interact with the Plug and Play subsystem and register device notification events. If your hardware device has a Plug and Play driver, it will be displayed by the Device Manager. The tabs that allow you to configure device properties are available in the Device Manager window.
- *Neither the device nor its driver support Plug and Play: no Plug and Play support.* Legacy drivers will function as usual, but they won't support Plug and Play functions. All newly developed drivers should support Plug and Play.

As you can see, Plug and Play support depends on both the hardware device and the device driver. For example, if you have a manually installed legacy device, you still can gain functionality and provide partial Plug and Play support by installing a Plug and Play driver.

Windows XP supports Plug and Play for monitors if only the monitor, the display adapter, and the display driver are Plug and Play; otherwise, the monitor is detected as a default monitor.

Plug and Play Architecture in Windows 2000 and Windows XP

The Windows 2000/XP kernel provides Plug and Play support at boot-time. It provides interfaces to interact with various operating system components, such as the Hardware Abstraction Layer (HAL), the Executive subsystem, and device drivers. User-mode functions interact with kernel-mode functions, thus providing capabilities of dynamic configuration and interface with all other components supporting Plug and Play, such as Setup program and Control Panel applets. Schematic representation of PnP architecture in Windows 2000/XP is shown in Fig. 5.1.

The Plug and Play modules shown in Fig. 5.1 will be discussed later in this chapter.

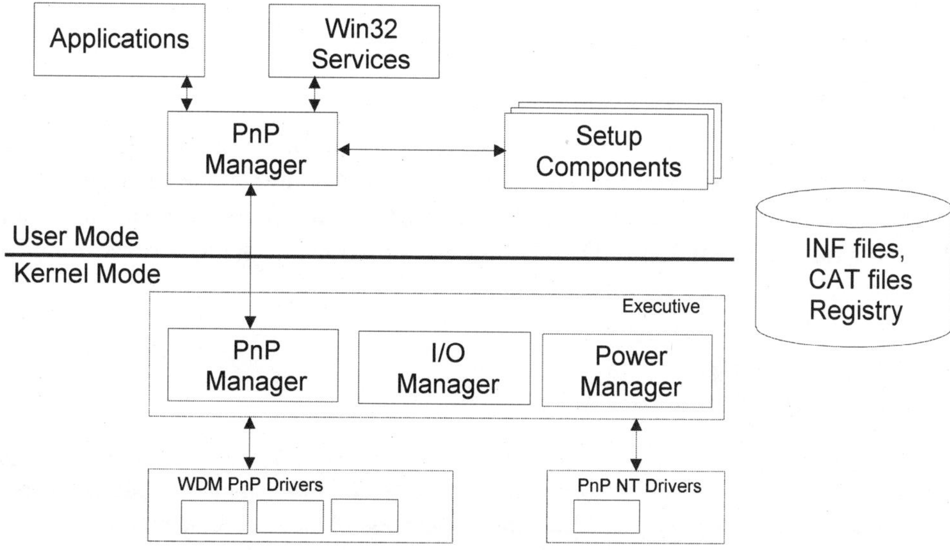

Fig. 5.1. Plug and Play architecture in Windows 2000 and Windows XP

Kernel-Mode Plug and Play Manager

The Kernel-mode Plug and Play Manager supports functions for centralized management, and manages bus drivers during enumeration. It also supports device drivers, which include adding or starting a new device.

For example, Plug and Play Manager requests if the device can be unplugged or removed, and allows the driver of this device to synchronize pending I/O requests with the newly received one. The kernel-mode Plug and Play Manager interacts with the user-mode Plug and Play Manager when identifying devices available for these operations.

Power Manager and Policy Manager

Power Manager is the kernel-mode component that works together with Policy Manager to process API calls, coordinate events, and generate I/O Request Packets (IRP). For example, if devices send requests for unplugging, Power Manager collects these requests, identifies which of them should be serialized, and generates the appropriate IRPs.

Policy Manager monitors the system activity and collects integrated status information on the users, applications, and device drivers. Under certain conditions (or by direct request) Policy Manager generates IRPs for changing device driver status.

Input/Output Manager

Input/Output manager provides basic services for device drivers. Input/Output Manager is the kernel-mode component that translates user-mode read and write commands to the appropriate IRPs. Besides, I/O Manager manages all the other basic operating system IRPs. These interfaces function the same way as those in Windows NT 4.0.

Windows XP enhances the I/O subsystem by adding new APIs that will be available to drivers developed according to the Windows XP Logo requirements. Device drivers written specially for Windows XP will take advantage of the new Windows XP functionality, including System Restore and Volume Snapshot Service, which were mentioned in *Chapter 2*. At the same time, Windows XP provides full backward compatibility with drivers developed for Windows 2000. Notice that despite the fact that all existing Windows 2000 drivers will work with Windows XP, it is strongly recommended that you check if Windows XP drivers are available. To obtain an updated driver, contact the device vendor or visit the Windows Update site.

WDM Interface for Plug and Play

The Input/Output system provides leveled driver architecture. This section discusses types of WDM (Win32 Driver Model) drivers, driver levels, and device objects. If you're interested in this topic and intend to develop device drivers, you can find all the necessary information in the documentation supplied with the latest version of Windows DDK.

Driver Types

From the Plug and Play system point of view, there are the following types of drivers:

- *Bus driver*—serves the bus controller, adapter, bridge, or any other device that has child devices. Bus drivers are required drivers and are normally supplied by Microsoft. Each type of the bus present in the system has its own bus driver.
- *Function driver*—this is the main device driver, which provides the operational interface for its device. It's a required driver unless the device is used raw (an implementation in which I/O is done by the bus driver and any bus filter drivers). The function driver for a device is typically implemented as a driver/minidriver pair. In these driver pairs, a *class driver* (usually written by Microsoft) provides the functionality required by all devices of that type, and a *minidriver* (usually written by the device vendor) provides device-specific functionality. The Plug and Play Manager loads one function driver for each device.
- *Filter driver*—sorts I/O requests for a bus, a device, or a class of devices. Filter drivers are optional and any number of them can exist placed above or below a function driver and above a bus driver. Usually, system original equipment manufacturers (OEMs) or independent hardware vendors (IHVs) supply filter drivers.

In most cases, lower-level filter drivers modify the behavior of the device hardware. For example, a lower-level class filter driver for mouse devices can provide acceleration, performing a non-linear conversion of mouse movement data.

Upper-level filter drivers usually provide value-added features for a device. For example, an upper-level device filter driver for a keyboard can enforce additional security checks.

Driver Layers

For any given device, there are two or more driver layers: a bus driver for the underlying I/O bus (or the Plug and Play Manager for root-enumerated devices) and a function driver for the device. Optionally, one or more filter drivers can be provided for the bus or device.

Device Objects

A driver creates a *device object* for each device it controls; the device object represents the device to the driver. From the Plug and Play perspective, there are three kinds of device objects: physical device objects (PDOs), functional device objects (FDOs), and filter device objects. PDOs represent a device on the bus; every Plug and Play API that refers to a device refers to the PDO. FDOs represent the functionality of a device to a function driver. Filter device objects represent a filter driver as a hook to add value. These three kinds of device objects are all of the `DEVICE_OBJECT` type, but are used differently and can have different device extensions.

Additional Windows NT/2000/XP Interfaces

Windows 2000/XP Plug and Play drivers aren't limited to using only the WDM interfaces. Drivers can call other interfaces to support legacy Windows NT drivers, detection, or other Windows NT-specific capabilities which aren't provided under WDM. Notice that if a driver is intended for work in both Windows 2000 and Windows 98, only WDM interfaces can be used.

WDM Bus Drivers

Bus power management and Plug and Play are controlled by WDM bus drivers, which are standard WDM drivers that expose bus capabilities. Notice that in this context, any device from which other devices are enumerated is referred to as a *bus*. A bus driver responds to new Plug and Play and power management I/O request packets (IRPs), and can be extended using filter drivers.

The bus driver is mainly responsible for the following tasks:

- Enumerating the devices on its bus
- Reporting dynamic events on its bus to the operating system
- Responding to Plug and Play and power management IRPs

- Multiplexing access to the bus (for some buses)
- Generically administering the devices on its bus

During enumeration, a bus driver identifies the devices on its bus and creates device objects for them. The method a bus driver uses to identify connected devices depends on the particular bus.

A bus driver performs certain operations on behalf of the devices on its bus, but usually doesn't handle reads and writes to the devices. (A device's function driver handles reads and writes to a device.) A bus driver acts as a function driver for its controller, adapter, bridge, or other device.

Microsoft provides bus drivers for most common buses, including PCI, Plug and Play ISA, SCSI, and USB. Other bus drivers can be provided by IHVs or OEMs. A bus driver can be implemented as a driver/minidriver pair, the way a SCSI port/miniport pair drives a SCSI host adapter. In these driver pairs, one driver is linked to the second driver, and the second driver is a DLL.

The ACPI driver plays the role of both bus driver and function driver. ACPI allows the system to learn about devices that either don't have a standard way of enumerating themselves (that is, legacy devices) or are newly defined ACPI devices to be enumerated by ACPI (for example, the embedded controller device). ACPI also installs upper-level filter drivers for devices that have functionality beyond the standard for their bus. For example, if a PCI bus driver installs a graphics controller with power controls not supported by the PCI bus, the device can access its added functionality if the ACPI driver loads an upper-level filter driver for it.

WDM Device Drivers

WDM device drivers are usually the function driver/minidriver pair and filter drivers. In addition to providing the operational interface for its device, function drivers play an important role in a power-managed system, contributing information as the policy owner for the device about power management capabilities and carrying out actions related to transitions between sleeping and fully-on power states.

User-Mode Plug and Play Components

The user-mode Windows 2000 APIs for managing and configuring Plug and Play devices are 32-bit extended versions based on the Configuration Manager API for Windows 95. Windows 95 Configuration Manager is a virtual device driver (VxD) that exposes these routines as services to both ring 0 and ring 3 components.

In Windows 2000/XP, these procedures extend the user-mode Plug and Play Manager functionality. Actually, they're exclusively user-mode APIs. Windows NT/2000/XP Setup program performs driver installation. The Setup program uses 32-bit device installation APIs, which represent a superset of the Windows 95 installation procedures.

Windows 2000/XP provides APIs that can be used by applications for customized hardware event management and creating new hardware events.

Plug and Play Device Tree

Plug and Play Manager supports the device tree that you can view using Device Manager (Fig. 5.2). This device tree keeps track of the active devices in the system and information about those devices. The Plug and Play Manager updates the device tree as devices are added and removed, or as resources are reallocated. The device tree is hierarchical, with devices on a bus represented as children of the bus adapter or controller. The registry is the central repository for static hardware information. Plug and Play system components and drivers build, maintain, and access new and existing subtrees in the registry.

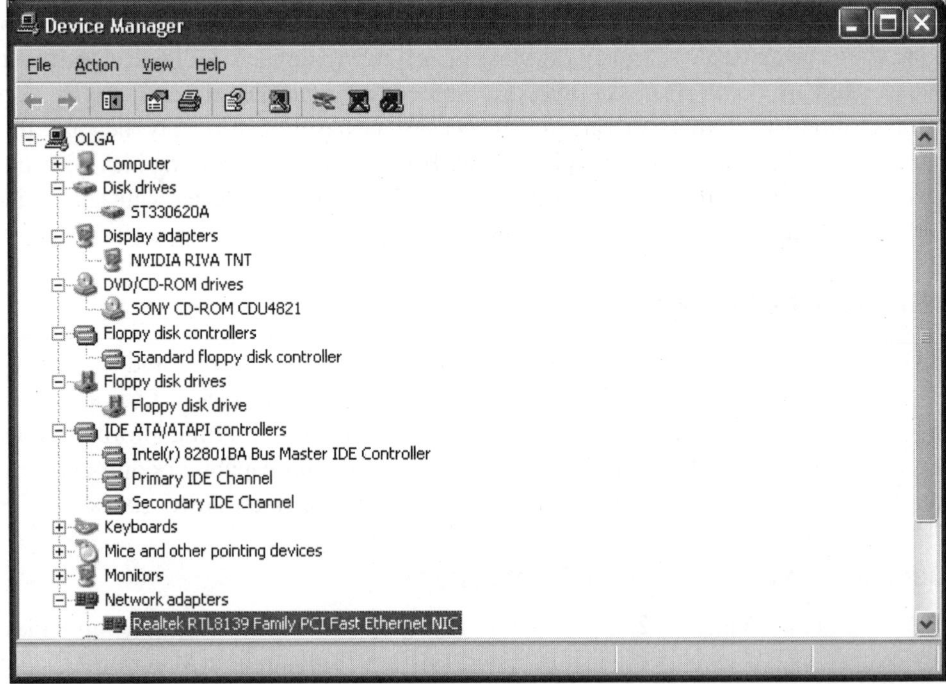

Fig. 5.2. The device tree displayed by the Device Manager is supported by the Plug and Play Manager

During enumeration, data for each device is stored under a new `HKEY_LOCAL_MACHINE\System\CurrentControlSet\Enum` key in the registry (this is the enum tree). Plug and Play makes decisions about which device drivers are loaded based on the results of enumeration. Thus, there's an important connection between the enum tree and the list of services under `HKEY_LOCAL_MACHINE\System\CurrentControlSet\Services`.

Notice that Device Manager allows you to view devices both by type and by connection. To view devices by connection, simply select the **Devices by connection** command from the **View** menu. The device tree displaying devices by connection is shown in Fig. 5.3.

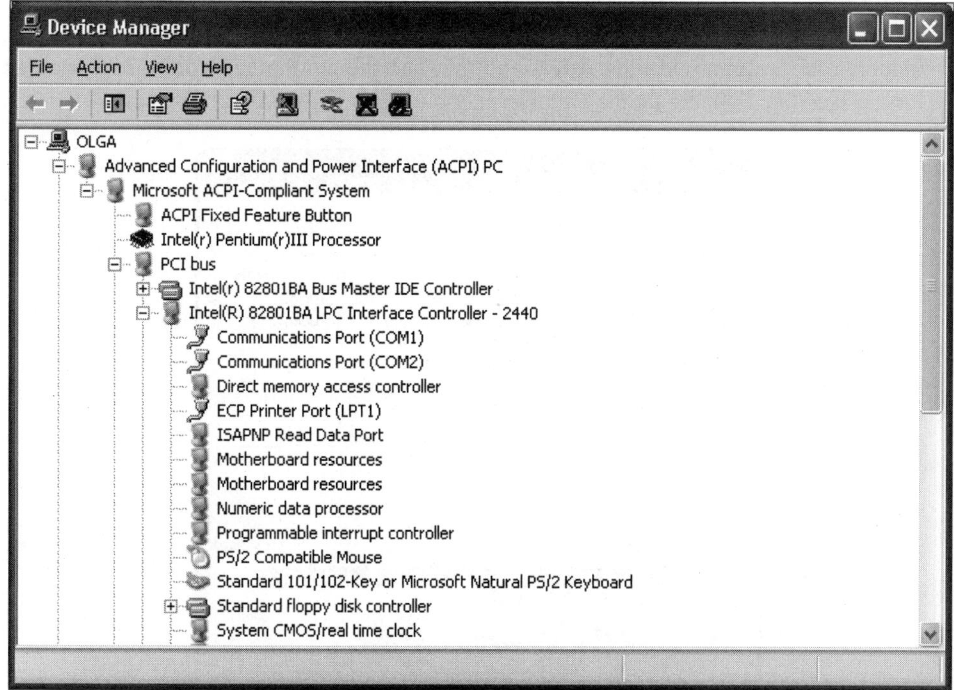

Fig. 5.3. Viewing devices by connection

Each branch in the tree defines a device node with the following requirements for system configuration:

- Device unique identifier (Device ID, DID), which is typically identified by a friendly name
- Resources such IRQs and DMAs, including resource type

- Allocated resources
- Indicates whether the device node is a bus, if applicable (each bus device has additional device nodes under it in the tree)

Specific icons indicate the device type and indicate any device conflict on the computer. Problem codes and icons for troubleshooting devices are also displayed.

Device Manager does not display all devices by default. Legacy devices, devices that are no longer attached to the computer, and some other devices are hidden. To view such hidden devices, select the **Show hidden devices** command from the **View** menu.

NOTE

You can set Device Manager to show a list of non-present devices. In Control Panel, double-click **System**, click the **Advanced** tab, and then in the **Environment Variables** dialog box (Fig. 5.4), create the variable `DEVMGR_SHOW_NONPRESENT_DEVICES=1`.

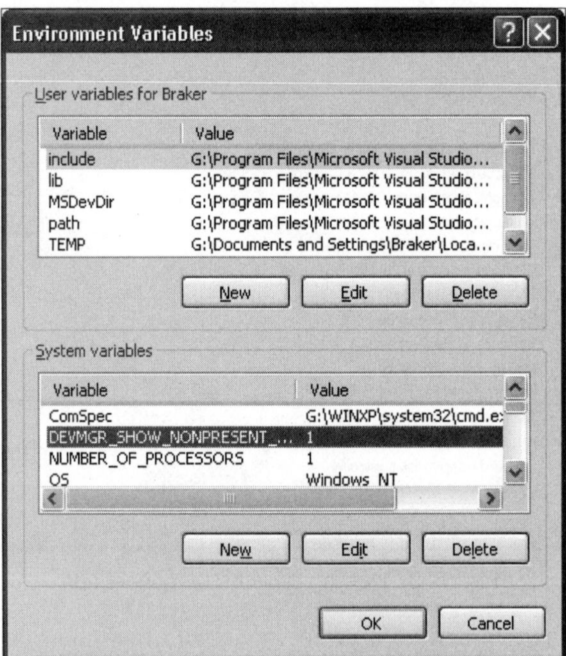

Fig. 5.4. The **Environment Variables** window

You can use Device Manager to enable or disable devices, troubleshoot devices, update drivers, use driver rollback, and change resources assigned to devices.

In order to scan for hardware changes, update the driver for the device, disable or uninstall the device, troubleshoot the device, or view its properties, right-click the appropriate device node in the device tree and then select the appropriate command from the popup menu.

Plug and Play Device Detection

Plug and Play implementation in the Windows XP operating system provides the following advantages:

- Detects and enumerates devices
- Allocates resources during detection
- Dynamically loads, initializes, and unloads drivers
- Notifies other drivers and applications when a new device is available
- Works with power management to insert and remove devices
- Supports a range of device types

After Windows XP detects a Plug and Play device, the device driver can be configured and loaded dynamically, requiring little or no user input. Some buses, such as PCI and USB, take full advantage of Plug and Play capability and are also automatically detected. After the device is detected, PnP Manager and Bus driver enumerate the device, load the required driver(s) and start the device. If the device is new (no information on this device is available in the registry), Windows XP will install and start driver(s) for this device.

As was already noted, Windows XP Setup inspects the hardware configuration of the computer and records information on the devices it had detected in the registry. Setup gets configuration information for system devices from the INF file associated with each device and, with Plug and Play devices, from the device itself.

On a PnP system, a device transitions through various PnP states as it is configured, started, possibly stopped to rebalance resources, and possibly removed. The transitions between various states of the PnP device are shown in Fig. 5.5.

When a new device is installed, Windows XP uses the device ID to search INF files for an entry for that device. Windows XP uses this information to create an entry for the device under the `Hkey_Local_Machine` branch in the registry, and it copies the drivers needed. Then the registry entries are copied from the INF file to the driver's registry entry.

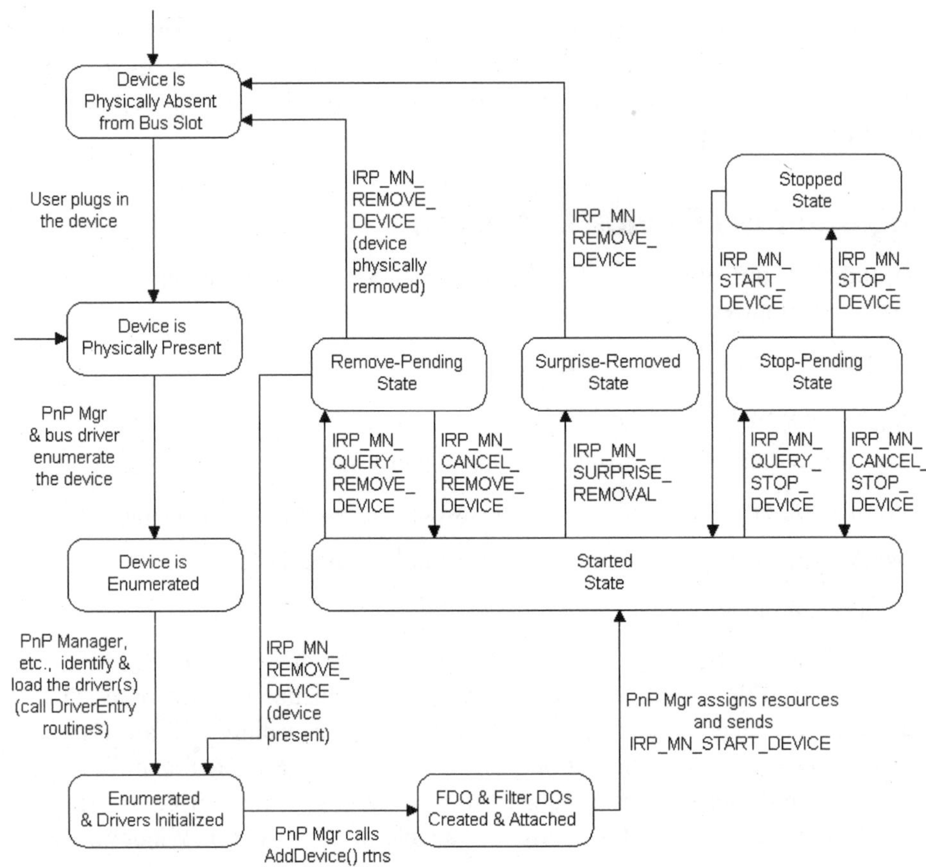

Fig. 5.5. PnP device states

Windows XP uses driver-ranking schemes to determine which driver to load when multiple drivers are available for a device. Drivers are ranked based on whether they are signed with a digital signature, and how closely they match the device's hardware ID (HW ID). If there are multiple drivers for a device, the driver with the highest ranking is selected for installation. The list of driver-ranking schemes from the highest to the lowest rank is as follows:

- Signed driver with a perfect four-part HW ID match to the driver
- Signed driver with a two-part HW ID match to the driver
- Unsigned driver with a perfect four-part HW ID match to the driver
- Unsigned driver with a two-part HW ID match to the driver

When you need to install a new device, rely first on Windows XP to detect and configure it. How you do it depends on what type of device you have, as the following list explains:

- For Plug and Play-compliant devices, plug the device in.
- For PCI and ISA Plug and Play cards, turn the computer off and then install the device. When you restart the computer, Windows XP detects the device and starts the Plug and Play installation procedures automatically.
- For legacy devices, run the Add Hardware wizard and let Windows XP detect the device. This requires administrator privileges.

Devices are installed after the user logs on to the computer.

Whenever possible, choose new Plug and Play devices, even for a computer that does not have an ACPI BIOS, to gain some Plug and Play functionality.

An example illustrating all the processes that take place in the system when the user installs new devices, and all the components required for successful installation is provided in Fig. 5.6. The sequence of action is as follows:

1. The user plugs the device into the computer. Note that if the device and its bus support the so-called *hot-plug notification*, you can plug the device in when the system is up and running.
2. PnP Manager and bus driver enumerate the new device. First, the bus driver with the support from the bus receives notification from the new device, and then notifies the kernel-mode PnP Manager on the change in the hardware configuration (in our case, a new device has been added). The kernel-mode PnP Manager then queries the bus driver for a list of devices physically present on the bus and compares the new list to the previous copy. Thus, PnP Manager determines which device has been added, and requests the bus driver for information on the new device (such as hardware ID, vendor ID, compatible IDs, and device capabilities).
3. The kernel-mode PnP Manager notifies the user-mode PnP Manager that there is a device to be installed. The user-mode PnP Manager creates a new process using *rundll32.exe* and launches *newdev.dll* to install the device.
4. The New Device DLL calls device installation functions (Setup API) and PnP Configuration Manager functions (CfgMgr API) to carry out its installation

tasks. The New Device DLL creates a list of possible drivers for the device, and if necessary displays the Found New Device wizard. Information on driver selection was provided earlier in this chapter.

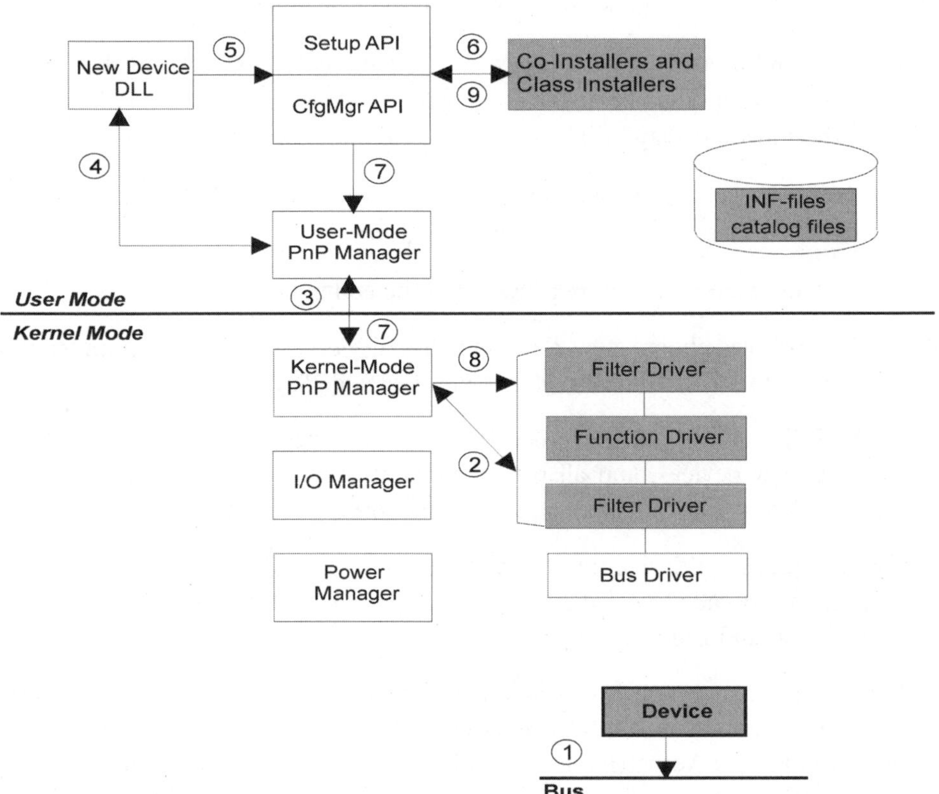

Fig. 5.6. Device Installation scheme

5. The class installer and co-installers, if there are any, can participate in the device installation.

6. Setup transfers control to kernel mode to load drivers and start the device. Once Setup has selected the best driver for the device, copied the appropriate driver files, registered any device-specific co-installers, registered any device interfaces, and so forth, it transfers control to kernel mode to load the drivers and start the device. The appropriate CfgMgr function sends a request to the user-mode PnP Manager, which passes it to the kernel-mode PnP Manager.

7. The PnP Manager loads the appropriate function driver and any optional filter drivers for the device.
8. Installers can supply wizard pages to change device settings.

Driver Rollback

This new feature, introduced with Windows XP, provides a useful reliability enhancement. Problems such as hardware conflicts, persistent STOP errors, or system instabilities occur after you install an incompatible driver. Needless to say, in such a situation it would be highly desirable to have the capability of replacing the driver that causes problems without reinstalling the operating system. Now, Windows XP provides this capability.

Driver RollBack is an indispensable troubleshooting tool when you need to restore a damaged system. It is also very useful when debugging beta-versions of drivers. For example, if after updating the driver version your system displays a STOP message during boot, you can try to boot the system in safe mode and perform rollback of the faulty driver.

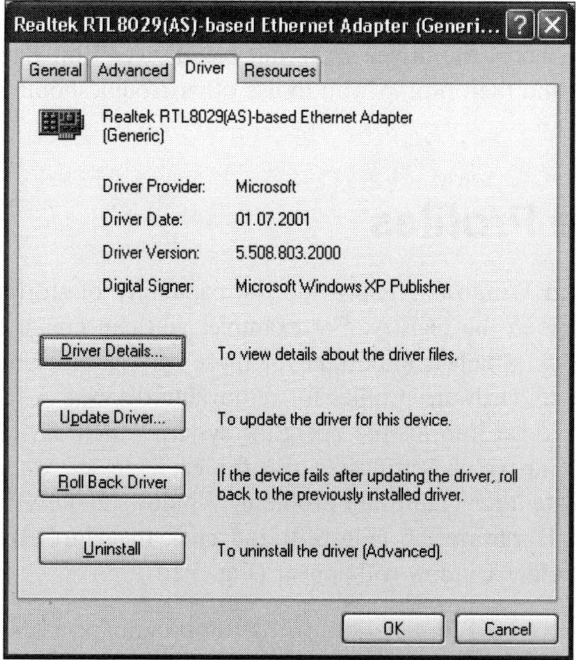

Fig. 5.7. The **Driver** tab of the device properties window now allows you to perform driver rollback

Fig. 5.8. The driver can't be rolled back, since there are no driver files backed up for the device

To use Driver RollBack, proceed as follows:

1. Start the System applet in Control Panel, go to the **Hardware** tab and click the **Device Manager** button.
2. Right-click the device whose updated driver is causing the problem, and select the **Properties** command from the context menu.
3. Go to the **Driver** tab (Fig. 5. 7). Click **Roll Back Driver**.
4. The Device Manager will prompt you to confirm driver rollback. Click **Yes**. If a previous version of the driver is unavailable, Driver Roll Back will display an error message and then prompt you to use other troubleshooting tools.

Hardware Profiles

Windows 2000 and Windows XP provide the capability of storing multiple hardware configurations in the registry. For example, you can create hardware profiles for docking stations, which is important for those of you with portable computers. You can also create hardware profiles for removable devices. A hardware profile is a set of instructions that informs the operating system which devices to start, which drivers to load, and which settings to use for each device when you start your computer. To create a new hardware profile in Windows 2000/XP, start the System applet, go to the **Hardware** tab (Fig. 5.9) and click the **Hardware Profiles** button. The **Hardware Profiles** window will appear (Fig. 5.10).

During Windows 2000/XP installation, the Setup program creates the default hardware profile, which includes all hardware detected on the computer during the installation.

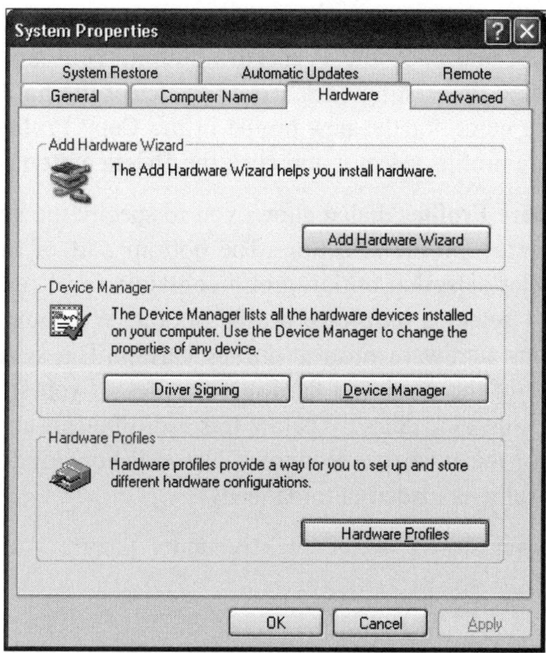

Fig. 5.9. The **Hardware** tab of the **System Properties** dialog

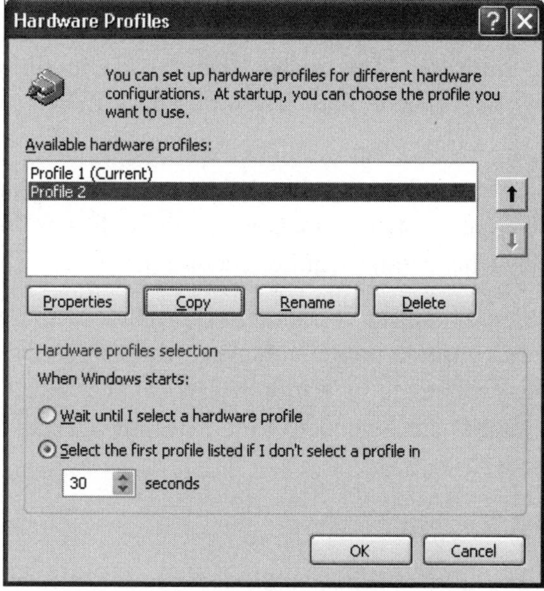

Fig. 5.10. Hardware profiles

To change the hardware profile properties, select its name from the **Available hardware profiles** list and click the **Properties** button. You can also create a new hardware profile based on existing ones. To do so, select the hardware profile, click **Copy**, and enter the name for the new profile in the **Copy Profile** dialog. To delete the existing hardware profile, select it and click the **Delete** button.

Finally, the **Hardware Profiles** dialog allows you to specify the system's behavior as related to the hardware profile selection. The bottom part of this dialog contains the **Hardware profiles selection** option group containing two radio buttons. If you set the **Wait until I select a hardware profile** option, Windows 2000/XP will display a list of existing hardware profiles during startup. The system will wait until the user selects one of the displayed hardware profiles. If you set the second radio button, navigate to the field directly below this radio button and specify the time interval (in seconds) that instructs Windows 2000/XP how long to wait before the default hardware profile is loaded automatically.

Hardware profiles are stored in the registry under `HKEY_LOCAL_MACHINE\System\CurrentControlSet\Hardware Profiles`.

Power Management

Power management implementation in Windows 2000 and Windows XP is an integrated approach to power management within the whole computer system (for both hardware and software). This means that the computer system supporting power management must include both hardware and software support for the following functions:

- Minimum time expenses for startup and shutdown. This means that the system may stay in a hibernation state as long as necessary. It may "wake up" from this mode very quickly (this doesn't require rebooting).
- Efficient and economic power consumption, increase of the working life of the hardware. Devices consume power only when they process a system request or perform operations requested by the user. Devices that aren't in use during the specified time period are switched to a "sleeping" state, and subsequently "wake-up" as needed.
- Silent operation.

Requirements to the power-aware hardware and software are defined by the OnNow initiative. Windows XP provides this support, and both the PC as a whole and each individual device consume minimum power (if the hardware meets the OnNow requirements). Notice that power management and PnP are interrelated and depend on each other.

This approach provides the following advantages:

- Intellectual behavior of the system. The operating system and applications work together to operate the PC, delivering effective power management in accordance with your current needs. For example, applications won't inadvertently keep the PC busy when it isn't necessary; instead, they'll proactively participate in shutting down the PC to conserve energy and reduce noise.
- Improved robustness and reliability.
- Higher level of integration.

By using the Power Options applet in the Control Panel, it's possible to decrease energy consumption for any device installed in the system. However, you can only achieve this if you have an ACPI-compliant computer system.

The *Power Schemes* Tab

To start the Power Options applet, proceed as follows:

1. From the **Start** menu, select **Settings** | **Control Panel**. Double-click **Power Management**.
2. The **Power Options Properties** window will appear (Fig. 5.11).
3. To reduce the power consumption of your computer devices, or of your entire system, choose a *power scheme*, which is a collection of settings that manage the power usage of your computer. You can select one of the existing power schemes or create a user-defined power scheme. For example, depending on your hardware, you can do the following:
   - Specify the conditions where the system will automatically turn off your monitor and hard disks to save power.
   - Put the computer on standby if it's idle for a long period of time. While on standby, your entire computer switches to a low power state, where devices such as the monitor and hard disks turn off and your computer uses less power. When you want to use the computer again, it comes out of standby

quickly, and your desktop is restored exactly as you left it. Standby is particularly useful for conserving battery power in portable computers.

- Put your computer in hibernation. The hibernate feature saves everything in memory on disk, turns off your monitor and hard disk, and then turns off your computer. When you restart your computer, your desktop is restored exactly as you left it. It takes longer to bring your computer out of hibernation than out of standby.

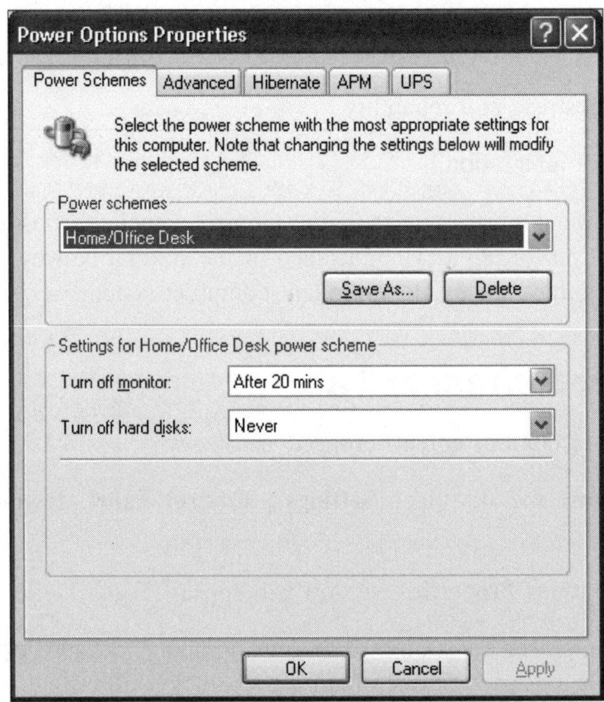

Fig. 5.11. The **Power Schemes** tab of the **Power Options Properties** window

Table 5.2 lists the registry keys that you can modify using the **Power Schemes** tab of the **Power Management Properties** window.

Table 5.2. Registry Keys Modified Using the Power Schemes Tab Controls

***Power Schemes* option**	**Registry key**
Power schemes	`HKCU\Control Panel\PowerCfg\CurrentPowerPolicy`

continues

Table 5.2 Continued

***Power Schemes* option**	**Registry key**
Standby detection threshold values (for the system, monitor, hard disk—**System hibernates**, **Turn off monitor**, **Turn off hard disks** fields, respectively)	Binary-encoded parameters `HKCU\Control Panel\PowerCfg\PowerPolicies\`*n*`\Policies`
Deleting the power scheme (the **Delete** button)	Deletes the following key `HKCU\Control Panel\PowerCfg\PowerPolicies\`*n*`\Policies` Decreases the following index counter: `HKLM\SOFTWARE\Microsoft\Windows\CurrentVersion\Controls Folder\PowerCfg\LastID`
Adding new power scheme (the **Save As** button)	Adds new subkey under the following key: `HKCU\Control Panel\PowerCfg\PowerPolicies\`*n*`\Policies` Increases the following index counter: `HKLM\SOFTWARE\Microsoft\Windows\CurrentVersion\Controls Folder\PowerCfg\LastID`

Usually, you need to turn off your monitor or hard disk for a short period of time to conserve power. The most convenient mode for this is the standby mode, which puts your entire system in a low-energy state.

The *Hibernate* Tab

Besides the standby mode, the Power Options applet allows you to put your system into hibernation mode. As I already mentioned, the hibernate feature saves everything in memory on disk, turns off your monitor and hard disk, and then turns off your computer. After rebooting the system, your desktop is restored exactly as you left it. It takes longer to bring your computer out of hibernation than out of standby.

If you're planning to be away from your computer for any length of time, I recommend that you put the system into hibernation. To activate hibernation support, proceed as follows:

1. Open the **Power Options Properties** window and go to the **Hibernate** tab (Fig. 5.12). If your system doesn't support this option, the tab will be unavailable.

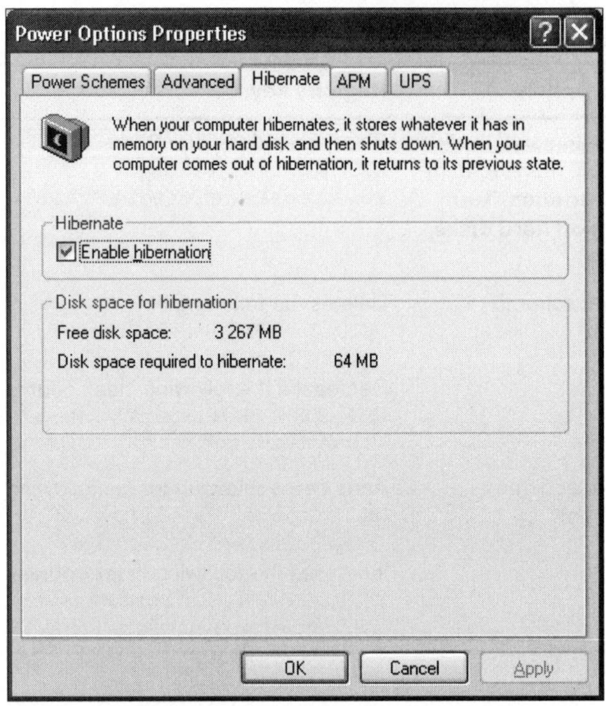

Fig. 5.12. The **Hibernate** tab of the **Power Options Properties** window

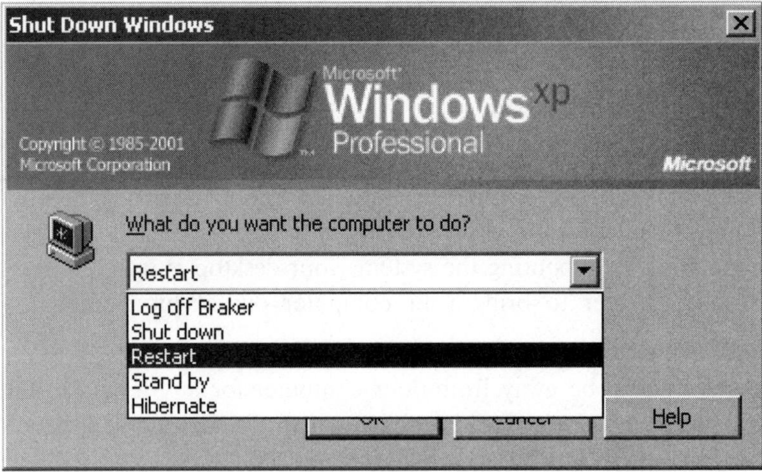

Fig. 5.13. When you enable hibernation support, the **Shut Down Windows** window will display a new option—**Hibernate**, allowing you to put the system to hibernation manually

2. Set the **Enable hibernate support** checkbox. Please note that when your computer is set to hibernation, everything in the physical memory is saved to the hard disk. Because of this, you need to have sufficient disk space on the hard disk (the file storing memory dump will be as large as your RAM memory).

After hibernation support is activated, the **What do you want the computer to do?** list in the **Shut Down Windows** dialog will contain a new option—**Hibernate**, which allows you to put the computer into hibernation manually (Fig. 5.13).

The *Advanced* Tab

The **Advanced** tab of the **Power Options Properties** window (Fig. 5.14) allows you to do the following:

- Enable and disable the power options indicator on the taskbar (Fig. 5.15). This indicator is a small icon that provides quick access to the Power Options applet.
- Enable and disable password protection for the standby mode.

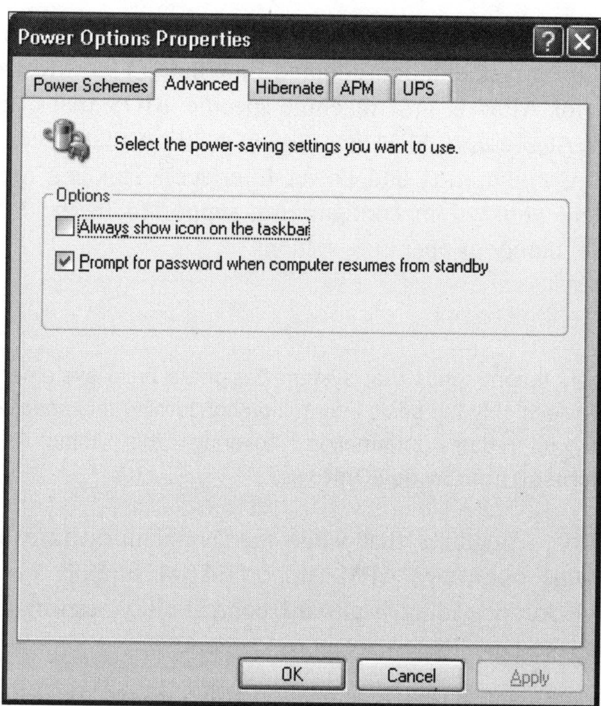

Fig. 5.14. The **Advanced** tab of the **Power Options Properties** window

Fig. 5.15. The taskbar indicator provides quick access to the Power Options applet

Registry keys that correspond to the parameters set using this tab are listed in Table 5.3.

Table 5.3. Registry Keys Modified by Setting Parameters of the Advanced Tab

Advanced **tab option**	**Registry key**
Always show icon on the taskbar checkbox	`HKCU\Control Panel\PowerCfg \GlobalPowerPolicy\Policies`
Display a prompt for a password when the computer goes off standby checkbox	`HKCU\Control Panel\PowerCfg \GlobalPowerPolicy\Policies`

The *APM* Tab

Advanced Power Management (APM) is the legacy scheme of power management based on the BIOS implementation adopted in Windows 95. Most of the interesting functionality for APM is in a machine-specific BIOS that's hidden from the operating system. At present, APM is a legacy solution that's been superseded by ACPI (Advanced Configuration and Power Interface). This is a robust scheme for power management and system configuration supported in the Windows 98 and Windows 2000/XP family of operating systems.

NOTE

Microsoft strongly recommends that system designers build systems based on ACPI. This chapter provides only the basic information concerning this specification. The most complete and up-to-date information covering this topic is available at: **http://www.microsoft.com/hwdev/OnNow**.

However, Microsoft recognizes that while many machines have both ACPI and APM support, some only have APM support. APM support was included with Windows 2000/XP for providing backward compatibility, especially for the convenience of users who have legacy notebook computers.

APM should *not* be used if the machine or BIOS is on the Windows 2000/XP "Disable APM" list. The system will refuse to run APM on these machines, because

Microsoft Development found that it *does not work* on them. Don't attempt to override this limitation.

You can try using APM if the system BIOS isn't ACPI-compliant or the ACPI BIOS isn't properly implemented.

NOTE

On some machines, the APM BIOS may make the system unstable. Enabling APM support in Windows 2000/XP (using the Ntapm.sys driver) may correct the problem, since this puts the operating system more in sync with the system's APM BIOS.

The classes of APM systems under Windows 2000 and Windows XP are:

- *"AutoEnable APM"*. This indicates that the system passed testing at Microsoft and was placed on the "AutoEnable APM List" that Windows 2000 Setup checks before installing the operating system. Windows 2000 Setup will install and enable APM support automatically on these systems. This list includes the APM system/BIOS combinations that Microsoft believes are stable and ready to support APM while running Windows 2000/XP.
- *"Disable APM"*. This means that Microsoft has determined that APM doesn't work properly on the system. Microsoft placed entries for specific system/BIOS combinations on the Disable APM List that malfunctioned in testing when APM was turned on. For system/BIOS combinations on the Disable APM List, Windows 2000/XP Setup won't install or enable APM support. Notice that it may still be necessary to disable the APM BIOS using the machine's BIOS setup utility to make things reliable.
- *Neutral systems*. This means that Microsoft doesn't know how well this system works with APM under Windows 2000/XP. Systems that aren't on the AutoEnable APM List or the Disable APM List are considered "neutral." In this case, Windows 2000/XP installs the Ntapm.sys software, but leaves it disabled. You can manually enable the APM support in Windows 2000/XP by using the Power Options applet in the Control Panel.

NOTE

The only approved or supported method of activating or disabling APM support manually is to use the Power Options applet from Control Panel. To enable APM support, go to the **APM** tab of the **Power Options Properties** window (Fig. 5.16), and set the **Enable Advanced Power Management support** checkbox. Notice that turning APM support off requires a reboot. Turning APM on doesn't require a reboot.

APM support is included only with Windows 2000 Professional, Windows XP Professional, and Home Edition. APM support isn't allowed on server products. This means that the APM tab won't appear and that there's no APM support in Windows 2000 Server, Windows 2000 Advanced Server, or Windows 2000 DataCenter.

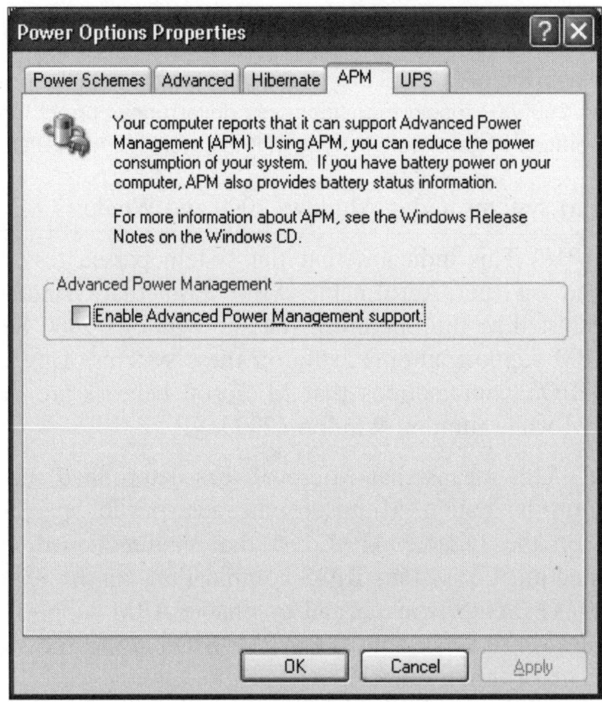

Fig. 5.16. The **APM** tab of the **Power Options Properties** window

APM Keys in the Registry

The data on APM support collected by the hardware recognizer (Ntdetect.com) is stored in the registry under the following key: `HKEY_LOCAL_MACHINE\HARDWARE\DESCRIPTION\System\MultifunctionAdapter`.

This key contains a set of subkeys named 0, 1, 2, 3, and so on. Each of them will have value entries named `Component Information`, `Configuration Data`, or `Identifier`. Find the key whose `Identifier` entry has a value of "APM" (Fig. 5.17). The `Configuration Data` entry of that key will contain the data on APM found and reported by Ntdetect.com. If the key is absent, then APM wasn't found.

APM support is provided for Intel platforms only (the HAL version is Halx86.dll). This information is stored in the registry under the following key: `HKEY_LOCAL_MACHINE\System\CurrentControlSet\Control\ApmLegalHal`. If the HAL is Halx86.dll, this registry key will have a value entry present with data of 1.

The results of machine-specific detection versus Biosinfo.inf are stored in `HKEY_LOCAL_MACHINE\System\CurrentControlSet\Control\BIOSInfo\APM`. If the "Attributes" value is 1, the machine's APM BIOS is "known good" and the machine is on the `AutoEnable APM` list. If the value is 2, the machine's APM BIOS is "known bad" and the machine is on the `Disable APM` list. Otherwise, the machine is neutral.

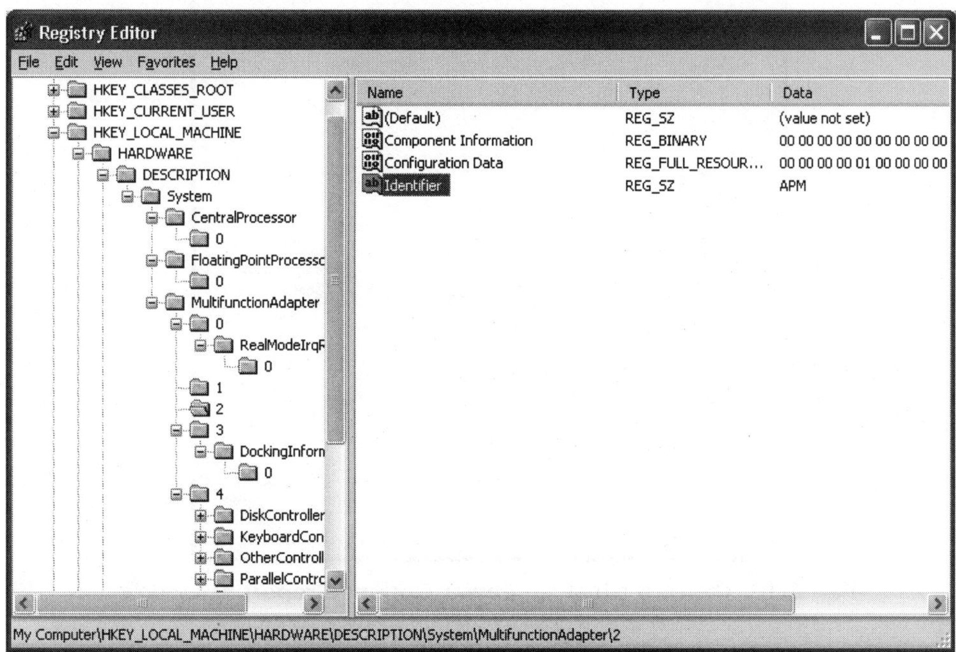

Fig. 5.17. APM data in the registry

If the machine is an ACPI machine, there will be a services entry for ACPI under `(HKLM\System\CurrentControlSet\Services\ACPI)` with a value of `Start` = 0. This is telling the system to load and run Acpi.sys at phase 0.

More detailed information on the boot process will be provided in *Chapter 6.*

If the ACPI key isn't present, the machine isn't being run as an ACPI machine, even if it should be.

The *UPS* Tab

If Uninterruptible Power Supply (UPS) is present in your system, it can also be managed via Power Options. To configure and manage the UPS service, start the Power Options applet in Control Panel, and go to the **UPS** tab (Fig. 5.18). This tab displays the current power status, details on your UPS equipment, and the current status of the UPS service.

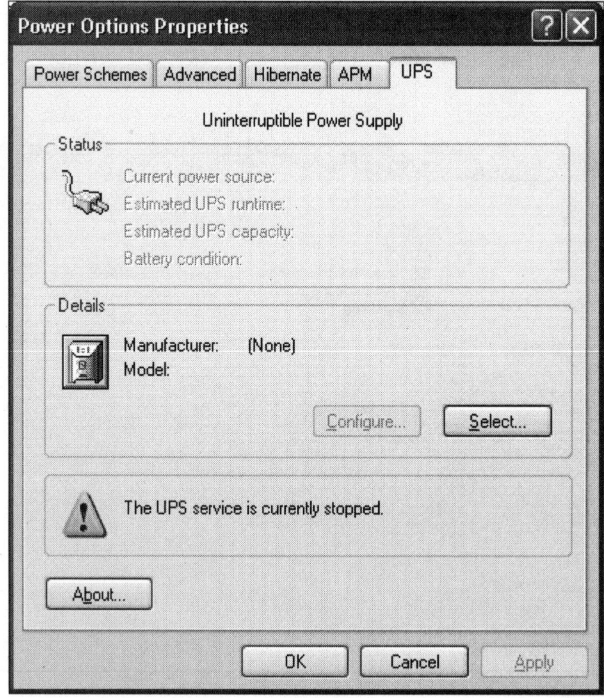

Fig. 5.18. The **UPS** tab of the **Power Options Properties** window

Windows 2000/XP Power Management Tools

Having already discussed the power management tools provided by the Windows 2000/XP operating system, let's now discuss the basic concepts that made it possible to implement these tools. Some of the concepts discussed in this section are applicable to both Windows 2000/XP and Windows 98.

The topics covered here include:

- Power management policies and power schemes

- Parameters included into the power scheme
- How power management settings specified by the Power Options Control Panel applet are stored in the registry

Power Schemes

Windows 2000/XP power management configuration is based on the concept of power schemes. A power scheme is a group of preset power options that are passed to the Power Policy Manager component of the operating system to control the machine's power management behavior.

Each power scheme consists of a global power policy structure and a power policy structure.

- Global power policy structures contain preset power options that are global across all power schemes.
- Non-global power policy structures contain power options that are unique to a particular power scheme.

These power policy structures are further divided into machine structures and user structures.

- Values in machine structures are stored in the `HKEY_LOCAL_MACHINE` registry key, and none of these values are exposed in the user interface. For example, you can't set any of these values using the Power Options applet in the Control Panel.
- Values in user structures are stored in the `HKEY_CURRENT_USER` registry key and some of these values are displayed in the user interface. Some of these parameters can be set using the Power Options applet in Control Panel.

The data structures defining power management policy are listed below:

- `GLOBAL_POWER_POLICY`—used to manage global power policies. This structure contains the data common across all power schemes. This structure is a container for a `GLOBAL_USER_POWER_POLICY` structure and a `GLOBAL_MACHINE_POWER_POLICY` structure, which contains elements that are read from and written to the registry.
- `GLOBAL_MACHINE_POWER_POLICY`—this structure is a part of the `GLOBAL_POWER_POLICY` structure; it contains the data common across all power schemes and users. The elements in this structure are read from and written to the `HKLM` key in the registry.

- GLOBAL_USER_POWER_POLICY—this structure is a part of the GLOBAL_POWER_POLICY structure; it contains the data common across all power schemes for the user. The elements in this structure are read from and written to the HKCU key in the registry.
- POWER_POLICY—used to manage non-global power policies. This structure contains the data unique across power schemes. This structure is a container for the USER_POWER_POLICY and MACHINE_POWER_POLICY structures that contain the elements to be read from and written to the registry. There's one POWER_POLICY structure for each power scheme on a machine.
- MACHINE_POWER_POLICY—this structure is a part of the POWER_POLICY structure; it contains the data unique to each power scheme, but common to all users. The elements in this structure are read from and written to the HKLM key in the registry.
- USER_POWER_POLICY—this structure is a part of the POWER_POLICY structure; it contains the data unique to each user and power scheme. The elements in this structure are read from and written to the HKCU key in the registry.

Registry Keys Intended for Power Management

In this section, we'll discuss the registry keys that are used for power management. You may edit any of them using one of the registry editors.

NOTE

Changing registry entries responsible for power management won't have an immediate effect. Windows only reads settings from the registry when you log on, when you click OK in Control Panel, or when a Powerprof.dll function is called to read the registry.

The registry keys used for power management are listed below.

- HKCU\AppEvents\EventLabels\LowBatteryAlarm—descriptive name of a low battery power alarm event.
- HKCU\AppEvents\EventLabels\CriticalBatteryAlarm—descriptive name of a critical battery power alarm event.
- HKCU\AppEvents\Schemes\Apps\PowerCfg\LowBatteryAlarm\.Current, HKCU\AppEvents\Schemes\Apps\PowerCfg\LowBatteryAlarm\.Default, HKCU\AppEvents\Schemes\Apps\PowerCfg\CriticalBatteryAlarm\.Current, HKCU\AppEvents\Schemes\Apps\PowerCfg\CriticalBatteryAlarm\.Default—filenames of the WAV files that will play as a low and critical power alarm events.

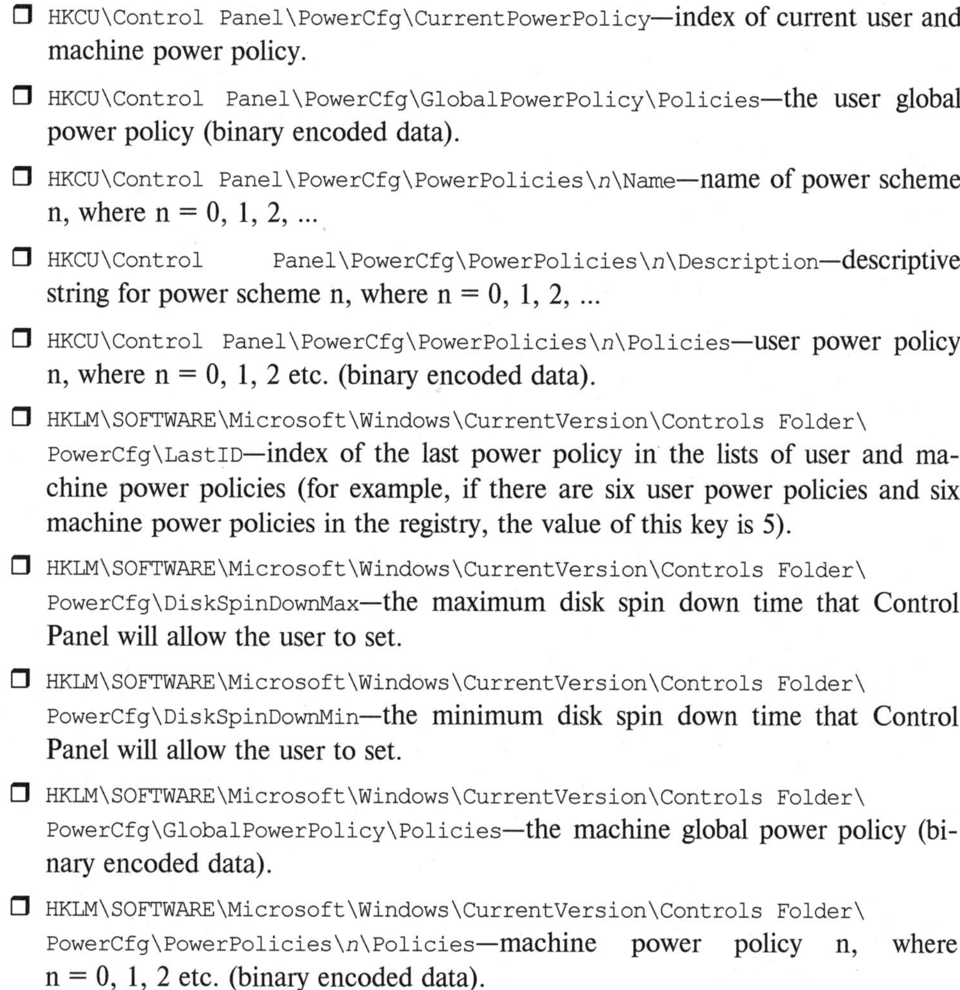

- `HKCU\Control Panel\PowerCfg\CurrentPowerPolicy`—index of current user and machine power policy.
- `HKCU\Control Panel\PowerCfg\GlobalPowerPolicy\Policies`—the user global power policy (binary encoded data).
- `HKCU\Control Panel\PowerCfg\PowerPolicies\n\Name`—name of power scheme n, where n = 0, 1, 2, ...
- `HKCU\Control Panel\PowerCfg\PowerPolicies\n\Description`—descriptive string for power scheme n, where n = 0, 1, 2, ...
- `HKCU\Control Panel\PowerCfg\PowerPolicies\n\Policies`—user power policy n, where n = 0, 1, 2 etc. (binary encoded data).
- `HKLM\SOFTWARE\Microsoft\Windows\CurrentVersion\Controls Folder\PowerCfg\LastID`—index of the last power policy in the lists of user and machine power policies (for example, if there are six user power policies and six machine power policies in the registry, the value of this key is 5).
- `HKLM\SOFTWARE\Microsoft\Windows\CurrentVersion\Controls Folder\PowerCfg\DiskSpinDownMax`—the maximum disk spin down time that Control Panel will allow the user to set.
- `HKLM\SOFTWARE\Microsoft\Windows\CurrentVersion\Controls Folder\PowerCfg\DiskSpinDownMin`—the minimum disk spin down time that Control Panel will allow the user to set.
- `HKLM\SOFTWARE\Microsoft\Windows\CurrentVersion\Controls Folder\PowerCfg\GlobalPowerPolicy\Policies`—the machine global power policy (binary encoded data).
- `HKLM\SOFTWARE\Microsoft\Windows\CurrentVersion\Controls Folder\PowerCfg\PowerPolicies\n\Policies`—machine power policy n, where n = 0, 1, 2 etc. (binary encoded data).

Summary

In this chapter, we briefly discussed the role of Plug and Play architecture in Windows 2000. You also learned how hardware information is stored in the Windows NT/2000 registry, and what happens to this information when you configure hardware using Device Manager, or add/remove devices. Next we discussed the OnNow initiative, ACPI specification, power management, and registry keys responsible for power management on the computer. If your system is ACPI-compliant, there shouldn't be any hardware conflicts when you install new devices in the system.

Chapter 6

Registry and the System Boot Process

"Complexity increases the possibility of failure; a twin-engine airplane has twice as many engine problems as a single-engine airplane."

Airplane rule

(THE JARGON FILE, VERSION 4.1.2)

If you knew what you will know
when your candle was burnt low
it would greatly ease your plight
while your candle still burns bright

P. Hein
Grooks

As I mentioned in *Chapter 1*, the Windows XP registry plays an extremely important role, because it actually manages the whole configuration of your system. Like in Windows NT/2000, the registry information also manages the Windows boot process. Proper understanding of the influence of the registry data on the system startup allows you to solve most startup problems, for example, when the system won't boot or starts incorrectly.

As I will show in this chapter, the Windows XP boot process closely resembles the Windows NT/2000 boot process. This is not surprising, because Windows XP is built on the basis of the Windows NT/2000 kernel. However, there are several improvements in this area, which will be emphasized later in this chapter. These include a logical prefetcher for faster boot, boot loader improvements, and operating system boot improvements.

You never can overestimate the role of the system registry, since it's required even in the early phases of the boot process (actually, when the operating system loader starts executing). For example, if the loader can't find the \System hive that's necessary for loading the drivers (or the hive happens to be corrupt), you'll see an error message like the one shown at the beginning of *Chapter 1*:

```
Windows XP could not start because the following file is missing
 or corrupt:
\WINNT\SYSTEM32\CONFIG\SYSTEM
You can attempt to repair this file by Starting Windows XP Setup using
the original Setup floppy disk of CD-ROM.
Select 'r' at the first screen to repair.
```

When Windows XP is up and running, the \System registry hive is visible under `HKEY_LOCAL_MACHINE`. This hive defines the loading order for all drivers installed in the system. Both the operating system loader (NTLDR) and I/O Manager access this hive.

Each driver installed in the system has its own key under `HKEY_LOCAL_MACHINE\System\CurrentControlSet\Services`. Each of the driver keys, in turn, contains a `Start` value entry. The value assigned to this entry defines the phase during the system boot process when the driver is loaded and initialized. We'll talk about the Start value in more detail later in the chapter.

What Happens When You Start Your Computer

As was stated earlier in this chapter, the Windows XP boot sequence closely resembles that of Windows NT/2000. Listed below are the processes that take place when Windows NT/2000/XP successfully starts on an *x*86-based computer:

- Power On Self Test (POST)
- Initial startup process
- Boot loader process
- Selects the operating system (if you have a multi-boot system)
- Detects the hardware
- Selects a hardware profile
- Loads the kernel
- Kernel initialization process
- Logs on

NOTE

The startup sequence described above applies to systems started or restarted after a normal shutdown. The startup processes begin when you do one of the following:

- Power on the computer
- Reboot the system by selecting the **Shutdown** option in the **Enter Password** window or the **Restart** option in the **Shut Down Windows** window (Fig. 6.1)

However, this startup sequence does not apply when resuming from hibernate or standby modes.

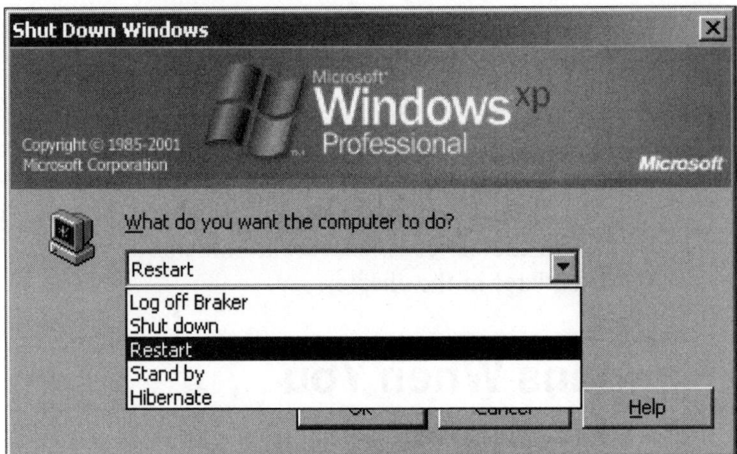

Fig. 6.1. The **Shut Down Windows** window

Windows XP also runs on Itanium-based systems, for which the following startup stages take place:

- Power-on self test (POST) phase
- Initial startup and boot manager phase
- Kernel loading phase
- Windows XP device driver and service initialization phase
- Windows XP logon phase

When you log on, the process of loading Windows NT/2000/XP is completed, as well as are most of the initialization procedures. However, the startup can be considered successfully completed only after you log on.

The following requirements need to be met to successfully begin the Windows NT/2000/XP startup:

- Correct initialization of all the hardware.
- Presence of all the files required for starting Windows NT/2000/XP. If any of these files aren't present in the correct folder or are corrupt, the startup will fail.

Power on Self Test

When you power on or restart your computer, it undergoes the Power On Self Test (POST) procedure. The POST routine is a set of tests performed by the CPU, which, as soon as the power is applied, starts to perform the code contained in the

motherboard system firmware. Firmware, known as the basic input output system (BIOS) on *x*86-based systems and internal adapters, contains the code necessary to start the computer.

The POST routine performs the following two tasks:

- Runs the POST diagnostic routine, which, depending on the firmware, might run some rudimentary hardware checks, such as determining the amount of memory present. The POST diagnostic routine also verifies that all hardware devices needed to start an operating system (such as a hard disk) are present and have been correctly initialized.
- After completing the diagnostic routine, POST retrieves the system configuration settings from the Complementary Metal Oxide Semiconductor (CMOS) memory, located on the motherboard. After the motherboard POST completes, each add-on adapter with built-in firmware (for example, video and hard drive controllers) runs a device-specific POST routine.

If there are problems related to the computer hardware or BIOS settings, POST will emit a series of beeps. POSTs are controlled by your computer's BIOS and may differ from machine to machine. Because of this, I recommend that you always have at hand the documentation supplied with your computer.

The topic of troubleshooting hardware problems goes beyond the range of problems discussed in this book. As a matter of fact, it deserves a separate comprehensive volume. However, I would like to recommend to you some helpful resources on the topic that would certainly help you make sense of the BIOS error codes:

- BIOS Survival Guide, available at: **http://burks.bton.ac.uk/burks/pcinfo/hardware/bios_sg/bios_sg.htm**
- Definitions and Solutions for BIOS Error Beeps and Messages/Codes, available at **www.earthweb.com**

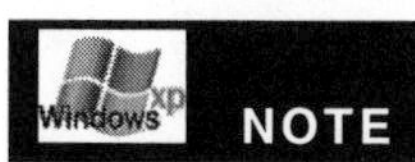

The POST process for Itanium-based systems is similar to *x*86-based systems. The Extensible Firmware Interface (EFI) performs rudimentary hardware checks, similar to those performed by BIOS, and verifies that the devices needed to start the system are present. The EFI specification, currently implemented for Itanium-based systems only, defines a new model for the interface between operating systems and platform firmware. For more information about EFI, see the EFI link on the Web Resources page at **http://www.microsoft.com/windows/reskit/webresources**.

Files Required to Start up Windows NT/2000/XP

If the POST routine was completed successfully, then your computer's hardware was initialized successfully as well. Now it's time to start the operating system. This process requires the presence of all the files necessary to boot the system. The Startup procedure will fail if any of these files are missing or corrupt.

The files required to start Windows NT/2000/XP (for *x*86 platforms) are listed in Table 6.1.

Table 6.1. Files Required to Start Up Windows NT/2000/XP (*x*86 Platforms)

File	Location
NTLDR	Root directory of the startup disk
Boot.ini	Root directory of the startup disk
Bootsect.dos*	Root directory of the startup disk
Ntdetect.com	Root directory of the startup disk
Ntbootdd.sys (for SCSI only)	Root directory of the startup disk
Ntoskrnl.exe	*%SystemRoot%%*\System32
Hal.dll	*%SystemRoot%*\System32
The \SYSTEM registry hive	*%SystemRoot%*\System32\Config
Device drivers	*%SystemRoot%*\System32\Drivers

* This file is required only in multi-boot systems, where MS-DOS, Windows 3.1*x*, or Windows 9*x* are used as alternative operating systems. (This file is needed for booting an alternative operating system.) You can also use the NT loader to boot UNIX or Linux. Copy the first sector of your native root Linux or FreeBSD partition into a file in the NT/2000 partition and name the file, for example, C:\Bootsect.inx or C:\Bootsect.bsd (by analogy to C:\Bootsect.dos). Then edit the `[operating systems]` section of the Boot.ini file by adding strings such as:

```
C:\BOOTSECT.LNX="Linux"
C:\BOOTSECT.BSD="FreeBSD"
```

NOTE

Due to the differences between Itanium-based and *x*86-based systems, certain files required for the *x*86-based startup process are not required for Itanium-based computers. These files include the following—Boot.ini, Ntdetect.com, and Ntldr. The boot.ini file is not required, since its information on Itanium-based systems is now stored in NVRAM. Ntdetect.com is not needed, because unlike *x*86-based systems, all Itanium-based systems are fully ACPI-compliant, and, therefore, there is no need for basic hardware detection. All hardware is detected and initialized by Windows XP according to the ACPI specification requirements. The Ntldr file is the *x*86-based loader. It is not needed, since Itanium-based systems use another loader—IA64ldr.efi.

The files required to load Windows XP on Itanium-based systems are listed in Table 6.2. These files are located in the EFI system partition, which is the first partition of the startup drive.

Table 6.2. Windows XP Startup Files for Itanium-Based Systems

File and Folder Names	Location on Drives	Description
FPSWA.efi	Resides on the root of the EFI system partition	Supports EFI floating point operations
MSUtil (folder)	Resides on the root of the EFI system partition	Contains EFI tools
IA64ldr.efi	EFI\Microsoft\WinNT50.x folder on the ESP	This is the operating system loader. This path depends on the number of operating systems installed
Ntoskrnl.exe	*%SystemRoot%*\System32	The core of the Whistler operating system, also known as the kernel. The operating system code that runs as part of the kernel does so in a special privileged processor mode, with direct access to system data and hardware
Hal.dll	*%SystemRoot%*\System32	Hardware abstraction layer (HAL) dynamic-link library file. The hardware abstraction layer (HAL) isolates, or abstracts, low-level hardware details from the rest of the operating system, and provides a common programming interface to devices of the same type (such as video adapters)
System registry file	*%SystemRoot%*\System32\Config\System	The registry `HKEY_LOCAL_MACHINE\SYSTEM` key
Device drivers	*%SystemRoot%*\System32\Drivers	Hardware driver files for various devices

NOTE

Windows NT, Windows 2000, and Windows XP define the "system" and "boot" partitions differently from other operating systems. These are the most important things that you should know. The system partition contains the files necessary to start Windows NT/2000/XP. The boot partition, which contains the *%SystemRoot%* and *%SystemRoot%*\System32 directories, can be another partition on the same or a different physical disk. The term *%SystemRoot%* is an environment variable.

Initial Startup Process

When the POST routine has successfully completed, the system BIOS tries to locate the startup disk. The search order for locating the startup disk is specified by the system BIOS. In addition to floppy disks and hard disks attached to SCSI or ATA controllers, firmware might support starting an operating system from other devices, such as CD-ROM, network adapters, or Zip or LS-120 disks.

The system BIOS allows you to reconfigure the search order (also known as the boot sequence). You can find detailed information concerning boot sequence editing in the documentation supplied with your computer. If drive A: is the first item in the boot sequence list, and there's a disk in it, the system BIOS will try booting from the disk. If there's no disk in drive A:, the system BIOS will check the first hard drive that's powered up and initialized. The first sector on the hard disk, which contains the Master Boot Record (MBR) and partition table, is the most critical data structure to the startup process.

The system BIOS reads the Master Boot Record, loads it into memory, and then transfers execution to the Master Boot Record. The code scans the partition table to find the system partition. When it's found, MBR loads sector 0 of the system partition and executes it. Sector 0 on the system partition is the partition boot sector, containing the startup code for the operating system. This code uses a method defined by the operating system.

NOTE

If the startup disk is a floppy disk, the first sector of this disk is the Windows NT/2000/XP partition boot sector. For a successful startup, this disk must contain all the boot files required for starting Windows NT/2000/XP.

If the first hard disk has no system partition, MBR will display one of the following error messages:

- `Invalid partition table`

- `Error loading operating system`
- `Missing operating system`

Generally, MBR doesn't depend on the operating system. For example, on *x*86 computers the same MBR is used to start Windows NT/2000/XP, Windows 9*x*, MS-DOS, and Windows 3.1*x*. On the other hand, the partition boot sector depends on both the operating system and the file system. On an *x*86 platform, the WindowsNT/2000/XP partition boot sector is responsible for the following actions:

- Detecting the file system used to find the operating system boot loader (NTLDR) in the root directory of the system partition. On FAT volumes, the partition boot sector is 1 sector long. On FAT32 volumes, this data structure takes up 2 physical sectors, because the startup code requires more than 512 bytes. On NTFS volumes, the partition boot sector data structure can consume up to 16 sectors, with the extra sectors containing the file system code required to find NTLDR.
- Loading NTLDR into memory.
- Executing the boot loader.

On *x*86 computers, the system partition must be located on the first physical hard disk. Don't confuse the system partition and the boot partition. The boot partition contains Windows NT/2000/XP system files and can be the same as the system partition. It can also be on a different partition or even on a different hard disk.

If the first hard disk has no system partition that should be used to start the computer, you need to power down this disk. This will allow the system BIOS to access another hard disk, which will be used to start the operating system.

If there's a disk in drive A:, the system BIOS will try loading the first sector of this disk into the memory. If the disk is bootable, its first sector is the partition boot sector. If the disk isn't bootable, the system will display errors such as:

```
Non-System disk or disk error
Replace and press any key when ready
```

(if the disk is DOS-formatted)

or

```
Ntldr is missing
Replace and press any key when ready
```

(if the disk is formatted under Windows NT/2000/XP).

If you need to boot the system from a bootable CD (for example, to install Windows XP from the distribution CD or use the CD-based Recovery Console), you must set the CD-ROM as the primary boot device—the first item listed in the boot order. When you start your system using the bootable Windows XP CD, Setup checks the hard disk for existing Windows XP installations. If Setup finds an existing installation, it provides you with the option of bypassing CD-ROM startup by not responding to the **Press any key to boot from CD-ROM** prompt. If you do not press a key within three seconds, Setup does not run and the computer passes control from the CD-ROM to the hard disk.

If you don't want to start Windows XP Setup to install this operating system or repair the damaged Windows XP installation, remove the CD from your CD drive, since this will allow you to minimize the time required to start Windows XP. Also note that the presence of a non-bootable CD in the CD-ROM drive can significantly increase the time required to start Windows XP.

Boot Loader Process

The boot loader allows you to select the operating system to be started and loads the operating system files from the boot partition. This process is different for *x*86 systems and RISC-based computers. The tasks performed at this phase include installing a 32-bit memory model with flat memory space, detecting hardware configuration data, generating its configuration in the memory, and transferring the handle of this description to the loader. NTLDR then loads the kernel image, the HAL, the device drivers, and the file system drivers for the volume, from which the operating system will start. Besides other tasks at this phase, the system loads the drivers for which the `Start` registry value is set to 0. The `Start` registry entry for device drivers is located in the registry under the following key:

```
HKEY_LOCAL_MACHINE\SYSTEM\CurrentControlSet\Services\ServiceName
```

The *ServiceName* here is the name of the service. For example:

```
HKEY_LOCAL_MACHINE\SYSTEM\CurrentControlSet\Services\atapi
```

NTLDR Functions

NTLDR controls the process of selecting the operating system to be loaded and detecting hardware prior to initializing the Windows NT/2000/XP kernel. NTLDR must be located in the root folder of the system partition. Besides the operating system loader, the partition must contain all the files listed in Table 6.1.

When NTLDR starts execution, it clears the screen and performs the following actions:

- Switches the processor to 32-bit flat memory mode. All *x*86-based computers first start in real mode, similar to an 8088 and 8086 start mode. Because NTLDR is a 32-bit program, it must switch the CPU to a 32-bit flat memory mode before it can perform any actions.
- Starts an appropriate minifile system. The code intended for accessing files on FAT and NTFS partitions is built into NTFS. This code enables NTLDR to access the files.
- Reads the Boot.ini file located in the root directory of the system partition and displays the boot menu. This screen is also known as a boot loader screen. If your computer is configured for starting multiple operating systems, and you select an alternative operating system (other than Windows NT/2000/XP), NTLDR will load the Bootsect.dos file and transfer all control to the code contained in this file. The alternative operating system will start as normal, because the Bootsect.dos file contains an exact copy of the partition boot sector necessary to start the operating system.
- If you select one of the Windows NT/2000/XP installations, NTLDR finds and executes Ntdetect.com to collect information on the hardware currently installed.
- NTLDR loads and starts the operating system kernel (Ntoskrnl.exe). After starting the kernel, NTLDR passes on the hardware information collected by Ntdetect.com.

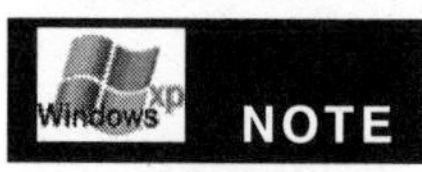

One of the most significant improvements introduced with Windows XP is the so-called Fast Boot feature, which was implemented by increasing the boot loader performance. The Ntldr version included with Windows XP is optimized for fast disk reading. When the system is loaded for the first time, all information on the disk configuration, including file system metadata, is cached. The Logical Prefetcher, which is new in Windows XP, brings much of this data into the system cache with efficient asynchronous disk I/Os that minimize seeks. During boot, the logical prefetcher finishes most of the disk I/Os that need to be done for starting the system in parallel with device initialization, providing faster boot and logon performance. Furthermore, each system file during boot is now read only once, within a single operation. As a result, Windows XP boot loader is approximately 4-5 times faster than Windows 2000 boot loader.

As you can probably guess, the prefetcher settings are also stored in the registry. You can find them under the following key (Fig. 6.2):

```
HKEY_LOCAL_MACHINE\SYSTEM\CurrentControlSet\Control\Session Manager\
Memory Management\PrefetchParameters
```

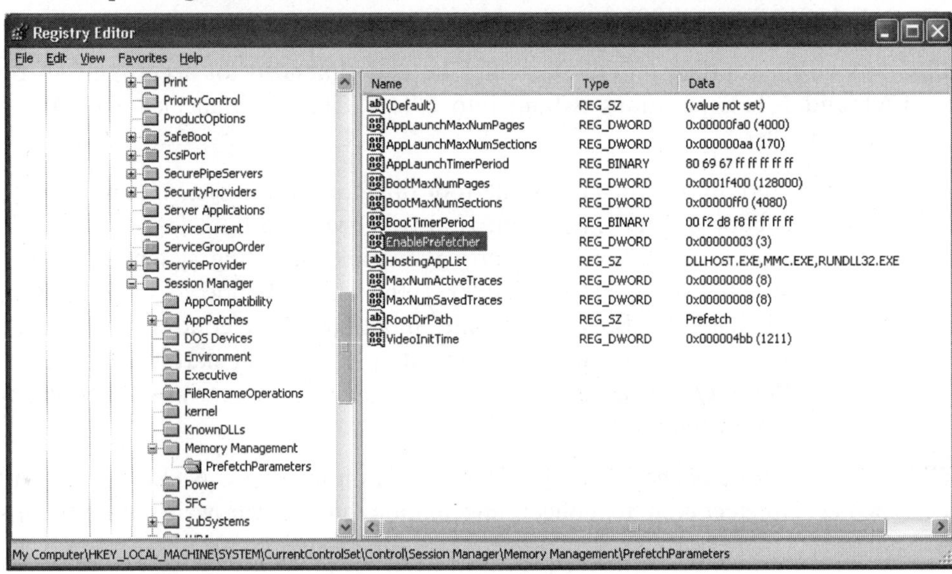

Fig. 6.2. Logical Prefetcher settings in the registry

The values that interest us the most are the `RootDirPath` (data type `REG_SZ`, the default value is `Prefetch`) and `EnablePrefetcher` (data type `REG_DWORD`). The `EnablePrefetcher` setting can take the following values:

- `0x00000001`—application launch prefetching
- `0x00000002`—boot prefetching

If both options are enabled, the setting would be `0x00000003`. The setting takes effect immediately. Note that in the Server product line, only the boot prefetch is enabled by default. Application prefetch can be enabled by the registry setting cited here. The system boot prefetch file is in the *%SystemRoot%*\Prefetch directory (and the path to it is specified by the `RootDirPath` parameter mentioned above). Although these prefetch-readable files can be opened using Notepad, they contain binary data that will not be recognized by Notepad. If you are going to view these files, make them read-only or copy them to a different location before opening.

Selecting the Operating System to Start

NTLDR displays a menu where you can select the operating system to be started. What you see on this screen depends on the information contained in the Boot.ini file, which was described in *Chapter 4*. An example of the screen is shown below:

```
Please select the operating system to start:
     Windows XP Professional
     Windows 2000 Professional
     Windows NT Server Version 4.0
     Windows NT Server Version 4.0(VGA mode)
Use ↑ and ↓ keys to move the highlight to your choice.
Press Enter to choose.
Seconds until highlighted choice will be started automatically: 29
   For troubleshooting and advanced startup options for Windows, press F8
```

The process of selecting the operating system to start is similar to the process for earlier Windows NT versions (for example, Windows NT 3.51 and Windows NT 4.0). The operating system that appears first in the list is the default operating system. To select another operating system, use the arrow keys (↑ and ↓) to move the highlight to the string you need. Then press <Enter>.

If you don't select an item from the boot menu before the counter specified in the following string reaches zero, you'll see the message:

```
Seconds until highlighted choice will be started automatically: 29
```

NTLDR will load the default operating system. Windows NT/2000/XP Setup specifies the most recently installed copy of the operating system as the default option. You can edit the Boot.ini file to change the default operating system. A detailed description of the Boot.ini file format was provided in *Chapter 4*.

NOTE

The startup menu does not appear if you only have one copy of Windows XP installed on your computer. In this case, Windows XP ignores the time-out value in the Boot.ini file and starts immediately.

Windows XP Advanced Startup Options

Any experienced Windows NT user will notice that there is one small but very significant difference between the boot loader screens in Windows 2000/XP and Windows NT 4.0. This is the string placed at the bottom of the screen:

```
For troubleshooting and advanced startup options for Windows 2000,
press F8
```

In Windows 95/98, there was a similar option. If you have any problems booting Windows 2000 and Windows XP, try using the advanced startup options menu displayed when you press the <F8> key.

The menu looks like this:

```
Windows Advanced Options Menu
Please select an option:

Safe Mode
Safe Mode with Networking
Safe Mode with Command Prompt

Enable Boot Logging
Enable VGA Mode
Last Known Good Configuration (your most recent settings that worked)*
Directory Services Restore Mode (Windows domain controllers only)
Debugging Mode

Start Windows Normally**
Reboot**
Return to OS Choices Menu**
```

---

*This option is improved in comparison to Windows 2000.

**Options that are new in Windows XP.

Notice that this menu will remain on screen until you select one of the available options.

When Windows 2000/XP boots in safe mode, it uses the standard settings (VGA driver, no network connections, default system services only). When the system starts in safe mode, only vitally important drivers necessary for starting Windows are loaded. The safe boot mode allows the system to boot even with an incompatible or corrupt service or driver. Thus, the safe mode increases the probability of successful booting, because you load the system with the minimum set of services and drivers. For example, if your Windows 2000 installation became unbootable after installing new software, it's highly probable that your attempt to boot the system in safe mode will be successful. After booting the system, you'll be able to change the settings that prevent Windows 2000/XP from booting correctly, or delete the software that caused the problem.

The options of Windows XP advanced startup menu are described below:

- **Safe Mode**

  As I mentioned, this option is similar to the one that was introduced with Windows 2000. If the user selects this option, only the basic Windows XP services and drivers will be loaded. These services and drivers are vitally important for the operating system (this set includes standard mouse, keyboard and mass storage drivers, base video, and default system services). If you can't start Windows XP using this mode, you'll probably need to restore the damaged system. More detailed information concerning this topic will be provided later in this chapter.

- **Safe Mode with Networking**

  Similar to the option that existed in Windows 2000, Windows XP will start in safe mode (very much like the previous option), but in addition, there will be an attempt to start networking services and restoring network connections.

- **Safe Mode with Command Prompt**

  When you select this option, Windows 2000/XP will start using only the basic set of drivers and services (just the same as safe mode except that a command prompt will be started instead of the Windows GUI).

- **Last Known Good Configuration (your most recent settings that worked)**

  In Windows NT 4.0/Windows 2000, there was a similar option. However, in Windows XP this option has an improvement that deserves special mention. If you select this option in Windows 2000, the operating system starts using registry information saved immediately after successful startup (the Windows NT/2000/XP system startup is considered to be successful if at least one user has successfully logged on to the system). It should be pointed out that in Windows NT/2000 this option only allows you to correct configuration errors, and won't always be successful. Use this option only when you're absolutely sure that you've made an error when configuring the system. The problems caused by missing or corrupt system files or drivers won't be corrected. Also note that if you use this option, all modifications introduced into your registry since the last successful boot of Windows NT/2000 will be discarded.

In Windows XP, this option was enhanced by additional functionality. In contrast to Windows NT/2000, Windows XP creates backup copies of the drivers before updating the currently used set of drivers. In addition to restoring the most recent registry settings, the **Last Known Good Configuration** startup option also restores the last set of drivers used after the last successful user logon. This allows you to recover from system errors such as unstable or improperly installed applications and drivers that prevent you from starting Windows XP.

- **Directory Services Restore Mode (Windows 2000 domain controllers only)**

  This option shouldn't be used with Windows XP Professional because it's intended for domain controllers running Windows 2000 Server or later versions. As you can tell from the name of this option, it's used for restoring directory services.

- **Debugging Mode**

  This option starts Windows XP and establishes the debugging mode.

- **Start Windows Normally**

  New in Windows XP, this option allows you to start Windows XP normally.

- **Reboot**

  When the user selects this option, the boot process will restart from the beginning (actually, with the POST routine). Like the previous option, this one was first introduced with Windows XP.

- **Return to OS Choices Menu**

  New in Windows XP, this option returns you to the boot loader screen, allowing you to select the operating system.

As was said, the last three options were first introduced with Windows XP. Of course, they don't provide anything totally new and are purely cosmetic improvements. However, they certainly make the Advanced Startup Options menu more convenient than the one in Windows 2000.

You may be wondering where the system stores safe mode configurations used to start the system when you select one of advanced boot options. Like everything else in the system, these parameters are stored in the registry under `HKEY_LOCAL_MACHINE\SYSTEM\CurrentControlSet\Control\SafeBoot` (Fig. 6.3). This key contains all configuration settings used to boot the system in safe mode. It contains two subkeys: `Network` and `Minimal`. The `Network` key contains the information necessary to boot the system using the **Safe Mode with Networking** option, while the `Minimal` key contains the same information, except for networking settings. The `SafeBoot` key contains the `AlternateShell` value entry, which specifies the name of the program used instead of the Windows GUI. Normally, this entry has a value of "cmd.exe" (Windows 2000/XP command processor), which corresponds to the **Safe Mode with Command Prompt** option.

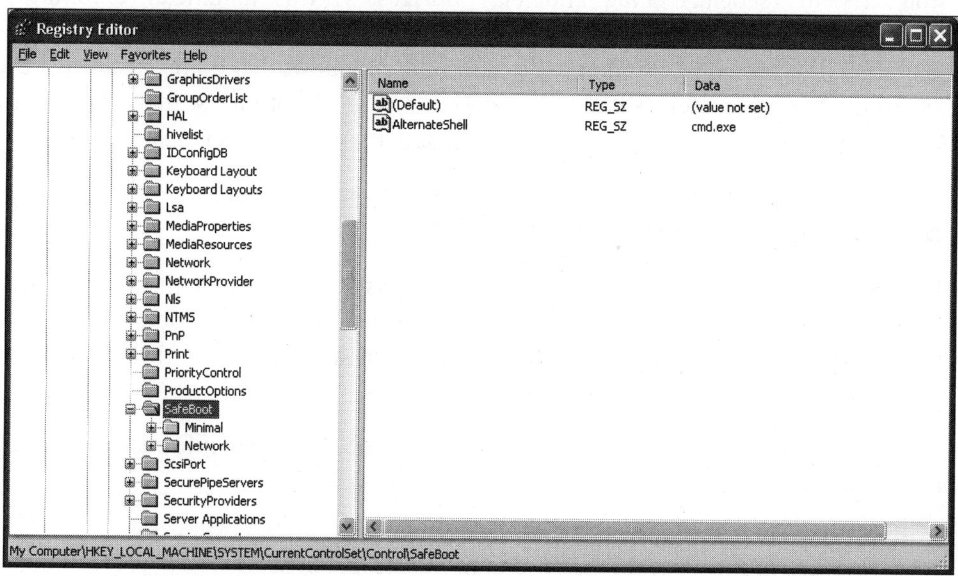

Fig. 6.3. The advanced startup menu options in Windows 2000/XP are specified by the `HKEY_LOCAL_MACHINE\SYSTEM\CurrentControlSet\Control\SafeBoot` registry key

Hardware Detection

When you select one of the Windows NT/2000 installations from the boot menu (or the default operating system starts loading after the timer has expired), NTLDR calls Ntdetect.com to collect information on the currently installed hardware. Ntdetect.com returns the collected information to NTLDR.

This phase of the initialization is different for Windows NT 4.0 and Windows 2000/XP. As I mentioned in *Chapter 5*, starting with Windows 2000, the system includes two new Executive subsystems: *Plug and Play Manager* and *Power Manager*. Plug and Play Manager is integrated with I/O Manager and doesn't participate in the initialization process. However, because Windows 2000 supports Plug and Play, PnP-aware drivers perform a certain part of hardware detection in the operating system. The main difference from Windows NT 4.0 is that it performs hardware detection using Ntdetect.com only. Because of this, a new Boot.ini parameter was introduced in Windows 2000—/FASTDETECT, which is used when Windows NT 4.0 and Windows 2000 co-exist on the same computer. If you have a configuration like this, the Windows 2000 version of Ntdetect.com will be used to load both operating systems. If the /FASTDETECT parameter is set, NTDETECT won't try to recognize Plug and Play devices. If this parameter is omitted, NTDETECT will enumerate all the hardware. So, if you have a multi-boot configuration where both Windows NT 4.0 and Windows 2000 are installed, the /FASTDETECT parameter should be set for the Boot.ini strings that start Windows 2000 and omitted for the strings that start Windows NT 4.0.

Selecting the Hardware Profile

If you've selected the option that starts Windows 2000/XP, and there's only one hardware profile in the system, Ntldr will continue the startup process by starting the operating system kernel (Ntoskrnl.exe) and passing on the hardware information collected by Ntdetect.com.

If Windows 2000 has several hardware profiles, the following information will be displayed on the screen:

```
Hardware Profile/Configuration Recovery Menu
This menu allows you to select a hardware profile
to be used when Windows is started.
If your system is not starting correctly, then you may switch to a
previous system configuration, which may overcome startup problems.
IMPORTANT: System configuration changes made since the last successful
startup will be discarded.

Profile 1
Profile 2
Profile 3

Use the up and down arrow keys to move the highlight
to the selection you want. Then press ENTER.
To switch to the Last Known Good Configuration, press 'L'.
To Exit this menu and restart your computer, press F3.
Seconds until highlighted choice will be started automatically: 5
```

After displaying this menu, the boot loader will allow you time to select among the available options. You can select one of the existing hardware profiles, switch to the **Last Known Good Configuration** option, or quit this menu and restart the computer.

The first hardware profile is highlighted. To select other hardware profiles, highlight the option you need and press <Enter>.

You can also select between the default configuration and LastKnownGood Configuration. If you select the **Last Known Good Configuration** option, Windows 2000/XP will load the registry information that was saved immediately after the last successful boot. If you don't select this option, Windows 2000 will use the default configuration that was saved in the registry the last time you performed a system shutdown. The Last Known Good Configuration is stored in the registry under `HKEY_LOCAL_MACHINE\SYSTEM\Select`. More detailed information concerning this topic will be provided later in the chapter.

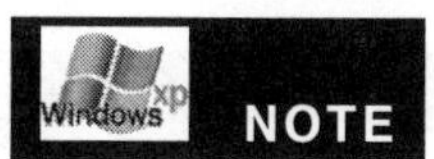

Windows XP creates the default hardware profile for desktop computers. This default profile includes all the hardware detected when you installed the system. For portable computers, Windows XP creates two default hardware profiles (Docked Profile and Undocked Profile), and selects the appropriate profile depending on the way you are using your computer (as a dock station or standalone). Notice that despite the fact that full-featured Plug and Play support has eliminated the necessity of manually configuring hardware profiles, they still can be very useful for troubleshooting hardware problems.

Loading the Kernel

When the boot loader obtains information on the currently installed hardware and selected hardware profile, it starts the operating system kernel Ntoskrnl.exe and passes on the hardware information collected by Ntdetect.com.

Information on the currently selected hardware profile is passed to the loader when you press <Enter> in the **Hardware Profile/Configuration Recovery Menu** screen. The loader can also make this choice automatically (if the timer has expired or if there's only one hardware profile).

When the kernel starts loading, you'll see several dots on the screen. These dots serve as a progress indicator displayed when the boot loader loads Ntoskrnl.exe and the hardware abstraction layer into the memory. At this phase, neither of these programs are initialized. Ntldr then scans the registry and retrieves information on the size of nonpaged pool and registry quota (for Windows NT/2000). Next, Ntldr loads the `HKEY_LOCAL_MACHINE\SYSTEM` registry hive from *%SystemRoot%*\System32\Config\System.

At this point, the boot loader enables the registry API and creates a control set that will be used to initialize the computer. Both of these tasks are preliminary steps necessary for preparing the drivers for loading. The value specified in the `HKEY_LOCAL_MACHINE\SYSTEM\Select` registry key (Fig. 6.4) defines which control set in `HKEY_LOCAL_MACHINE\SYSTEM` should be used to load the system. By default, the loader will select the `Default` control set. If you select the LastKnownGood configuration, the loader will use the `LastKnownGood` control set. Based on your selection and on the value of the `Select` key, the loader will determine which control set (`ControlSet00x`) will be enabled. The loader will then set the `Current` value of the `Select` key to the name of the control set it will be using.

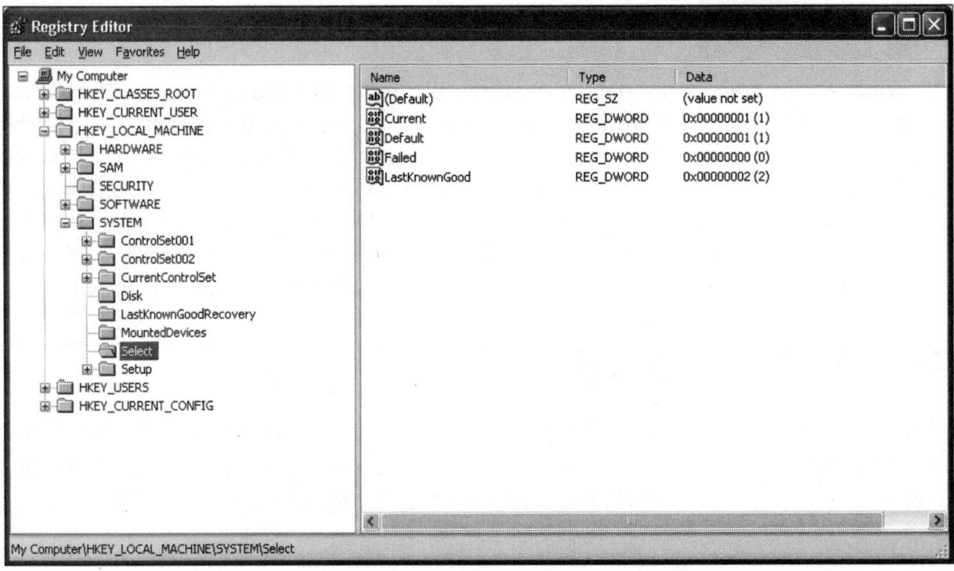

Fig. 6.4. The `HKEY_LOCAL_MACHINE\SYSTEM\Select` registry key

The loader then scans all the services defined by the `HKEY_LOCAL_MACHINE\SYSTEM\CurrentControlSet\Services` registry key and searches device drivers with a `Start` value of 0x0 (this means that the drivers should be loaded, but not initialized). Normally, drivers with these values are low-level device drivers (for example, disk drivers). The `Group` value for each device driver defines its load order. The `HKEY_LOCAL_MACHINE\SYSTEM\CurrentControlSet\ControlServiceGroupOrder` registry key defines the loading order.

When this phase is completed, all of the basic drivers are loaded and active. If one of the critical drivers can't be initialized though, the system starts rebooting.

Initializing the Kernel

When the Windows NT 4.0 kernel starts initializing, the screen turns blue, and a text similar to the one presented below appears:

```
Microsoft ® Windows NT (TM) Version 4.0 (Build 1345)
1 System Processor (64 MB Memory)
```

If this message appears, it means that all of the previous stages of the boot sequence have completed successfully. One obvious difference between Windows 2000/XP and Windows NT 4.0 is the fact that all system messages that appear during the Windows NT 4.0 boot process are displayed in 80×50 text mode, while Windows 2000 and Windows XP display these messages in VGA mode. The Windows NT 4.0 Hardware Abstraction Layer (HAL) provides all the support for this mode and is also responsible for displaying the messages. Windows 2000 has a special driver—Bootvid.sys—which performs these tasks. In Windows 2000 and Windows XP, you know that the Kernel is initializing when the animated screen displaying the OS logo appears. This cosmetic improvement doesn't change the basic principles of the loading process in comparison to the previous versions of the Windows NT operating system.

If you want to check things out for yourself, add the `/SOS` option to the Boot.ini file string that starts Windows 2000/XP. Then save your changes and reboot the system. You'll see the whole sequence of loading for all the drivers. The graphics logo will be used as a background, and in the foreground you'll see something very much like the following:

```
Microsoft ® Windows XP Professional (TM) (Build 2600)
1 System Processor (256 MB Memory)
```

The kernel creates the `HKEY_LOCAL_MACHINE\HARDWARE` registry key based on information obtained from the boot loader. The `HKEY_LOCAL_MACHINE\HARDWARE` key contains hardware data collected when the system starts. This data includes information on the hardware components and IRQs used by each hardware device.

The kernel then creates a `Clone` control set by making a copy of the control set indicated by the `Current` value.

NOTE

In Windows NT 4.0, the `Clone` control set was visible; but after a successful boot, it became unavailable (the system displayed an error message any time an attempt was made to open this key). In Windows 2000/XP, the registry editors simply don't display this.

The `Clone` control set should never be modified, since it must be an identical copy of the data used for configuring the computer. It shouldn't contain any changes introduced in the course of system startup.

As the kernel initializes, it performs the following operations:

- Initializes low-level device drivers loaded at the previous stage
- Loads and initializes other device drivers
- Starts programs, such as Chkdsk, which should run before starting any services
- Loads and initializes system services
- Creates the paging file (Pagefile.sys)
- Starts all the subsystems necessary for Windows 2000/XP

Loading and Initializing the Device Drivers

Now the kernel initializes the low-level device drivers that were loaded at the previous stage (kernel loading). If any of these drivers can't be initialized, the system performs corrective action based on the data defined by the following registry entry:

```
HKEY_LOCAL_MACHINE\SYSTEM\CurrentControlSet\Services
\DriverName\ErrorControl
```

Ntoskrnl.exe then scans the registry, this time for device drivers that have an `HKEY_LOCAL_MACHINE\SYSTEM\CurrentControlSet\Services\`*`DriverName`*`\Start` value of 0x01. The `Group` value for each device driver defines the order in which the drivers are loaded. The `HKEY_LOCAL_MACHINE\SYSTEM\CurrentControlSet\Control\ServiceGroupOrder` registry subkey defines the loading order.

In contrast to the kernel loading phase, device drivers that have a `Start` value of 0x01 aren't loaded using BIOS calls. Instead, they use device drivers loaded and initialized at the kernel loading phase. Error handling for device drivers belonging to this group is based on the `ErrorControl` value for each device driver.

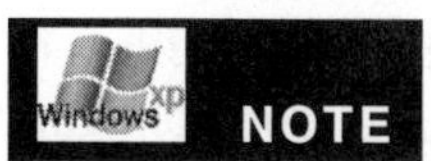

Windows XP initializes device drivers simultaneously to improve boot time. Instead of waiting for each device to initialize separately, many can now be brought up concurrently. The slowest device has the greatest effect on boot time.

Loading Services

The Session Manager (Smss.exe) starts the higher-level subsystems and services of the operating system. All information used by the Session Manager is also stored in the registry under the following key: `HKEY_LOCAL_MACHINE\SYSTEM\CurrentControlSet\Control\Session Manager`. The Session Manager uses information stored under the following registry items:

- The `BootExecute` data entry
- The `Memory Management` key
- The `DOS Devices` key
- The `SubSystems` key

The *BootExecute* Data Entry

The `BootExecute` registry entry contains one or more commands that the Session Manager has to run before it starts loading services. The default value for this registry item is Autochk.exe, which is simply the Windows NT/2000/XP version of the Chkdsk.exe program. The example shown below shows the default setting for this registry item:

```
BootExecute: REG_MULTI_SZ: autochk autochk*
```

The Session Manager is capable of running more than one program. The example shown below shows how to start the Convert utility, which will convert the `x` volume to NTFS format next time the system starts:

```
BootExecute: REG_MULTI_SZ: autochk autochk* autoconv \DosDevices\x:
/FS:ntfs
```

When the Session Manager executes all the commands specified, the kernel will load the other registry hives stored in the *%SystemRoot%*\System32\Config directory.

The *Memory Management* Key

For the next step, the Session Manager needs to initialize the information in the paging file, which is necessary to the Virtual Memory Manager. The configuration information is stored in the following data items:

```
PagedPoolSize: REG_DWORD 0
NonPagedPoosSize: REG_DWORD 0
PagingFiles: REG_MULTI_SZ: c:\pagefile.sys 32
```

In versions of Windows earlier than Windows XP, as device drivers, system services, and the user shell load, the required memory pages will not be in memory until loaded from the disk drive. Another key improvement in Windows XP is the overlap of pre-fetching these pages before loading the device drivers that require them.

The prefetcher in Windows XP has the following functions:

- Dynamically traces each boot to build a list of what to prefetch. Boot files are laid out together on disk during the idle time, or when the Bootvis.exe tool is used to arm boot traces. The prefetcher needs at least two boots after installation to learn which files to lay out. The prefetcher monitors the previous eight boots on an ongoing basis.
- Enables fast asynchronous I/O during boot to load required files in highly efficient transfers.

As was already mentioned, the prefetcher settings are stored in the registry under `KEY_LOCAL_MACHINE\SYSTEM\CurrentControlSet\Control\Session Manager\Memory Management\PrefetchParameters` key.

The *DOS Devices* Key

The Session Manager needs to create symbolic links that direct certain command classes to the appropriate file system components. The configuration data resides in the following registry entries:

```
PRN: REG_SZ:\DosDevices\LPT1
AUX: REG_SZ:\DosDevices\COM1
NUL: REG_SZ:\Device\Null
```

```
UNC: REG_SZ:\Device\Mup
PIPE:\REG_SZ:\Device\NamedPipe
MAILSLOT:\REG_SZ\Device\MailSlot
```

The *SubSystems* Key

Since the architecture of all Windows NT/2000/XP subsystems is message-based, it's necessary to start the Windows (Win32) subsystem that controls all input/output operations and video display access. The process of this subsystem is called CSRSS. The Win32 subsystem starts the WinLogon process, which, in turn, starts other important subsystems.

Configuration information for subsystems is defined by the `Required` value under the following registry key: `HKEY_LOCAL_MACHINE\SYSTEM\CurrentControlSet\Control\SessionManager\SubSystems`.

Logging on

The Win32 subsystem starts the Winlogon.exe process, which, in turn, starts the Local Security Administration process (LSA)—Lsass.exe. When the kernel initializes successfully, it's necessary to log on to the system. The logon procedure may be done automatically, based on the information stored in the registry, or it can be done manually. When you log on manually, the system displays the **Begin Logon** dialog or the Welcome screen (Windows XP-specific new feature). The Graphical Identification and Authentication (GINA) component collects your user name and password, and passes this information securely to the LSA for authentication. If you supplied valid credentials, you are granted access using either Kerberos V5 (for network) or NTLM (local machine) authentication.

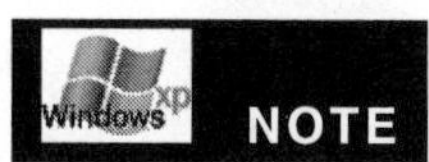

Windows NT/2000 may continue initializing network drivers, but you can now log on to the system. As for Windows XP, if your PC doesn't belong to a domain, network initialization will be done at the same time as boot. However, the PCs that are members of a domain will still wait.

At this stage, the Service Control Manager loads the services that start automatically. The `Start` value under `HKEY_LOCAL_MACHINE\SYSTEM\CurrentControlSet\Services\`*`DriverName`* is set to 0x2. Now the services are loaded according to their dependencies, which are described by the values `DependOnGroup` and `DependOnService` under the `HKEY_LOCAL_MACHINE\SYSTEM\CurrentControlSet\Services\DriverName` registry key.

NOTE

As with Windows NT/2000, Windows XP isn't successfully loaded until you log on to the system. After that, the `Clone` control set will be copied to the **LastKnownGood** configuration.

The services listed in the following registry keys start and run asynchronously with the **Welcome to Windows** and **Log On to Windows** dialog boxes:

- `HKEY_LOCAL_MACHINE\Software\Microsoft\Windows\CurrentVersion\RunServicesOnce`
- `HKEY_LOCAL_MACHINE\Software\Microsoft\Windows\CurrentVersion\RunServices`

The Plug and Play device detection process also runs asynchronously with the logon process and relies on system firmware, hardware, device drivers, and operating system features to detect and enumerate new devices. When these components are properly coordinated, Plug and Play allows for device detection, system resource allocation, driver installation, and device installation with minimal user intervention. Detailed information on the Plug and Play detection process was provided in *Chapter 5.*

After you log on, the following events occur:

- *Control sets are updated.* The control set referenced by the `LastKnownGood` entry is updated with the contents in `Clone`. `Clone`, a copy of the `CurrentControlSet` entry, is created each time you start your computer.
- *Group Policy settings take effect.* Group Policy settings that apply to the user and computer take effect. For more information about Group Policy, see *Chapter 10.*
- *Startup programs run.* Windows XP starts logon scripts, startup programs, and services referenced in these registry and folder locations:
  - `HKEY_LOCAL_MACHINE\Software\Microsoft\Windows\CurrentVersion\RunOnce`
  - `HKEY_LOCAL_MACHINE\Software\Microsoft\Windows\CurrentVersion\Policies\Explorer\Run`

- `HKEY_LOCAL_MACHINE\SOFTWARE\Microsoft\Windows\CurrentVersion\Run`
- `HKEY_CURRENT_USER\SOFTWARE\Microsoft\Windows\CurrentVersion\Run`
- *%systemdrive%*\Documents and Settings\All Users\Start Menu\Programs\Startup
- *%systemdrive%*\Documents and Settings*%username%*\Start Menu\Programs\Startup
- *%windir%*\Profiles\All Users\Start Menu\Programs\Startup
- *%windir%*\Profiles*%username%*\Start Menu\Programs\Startup

NOTE

The last two *%windir%* folders exist only on Windows 2000/XP systems upgraded from Windows NT 4.0.

Loading Other Services and Drivers

As I mentioned before, the system may continue loading and initializing certain services and drivers from the moment you log on. Future sections of this chapter concentrate on the following important topics:

- Control sets in the registry. Control sets contain information on the system configuration used during system startup. Proper understanding of control sets is necessary to appropriately use the **LastKnownGood** configuration.
- How the registry data specifies the loading order of services and drivers. We'll discuss the Start value that specifies the loading order of the service or driver. We'll also discuss the `Error Control` value that defines the default behavior of the system in case the driver or service can't be loaded or initialized correctly.

Control Sets in the Registry

The Control set contains system configuration data, including information on the device drivers that need to be loaded and the services that need to be started. Control sets are stored in the registry under the `HKEY_LOCAL_MACHINE\SYSTEM` registry key. The system may have several control sets, and their number depends on how frequently you modify the system settings or how often problems arise. A typical Windows NT/2000 installation contains the following control sets:

- Clone
- ControlSet001
- ControlSet002
- ControlSet003
- CurrentControlSet

The CurrentControlSet subkey points to one of the ControlSet00x subkeys. The Clone control set is an exact copy of the control set used for starting and initializing the system (Default or LastKnownGood). The kernel initialization process creates this control set at each system startup. The Clone control set becomes inaccessible after the first successful logon.

The HKEY_LOCAL_MACHINE\SYSTEM\Select registry key contains the following entries:

- Current
- Default
- Failed
- LastKnownGood

These parameters contain REG_DWORD data that point to a specific control set. For example, if the Current value is set to 0x1, then the CurrentControlSet points to ControlSet001. Similarly, if the LastKnownGood value is set to 0x2, it points to the ControlSet002. Usually, the Default value is the same as the Current value. The Failed parameter indicates the control set specified by the Default parameter when the user last used the LastKnownGood control set.

Earlier in the chapter, we discussed the process of system initialization using the Default and LastKnownGood configuration. When the kernel uses the default configuration, it uses the Default value to identify the control set that should be used for initialization.

There are only two situations when the kernel uses the LastKnownGood configuration.

- During system recovery after a critical failure (for example, if one of the critical device drivers couldn't be loaded or initialized). We'll discuss this topic in greater detail later in the chapter.

- When the user selects the **LastKnownGood configuration** from the **Hardware Profile/LastKnownGood** menu.

If you have either of the following problems, using the `LastKnownGood` control set may help you recover the damaged system:

- Problems caused by a device driver added into the system since the last successful startup
- Boot problems caused by invalid registry modifications

The `LastKnownGood` control set can help you recover from configuration errors.

NOTE

If you suspect that changes made since the last successful user logon process are causing problems, do not log on, since this causes the `LastKnownGood` control set to be overwritten. Instead, restart the computer, and press **F8** when prompted. Select **Last Known Good Configuration** from the **Advanced Options** startup menu. If you select the **Last Known Good** option during startup, all modifications introduced since the last successful startup will be discarded.

After the first user logs on, all configuration changes introduced using Control Panel applets will be reflected only by the `CurrentControlSet` control set. Thus, if you need to modify the control set, the only control set worth editing is the `CurrentControlSet`.

If you have problems finding subkeys of the `CurrentControlSet`, use the **Find Key** command from the **View** menu of the registry editor (Regedit.exe).

The *Start* Value

Each of the `HKEY_LOCAL_MACHINE\SYSTEM\`*`<control set>`*`\Services\`*`<DriverName>`* (where *`DriverName`* is the name of specific driver) keys contains the Start value that defines the loading order for the driver or service. The Start parameter can take one of the following values:

- *0x0* (*Boot*). The driver or service is loaded by the operating system boot loader before the kernel initialization phase starts. Disk drivers, for example, belong to this group.
- *0x1* (*System*). The service or driver is loaded by the I/O subsystem during kernel initialization. This value type is used by mouse drivers, for example.

- *0x2* (*Auto load*). The service or driver is loaded by the Service Control Manager. This type of loading order is generally used for services that start automatically under any conditions, independent of the service type. This type of value is used, for example, by parallel port device drivers. An example of a service that uses this value is the Alerter service.
- *0x3* (*Load on Demand, Manual*). The Service Control Manager will load this service only after obtaining explicit instructions to do so. Services of this type are always available, but load only when the user starts them manually.
- *0x4* (*Disabled*). This service or driver will never be loaded. Windows NT/2000 disables services or drivers if they can't be loaded by the Service Control Manager (for example, if the appropriate hardware isn't installed). If the Start parameter is set to this value, the Service Control Manager never tries to load the service or driver. The only exception to this rule is represented by the file system drivers, which the system always tries to load, even when the Start entry for these drivers is set to 0x4.

The ErrorControl Value

The list shown below provides brief descriptions of all the possible values of the `ErrorControl` registry entry located under `HKEY_LOCAL_MACHINE\SYSTEM\<control set>\Services\<DriverName>`.

- *Ignore* (*0x0*). If an error occurs when loading or initializing the device driver, the startup procedure continues without displaying an error message.
- *Normal* (*0x1*). If an error occurs while loading or initializing the device driver, the startup procedure will continue after displaying an error message. The ErrorControl value entries for most device drivers are set to this value.
- *Severe* (*0x2*). If the kernel detects an error while loading or initializing the driver or service, it switches to the `LastKnownGood` control set. The startup process then restarts. If the `LastKnownGood` control set is already in use, the startup procedure continues, and the error is ignored.
- *Critical* (*0x3*). The procedure used in this case is similar to the one used for Severe errors, with one exception. If the system has already switched to the `LastKnownGood` control set and this didn't eliminate the error, the boot process stops, and the system displays a failure message.

Preventing System Failures

Now it's time to discuss the measures that will help you prevent system failures. Naturally, all emergency planning should be done beforehand.

Performing maintenance procedures on a regular basis allows you to prevent possible problems or, at least, minimize their negative effect. The general procedures are listed below:

- Most of the time, system malfunctions or even boot failures are caused by overwritten system files or by incompatible drivers. This usually happens when you install incompatible third-party software. This problem exists not only in Windows 2000/XP, but in all earlier versions of the Windows NT operating system as well. Windows 2000 and Windows XP implement additional tools, though, which protect system files and drivers with a digital signature. The digital signature guarantees that the system file or driver is Windows-compatible. If you want to avoid any possible problems, I recommend that you use these tools. This topic will be covered in greater detail later in the chapter.
- Backup the System State data and prepare for the Automated System Recovery process (ASR) on a regular basis. Don't forget to perform these operations before introducing significant modifications into the system configuration (including new hardware and software installations). A usable and up-to-date backup copy of all your important data will also be helpful.
- Don't disable System Restore. Despite the fact that some users may think that this tool consumes too much free disk space, it still can be very useful if you need to restore the damaged system.

Detailed instructions on performing these operations were provided in *Chapter 2.*

- View system event logs on a daily basis (at the very least, view the system and application logs). Pay close attention to the messages generated by the FtDisk driver and hard disk drivers, because they may report possible file system errors. If you don't follow this rule, file system errors may remain unnoticed until the Chkdsk utility detects them. Notice that, in this case, the damaged data may even be included into the backup copy, since most backup utilities (including the Backup program supplied with Windows 2000/XP) don't recognize errors in user data.
- Check your disks on a regular basis for early detection of possible file system errors. I also recommend that you defragment your disks regularly to eliminate any possible performance problems. Use only Windows 2000/XP built-in tools or third-party disk utilities certified for Windows 2000/XP. An official list of third-party software products tested for compatibility with Windows 2000/XP can be downloaded from **http://www.microsoft.com**.
- Install a parallel copy of the operating system to improve reliability.

If the POST procedure has completed successfully, this means that the hardware initialized correctly. If the Windows XP boot process still fails, the boot problem may come from one of the following sources:

- Problems with the hard disk containing the system partition.
- Corruption of the Master Boot Record (MBR) or partition boot sector.
- One of the Windows XP boot files may be missing or corrupt. A list of the files necessary to boot Windows XP was provided earlier in this chapter.

Windows XP includes several advanced tools that help restore the damaged system. These tools are briefly described in the list below.

- *Windows file protection with a digital signature.* Windows 2000 and Windows XP provide a set of tools that protect system files and device drivers from being overwrittten during software installation procedures. Previous versions of Windows NT didn't provide protection for system files (which also include dynamically loaded libraries (DLL) and executables (EXE)). If these files were accidentally overwritten by incompatible versions, the possible consequences range from performance degradation to catastrophic failures. Windows 2000/XP includes the following system file protection tools: System File Protection (SFP), System File Checker (SFC), and File Signature Verification (FSV).
- *Automatic Updates.* Automatic Updates automates the process of downloading updates from the Windows Update website. You can configure Automatic Updates to check for and download updates.
- *Safe mode.* This option closely resembles a similar boot option implemented in Windows 95/98. It's one of the most important and useful features introduced in Windows 2000 and further enhanced in Windows XP. When the system boots in safe mode, it loads the minimum set of device drivers and services. Safe mode improves reliability and provides an easy way to recover a system damaged by incorrect software installation. Notice, however, that the safe mode option isn't a universal tool that helps in all cases. For example, this option is almost useless if there's a problem with your hard disk, or if any of the system files are missing or corrupt.
- *Automated System Recovery.* Automated System Recovery (ASR) is a two-part recovery system that allows you to restore a damaged Windows XP installation by using files saved to tape media, and hard disk configuration information saved to a floppy disk. It replaces the Emergency Repair Disk (ERD) functionality that was used in earlier Windows NT versions and, with some improvements, was also included with Windows 2000. The step-by step descriptions

of actions that you are required to take in order to prepare and perform the Automated System Recovery are provided in *Chapter 2*.

- *Driver Rollback*. This is probably one of the most useful recovery tools introduced with Windows XP. Now, if you have installed an updated version of the driver after installing Windows XP, and suspect that this operation has caused system instability or even boot problems, you can replace a specific device driver with a previously installed version. Replacing a driver is the simplest way of restoring the system, provided, of course, that it is the driver that is causing the problem. The **Roll Back Driver** button in Device Manager enables you to revert to an older driver while you investigate issues with the new one. The procedure of performing Driver Rollback are described in *Chapter 5*. Note that if you update several drivers during a single session, it might be more convenient to use the **Last Known Good Configuration** startup option or System Restore instead of rolling back individual drivers.
- *Error Reporting*. Error Reporting, if enabled, monitors your system for problems that affect Whistler components and applications. When a problem occurs, you can send a problem report to Microsoft and receive a response with more information.
- *Recovery Console*. Windows 2000/XP Recovery Console provides a command line interface to perform the recovery of a damaged system. Like the previous option, Recovery Console is also a new feature introduced in Windows 2000. Using Recovery Console, you can enable or disable services, restore damaged Master Boot Records and/or partition boot sectors, and replace damaged system files. This is a powerful recovery tool, available only for users with administrative rights in the local system. The syntax of the Recovery Console commands will be discussed later in this chapter.

System File Protection in Windows 2000 and Windows XP

All system files and device drivers in Windows 2000 and Windows XP are protected by a digital signature, which confirms that these system files and drivers are compatible with the operating system. A Microsoft digital signature verifies that the signed file was successfully tested for compatibility at Windows Hardware Quality Labs (WHQL), and wasn't modified or overwritten when installing add-on software.

According to the configuration settings, Windows 2000/XP may ignore drivers that aren't digitally signed, display a warning message when detecting these drivers (this option is set by default), or simply prohibit their installation. To configure system file protection options in Windows 2000/XP, proceed as follows:

1. Open Control Panel and start the **System** applet. The **System Properties** window will open. Go to the **Hardware** tab (Fig. 6.5).

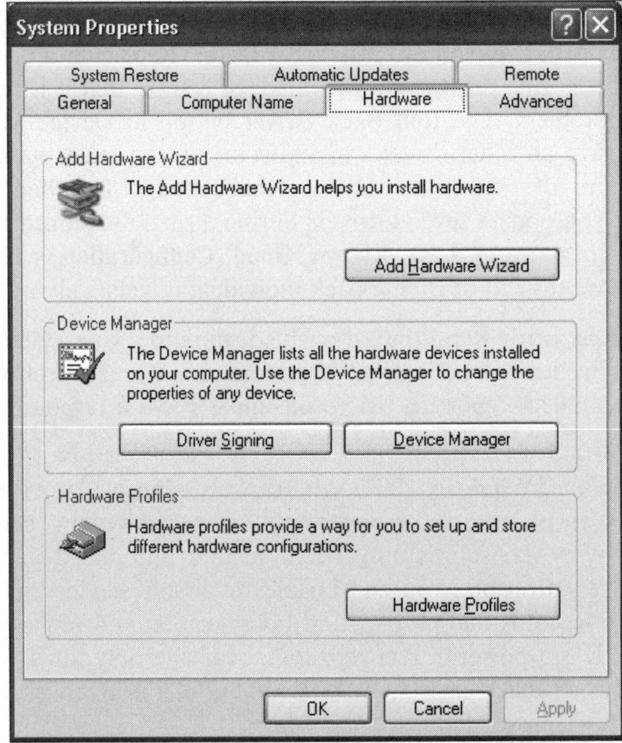

Fig. 6.5. The **Hardware** tab of the **System Properties** window

2. Click the **Driver Signing** button. The **Driver Signing Options** window will appear (Fig. 6.6). This window contains the **What action do you want Windows to take?** option group that allows you to specify the following options:

   - If you set the **Ignore** radio button, the system will allow you to install any of the drivers. However, it won't check if the driver you're going to install has a digital signature. (If this option is installed, Windows 2000/XP behaves like Windows NT 4.0). I mentioned that the presence of a digital signature confirms that the file was officially tested for compatibility. If the system file or device driver doesn't have a digital signature, this means that the file isn't officially guaranteed to be compatible.

- If you set the **Warn** radio button, the system will display warning messages any time an attempt is made to install a system file or driver that isn't digitally signed. Notice that despite this warning, the system file or driver will be installed
- If you set the **Block** radio button, the system won't allow anyone to install drivers without a digital signature.

NOTE

Users with administrative rights (Administrator and members of the Administrators group) can specify the default option, which will be used by default for all users who log on to the computer. To establish this mode, set the **Apply setting as system default** checkbox in the **Administrator option** group.

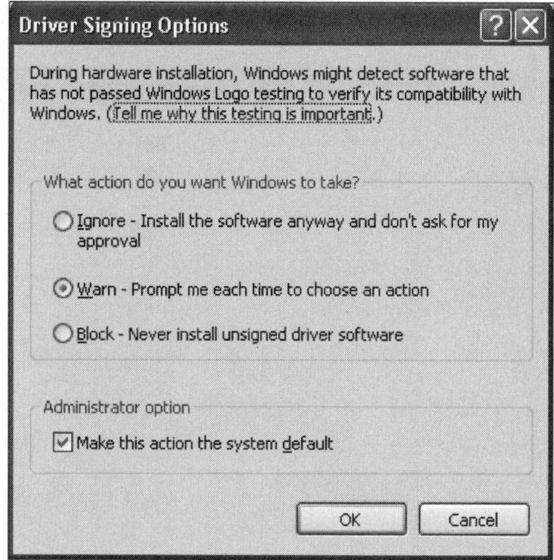

Fig. 6.6. The **Driver Signing Options** dialog

Mechanism of Driver Protection by a Digital Signature

How do Windows 2000 and Windows XP install drivers? There are two methods:

- Automatic driver installation by the PnP subsystem. This method, first introduced in Windows 2000, was further streamlined in Windows XP and is the recommended one. More detailed information on this topic was provided in *Chapter 5*. Here, I would only remind you that Windows 2000 and Windows XP attempt driver installation after the Plug and Play subsystem (PnP subsystem) discovers a new device. The user-mode Plug and Play Manager (UMPNPMGR, which is the system DLL: *%SystemRoot%*\System32\Umpnpmgr.dll) waits until the kernel-mode PnP subsystem notifies it that a new device was detected. When the notification arrives, UMPNPMGR searches the INF file for a device driver that contains the necessary installation information. All INF files for drivers included with Windows 2000/XP are located in the *%SystemRoot%*\INF folder. If you're installing an OEM driver, then the INF file will probably be located on the floppy disk or CD supplied by the vendor.

- There's also another method of installing device drivers—using the Hardware Installation Wizard located at *%SystemRoot%*\System32\Newdev.dll. The Hardware Installation Wizard performs the same operations as the user-mode PnP Manager. It also searches the INF file for the device driver to be installed.

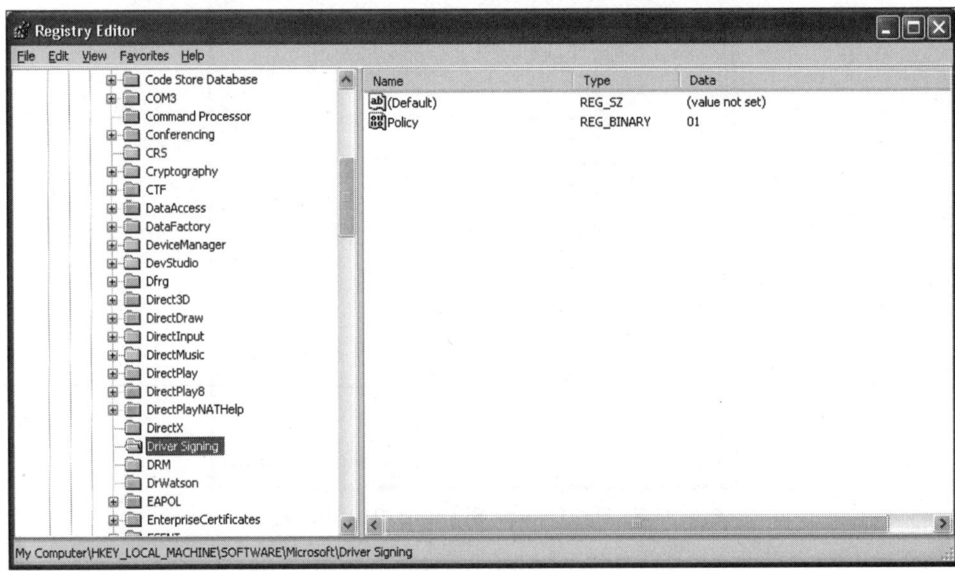

Fig. 6.7. The `HKEY_LOCAL_MACHINE\SOFTWARE\Microsoft\Driver Signing` registry key

Both UMPNPMGR and Hardware Installation Wizard use Setup API (SETUPAPI—*%SystemRoot%*\System32\Setupapi.dll) for reading the information contained in the INF file. Besides handling driver installation instructions, Windows 2000 checks the `Policy` value under `HKEY_LOCAL_MACHINE\`

SOFTWARE\Microsoft\Driver Signing (Fig. 6.7). If this entry is missing, Windows 2000 and Windows XP will check the Policy value under HKEY_CURRENT_USER\Software\Microsoft\Driver Signing (Fig. 6.8). Notice that you set these parameters using the **Driver Signing Options** dialog. If you've logged in to the system as an Administrator, and you instruct the system to use this option by default, the system will set the Policy setting under HKEY_LOCAL_MACHINE; otherwise, it will set this parameter under HKEY_CURRENT_USER. When the system checks these settings, it first checks the Policy setting under HKEY_LOCAL_MACHINE (if this value is set, it will have priority over the parameters set for individual users). If the Policy value is set to 0, the system will install all of the drivers, including those with no digital signature. If this value is set to 1, the system will allow you to install drivers without a digital signature, but a warning message will be displayed. If this value is set to 2, all of the drivers that aren't digitally signed will be ignored.

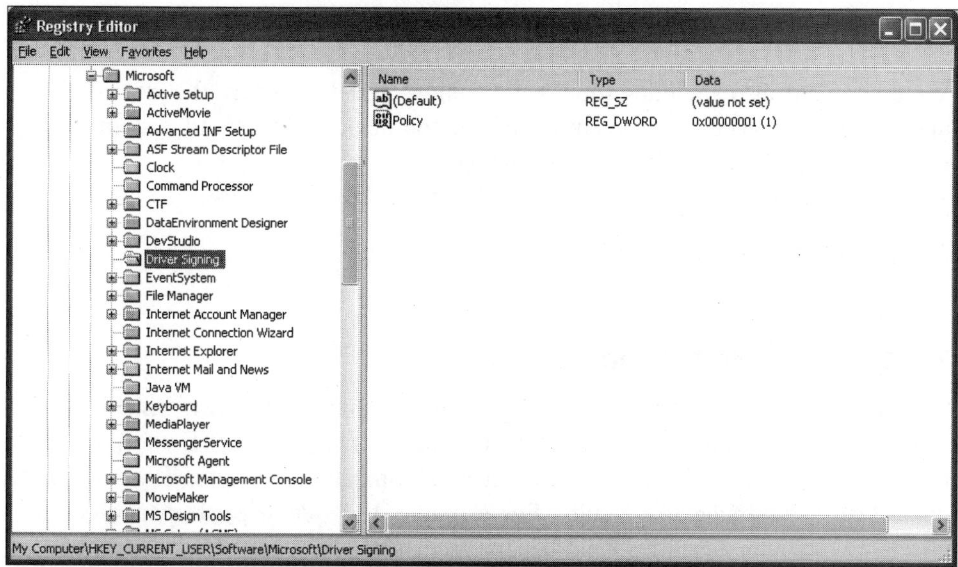

Fig. 6.8. The HKEY_CURRENT_USER\Software\Microsoft\Driver Signing registry key

If the policy on unsigned drivers makes it necessary to check the digital signature, Setupapi.dll calls CryptoAPI services to decrypt the signature using the VeriSign open key.

But where does the system store the digital signatures that protect Windows 2000/XP device drivers and system files? Microsoft stores all the digital signatures protecting Windows 2000 distribution files in special catalog files that reside in the

%SystemRoot%\System32\Catroot directory. OEM device drivers should be supplied along with their individual catalog files. Microsoft supplies these files to the device supplier after the device has been successfully tested and included into the Hardware Compatibility List (HCL). The \Catroot directory contains the master index of the device driver catalog files (sysmast.cbd and sysmast.cbk) and the nested folder. The nested folder name represents a long combination of digits and characters. When you open this folder, you'll find catalog files for all the operating system's built-in components. The Nt5.cat and Nt5inf.cat files deserve special attention, because they store the digital signatures for all of the Windows 2000/XP system files included into the distribution set.

If the result of decrypting the digital signature of a device driver or system file doesn't coincide with the digital signature contained in the driver catalog file, or if the driver has no catalog file, you'll either get a warning message, or (if the option has been set) the driver installation will fail.

Other Tools of Protecting Windows 2000 System Files

Windows 2000 also includes tools which allow you to protect the device drivers and system files. These tools guarantee that the device drivers and system files remain unchanged, and include the following:

- Windows File Protection
- System File Checker
- File Signature Verification

Windows File Protection

All earlier versions of Windows had one common drawback—when installing third-party add-on software, all shared files (including DLL and EXE files) could be changed or even overwritten by incorrect or incompatible versions. This, of course, could lead to unpredictable results. For example, the system performance could be affected, certain applications could behave incorrectly, or STOP errors could become persistent. In some cases, this could even make your system unbootable.

Windows 2000 is the first Windows operating system where an attempt was made to correct this situation. Certainly, this functionality is also present in Windows XP. The Windows File Protection feature contains the following two components:

- Windows File Protection service
- The System File Checker command-line utility (Sfc.exe)

Windows File Protection service (WFP) is based on the principle of detecting the digital signatures of all protected system files (such as SYS, DLL, OCX, TTF, FON, EXE files) and protecting these files from being accidentally modified or replaced. Windows File Protection services runs in background mode and protects all files installed by the Setup program during installation of the operating system.

WFP detects any attempts made by other programs to replace the protected system files. It performs this task by checking to make sure that the file intended to replace the protected version is digitally signed. The presence of a digital signature verifies that the version is Windows XP-compatible. If the newer version is incorrect, Windows File Protection replaces this file with the one from the backup copy of the *%SystemRoot%*\System32\Dllcache folder or from the Windows XP distribution CD. If the Windows File Protection function can't locate a correct version of the file, it prompts you to specify the path to a directory that stores this version. It also registers any attempt at system file replacement in the system event log. This function is enabled by default, which means that it will allow you to replace protected system files only when you're installing the following types of software:

- Windows 2000 and Windows XP Service Packs (using the Update.exe program)
- Hotfix packs (using the Hotfix.exe program)
- Operating system upgrades (using the Winnt32.exe program)
- Any Windows Update software

System File Checker

Windows 2000 and Windows XP include a special utility for checking the system files (System File Checker, Sfc.exe). This is a command-line utility, which scans all installed system files and checks their versions when rebooting the system. If this utility detects replaced versions of any protected system file, it will find the correct version in the *%SystemRoot%*\System32\Dllcache directory and will replace the modified file with this version.

This utility uses the following syntax:

```
sfc [/scannow] [/scanonce] [/scanboot] [/cancel] [/quiet] [/enable]
[/purgecache] [/cachesize=x]
```

where:

`/scannow`—if this parameter has been specified, SFC will perform the check immediately.

`/scanonce`—if you specify this parameter, SFC will scan all protected system files only once.

`/scanboot`—if you specify this parameter, a scan will take place each time you reboot the system.

`/revert`—returns scan to the default settings.

`/purgecache`—this switch clears the file cache of the System File Protection function and scans all protected system files immediately.

`/cachesize=x`—allows you to specify the size of the file cache of the System File Protection function (in MB).

NOTE

To use the Sfc.exe utility, you need to log on as an Administrator or member of the Administrators group.

If the contents of the *%SystemRoot%*\System32\Dllcache folder become corrupt, use `Sfc /scanonce`, `Sfc /scannow` or `Sfc /scanboot` commands to restore the contents of the \Dllcache folder.

Now, let's answer the question "Where does the system store all the settings that control SFC?". You won't be too surprised when I tell you that they're stored in the registry. All registry settings that control SFC behavior are located under `HKEY_LOCAL_MACHINE\SOFTWARE\Microsoft\Windows NT\CurrentVersion\Winlogon`. These settings are listed below:

- `SFCDisable`—the first registry setting read by SFC. If this value isn't set to 0 and the system is running in debugging mode (WinDbg kernel debugger is active), SFC disables all the functions of protecting Windows 2000 system files and device drivers.
- `SFCScan`. If this value is set to 1, SFC will scan the system files immediately after system initialization. If the `SFCScan` value is set to 2, SFC will reset it to 0 immediately after performing the scan. The default value for this setting is 0, and the value instructs SFC to protect system files (however, without scanning immediately after system initialization).
- `SfcDllCacheDir`—specifies the path to the \Dllcache folder.
- `SFCQuota`—this value specifies the total size of the system files that need to be scanned and protected.

NOTE

None of the registry settings listed above are mandatory, nor are they present in the registry by default. If any of these settings are missing, SFC behaves as if the missing parameters are present and are set to default values (the default value for `SFCQuota` is equal to –1; this value specifies an unlimited size of data to be checked).

File Signature Verification

As I mentioned before, there are some cases when the system file gets replaced by incorrect or incompatible versions during the installation procedures of third-party add-on software that aren't digitally signed. This replacement can make your system unstable (and be a potential source of persistent boot problem STOP errors).

To avoid this kind of problem, all of the system files installed during Windows 2000/XP Setup are protected by Microsoft digital signatures. This guarantees that the digitally signed files are Windows 2000-compatible. The digital signature also verifies that the signed file is either the original version developed by Microsoft, or has been tested for compatibility. Verification of the files' digital signatures allows you to identify all the files installed on the computer that aren't digitally signed. The File Signature Verification utility also displays the following information on the detected files:

- Name and fully qualified path to the file
- Date of modification to the file
- File type and version number

To start the verification procedure, click the **Start** button, select **Run,** and enter the following command: `sigverif`.

This tool will prove to be very useful for troubleshooting problems related to incorrect versions of system files, if you save the information collected by `sigverif` in the log file. To log this information, proceed as follows:

1. Start the `sigverif` program. The **File Signature Verification** window will open (Fig. 6.9). Click the **Advanced** button.

2. The **Advanced File Signature Verification Settings** window will open. Go to the **Logging** tab (Fig. 6.10) and set the **Save the file signature verification results to a log file** checkbox.

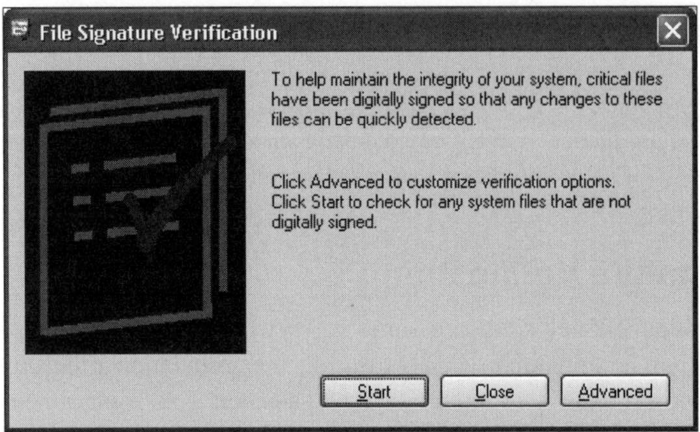

Fig. 6.9. The initial dialog of **the File Signature Verification** program

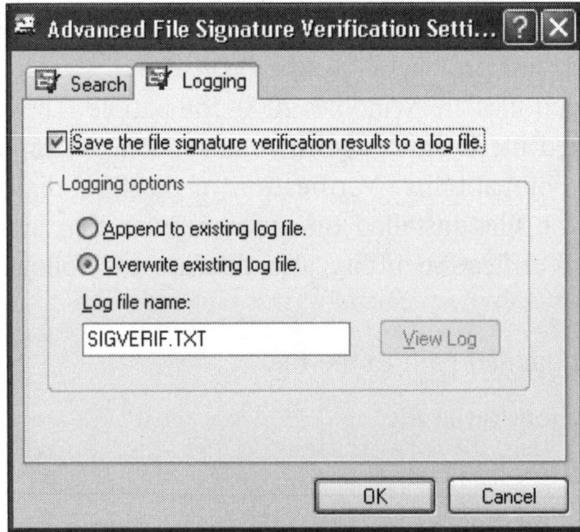

Fig. 6.10. The **Logging** tab of **the Advanced File Signature Verification Settings** window

3. Go to the **Logging options** group, which provides you with the following logging options:

   - **Append to existing log file**: if you set this radio button, the results of the new scanning operation will be added to the end of the existing log file.
   - **Overwrite existing log file**: if you select this option, the existing log file will be overwritten by the results of the new scanning.
   - You can manually enter the log file name into the **Log file name** field.

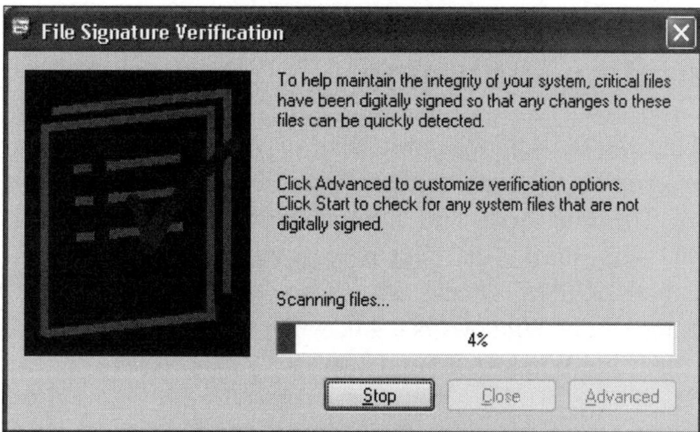

Fig. 6.11. Scanning is in progress

4. Click **OK**. You'll return to the **File Signature Verification** window. To start scanning, click the **Start** button in this window. The **Scanning files...** progress indicator will indicate the scanning progress (Fig. 6.11). To cancel scanning, click **Stop**. When finished, the program will display the **Signature Verification Results** window (Fig. 6.12), containing a complete list of all the unsigned files the program has detected.

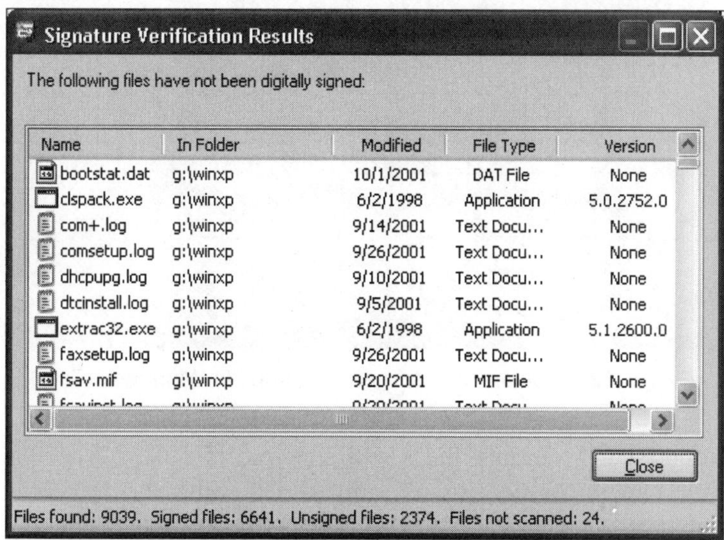

Fig. 6.12. The **Signature Verification Results** window

Starting the System With Configuration Problems

When the Windows NT 4.0, Windows 2000, or Windows XP operating system detects a severe error that it can't correct, it generates a system message known as a "blue screen". The Blue Screen of Death (BSOD) may also appear when Windows NT/2000 stops during the boot process to prevent further data corruption. Typical examples of these screens are shown below: Fig. 6.13 shows the "blue screen" as it appears in Windows NT 4.0, while Fig. 6.14 shows the "blue screen" in Windows 2000 and Windows XP.

```
             DSR CTS
*** STOP:  0x0000000A  (0x00000000, 0x0000001a, 0x00000000, 0x00000000)
IRQL_NOT_LESS_OR_EQUAL

p4-0300 irql:1f  SYSVER:0xf000030e

Dll Base DateStmp - Name                Dll Base DateStmp - Name
80100000 2e53fe55 - ntoskrl.exe         80400000 2e53eba6 - hal.dll
80010000 2e41884b - Aha154x.sys         80013000 2e4bc29a - SCSIPORT.SYS
8001b000 2e4e7b6b - Scsidisk.sys        80220000 2e53f238 - Ntfs.sys
fe420000 2e406607 - Floppy.SYS          fe430000 2e406618 - Scsicdrm.SYS
fe440000 2e406659 - Fs_Rec.SYS          fe450000 2e40660f - Null.SYS
fe460000 2e4065f4 - Beep.SYS            fe470000 2e406634 - Sermouse.SYS
fe480000 2e42a4a4 - i8042prt.SYS        fe490000 2e40660d - Mouclass.SYS
fe4a0000 2e40660c - Kbdclass.SYS        fe4c0000 2e4065e2 - VIDEOPRT.SYS
fe4b0000 2e53d49d - ati.SYS             fe4d0000 2e4065e8 - vga.sys
fe4e0000 2e406655 - Msfs.SYS            fe4f0000 2e414f30 - Npfs.SYS
fe510000 2e53f222 - NDIS.SYS            fe500000 2e40719b - elnkii.sys
fe550000 2e406697 - TDI.SYS             fe530000 2e47c740 - nbf.sys
fe560000 2e5279d9 - nwlnkipx.sys        fe570000 2e53a89e - nwlnknb.sys
fe580000 2e494973 - tcpip.sys           fe5a0000 2e5256b8 - afd.sys
fe5b0000 2e5279d3 - netbt.sys           fe5d0000 2e4167f7 - netbios.sys
fe5e0000 2e4066b3 - mup.sys             fe5f0000 2e4f9f51 - rdr.sys
fe630000 2e53f24a - srv.sys             fe660000 2ef16062 - nwlnkspx.sys

Address    dword dump Build [1057]                              - Name
FF541E4c   fe5105df fe5105df 00000001 ff640128 fe4a8228  000002fe - NDIS.SYS
ff541e60   fe501368 fe501368 00000246 00004002 00000000  00000000 - elnkii.sys
ff541eb4   fe481509 fe481509 ff6688c8 ff668288 00000000  ff668138 - i8042prt.SYS
ff541ee0   fe481ea8 fe481ea8 fe482078 00000000 ff541f04  8013c58a - i8042prt.SYS
ff541ee4   fe482078 fe482078 00000000 ff541f04 8013c58a  ff6688c8 - i8042prt.sys
ff541ef0   8013c58a 8013c58a ff6688c8 ff668040 80405900  00000031 - ntoskrnl.exe
ff541efc   80405900 80405900 00000031 06060606 06060606  06060606 - hal.dll

Restart and set the recovery options in the system control panel
or the /CRASHDEBUG system start option if this message reappears,
contact your system administrator or technical support group.
CRASHDUMP: Initializing miniport driver
CRASHDUMP: Dumping physical memory to disk:   2000
CRASHDUMP: Physical memory dump complete
```

Fig. 6.13. Typical "blue screen of death" in Windows NT 4.0

In earlier Windows NT versions, the STOP consisted of 5 parts. The Windows 2000 STOP screen (Fig. 6.14) consists of only three parts: the bugcheck information, recommended user action, and debug port information. Even so, interpretation of the STOP message and identification of the true source of the problem still remains a difficult task. If the STOP message appears during the startup process, the most probable source of the problem may be one of the following:

- The user has installed add-on software that's destroyed one of the most important parts of the system registry—the `HKEY_LOCAL_MACHINE` root key. This usually happens when an application program attempts to install a new system service or device driver. As a result, the "blue screen" either informs you that the system couldn't load the registry, or, one of the registry files will be indicated.
- The user configured the system hardware incorrectly. As a result, critical system files were overwritten or became corrupt.
- The user tried to install a system service or device driver, and the newly installed service or driver isn't compatible with the hardware installed on the computer. When the user tries to reboot the system, it will attempt to load the incorrect file. This will destroy the correct version of this system file that was loaded before the failure.

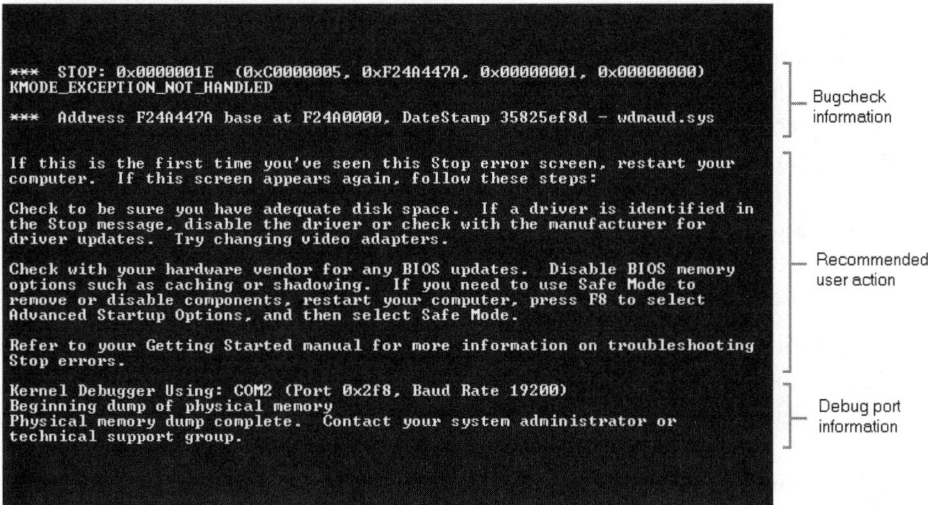

*** STOP: 0x0000001E (0xC0000005, 0xF24A447A, 0x00000001, 0x00000000)
KMODE_EXCEPTION_NOT_HANDLED
*** Address F24A447A base at F24A0000, DateStamp 35825ef8d - wdmaud.sys
If this is the first time you've seen this Stop error screen, restart your computer. If this screen appears again, follow these steps:
Check to be sure you have adequate disk space. If a driver is identified in the Stop message, disable the driver or check with the manufacturer for driver updates. Try changing video adapters.
Check with your hardware vendor for any BIOS updates. Disable BIOS memory options such as caching or shadowing. If you need to use Safe Mode to remove or disable components, restart your computer, press F8 to select Advanced Startup Options, and then select Safe Mode.
Refer to your Getting Started manual for more information on troubleshooting Stop errors.
Kernel Debugger Using: COM2 (Port 0x2f8, Baud Rate 19200)
Beginning dump of physical memory
Physical memory dump complete. Contact your system administrator or technical support group.
Bugcheck information
Recommended user action
Debug port information

Fig. 6.14. Typical "blue screen" in Windows 2000 and Windows XP

NOTE

Active usage of the Windows 2000/XP system file protection features described in the previous section is one of the most efficient and reliable methods of preventing boot-time STOP screens. If you really want to avoid Windows 2000 startup problems, don't neglect these tools!

However, what can be done if a problem already exists? Sometimes the message displayed in case of a boot failure may explicitly refer to the missing or corrupt registry file (the message that informs you of a missing or corrupt SYSTEM hive file, shown at the beginning of this chapter, is an example). In certain cases, STOP messages may also inform you of a registry corruption that's preventing the system from booting. Unfortunately, this isn't always true. If you suspect that the boot problems relate to the registry, first try to restore the damaged system using the LastKnownGood configuration.

NTLDR displays a boot menu that allows you to select the operating system to be started. For *x*86-based computers, this menu depends on the contents of the Boot.ini file. To use the **LastKnownGood configuration** in Windows NT 4.0, press the <Space> key when the boot menu appears, then select the **LastKnownGood Configuration** option. To use the **LastKnownGood configuration** in Windows 2000, press <F8> to display the Advanced startup menu, which was described earlier in this chapter.

If you're an experienced Windows NT 4.0 user, you'll remember that most of the boot problems in the system were caused by incompatible or incorrect device drivers. Incompatible drivers can either result in a system crash immediately after installation, or after a certain period of time, during which they seem to work correctly. The second situation, when the corrupt driver works for some time without causing any problems, has always been difficult to explain. After all, why did it work at all, and what actually caused the problem? Sometimes it may even seem that there are no reasonable explanations. However, remember the Original Murphy's Law: "If there are two or more ways to do something, and one of those ways can result in a catastrophe, then someone will do it".

Suppose there's a bug in the driver (after all, "there's always one more bug"), which remained unnoticed and didn't reveal itself right away. Both the hardware and software configuration of your computer may change with time, and these changes may wake the wretched thing up (because if something can go wrong, it will). Remember, Windows 2000/XP can also be prevented from booting by an incompatible driver. However, Windows 2000/XP is actually more reliable and robust than Windows NT 4.0, because booting the system in the safe mode (the concept borrowed from Windows 9*x*) presents a more convenient means of quick recovery after such errors.

If an incompatible driver causes a problem when you reboot the system for the first time after installing it, you're lucky. In this case, the **LastKnownGood Configuration** will be very helpful. When you select this option from the safe boot menu, the system will use the HKEY_LOCAL_MACHINESYSTEM\CurrentControlSet registry key and restore all the configuration information stored since the last successful boot. If using the **LastKnownGood Configuration** option didn't help, and you know for certain which driver has caused the problem (the sigverif utility discussed earlier in the chapter gives you a list of these drivers), you can try other methods of quick recovery. For example, try using safe mode options such as **Safe Mode**, **Safe Mode with Networking**, or **Safe Mode with Command Prompt**. After the system boots with the minimum set of services and drivers, you can try deleting the corrupt driver using Windows 2000 administrative tools such as Hardware Wizard or Device Manager. If both system and boot partitions are formatted using the FAT file system, you can try booting from an MS-DOS system disk and manually delete or rename the driver that's causing the problems.

NOTE

The **LastKnownGood Configuration** option provides the quickest and easiest method of recovering a corrupt registry for both Windows NT 4.0 and Windows 2000/XP (if it works, of course). Unfortunately, this method has some limitations. For example, it restores only one part of the registry (namely, the ControlSet00x branch under HKEY_LOCAL_MACHINE\SYSTEM). So, it will help you to recover the damaged system only if the problem is limited to this registry branch and if you use this method immediately. Notice that all configuration changes introduced into the system since the last successful boot will be lost if you use this method.

If the information mentioned above didn't help you to solve the problem, then it's time to use one of the methods for restoring the corrupt registry that we discussed in *Chapter 2.* If you're working with Windows NT 4.0, try to restore the system by using an ERD and select the **Inspect Registry Files** option. After you select this option, the system will display a list of registry files where you can select the hives to be restored.

In contrast to the emergency repair process in Windows NT 4.0, neither the manual nor the automatic recovery of Windows 2000 using an ERD can repair registry errors. To tell you the truth, the Windows 2000 emergency recovery process does recover the system registry, but this recovery is awkward, because the ERD process uses a registry backup copy created by the Setup program during system installation. As you already know, the backup copy is stored in the *%SystemRoot%*\Repair folder. Because of this, I recommend that you use the Windows 2000 Recovery Console for registry recovery (and never forget to backup the registry). As I mentioned in *Chapter 2*, which is entirely dedicated to various methods of registry backup and recovery, the Backup program creates registry backup while performing the System State data backup. This backup copy is stored in the *%SystemRoot%*/Repair/Regback folder. Advanced users may use these registry backup files to restore the system without going through the whole routine of restoring the system state data.

Also, don't neglect the Resource Kit utilities for registry backup and recovery (`Regback/Regrest` in Windows NT 4.0 and `REG` in Windows 2000 Resource Kit).

NOTE

A disk partition different from the boot partition is a safe place for storing the backup copies of your registry (ideally, you should store registry backups on another physical disk). This will help you to safeguard the registry backups from hardware failures, which might make your backup copies unavailable.

Recovery Console

Windows 2000/XP Recovery Console provides a command-line interface, allowing administrators and users with administrative privileges the capability of recovering a system that doesn't boot. Using the Recovery Console, you can start and stop system services, read and write data to the local hard drives (including NTFS drives), and repair damaged boot sectors and MBR.

This new functionality is especially useful when you need to copy one or more system files to the local hard drive in order to recover a damaged system. You can copy these files from a CD or disk. Recovery Console will also be very helpful if you need to reconfigure a service or driver that causes boot problems.

NOTE

You need to log in as an Administrator to access the Recovery Console.

Methods of starting, installing, or deleting the Recovery Console were discussed in detail in *Chapter 2.* In this chapter, we'll concentrate on using this tool for recovering a system that has configuration problems.

Using Recovery Console

Recovery Console provides an MS-DOS-like command-line interface. Like any other tool of this sort, Recovery Console has a `help` command that displays a list of available commands. You can also find a complete list of Recovery Console commands in the Windows 2000/XP online Help system (search using the keywords "Recovery Console").

A brief listing of Recovery Console commands is provided below:

- `Attrib`—changes file or folder attributes
- `Batch`—executes commands contained in the text file you specify
- `ChDir (CD)`—changes to the other directory
- `Chkdsk`—starts the Chkdsk program
- `Cls`—clears the screen
- `Copy`—copies a single file you've specified
- `Delete (DEL)`—deletes a single file
- `Dir`—lists the contents of the current directory
- `Disable`—disables the system service or driver
- `Diskpart`—manages partitions on your hard disk
- `Enable`—enables the service or driver
- `Exit`—exits Recovery Console and reboots the computer
- `Expand`—expands the compressed file
- `Fixboot`—repairs the corrupt boot sector on the system partition
- `Fixmbr`—repairs the corrupt Master Boot Record
- `Format`—formats the hard drive
- `Help`—displays a list of Recovery Console commands
- `Listsvc`—displays a list of all the available services and drivers
- `Logon`—allows you to log on to the Windows 2000/XP system
- `Map`—displays a list of drive mappings
- `MkDir (MD)`—creates a new directory
- `More`—displays text files in screen-size portions
- `Rename (REN)`—renames the file
- `RmDir (RD)`—deletes the directory

- `Set`—displays and sets the Recovery Console environment variables
- `SystemRoot`—marks the current directory as *SystemRoot*
- `Type`—prints the text file on the screen

To display information concerning the use of a certain command, use the following syntax:

```
HELP command name
```

(for example, `HELP FIXBOOT`) or

```
command name /?
```

(for example, `LISTSVC /?`).

NOTE

There are certain limitations that restrict usage of the Recovery Console. For example, in Win2K, you could copy the files from disks to the local hard disk, but any attempt at copying the files from the hard drive to disk failed. You can only create a new directory within the *%SystemRoot%* folder (\WINNT, for example), but this operation fails if you attempt to create a new directory at the root level (C:\). You can only copy files to the root folder or to the *%SystemRoot%* directory. Finally, the copy command doesn't support wildcard characters, and, consequently, doesn't allow you to copy multiple files.

Error Reporting

Windows XP now includes a new feature named Error Reporting service. As Microsoft declares, this service is intended to help you troubleshoot error in your system, and at the same time help Windows XP developers improve future versions of the product. The Error Reporting service monitors your system for user and kernel-mode faults that affect Windows XP components and applications.

When a user mode error occurs (such as an application error), the Error Reporting service does the following:

- *Displays an alert* stating that Windows XP has detected a problem (Fig. 6.15). You have the option of reporting the error to Microsoft by clicking the **Send Error Report** button or declining the action by clicking the **Don't Send**; or you can click **click here** to view technical information about the problem before sending a report to Microsoft. Notice that you can also debug the application by clicking the **Debug** button.

- *Sends a problem report to Microsoft.* If you click **Send Error Report**, the Error Reporting service sends the report to Microsoft through an Internet connection. You might be prompted to provide additional information to complete your error report. When the process is complete, the Error Reporting service enables you to obtain more details by clicking **More Information**.
- An automated process then searches a database of known issues for matching conditions. If a match exists, an on-screen message appears with information containing Internet links to updated drivers, patches, or Microsoft Knowledge Base articles with troubleshooting and support information.

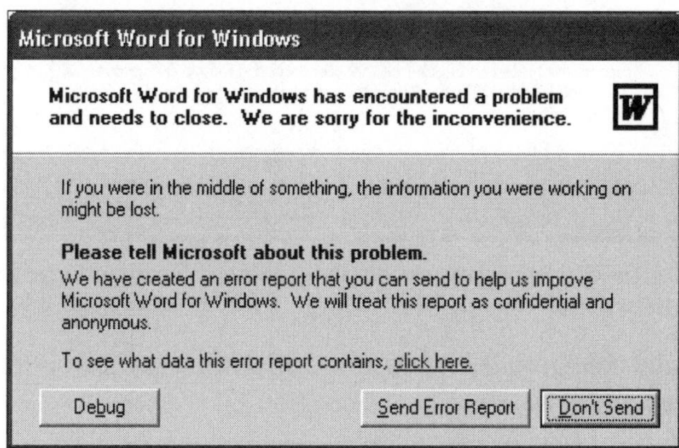

Fig. 6.15. Error Reporting service displays an alert when a user-mode error, such as an application error, occurs

When a kernel mode error occurs (such as the STOP message, which we briefly discussed in the previous section), Windows XP writes a small memory dump file to disk. After you reboot the system either in normal mode or safe mode with networking and logon, the Error Reporting service does the following:

- *Displays an alert* stating that Windows XP has encountered a serious problem (Fig. 6.16). As in the previous case, you have the option of reporting this error to Microsoft. You can also choose not to send an error report. To view technical details on the problem, follow the **click here** link.
- *Sends a problem report to Microsoft.* If you choose to report the problem, the Error Reporting service sends the report to Microsoft (which includes the information in the small memory dump file) through an Internet connection. You might be prompted to provide additional information to complete your error report. When the process is complete, the Error Reporting service enables you to obtain more details by clicking **More Information**.

- An automated process then searches a database of known issues for matching conditions. If a match exists, an on-screen message appears with information containing Internet links to updated drivers, patches, or Microsoft Knowledge Base articles with troubleshooting and support information.

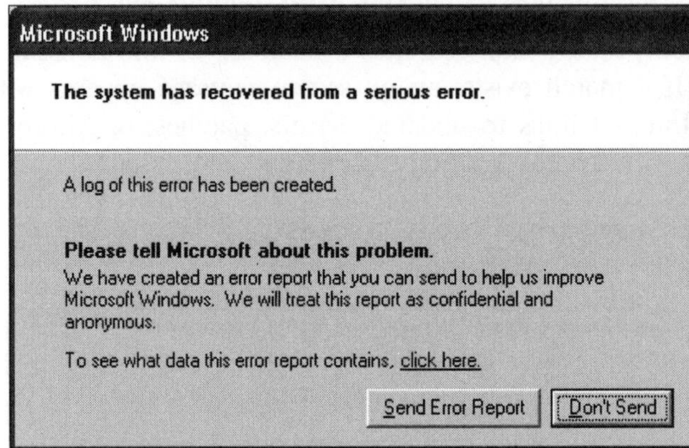

Fig. 6.16. The Error Reporting service displays an alert informing you that Windows XP has encountered a serious problem (a STOP message, in this case)

You can manually configure Windows Error Reporting service options. To perform this task, proceed as follows:

1. Start the System applet in Control Panel. Go to the **Advanced** tab and click the **Error Reporting** button to display the **Error Reporting** window (Fig. 6.17).
2. In this window, you can set the following Error Reporting options:
   - Completely disable the Error Reporting service by setting the **Disable error reporting** radio button. Notice that in this case you can still instruct the service to display notification in case of severe errors, such as STOP errors. To do so, set the **But notify me when critical errors occur** checkbox directly below the above mentioned radio button.
   - Enable the Error Reporting service by setting the **Enable error reporting** radio button. If you set the **Windows operating system** checkbox directly below this radio button, the service will always report problems with Windows XP kernel-mode components. You can also choose to report problems with individual applications by setting the **Programs** checkbox.

Windows XP always writes a small memory dump file when a STOP message appears. Therefore, the Error Reporting service is able to send a problem report with the information from the small memory dump file, even if you have configured your system to generate kernel or complete memory dump files.

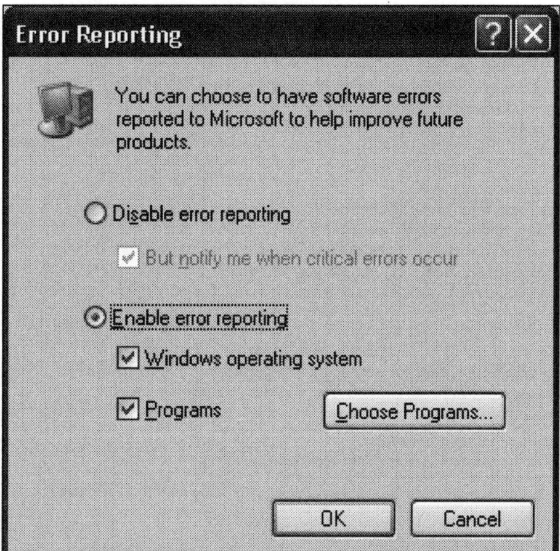

Fig. 6.17. The **Error Reporting** window

To configure Windows Error Reporting for individual applications, proceed as follows:

1. Open the **Error Reporting** window (Fig. 6.17). If error reporting is disabled, enable this service by setting the **Enable error reporting** radio button, and make sure that the **Programs** checkbox is set.
2. Click the **Choose Programs** button to open the **Choose Programs** window (Fig. 6.18). In this window, you have the following options:
   - If you set the **All programs** radio button, the service will report errors and problems with all applications installed in the system.
   - If you set the **All programs in this list** radio button, you will be able to enable or disable error reporting for Windows components and Microsoft applications by setting or clearing the appropriate checkboxes.
   - Finally, you'll be able to create an exception list for error reporting service. To do so, click the **Add** button at the bottom of this window, then select one or more applications for which you want error reporting to be disabled. Applications added to the exception list will be displayed in the **Do not report errors for these programs** field. To remove programs included into this list, select the program from this list and click the **Remove** button.

You can optionally change error report destinations from the default value (sent directly to Microsoft) or to a network path by changing Group Policy settings or by editing the registry.

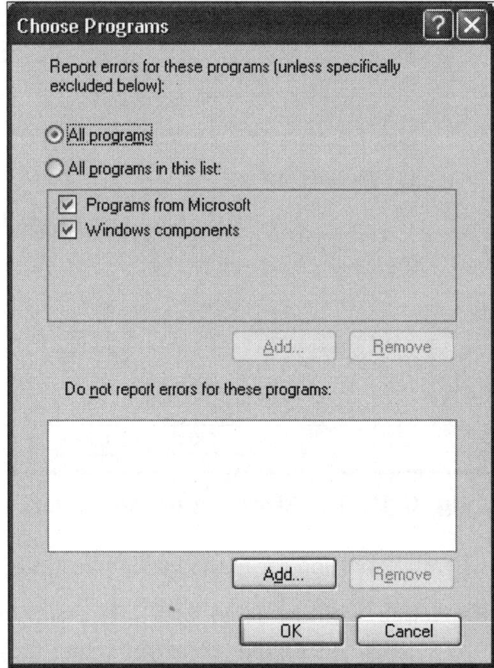

Fig. 6.18. The **Choose Programs** window

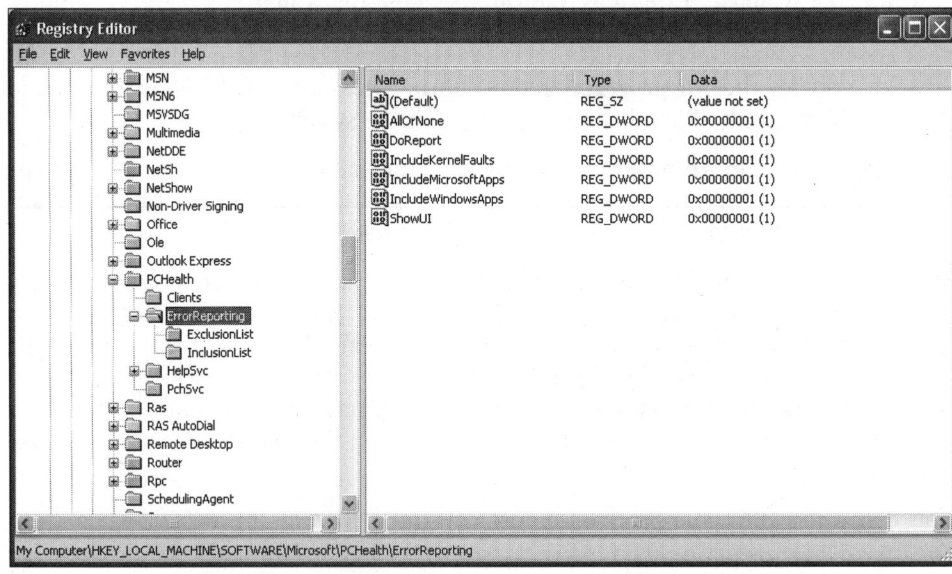

Fig. 6.19. The Error Reporting options parameters in the registry

To change the error report destination:

1. Start Regedit.exe and expand the `HKEY_LOCAL_MACHINE\SOFTWARE\Microsoft\PCHealth\ErrorReporting` key (Fig. 6.19). If this key doesn't contain the nested DW key, create it.

2. Create another nested key named `DWNoSecondLevelCollection`, and under this key create a string value named `ER_Report_path`. To change the error report destination, specify a path to the new location. For example, \\myserver\myshare\my_dir.

3. Click **OK** and close the Registry Editor.

4. To restore the original configuration and send reports directly to Microsoft, delete the `ER_Report_Path` entry.

Summary

This chapter concentrated mainly on the role of the system registry in the startup process, methods of preventing boot failures, and the most common procedures for recovering a system with configuration problems related to a corrupt registry.

Chapter 7

Registry Key Reference

Put up in a place
where it's easy to see
the cryptic admonishment
T.T.T.
When you feel how depressingly
slowly you climb,
it's well to remember that
Things Take Time.

Piet Hein
Grooks

The everyday tasks of system administrators are extremely difficult; they need to manage all the hardware, operating systems, and applications installed on the organization's computers. They often need to administer the registry as well. A very short description of the root registry keys existing in Windows NT/2000 and Windows XP registries was provided in *Chapter 1.* This chapter considers the topic in more detail. Since it was written as a brief reference on the main registry keys existing in all Windows NT/2000/XP operating systems and emphasizes the new keys that have been added to Windows XP, the system administrator can greatly benefit from it.

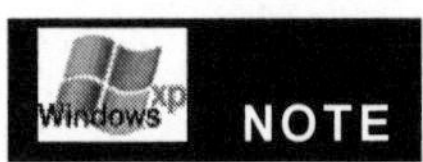

Like many other Windows XP system components, the Registry is very similar to the Windows NT/2000 registry, and has significant differences from the Windows 9*x*/ME registry. This is due to the fact that Windows XP is based on the Windows NT/2000 kernel. However, because of new functionality that was first introduced with Windows XP, and of enhancements introduced into the Windows XP kernel, there appeared new registry keys and value entries. This is not surprising, since all new features must be reflected in the registry.

The *HKEY_LOCAL_MACHINE* Key

`HKEY_LOCAL_MACHINE` is one of the most important, and most interesting, root keys of the registry. It contains configuration data for the local computer. Information stored in this registry key is used by applications and device drivers, and by the operating system itself for obtaining information on the configuration of the local computer. The information doesn't depend on the user who's logged in to the system.

The HKEY_LOCAL_MACHINE root key contains five subkeys, briefly described in Table 7.1. The rest of this section describes the subkeys in greater detail.

NOTE

You can read the information contained in any of these subkeys, but it only makes sense to edit the contents of the Software and System keys.

Table 7.1. Subkeys Contained within the *HKEY_LOCAL_MACHINE* Root Key

Subkey	Contents
HARDWARE	This subkey contains the database describing all the hardware devices installed on the computer, the method of interaction between device drivers and hardware devices, and the data that connects kernel-mode device drivers with user-mode code. All the data contained within this subkey are volatile. The system re-creates these data each time it starts The Description subkey describes all the hardware physically present on the computer. The hardware recognizer collects this information at system startup and the kernel stores this information under the HKEY_LOCAL_MACHINE\HARDWARE\DESCRIPTION registry key The DeviceMap subkey contains various data in formats defined by certain device driver classes. As device drivers are loading, they pass their information to the system so that it can associate specific hardware devices and their drivers The ResourceMap subkey contains information on the system resources allocated to each device (including ports, DMA addresses, IRQs). Notice that all Windows NT-based operating systems, including Windows 2000 and Windows XP, provide a much more convenient way to view the contents of this subkey. To view (and possibly change) this data, it is recommended that you use various administrative tools. For example, if you're using Windows NT 4.0, you can view the information using the Windows NT Diagnostics utility (Winmsdp.exe). In Windows 2000 and Windows XP, you can use the MMC console or Device Manager for the same purpose
SAM	This subkey contains the directory services database, which stores information on user and group accounts and security subsystems. (SAM stands for the Security Account Manager). By default, you can't view this key using registry editors even if you're logged in as an Administrator. The data contained within the HKLM\SAM registry key isn't documented, and user passwords are encrypted. Note that for Windows NT domains the SAM database also stores a domain directory services database. In native-mode Windows 2000 domains, the directory services database is stored in the Ntds.dit file on domain controllers. However, the SAM database remains important, since it stores local accounts (required to log on locally). If your computer that is running Windows XP does not participate in a domain, SAM database is the main storage of the user and group accounts information

continues

Table 7.1 Continued

Subkey	Contents
SECURITY	This database contains the local security policy, including user rights and permissions. The key is only used by the Windows NT/2000/XP security subsystem. For example, it contains information that defines whether or not an individual user can reboot the computer, start or stop device drivers, backup/recover files, or access the computer through the network. Information contained within this key is also encrypted. The HKLM\SAM key is the link to the HKLM\SECURITY\SAM key
SOFTWARE	This database contains information on the software products installed on the local computer, along with various configuration data
SYSTEM	This database contains information on controlling the system startup, the loading order of device drivers and system services, and on the operating system behavior

If the HKEY_CURRENT_USER registry key contains data similar to that contained under HKEY_LOCAL_MACHINE, then the HKEY_CURRENT_USER data has priority by default.

NOTE

If you read the previous chapter carefully, you'll remember that the Policy setting under HKEY_LOCAL_MACHINE has priority over the individual settings specified for each user. This is only true if you logged in to the system as an Administrator and specified the default value for the power policy, as described in *Chapter 5*.

However, the settings under this key may also extend the data under HKEY_LOCAL_MACHINE rather than replace them. Furthermore, there are certain settings (for example, those that manage the device driver loading order) that have no meaning outside the HKEY_LOCAL_MACHINE root key.

The *HKEY_LOCAL_MACHINE\HARDWARE* Key

The HKEY_LOCAL_MACHINE\HARDWARE registry key contains hardware data recreated during each system startup. This data includes information about the devices on the motherboard and the data on the IRQs used by individual device drivers.

The HARDWARE key contains important data sets subdivided between the following three subkeys: DESCRIPTION, DEVICEMAP, and RESOURCEMAP.

All the information contained under HKEY_LOCAL_MACHINE\HARDWARE is volatile. This means that the settings are computed and recreated each time the system starts up, and are lost when you shut the system down. All drivers and applications use this subtree for obtaining information on system components and for storing the data directly under the DEVICEMAP subkey and indirectly under the RESOURCEMAP subkey (Fig. 7.1).

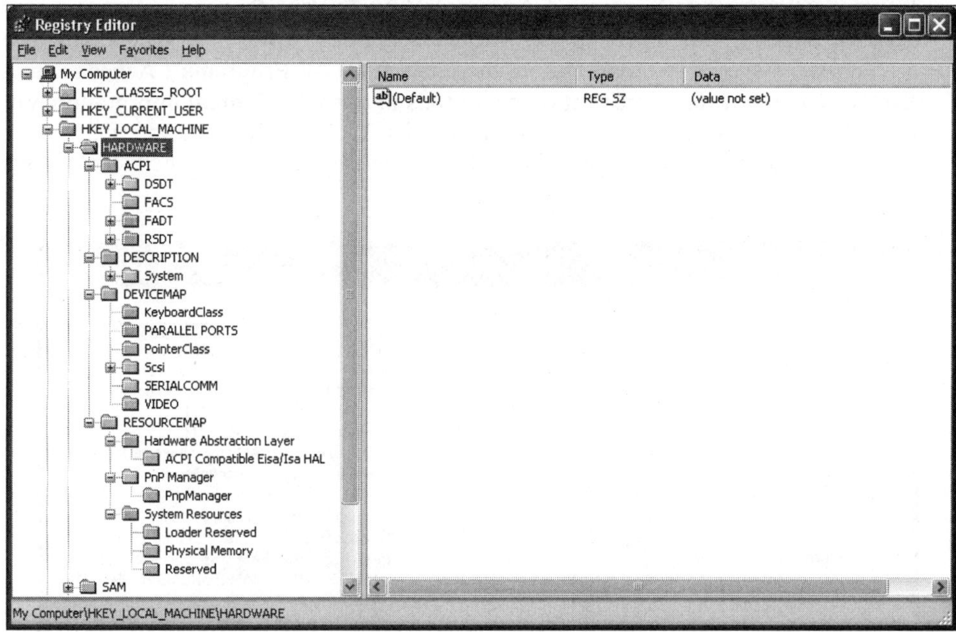

Fig. 7.1. The HKEY_LOCAL_MACHINE\HARDWARE registry key

NOTE

As was explained in *Chapter 5*, integrated support for Plug and Play and power management in Windows 2000/XP is available only on computers that have an Advanced Configuration and Power Interface (ACPI) BIOS. At boot time, the operating system loader checks whether such a BIOS is loaded. If so, ACPI is enabled in the operating system. If such a BIOS is not loaded, ACPI is disabled and the less reliable Advanced Power Management (APM) model is used instead. Microsoft supplies the ACPI driver as part of the operating system. On systems that have an ACPI BIOS, the HAL causes the ACPI driver to be loaded during system start-up at the base of the device tree, where it acts as the interface between the operating system and the BIOS. The ACPI driver is transparent to other drivers. If your system has ACPI BIOS, the HKEY_LOCAL_MACHINE\HARDWARE registry tree will contain the nested ACPI subkey (Fig. 7.1).

Don't try to edit the data under HKEY_LOCAL_MACHINE\HARDWARE directly. This information is usually stored in binary format and is difficult to understand if you can't interpret binary data.

TIPS

If you are working with Windows 2000, and need to view the hardware data in user-friendly format, select **Programs | Administrative Tools | Computer Management** from the **Start** menu and expand the MMC console tree. To view the same information in Windows XP, click the **Start** button, then select the **All Programs | Accessories | System Tools | System Information** commands to open the **System Information** window (Fig. 7.2). Like Windows 2000 hardware data, Windows XP hardware information will be represented in user-friendly format (the system also reads it from the system registry).

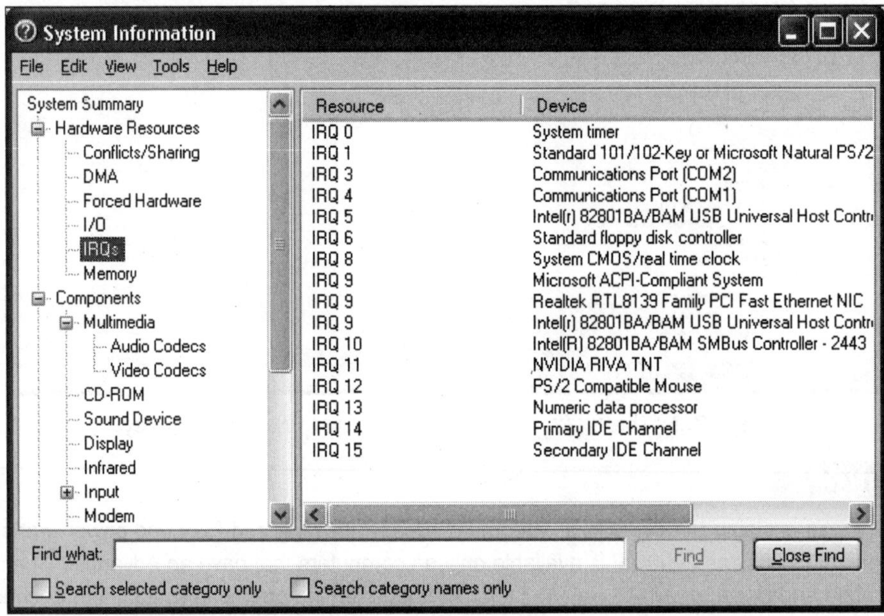

Fig. 7.2. Viewing Windows XP hardware information using the System Information utility

The *DESCRIPTION* Subkey

The DESCRIPTION subkey under HKEY_LOCAL_MACHINE\HARDWARE displays information from the hardware database. For *x*86 computers, this information contains data on the devices detected by Ntdetect.com and Ntoskrnl.exe.

Ntdetect.com is the standard DOS-style program that uses BIOS calls for selecting hardware information and configuring hardware devices. This includes date and time information stored in the CMOS chip; bus types (for example, ISA, PCI, EISA) and identifiers of the devices on these buses; data on the number, type, and capacity of the hard drives installed in the system; and the number and types of parallel ports. Based on this information, the system creates internal data structures that Ntoskrnl.exe stores under `HKEY_LOCAL_MACHINE\HARDWARE\DESCRIPTION` during system startup.

A specific feature of the Ntdetect.com version included with Windows 2000 and Windows XP is that PnP detection functions are delegated to PnP drivers. In contrast, the Windows NT 4.0 version of Ntdetect.com detects all installed hardware (due to limited PnP support in Windows NT 4.0).

Ntdetect.com detects the following hardware:

- Type of bus/adapter
- Keyboard
- SCSI adapters
- COM-ports
- Machine ID
- Video adapter
- Arithmetic co-processor
- Mouse
- Floppy drives
- Parallel ports

NOTE

Network adapters aren't detected at this phase. The system detects network adapters either during Windows NT/2000/XP installation, or when you install a new network adapter.

There are more subkeys, each of them corresponds to a certain bus controller type. These subkeys are located under `HKEY_LOCAL_MACHINE\Hardware\Description\System\MultifunctionAdapter`. Each of these keys describes a specific controller class (including hard disk controllers, display controllers, parallel port controllers, and SCSI controllers.) The path to the subkey describes the component type. All physical devices are numbered, beginning from 0.

Each detected hardware component has `Component Information` and `Configuration Data` settings, which contain binary data on the version of a specific component and its configuration (Fig. 7.3). The `Identifier` setting contains the component name (if specified).

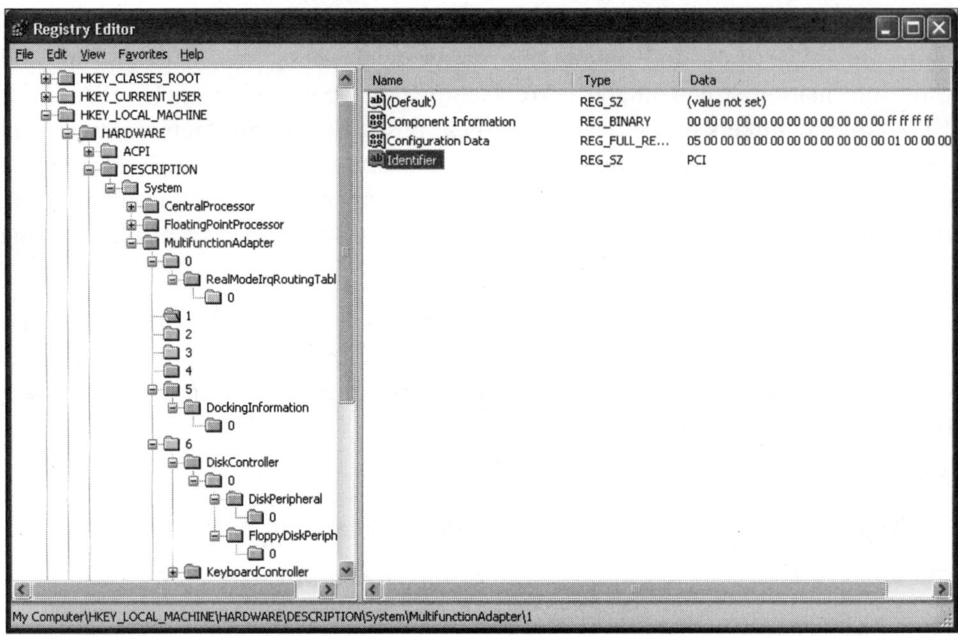

Fig. 7.3. The `HKEY_LOCAL_MACHINE\HARDWARE\DESCRIPTION\System\MultifunctionAdapter` registry key

The *DEVICEMAP* Subkey

The `HKEY_LOCAL_MACHINE\HARDWARE\DEVICEMAP` registry key contains a set of subkeys. The subkeys contain one or more settings that specify the path to the drivers required by each device. Let's consider using this information for searching for device drivers. For example, how does the registry store information on the video drivers? Fig. 7.4 shows an example illustrating the contents of the `VIDEO` subkey under the `DEVICEMAP` key (the information you'll see when you open the registry key will differ from what's shown in this figure). However, the information will show you what you'll see in general.

The `HKEY_LOCAL_MACHINE\HARDWARE\DEVICEMAP\VIDEO` registry key contains settings that are actually links to currently active devices. These registry items use an ordinal naming scheme (for example, in Fig. 7.4 it's `\Device\Video`*N*, where *N* is an ordinal number (0, 1, 2). The values of each of these registry settings are `REG_SZ` strings that reference particular device drivers.

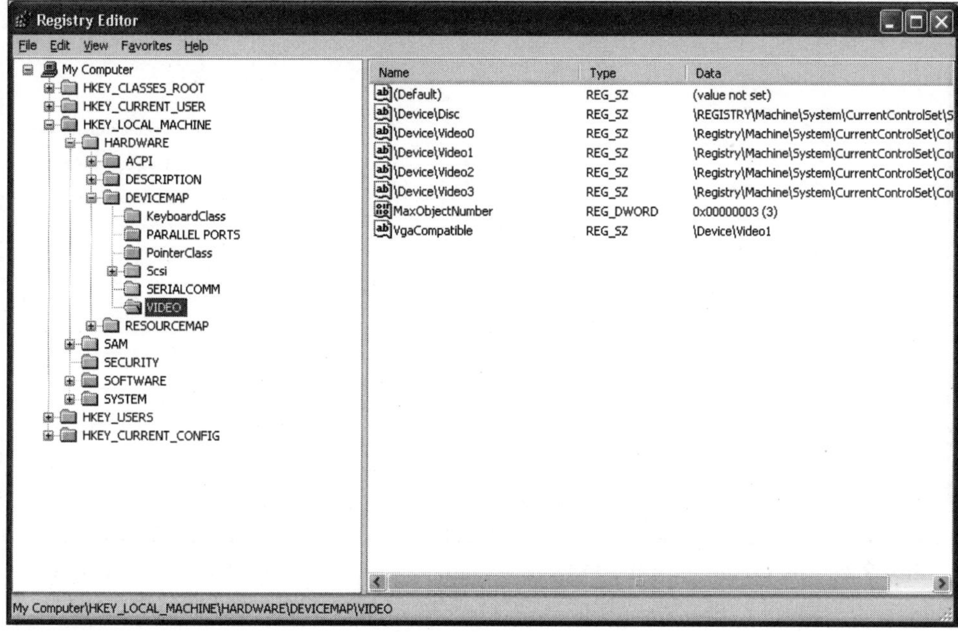

Fig. 7.4. The `HKEY_LOCAL_MACHINE\HARDWARE\DEVICEMAP\VIDEO` registry key

NOTE

Notice that these strings have a specific data format. For example, the `Device\Video0` setting represented in Fig. 7.4 is set to `\Registry\Machine\System\CurrentControlSet\Control\Video\{AFCB39E1-9FBB-4404-A3AE-29492CF7D79D}\0000` value. This format is different from the one that's normally used (for example, `HKEY_LOCAL_MACHINE`, `HKEY_CURRENT_USER`). What does it mean?

All Windows NT-based operating systems, including Windows 2000 and Windows XP, are object-oriented, which means that they manipulate several object types, including devices, ports, events, directories, and symbolic links. Registry keys are objects of special types. The registry root key is the object of the Key type named `REGISTRY`. In the DDK (Device Driver Kit) documentation, the names of all the registry keys begin with the `\REGISTRY` string (for example, `\REGISTRY\Machine\CurrentControlSet\Services`). Thus, the `HKEY_LOCAL_MACHINE` handle is the key named `\REGISTRY\Machine`, and the `HKEY_USERS` handle is the key named `\REGISTRY\User`.

Now let's expand the `\HKEY_LOCAL_MACHINE\SYSTEM\CurrentControlSet\Control\Video\{AFCB39E1-9FBB-4404-A3AE-29492CF7D79D}\0000` registry key (Fig. 7.5). Notice that it contains quite a lot of entries, mostly in binary format.

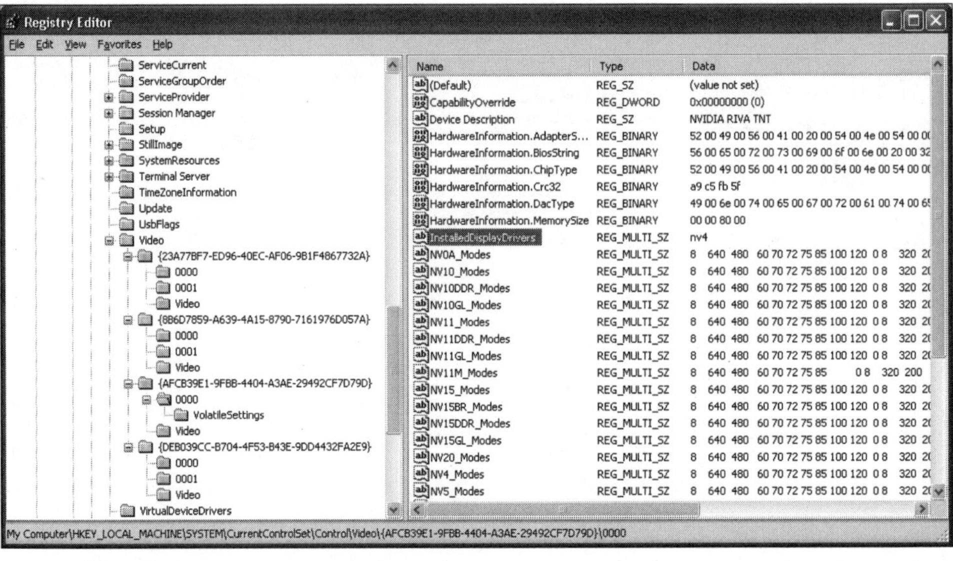

Fig. 7.5. The contents of the `HKLM\SYSTEM\CurrentControlSet\Control\Video\{AFCB39E1-9FBB-4404-A3AE-29492CF7D79D}\0000` registry key

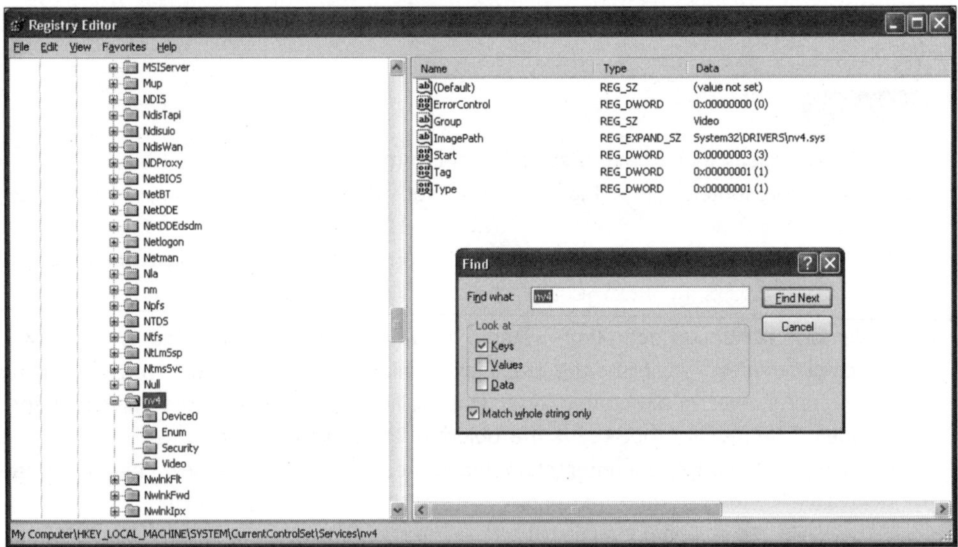

Fig. 7.6. The contents of the `HKEY_LOCAL_MACHINE\SYSTEM\CurrentControlSet\Services\nv4` registry key

However, among these entries there is the `Device Description` value (data type `REG_SZ`), which, as its name implies, contains the device description (`NVIDIA

`RIVA TNT`, in our example). Besides, it also contains another value, `InstalledDisplayDrivers`, which references the driver for this device. In our case it references the `nv4` service. The information on this service can be found in the registry under `HKEY_LOCAL_MACHINE\SYSTEM\CurrentControlSet\Services` registry key, which must contain a nested key with the same name (`nv4` in our example). Let us expand the `HKEY_LOCAL_MACHINE\SYSTEM\CurrentControlSet\Services` key; there we'll find a nested key named `nv4` (Fig. 7.6). It must exist for the device to function properly, and you'll certainly find it.

TIP

Use Regedit.exe searching capabilities to find the key, since in our case this is the easiest way to locate the required key.

The key that you'll locate contains standard settings that specify the start mode for the driver: `Start`, `Tag`, `Type`, `ErrorControl`, and `Group`. Depending on the driver type, its key may contain several other settings, such as the `ImagePath` setting that specifies an actual path to the directory where the driver resides.

NOTE

Notice how the image path has been specified. The loading order for the driver is specified by the `Start` setting (as we saw in the previous chapter). Sometimes the system doesn't assign drive mappings at the time the driver's loaded. Because of this, an error may result if you specify, for example, "C:\WINNT\System32\DRIVERS\<*YourDriver*>" as a value for ImagePath.

The HKEY_LOCAL_MACHINE\SYSTEM\ControlSet*nnn*\Services\<*Driver*> key may contain an optional `REG_SZ` setting named `DisplayName`. The value assigned to this parameter is a text string displayed by administrative utilities like the Devices Control Panel applet (Windows NT 4.0) or the MMC console (Windows 2000 and Windows XP). If the `DisplayName` setting is omitted, then the actual name of the service or driver will be displayed in the list (in our example, the list will display the nv4 driver name).

In addition to the settings listed above, the video driver key under HKEY_LOCAL_MACHINE\SYSTEM\ControlSet*nnn*\Services contains several subkeys. One of the most important subkeys within this key is Device*N*—in our example, this is the `Device0` subkey (Fig. 7.7).

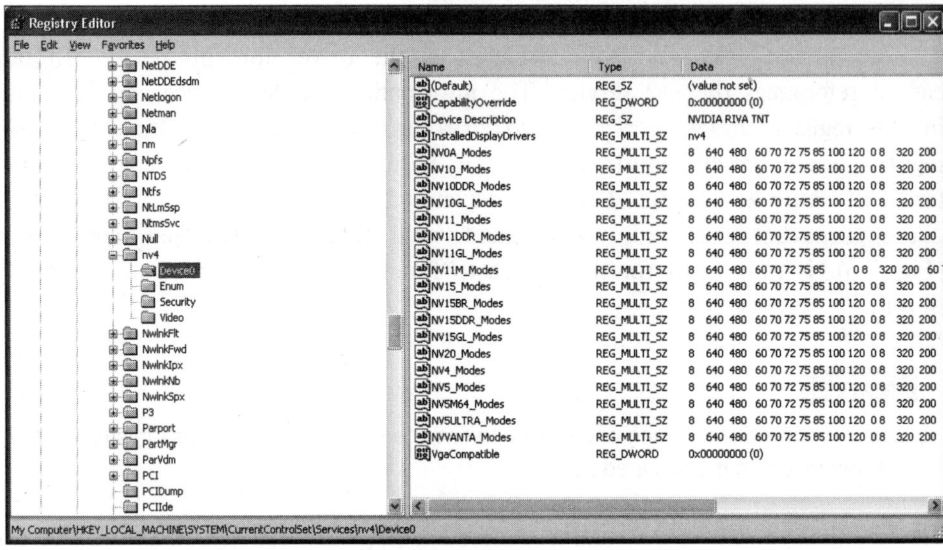

Fig. 7.7. An example of the contents of the `DeviceN` nested key for the device driver subkey under `HKEY_LOCAL_MACHINE\SYSTEM\ControlSetnnn\Services`

Depending on the video driver implementation, this key may contain a variety of parameters, including the `VgaCompatible` standard setting, which is set to `FALSE` for most modern drivers. If the parameter is set to `FALSE`, the driver is based on the MS VGA miniport driver.

The following `REG_BINARY` settings under the `HKEY_LOCAL_MACHINE\SYSTEM\CurrentControlSet\Control\Video\{AFCB39E1-9FBB-4404-A3AE-29492CF7D79D}\0000`:

```
HardwareInformation.ChipType,
HardwareInformation.Crc32,
HardwareInformation.DacType
HardwareInformation.MemorySize
```

contain hardware information displayed by administrative utilities. Notice that these settings are present in both the Windows NT 4.0/Windows 2000 and in Windows XP registries, but under different locations.

When Windows GUI starts, the system reads the video settings contained under the following registry key (Fig. 7.8):

```
HKEY_LOCAL_MACHINE\SYSTEM\CurrentControlSet\Hardware Profiles\
Current\System\CurrentControlSet\Control\VIDEO\
{AFCB39E1-9FBB-4404-A3AE-29492CF7D79D}\0000
```

After reading these settings, the system checks whether the display driver supporting the specified mode is present. As soon as the appropriate driver has been found, the startup procedure continues. What happens, though, if the system can't find an appropriate driver? The answer's simple: the system will use standard VGA mode (16 colors).

Thus, we have considered the usage of the `HKEY_LOCAL_MACHINE\HARDWARE\DEVICEMAP` information for searching for specific device driver data. We've used the video adapter as an example, but the system uses a similar algorithm for locating the appropriate drivers for any other device. To summarize, let's note that the `HKEY_LOCAL_MACHINE\HARDWARE\DEVICEMAP` data describes either an actual port name or the path to the appropriate subkey under `HKEY_LOCAL_MACHINE\System\ControlSet`*`nnn`*`\Services`. This, in turn, contains the necessary information on the device driver. Sometimes system administrators may need this information for troubleshooting purposes. It should be noted again that administrative utilities, such as Device Manager, display the same information presented in user-friendly format rather than raw binary data.

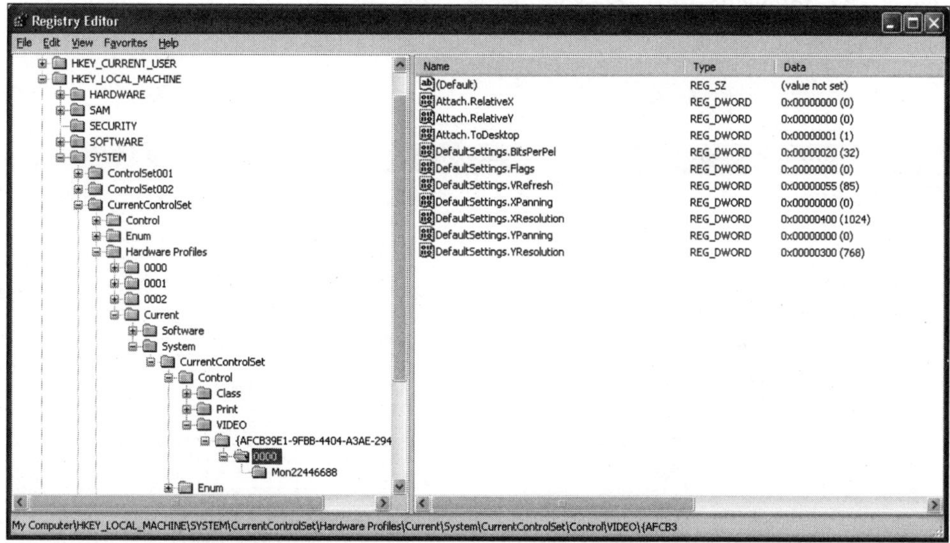

Fig. 7.8. Registry settings that specify the video mode

The *RESOURCEMAP* Subkey

The `RESOURCEMAP` subkey under `HKEY_LOCAL_MACHINE\HARDWARE` maps device drivers and hardware resources allocated to these drivers. Each setting stored within the

RESOURCEMAP key contains the data reported by the device driver concerning memory addresses, IRQs, and DMA channels requested by respective drivers. All the data contained within this key is volatile. Windows NT/2000 and Windows XP recreate the key during every system startup.

Because Windows 2000 and Windows XP implement full-featured Plug and Play support and include a new kernel-mode component (Plug and Play Manager), the contents of the HKEY_LOCAL_MACHINE\HARDWARE\RESOURCEMAP registry key are different for Windows 2000/XP from what they are for Windows NT 4.0. In the Windows NT 4.0 registry, the RESOURCEMAP key contains multiple *<DeviceClass>* subkeys, which are used to store information on specific device driver classes. Each of these keys contains one or more *<DriverName>* subkeys that store information related to individual drivers.

The RESOURCEMAP key in Windows 2000/Windows XP registries looks somewhat different (Fig. 7.9). The kernel-mode Plug and Play Manager now controls all the hardware devices. Because of this, the data concerning system resources is stored under the following registry key: HKEY_LOCAL_MACHINE\HARDWARE\RESOURCEMAP\PnP Manager\PnpManager.

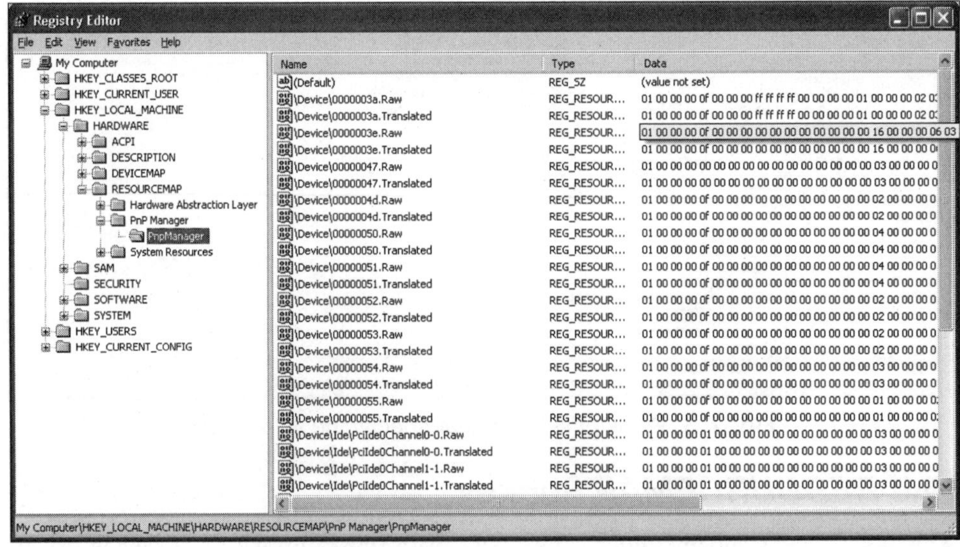

Fig. 7.9. The RESOURCEMAP key in Windows XP

The *HKEY_LOCAL_MACHINE\SAM* Key

The HKEY_LOCAL_MACHINE\SAM registry key contains information on user and group accounts stored in the directory database (which was formerly known as the SAM database) on the local computer. For Windows NT/2000 Server computers, this key also contains security data for the domain that the local computer belongs to.

This key references the HKEY_LOCAL_MACHINE\Security\SAM key, and any modification introduced into one of these keys is immediately introduced into the other one.

The *HKEY_LOCAL_MACHINE\SECURITY* Key

The HKEY_LOCAL_MACHINE\SECURITY registry key contains information on the security subsystem on the local computer, including user rights and permissions, password policies, and local group membership. All of this information is specified using administrative utilities such as User Manager (Windows NT 4.0 Workstation), User Manager for Domains (Windows NT 4.0 Server), and User Management MMC snap-in (Windows 2000).

The HKEY_LOCAL_MACHINE\SECURITY\SAM key references the HKEY_LOCAL_MACHINE\SAM key; because of this, any modification introduced into one of these keys will immediately appear within the other one.

The *HKEY_LOCAL_MACHINE\SOFTWARE* Key

The HKEY_LOCAL_MACHINE\SOFTWARE registry key contains configuration data concerning the software installed on the local computer. Settings that reside under this key contain settings for the software installed on the local PC and are in force for any user who's logged on to the local system.

The HKEY_LOCAL_MACHINE\SOFTWARE\Classes key contains filename extension association data. It also stores registry data associated to COM objects. The data stored under the Classes key is also displayed under HKEY_CLASSES_ROOT. Fig. 7.10 shows the typical contents of the HKEY_LOCAL_MACHINE\Software registry key.

The HKEY_LOCAL_MACHINE\SOFTWARE subtree contains several nested keys, the most important being the Classes, Program Groups, and Secure subkeys.

Later in this chapter, we'll discuss several *<Description>* subkeys that may appear in the registry.

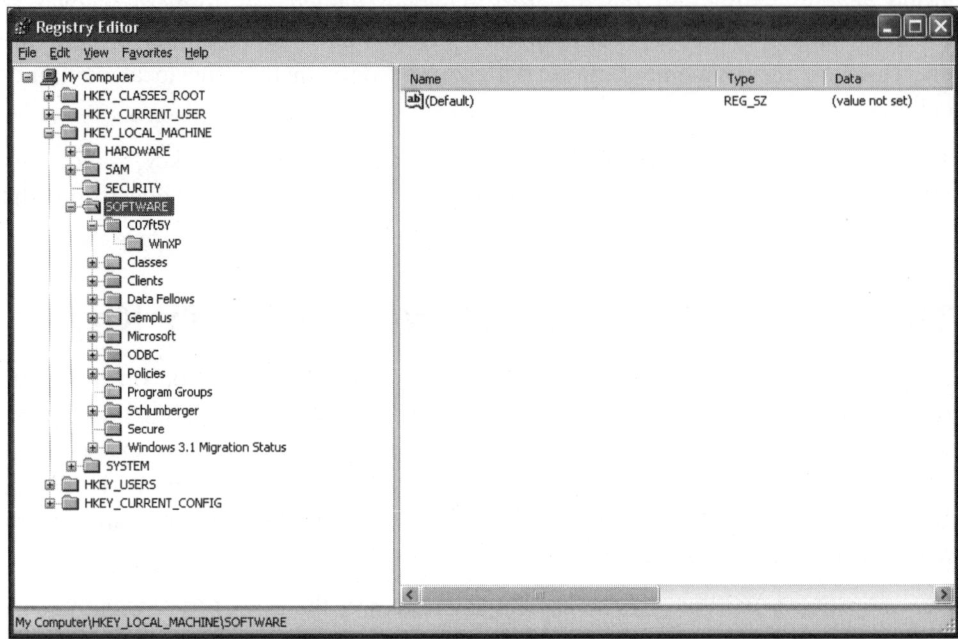

Fig. 7.10. Typical contents of the `HKEY_LOCAL_MACHINE\SOFTWARE` key

The *Classes* Subkey

The parameters contained under this key are the same as the parameters stored under `HKEY_CLASSES_ROOT`. Detailed information on the contents of this key is provided in the "OLE Programmer's Reference" document included with Windows Platform Software Development Kit. The `HKEY_LOCAL_MACHINE\SOFTWARE\Classes` key contains subkeys of the following types:

- Subkeys of the *<Filename-extension>* type associate applications installed on local computers with file types (identified by filename extensions). These subkeys contain data that you can add using the **File Types** tab of the **Folder Options** window (Fig. 7.12), as well as information added by the Setup programs that install Windows applications. The keys also contain information on the applications installed by Windows NT/2000 applications. The example shown in Fig. 7.11 shows the file association between AVI files and the

Windows Media Player application. The screenshot (Fig. 7.12) shows the registry key that corresponds to the association (`HKEY_LOCAL_MACHINE\SOFTWARE\Classes\.avi`).

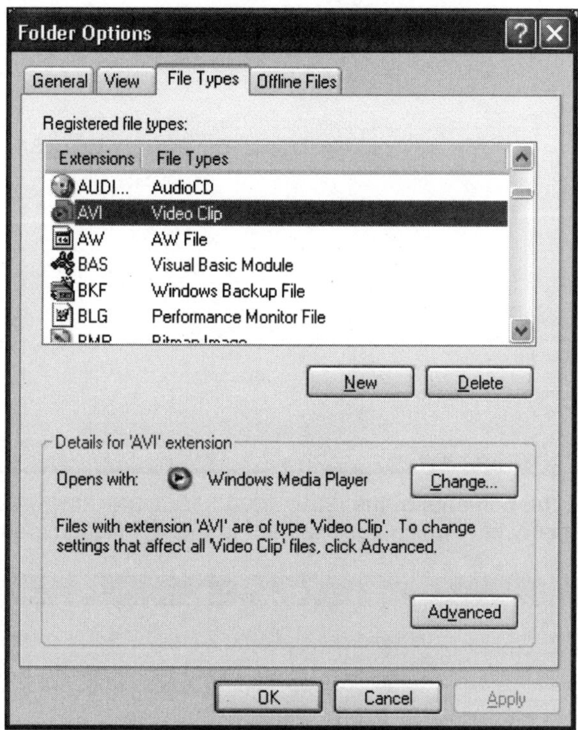

Fig. 7.11. The **File Types** tab of the **Folder Options** window

- *`<Class-definition>`* subkeys. These subkeys contain information associated with COM objects. The data contained within these keys specifies the shell and OLE (COM) properties for specific objects. If the application supports DDE (Dynamic Data Exchange), the `Shell` subkey may, in turn, contain other subkeys such as `Open` and `Print`. The subkeys define DDE commands for opening and printing files. Notice that the information contained under these keys is very similar to the information stored in the registry database of previous Windows versions, such as Windows 3.1*x*. Fig. 7.13 illustrates the shell properties for the AVI file.

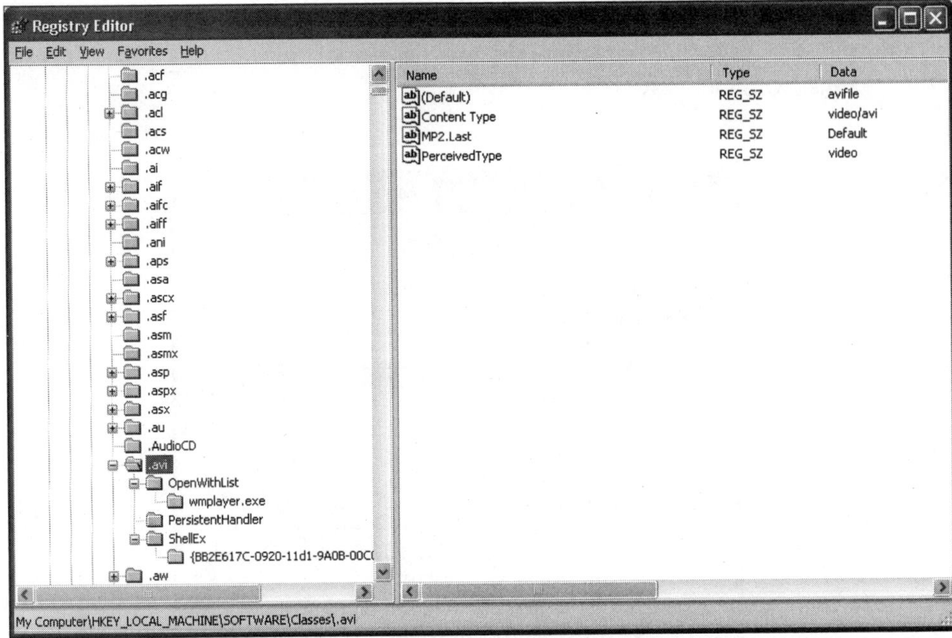

Fig. 7.12. The contents of the `HKEY_LOCAL_MACHINE\SOFTWARE \Classes\.avi` registry key, which corresponds to the AVI filename association

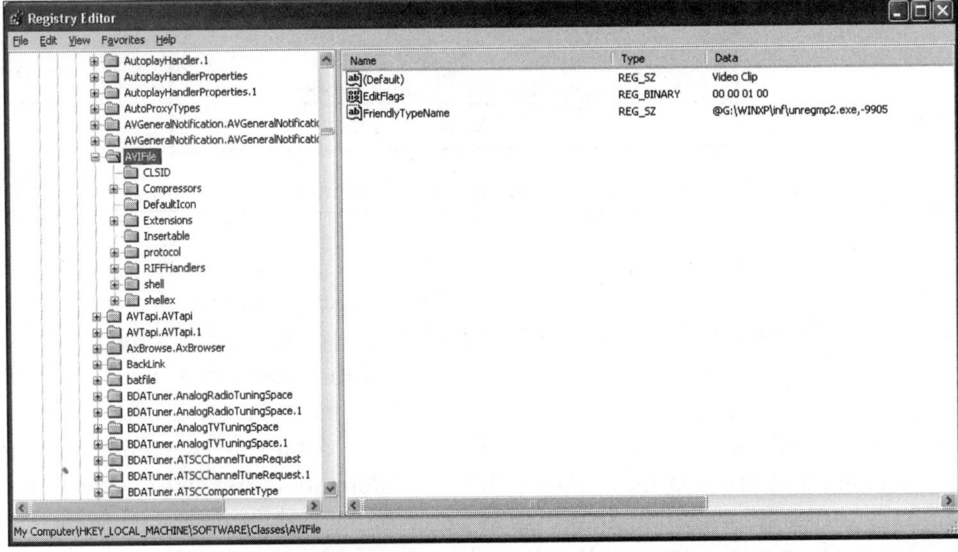

Fig. 7.13. The shell properties for the `AVIFile` class under `HKEY_LOCAL_MACHINE\Classes`

NOTE

The COM object information contained in the registry must be created by an application supporting COM. Direct registry editing can't be considered the easiest method of editing the information. If you need to perform this task in Windows NT 4.0, select the **Options** command from the **View** menu in Windows NT Explorer, then go to the **File Types** tab of the **Options** dialog. If you need to perform the same task in Windows 2000 or Windows XP, start the Folder Options applet from the Control Panel, or select the **Folder Options** command from the **Tools** menu in Windows Explorer; then go to the **File Types** tab in the **Folder Options** window.

The *Description* Subkeys

The `HKEY_LOCAL_MACHINE\Software\Description` keys contain names and version numbers of the software installed on the local computer. (Configuration settings specified for individual users are stored under `HKEY_CURRENT_USER`.)

During installation, applications register this information in the following form:

```
HKEY_LOCAL_MACHINE\Software\Description\CompanyName\ProductName\
Version.
```

NOTE

Version information for each application must be added to the registry by the appropriate application. Don't edit values under these keys except when the application vendor instructs you to do so.

An example illustrating how the registration information of an application (F-Secure anti-virus in our case) is stored under the `HKEY_LOCAL_MACHINE\SOFTWARE` registry key is presented in Fig. 7.14.

The *Microsoft* Subkey

The `HKEY_LOCAL_MACHINE\SOFTWARE\Microsoft` subkey contains configuration settings for Microsoft software products installed on the local computer.

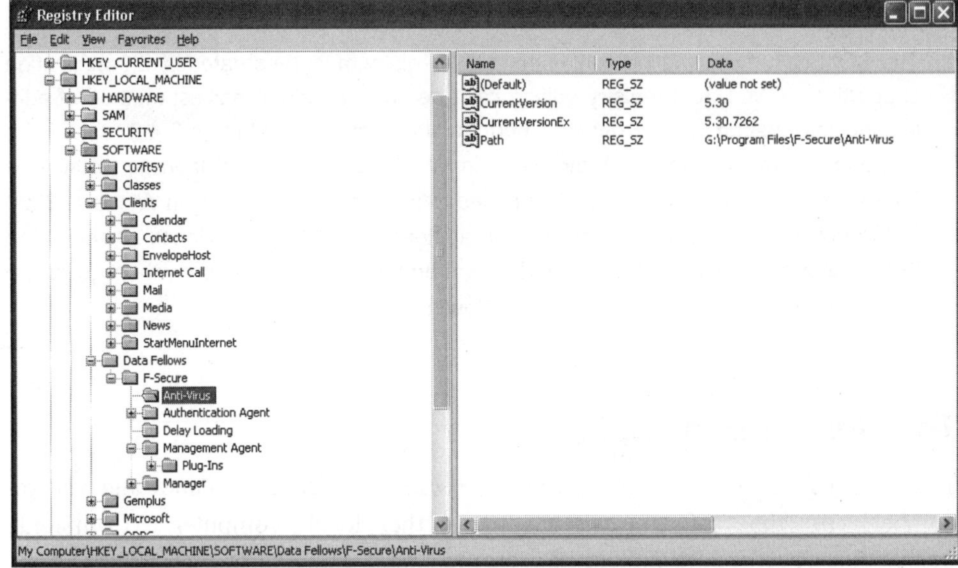

Fig. 7.14. An example of application registration information under `HKEY_LOCAL_MACHINE\Software` registry key

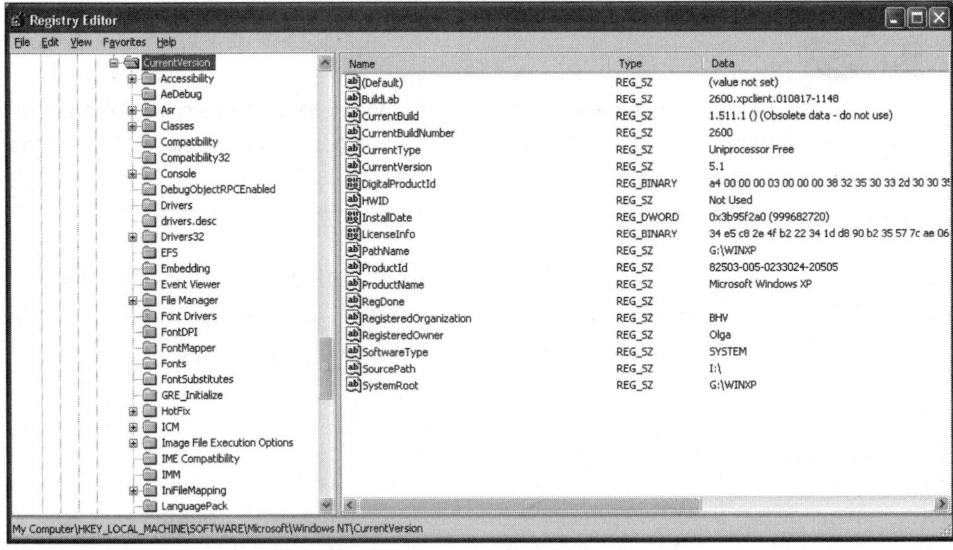

Fig. 7.15. The `HKEY_LOCAL_MACHINE\SOFTWARE\Microsoft\Windows NT\CurrentVersion` registry key

One of the most important subkeys under HKLM\SOFTWARE\Microsoft is the HKLM\SOFTWARE\Microsoft\Windows NT\CurrentVersion key. This key contains information on the software that supports Windows built-in services and the type and version number of the current Windows NT/2000/XP installation (for example, the data specifies whether the system has a multiprocessor kernel). Obviously, a single-processor Windows NT/2000/XP kernel will work on a multi-processor computer, but it won't provide any advantages over the single-processor configuration. To identify the kernel type, view the following registry key: HKEY_LOCAL_MACHINE\SOFTWARE\Microsoft\Windows NT\CurrentVersion (Fig. 7.15).

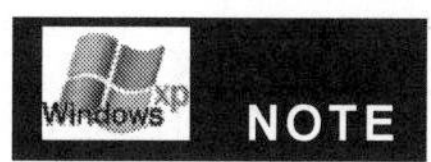

When speaking about the HKEY_LOCAL_MACHINE\SOFTWARE\Microsoft\Windows NT\CurrentVersion registry key, it is simply impossible not to mention one of the most appreciated Windows XP performance enhancements introduced with this version of the operating system. Windows XP provides built-in user mode heap-leak detection. The problem is that poorly written or miscoded applications can "leak" heap memory. In versions before Windows XP when this situation arose, special tools were needed to help identify the cause of the memory leak. To enable leak detection, set the following registry key:

```
[HKEY_LOCAL_MACHINE\SOFTWARE\Microsoft\Windows NT\CurrentVersion\
Image File Execution Options\ImageName]

"ShutdownFlags"="3"
```

The *Program Groups* Subkey

The Program Groups subkey, residing under the HKEY_LOCAL_MACHINE\Software registry key, has undergone some changes in comparison to previous versions of Windows NT (Windows NT 3.51 and earlier). In Windows NT 4.0, this key was redefined. In earlier Windows NT versions, the key contained a list of program groups used by all users of the local computer. In Windows NT 4.0 and Windows 2000/XP, this key is only used to specify whether or not all the program groups that existed in the previous operating system (for upgraded systems) were converted to a new format.

The Program Groups key contains a single entry named ConvertedToLinks, which determines whether the program groups have been converted. If the ConvertedToLinks value is set to 1, the conversion has been completed successfully.

If you install a fresh copy of the operating system rather than upgrade an earlier version to Windows XP, the `Program Groups subkey` won't contain any subkeys. If you've performed an upgrade, the `Program Groups` key will contain subkeys containing binary data defining general program groups.

The *Secure* Subkey

Applications can use the `Secure` subkey for storing configuration settings that can only be changed by the system administrator.

The *Windows 3.1 Migration Status* Subkey

The `Windows 3.1 Migration Status` subkey contains data only if the current operating system was installed as an upgrade from Windows 3.1. The parameters contained in this key specify if all INI files and the registry database (Reg.dat) were successfully converted to the Windows NT 4.0/Windows 2000 registry format. If you delete this key, Windows will make another attempt to convert these files after reboot.

Windows 3.1 Migration Status also exists under `HKEY_CURRENT_USER`. It specifies the conversion status of the program groups files (GRP files) to the Windows Explorer program group format.

The *HKEY_LOCAL_MACHINE\System* Key

All the data related to the startup process, which the system needs to read rather than calculate, are stored in the System hive. The System.alt file also contains a complete copy of these data. The data stored under `HKEY_LOCAL_MACHINE\System` are organized into Control Sets, each containing a complete set of the settings for device drivers and system services. From time to time, the system administrator may need to edit the items stored under the `CurrentControlSet` subkey.

Detailed information on the contents of the `CurrentControlSet` subkey was presented in *Chapter 6.*

The *ControlSet*nnn, *Select*, and *CurrentControlSet* Subkeys

The registry, in particular the System hive, has the most important role at system startup. To guarantee that the system will start, Windows NT/2000 saves the backup copy, allowing you to discard any configuration modifications that have led to unexpected results. In this section, we'll discuss the mechanism used for this purpose.

All data necessary to control the startup process are organized in subkeys called Control sets. Each control set contains the following four subkeys:

- The `Control` subkey that contains configuration settings used for system management, including the network name of the local computer and subsystems that should start.
- The `Enum` subkey contains hardware data, including data on the hardware devices and drivers to be loaded.
- The `Hardware Profiles` subkey contains hardware settings and driver configurations related to the individual hardware profile. You can create individual hardware profiles for each control set. The `Hardware Profiles` subkey will contain any data if only the data are different from the standard settings for device drivers and system services. The current hardware profile stored under `CurrentControlSet` is also stored under the `HKEY_CURRENT_CONFIG` root key.
- The `Services` subkey contains a list of drivers, file systems, and service programs that run in user mode, together with virtual hardware keys. The data contained in this key define the drivers to be loaded and specifies their loading order. The data also define the methods used by the services to call each other.

Multiple control sets are stored as subkeys under the `HKEY_LOCAL_MACHINE\System` registry keys under the names from `ControlSet001` to `ControlSet003`. There can be as many as four control sets, but normally there are only two. This mechanism is similar to the one used to create the Config.sys backup copies for MS-DOS computers. Normally, there's one copy of Config.sys used to start the system, and the backup copy. In our case, however, the whole job of creating and maintaining the backup copies is performed automatically by the system.

The `Select` subkey, shown in Fig. 7.16, contains four parameters, which describe the control set usage:

- The `Default` setting identifies the number of the control set (for example, `001=ControlSet001`) that the system should use next time it starts up. This may happen when a system error prevents the system from booting or when you manually select the **LastKnownGood** option.
- The `Current` setting specifies the ordinal number of the control set that's actually been used to start the computer.

- The LastKnownGood setting specifies the ordinal number of the control set that was used the last time you successfully started up the system.
- The Failed setting specifies the control set that was replaced by the LastKnownGood control set (if it was used to start up the system). You can also examine this control set to identify the source of the problem, which you have to do in order to replace the current control set with the last known good one.

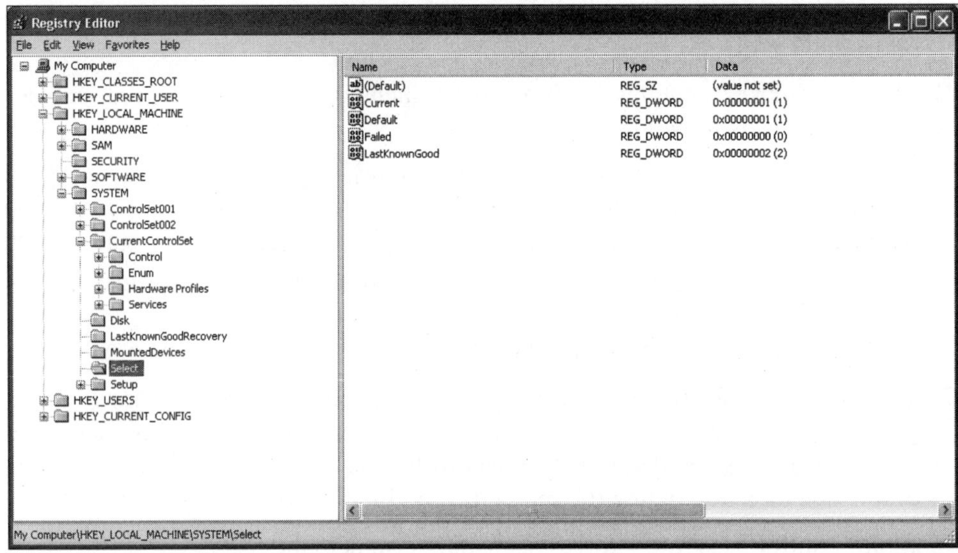

Fig. 7.16. The contents of the HKEY_LOCAL_MACHINE\SYSTEM\Select registry key

The CurrentControlSet key is actually a symbolic link to the control set specified by the Current setting under HKEY_LOCAL_MACHINE\SYSTEM\Select. This is necessary so that constant paths can be used to refer to subkeys in the currently used control set, even though its name may change.

Any time you start the system, the control set used to start up the system is stored under HKEY_LOCAL_MACHINE\System\Clone. If the system started successfully, this control set is considered "good", and the system discards the existing LastKnownGood control set. Actually, the system replaces the existing LastKnownGood control set with a copy of the Clone key. The system administrator can change this requirement at the startup process. Normally, startup is considered successful if no severe errors occurred and at least one user was able to log on to the system.

The LastKnownGood configuration is used when you select the **LastKnownGood** option during startup, or if the startup process fails (in this case, the control set won't be considered "good"). If this happens, the system creates a new control set by copying the `LastKnownGood` control set. The values under `HKEY_LOCAL_MACHINE\System\Select` will change as follows:

- The control set identified as `Default` will became the `Failed` control set
- The control set that was identified as `LastKnownGood` will become the `Default` control set

User profile data are stored under other registry keys, and these modifications won't be reflected in user profiles.

TIP

If you need to identify the control set used to start up your system, view the `Select` subkey.

Using administrative utilities and Control Panel applets is the easiest method of modifying the data stored under the keys previously discussed.

It's the `CurrentControlSet` subkey that you need to edit when modifying the configuration settings using one of the registry editors.

Control Subkeys for Controls Sets

Each control set contains a `Control` subkey. This subkey stores the startup parameters, including information on the subsystems to be loaded, environment variables, and the size and location of the paging file. The most important subkeys located under the `Control` key present in the control set are listed in Table 7.2. Fig 7.17 shows a typical configuration of the `Control` subkey.

Table 7.2. Typical subkeys of the *Control* Key for All Control Sets

Subkey	Description
`BackupRestore`	This key contains nested keys that specify parameters for the Ntbackup program, including subkeys such as `FilesNotToBackup` and `KeysNotToRestore` (Fig. 7.18), which contain exclusion lists for files and registry keys not to be included into backup or restore processes. The contents of the `BackupRestore` subkey can be used for customizing the built-in Microsoft Backup utility. Also notice the `AsrKeysNotToRestore` nested key, which is new to Windows XP. This key relates to the Automated System Recovery

continues

Table 7.2 Continued

Subkey	Description
	process, which in Windows XP has the Emergency Repair Disk functionality included with Windows NT and Windows 2000. By default, it contains a single value entry named `Plug & Play` (data type `REG_MULTI_SZ`, value `CurrentControlSet\Control\CriticalDeviceDatabase\`). This information will not be restored during the ASR process, which is not surprising, since such information must be re-created by the Setup program when it inspects the hardware configuration of your system
`BootVerificationProgram`	This value can be used to specify a non-standard mechanism of declaring the system startup as successful ("good"). If an additional verification mechanism hasn't been specified, this subkey won't contain any settings
`ComputerName`	Default computer names and active computer names are stored under `ComputerName` and `ActiveComputerName` subkeys. To set the computer name, use the **Network** option in the **Control Panel** (Windows NT 4.0), the **Network Identification** tab in the **System Properties** window (Windows 2000) or the **Computer Name** tab of the **System Properties** window (Windows XP)
`CrashControl`	This key contains value entries that manage system behavior in case of a system crash, including options for creating a memory dump file. Notice the `MinidumpDir` string value, which is new to Windows XP. As its name implies, this setting specifies the path to the directory where the small dumps, mainly used by the Error Reporting service, are stored. You can specify these settings in the **Startup and Recovery** window
`GroupOrderList`	Specifies the order in which the system should load the services for all groups that have one. This option is used in combination with the `Tags` option. The `ServiceGroupOrder` setting specifies the loading order for the groups
`ServiceGroupOrder`	Specifies the order in which to load various groups of services. The services loading order within a group is defined using the Tags and `GroupOrderList` settings
`HiveList`	This setting specifies the location of the registry hive files (the contents of this key are shown in Fig. 7.19) The value is maintained by the system because the settings under this key show the exact location of the registry hive files (if these files can't be loaded, the startup process will fail)

continues

Table 7.2 Continued

Subkey	Description
	Pay attention to the format used to represent the names of these settings (Fig. 7.19). Note that the are represented as follows: `\REGISTRY\MACHINE\`*<hivename>*, where the *<hivename>* is the name of appropriate registry hive. Also note the following schema: `\Device\HarddiskVolumeN\`*%SystemRoot%*`\System32\Config\`*<hive>*, which is adopted because when an appropriate registry file needs to be loaded, the system has not yet created drive mappings for logical disks
`KeyboardLayout`	DLL for the keyboard layout, the default language used as a default, plus a subkey named `DosKeybCodes`, which lists all other available keyboard layouts
`LSA`	The authentication packages for the Local Security Authority (LSA). This value is maintained by the system. If you make an error editing this value, it may prevent everyone from logging in to the local system
`NetworkProvider`	This key can contain subkeys that specify network providers and the order in which to load them. You can manage the settings for network providers using the **Network** option in the **Control Panel** (Windows NT 4.0) or the **Network and Dial-up Connections** option (Windows 2000)
`NLS`	This subkey contains information on national language support (NLS). You can manage the national language support using the **Regional Settings** option in **Control Panel** (Windows NT 4.0) or the **Regional Options** applet in **Control Panel** (Windows 2000)
`Print`	This subkey contains information on the currently installed printers and printing environment. It has the following important subkeys: `Environments`—this subkey contains other subkeys that define drivers and print processors for various system environments `Monitors`—this subkey contains other subkeys that store data for specific network printing monitors `Printers`—this subkey contains other subkeys that describe the settings for each installed printer `Providers`—this key can contain subkeys describing print services' DLLs To modify the printer settings, click the **Start** button, then select **Settings** | **Printers**

continues

Table 7.2 Continued

Subkey	Description
`PriorityControl`	This subkey specifies the priority separation in Win32. You should only set this value using the **System** option in **Control Panel**
`ProductOptions`	This subkey defines the software product type (Windows NT, for example). These values are maintained by the system. Notice one especially interesting fact: the ProductType value in Windows 2000 registry is set to "WinNT"
`SessionManager`	This subkey specifies global variables used by Session Manager. This key can, in turn, contain the following subkeys: `DOS Devices`—the subkey that identifies various DOS devices such as `AUX`, `MAILSLOT`, `NUL`, `PIPE`, `PRN`, and `UNC` `Environment`—this key identifies environment variables such as `ComSpec`, `Path`, `Os2LibPath`, and `WinDir`. These variables are set using the **System** option in Control Panel (this is the same for both Windows NT 4.0 and Windows 2000) `FileRenameOperations`—this key is used during the startup process. It allows you to rename certain files in order to replace them. These values should be maintained only by the operating system `KnownDLLs`—this key defines the directories and filenames for Session Manager DLLs. Again, all these values are maintained by the operating system `MemoryManagement`—this key defines the paging options. Normally, you specify the paging file parameters using the System applet in the Control Panel. Notice that in Windows NT/2000 this key contains the `RegistrySizeLimit` setting mentioned in *Chapter 1*. Also notice that in Windows XP this setting has become obsolete `SubSystems`—this key defines information intended for Windows NT/2000/XP subsystems. The values under this key are maintained by the system
`Setup`	This key specifies hardware setup options. Once again, all the values under this key are maintained by the operating system. If you need to modify these settings, the easiest way is to start Windows NT/2000 Setup

continues

Table 7.2 Continued

Subkey	Description
`TimeZoneInformation`	This key contains the values that define the time zone information. Normally, you set these values using the **Date/Time** option in the **Control Panel**
`VirtualDeviceDrivers`	This subkey contains virtual device drivers. These values must be maintained by the system
`Windows`	This subkey specifies the paths to the Windows NT/2000 directory and system directory
`WOW`	The settings stored under this key define options for 16-bit Windows applications. Once again, these settings should be maintained by the system

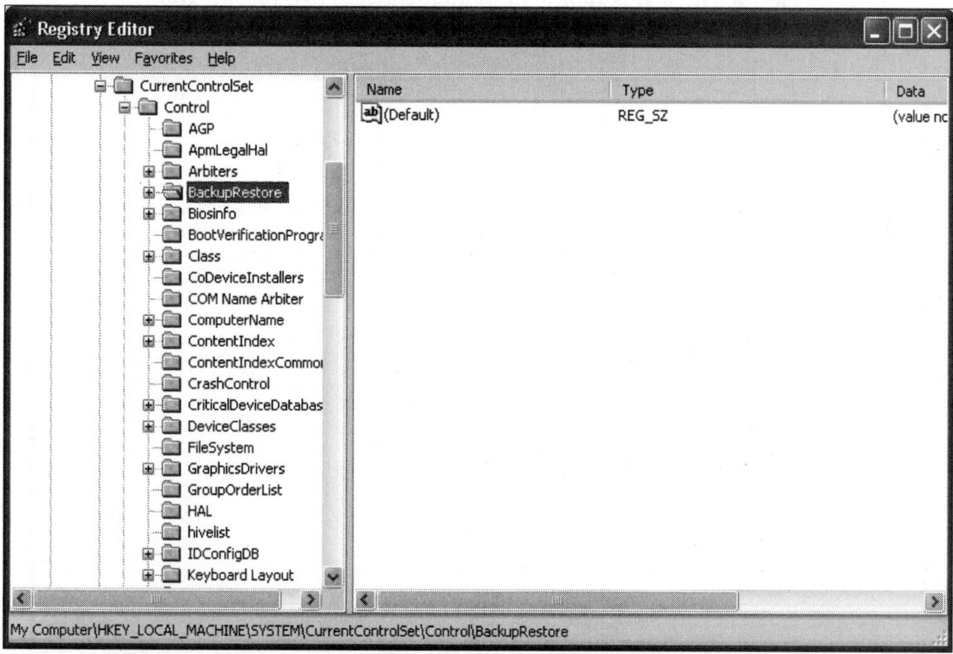

Fig. 7.17. Typical configuration of the `Control` subkey for the `CurrentControlSet`

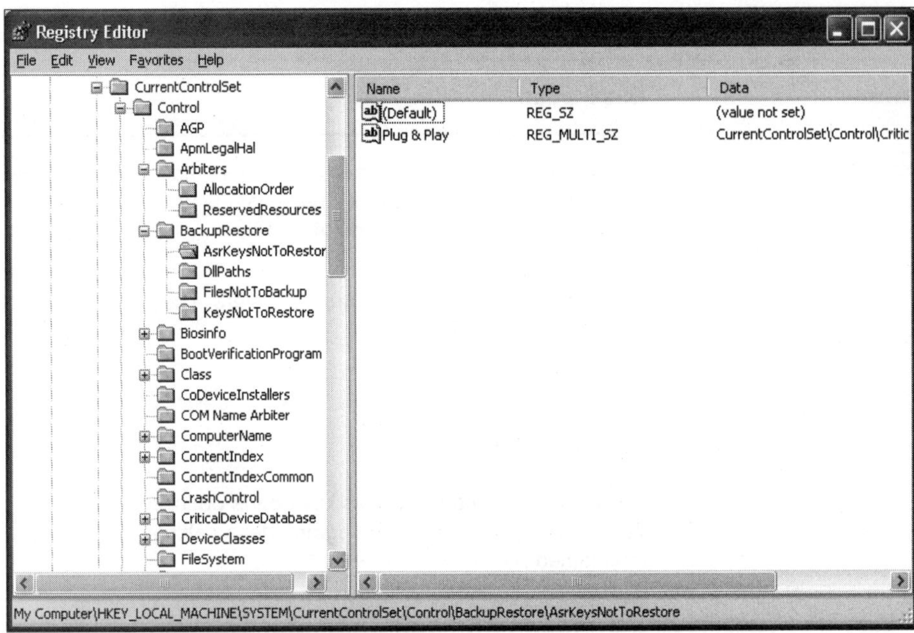

Fig. 7.18. The contents of the `BackupRestore` nested key

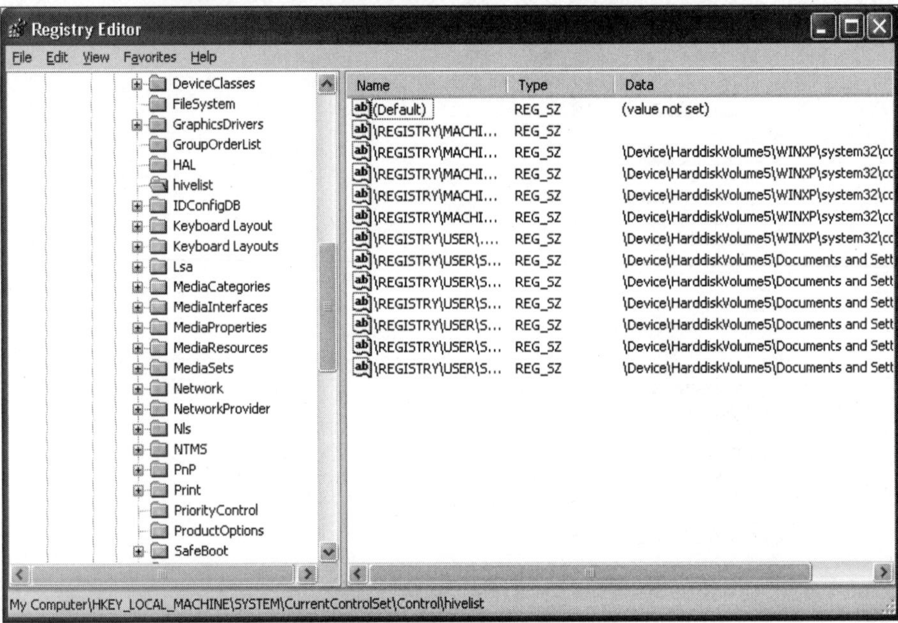

Fig. 7.19. The `hivelist` subkey

The *Enum* Subkey for All Control Sets

The `Enum` subkey contains configuration data for all hardware devices, independent of the drivers these devices use.

This subkey was first introduced in Windows NT 4.0. It was added to enable Windows NT to access devices and their drivers and manage them using methods similar to those used in Windows 95. (Notice that these methods are similar, but not the same, because Windows NT architecture is different from that of Windows 95.)

These changes were intended to prepare the ground for providing support for new Plug and Play devices in future versions of Windows NT. As we saw in *Chapter 5*, full-featured PnP support was first implemented in Windows 2000, and further enhanced in Windows XP.

NOTE

Don't use registry editors to modify this key. If you make an error, neither Windows NT/2000 nor Windows XP will be able to detect hardware devices.

Normally, the `Enum` key contains configuration data for hardware devices. The subkeys under the `Enum` key form a hierarchical structure known as the hardware device tree. The hardware tree starts at the tree root and ends at the lowest branch containing configuration data for a specific instance of the device (for example, the keyboard on the local computer).

The `Enum` key itself can be considered as a container that isn't associated with any value. This key contains at least two subkeys: the `Htree` subkey, which represents the hardware tree; and one or more enumerators, which are used by Windows NT/2000/XP to get information about specific devices.

The `Htree\Root\0` key is a reserved registry space representing the root of the hardware tree (this is the same for Windows NT 4.0, Windows 2000, and Windows XP). Since Windows 2000/XP implements full-featured Plug and Play support, the contents of the `Enum` key has become more complicated compared to those of Windows NT 4.0. The screenshot shown in Fig. 7.20 shows the `Enum` key structure for Windows XP.

The remaining subkeys directly under the `Enum` key represent enumerators and contain subkeys for devices on the same enumerator. According to Plug and Play requirements, each enumerator has its respective device bus (for example, PCI or ISAPNP). The default enumerator (`Root`) is used for non-PnP (legacy) devices. Fig. 7.21 shows a typical `Root` enumerator for Windows XP.

Each subkey of the enumerator contains multiple subkeys that represent various device types and models. The subkeys representing device types, in turn, contain their own subkeys that identify specific instances of the devices of this type. The name of each device type subkey identifies the device as a legacy device or as a Plug and Play device.

For most non-Plug and Play devices, Windows NT/2000 creates a device-type ID in the LEGACY_<*DriverName*> format. This subkey contains data for all the devices managed by this driver.

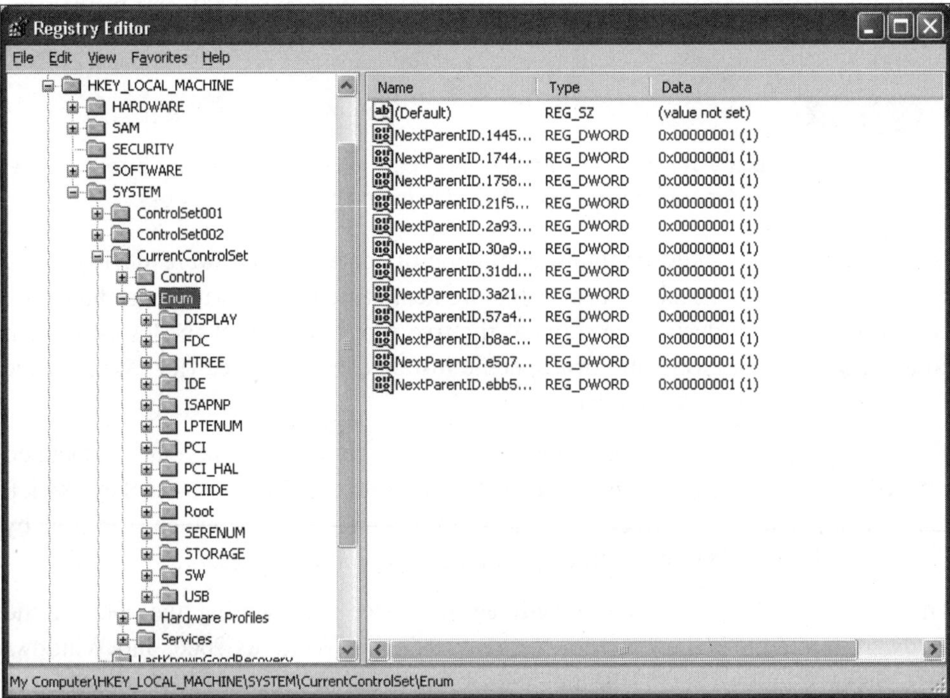

Fig. 7.20. The `HKEY_LOCAL_MACHINE\SYSTEM\CurrentControlSet\Enum` key structure

The subkeys below the device type keys are keys representing specific device instances. They contain the setting specifying device configuration.

The settings and subkeys directly below the device instance keys may be different, and vary depending on the devices and their drivers.

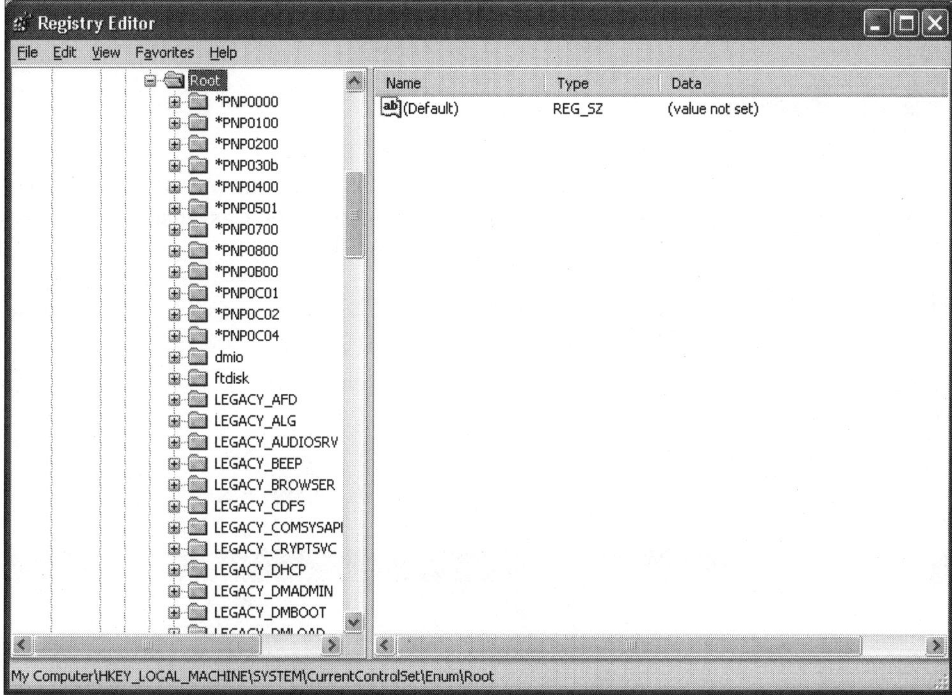

Fig. 7.21. The `Root` enumerator for a typical Windows XP computer

The *Services* Subkey for All Control Sets

Each control set contains a `Services` subkey that lists the device drivers, file system drivers, and Win32 service drivers. All the drivers listed under this key may be loaded by the operating system boot loader (Ntldr), I/O Manager, or Service Control Manager.

As I already mentioned earlier in this chapter when we discussed the `HKEY_LOCAL_MACHINE\HARDWARE\DEVICEMAP` registry key, all the subkeys under this key contain the settings that reference the entries under the `Services` key within the control set. For example, in Windows NT/2000, the following entry may be present in the `DeviceMap\PointerPort` subkey for the parallel port mouse:

```
\Device\PointerPort0:
\REGISTRY\Machine\System\ControlSet001\Services\Sermouse
```

The `Services` key must contain the key corresponding to this link, which is named `Sermouse`. This subkey identifies the mouse driver settings. This mechanism is called device mapping, which explains why the registry key is called DEVICEMAP.

In Windows XP, to facilitate device installation, devices are set up and configured using device setup class grouping. The device setup class defines the class installer and class co-installer components that are involved in installing the device.

Therefore, there will be the following entry for the parallel port mouse under HKEY_LOCAL_MACHINE\HARDWARE\DEVICEMAP\PointerClass (Fig. 7.22). Notice that the key name is PointerClass and not PointerPort, as it was in Windows NT/2000:

```
\Device\PointerClass0:
\REGISTRY\MACHINE\SYSTEM\ControlSet001\Services\Mouclass
```

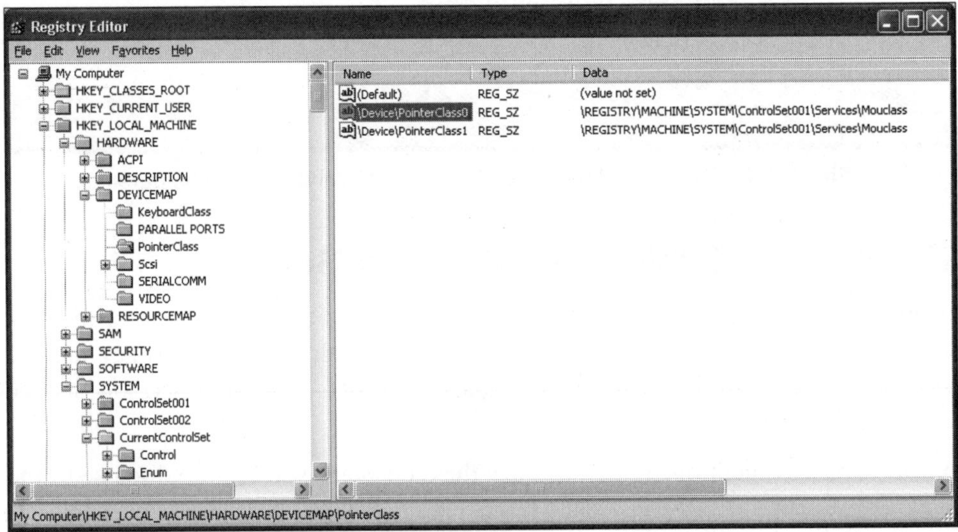

Fig. 7.22. An example of the contents of the HKEY_LOCAL_MACHINE\HARDWARE\DEVICEMAP\PointerClass registry key in Windows XP

Like in Windows NT/2000, the Services key contains the key corresponding to this link, which is named Mouclass. This subkey identifies the mouse driver settings (Fig. 7.23). At the beginning of the chapter, we discussed this mechanism in the example on video drivers.

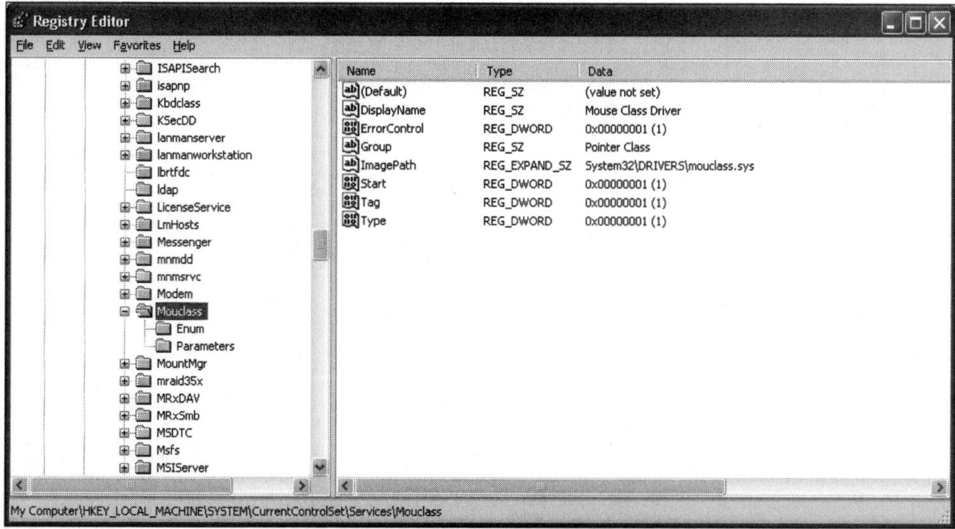

Fig. 7.23. The Services key contains the key corresponding to the link provided under `DEVICEMAP` registry key

Microsoft defines setup classes for most devices. IHVs and OEMs can define new device setup classes, but only if none of the existing classes apply. For example, a camera vendor doesn't need to define a new setup class because cameras fall under the `Image` setup class. Similarly, uninterruptible power supply (UPS) devices fall under the `Battery` class.

Class installer defines the class of the component to be installed by the `ClassGuid` value. There is a GUID associated with each device setup class. The `ClassGuid` value is the Globally Unique Identifier (GUID) for the class. You can generate GUID values using the Uuidgen.exe utility. More detailed information about this utility is provided in Platform SDK supplementary documents.

The device setup class GUID defines the `...\CurrentControlSet\Control\Class\`*`ClassGUID`* registry key under which to create a new subkey for any particular device of a standard setup class.

Each subkey under the `Services` key may contain several optional settings. For example, the content of the `Alerter` key (Fig. 7.24) specifies the Alerter service parameters.

Settings such as `ErrorControl`, `Group`, `DependOnGroup`, `DependOnService`, `ImagePath`, `ObjectName`, `Start`, `Tag`, and `Type` manage the service behavior.

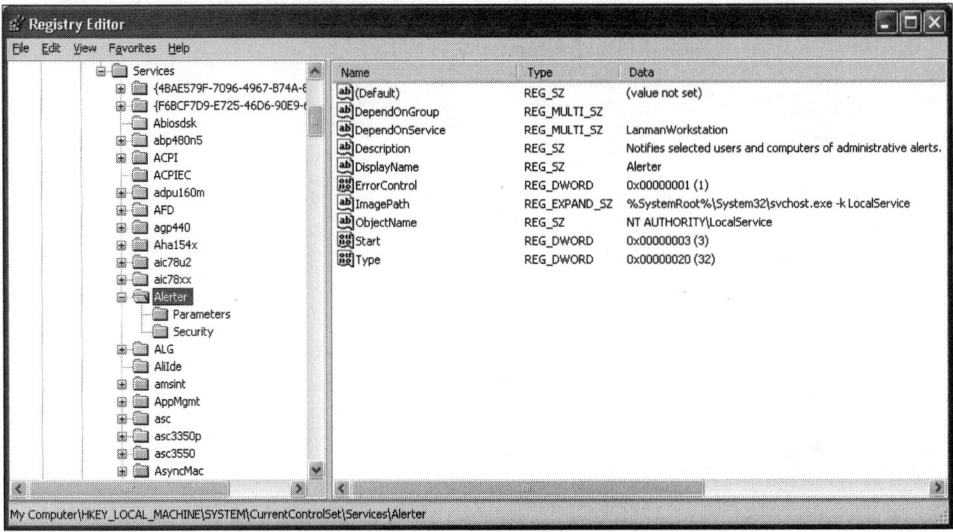

Fig. 7.24. The Alerter service parameters in Windows XP registry

The loading order for services and drivers is specified by the `\Control\ServiceGroupOrder` key under the control set key.

The *Hardware Profiles* Key for All Control Sets

The `Hardware Profiles` subkey is present in any control set. These subkeys contain configuration data for all hardware profiles created in Windows NT/2000/XP. This key was first introduced in Windows NT 4.0.

As you know already, the hardware profile is a set of modifications introduced to the standard device and service configuration (including Win32 services and drivers) loaded at system startup.

Windows NT/2000 creates a default hardware profile based on the original configuration detected during Windows NT/2000 Setup. You can create multiple hardware profiles and select existing profiles at boot time.

Fig. 7.25 shows a typical structure of the `HKEY_LOCAL_MACHINE\SYSTEM\CurrentControlSet\Hardware Profiles` registry key.

Each subkey under the `Hardware Profiles` key contains configuration data for its respective hardware profile. If the system has more then one hardware profile, it identifies the hardware profile as current when you select it at boot time. The

HKEY_LOCAL_MACHINE\SYSTEM\CurrentControlSet\Hardware Profiles\Current registry key represents a symbolic link to one of the keys named 0000, 0001, ...

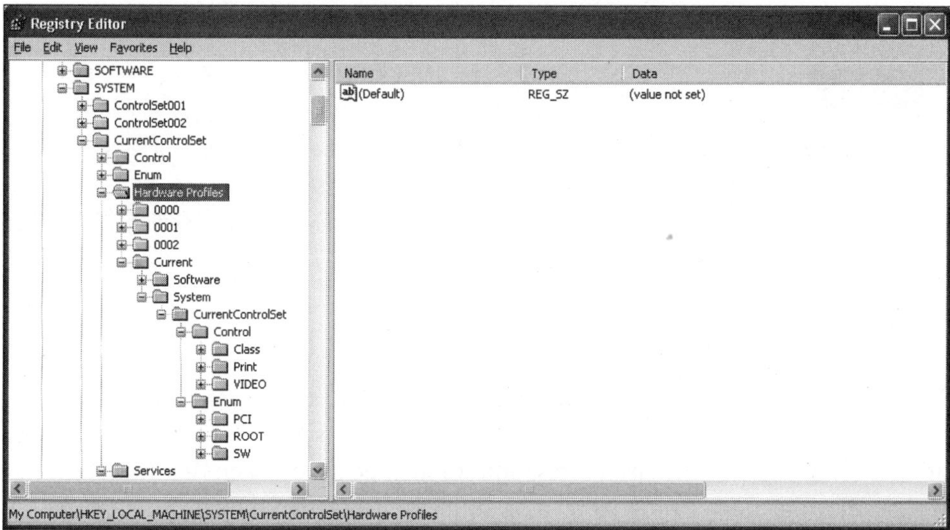

Fig. 7.25. The contents of a typical HKEY_LOCAL_MACHINE\SYSTEM\CurrentControlSet\Hardware Profiles key

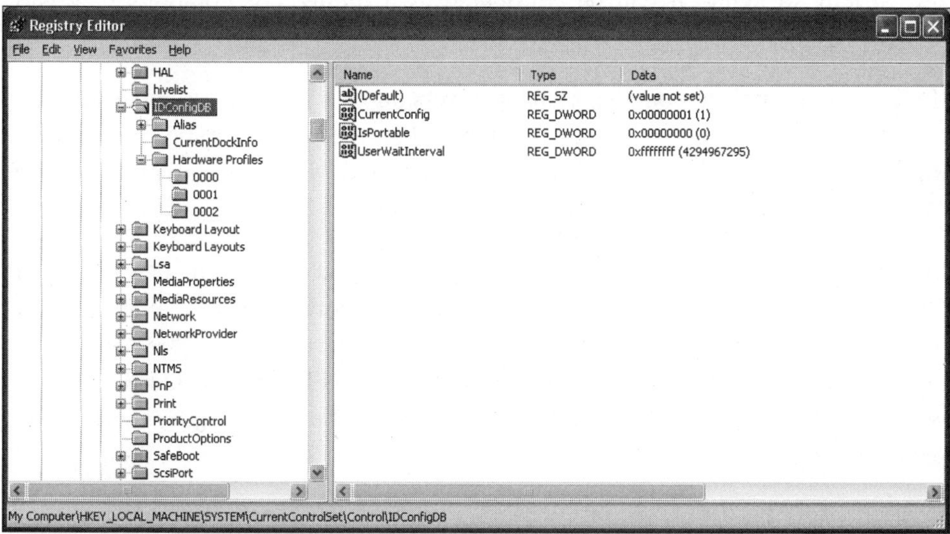

Fig. 7.26. The contents of the IDConfigDB subkey

The `HKEY_CURRENT_CONFIG` tree is an alias that references the `Hardware Profiles\Current` key under the `CurrentControlSet`. The contents of the `Current` key also appears under the `HKEY_CURRENT_CONFIG` tree.

TIP

To define which of the `0000`, `0001`, ... `000`*n* keys under the Hardware Profiles keys is selected as the current one, view the `HKEY_LOCAL_MACHINE\System\CurrentControlSet\Control\IDConfigDB` key. This key contains the `CurrentConfig` setting (Fig. 7.26), whose value specifies the number corresponding to the key that contains the current hardware profile.

The settings contained within each hardware profile subkey represent individual modifications of the standard configuration of the system services and device drivers. These modifications correspond to the goals of each hardware profile. Notice that these keys only store data different from the standard configuration, which is defined by the data stored under the `Software` and `System` subkeys under `HKEY_LOCAL_MACHINE`. Consequently, the hardware profile structure is modeled based on the structure of the `HKEY_LOCAL_MACHINE` registry key. Strictly speaking, it can be considered as a limited, or compressed, version of this key.

If the hardware profile contains a changed version of a value entry under the Software or System keys of `HKEY_LOCAL_MACHINE`, then the original value isn't changed. Rather, the changed version of this value is stored within a similar key of the `Hardware Profiles\`<*Number*> subtree.

For example, let's look at a situation when you create a new hardware profile that excludes the Iomega Parallel Port Legacy Filter Driver (ppa3). The `HKEY_LOCAL_MACHINE\System\CurrentControlSet\Enum\Root\LEGACY_PPA3` key won't be changed in Windows NT 4.0, Windows 2000, or Windows XP. On the contrary, this modification will be stored under the following key (Fig. 7.27):

```
HKEY_LOCAL_MACHINE\System\CurrentControlSet\Hardware Profiles
\<Number>\System\CurrentControlSet\Enum\Root\LEGACY_PPA3.
```

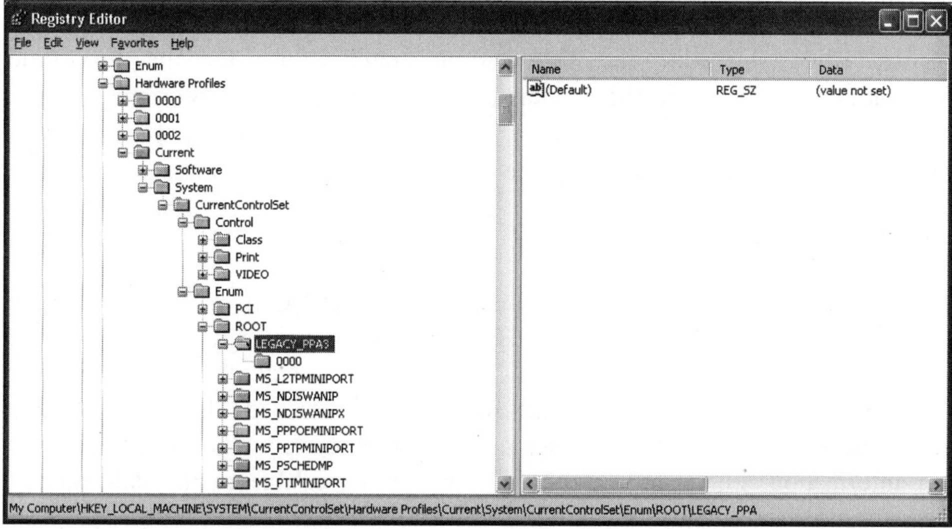

Fig. 7.27. Hardware profiles store only changes introduced to the original configuration

The *Setup* Subkey

The Setup subkey under the `HKEY_LOCAL_MACHINE\System` tree is intended for internal use by the Setup program. You need not (and should not) change the value entries under this key, because they need to be maintained by the operating system.

The *Disk* Subkey

The `HKEY_LOCAL_MACHINE\SYSTEM\Disk` subkey has undergone significant changes from its Windows NT 4.0 version. In the Windows NT 4.0 registry, this key contained all the information need to manage the volumes. This key is created by the Disk Administrator built-in Windows NT utility. The key contains the `Information` setting (data type is `REG_BINARY`). This setting contains all configuration information, including the data on the hard disk partitions that were recognized, drive mappings, and the data concerning fault-tolerant disk configurations (mirror sets, stripe sets with or without parity), if you've configured the fault tolerant disk configurations. Detailed information concerning fault-tolerant disk configurations is provided in the documentation supplied with the Windows NT 4.0 Workstation Resource Kit software.

The HKEY_LOCAL_MACHINE\System\Disk key is created in the Windows NT 4.0 registry when you start the Disk Administrator utility for the first time. This utility creates both the key and the Information binary setting, which stores all the data on the hard disks present in the system. As you create or delete hard disk partitions using the Disk Administrator utility, or configure fault-tolerant volumes, the program stores all configuration changes in the Information setting.

If you explicitly establish drive mapping for the CD-ROM drive (for example, you need to map this drive as "H:"), the Disk key will contain another setting named \device\CdRom0. This string setting will have a value that corresponds to the drive mapping that you've specified. Besides the Disk Administrator utility, there are other drivers and subsystems that access the Disk key information. For example, this information is available to the fault-tolerant file system driver (Ftdisk.sys) and to the Win32 subsystem. The Ftdisk.sys driver identifies whether or not there are fault tolerant disk configurations in the system, such as mirror or stripe sets. The driver does this by reading the Information setting. The Win32 subsystem needs the Information setting data for establishing drive mappings.

NOTE

The Information setting is a variable-length setting, because the number of logical disks and fault tolerant volumes in each individual Windows NT 4.0 system are also variable.

With the release of Windows 2000, the disk management subsystem has undergone significant changes (for example, a new type of volume was introduced—dynamic volume). The HKEY_LOCAL_MACHINE\SYSTEM\Disk\Information setting is present in the registry (in order to provide backward compatibility), but it no longer stores information on fault-tolerant volumes.

Windows 2000 and Windows XP store the information on fault-tolerant volumes directly on the hard disk. There's a noticeable difference, though. The Ftdisk.sys driver in Windows 2000 manages all disk partitions, including the fault-tolerant volumes and all other partitions that exist on the hard disks. So, even if you don't configure the fault-tolerant volumes in your Windows 2000/XP system, Ftdisk.sys loads anyway and detects all requests to the hard disks.

The *HKEY_CLASSES_ROOT* Key

The HKEY_CLASSES_ROOT root key contains information on all existing filename associations and data associated with COM objects. As I mentioned earlier, these data are the same as that contained under the Classes subkey of the HKEY_LOCAL_MACHINE\Software hive.

The only purpose for the HKEY_CLASSES_ROOT registry root key is to provide backward compatibility with the Windows 3.1*x* registry database.

The HKEY_CLASSES_ROOT key contains the data that associates file types (by filename extensions) with specific applications supporting formats of these files.

The *HKEY_CURRENT_CONFIG* Key

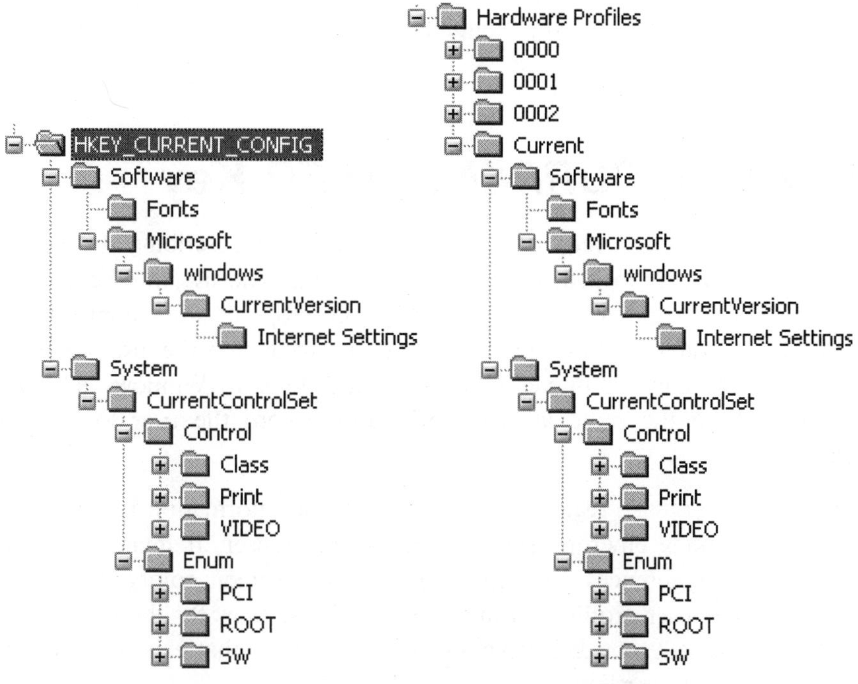

Fig. 7.28. The HKEY_CURRENT_CONFIG and HKEY_LOCAL_MACHINE\System\CurrentControlSet\Hardware Profiles\Current registry keys

The HKEY_CURRENT_CONFIG registry root key was first introduced with the release of the Windows NT 4.0 operating system. This key contains configuration data for the currently used hardware profile. Actually, this key is an alias that references the HKEY_LOCAL_MACHINE\System\CurrentControlSet\Hardware Profiles\Current registry key.

The HKEY_CURRENT_CONFIG registry key was introduced with the release of Windows NT 4.0 in order to provide backward compatibility with the HKEY_CURRENT_CONFIG root key present in Windows 95. Now that the HKEY_CURRENT_CONFIG tree is present both in Windows 9*x* and Windows NT/2000 registries, all applications designed for Windows 95 will also work under Windows NT/2000.

Fig. 7.28 illustrates the HKEY_CURRENT_CONFIG registry key structure. This screenshot demonstrates that the HKEY_CURRENT_CONFIG key simply represents a symbolic link to the HKEY_LOCAL_MACHINE\System\CurrentControlSet\Hardware Profiles\Current registry key.

The HKEY_CURRENT_CONFIG key contains data describing the current hardware profile.

The *HKEY_CURRENT_USER* Key

The HKEY_CURRENT_USER registry key contains the data describing the user profile for the user currently logged on to the local system. The user profile contains information defining individual settings for the desktop, network connections, and environment variables. Provided that the user profile for the user exists and is available on the local computer or in the same domain, Windows NT/2000 will look and behave the same at any workstation where the user logs on to the network.

The HKEY_CURRENT_USER registry key contains all the information necessary for setting up the working environment for that particular user. It includes the settings and individual preferences for various applications, screen colors, and other user preferences. The user profile also includes security settings for the user. Many settings existing in HKEY_CURRENT_USER are similar to those that existed in the Win.ini for earlier Windows versions.

Standard subkeys of the HKEY_CURRENT_USER are listed in Table 7.3.

Table 7.3. Standard Subkeys of the *HKEY_CURRENT_USER* Registry Key

Subkey	Description
`AppEvents`	Subkeys defining application events, including sound scheme events, the set of relationships between user actions, and the sounds produced by your computer as a reaction
`Console`	The `Console` subkey contains nested subkeys that define console window size and other settings for console applications. A console represents the interface between user-mode and character-mode applications. This key also includes the settings for the Windows NT/2000 command prompt sessions. In Windows 2000, you set command prompt default options–such as window color, cursor size, and font size and style–directly in the command prompt window. You can also specify whether the options you set are used for every session or for the current session only
`Control Panel`	The subkeys under the `Control Panel` subkey correspond to the parameters that can be changed using Control Panel applets. These data also include the information that was stored in the Win.ini file in earlier Windows versions
`Environment`	These settings correspond to the environment variable settings specified for the individual user who's currently logged on to the system. The value entries contain information which under earlier Windows versions was stored in the Autoexec.bat file. Normally, you can set these values using Control Panel applets
`Keyboard Layout`	The subkeys under this key specify the national language used for the current keyboard layout
`Printers`	The subkeys under this key describe currently installed printers that are available for the user currently logged on to the system. To change these settings, click the **Start** button, then select **Settings | Printers**
`Software`	This key contains subkeys that describe configuration settings for the software installed on the local computer and available to the user who's currently logged on to the system. This information has the same structure as the `HKEY_LOCAL_MACHINE\Software` registry key. The information also includes application-specific data that was previously stored in the Win.ini file or in application-specific INI files

continues

Table 7.3 Continued

Subkey	Description
UNICODE Program Groups	This key is provided for backward compatibility. It wasn't used in Windows NT 4.0. If your system was upgraded from earlier versions of the Windows NT operating system (for example, from Windows NT 3.51 to Windows NT 4.0), this key may contain some subkeys inherited from the previous versions and store binary data. However, neither this key nor its subkeys contain any data needed by Windows NT 4.0/Windows 2000 or Windows XP
Windows 3.1 Migrations Status	This key will contain data only if you've upgraded your operating system from an earlier Windows version (for example, from Windows 3.*x* to Windows NT 4.0). The subkeys present within this key specify whether the process of upgrading program group files (GRP files) and initialization files (INI files) has completed successfully. If you delete this key, Windows NT/2000/XP will attempt the conversion next time you reboot the system. Note that the `Windows 3.1 Migration Status` subkey also exists within the `HKEY_LOCAL_MACHINE \Software` key

As I mentioned earlier in the section dedicated to the `HKEY_LOCAL_MACHINE` root key, the `HKEY_CURRENT_USER` data normally has priority over similar data existing under `HKEY_LOCAL_MACHINE`. For example, let's look at how this convention works for environment variables. The environment variable settings defined for the currently logged on user have priority over the system environment variables (use the System applet in Control Panel to set environment variables).

The `HKEY_CURRENT_USER` key references the `HKEY_USERS\<SID_#>` registry key, where the `<SID_#>` is the string containing the security identifier (SID) of the user who's currently logged on to the system. The logon process creates the user profile environment based on the data found under the `HKEY_USERS\<SID_#>`. If this data is unavailable, the `HKEY_CURRENT_USER` is built based on the data contained in the *%SystemRoot%*\Profiles\Default User\Ntuser.dat file (Windows NT 4.0) or in the *%SystemRoot%*\Documents and Settings\Default User\Ntuser.dat file (Windows 2000).

NOTE

To find the file supporting the registry hive, view the `HiveList` subkey under the `HKEY_LOCAL_MACHINE\System\CurrentControlSet\Control` key. To find the user profile hive (whether or not this user is currently logged on), view the ProfileList subkey under the HKEY_LOCAL_MACHINE\Software\Microsoft\Windows NT\CurrentVersion key.

The *HKEY_USERS* Key

The HKEY_USERS key contains all actively loaded user profiles. In this case, the key contains at least two subkeys: the .DEFAULT subkey and the *<Security ID>* subkey for the currently logged on user (Fig. 7.29). The data from the .DEFAULT subkey is used if no one is currently logged on to the system.

The .DEFAULT subkey contains the same subkeys as the HKEY_CURRENT_USER key. These keys were listed in Table. 7.3.

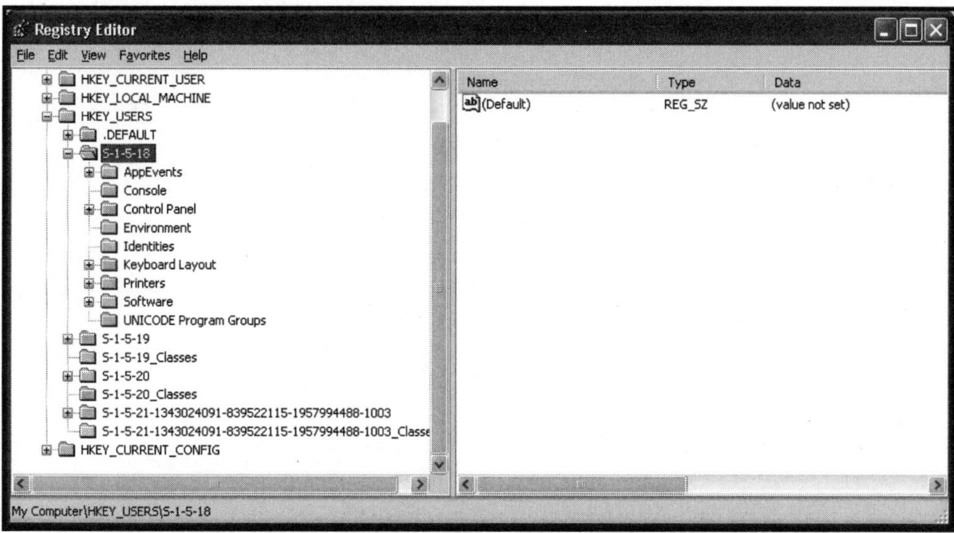

Fig. 7.29. The HKEY_USERS key structure

Summary

In this chapter we discussed the most important keys that in exist in the Windows NT/2000 registries. The description provided here is more detailed than that provided in Chapter 1 and was mainly intended as a brief overview. Unfortunately, it would be impossible to create a complete reference on all the registry keys and make it fit in a single chapter (or else this chapter would become a book by itself). However, the information presented here is a "must-know" for any system administrator or support specialist who intends to use and support Windows NT/2000/XP.

Chapter 8

Network Settings in the Registry

A new system creates new problems.

Technological Murphy's Law

A bit beyond perception's reach
I sometimes believe I see
that Life is two locked boxes, each
containing the other's key

Piet Hein
Grooks. The Paradox of Life

Windows XP networking is mainly based on similar functionality provided by Windows 2000, including local networking, dial-up, and remote connectivity. Like Windows NT4.0/2000, the basic network settings in Windows XP registry are normally set during system setup. Most installation problems, caused by network adapters installed on the computer, occur at this time. Many Windows NT 4.0/2000 drawbacks were eliminated in Windows XP. One remaining problem, though, is incorrect detection of network adapters during installation. This wasn't completely eliminated, and still can occur during Windows XP setup. Unfortunately, the Setup program doesn't provide any other options for installing network adapters, except for automatic detection.

There's a solution, though: simply install the operating system without the network adapter (you should physically remove it from the computer). When the installation procedure has successfully completed, you add the network adapter using the Add Hardware applet in Control Panel, and then install the network components.

Installing Network Components Using Control Panel Applets

When you install network components and configure network settings, new entries are added into the system registry. Before we open the registry editor and start exploring these entries, let's discuss an easy method of installing network components and specifying their settings.

In Windows NT 4.0, you use the Network applet in the Control Panel. When the applet starts, the **Network** window opens. This window has the following 5 tabs:

- **Identification**—allows you to view or modify the computer name and the name of the workgroup or domain the local system belongs to.

- **Services**—this tab allows you to view the list of network services installed on the computer. You can also add, delete, or configure additional network services.
- **Protocols**—this tab is used to view the list of installed network protocols, view and modify the properties of individual protocols, and add or remove network protocols.
- **Adapters**—this tab lists the network adapters installed on the computer, allowing you to view or modify their settings.
- **Bindings**—displays bindings of the protocols to network adapters. You can enable or disable individual bindings and change their order.

In Windows 2000, the Network and Dial-up Connections Control Panel applet has replaced two independent Windows NT 4.0 administrative tools: the Network applet and the Dial-up Connections applet, by combining their functionality. In Windows XP, this situation has not changed significantly. To start configuring network connections, start the Network Connections applet in Control Panel to open the **Network Connections** window. Provided that you have installed network adapter, and the system has correctly detected it, the **Network Connections** window will look as shown in Fig. 8.1.

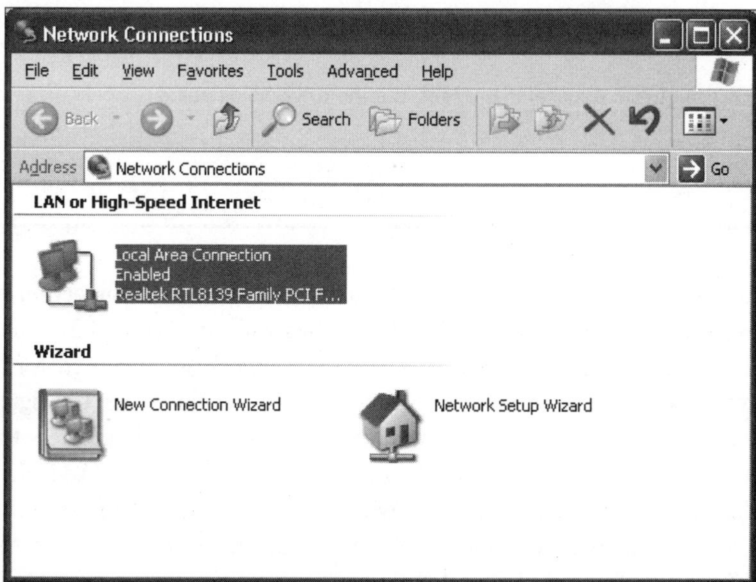

Fig. 8.1. The **Network Connections** window

NOTE

Certain conditions, such as a malfunctioning network adapter card, can keep your LAN connection from appearing in the Network Connections folder.

Notice that the appearance of the **Local Area Connection** icon in this window changes according to the status of the connection. By design, if your computer doesn't detect a network adapter, a local area connection icon does not appear in the Network Connections folder. Possible states of your LAN connections and their respective icons are summarized in Table 8.1.

Table 8.1. Local Area Connection Icons

Icon	Description
Local Area Connection	Network adapter has been correctly installed and detected by your computer. You are connected to the LAN (the LAN connection is active)
Local Area Connection	Network adapter is physically present, but the cable is unplugged from your computer
	The cable is unplugged from your computer, or from the hub. This icon appears at the taskbar at the same time as the previous one
Local Area Connection	Network adapter is present, but the driver is disabled
None	The network adapter was not detected

To view or modify network settings, right-click the **Local Area Connection** and select **Properties**. The **Local Area Connection Properties** will open (Fig. 8.2). The **Connect using** field at the top of the window specifies the network adapter used for local area connections. You can configure network adapters by clicking the **Configure** button below the field. Notice that this method only configures network adapters that you've already installed. If you need to install a new network adapter, use Add Hardware in Control Panel. The dialog that appears when you click the **Configure** button is the same as the network adapter properties window that opens when you use the Device Manager (Fig. 8.3). This window only allows you to configure network adapter properties (if the driver has already been installed).

Fig. 8.2. The **Local Area Connection Properties** window

The **This connection uses the following items** list contains network services and protocols used by the adapter. The **Install**, **Uninstall**, and **Properties** buttons allow you to install, delete, or configure network protocols and services.

The **Show icon in taskbar when connected** checkbox at the bottom of the **Local Area Connection Properties** window (Fig. 8.2) allows you to specify a mode in which you can view the local area connection status using the taskbar indicator (Fig. 8.4).

As I already mentioned, the Network and Dial-up Connections applet (Windows 2000) and Network Connections applet (Windows XP) combine the functionality of two Windows NT 4.0 Control Panel applets. This change reflects the fact that certain components of the Windows 2000/XP network subsystem, such as Remote Access Service (RAS) and Dial-up Networking (DUN) have undergone modifications. The improvements are listed below.

- The Remote Access Service (RAS) is now closely integrated with other components of the network subsystem. Thus, this service is easier to use. In contrast to the method used in Windows NT 4.0 where RAS management was done using a separate utility, both local and remote network connections in Windows 2000 and Windows XP are managed using the same utility (Network and Dial-up Connections in Windows 2000, Network Connections in Windows XP). This enhancement simplifies the tasks for both system administrators and end-users.

Fig. 8.3. The network adapter properties window

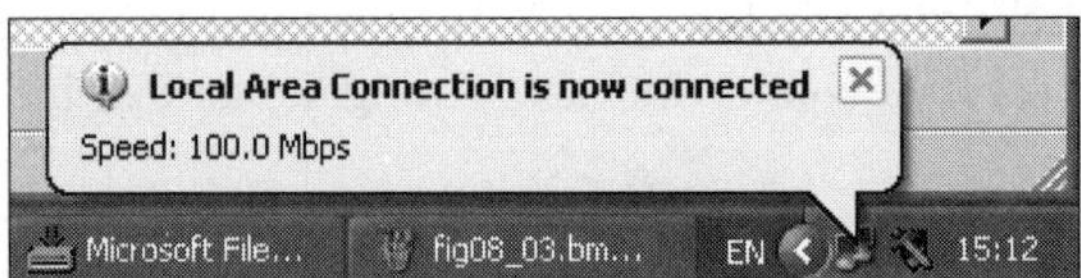

Fig. 8.4. The taskbar indicator displays the local area connection status

- The procedure for establishing and managing network connections is now much easier. Windows 2000 has introduced a special wizard for this purpose, and Windows XP continues this tradition (Fig. 8.5). This program contains a large list of configuration options displaying a series of dialogs that show available options and step-by-step instructions for configuring connections. The New Connection Wizard provides the capability of establishing and configuring various types of network connections (Fig. 8.6), including VPN (Virtual Private Network) connections, Internet connections, corporate network connections, and RAS server.

Fig. 8.5. The **New Connection Wizard** welcome window

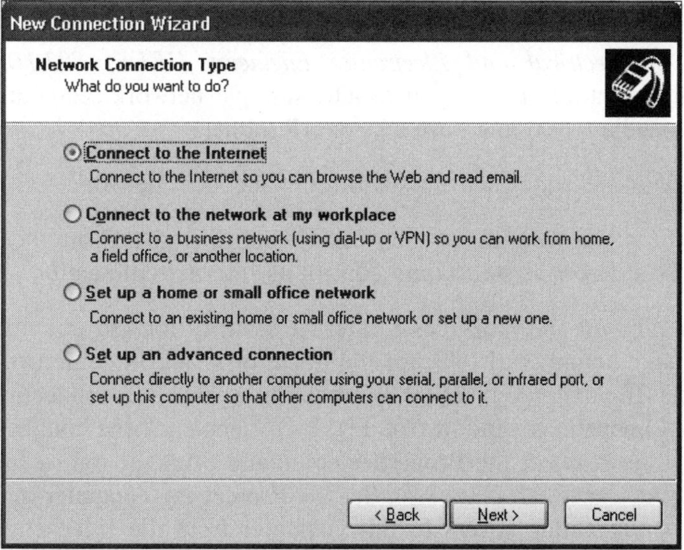

Fig. 8.6. The Network Connection Wizard provides capabilities of establishing various connections

- New Windows 2000/XP functions include network connection sharing. A user can now establish a remote connection (for example, an Internet connection), and then allow other users to connect to the Internet using this connection. This is convenient for small networks (especially home networks). Although this functionality allows you to share a connection with any remote network, it's most frequently used for sharing Internet connections.
- Windows 2000/XP provides support for Virtual Private Networks (VPN). In addition to the PPTP protocol for accessing virtual private networks (also supported in Windows NT 4.0), Windows 2000/XP supports various new VPN technologies, including Layer 2 Tunneling Protocol (L2TP) and IP Security (IPSec). IPSec is an open standard using Level 3 encryption technology.
- Increased stability of RRAS (Routing and Remote Access). Windows 2000/XP also combines RAS and RRAS features.
- In comparison to Windows NT 4.0, Windows 2000 and Windows XP provide an extended set of functions for customizing dial-up connections.

Besides these functions, which are provided by both Windows 2000 and Windows XP, Windows XP also introduces several improvements and new features, the most important among which are:

- *Institute of Electrical and Electronics Engineers (IEEE) 802.1D Transparent Bridge*—this feature enables you to add multiple network segments (usually, of different media types) and have a single IP subnet.
- *DNS resolver*—provides name resolution for the local network.
- *Discovery and Control*—allows network clients to find the Internet Connection Sharing host, know its status, and control its Internet connection.
- *Personal Firewall*—provides basic Internet security for the computer, or when used in conjunction with ICS, for the home or small office network. To enable or disable Internet Connection Firewall for a specific connection, open the **Network Connections** window (see Fig. 8.1), right-click the connection that you want to protect, select the **Properties** command from the right-click menu, and go to the **Advanced** tab (Fig. 8.7). Set the **Protect my computer and network by limiting or preventing access to this computer from the Internet** checkbox. To configure the Internet Connection Firewall, click the **Settings** button at the bottom of this window.

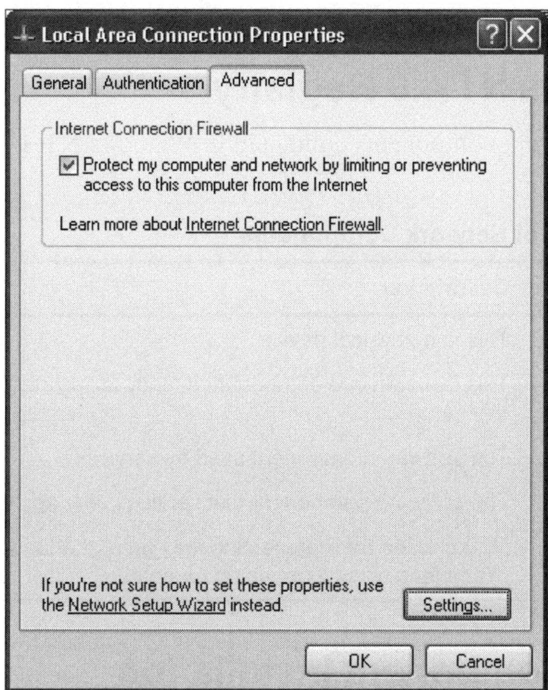

Fig. 8.7. Enabling Internet Connection Firewall

Network Settings in Windows NT 4.0 Registry

When you install new network components, the appropriate information is added to the registry. In Windows NT 4.0, each network component is represented in the following two parts of the registry:

- Software registration keys for the component driver and network adapter driver under `HKEY_LOCAL_MACHINE\Software`
- Service registration keys for the component driver and network adapter driver under `HKEY_LOCAL_MACHINE\System`

This section describes the general organization and contents of the software registration and service registration keys for network components. Next, we'll discuss bindings and dependency handling.

Types of Network Components in Windows NT 4.0 Registry

The types of network components contained in Windows NT 4.0 registry are listed in Table 8.2.

Table 8.2. Types of Network Components

Component type	Description
Adapter	This is a physical device
Driver	This is a software component directly associated with the physical device
Transport	The software component used by services
Service	The software component that services user applications
Basic	Marker used for representing the name of a fundamental class (for example, a class that has no parents)

Network Component Installation and Windows NT 4.0 Registry

When you install any type of network component, the installation program creates registry subkeys for both the services and network software. Thus, if you install a single networking component, the following keys will be created in the Windows NT 4.0 registry:

- The software registration subkey for the driver, located under `HKEY_LOCAL_MACHINE\Software\`*`Company`*`\`*`ProductName`*`\`*`Version`*. For example, the registry path to the Etherlink adapter driver will look like the following: `HKEY_LOCAL_MACHINE\Software\Microsoft\Elinkii\CurrentVersion`. In Windows 2000/XP registry, there's no `CurrentVersion` key.
- The software registration subkey of the network adapter card has the following registry path: `HKEY_LOCAL_MACHINE\Software\Microsoft\Windows NT\CurrentVersion\NetworkCards\`*`Netcard#`*.
- The service registration key for the driver, located under `HKEY_LOCAL_MACHINE\System\CurrentControlSet\Services`.
- The service registration subkey for the network adapter, located under `HKEY_LOCAL_MACHINE\System\CurrentControlSet\Services`.

Software Registration Data for Network Components

When you install the network adapter, the installation program creates separate registry entries for both the driver and the adapter. Because of this, the `Software` key must contain several subkeys describing the network component. For each network component, registration keys for the driver and the adapter contain a special subkey named `NetRules`, which identifies the component as part of a set of networking components.

For example, the standard registration item for the Etherlink II driver is stored under `HKEY_LOCAL_MACHINE\Software\Microsoft\Elinkii\CurrentVersion`.

The standard settings for this driver may include the following:

```
Description = 3Com Etherlink II Adapter Driver
InstallDate = 0x2a4e01x5
...
RefCount = 0x1
ServiceName = Elnkii
SoftwareType = driver
Title = 3Com Etherlink II Adapter Driver
```

The `NetRules` subkey associated with the Etherlink II driver may contain the following settings:

```
bindable = elnkiiDriver elnkiiAdapter non exclusive
bindform = "ElnkIISys" yes no container
class = REG_MULTI_SZ "elnkiiDriver basic"
Infname = OEMNADE2.INF
InfOption = ELNKII
type = elnkiiSys ndisDriver elnkiiDriver
use = driver
```

Detailed descriptions of the registry settings under `NetRules` keys are provided in the Regentry.hlp file included with the Windows NT 4.0 Workstation Resource Kit. This data is maintained by the system, and users shouldn't modify these settings.

The adapter (Etherlink, in our example) is described by the `NetworkCards` key under `HKEY_LOCAL_MACHINE\Software\Microsoft\Windows NT\CurrentVersion\NetworkCards\`*`Netcard#`*.

Standard settings for the network adapter may look like the following:

```
Description = 3Com Etherlin II Adapter Driver
InstallDate = 0x2a4e01x5
Manufacturer = Microsoft
ProductName = Elnkii
ServiceName = Elnkii02
Title = [01] 3Com Etherlink II Adapter
```

Service Registration Information for Network Components

The `HKEY_LOCAL_MACHINE\System\CurrentControlSet\Services` registry key represents the registration area for the services (including network services). The service registration information is used when you load the service into the memory. Registry subkeys under this key contain all the data needed to load the service, including the path to the executable file, service type, and startup criteria.

Software registration keys for network components, described in the previous section, contain mandatory `ServiceName` parameters. Each `ServiceName` setting has a value that represents the name of the service for the appropriate network component. This name is used as a symbolic link to the settings of the service located under `HKEY_LOCAL_MACHINE\System\CurrentControlSet\Services\`<*ServiceName*>.

Some network components represent a set of services rather than a single service. In this case, each of the services has its own subkey under `HKEY_LOCAL_MACHINE\System\CurrentControlSet\Services`. Usually, these network components contain a "main" service. All other services included in the set depend on it.

To illustrate this, let's discuss our example (registry settings for the Etherlink adapter). The `ServiceName` setting for the Etherlink adapter driver has a value set to `Elnkii`. The `HKEY_LOCAL_MACHINE\System\CurrentControlSet\Services` key contains the subkey with this name, and information contained under this subkey will define the path to the driver file, dependent services (dependencies), and other data needed to start the service. The `Elnkii` subkey may contain other subkeys that define settings and rules for binding this driver.

In our example, the `ServiceName` setting for the Etherlink adapter has a value set to `Elnkii02`, which is also the name of the subkey under the `Services` key. This key defines the binding rules and physical settings of the network adapter (for example, the I/O address and IRQ). Normally, you set these parameters using the **Adapters** tab of the **Network** window.

Binding Network Components

For the networking software to function correctly, it's necessary to load all the required software components. It's also necessary to establish appropriate relationships between all the components. These relationships are also known as bindings. To establish an optimum set of bindings, the system searches the following registry information:

- The set of configurable network components
- Types of network components included into this set
- Restricting settings for network components and their bindings
- Possible bindings that can be established
- The appropriate method of informing network components about their bindings

During the system startup, the kernel scans the `HKEY_LOCAL_MACHINE\SYSTEM\CurrentControlSet\Services` key to find binding information for each service. If it finds such information, it creates the `Linkage` subkeys to store these data. For example, the `Bind` setting under `HKEY_LOCAL_MACHINE\SYSTEM\CurrentControlSet\Services\LanmanWorkstation\Linkage` may contain the following string:

```
Bind\Device\Nbf_Elnkii01\Device\Nbf_Elnkii02
```

The `Bind` setting describes the binding information used by Windows NT redirector if there are two network adapters installed on the computer. In this case, the network card number is added as an index to the symbolic name of the adapter. This name is added to the name of the transport that provides access to the network card. These names are generated by the system according to restrictions that are put in effect by the network components.

All bindings must meet a usability requirement, which means that the binding must end with an adapter (physical device) or with a logical end point, which may represent a program component that manages all other information interactions. This requirement allows you to avoid loading unnecessary software components. For example, you can work with the network before deciding to remove the network card. Without the usability restriction, bindings continue to bind the components that need to be loaded (for example, without a network adapter, it's no use of loading its driver).

The example shown below illustrates the working principles of the Nbf.sys and Srv.sys software components with two Etherlink II adapters and one IBM Token Ring adapter. The `HKEY_LOCAL_MACHINE\SYSTEM\CurrentControlSet\Services\Nbf\Linkage` registry key contains the following settings:

```
Bind = "Device\ElnkII1"
       "Device\ElnkII2"
       "Device\IbmTok11
Export = "\Device\Nbf\ElnkII1"
         "\Device\Nbf\ElnkII2"
         "\Device\Nbf\IbmTok1"
Route = "ElnkIISys ElnkII1"
        "ElnkIISys ElnkII2"
        "IbmtokSys IbmTok1"
```

Under the `HKEY_LOCAL_MACHINE\SYSTEM\CurrentControlSet\Services\Srv\Linkage`, the following settings may be present:

```
Bind = "Device\Nbf\ElnkII1"
       "Device\Nbf\ElnkII2"
       "Device\Nbf\IbmTok11
Export = "\Device\Srv\Nbf\ElnkII1"
         "\Device\Srv\Nbf\ElnkII2"
         "\Device\Srv\Nbf\IbmTok1"
Route = "Nbf ElnkIISys ElnkII1"
        "Nbf ElnkIISys ElnkII2"
        "Nbf IbmtokSys IbmTok1"
```

The names in the `Bind` and `Export` settings are created based on object names defined under `NetRules` keys for the respective components. Consequently, these settings may be different from the actual names of the services (in our example, similar names are used in order to simplify the description). The names contained in the `Route` settings are the names of the subkeys under the `Services` key, including the whole downward route along the binding hierarchy.

When the system completes the binding procedure for network components, and the results of this procedure have been saved in the registry, you may need to inform certain network components about modifications that have been introduced. For example, TCP/IP may require you to enter the IP address for each newly configured network adapter. If the `NetRules` key for a network component contains a `Review` setting that has a nonzero value, then the INF file for this network component will be checked each time the bindings are modified.

Dependency Handling for Network Components

Network services may depend on other services or drivers. These, in turn, may depend on yet other services or drivers. The system will establish the following types of dependencies:

- Specific dependencies represented by the names of the services the current service is dependent on
- Group dependencies
- Static dependencies that are required under any condition and in any situation

Specific Dependencies

Specific dependencies simply represent the name of the required service. By default, the system generates explicit names for all dependent services detected when generating bindings. Specific dependencies are marked by the `Use` setting, which, in our case, appears under the `NetRules` key of the respective component.

For example, suppose that the Workstation service depends on NBF, which binds to the two network adapters, and, consequently, depends on their drivers. The system marks NBF as a service dependent on the two network card drivers, and the Workstation service as a service dependent on both the network card drivers and on the NBF.

Group Dependencies

This service needs to be loaded only if one of the members of the dependency set has been loaded successfully. In the previous example, the Workstation service didn't need to be loaded if the drivers for both network adapters couldn't be initialized.

The easiest approach, in this case, is using group dependencies. Each service (driver, transport, or other) can identify itself as a member of a service group. For example, all Windows NT drivers for network adapters are handled as members of the NDIS group.

In the registry, all group dependencies are marked by the `Use` setting, which appears under the `NetRules` key for the appropriate component. The groups are the symbolic names listed under `HKEY_LOCAL_MACHINE\SYSTEM\CurrentControlSet\Control\GroupOrderList`.

Static Dependencies

A static dependency is a required service that needs to be loaded under any condition.

To configure a service as statically dependent on another service, create the `OtherDependencies` setting under the `Linkage` key for appropriate component. The `OtherDependencies` setting has a `REG_MULTI_SZ` data type, and it can contain as many service names as necessary.

Windows 2000 and Windows XP Network Parameters in the Registry

Windows 2000/XP networking features include several improvements. These improvements have also influenced the method of storing network data in the registry. The main improvements introduced into the networking are: support for NDIS 5.0 (Windows 2000) and NDIS 5.1 (Windows XP), Plug and Play support, power management, and the new INF file format used for installing network components.

Installing Network Components in the Windows 2000/XP Registry

To install Windows 2000/XP networking components, the operating system requires the following:

- *Class installer and optional co-installer*

  Class installer is a dynamically loaded library (DLL) that installs, configures, or deletes devices of a specified class. Networking components in Windows 2000/XP must be installed by Windows 2000/XP network class installer or by a vendor-supplied class installer.

  If the standard class installer doesn't provide all of the necessary functionality for an individual device, the device vendor may develop an optional co-installer. This co-installer is a Win32 DLL that implements all the necessary functions for the individual device.

A list of existing network components is provided below:

- `Net`—this class defines network adapters.
- `NetTrans`—this class defines network protocols (such as TCP/IP and IPX) and connection-oriented network clients.
- `NetClient`—this class specifies network clients, such as Microsoft Client for Networks or NetWare Client. The `NetClient` component is considered a network provider. It also can be used to provide print services (in this case, it's also the print provider).
- `NetService`—this class specifies network services, such as the file service or the print service.

  The network class installer defines the class of the network component to be installed by the `ClassGuid` value. The `ClassGuid` value is the Globally Unique Identifier (GUID) for the class. You can generate GUID values using the Uuidgen.exe utility. More detailed information about this utility is provided in Platform SDK supplementary documents.

  All standard network component classes and their respective `ClassGuid` values are listed in Table 8.3.

Table 8.3. Network Component Classes and Their Respective ClassGuid Values

Network component class	ClassGuid value
Net	{4D36E972-E325-11CE-BFC1-08002BE10318}
NetTrans	{4D36E973-E325-11CE-BFC1-08002BE10318}
NetClient	{4D36E974-E325-11CE-BFC1-08002BE10318}
NetService	{4D36E975-E325-11CE-BFC1-08002BE10318}

Class installer information is stored in the registry under `HKEY_LOCAL_MACHINE\SYSTEM\CurrentControlSet\Control\Class`. For each class installer, this key contains a subkey named... No, it won't have the name you're expecting it to have. And it won't be something like "Net", either. Rather, it will be the `ClassGuid` value (Fig. 8.8). Compare this name to the `ClassGuid` values listed in Table 8.3.

- ❐ *One or more INF files*

INF files contain information that's necessary to the class installer of the network component to install this component. A detailed description of the INF file format is provided in the documents supplied with Windows Driver Development Kit (DDK).

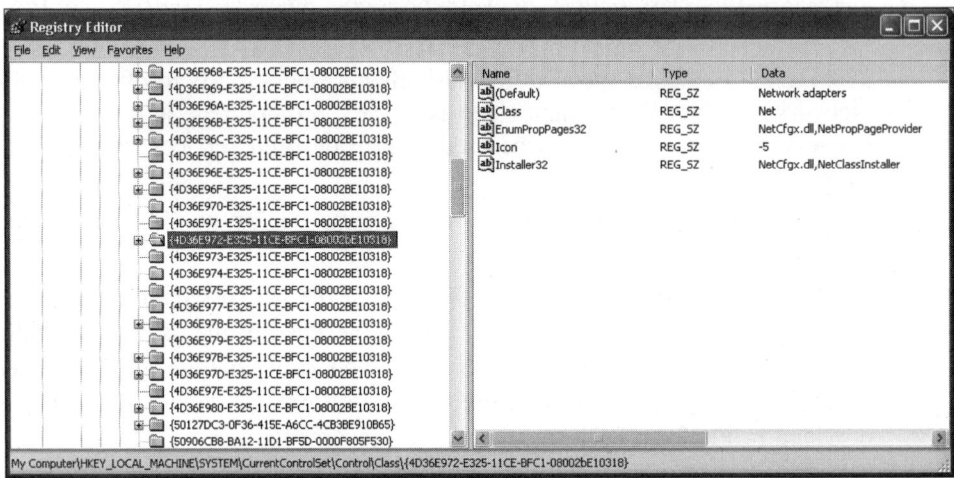

Fig. 8.8. The contents of the `HKEY_LOCAL_MACHINE\SYSTEM\CurrentControlSet\Control\Class\{4D36E972-E325-11CE-BFC1-08002BE10318}` registry key defines the settings of the class installer for the network adapter class

❒ *Optional notify object*

Network software components, such as network protocols, services, or network clients, may have notify objects that allow you to display the user interface for manual configuring of the network components. For example, the UI provides capabilities for manual control over the binding process. Notice that hardware components, such as network adapters, may also provide both UI and software control over the binding process. However, all these tasks are performed by the INF file or coinstaller, rather than by notify objects. Fig. 8.9 shows information on the notify object that provides the capability of manually configuring the NWLink protocol, Migration DLL, and its associated files.

If the device driver isn't included with the standard Windows 2000/XP distribution package, then the device vendor should provide the support.

In addition to the files listed above, the following files are needed to install network components:

❒ *One or more device drivers.* Normally, each driver contains a driver image (the SYS-file) and a driver library (DLL).

- *The driver catalog file* is optional, but highly desirable. We discussed catalog files in *Chapter 6*. Here, we'll only note that if the device vendor needs to include a device into the Hardware Compatibility List (HCL), it's necessary to test both the device and its driver in the Windows Hardware Quality Lab (WHQL). If the test results are satisfactory, WHQL includes the device into the HCL and provides the catalog file (CAT file) for the driver. The CAT file contains the digital signature.
- *The optional Txtsetup.oem file.* This file contains the data needed by the Windows 2000/XP Setup program to install the device driver during the earliest phases of the setup process (the text-mode setup).

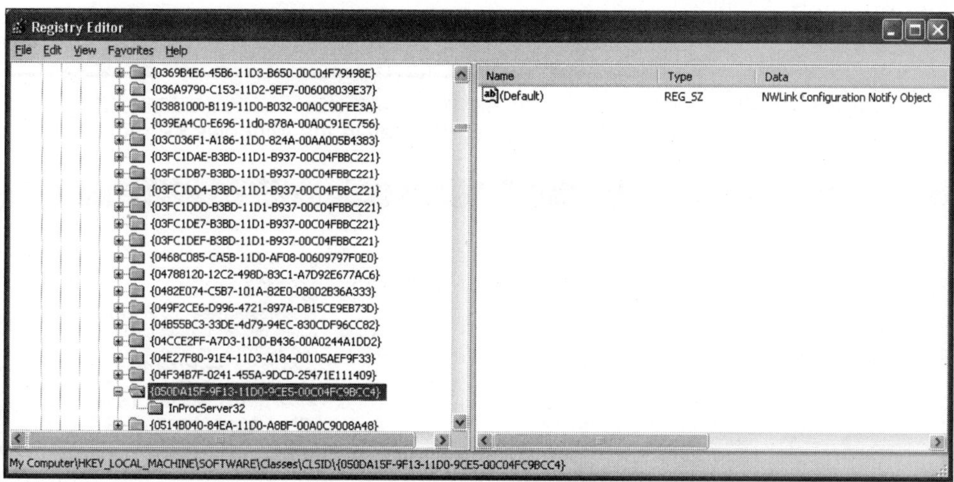

Fig. 8.9. Information on the notify object that configures the NWLink protocol

Network Adapter Registration Information

Like Windows NT 4.0, Windows 2000/XP also has software registration subkeys for all of the installed network adapter cards. These keys are stored under `HKEY_LOCAL_MACHINE\SOFTWARE\Microsoft\Windows NT\CurrentVersion\NetworkCards\`*`Netcard#`* (Fig. 8.10).

NOTE

Notice that network adapters are numbered beginning from 1, rather than from 0 as usual.

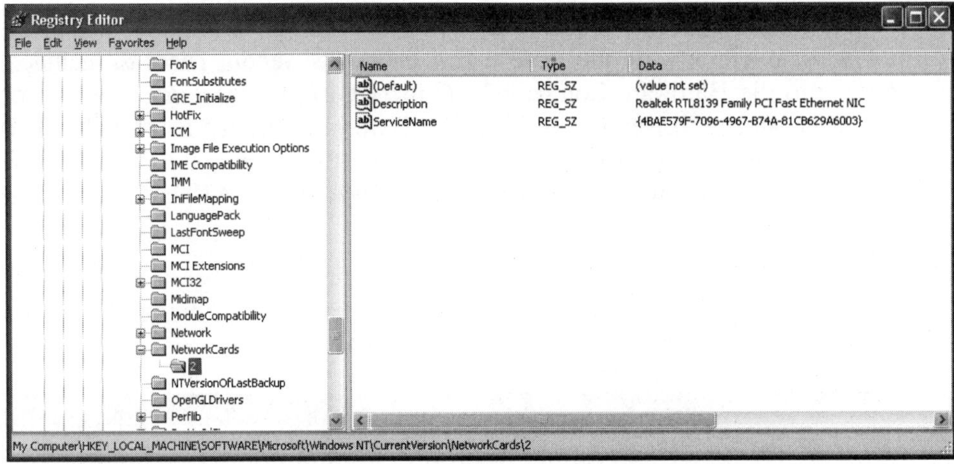

Fig. 8.10. The `HKEY_LOCAL_MACHINE\SOFTWARE\Microsoft\Windows NT\CurrentVersion\NetworkCards\2` registry key in the Windows XP registry

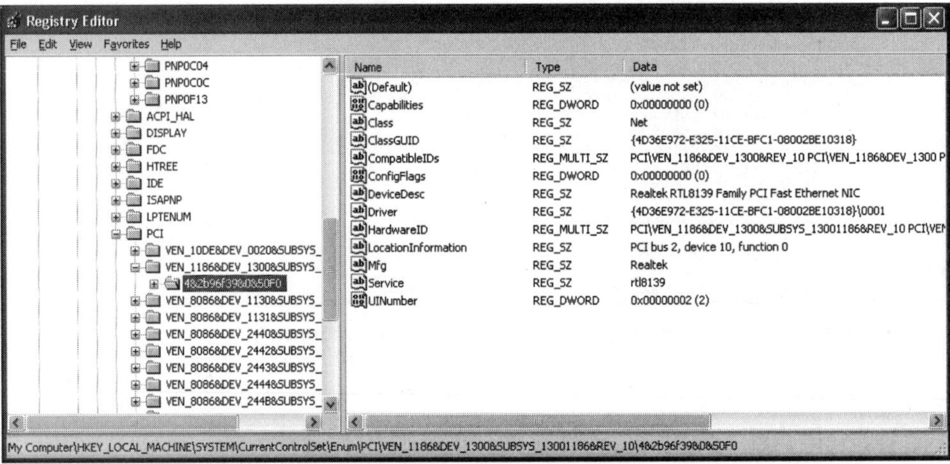

Fig. 8.11. Information on the Realtek RTL8139 Family PCI Fast Ethernet network adapter under `HKEY_LOCAL_MACHINE\SYSTEM\CurrentControlSet\Enum`

The `HKEY_LOCAL_MACHINE` root key also contains two more subkeys containing data on the network adapter:

- `HKEY_LOCAL_MACHINE\SYSTEM\CurrentControlSet\Enum`. Here, Plug and Play enumerators store the data concerning individual devices, such as device identifiers (device ID) and identifiers of compatible devices (if they exist). Fig. 8.11 provides information about the Realtek RTL8139 Family PCI Fast Ethernet

NIC stored under `HKEY_LOCAL_MACHINE\SYSTEM\CurrentControlSet\Enum`. Fig. 8.12. shows how some of this information (including the device description and its type) is displayed by the Network Connections applet in Control Panel.

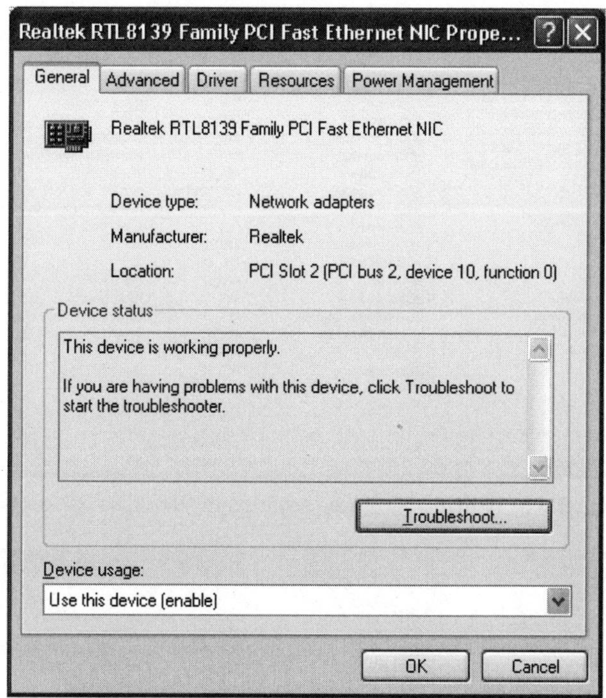

Fig. 8.12. The Network Connections applet in Control Panel displays the registry information stored under `HKEY_LOCAL_MACHINE\SYSTEM\CurrentControlSet\Enum`

- `HKEY_LOCAL_MACHINE\SYSTEM\CurrentControlSet\Class\<ClassGUID>`. Here, device installers store data on each individual class of devices, its respective class installer, and coinstallers (if present). For each installed driver, there's a subkey under the key, named "0000", "0001", ... These subkeys contain information on individual drivers, including a description string, the path to the driver's INF file, and vendor information. Fig. 8.13 shows the contents of the registry key containing data on the driver we're discussing—the network driver for Realtek RTL8139 Family PCI Fast Ethernet adapter.

Each of the driver keys also contains a set of required subkeys: `Linkage` and `Ndi`. The typical contents of the `Linkage` subkey for the network adapter driver are shown in Fig. 8.14. As you can see, this subkey contains the following standard settings: `Export`, specifying the list of created objects; `RootDevice` (the setting that specifies the root device); and `UpperBind` (the setting that specifies protocol binding).

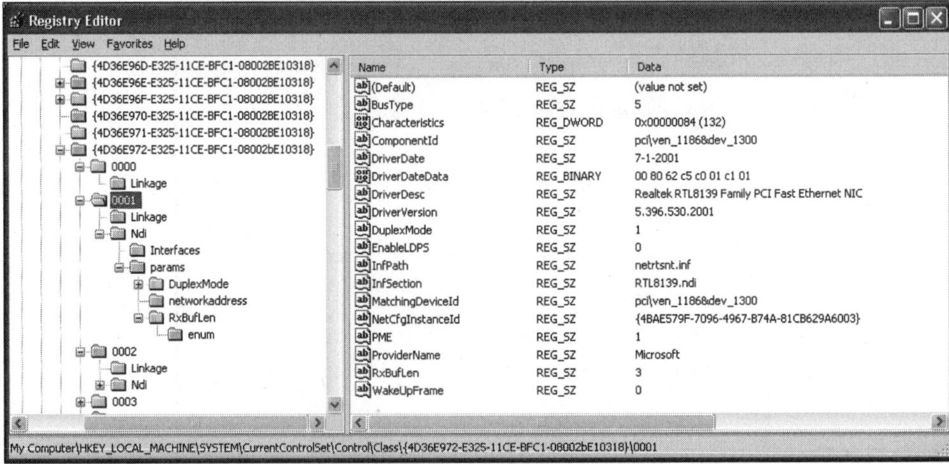

Fig. 8.13. Network adapter settings in Windows XP registry

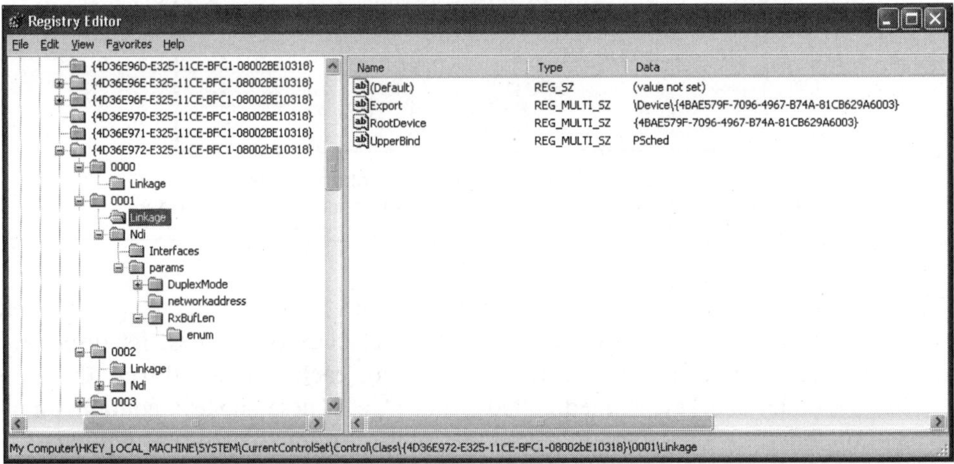

Fig. 8.14. Typical contents of the `Linkage` key for the network adapter driver

The `Ndi` key contains subkeys and settings that depend on the type of installed network component. If the network component has an associated service or device driver, then the `Ndi` key will contain a `Service` setting. This setting specifies the name of the appropriate service or driver (Fig. 8.15). If there are several services associated to a given network component, then the `Ndi` key will contain the required `CoServices` setting (`REG_MULTI_SZ` data type). This setting will list all services associated with the component, including the main service specified by the `Service` setting. This setting is required for all `NetTrans` components (transport protocols), `NetClient` components (network clients), and `NetService` components (network services). The components of the `Net` type (network adapters) have no such setting (Fig. 8.15). As you can see, only the RTL8139 device driver has been associated with the network adapter.

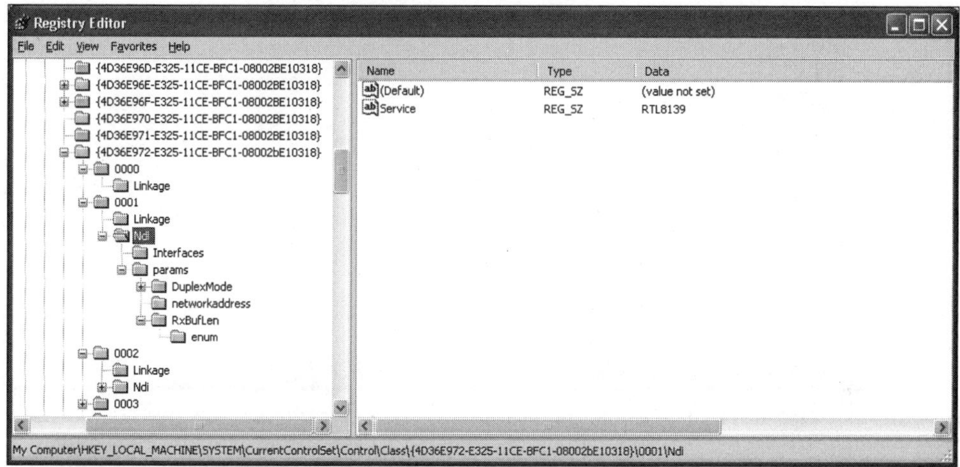

Fig. 8.15. The `..\Ndi\Service` setting specifies the name of the service or driver associated with the network component

All further configuration information on Windows 2000/XP network components is stored in the registry under `HKEY_LOCAL_MACHINE\SYSTEM\CurrentControlSet\Control\Network`. Notice the subkeys, long strings composed of characters and digits and enclosed in braces (Fig. 8.16). If you look at these keys carefully, you'll immediately notice that their names are actually the `ClassGuid` values listed in Table. 8.3.

If you open these keys sequentially and explore their contents, you'll find everything you need to understand how network components are configured. For example, if you open the subkey named `{4D36E972-E325-11CE-BFC1-08002BE10318}` (if you remember, this `ClassGuid` value specifies network adapters), you'll notice the `Connection` key at the lowest level of hierarchy (Fig. 8.17). It's not difficult to see that this key specifies the LAN connection properties. First, the `Name` string setting specifies the "Local Area Connection" string that you see in the **Network and Dial-up Connections** window. Next, the string setting named `PnPInstanceID` is the link to the subkey under the `Enum` key, which contains the data concerning the network adapter. Finally, the binary setting named `ShowIcon` specifies if the toolbar indicator is enabled. The relationship between registry settings and Control Panel applets is illustrated by Fig. 8.18.

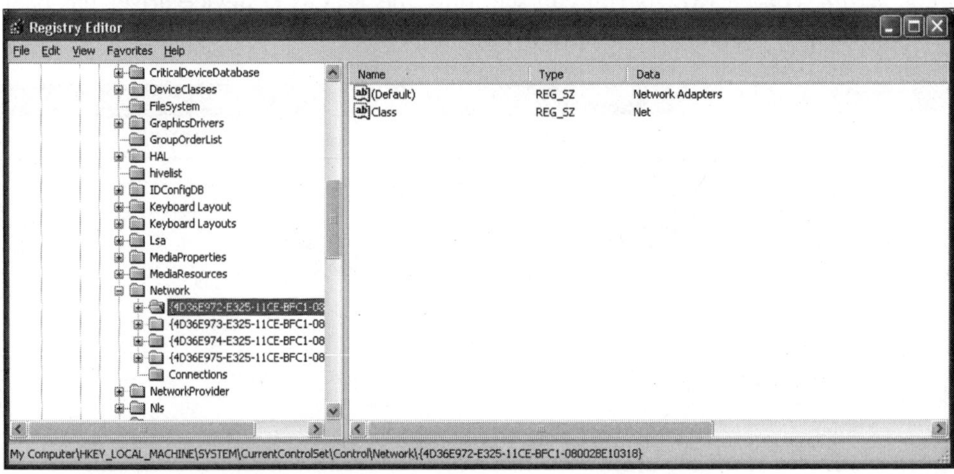

Fig. 8.16. The contents of the `HKEY_LOCAL_MACHINE\SYSTEM\CurrentControlSet\Control\Network` registry key

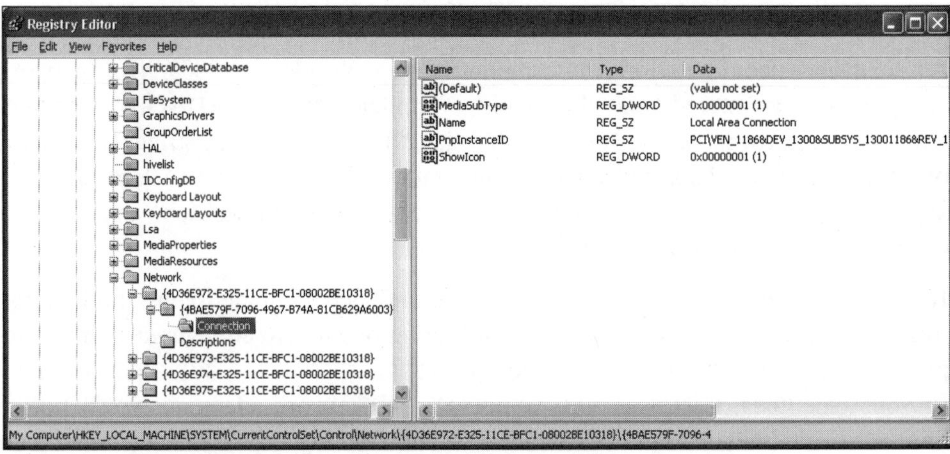

Fig. 8.17. Local Area Connection properties in the system registry

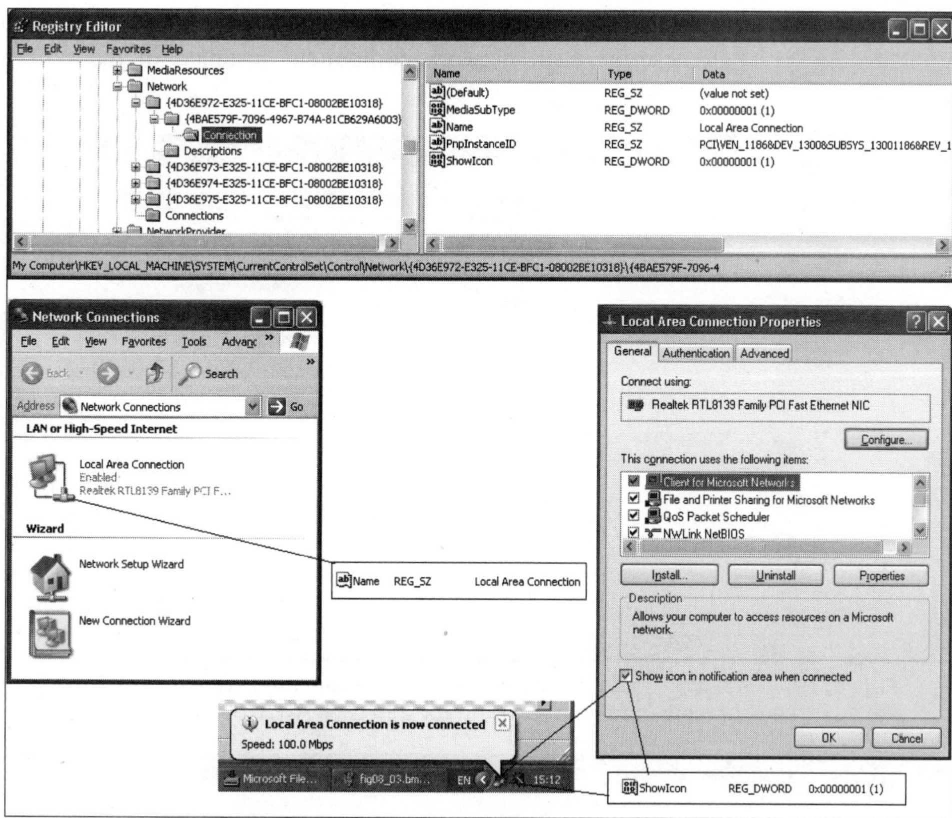

Fig. 8.18. Relationship between registry information and the Network and Dial-up Connections applet in Control Panel

Registration Information on the Network Components

Registration information for the network services is stored in the system registry under `HKEY_LOCAL_MACHINE\SYSTEM\CurrentControlSet\Services`. This registry key contains the service registration keys for network components (including network adapters). To continue our discussion, notice that the `HKEY_LOCAL_MACHINE\SYSTEM\CurrentControlSet\Control\Class\{4D36E972-E325-11CE-BFC1-08002BE10318}\0000\Ndi` key contains the `Service` setting, which specifies the name of the respective service or driver (in our example, `RTL8139`). The `RTL8139` subkey that describes the settings for the service associated with the Realtek RTL8139 Family PCI Fast Ethernet adapter is shown in Fig. 8.19.

The HKEY_LOCAL_MACHINE\SYSTEM\CurrentControlSet\Services registry key also contains subkeys that describe each network component installed in the system (Fig. 8.20).

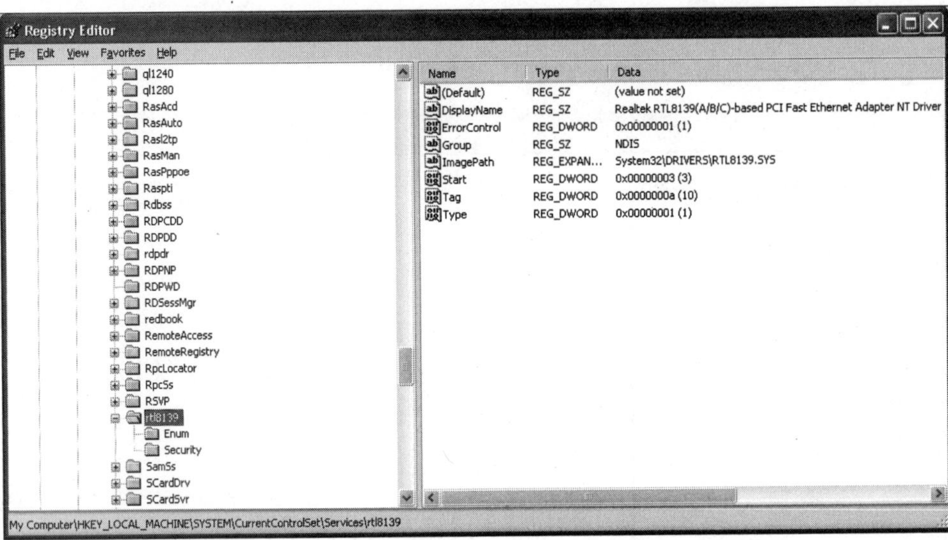

Fig. 8.19. The HKEY_LOCAL_MACHINE\SYSTEM\CurrentControlSet\Services \RTL8139 key contains configuration data for a Realtek RTL8139 network adapter

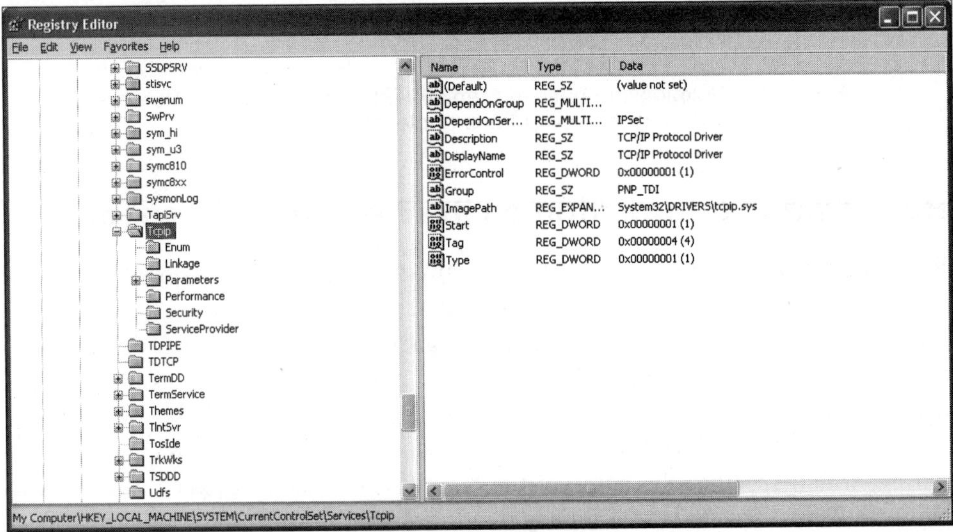

Fig. 8.20. The HKEY_LOCAL_MACHINE\SYSTEM\CurrentControlSet\Services registry key contains subkeys for all installed network components

Customizing a Network Using the Registry

It's impossible to provide a complete reference for all of Windows NT/2000/XP networking in a single chapter (for example, the Resource Kits usually include a comprehensive volume entitled "Windows NT Networking"). This topic certainly deserves a separate book. However, I hope that this chapter helps you to understand how network settings are stored in the registry, and how these settings are related to the data displayed by Control Panel applets. This topic is one of the most interesting ones, and if you explore it, you'll make many discoveries and invent many new ways of customizing network settings.

The remaining sections of this chapter will describe various methods of customizing network settings using the registry.

Automatic Configuration of IP Addresses

Windows 2000/XP includes many improvements, some of which were noticed immediately and cause heated debates among users. Many of the improvements that simplify administrative procedures, however, aren't as obvious. Automatic configuration of IP addresses is one such feature (Beginning with Windows 2000 Release Candidate 2, this function was called "Automatic Private IP Addressing" or APIPA). Let's see how it works.

When you install Windows 2000 or Windows XP, the standard set of network capabilities includes the TCP/IP protocol. By default, it's assumed that the client computer will get the IP address and subnetwork mask from the DHCP server. Most users who have at least some experience configuring TCP/IP in Windows NT 4.0 networks, know that problems can occur if there is an IP address conflict (or if the DHCP server is unavailable for a time). The APIPA functionality introduced in Windows 2000/XP allows DHCP clients to configure the IP address and subnetwork mask automatically (if the DHCP server is down or unavailable for some reason).

To configure the local computer as a DHCP client, set the **Obtain an IP address automatically** option on the **General** tab of the **Internet Protocol (TCP/IP) Properties** window (Fig. 8.21).

NOTE

All client computers running Windows 2000/XP are configured as DHCP clients by default. If you select the standard networking options when you install the operating system, your computer is already configured as a DHCP client. No additional operations are required.

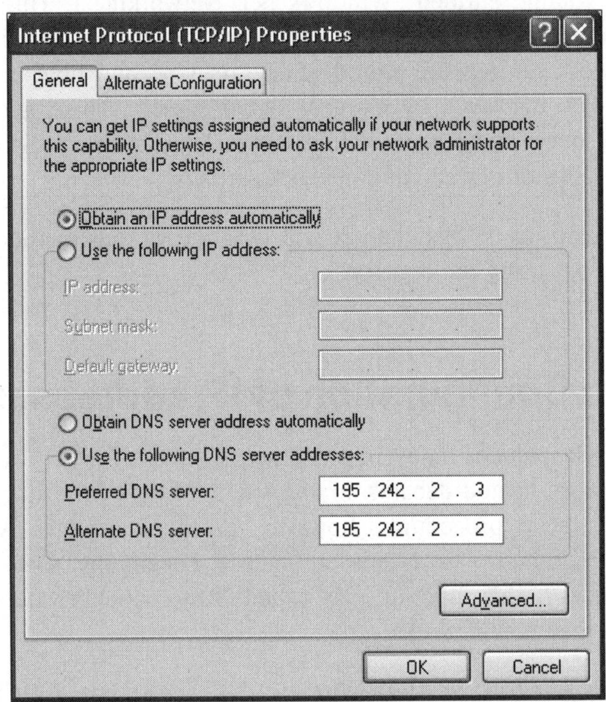

Fig. 8.21. The **General** tab of the **Internet Protocol (TCP/IP) Properties** window

When the DHCP client starts, it searches for the DHCP server to obtain TCP/IP configuration information (usually, these data include an IP address, a subnet mask, and other DHCP settings). If the client can't get this information from the DHCP server, it will use the APIPA functionality, which automatically assigns it an IP address within a range from 169.254.0.1 to 169.254.255.254. The address range is especially reserved for this purpose and isn't used anywhere else in the Internet. The standard class B subnet mask will be used: 255.255.0.0. Since the client selects an arbitrary IP address from the range just specified, IP address conflicts may occur in the network. If this happens, Address Resolution Protocol (ARP) is used to resolve the conflicts. If the client selects an arbitrary IP address from the reserved range, it then sends an ARP frame to the network. If it doesn't get an answer to this request, the client retains the IP address it's selected. If the selected IP address is already in use, the client will make up to 10 attempts to select another IP address. The client will use this configuration data until the DHCP server becomes available. Obviously, the APIPA feature is very convenient for small networks without routing.

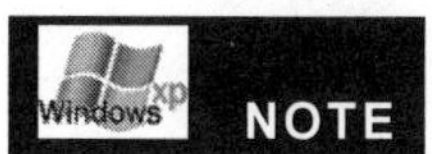

If you carefully look at the **Internet Protocol (TCP/IP) Properties** window shown in Fig. 8.21, you'll certainly notice one of the most appreciated new features introduced with Windows XP—so-called Alternate Addressing—which certainly will be most appreciated by users of mobile computers. The problem is that laptops often participate in more than one network, and are using a static IP address at one location and a dynamically assigned IP address at another. Moving between locations, therefore, each time requires reconfiguring of IP settings. Windows XP has eliminated this problem. Now the user can configure his or her laptop to first use dynamically assigned IP address, and then try alternate IP address, if the DHCP server is unavailable. To use this feature, open the **Internet Protocol (TCP/IP) Properties** window and set the **Obtain an IP address automatically** radio button, then go to the **Alternate Configuration** tab (Fig. 8.22) and configure an alternate IP address. Note that a second address may be either static or APIPA.

It may happen, though, that you need to disable APIPA completely. To accomplish this, edit the registry as follows:

1. Start Regedit.exe (if you work with Windows 2000, start Regedt32.exe).
2. Open the following registry key: `HKEY_LOCAL_MACHINE\SYSTEM\CurrentControlSet\Services\Tcpip\Parameters\Interfaces`.
3. Select the subkey for the adapter that you'll need to disable APIPA, add the `IPAutoconfigurationEnabled` `REG_DWORD` value, and set it to 0 (the default value is 1). Initially this value is omitted, and the system assumes the default value (which means that APIPA is enabled).

NOTE

Add the `IPAutoconfigurationEnabled` value only if you need to disable APIPA. If there's more than one network adapter on the computer, and you need to disable the APIPA function for each adapter, add the `IPAutoconfigurationEnabled` setting under the `HKEY_LOCAL_MACHINE\SYSTEM\CurrentControlSet\Services\Tcpip\Parameters` key and set it to 0.

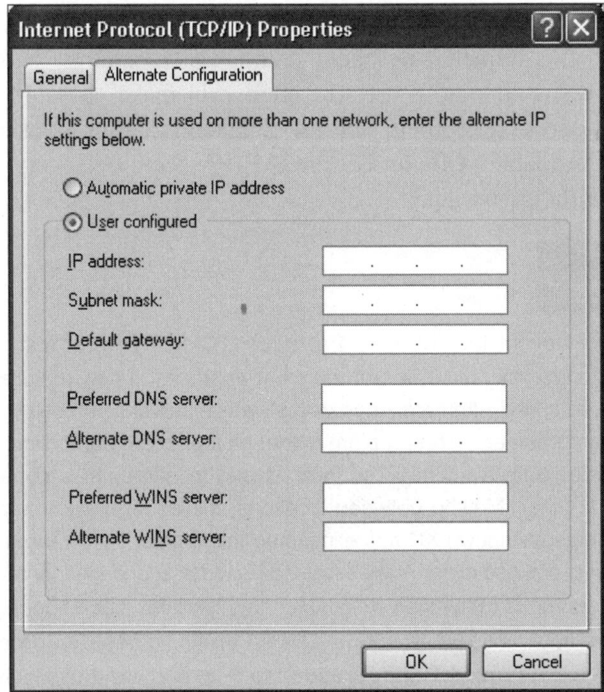

Fig. 8.22. The **Alternate Configuration** tab of the **Internet Protocol (TCP/IP) Properties** window

Disabling Dynamic DNS Registration

By default, all Windows 2000/XP computers attempt to dynamically register on the DNS servers specified on the **General** tab of the TCP/IP properties window. To disable this feature, click the **Advanced** button on the **General** tab of the **Internet Protocol (TCP/IP) Properties** window. The **Advanced TCP/IP Settings** window will open. Go to the **DNS** tab (Fig. 8.23) and clear the **Register this connection's addresses in DNS** checkbox.

In case you want to do the same operation using the registry, open the `HKEY_LOCAL_MACHINE\SYSTEM\CurrentControlSet\Services\Tcpip\Parameters\Interfaces` key, and set the `DisableDynamicUpdate` value (of `REG_DWORD` data type) to 1.

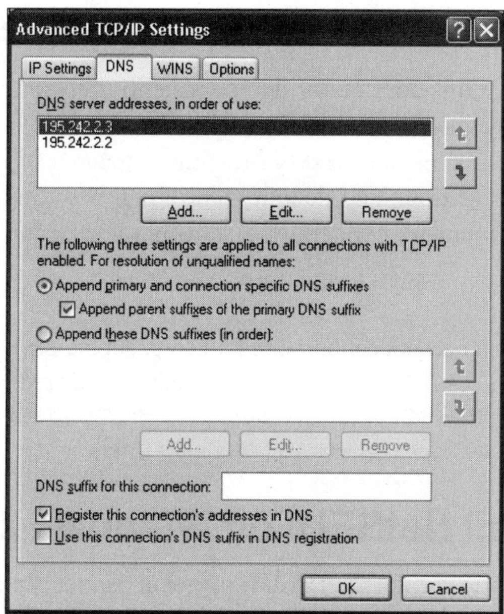

Fig. 8.23. The **DNS** tab of the **Advanced TCP/IP Settings** window

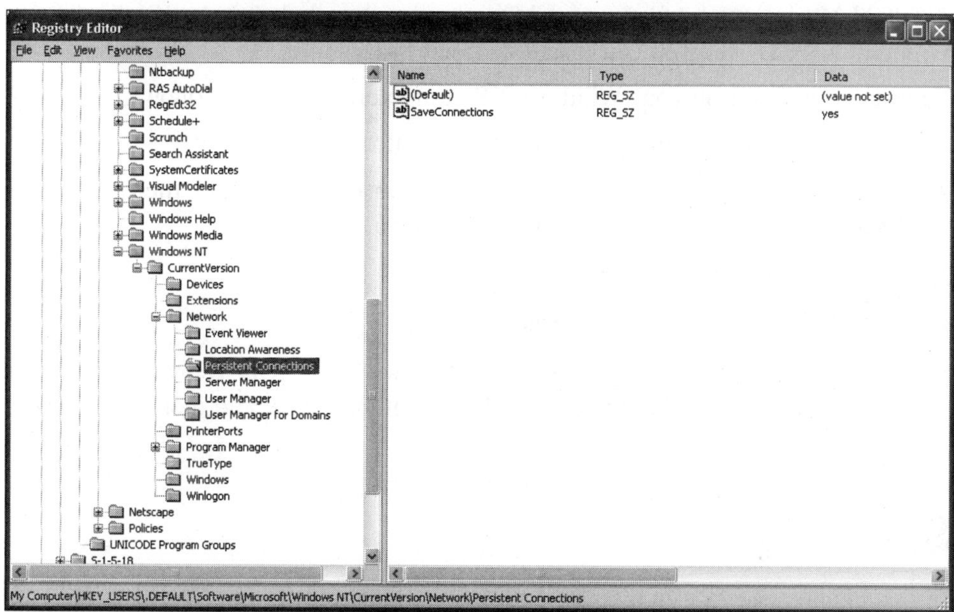

Fig. 8.24. The `HKEY_USERS\.DEFAULT\Software\Microsoft\WindowsNT\CurrentVersion\Network\Persistent Connections` registry key

Disabling Persistent Network Connections

To disable the option for restoring persistent network connections, start the registry editor, open the `HKEY_USERS\.DEFAULT\Software\Microsoft\WindowsNT\CurrentVersion\Network\Persistent Connections` key, and locate the `SaveConnections` setting. The default value for this setting is "yes" (Fig. 8.24). To disable persistent network connections, set this value to "no".

NOTE

To disable persistent network connections for users, set the `SaveConnections` value to "no" in all existing user profiles. This information is stored in the registry under the following keys: `HKEY_USERS\<User_SID>\SOFTWARE\Microsoft\WindowsNT\CurrentVersion\Network\Persistent Connections`.

How to Install NetBEUI on Windows XP

As you probably noticed, the NetBEUI protocol is not included in the list of installable protocols in Windows XP. This is because the NetBEUI protocol is no longer supported on Windows XP. However, the files that are required to install NetBEUI (Netnbf.inf and Nbf.sys) are still included with the distribution Windows XP CD, and you can install it, if necessary.

To install NetBEUI on your Windows XP computer, proceed as follows:

1. Start the Network Connections applet in Control Panel.
2. Right-click the adapter you want to add NetBEUI to, and then select the **Properties** command from the right-click menu.
3. On the **General** tab, click **Install**.
4. Click **Protocol**, and then click **Add**.
5. Click **Have Disk**, insert your Windows XP CD-ROM, open the Valueadd\msft\net\netbeui folder, click the Netnbf.inf file, and then click **Open**.
6. Click **OK**.

Summary

In this chapter, we briefly discussed the network settings in the Windows NT 4.0, Windows 2000, and Windows XP registries. In the next chapter, we'll discuss important topics concerning registry protection and security.

Chapter 9

Securing the Registry

> This is a secret, top secret! The testament was enclosed in seven envelopes by seven seals. When the princess opened and read it, she was absolutely alone. The doors and the windows were guarded by the armed guards who closed their ears (though the princess did not read the testament aloud). The content of this top-secret document is well known only to the princess and to our whole town.
>
> *E. Schwarz*
> *"The Shadow"*

Naturally, you wouldn't like your plans of securing the registry to look like the "top secret" ones described above (although you certainly need to protect and secure your registry). This chapter is dedicated to measures that will allow you to protect the registry. At the same time, these security measures won't create any difficulties for you when performing everyday tasks. Notice that while this chapter can't be considered to be a complete security reference, the measures of protecting the system registry discussed here are important, and each system administrator must know them.

In nearly all the chapters of this book, I tried to emphasize that Windows XP is based on the Windows NT/2000 kernel. And, as a matter of fact, Windows NT/2000 is the first Microsoft operating system where security requirements were taken into account at the earliest stages of development. From the very beginning, Windows NT developers knew they would have to create an operating system that would meet the C2-level requirements for protected operating systems. The set of criteria, developed by the U.S. National Security Agency NSA for evaluating the level of security for computer systems and software, was published as a series of books. Each of these books' covers had a different color, and because of this, the set of these security standards became known as the Rainbow Series. The "C2 security level" is one of the most commonly used terms in the Rainbow Series. Certification of software for C2 security requirements is performed using the Trusted Computer System Evaluation Criteria, TCSEC. The TCSEC criteria, known as the Orange Book, provides specifications for the procedure of evaluating the security level of information systems for governmental organizations. The C2 security class is considered to be the highest security class, by which any general-purpose operating system can be certified.

NOTE

It's also necessary to mention an alternative point of view. The C2 class is regarded as the highest security level for general-purpose operating systems. It can't be considered the highest security level, though, if you take into account all of the existing operating systems. Notice that if it's necessary to provide the highest security level, you should use specialized operating systems (and all widely used operating systems such as Novell NetWare, Windows NT/2000/XP, UNIX and Linux can't be considered as such). For certification of the most secure operating systems used by military organizations (for example, nuclear power stations) there are other higher security classes, the highest being the A class. A lower level of security (in comparison to the C2 level) is provided by the C1 and D classes. Notice that there isn't any certification for the C1 class. As for the D class, it includes all the operating systems that don't meet the requirements of other classes. If you're interested in more detailed information concerning the Rainbow Series, download it from **http://www.radium.ncsc.mil/tpep/library/rainbow**.

Certification and testing of any operating system for the C2 security class includes evaluation and testing the security functions implemented by the operating system. This testing will determine if this function has been implemented satisfactorily and if it works correctly. The C2 security level requirements include the following:

- Required identification and authentication of all operating system users. The system must provide the capability to identify each user who has authorized access to the system, and provide access for only those users.
- Discretionary access control—users must be able to protect their data.
- Auditing capabilities—the system must have the capacity to audit all actions performed by the users and operating system itself.
- Protecting the system objects against reuse—the operating system must be capable of preventing user access to the resources released by another user (for example, preventing users from reading and reusing released memory or reading deleted files).

The process of certifying the operating system according to the C2 security class includes the following procedures:

- Investigating the source code
- Study of the documentation concerning implementation details provided by the software developers
- Repeated testing in order to eliminate errors discovered during the previous phases

NOTE

More detailed description of the certification procedure is provided at **http://www.radium.ncsc.mil/tpep**.

In the past, many reliable sources often stated that Windows NT 4.0 didn't meet the C2 class requirements, and wasn't actually certified. At the time, this was true, because only Windows NT 3.5 (with Service Pack 3) was certified by the C2 security level. However, by the time this book was written, the long-awaited event happened. Windows NT 4.0 Workstation and Windows NT 4.0 Server were finally certified to the C2 security level (this was declared on February 2, 1999). The certification tests involved both servers and a workstation, and both local (without network adapters) and networked environments (TCP/IP networks). The official press release covering this topic can be found on the Microsoft Web-site.

As for the Windows 2000 and Windows XP Professional operating systems, they're just about to be certified to the C2 level.

Cases of unauthorized access to computer networks are the reality of today life. The most common case of this can be seen when users themselves damage the computer. This usually happens when a user has just enough knowledge to be dangerous. If such users find one of the registry editors (Regedit.exe or Regedt32.exe), and you didn't take any precautions, they'll only become "worried" when the operating system stops booting.

The Easiest Methods of Restricting the Registry Access

The easiest way to avoid problems caused by unskilled users who damage the registry is to simply prevent their access to the registry. If Windows NT/2000/XP is installed on the NTFS partition, restricting registry access can be done by setting permissions to critically important files, including registry editors, registry hives, and user profiles. Unfortunately, using NTFS isn't always possible. For example, sometimes it's necessary to use the FAT file system because of legacy applications (most Windows NT/2000 computers use FAT for this reason). Thus, if it's necessary to use the FAT, you'll need to develop alternative measures of protecting the registry.

Additional Protection in Windows 2000 and Windows XP

As I already mentioned, the Windows 2000/XP user interface is oriented towards beginners, who may need protection from their own errors. Because of this, Windows 2000/XP provides the so-called "super-hidden" files.

In *Chapter 1*, we discussed the protected operating system files (which shouldn't be edited, or even seen, by the ordinary user). These files are sometimes called "super hidden". Actually, there's no such attribute. The files simply have a combination of Hidden and System attributes. By default, Windows Explorer doesn't display these files. You may set Hidden and System attributes for registry editors. Thus, you'll "hide" them from beginner users, who may be afraid of command lines such as `dir /a`.

If you decide to take this simplest protective measure, don't forget to restore the default system options in relation to displaying protected operating system files. From Windows Explorer or My Computer, select the **Folder Options** command from the **Tools** menu, then click the **View** tab (Fig. 9.1). In the **Advanced settings** list, set the **Do not show hidden files and folders** radio button. Also, don't forget to set the **Hide protected operating system files (Recommended)** option.

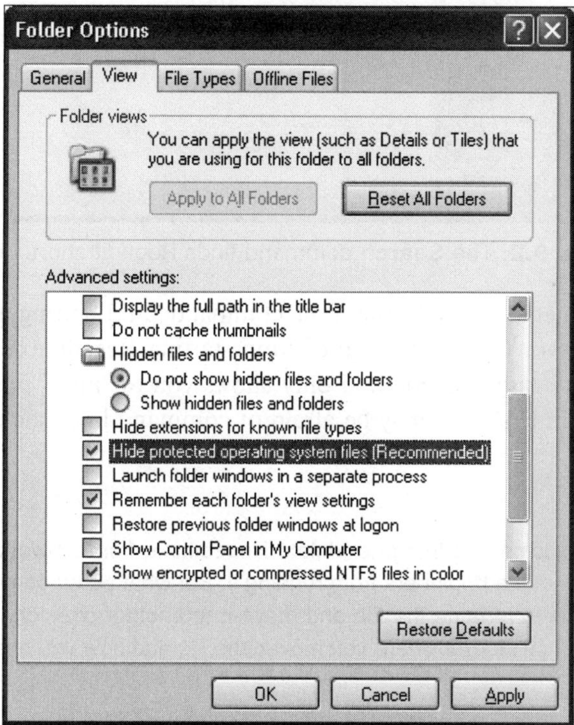

Fig. 9.1. Default operating system options in relation to protected operating system files

NOTE

Did you place the Regedit shortcut to the desktop or to the **Start** menu (just for convenience)? Well, don't forget to remove them, or otherwise the user can find them with the **Search** command (Fig. 9.2).

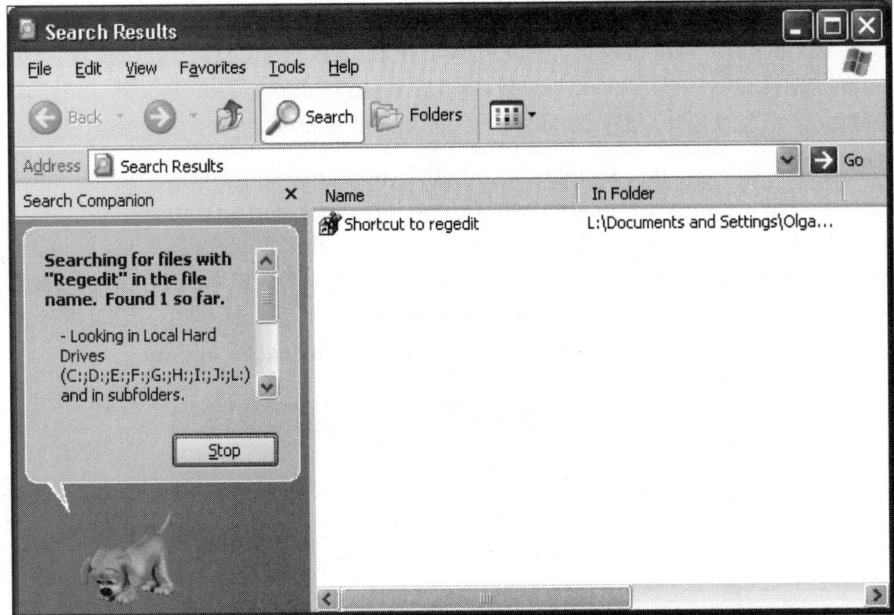

Fig. 9.2. The **Search** command finds Regedit shortcuts

Also, the **Start** menu contains the **Run** command, and setting the Hidden and System attributes won't prevent the user from starting Regedit.exe using this command. And, in any case, this method only allows you to "hide" potentially dangerous files from beginners, who may be afraid of command lines such as `dir /a`.

TIP

Some authors recommend that one "delete Regedit.exe from all workstations". This, of course, will prevent the beginners from running it. But what about convenience? A better solution would be to rename the file and move it to another directory. Of course, if you decide to do so, don't forget where you moved the file and how you named it.

Editing Access Rights to the Registry Keys

If have some previous experience working with Windows NT/2000, you'll certainly notice that many of the security features in Windows XP Professional will be quite familiar to you.

For example, similar to Windows NT/2000, Windows XP identifies users and groups using security identifiers (Security Ids, SIDs). Security identifiers are quite long, and are unique for each user (even for the user accounts in different systems). If you first delete the user account on the local computer or in the domain, and then create a new user account with the same login name, the system will generate a new security ID for that account. There's no possibility of having two identical security Ids. SIDs have the following format: S-1-XXXXX_1-$YYYYY_2$-....-RID, where: S-1—security ID, version 1; XXXXX—authority number, YYYYYn—sub-authority numbers, RID—relative identifier (Relative ID). Notice that the Relative ID (RID) won't be unique for each computer.

NOTE

Also notice that many Windows NT/2000/XP users, even experienced ones, often think that the system identifies each user by his or her credentials—username (or login name) and the password. This isn't so; it's the SID that uniquely identifies the user to the system. User profiles, which will be discussed in detail in *Chapter 10*, are also identified by their associated SIDs.

As aforementioned, most of the user SIDs are unique. However, there are so-called well-known SIDs, whose values are constant for all systems. For example, such SIDs include the following users and groups:

- *Everyone (S-1-1-0)*. The Everyone group will be discussed later in this chapter. For now, let us take notice of the fact that it automatically includes everyone who uses the computer, even users with anonymous guest accounts. The identifier authority value for this SID is 1 (World Authority), while its subauthority value is 0 (Null RID).
- *Creator Owner (S-1-3-0)*. This is the Creator Owner user, serving as a placeholder in an inheritable Access Control Entry (ACE). When the ACE is inherited, the system replaces the SID for Creator Owner with the SID for the object's current owner. The identifier authority value for this SID is 3 (Creator Authority). It has only one subauthority value, 0 (Null RID).

NOTE

A complete list of well-known SIDs in Windows 2000 and Windows XP is provided in the Microsoft Knowledge Base article Q243330—"*Well Known Security Identifiers in Windows 2000 and Windows XP*".

On all computers running Windows NT/2000/XP, access to resources is controlled by Access Control Lists (ACLs) and SIDs. Like Windows NT/2000, Windows XP supports Access Control Lists (ACL) for the registry. You can use ACL to protect registry keys. Actually, ACL represents the database supporting information on access rights to individual operating system objects (in our case, the objects are registry keys).

Notice that in Windows NT/2000 only Regedt32.exe provided access to the ACL for the registry keys. The Regedit.exe version supplied with Windows NT/2000 didn't provide this capability. As compared to Windows NT/2000, Windows XP also provides an improvement in this area. The Regedit.exe version included with this new release now integrates its traditional strong points with the functionality that was earlier available only in Regedt32.exe, including, of course, access to the ACLs and auditing registry key access. Detailed, step-by-step instructions on setting access rights to the registry keys were provided in *Chapter 3*. In this chapter, we'll concentrate on practical tips rather than administrative operations.

First of all, we'll specify the registry keys that have to be secured in order to secure and protect the whole registry.

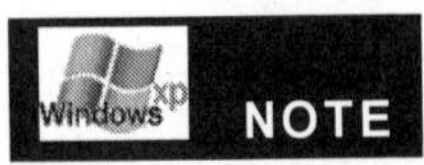

When you're working with Windows XP Professional as part of a workgroup or in a standalone environment, and you have administrator rights to your computer, you'll have access to all of the operating system's security features. If your Windows XP Professional-equipped computer is a part of a domain, your options will be determined by the policies set by the IT administrator.

Standard Access Rights in Windows XP

Standard security settings in Windows XP are defined by default access rights that are set for the following built-in local security groups:

- *Administrators*. Similarly to Windows 2000, members of the Administrators group have full control of the local computer. They can create or delete user accounts and modify permissions for users and resources. Notice that, by default, this group will include the first user account created when you perform a clean installation of the operating system. If you are performing an upgrade from an earlier Windows NT/2000 version, this group will include existing members of the Administrators group. If your Windows XP computer joins a domain, this group will also include the members of the domain Administrators group.

NOTE

It is strongly recommended that you limit the number of users who belong to the Administrators group, no matter what system you are running—Windows NT/2000 or Windows XP. The reason for this tip is straightforward—the greater the number of members in the Administrators group, the more vulnerable your system will be, because all these accounts (especially if they aren't properly protected with strong passwords) can potentially be used to gain unauthorized access to a computer.

- *Power Users*. Similarly to Windows 2000, this group has fewer rights than Administrators; but at the same time, they have wider access rights and permissions than the Users group. By default, members of this group have Read/Write permissions to other parts of the operating system in addition to their own user profiles. Security settings for this group are similar to the settings that existed in Windows NT 4.0 for the Users group. In Windows 2000 and Windows XP, Power Users can install applications that can later be run by all users, including the Users group. They perform limited sets of administrative tasks, including setting the system date and time, specifying the screen setting, installing printers and configuring power management. Members of this group can also run non-certified applications that will not run successfully under the Users. When computers running Windows NT 4.0 are upgraded to Windows XP, all users are added to the Power Users group.
- *Users*. As with Windows 2000, when you install a new copy of the Windows XP operating system (instead of upgrading from a previous version) on the NTFS partition, the standard settings of the security subsystem are configured so that the users from this group can't break the integrity of the operating system and installed applications. For example, users have Read/Write access only to their own user profiles, they can't modify registry settings that influence the whole configuration or change the operating system files. Users belonging to this group have no rights to install applications that can be used by others in this group (this is one of the measures used to protect against worms and Trojans). Microsoft also recommends that you include all end users into the Users group to protect your system integrity. Each application needed for everyday work must be installed by Administrators or Power Users. Members of the Users

group can't install most legacy applications. Typically, only applications that are certified for Windows XP run successfully under the secure Users context. With regard to the applications certified for use with Windows 2000, users might need to have Power Users privileges; therefore, it is necessary to test all your applications at the privilege levels of the users who need to run them.

- *Guests*. Default Windows XP security settings deny access to the application and system event logs for the members of the Guests group. In all other aspects, members of the Guests group have the same access rights as members of the Users group. This allows occasional or one-time users to log on to a workstation's built-in Guest account and be granted limited abilities. Members of the Guests group can also shut down the system.
- *Backup Operators*. Members of this group can back up and restore files on the computer, regardless of the permissions that protect those files. They can also log on to the computer and shut it down, but they cannot change security settings.
- *Replicators*. Members of this group are allowed to replicate files across a domain.
- *Network Configuration Operators*. Members of this group have limited administrative privileges that allow them to configure networking features, such as IP address assignment.
- *HelpServicesGroup*. Members of this group can utilize helper applications to diagnose system problems. This account can be used by members of Microsoft Help and Support Services to access the computer from the network and to log on locally.
- *Remote Desktop Users*. Members of this group have the right to log on locally.

As mentioned earlier, if your Windows XP Professional-based computer participates in a domain, your options will be determined by the security policies set by the domain administrator. Domain controllers contain local versions of all groups listed above and a number of additional server-specific built-in groups.

Default Access Rights to the Windows 2000 and Windows XP File System Objects and Registry Keys

Standard security settings are specified by Security Configuration Manager during the operating system installation when the GUI setup starts. If you perform a clean

installation of Windows XP, the *%SystemRoot%*\inf\defltwk.inf security template will be used (notice that upgrades from Windows 9*x* platforms are treated as clean installs). If you are upgrading from Windows NT/2000, Security Configuration Manager will use the *%SystemRoot%*\inf\DWUp.inf security template.

Notice that security settings for the file system objects can be set only if you choose to install Windows 2000 or Windows XP on the NTFS partition, and are unavailable with the FAT or FAT32 file systems.

As was already discussed, for standalone computers or computers participating in a workgroup, users belonging to the Administrators group have unlimited access to all file system and registry objects. Users and Power Users have a more restricted set of access rights. Access rights to the file system objects assigned by default to the Users and Power Users groups are listed in Table 9.1. These standard access rights to the file system objects are assigned to Power Users and Users groups only if you install Windows 2000/XP fresh on the NTFS partition. If not mentioned specifically, access rights specified in the table are applicable to the directory, all subdirectories, and files.

Here: *%SystemDir%* is the *%SystemRoot%*\System32 folder, RX means "Read and Execute", and the *.* mark specifies all the files contained within current directory (but not other nested directories).

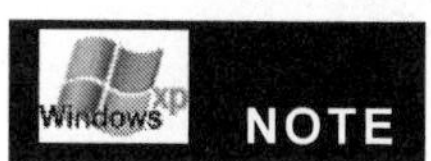

Windows XP includes a new root ACL, which is also implemented by `Format` and `Convert` commands. In addition to the previous releases, the Security Configuration Manager now secures the root directory during setup, if the current root security descriptor grants the Everyone group the Full Control permission. This provides increased security for non-Windows directories. The new Windows XP root ACL is as follows:

- Administrators, System: Full Control (Container Inherit, Object Inherit)
- Creator Owner: Full Control (Container Inherit, Object Inherit, Inherit Only)
- Everyone: Read\Execute (No Inheritance)
- Users: Read\Execute (Container Inherit, Object Inherit)
- Users: Create Directory (Container Inherit)
- Users: Add File (Container Inherit, Inherit Only)

Table 9.1. Default Windows 2000/XP Access Rights to File System Objects

File system object	Default access rights for Power Users	Default access rights for Users
c:\boot.ini	RX	None
c:\ntdetect.com	RX	None
c:\ntldr	RX	None
c:\ntbootdd.sys	RX	None
c:\autoexec.bat	Modify	RX
c:\config.sys	Modify	RX
\ProgramFiles	Modify	RX
%SystemRoot%	Modify	RX
*%SystemRoot%**.*	RX	RX
%SystemRoot%\config*.*	RX	RX
%SystemRoot%\cursors*.*	RX	RX
%SystemRoot%\Temp	Modify	Synchronize, Traverse, Add File, Add Subdir
%SystemRoot%\repair	Modify	List
%SystemRoot%\addins	Modify (directories and subdirectories); RX (files)	RX
%SystemRoot%\Connection Wizard	Modify (directories and subdirectories); RX (files)	RX
%SystemRoot%\fonts*.*	RX	RX
%SystemRoot%\help*.*	RX	RX
%SystemRoot%\inf*.*	RX	RX
%SystemRoot%\java	Modify (directories and subdirectories); RX (files)	RX
%SystemRoot%\media*.*	RX	RX
%SystemRoot%\msagent	Modify (directories and subdirectories); RX (files)	RX

continues

Table 9.1 Continued

File system object	Default access rights for Power Users	Default access rights for Users
%SystemRoot%\security	RX	RX
%SystemRoot%\speech	Modify (directories and subdirectories); RX (files)	RX
%SystemRoot%\system*.*	Read, Execute	RX
%SystemRoot%\twain_32	Modify (directories and subdirectories); RX (files)	RX
%SystemRoot%\Web	Modify (directories and subdirectories); RX (files)	RX
%SystemDir%	Modify	RX
*%SystemDir%**.*	RX	RX
%SystemDir%\config	List	List
%SystemDir%\dhcp	RX	RX
%SystemDir%\dllcache	None	None
%SystemDir%\drivers	RX	RX
%SystemDir%\CatRoot	Modify (directories and subdirectories); RX (files)	RX
%SystemDir%\ias	Modify (directories and subdirectories); RX (files)	RX
%SystemDir%\mui	Modify (directories and subdirectories); RX (files)	RX
%SystemDir%\OS2*.*	RX	RX
%SystemDir%\OS2\DLL*.*	RX	RX
%SystemDir%\RAS*.*	RX	RX
%SystemDir%\ShellExt	Modify (directories and subdirectories); RX (files)	RX

continues

Table 9.1 Continued

File system object	Default access rights for Power Users	Default access rights for Users
%SystemDir%\Viewers*.*	RX	RX
%SystemDir%\wbem	Modify (directories and subdirectories); RX (files)	RX
%SystemDir%\wbem\mof	Modify	RX
%UserProfile%	Full Control	Full Control
All Users	Modify	Read
All Users\Documents	Modify	Read, Create File
All Users\Application Data	Modify	Read

Power Users can write new files into directories (the list is provided below), but can't modify files that were written to these directories during Windows 2000 installation. All members of the Power Users group inherit Modify access to all the files created in these directories by a member of their group.

- *%SystemRoot%*
- *%SystemRoot%*\Config
- *%SystemRoot%*\cursors
- *%SystemRoot%*\fonts
- *%SystemRoot%*\help
- *%SystemRoot%*\inf
- *%SystemRoot%*\media
- *%SystemRoot%*\system
- *%SystemDir%*
- *%SystemDir%*\OS2
- *%SystemDir%*\OS2\DLL
- *%SystemDir%*\RAS
- *%SystemDir%*\Viewers

Power Users can write new files to all the directories, subdirectories, and RX files that they have Modify access to (see Table 9.1). All other members of the Power Users group will have Read access to these files.

Table 9.2 lists Windows 2000/XP registry key permissions, assigned by default to members of the Users and Power Users groups. Access rights to individual registry objects are inherited by its child objects, except when the child object itself is listed in this table.

Table 9.2. Windows 2000 Default Registry Key Permissions Assigned to Users and Power Users

Registry object	Permissions for Power Users	Permissions for Users
HKEY_LOCAL_MACHINE		
HKLM\Software	Modify	Read
HKLM\SW\Classes\helpfile	Read	Read
HKLM\SW\Classes\.hlp	Read	Read
HKLM\SW\MS\Command Processor	Read	Read
HKLM\SW\MS\Cryptography	Read	Read
HKLM\SW\MS\Driver Signing	Read	Read
HKLM\SW\MS\EnterpriseCertificates	Read	Read
HKLM\SW\MS\Non-Driver Signing	Read	Read
HKLM\SW\MS\NetDDE	None	None
HKLM\SW\MS\Ole	Read	Read
HKLM\SW\MS\Rpc	Read	Read
HKLM\SW\MS\Secure	Read	Read
HKLM\SW\MS\SystemCertificates	Read	Read
HKLM\SW\MS\Windows\CV\RunOnce	Read	Read
HKLM\SW\MS\W NT\CV\DiskQuota	Read	Read
HKLM\SW\MS\W NT\CV\Drivers32	Read	Read
HKLM\SW\MS\W NT\CV\Font Drivers	Read	Read
HKLM\SW\MS\W NT\CV\FontMapper	Read	Read
HKLM\SW\MS\W NT\CV \Image File Execution Options	Read	Read
HKLM\SW\MS\W NT\CV\IniFileMapping	Read	Read
HKLM\SW\MS\W NT\CV\Perflib	Read (through Interactive)	Read (through Interactive)
HKLM\SW\MS\W NT\CV\SecEdit	Read	Read
HKLM\SW\MS\W NT\CV\Time Zones	Read	Read
HKLM\SW\MS\W NT\CV\Windows	Read	Read

continues

Table 9.2 Continued

Registry object	Permissions for Power Users	Permissions for Users
HKLM\SW\MS\W NT\CV\Winlogon	Read	Read
HKLM\SW\MS\W NT\CV\AsrCommands	Read	Read
HKLM\SW\MS\W NT\CV\Classes	Read	Read
HKLM\SW\MS\W NT\CV\Console	Read	Read
HKLM\SW\MS\W NT\CV\ProfileList	Read	Read
HKLM\SW\MS\W NT\CV\Svchost	Read	Read
HKLM\SW\Policies	Read	Read
HKLM\System	Read	Read
HKLM\SYSTEM\CCS\Control \SecurePipeServers\winreg	None	None
HKLM\SYSTEM\CCS\Control \Session Manager\Executive	Modify	Read
HKLM\SYSTEM\CCS\Control \TimeZoneInformation	Modify	Read
HKLM\SYSTEM\CCS\Control\WMI\Securi ty	None	None
HKLM\Hardware	Read (through Everyone)	Read (through Everyone)
HKLM\SAM	Read (through Everyone)	Read (through Everyone)
HKLM\Security	None	None
HKEY_USERS		
USERS\.DEFAULT	Read	Read
USERS\.DEFAULT\SW\MS\NetDDE	None	None
HKEY_CURRENT_CONFIG	= HKLM\System\CCS\HardwareProfiles \Current	
HKEY_CURRENT_USER	Full Control	Full Control
HKEY_CLASSES_ROOT	= HKLM\SW\Classes	

Here:

- HKLM = HKEY_LOCAL_MACHINE
- SW = Software

- MS = Microsoft
- CV = CurrentVersion
- CCS = CurrentControlSet
- W NT = Windows NT

File Sharing and Permissions in Windows XP

Like previous releases of Windows NT/2000, Windows XP enables you to share files with other users on your local system and across the network. However, Windows XP Home Edition and Windows XP Professional introduces new user interface known as Simple File Sharing (Fig. 9.3), and also includes a new Shared Documents feature, which we will consider here in detail.

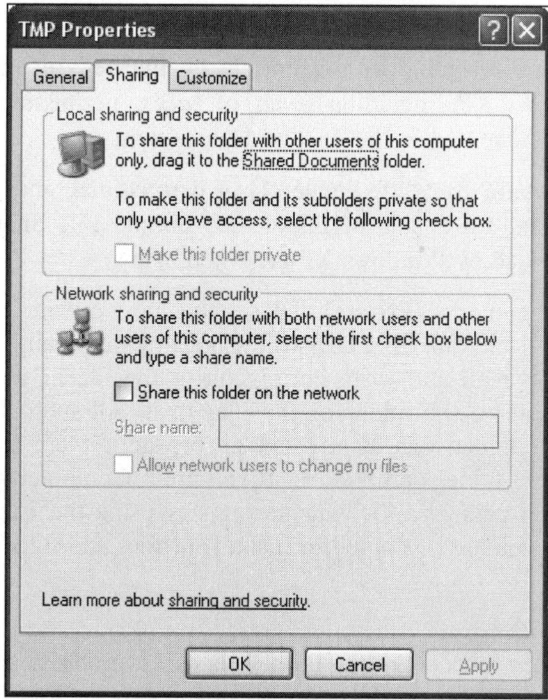

Fig. 9.3. The Simple File Sharing user interface

The Simple File Sharing is enabled by default for computers running Windows XP Home Edition and for Windows XP Professional-based computers that participate in a workgroup. However, the interesting point is, if you start in the Safe mode, the classic ACL editor is displayed instead of Simple File Sharing. Also, if you join your Windows XP Professional-based computer to a domain, only the classic Windows 2000-style file sharing and security interface will be available.

However, you can disable the Simple File Sharing UI by simply starting the Folder Options applet in Control Panel, navigating to the **View** tab and clearing the **Use Simple File Sharing (Recommended)** checkbox.

NOTE

If you disable Simple File Sharing, you'll get more control over the permissions to individual users. Notice, however, that in this case you must have advanced knowledge of NTFS and share permissions to keep your folders and files secure. Also note that the Shared Documents feature is not turned off by disabling the Simple File Sharing.

The tip explaining how to disable Simple File Sharing was already provided in *Chapter 4.* Here, we are going to concentrate on the new security features introduced with Windows XP, including levels of access permissions, which, by the way, are poorly documented in the on-line Help system.

Windows XP allows for five different levels of permissions, and this configuration is not affected when you enable or disable the Simple File Sharing feature. Permission levels provided by Windows XP are listed below:

- *Level 1:* My Documents (Private). This is the most private and secure setting. This level is available only to a user who is logging on locally. The owner of the file or folder has read and write permission to the file or folder. Nobody else may read or write to the folder or the files in it. All subfolders that are contained within a folder that is marked as private remain private unless you change the parent folder permissions. If you are a Computer Administrator and you create a user password for your account by using the User Accounts Control Panel tool, you are prompted to make your files and folder private.

NOTE

The option to make a folder private (Level 1) is only available to a user account in its own My Documents folder. To configure a folder and all of the files in it to Level 1, right-click the folder, then click **Sharing and Security**, then set the **Make this Folder Private** checkbox and click **OK**. When you make a folder private, it will have the following local NTFS permissions: Owner—Full Control, System—Full Control, the folder is not shared across the network.

- *Level 2:* Default sharing. Files stored in My Documents folders are at this level by default. Level 2 folders are available only to a user who logs on locally. The owner of the file or folder and local Computer Administrators have read and write permission, and no other user can read or write to the folder or the files in it. This is the default setting for all of the folders and files in each user's My Documents folder. To configure a folder and all of the files in it to Level 2, right-click the folder, go to the **Sharing and Security** tab, and ensure that both the **Make this Folder Private** and the **Share this folder on the network** checkboxes are cleared, and then click **OK**. When you configure the folder at Level 2, the following local NTFS permissions are set: Owner—Full Control, Administrators—Full Control, System—Full Control, the folder is not shared across the network.
- *Level 3:* Files in shared documents available to local users. To configure Level 3, simply copy a file or folder into the Shared Documents folder under My Computer. Level 3 folders are available only to a user who is logging on locally. When you configure a folder at Level 3, the files are shared with users who log on locally. Local Administrators will be able to read, write, and delete the files in such folders, while restricted users will be able only to read the files. The Power Users group is only available in Windows XP Professional. Remote users cannot access folders or files at Level 3. When you configure the folder to Level 3, the following local NTFS permissions will be set: Owner—Full Control, Administrators—Full Control, Power Users—Change, Restricted Users—Read, System—Full Control. The folder will not be shared across the network
- *Level 4:* Shared Files on the Network (Readable by Everyone) Level 4 folders are available both to the users who log on locally and to the users who log on via the network. Files are shared for everyone to read on the network. All local users, including the Guest account, can read the files, but they cannot modify the contents. Any user that can connect to your computer on the network is able to read and change your files. To configure a folder and all of the files in it to Level 4, right-click the folder, select **Sharing and Security**, click to select the **Share this folder on the network** checkbox, but don't set the **Allow network users to change my files** check box. When you configure the folder at Level 4, the following local NTFS permissions will be set: Owner—Full Control, Administrators—Full Control, System—Full Control, Everyone—Read. The folder will be shared across the network with the following network share permissions: Everyone—Read.
- *Level 5:* Shared Files on the Network (Readable and Writable by Everyone)—the most public and changeable (non-secure) setting. Level 5 folders are available both to the users who log on locally and to the users who log on via the networking. This level is recommended only for a closed protected network

working. This level is recommended only for a closed protected network that has a firewall configured. All local users, including the Guest account, can read and modify the files as well. To configure a folder and all of the files in it to Level 5, right-click the folder, select **Sharing and Security**, then set the **Share this folder on the network** and **Allow network users to change my files** check-boxes. When you configure the folder at Level 5, the following local NTFS permissions will be set: Owner—Full Control, Administrators—Full Control, System—Full Control, Everyone—Change. The folder will be shared across the network, and the Everyone group will have Full Control access to it.

NOTE

Users who log on locally include a user who logs on to a Windows XP Professional-based computer from a Remote Desktop (RDP) session.

Levels of permissions provided by Windows XP are described in Table 9.3.

Table 9.3. Levels of Permissions Provided by Windows XP

Access Level	Everyone (NTFS/File)	Owner	System	Administrators	Everyone (Share)
Level 1	Not available	Full Control	Full Control	Not available	Not available
Level 2	Not/available	Full Control	Full Control	Full Control	Not available
Level 3	Read	Full Control	Full Control	Full Control	Not available
Level 4	Read	Full Control	Full Control	Full Control	Read
Level 5	Change	Full Control	Full Control	Full Control	Full Control

NOTES

All NTFS permissions that refer to the Everyone group include the Guest account. All of the levels that are described above are mutually exclusive. Private folders (Level 1) cannot be shared unless they are no longer private. Shared folders (Level 4 and 5) cannot be made private until they are unshared. If you create a folder in the Shared Documents folder (Level 3), share it on the network, and then allow network users to change your files (Level 5), the permissions for Level 5 are effective for the folder, the files in that folder, child folders, and so on.

Advanced users note that NTFS permissions are not maintained on file move operations when you use Windows Explorer with Simple File Sharing enabled.

If you enable and disable Simple File Sharing, the permissions on files are not changed. The NTFS and share permissions do not change until you change the permissions in the interface. If you set the permissions with Simple File Sharing enabled, only Access Control Entries (ACEs) on files that are used for Simple File Sharing are affected. The following ACEs in the Access Control List (ACL) of the files or folders are affected by the Simple File Sharing interface:

- ❒ Owner
- ❒ Administrators
- ❒ Everyone
- ❒ System

Registry Setting to Show the Classic Security UI

When security settings are set in Windows XP, the following registry key is used (Fig. 9.4):

```
HKEY_LOCAL_MACHINE\SYSTEM\CurrentControlSet\Control\Lsa
```

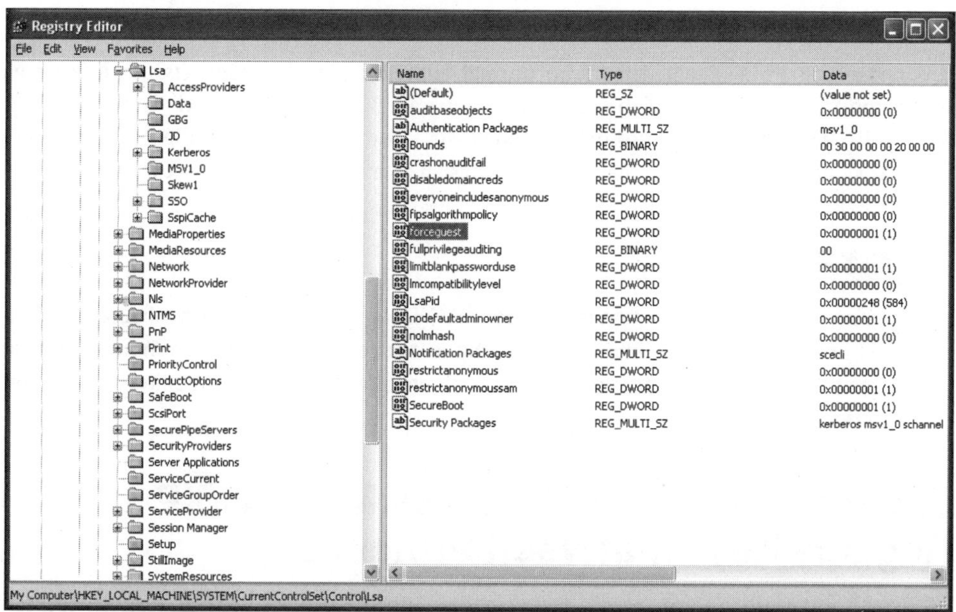

Fig. 9.4. The contents of the `HKEY_LOCAL_MACHINE\SYSTEM\CurrentControlSet\Control\Lsa` registry key

Find the `forceguest` value with the `REG_DWORD` data type. This value entry can take the values of 1 (force guests on) or 0 (force the guests off), which influences the behavior of the Sharing UI and ACL editor behavior.

The default value for the `ForceGuest` registry entry and its influence on the Sharing UI and ACL editor behavior.

Table 9.4. Influence of the ForceGuest Registry Value on the Sharing UI and ACL Editor Behavior

Operating system and mode	ForceGuest	Sharing UI	ACL editor
Windows XP Home Edition	1 (no choice)	Simple	Not available
Windows XP Home Edition in Safe mode	1 (no choice)	Classic	Available
Windows XP Professional	0*	Classic	Available
Windows XP Professional	1	Simple	Not available
Windows XP Professional in Safe mode	0	Classic	Available
Windows XP Professional in Safe mode	1	Classic	Available

* Windows XP Professional defaults to normal authentication but supports the **Log on as Guest** option. For example, if the computer is upgraded from Windows XP Home Edition, Microsoft Windows 95, Microsoft Windows 98, and Microsoft Windows 98 Second Edition, Windows XP Professional uses the **Guest if in a workgroup** option by default.

NOTE

You cannot share a folder that is located in My Documents after you configure the simple Sharing and Security setting to **Only I have access to this folder**. When security is set for the parent folder, security is set on all child folders; security settings cannot be changed from the child folders.

The Most Important Windows NT/2000/XP Registry Keys that Need Protection

Microsoft officially recommends that system administrators restrict user access to certain subkeys under `HKEY_LOCAL_MACHINE\SOFTWARE`. The purpose of this restriction is to prevent unauthorized access to the software settings.

NOTE

Microsoft officially recommends system administrators to restrict user access to the following registry keys:

HKEY_LOCAL_MACHINE\SOFTWARE\Microsoft\Windows NT\CurrentVersion and HKEY_LOCAL_MACHINE\SOFTWARE\Microsoft\Windows\CurrentVersion.

For the Everyone group, it's sufficient to have the Query Value, Enumerate Subkeys, Notify and Read Control rights to the HKEY_LOCAL_MACHINE\SOFTWARE\Microsoft\Windows NT\CurrentVersion registry key and the following subkeys under this key: AeDebug, Compatibility, Drivers, Embedding, Font Drivers, FontCache, FontMapper, Fonts, FontSubstitutes, GRE_Initialize, MCI, MCI Extensions, Ports (and all its subkeys), Type 1 Installer, Windows 3.1 MigrationStatus (and all its subkeys), WOW (and all its subkeys).

The same set of access rights (Query Value, Enumerate Subkeys, Notify and Read Control) needs to be assigned to the Everyone group for the Uninstall, Run, and RunOnce subkeys under HKEY_LOCAL_MACHINE\SOFTWARE \Microsoft\Windows\CurrentVersion.

Microsoft also recommends that you restrict user access to the HKEY_LOCAL_MACHINE\SOFTWARE\Microsoft\Windows NT\CurrentVersion\Perflib key that stores the data, which governs the system performance. In Windows NT 4.0, the Everyone group by default has Read access to this key (it's recommended that you delete this group from the Perflib ACL). As shown in Fig. 9.5, this key can be accessed only by the operating system (System), the user who created the key (Creator owner), and system administrators and users who've logged on to the system interactively (Interactive).

The Everyone group has restricted access rights (only Query Value, Enumerate Subkeys, Notify and Read Control) to other registry keys, including HKEY_CLASSES_ROOT root key and all its subkeys, and for the HKEY_USERS\.DEFAULT key. By protecting these keys, you protect important system settings from changes (for example, this will prevent users from changing the filename extension associations or specifying new security settings for Internet Explorer).

Furthermore, it's necessary to restrict the Everyone group access to keys such as HKEY_LOCAL_MACHINE\SYSTEM\CurrentControlSet\Services\LanmanServer\Shares and HKEY_LOCAL_MACHINE\SYSTEM\CurrentControlSet\Services\UPS. The Everyone group only needs the rights to the following keys: Query Value, Enumerate Subkeys, Notify and Read Control. By setting these restrictions, you'll prevent unauthorized access to shared system resources and to using the ImagePath setting under the UPS key for starting undesirable software. Only the operating system (System) and members of the Administrators group need Full Control access to these keys.

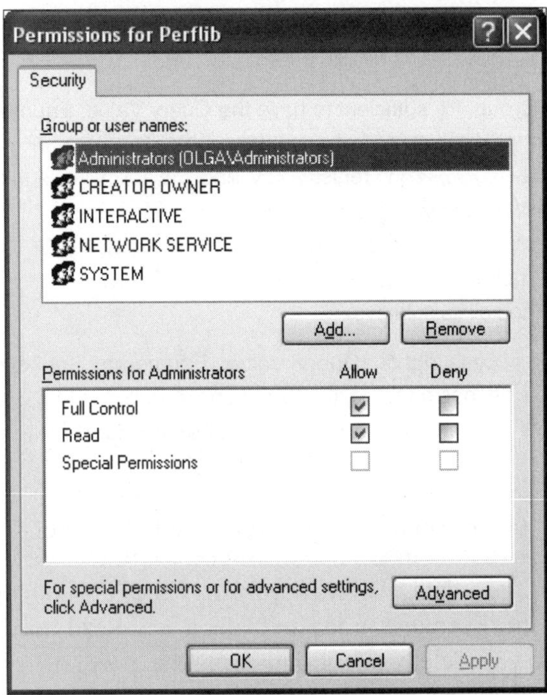

Fig. 9.5. Restricting access to the `HKEY_LOCAL_MACHINE\SOFTWARE\Microsoft\Windows NT\CurrentVersion\Perflib` registry key

Finally, pay close attention to the `Run`, `RunOnce`, and `RunOnceEx` registry keys under `HKEY_LOCAL_MACHINE\SOFTWARE\Microsoft\Windows\CurrentVersion`. For example, the system runs all the programs listed under the `RunOnceEx` key only once, and then deletes the settings specifying the starting parameters for these programs. It's easy to see that these registry settings may allow users to run undesirable software on the local computer. Thus, Full Control access to this key should only be provided to the operating system (System) and members of the Administrators group.

NOTE

It's necessary to mention one more registry key, which is also very important in terms of security. When you work with the Remote Access Service (RAS), the system sometimes displays dialogs prompting you to enter a login name and password. These dialogs often contain checkboxes, which allow you to save the password (for example, **Save This Password** or **Remember This Password**). Although this feature is very convenient for end users, it can possibly be very dangerous, because the passwords are stored in such a way that they can be easily retrieved by the system (and, for that matter, by anyone else). This is especially important for those of you working with laptops and other portable computers, because if your machine is lost or stolen, the person who finds (or steals) it will have access to all your networks.

The easiest method of protecting yourself against this risk is to disable the feature for saving RAS passwords on RAS clients. Open the `HKEY_LOCAL_MACHINE\SYSTEM\CurrentControlSet\Services\RemoteAccess\Parameters` key and add the `REG_DWORD` setting named DisableSavePassword. Now the system won't prompt you to save your RAS password.

Protecting the Registry Against Unauthorized Remote Access

The remote access to the registry is very convenient when the system administrator needs to support end users from his own workplace. However, in some cases, this capability may be potentially dangerous, that's why remote access must be authorized.

When you attempt to connect the registry of the remote Windows NT/2000 system, the Server service will check if there's an `HKEY_LOCAL_MACHINE\System\CurrentControlSet\Control\SecurePipeServers\Winreg` key in that registry (Fig. 9.6). Getting remote access to the registry is made possible with the following factors:

- If there isn't a \Winreg key in the registry you want to protect, then any remote user will have access to the registry. This user will be able to manipulate your registry within the limits defined by its ACL.
- If there's a \Winreg subkey, then the Access Control List defined for this key will specify who can access the registry remotely. (But remember that Back Orifice 2000, or BO2K, allows remote access to the registry. However, someone must install its server part on your system).

This means that to protect your system from unauthorized remote access, you need to configure the ACL for the following registry key `HKEY_LOCAL_MACHINE\System\CurrentControlSet\Control\SecurePipeServers\Winreg`.

If the ACL for `Winreg` key provides the remote user's read or write access (explicitly or through group membership), the user will be able to connect to the

Windows NT/2000/XP registry remotely. After establishing the connection, the user rights will be restricted only by his access rights to individual keys. Thus, if the user has Read access to the Winreg key, this will provide him access to other registry keys (if this is allowed by their ACLs).

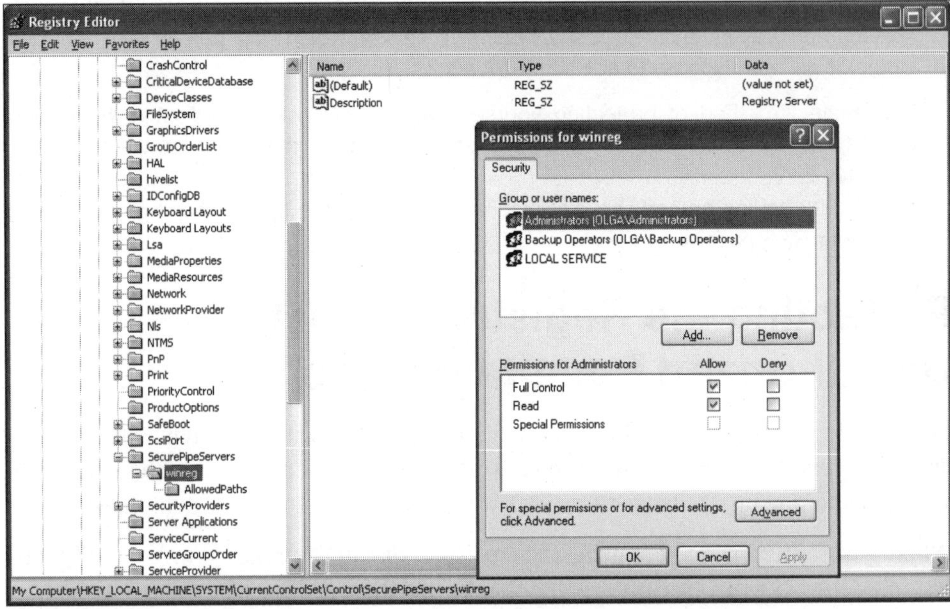

Fig. 9.6. Configuring the Access Control List for `HKEY_LOCAL_MACHINE\SYSTEM\CurrentControlSet\Control\SecurePipeServers\Winreg`

NOTE

You only need to create the \Winreg key on the computers running Windows NT 4.0 Workstation. Windows NT 4.0 Server, Windows 2000 Professional and Windows 2000 Server contain this key by default, and system administrators have Full Control access to this key.

Protecting SAM and Security Hives

Windows NT/2000/XP security information is stored in the SAM (Security Accounts Manager) and Security registry hives. The SAM hive contains user passwords as a table of hash codes; the Security hive stores security information for the local system, including user rights and permissions, password policies and group membership.

NOTE

The SAM information is encrypted. However, there are many utilities that allow you to crack the SAM hive. The most common examples are PWDUMP, NT Crack, and L0phtCrack (the latest version is LC3).

How to Protect the SAM Hive

Microsoft officially states that the best method of protecting Windows NT/2000/XP is protecting administrative passwords. This, however, isn't enough. Many users can access the SAM and Security hives, including members of the Backup Operators group, whose responsibility is registry backup.

By default, no user (even the Administrator) has necessary access rights that would allow them to access or view the SAM database using the registry editor. However, the SAM and Security hives are stored on the hard disk, the same as all the other files. All you need to do is to get the copies of these files. Of course, you can't do it by simply copying the registry of the running Windows NT/2000/XP system. If you make such an attempt, you'll get an error message (Fig. 9.7).

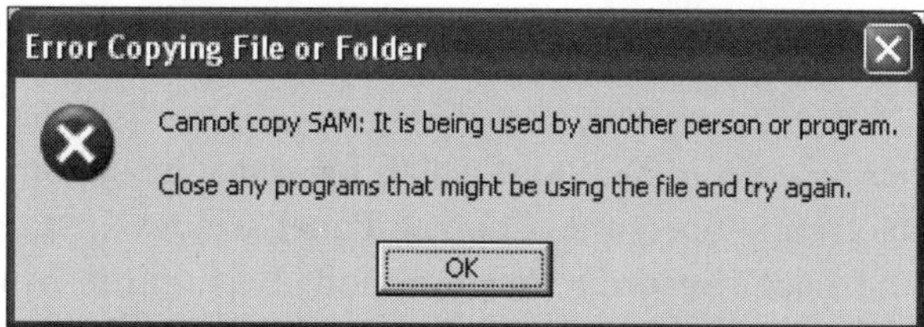

Fig. 9.7. When an attempt to copy the registry of the running Windows NT/2000/XP is made, the system displays an error message

However, there are tools such as Regback included with Windows NT 4.0 Resource Kit and REG included with Windows 2000 Resource Kit. By using these tools, members of Administrators or Backup Operators groups can obtain copies of the registry even if the system is up and running.

If Windows NT/2000 is installed on the FAT volume, then anyone who can reboot the system and has physical access to the computer can copy the Windows NT/2000 registry. They need only to reboot the system, start MS-DOS or Windows 95/98, and copy the SAM and Security hives from the *%SystemRoot%*\System32\Config folder.

NOTE

If Windows NT/2000 is installed on NTFS volume, you can use the NTFSDOS utility for copying the SAM and Security hives (you can download it from **http://www.sysinternals.com/ntfs30.htm**). NTFSDOS mounts NTFS volumes under DOS. This utility and its clones (for example, NTFS for Windows 98) causes different, and sometimes negative, reactions (because of the potential risk to the security subsystem). When the first version of NTFSDOS appeared, Microsoft had to state officially that "true security is physical security". NTFSDOS, though, is one of the most useful tools for registry backup and recovery and may be very helpful when performing emergency recovery (especially if this has to be done very quickly).

To summarize, in order to protect the SAM and Security files from unauthorized copying, you need to provide true physical security for the computers you need to protect. Also, don't assign every user the right to reboot the system.

NOTE

By default, this privilege is assigned to Administrators, Backup Operators, Power Users, and Users on Windows 2000/XP workstations. On member servers, it is assigned to Administrators, Power Users, and Backup Operators. On domain controllers, it is assigned to Administrators, Account Operators, Backup Operators, Print Operators, and Server Operators.

To edit the user permissions in Windows 2000, log onto the system as a member of the Administrators group, open the **Control Panel** windows, start **Administrative Tools** and select the **Local Security Policy** option. Expand the MMC tree and select the **User Rights Assignment** option. The list of user rights will appear in the right pane of this window (Fig. 9.8).

Now, can we say that the Windows NT/2000/XP is secure? No, we can't, because there are backup copies of the registry. In Windows NT 4.0, backup copies of the registry are created immediately after a successful setup or whenever you start the `Rdisk/s` command. The backup copies of the registry are stored in the *%SystemRoot%*\Repair directory. Backup copies of the Windows 2000 registry are created whenever you backup the System State Data. As you may recall, all this information is stored in the *%SystemRoot%*\Repair\Regback folder. These files aren't in use by the system, and any user who has appropriate access rights can copy them. In Windows NT 4.0, systems NTFS access rights don't protect the *%SystemRoot%*\Repair directory. Every user has Read access to this directory, and that's enough to copy the files. In Windows 2000, the Users group by default only has the List permission for this directory, and this permission doesn't allow you to copy the files. If you installed your system as an upgrade from earlier versions of Windows NT, though, access rights to the registry and file system objects will be inherited from the previous system.

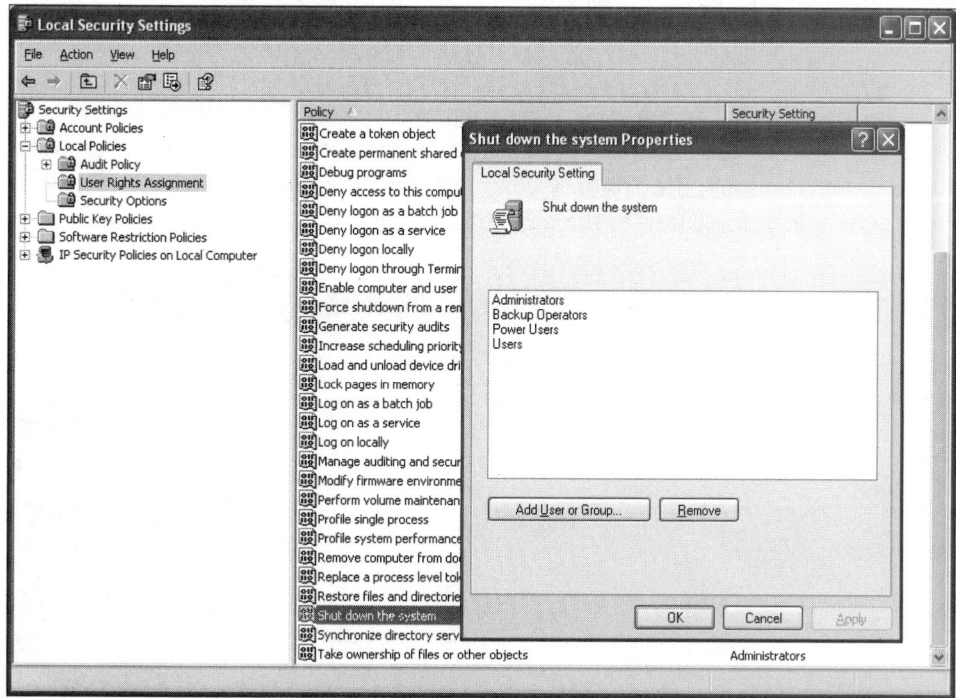

Fig. 9.8. Editing the list of Windows 2000/XP user groups allowed to reboot the system

Thus, to prevent unauthorized copying of the SAM and Security files, you need to do the following:

- Don't assign end users permission to log on locally on the servers
- Whenever possible, use NTFS file system
- Provide physical security for all servers
- In Windows NT 4.0 and in Windows 2000/XP systems upgraded from earlier Windows NT versions, restrict access rights to the *%SystemRoot%*\Repair folder
- Secure the backup copies of the registry and emergency repair disks (Windows NT 4.0) or System State Data (Windows 2000 and Windows XP)

You may ask "But what happens if someone steals my SAM and Security hives?" The answer is very simple: You don't need serious hacking skills to crack the stolen SAM. If you have these files at your disposal, you can make any number of dictionary or brute force attacks. And if you have LC3 at your disposal (which can be downloaded from **http://www.atstake.com/lc3** and represents a new version of the well-known L0phtCrack password-auditing tool), your success mainly depends on the quality of the dictionary you use (Fig. 9.9).

Thus, to protect the system, you need to prevent users from setting blank passwords and restrict the password policy. (Or at least require that passwords be at least 8 characters long, use arbitrary combinations of letters and digits, and specify the system policy in relation to the password complexity).

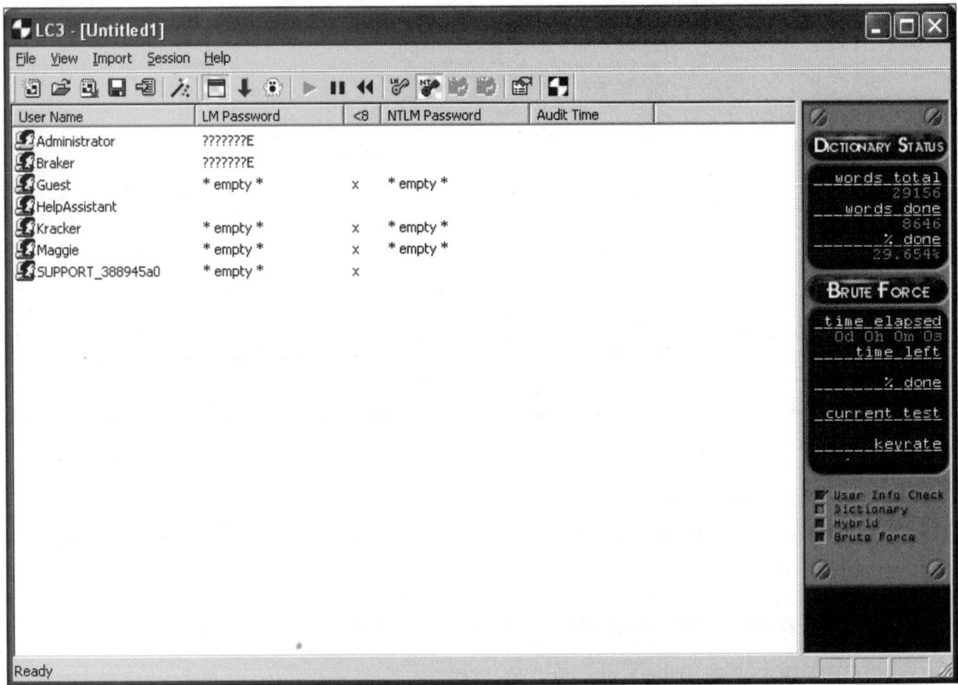

Fig. 9.9. Weak passwords are cracked by LC3 within a matter of minutes

NOTE

Imagine that you want to hack your own SAM hive (and then try to do it). Remember, your tasks are significantly easier than those of the hacker, because you don't need to plan a remote attack to steal the SAM and Security hives. If you can crack some passwords automatically, explain to the users who've specified these passwords that they're compromising the system security.

Restricting Anonymous Access to the Computer

As was previously mentioned, on Windows NT/2000/XP computers all access to resources is controlled by ACLs and SIDs. Each resource has an ACL containing SIDs of all users and groups who have been granted permissions to access that resource. When the users log on, either locally or over the network, they obtain access tokens containing the SIDs of their user account and of all security groups their accounts are members of. When the user tries to access a resource, Windows checks the SIDs in the access token to the ACL of the resource. If the SIDs match, access is granted, otherwise the user is denied access.

Restricting Anonymous Access in Windows 2000

Anonymous users or services that log on anonymously are automatically added to the Anonymous Logon built-in security group. In earlier versions of Windows NT, such users or services were able to access many resources (sometimes the ones access to which should be granted only to authenticated users). Windows 2000 introduced stricter security settings than the ones available in Windows NT 4.0. The Windows 2000 system may be configured in such a way as to prevent anonymous access to all resources, except for those who were explicitly assigned access. You can do this by using the Local Security Policy MMC snap-in or by editing the registry directly.

Using the Local Security Policy MMC Snap-In

1. From the **Start** menu select **Programs | Administrative Tools | Local Security Policy**.
2. Select **Security Settings | Local Policies | Security Options**.
3. Go to the right pane of this window and double-click the **Additional restrictions for anonymous connections** option. In the window that opens next, set the

No access without explicit anonymous permissions under Local policy setting option (Fig. 9.10).

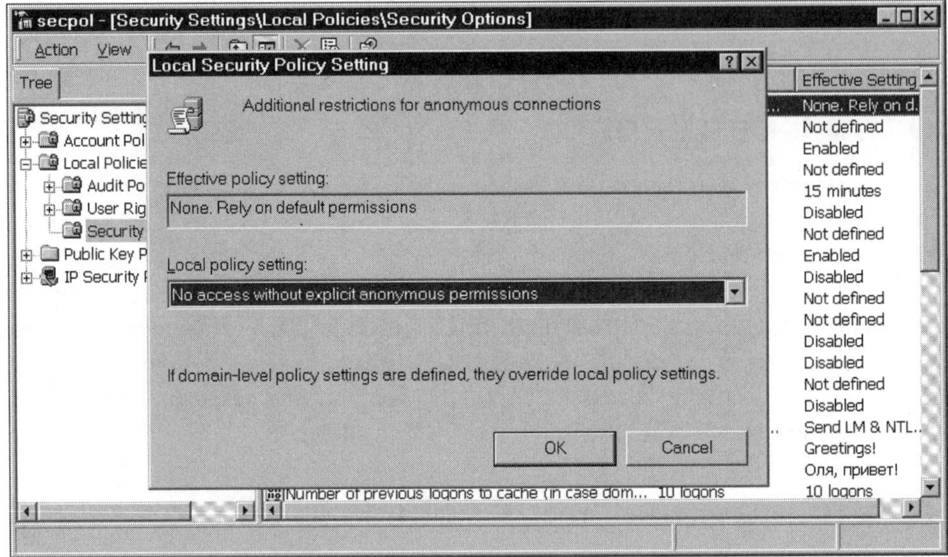

Fig. 9.10. Restricting anonymous access using Local security Policy MMC snap-in (Windows 2000)

Using the Registry Editor

Launch Regedt32.exe, find the `HKEY_LOCAL_MACHINE\SYSTEM\CurrentControlSet\Control\LSA` registry key and create the `REG_DWORD` setting named `RestrictAnonymous`. Set its value to 0x2 (Hex).

If the `RestrictAnonymous` setting is set to this value, then the access token for users who haven't been authenticated isn't included into the Everyone group. The system will deny access to resources that are available for the Everyone group by default.

NOTES

- Before restricting anonymous access to the system, Microsoft recommends that you analyze all the advantages provided by this setting (from a security point of view) in comparison to the possible problems that may be caused by the restriction of anonymous user rights. Some Windows 2000 services and legacy applications depend on the anonymous user. For example, if you have a mixed environment, where you also have Windows NT 4.0 Workstation and Server computers (and even Windows 95/98 systems), it's recommended that you don't set the RestrictAnonymous value to 0x2. If you only have Windows 2000 systems in your network, you can use this setting, but only after carefully testing all of the system services and application programs.

- The standard security template High Secure includes this restriction. If you use this security template in a mixed environment, this may cause problems.
- To be compatible with services that require anonymous access to certain domain data, Windows 2000 has provided a way to switch between high-security settings (the preferred configuration when backward compatibility is not required) to backward compatible security settings that grant anonymous users access as it is required by systems running Windows NT 4.0 and earlier versions of Windows. The Pre-Windows 2000 Compatible Access security group, that was introduced in Windows 2000, controls this security choice. Backward compatibility is achieved on computers that are running Windows 2000 by making the Everyone security group a member of the Pre-Windows 2000 Compatible Access security group. You are able to configure high-security settings by removing all members from the Pre-Windows 2000 Compatible Access group.

Windows XP Enhancements and Compatibility Issues

Windows XP has gone even further than Windows 2000. In contrast to previous versions of Windows, the access token for anonymous users no longer includes the Everyone security group. Therefore, the access token for anonymous users contains SIDs for:

- Anonymous Logon
- The logon type (usually Network)

When an anonymous user tries to access a resource on a computer that is running Windows XP, the anonymous user is not granted permissions or group memberships that are available to the Everyone security group. The SID for the Everyone security group is present in the anonymous user's access token. It should be noted that in most cases this restriction is desirable and appropriate. However, in some situations, for the sake of backward compatibility, you may need to include the Anonymous Logon security group into the Everyone group. For this very purpose Windows XP introduces a new registry value, EveryoneIncludesAnonymous, which can be set using the methods described below.

Using Local Security Policy

To enable anonymous access via MMC, proceed as follows:

1. Start the Administrative Tools applet in Control Panel, and then select either **Local Security Policy** or **Domain Security Policy** (on domain controllers only).
2. Expand the **Security Settings** tree, select **Local Policies**, and then click **Security Options**.
3. Double-click **Network access: Let Everyone permissions apply to anonymous users**. By default, this policy setting is disabled (Fig. 9.11).
4. To enable anonymous users to be members of the Everyone security group, click **Enabled**. To prevent the inclusion of the Everyone security group SID in the anonymous user's access token (the Windows XP default), click **Disabled**.

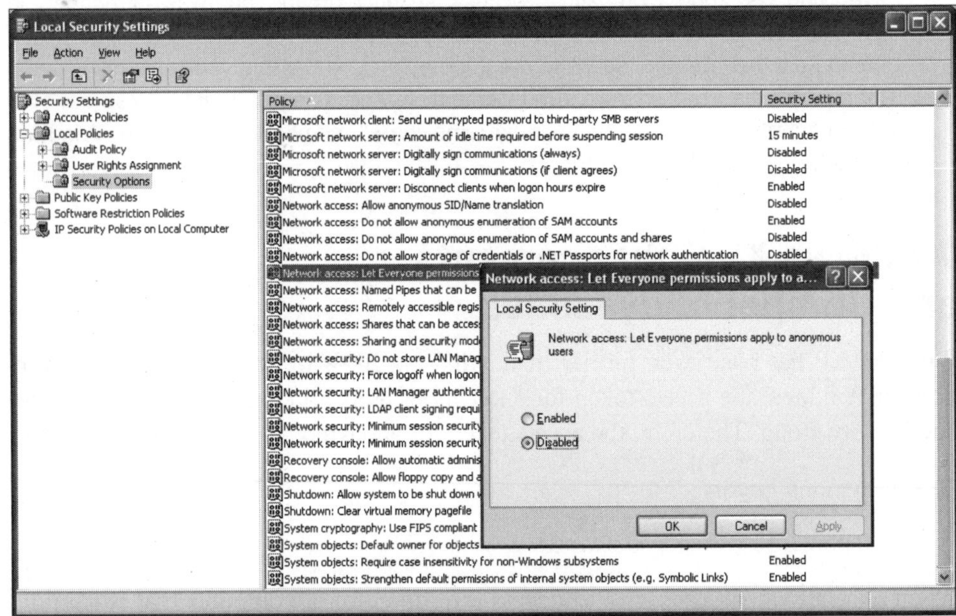

Fig. 9.11. Setting EveryoneIncludesAnonymous registry value via Local Security Policy

Using Registry Editor

To set the EveryoneIncludesAnonymous registry value by using Registry Editor:

1. Start Regedit.exe and locate the following registry key (Fig. 9.12):

```
HKEY_LOCAL_MACHINE\SYSTEM\CurrentControlSet\Control\Lsa
```

2. Right-click `EveryoneIncludesAnonymous`, and then click **Modify**.
3. To enable anonymous users to be members of the Everyone security group, in the **Value data** box, type `1`. To prevent the inclusion of the Everyone security group SID in the anonymous user's access token (the Windows XP default), in the **Value data** box, type `0`.
4. Quit Registry Editor.

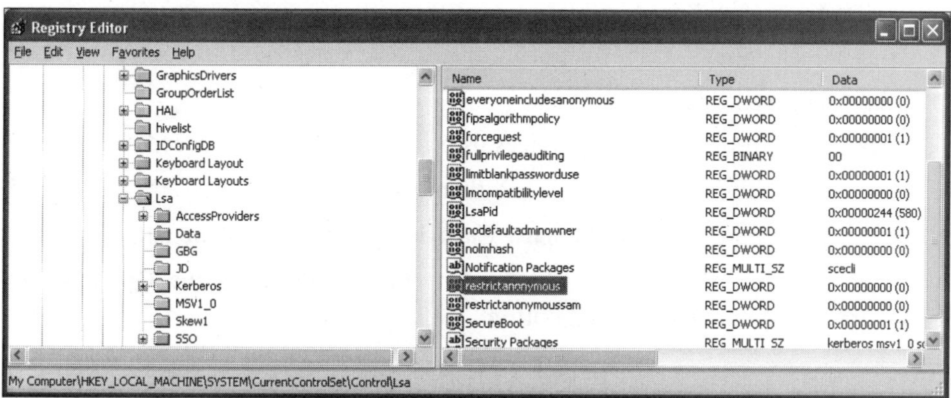

Fig. 9.12. The contents of the `HKEY_LOCAL_MACHINE\SYSTEM\CurrentControlSet\Control\Lsa` registry key

System Scheduler as a Potential Security Risk

The system scheduler (Task Scheduler), which is included with Windows NT/2000/XP, may be used for starting certain undesirable programs in the context of the SYSTEM account (which is present in all Windows NT/2000 systems). However, you won't see this account in either User Manager/User Manager for Domains utilities (Windows NT 4.0), or in MMC snap-ins (Windows 2000/XP). This account and the Task Scheduler allow the system administrator to provide an ordinary user the one-time use of certain administrative tasks without providing them administrative rights. For example, to allow them to run the MMC Disk Management snap-in:

```
at <\\machine_name> 1:00pm /interactive
%SystemRoot%\system32\diskmgmt.msc
```

where `<\\machine_name>`—is the name of the client system.

However useful this is, it's also risky, because running the Task Scheduler in the SYSTEM context will provide any program using this method the whole set of the system privileges, including access to the SAM database.

To protect the system against this possible danger, you can either lock the Task Scheduler service (this service is sometimes needed to run other jobs, though), or configure it in such a way as to log on with an ordinary user account.

You can also block user access to the Schedule services using one of the following two methods:

- Using Local Policy
- Using Registry Editor

To block access to the Schedule services using a Local Policy, proceed as follows:

1. Click **Start**, click **Run**, type `mmc`, and then click **OK**.
2. On the **File** menu, click **Add/Remove Snap-in**. On the **Standalone** tab, click **Add**.
3. In the **Available Standalone Snap-ins** list (Fig. 9.13), select the **Group Policy** options and then click the **Add** button.

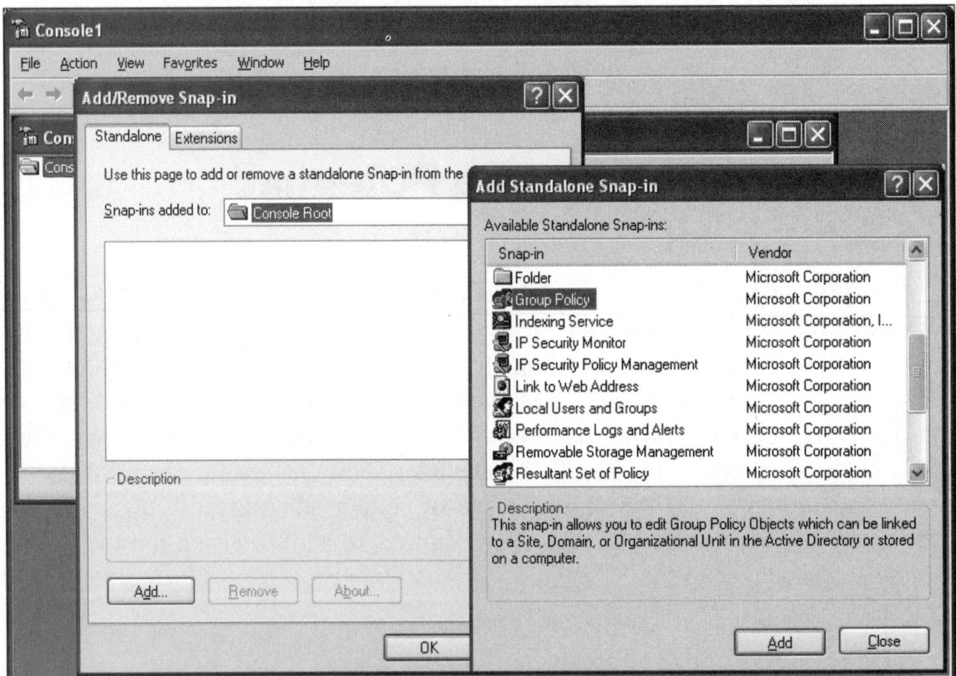

Fig. 9.13. Adding the Group Policy snap-in to the custom console

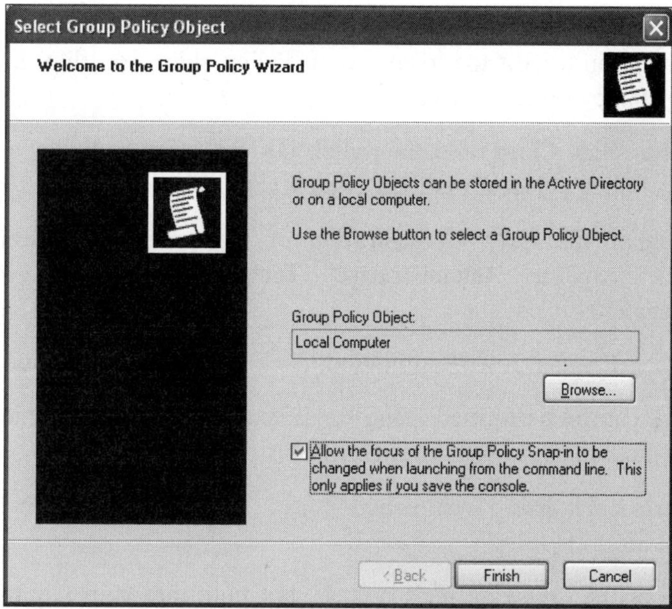

Fig. 9.14. The **Select Group Policy Object** window

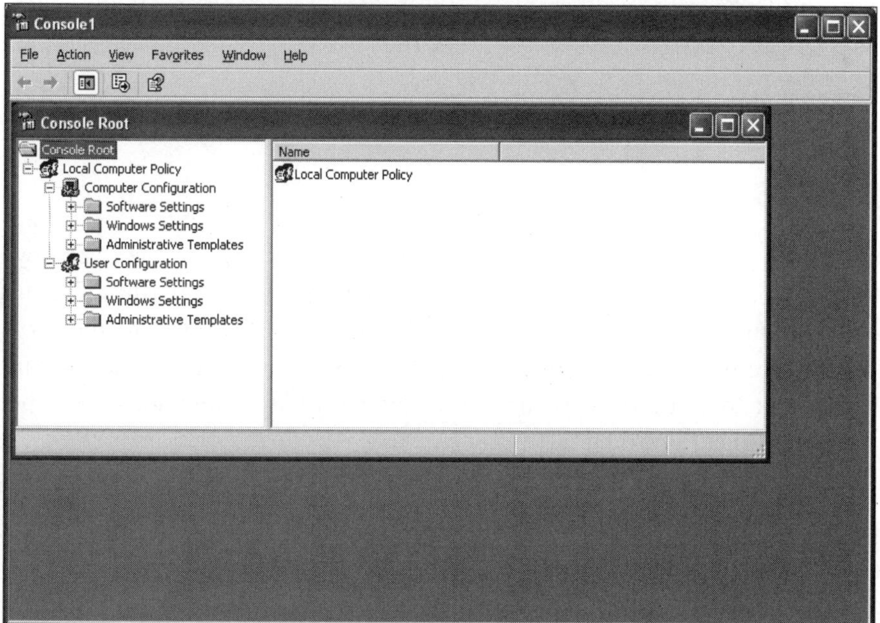

Fig. 9.15. The Group Policy Object opened for editing

4. The **Select Group Policy object** window will open (Fig. 9.14). Click **Local Computer** option to edit the local Group Policy object, or click **Browse** to find the Group Policy object that you want.
5. Click **Finish**, click **Close**, and then click **OK**. The Group Policy snap-in opens the Group Policy object for editing (Fig. 9.15).
6. Expand either the **User Configuration** or **Computer Configuration** branch, and then expand **Administrative Templates**, **Windows Components**, **Task Scheduler**.
7. Double-click **Prevent Task Run or End**, click **Enabled**, and then click **OK**.

The same task can be performed using Registry Editor (and experienced users can consider this method as faster than the previous one).

1. Click **Start**, click **Run**, type `regedit.exe`, and then press ENTER to start Registry Editor.
2. Open one of the following registry keys, but note that you may have to create the key:

   `HKEY_LOCAL_MACHINE\SOFTWARE\Policies\Microsoft\Windows\Task Scheduler5.0`

   `HKEY_CURRENT_USER\Software\Policies\Microsoft\Windows\Task Scheduler5.0`
3. Create a new `DWORD` value, name it `Execution`, and set it to `1`.

Summary

When writing this chapter, I didn't want to provide you with detailed, step-by-step instructions on the methods of cracking Windows NT/2000/XP (this information wouldn't be sufficient, anyway). Rather, this chapter is addressed to those of you who are interested in security in general (and in Windows NT security in particular) and want to restrict the security of their networks. Remember: "The person who's been warned, is armed".

Of course, this chapter isn't a complete reference on computer security. This topic deserves a separate book (and there are volumes of these in libraries). Additional information sources are provided in the bibliographical reference at the end of this book.

Chapter 10

Managing the User Working Environments

Let every hour be in its place
Firm fixed, nor loosely shift,
And well enjoy the vacant space,
As though a birthday gift.

Lewis Carroll.
"Punctuality"

The user work environment includes various desktop settings, including color scheme, mouse settings, size and position of the windows, network connections and printers, environment variables, registry settings and available applications. There are many conventional methods for managing user work environments, including the following:

- *User profiles*

  User profiles contain all the settings for the user-specific Windows work environment, including user documents, mail messages, application configuration settings and preferences, screen settings, network connections and so on.

- *Scripts*

  Logon script is the batch (BAT) or executable (EXE) file that runs any time you log onto the network from any of the workstations connected to it. Logon scripts can contain various operating system commands; for example, ones that restore network connections and start applications, or set environment variables (such as set paths using the `PATH` variable or specify the folder to store temporary files using the `TEMP` variable).

- *System policies*

  The system policy is used for managing user work environments and their permissions within the network. System administrators can use the system policies for managing user workstations both in local and global networks.

In this chapter, we'll discuss user profiles and system policies. I'll also provide some instructions on their usage to modify the system registry.

Basic Information on the User Profiles

All users of the modern operating systems from the Windows NT/2000/XP family has many customizable settings at their disposal, including wallpapers and screen savers, desktop settings, and many application settings which can be customized. These settings are only a small part of a large variety of the customizable settings. There are many reasons users may need these customizations (after all, individual preferences are always different).

Before the registry concept was introduced, there was always one common problem: any time you logged onto the network from another computer, you always needed to customize its settings.

A new user profile is created automatically each time you log onto Windows NT/2000 or to Windows XP for the first time. By default, Windows NT/2000/XP user profiles support desktop settings for the user environment on the local computer.

NOTE

It is necessary to distinguish user profiles from the policies. Profiles are not user policies, and each user has a profile even if they don't use Group Policy.

Advantages of the User Profile

User profiles provide the following advantages:

- After a successful logon, the users start working with their own working environment (including desktop settings) that existed at the time he/she last logged out.
- Many users can share a single computer, and each user will get individual settings for working environment.
- User profiles can be stored on the server; they may be used independently from the workstation where the user logs on to the network. These user profiles are called roaming user profiles.
- Starting with Windows 2000, Microsoft has implemented a whole range of new technologies called IntelliMirror (as a part of the Zero Administration Initiative), which in Windows XP was further improved and enhanced. These technologies simplify the process of network administration and improve its efficiency. This

set of functions allows system administrators and users to create mirror copies of the user profile data stored on the server, thus protecting critically important user data stored in the local system. The main idea of IntelliMirror technologies is that all information on the user profile and the software installed by the user is stored on the server in a personal cache.

Using IntelliMirror, the system administrator may install and support application software on the user workstations without interrupting their everyday work. Because the server always has a mirror of the user's working environment, the administrator can quickly replace the user workstation and restore the working environment, including data, installed software, and the administrative policy.

From the administrator's point of view, user profiles provide specific advantages and are capable of:

- creating customized user settings
- specifying common settings for each user group
- assigning mandatory user profiles, which can't be changed by the users and don't allow users to change the system configuration

As was already mentioned in *Chapter 1*, Windows XP provides the following types of user profiles:

- *Local User Profiles*. User profiles of this type are stored on the local computer's hard disk. Any changes that you might introduce to the local user profile are computer-specific and apply only to the computer on which these changes are made.
- *Roaming User Profile*. Roaming user profiles are stored on a server, and are available any time when the user logs onto a network. Any changes made to a roaming user profile are updated on the server.
- *Mandatory User Profile*. This type of user profile can be created or updated only by system administrators. Any changes put in place by the user to this type of profile are lost when the user logs off.

NOTE

The mandatory user profiles are included with Windows XP only in order to provide backward compatibility with existing Windows NT 4.0 domains. If you have Windows 2000 domains in native mode and need to provide managed desktop configurations for users and groups, it is recommended that you use Group Policy rather than mandatory user profiles. Group Policy basics will be discussed later in this chapter.

The Settings Stored in the User Profile

Each user profile contains configuration settings and options customized for each individual user. In practice, the user profile can be considered a "snapshot" of the user's working environment.

Main settings stored in the user profile are listed in Table 10.1.

Table 10.1. User Profile Settings

Working environment item	User profile settings
Windows GUI (Windows Explorer or My Computer)	All user-specified settings of the Windows Explorer application
Taskbar	All personal program groups and their properties, all personal programs and their properties, all individual settings of the taskbar
Printer settings	All connections to network printers
Control Panel	All individual user-specific settings specified using Control Panel applets
Accessories	All user-specific customized settings of the applications that influence Windows NT/2000 working environments, including individual settings for Calculator, Clock, Notepad, Paint, and HyperTerminal
Application settings	All Windows NT applications allow individual settings in relation to each individual user. If this information exists, it's stored in the user's registry hive (`HKEY_CURRENT_USER`)
Bookmarks in the online Help system	All Help bookmarks set by the user
Favorite registry key	All registry keys marked by the user as Favorites

User Profile Structure

Each user profile consists of a registry hive (NTUser.dat file, which is mapped to the `HKEY_CLASSES_ROOT` registry key when the user logs on) and a set of folders in the file system of your computer. Since the release of Windows NT 4.0, the default location of user profiles has changed in order to allow administrators to provided better security for the operating system folders without affecting the user data. Let us consider the default location of user profiles in more detail.

All Windows NT user profiles are stored in the *%SystemRoot%*\Profiles folder. When you log into the system for the first time, the system creates a new profile for you based on the Default User profile, present on each Windows NT Workstation or Windows NT Server computer. The \Default User folder and profile folders for individual users contain the Ntuser.dat and Ntuser.dat.log files (user profile hive and its log) together with the desktop shortcuts.

The naming conventions for the user profile folders have changed with Windows 2000. In general, the location of Windows 2000/XP user profiles depends on the method used to install the operating system:

- If Windows 2000 or Windows XP was installed fresh or as an upgrade from Windows 95/98, the Setup program will create a new folder for storing user profiles: *%SystemDrive%*:\Documents and Settings (for example, C:\Documents and Settings).
- If Windows 2000 or Windows XP was installed as an upgrade from the previous Windows NT versions, user profile folders will be located in the *%SystemRoot%*\Profiles folder (like in Windows NT 4.0).

NOTE

Later in this chapter, we'll use the *%ProfilePath%* variable to specify the path to the folder that contains user profiles.

The locations of user profiles for each of the possible types of Windows XP installation are briefly described in Table 10.2.

Table 10.2. User Profile Locations

Windows XP installation type	User profiles location
Clean installation of Windows XP (no previous operating system)	*%SystemDrive%*\Documents and Settings; for example, C:\Documents and Settings
Upgrade from Windows 2000	*%SystemDrive%*\Documents and Settings; for example, C:\Documents and Settings
Upgrade from Windows NT 4.0	*%SystemRoot%*\Profiles; for example, C:\WinNT\Profiles
Upgrade from Windows 9x/ME	*%SystemDrive%*\Documents and Settings; for example, C:\Documents and Settings

Windows XP, like the previous versions of Windows NT/2000, automatically creates a user profile when the new user first logs onto the system. To store this profile, the system creates a new nested folder named after the login name of the new user and located under the *%ProfilePath%* folder. The path to this folder will be saved in the system registry and associated with the user's security identifier (Security ID, SID).

NOTE

Windows NT/ 2000/XP operating systems identify users and groups using security identifiers (Security IDs, SIDs). Security identifiers are quite long, and are unique for each user (even for the user accounts in different systems). If you first delete the user account on the computer or in the domain, and then create a new user account with the same login name, the system will generate a new security ID for that account. It is impossible to have two identical security Ids. SIDs have the following format: S-1-XXXXX_1-$YYYYY_2$-....-RID, where: S-1—security ID, version 1; XXXXX—authority number, YYYYYn—subauthority numbers, RID—relative identifier (Relative ID). Notice that the Relative ID (RID) won't be unique for each computer.

Also notice that many Windows NT/2000/XP users, even experienced ones, often think that the system identifies each user by his or her username (or login name) and the password. This isn't so; it's the SID that uniquely identifies the user to the system. User profiles are also identified by their associated SIDs (Fig. 10.1).

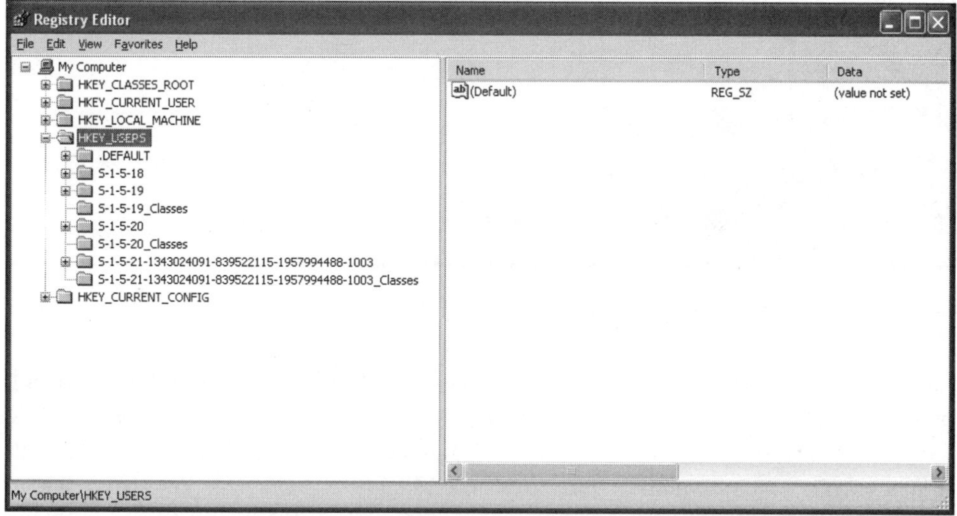

Fig. 10.1. The `HKEY_USERS` registry key contains a complete list of all existing user profiles identified by their associated SIDs

When the user logs into the local system using a local or domain user account, and the *%ProfilePath%* folder doesn't contain a subfolder with a name like the user's login name, the system will create such a folder. The path to this folder will be saved in the registry and associated with the user's SID. For example, if "Maggie" logs in to the Windows 2000/XP system, the system will create a folder named *%SystemDrive%*:\Documents and Settings\Maggie to store a new user profile (Fig. 10.2).

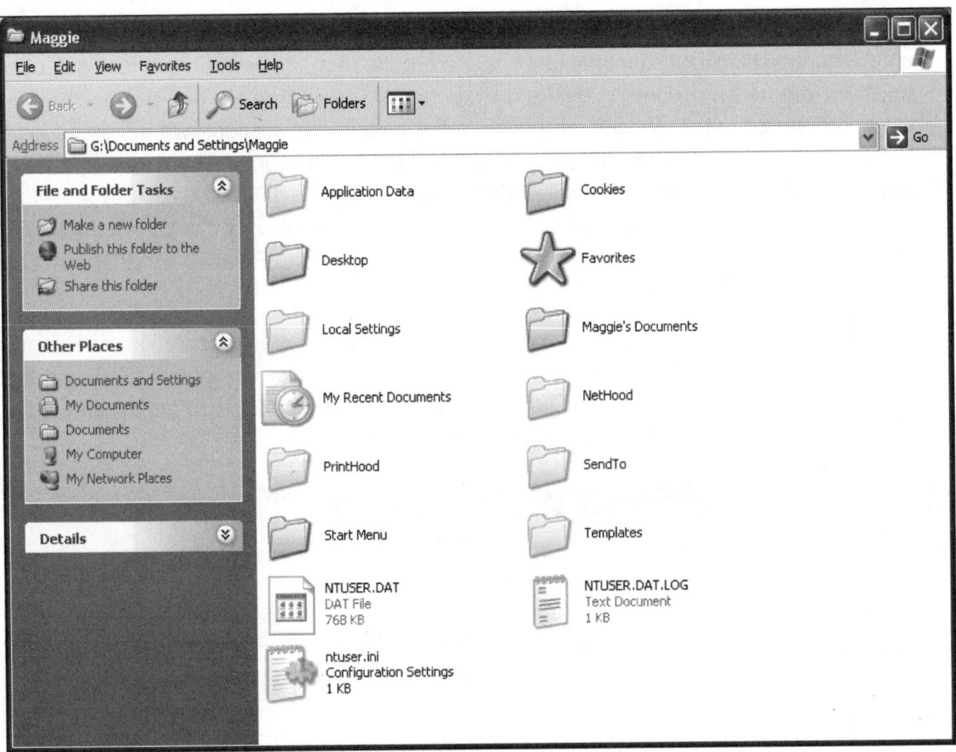

Fig. 10.2. Typical contents of the user profile folder

Later, if a user from another domain, having the same login name, attempts to log onto the network from this computer, the system will create another user profile folder for them. The folder will be named using the following format: *%SystemDrive%*:\Documents and Settings\Maggie [*DOMAIN_NAME*], where [*DOMAIN_NAME*] is the name of the domain to which the user account with the duplicated user name belongs to.

If both the login and domain names are the same, but the SIDs of two user accounts are different (this may happen when you delete a user account, and then create another one with the same name belonging to the same domain), the system will create a new user profile folders named as follows: *%SystemDrive%*:\Documents and Settings\Maggie [*DOMAIN_NAME*].000, *%SystemDrive%*:\Documents and Settings\Maggie [*DOMAIN_NAME*].001 etc.

NOTE

As I mentioned before, Windows NT 4.0 stores all locally cached user profiles in the *%SystemRoot%*\Profiles folder. If you've installed Windows 2000 or Windows /XP as an upgrade of the previous Windows NT version, the system will continue using this folder for storing user profiles. If you've installed a new copy of the Windows 2000/XP operating system, the Setup program will create a new "Documents and Settings" folder for storing user profiles. This folder will be located on the same partition with the Windows 2000 operating system.

Notice that some applications use hard-coded pathnames to access locally cached user profiles. This may cause a problem in mixed environments. For example, if the path to the user profile is coded "*%SystemRoot%* \Profiles", the program may behave as expected in Windows NT 4.0, but it will fail to find the user profile in Windows 2000 and Windows XP.

Now let us consider the preferences stored in the profile directories in more detail. The screenshot shown in Fig. 10.3 illustrates the typical structure of the user profile, which in Windows XP contains the following folders:

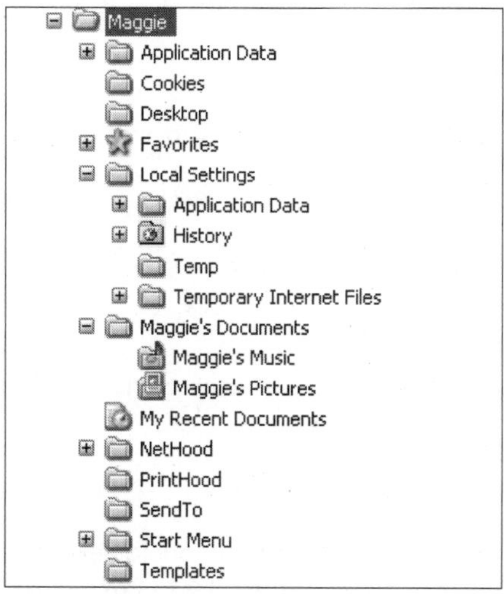

Fig. 10.3. The user profile structure

- *Application data**. Application-specific data, such as a custom dictionary for a word processing program. Application vendors decide what data to store in this directory.
- *Cookies*. Internet Explorer cookies.
- *Desktop*. Desktop items, including files and shortcuts.
- *Favorites*. Internet Explorer favorites.
- *Local Settings**. Application settings and data that *do not roam* with the profile. Usually either machine specific, or too large to roam effectively.
  - *Application data*. Computer specific application data.
  - *History*. Internet Explorer history.
  - *Temp*. Temporary files.
  - *Temporary Internet Files*. Internet Explorer offline cache.
- *My Documents*. The new default location for any documents that the user creates. Applications should be written to save files here by default.
  - *My Pictures*. Default location for user's pictures.
  - *My Music*. Default locations for user's music files.
- *NetHood**. Shortcuts to Network Neighborhood items.
- *PrintHood**. Shortcuts to printer folder items.
- *Recent*. Shortcuts to the most recently used documents.
- *SendTo*. Shortcuts to document storage locations and applications.
- *Start Menu*. Shortcuts to program items.
- *Templates**. Shortcuts to template items.

* These directories are hidden by default. To see these directories, change the View Options.

NOTE

By default, the **Local Settings** folder and its subfolders do not roam with the profile. This folder contains application data not required to roam with the user, such as temporary files, non-critical settings, and data too large to roam efficiently.

The Ntuser.dat File

The Ntuser.dat file is the part of the registry that actually supports the user profile. This file is the cached copy of the local `HKEY_CURRENT_USER` subtree. This key, shown in Fig. 10.4, stores the settings which define the working environment for the currently logged on user.

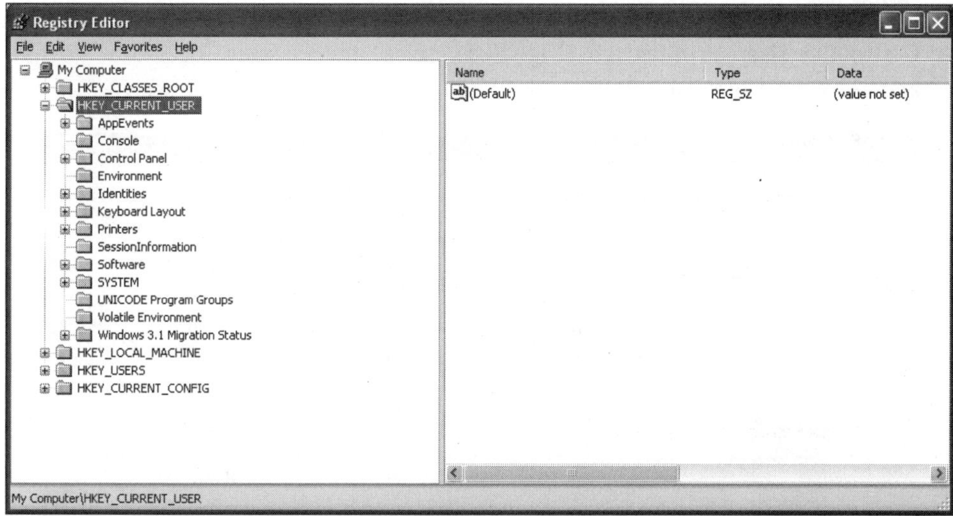

Fig. 10.4. The settings defining the working environment for the currently logged on user are stored under `HKEY_CURRENT_USER`

Roaming User Profiles in the Mixed Environments

Users who have roaming user profiles can use these profiles in a mixed environment to log on to both Windows NT 4.0 and Windows 2000. Both operating systems can read and use the same user profile. If you need to use the roaming profile in a mixed environment, proceed as follows:

1. Create an account for the administrative user on the Windows 2000 Server computer (use Active Directory Users and Computers for this purpose). This user will be the administrator of the user profiles. Also create the shared directory for storing user profiles.

2. Create a new user account for the roaming user, then open the **User Properties** window. Go to the **Profiles** tab and specify the path to the user profile in the following format: *server name**share name*\%*user name*%, where server name is the name of the server, share name is the name of the shared folder where you intend to store user profiles, and user name is the name of the roaming user.
3. From the **Start** menu, select **Settings** | **Control Panel**, and launch the System applet.
4. Go to the **User Profiles** tab (Fig. 10.5), select the existing local user profile, and click the **Copy To** button.

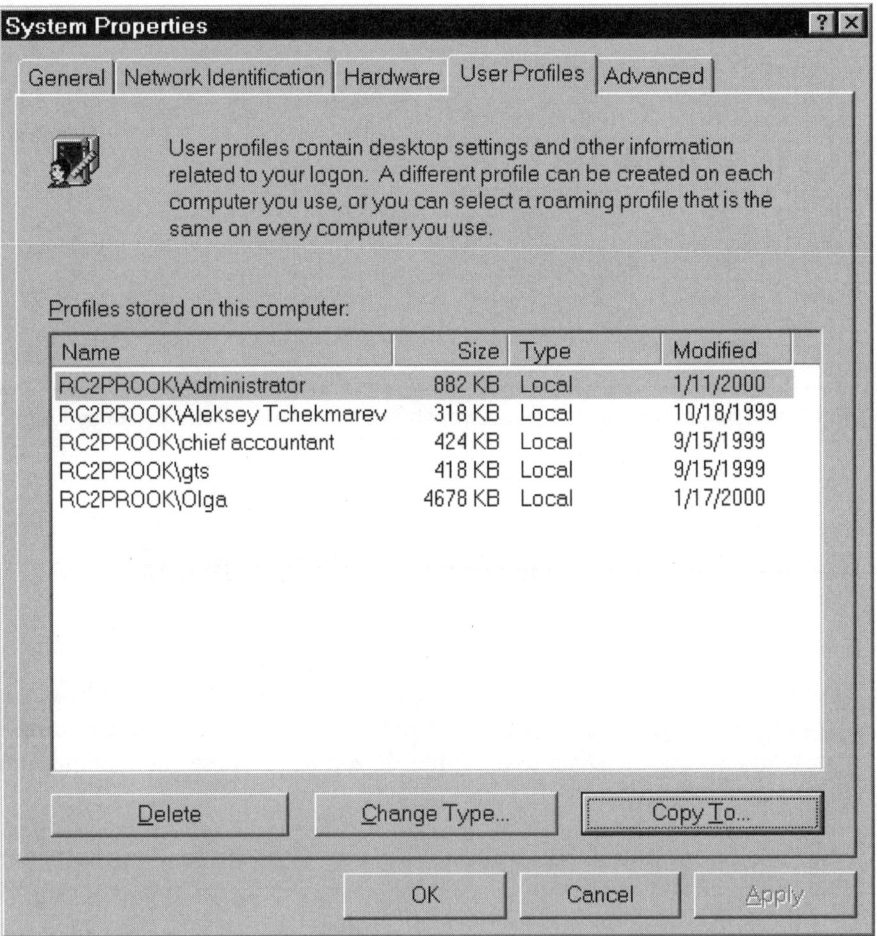

Fig. 10.5. The **User Profiles** tab of the **System Properties** window

5. The **Copy To** window will open (Fig. 10.6). Enter the path to the shared user profile folder into the **Copy profile to** field. Specify the path using the UNC (Universal Naming Convention) format (for example: *server name*\ *share name*\ *user profile folder*). If the folder doesn't exist, it will be created.
6. Select a user whom you'll allow to work with this profile. To copy the profile, click **OK**. You'll return to the **System Properties** window. Click **OK** to confirm the changes.
7. Logon to the network from the client workstation. From the **Start** menu, select **Settings** | **Control Panel**, then launch the System applet and go to the **User Profiles** tab. The profile type for the user whom you've assigned the roaming profile will change to **Roaming**.

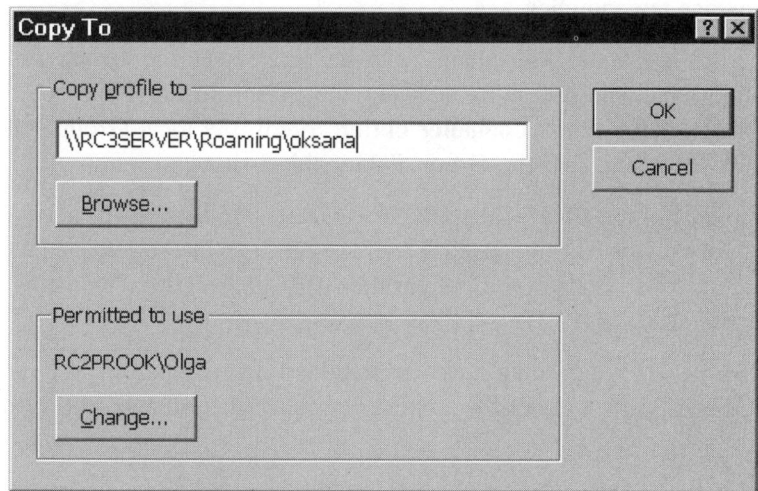

Fig. 10.6. The **Copy To** window

NOTE

Starting with Windows 2000, standard access rights to the roaming profiles have changed in comparison to those in Windows NT 4.0. For example, administrators no longer have Full Control access to all user profiles. Consequently, if an administrator needs access to the contents of the user profile, he'll need to take ownership for the appropriate file system objects (if the user profiles are stored on the NTFS partition). He'll also need to take ownership for the respective registry hives. From a security point of view, this is a wise thing to do, because the operation of taking ownership is an event that can be audited.

Windows XP Enhancements to Roaming User Profiles

Windows XP introduces several enhancements to the user settings management, including more reliable roaming, improved user profile merge algorithm and several new group policy settings. Let us consider these enhancements in more detail.

First of all, user profile policies in Windows XP have their own node in Group Policy Editor (Fig. 10.7). Furthermore, there are three new policies. To view these policies, proceed as follows:

1. Click **Start**, click **Run**, type `mmc`, and then click **OK**.
2. From the **File** menu, select the **Add/Remove Snap-in** command, go to the **Standalone** tab and click **Add**.
3. From the **Available Standalone Snap-ins** list, select the **Group Policy** option and then click the **Add** button. When the **Select Group Policy object** window opens, select the **Local Computer** option to edit the local Group Policy object, or click **Browse** to find the Group Policy object that you want.
4. Click **Finish**, then **Close**, then **OK**. The Group Policy snap-in opens the Group Policy object for editing. Expand the console tree in the left pane of this window as follows: **Computer Configuration | Administrative Templates | System | User Profiles** (Fig. 10.7).

The three new policies that have been added with Windows XP are the last ones in the list of the available policies in the right pane of the Group Policy window:

- **Prevent Roaming Profile Changes From Propagating to the server**. As its name implies, this policy specifies whether the changes made by the users to their roaming profiles are merged with the copies of their roaming profiles stored on the server. If you set this policy, the users at login will receive the copies of their roaming profiles, but the changes they introduce will not be merged to their roaming profiles.
- **Add the Administrator security group to the roaming user profile share**. As was aforementioned, starting with Windows 2000, the default permissions for newly created roaming profiles provide full control permissions for the user, and no access to the Administrators group. If you want to reset this behavior in a way compatible to Windows NT 4.0, where the Administrators group has full control of the user's profile directories, you should set this policy.

- **Do Not Allow users to change profile type.** Allows an administrator to control whether a user is allowed to change their profile type from a Roaming Profile to a Local profile.

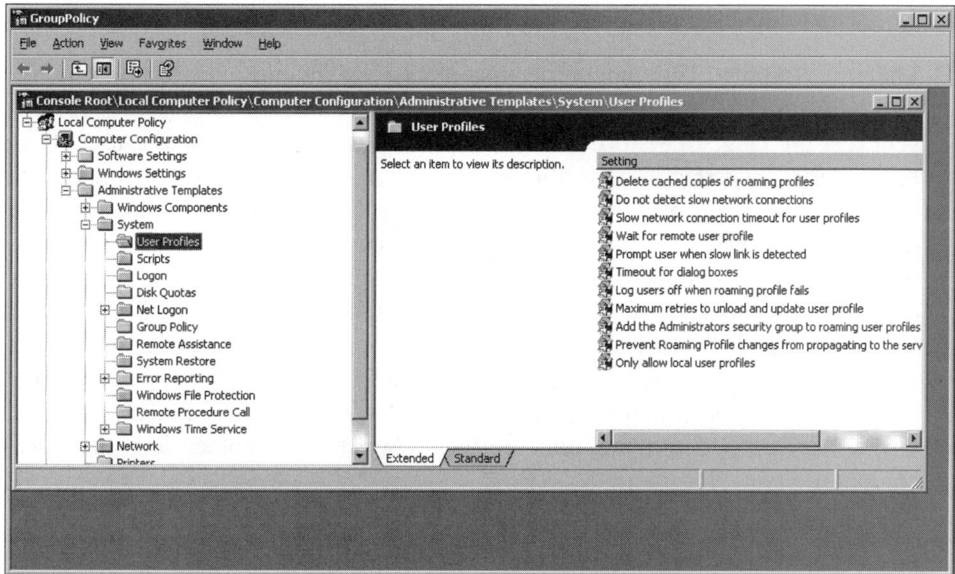

Fig. 10.7. User Profile Policies have their own node in Group Policy Editor

Besides new policies, Windows XP provides other improvements to roaming profiles management. For example, in Windows 2000 there may be situations, when applications and services keep registry keys open during logoff. This prevents Windows from unloading the user's registry hive and saving the user profiles modifications to the server. As a result, such "locked" user profiles never get unloaded, and take up a large amount of memory on a server that has many users logging on. If such a profile is marked for deletion at logoff in order to clean up the disk space on the server, it also never gets deleted. In Windows XP this problem was not an issue. Now Windows saves the user's registry hive at the end of the 60-second delay and roams the profile correctly. In contrast to Windows 2000, when the application or service closes the registry key that locks the user profile, Windows XP unloads the hive and frees the memory consumed by the user profile. In cases where the application or service never releases the registry key, Windows XP will delete all profiles marked for deletion at the next reboot.

Non-Roaming Folders and Quotas on Profile Size

The way the users get their profiles depends on the profile type configured for them. Let us consider this process in more detail. For local profiles the procedure comprises the following steps:

- The user logs on. The operating system checks the list of user profiles located in `HKEY_LOCAL_MACHINE\SOFTWARE\Microsoft\WindowsNT\CurrentVersion\ProfileList` (Fig. 10.8) to determine if a local profile exists for the user. If an entry exists, then this local profile is used. If a local profile is not found, and the computer is part of a domain, the operating system checks if a domain-wide default profile exists (it must be located on the domain controller's `NETLOGON` share in a folder named Default User). If a default domain-wide user profile exists, it will be copied to the following subfolder on the local computer: *%SystemDrive%*\Documents and Settings*Username*. If a default domain-wide user profile does not exist, then the local default profile is copied from the *%Systemdrive%*\Documents and Settings\Default User folder to the *%SystemDrive%*\Documents and Settings*Username* subfolder on the local computer.
- The user's registry hive (NTUser.dat) is mapped to the `HKEY_CURRENT_USER` portion of the registry.
- When the user logs off, a profile is saved to the local hard disk of the computer.

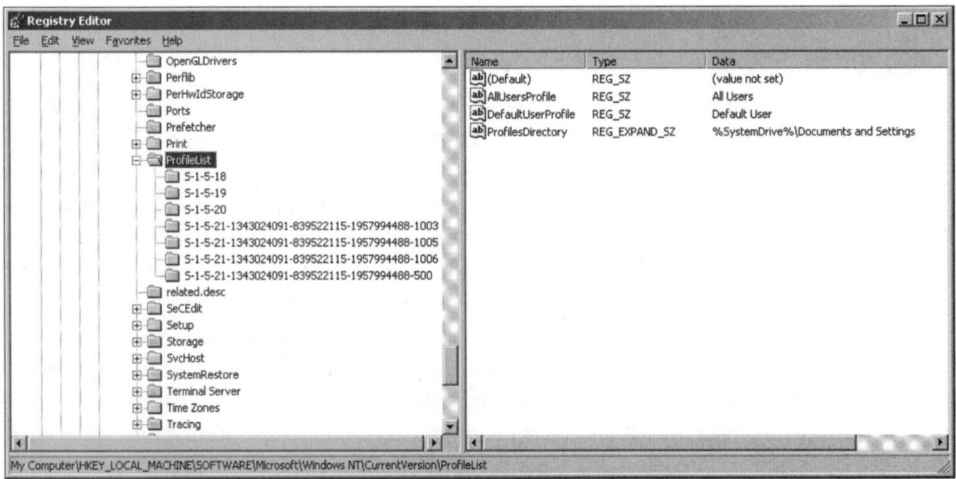

Fig. 10.8. The list of user profiles is stored in the registry under the `HKEY_LOCAL_MACHINE\SOFTWARE\Microsoft\Windows NT\CurrentVersion\ProfileList` key

For roaming profiles this process is as follows:

- The user logs on, and Windows checks the list of user profiles stored in the registry under `HKEY_LOCAL_MACHINE\SOFTWARE\Microsoft\WindowsNT\CurrentVersion\ProfileList` key to determine if a cached copy of the profile exists. If a local copy of the profile is not found, and the computer is part of a domain, Windows checks to determine if a domain-wide default profile exists in the Default User folder on the domain controller's NETLOGON share. If a default domain-wide user profile exists, it will be copied to the following subfolder on the local computer: *%SystemDrive%*\Documents and Settings*Username*. If a default domain-wide user profile does not exist, then the local default profile is copied from the *%Systemdrive%*\Documents and Settings\Default User folder to the *%SystemDrive%*\Documents and Settings*Username* subfolder on the local computer.
- The user's registry hive (Ntuser.dat) is copied to the local cached copy of their user profile, and is mapped to the `HKEY_CURRENT_USER` portion of the registry. The contents of the local cached profile are compared with the copy of the profile on the server, and the two profiles are merged.
- The user can then run applications and edit documents as normal. When the user logs off, their local profile is copied to the path configured by the administrator. If a profile already exists on the server, the local profile is merged with the server copy.

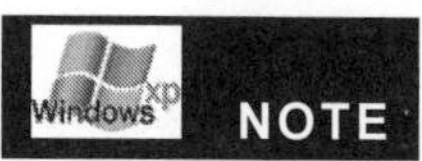

In Windows NT 4.0, the merge algorithm was based on the `Xcopy` command with full synchronization support. That means, that there is only one master copy of the profile at any given time. When the user is logged on, the master profile is on the local computer, and when the user is not logged on, the master copy of his or her profile is on the server. This algorithm works fine in most cases, where a user logs on to only a single computer. However, a user who logs on to multiple computers at the same time might experience unexpected behavior.

Windows XP eliminates this problem by introducing the profile merging at the file level. When a document or file is updated, the new algorithm compares the timestamp of the destination file with the timestamp of the source file. If the destination file is newer, it is not overwritten.

As was mentioned earlier, roaming user profiles are copied from the server to the client when the user logs on, and copied back when the user logs off. However,

Windows 2000/XP includes the per-user Local Settings folder within the user profile that is not copied during log on or log off sessions. Operating system components and other applications can store non-roaming per-user data in this folder. On the other hand, the IntelliMirror technology includes the Folder Redirection feature that allows administrators to redirect the location of specific user profile folders to a network location (from the user's point of view, this looks just like roaming, but in this case the user settings actually remain on the network share). Folder redirection can be used with all types of profiles, including local, roaming, or mandatory. Combining Folder Redirection with roaming profiles allows you to get all the benefits of roaming profiles and at the same time to minimize network traffic.

Table 10.3. lists the folders that roam with the profile by default, and indicates whether they can be redirected using Group Policy.

Table 10.3. Folders that Roam with the Profile

Folder Name	Description	Roams with Profile by default	Redirect with Group Policy
Application Data	Per-user roaming application data	Yes	Yes
Cookies	User's Internet Explorer cookies	Yes	No
Desktop		Yes	Yes
Favorites	User's Internet Explorer favorites	Yes	No
Local Settings	Temporary files and per-user non-roaming application data	No	No
My Documents	User's documents	Yes	Yes
NetHood		Yes	No
PrintHood		Yes	No
Recent	Shortcuts to recently used documents	Yes	No
Send To		Yes	No
Start Menu	User's personal start menu	Yes	Yes
Templates	Per-user customized templates	Yes	No

Scripts

A logon script is a batch (BAT) or executable (EXE) file that runs any time the user logs on to the network from any of the networked workstations. A logon script may contain operating system commands (for example, the ones that restore network connections or run applications). Logon scripts may also specify the environment variables, such as `PATH` or `TEMP`.

Windows 2000 has made an improvement in this area—Windows Script Host (WSH) 2.0. WSH 2.0 is capable of creating simple, but flexible and powerful scripts to automate network administration. Because WSH is language-independent, you're free to select any scripting language you prefer: Visual Basic Scripting Edition (VBScript), JScript and Perl. WSH also supports COM, allowing you to enjoy the advantages of new technologies such as Windows Management Instrumentation (WMI) and Active Directory Services Interface (ADSI).

Using WSH in Logon Scripts

We won't dive into the details here; instead, let's look at a small example of the logon script, which edits the registry (after all, this is a book on the registry). Most end users are afraid of registry editing procedures. Because of this, you can write a small logon script for these users that customizes the system registry. WSH provides a convenient and easy technique for manipulating the registry using the following methods: `regRead`, `regWrite`, and `regDelete`.

An example of the code provided below changes the proxy settings stored in the registry under `HKCU\Software\Microsoft\Windows\CurrentVersion\Internet Settings\ProxyServer`. First of all, you need to read these settings using the `regRead` method. Then, using the `regWrite` method, you can overwrite the existing value (for example, replace the existing value by `NEWPROXY:80`). Finally, you need to make sure that the changes you've introduced are correct. This is done using the `regRead` method:

```
...
   sub regProxy
     prefix = _
         "HKCU\Software\Microsoft\Windows\CurrentVersion\Internet Settings\"
         WScript.Echo "Old ProxyServer settings: " & wshShell.regRead(prefix & _
          "ProxyServer")
```

```
    wshShell.regWrite prefix & "ProxyServer", "MYPROXY:80"
    WScript.Echo "New ProxyServer settings: " & wshShell.regRead(prefix & _
      "ProxyServer")
end sub
...
```

System Policy Overview

The System policies provide another instrument to help system administrators control user access to the network and manage desktop settings, including data sharing and configuring system settings. The system policy represents registry settings that are automatically loaded when the user logs on to the system. The main difference between system policies and user profiles is that the system policy is applicable to users, user groups, and individual computers. Administrators can specify, modify, and support registry settings for each of the components just listed. By combining system policies for individual users, specific computers from which the user logs on, and for user groups, to which the user may belong, the administrator can get complete control over the types of user environments and user rights and permissions. To define the system policy settings, the administrator simply creates system policy templates.

The System Policy Editor tool was first introduced in the Windows NT 4.0 operating system. It allowed administrators to specify configuration settings for users and computers, and store these settings in the Windows NT registry. Using this utility, administrators could manage user work environments and specify configuration settings for all Windows NT 4.0 computers (both Workstation and Server). In Windows 2000, this tool was replaced by the Group Policy MMC snap-in, which extends the capabilities of the System Policy Editor (SPE) and provides many additional options for managing client computer configurations, including registry based policies, security settings, scripts and folder redirection. Group policy settings specified by the administrator are stored in the Group Policy Object (GPO), which, in turn, is associated with one of the Active Directory objects (site, domain, or organizational unit).

Windows 2000 group policy has many significant advantages over the Windows NT 4.0 system policy (not to mention Windows 95/98). These advantages include:

- The possibility of associating with the Active Directory objects (sites, domains, or organizational units). The policy associated with the Active Directory container influences all other computers and all the users within that container (site, domain, or organizational unit).

- Extended configuration capabilities. Both users and computers may be joined into groups.
- Improved security in comparison to Windows NT 4.0.
- Windows NT 4.0 policies were stored in the user profiles (this was sometimes called "*tattooing* the registry"). The specified registry setting using the System Policy Editor retained its value until it was changed by the administrator for the given policy, or manually changed by the user who edited the registry directly. This situation represented a problem (for example, when you decided to change group membership). Windows 2000 solved this problem, though, because registry settings, specified by the group policy, are written to the protected registry keys (`\Software\Policies` and `\Software\Microsoft\Windows\CurrentVersion\Policies`). When the group policy object (GPO) is no longer applicable, these settings are cleared.

Administrative Templates

The System Policy Editor utility included with Windows NT 4.0 Server uses administrative templates (ADM files). These templates allow you to define which registry settings are available for editing using the System Policy Editor.

Windows 2000 ADM files also specify registry settings that can be modified using the UI provided by the MMC Group Policy snap-in. The policy settings related to the user who logs on are written to the registry under the `HKEY_CURRENT_USER` root key (`HKCU`). The policy settings that relate to the software installed on the computer, and to computer itself, are written to the registry under the `HKEY_LOCAL_MACHINE` root key (`HKLM`).

ADM files are text files containing the hierarchy of categories and subcategories. These categories and subcategories define fully qualified registry settings that can be modified using the Group Policy user interface. The term "fully qualified registry setting" means that these settings also specify registry paths to the settings that will be modified using the Group Policy snap-in when you select the appropriate option.

Security Settings

The Group Policy MMC snap-in allows you to specify the security configuration applicable to one or more security areas supported by Windows 2000 Professional or Windows 2000 Server. The security configuration specified using Group Policy is then applied to all computers within Active Directory container.

The Group Policy allowing administrators to specify security settings extends the existing operating system functionality. For example, the following capabilities are provided:

- *Account Policies.* These are security settings related to the passwords, the account lockout policy and Kerberos-related policy (within Windows 2000 domains).
- *Local Policies.* This is a group of settings that specify the auditing policy, user permissions and other security settings. The Local policies allow administrators to configure access to the computer both locally and through the network, and specify the events that should be audited.
- *Event Log.* These are security settings that control the security of the system event logs (Application, Security, and System), accessed using Event Viewer.
- *Restricted Groups.* These settings allow you to specify the users who belong to restricted groups. Thus, the administrator can enforce the security policy in relation to the groups like Enterprise Administrators, for example. If another user is added to this restricted group (for example, when there's an emergency and it's necessary to perform an urgent job), the user will automatically be deleted from this group when the group policy comes into force next time.
- *System Services.* These options manage the starting mode and security handles for the system and network services.
- *Registry.* Used for configuring the security settings for registry keys, including access control, auditing, and owner rights. Security settings for the registry keys are specified according to the same inheritance modes that are used in all Windows 2000 hierarchical structures. Microsoft officially recommends using access rights inheritance when defining security settings for top-level objects, and redefine security settings for child objects only when necessary.
- *File System.* Used for configuring security settings related to the file system objects, including ACLs, auditing, and owner rights.

Incremental Security Templates

Windows 2000/XP includes incremental security templates. By default, these templates are stored in the *%SystemRoot%*\Security\Templates folder. These predefined templates may be further customized using the Security Templates MMC snap-in, and then imported into the Security Settings extension of the MMC Group Policy snap-in.

Incremental security templates were developed for step-by-step modifications of the standard security settings that exist in Windows 2000.

NOTE

Incremental security templates may be applied only if you've installed a new copy of the Windows 2000 operating system, and only when you've installed it on the NTFS partition. If you've installed Windows 2000 on the NTFS partition as an upgrade of Windows NT 4.0 or an even earlier Windows NT version, use the standard security template (Basic). The Basic security template is used to configure the system according to the standard security requirements applied by default. Windows 2000/XP systems installed on FAT partitions can't be protected.

Windows 2000 incremental security templates are listed in Table 10.4.

Table 10.4. Windows 2000 Incremental Security Templates

Configuration	Computer Type	Template	Description
Compatible	Workstations and servers	Compatws.inf	Intended for organizations where most users don't need to be included into the Power Users group
Secure	Workstations, servers, and domain controllers	Securews.inf and Securedc.inf	This configuration provides a higher level of security, including account policy, auditing, and access rights to certain registry keys that directly relate to the system security
High Secure	Workstations, servers, and domain controllers	Hisecws.inf and Hisecdc.inf	This configuration is intended for Windows 2000 computers that work in a pure Windows 2000 environment. It requires that all network communications be signed by a digital signature and encrypted (the level of encryption is supported only by Windows 2000). Thus, Windows 2000 computers that are configured using the High Secure template can't interact with earlier Windows NT versions

How the Group Policy is Stored

Group Policy Objects (GPO) store their information in the Group Policy Container and in the Group Policy Template. The Group Policy Container (GPC) is an Active Directory container that stores Group Policy Object (GPO) properties. It can include nested containers for storing information of the group policy related to both users and computers.

Group Policy Templates

Group Policy Objects (GPOs) store their policy information in the folder structure called Group Policy Template (GPT). GPTs are stored in the \Policies subfolder within the \Sysvol folder on domain controllers.

When modifying the GPO, the template is assigned the name of the directory, which is actually a Globally Unique Identifier (GUID) of the Group Policy Object that was modified. An example of the name of the Group Policy Template folder is shown below:

> *%SystemRoot%*\sysvol\<SYSVOL>\<*Domain_Name*>\Policies
> \{47636445-af79-11d0-91fe-080036644603}

Notice that the \<SYSVOL> folder becomes a shared directory named SYSVOL.

The Gpt.ini File

The root level of each GPT folder contains the Gpt.ini file, which keep the following information for all valid group policy objects:

- Client extensions of the Group Policy snap-in that contain the user or computer data within the group policy object
- Whether or not the settings specifying the user or computer policy are disabled
- Version number for the Group Policy snap-in extension used to create the Group Policy Object

Local Group Policy Objects

Local Group Policy Objects exist on each computer. By default, they contain only the security policy. Local Group Policy Objects are stored in the

%SystemRoot%\System32\GroupPolicy folder, and users only have Read access to the folder (administrators and the operating system have full control access to this folder).

Group Policy Template Folders

The Group Policy Template folder contains the following subfolders:

- *Adm*—contains all ADM-files used by the Group Policy Template (GPT).
- *Scripts*—contains all the scripts used by the GPT.
- *User*—contains the Registry.pol file, which lists all registry settings that should be in force in relation to the users. When the user logs on, the system reads this file and loads it to the `HKEY_CURRENT_USER` registry key. The folder contains the following subfolders:
    - *Apps*—contains all files used by Windows Installer.
    - *Files*—contains a list of files that need to be installed.
- *Machine*—contains the Registry.pol file that lists all the registry settings, which should be in force in relation to the computers. When the computer is initialized, the Registry.pol file is loaded into the `HKEY_LOCAL_MACHINE` root key. This folder contains the following subfolders:
    - *Apps*—contains all the files that are used by Windows Installer.
    - *Files*—contains a list of files that need to be installed.
    - *Microsoft\Windows NT\SecEdit*—stores the file that contains security settings (Gpttmpl.inf).

The \User and \Machine subfolders are created automatically during installation, and all the other folders are created when you install the group policy.

The Registry.pol Files

The Administrative Templates extension of the MMC Group Policy snap-in contains information about the group policy templates such as ASCII formatted files like the one named Registry.pol. These files contain individual registry settings specified by the system administrator using the Group Policy snap-in. As I discussed earlier, these settings must be loaded into the registry under `HKLM` and `HKCU` keys.

For each group policy template, there are two Registry.pol files: one for computer configuration in the \Machine folder, and another for user configuration in the \User folder.

NOTE

Format of the Registry.pol files in Windows 2000/XP is different from the Registry.pol format in Windows NT 4.0 and Windows 95. Notice that you need to use Registry.pol files only with the operating system for which these files were created.

The Registry.pol files created in Windows NT 4.0 using the System Policy Editor tool were binary files. In contrast, Registry.pol files created by the Group Policy snap-in in Windows 2000 are text files that contain binary strings.

Registry.pol files created in Windows 2000/XP contain the header and registry settings. The header contains version data and the signature, and it has a `DWORD` format.

Registry settings are specified in the following format:

```
[key;value;type;size;data]
```

where:

`key`—the path to the registry key (notice that you don't need to specify the root key; for example, `HKEY_LOCAL_MACHINE` or `HKEY_CURRENT_USER`). That's because the file location itself (in the \User or \Machine folders) specifies the root key where this key should be loaded.

`value`—list of the registry keys to be deleted (semicolon used as a separator), for example: ***DeleteKeys NoRun;NoFind.*

`type`—data type. Notice that the file format supports all registry data types (see *Chapter 1*). However, the Administrative Templates snap-in only distinguishes between `REG_DWORD`, `REG_EXPAND_SZ`, and `REG_SZ`.

`size`—the size of the data field (in bytes).

`data`—this is the data itself.

Summary

In this chapter, we discussed the user profile files and system policies. Also provided were the necessary instructions (a survival guide) on the use of system policies to introduce registry modifications.

Chapter 11

Troubleshooting Common Problems

"Anything that can go wrong, will."

Murphy's Law

Now that we have discussed nearly all aspects of the registry, it is time to consider some problems that frequently arise when working with Windows NT/2000/XP and that can be eliminated using the registry.

Where shall we start? Obviously, it would be logical to begin with the startup problems and the problems that prevent you from logging onto the system. Why? Because if the system stops immediately after rebooting, it will be impossible to do any other work. Just imagine the situation: your work is urgent and you need to do it right away. (By the way, how many times will it take you to troubleshoot this problem?).

Detailed instructions on backing up and recovering the Windows NT 4.0/2000/XP registry were provided in *Chapter 2.* In this chapter, we'll concentrate on several additional and rarely used procedures that may help you get the system up and running after boot failures.

Troubleshooting Startup Problems

Windows XP is certainly the most reliable Windows, possessing a level of robustness that is simply lacking in its predecessors, including even Windows 2000. Does this all mean that startup problems cannot possibly occur in Windows XP? No, it doesn't. Any operating system can be rendered unbootable, and Windows XP is no exception. So, you must be prepared in order not to feel helpless, if something goes terribly wrong. A significant part of this chapter is dedicated to troubleshooting Windows XP startup problems, which, one should admit, are the most frustrating ones (especially if your system won't boot when you have a lot of work that needs to be done). So, what should you do in case of emergency? First of all, don't panic. Next, try to detect what is preventing Windows XP from booting.

Since Windows XP boot sequence closely resembles that of Windows 2000, most (but not all) techniques described here are also applicable for Windows 2000. A detailed description of Windows 2000/XP boot sequence was provided in *Chapter 6*. Therefore, I will only provide a brief description of the boot sequence, and then we will proceed with problem detection and troubleshooting.

Table 11.1 lists Windows XP startup phases with brief descriptions of the processes that take place at each stage of the normal boot process.

Table 11.1. Brief Description of Windows XP Startup Process

Startup Stage	Description (*x*86-Based Systems)
POST routine	CPU initiates system board POST routines. POST routines of the individual adapters start after the motherboard POST is accomplished successfully
Initial startup process	The system searches for a boot device according to the boot order setting stored in CMOS. If the boot device is a hard disk, Ntldr starts
Operating system load	Ntldr switches the CPU to protected mode, starts the file system, and then reads the contents of the Boot.ini file. This information determines the startup options and initial boot menu selections
Hardware detection and configuration selection	Ntdetect.com gathers basic hardware configuration data and passes this information to Ntldr. If more than one hardware profile exists, Whistler attempts to use the one that is correct for the current configuration. Notice that if your computer is ACPI-compliant, Windows XP ACPI functionality will be used for device enumeration and initialization (more detailed information on this topic was provided in *Chapter 5*)
Kernel loading	Ntldr passes the information collected by Ntdetect.com to Ntoskrnl.exe. Ntoskrnl then loads the kernel, HAL, and registry information. A status bar at the bottom portion of the screen indicates progress
Operating system logon process	Networking-related components (such as TCP/IP) load asynchronously with other services and the **Begin Logon** prompt appears on screen. After a user logs on successfully, Windows XP updates the Last Known Good Configuration information to reflect the current state
New devices are detected by Plug and Play	If Windows XP detects new devices, they are assigned system resources. Windows XP extracts the required driver files from the Driver.cab file. If this file is not found, Windows XP prompts the user to provide them. Device detection occurs asynchronously with the operating system logon process

Diagnosing Startup Problems

Fortunately, Windows XP boot failures are quite rare, especially if you perform regular maintenance and take preventive measures against disaster. However, the problems still have a chance to arise, and, as with any other operating system, they might be caused both by hardware malfunctions and by software errors. If the problem is severe enough, the system stops booting and displays an error message. Quite a brief listing of error messages and their meanings is presented in Table 11.2.

Table 11.2. Startup Problem Symptoms

Startup Problem Symptom	Possible Cause

The POST routine emits a series of beeps and displays error messages, for example:
`Hard disk error.`
`Hard disk absent/failed.`
	The system self-test routines halted due to improperly installed devices.
	
	To recover from hardware problems, carefully review the documentation supplied with your system, and then perform the basic hardware checks. Verify that all cables are correctly attached, and all internal adapters are installed correctly. Make sure that all peripheral devices (such as keyboards) required to complete the POST without error messages are installed and functioning. If applicable, verify that you have correctly configured all jumpers or dual in-line package (DIP) switches. Jumpers and DIP switches are especially important for hard disks. Run diagnostic software to detect hardware malfunction, and replace the faulty device.
	
	Unfortunately, the topic of troubleshooting hardware problems goes beyond the range of problems discussed in this book. As a matter of fact, it deserves a separate comprehensive volume. However, I would like to recommend some helpful resources on the topic that would certainly help you make sense of the BIOS error codes:
	
	BIOS Survival Guide, available at: **http://burks.bton.ac.uk/burks/pcinfo/hardware/bios_sg/bios_sg.htm**
	
	Definitions and Solutions for BIOS Error Beeps and Messages/Codes, available at **www.earthweb.com**

continues

Table 11.2 Continued

Startup Problem Symptom	Possible Cause

Master boot record (MBR)–related error messages similar to the following:
`Missing operating system.`
`Insert a system diskette and restart the system.`
	The MBR is corrupt.
	The easiest method of recovering the damaged MBR is provided by Recovery Console (the methods of starting Recovery Console were discussed in detail in *Chapter 2*). Once you are in Recovery Console, use the `FIXMBR` command to repair the MBR.
	The `FIXMBR` command uses the following syntax:
	`Fixmbr [device_name]`
	where *`device_name`* parameter specifies the drive on which you need to repair the damaged MBR. For example:
	`fixmbr \Device\HardDisk0`
	If the *`device_name`* parameter is omitted, the new MBR will be written to the boot device, from which your primary system is loaded. Notice, that you'll be prompted to confirm your intention to continue, if an invalid partition table is detected

Partition table related error message similar to the following:
`Invalid partition table.`
`A disk-read error occurred.`
	The partition table is invalid.
	You can recover from this problem using the DiskProbe Resource Kit utility or any third-party low-level disk editor. Please take note of the fact that to prevent this problem, you must create a backup copy of the MBR beforehand (for example, use the DiskProbe tool for this purpose). More detailed information on this topic can be found in the Windows XP Resource Kit documentation.
	If the MBR on the disk used to start Windows XP is corrupt, then you'll most likely be unable to start Windows XP (and, consequently, DiskProbe). Therefore, before proceeding any further, you'll have to start Windows XP Recovery Console to replace the damaged MBR

Windows XP cannot start after you have installed another operating system	Windows XP boot sector overwritten by the other operating system's setup program. Windows XP Recovery Console provides the `FIXBOOT` command that enables you to restore the overwritten boot sector
Missing Boot.ini, Ntoskrnl.exe, or Ntdetect.com files (*x*86-based systems)	Required startup files are missing, damaged, or entries in the Boot.ini are pointing to the wrong partition

continues

Table 11.2 Continued

Startup Problem Symptom	Possible Cause

Bootstrap loader error messages similar to the following:
`Couldn't find loader`
`Please insert another disk.`
	Ntldr is missing or corrupt.
	If Ntldr or any other file required to boot the system is missing or corrupt, start Recovery Console and copy the required file

CMOS or NVRAM settings are not retained	The CMOS memory is faulty, data is corrupt, or the battery needs replacing
Stop messages appear	Many possible causes due to software or hardware issues

As I mentioned in *Chapter 6*, both Windows NT/2000 and Windows XP generate system messages known as "blue screens" or "Blue Screens of Death" (BSOD) if they encounter serious errors which they can't correct. The Blue Screen of Death may also appear when Windows NT/2000 stops loading in order to prevent further data corruption. If the STOP message appears during system startup, it's quite likely that the cause of the problem is among the following:

- The user has installed third-party software that's destroyed part of the system registry (that is, the `HKEY_LOCAL_MACHINE` root key). This may happen if the application attempts installation of new service or driver. As a result, the blue screen will appear, informing the user that the registry or one of its hives couldn't be loaded.
- The user has incorrectly modified the hardware configuration and, as a result, one of the critically important system files was overwritten or became corrupt.
- The user has installed a new service or system driver, which is incompatible with the hardware (as a result, the blue screen appears after rebooting). Strictly speaking, it's the attempt to load an incompatible file that leads to the corruption of a correct system file.

NOTE

One of the common drawbacks of Windows NT 4.0 and earlier versions of the Windows NT operating system was caused by shared system files, which could be overwritten during installation of third-party software that was incompatible with the operating system. In Windows 2000/XP, this drawback was eliminated by providing appropriate protection for the critical system files. This new Windows 2000 functionality was discussed in *Chapter 6*. If you wish to avoid startup problems, I recommend that you use these tools on a regular basis.

Parallel Installation of the Operating System

What else can be done to provide universal troubleshooting tools for the startup problems? There's another traditional method of increasing the probability of quick and easy recovery. This method is known as the "parallel installation of the operating system". The parallel installation is just another copy of the Windows NT/2000/XP operating system installed on the same computer. If the main operating system (the one you use most frequently) fails to boot, an additional copy of the operating system will allow quick access to NTFS volumes, system files, and registry hives. Another method of providing access to NTFS volumes after system failures is using the NTFSDOS utility, which will be discussed in the next chapter.

NOTE

Notice that the parallel installations generally weaken the system security (like NTFSDOS, parallel installations provide a backdoor entrance to your main operating system). Thus, from a reliability and recoverability point of view, both parallel installations and NTFSDOS are beneficial. From a security point of view, they're not as good as they may seem to be.

How should you install the parallel system? First of all, do it in advance, since the installation procedure is time-consuming; and, as a general rule, when problems occur, most people are short of time. The next thing you should take into account is that you can only install the minimum set of options in the parallel operating system.

Additional Hardware Profiles

Besides a parallel installation of the operating system, there's another method of performing quick recovery. If you experiment with various hardware devices, and aren't sure if the device you're going to install is listed in the HCL (Hardware Compatibility List), you may use additional hardware profiles for the system recovery. Proceed as follows:

1. Before installing a new device which may cause a problem (including the startup problems), create a new ERD (Windows 2000) or prepare for ASR

(Windows XP) and back up the registry using the method described in *Chapter 2.* Both the ERD (ASR backup) and registry backup copies will be useful in this case.

2. Create a new hardware profile. Launch the System applet in Control Panel, go to the **Hardware** tab and click the **Hardware Profiles** button. The **Hardware Profiles** window will open (Fig. 11.1). Click the **Copy** button and create a new hardware profile by copying one of the existing profiles. The best way to name hardware profiles is to use "speaking names", which explain their usage (for example, Working—the current hardware profile, free of errors; and Experimental—the new hardware profile, where you'll do experiments). In the **Hardware profiles selection** group of options, set the **Wait until I select a hardware profile** radio button.

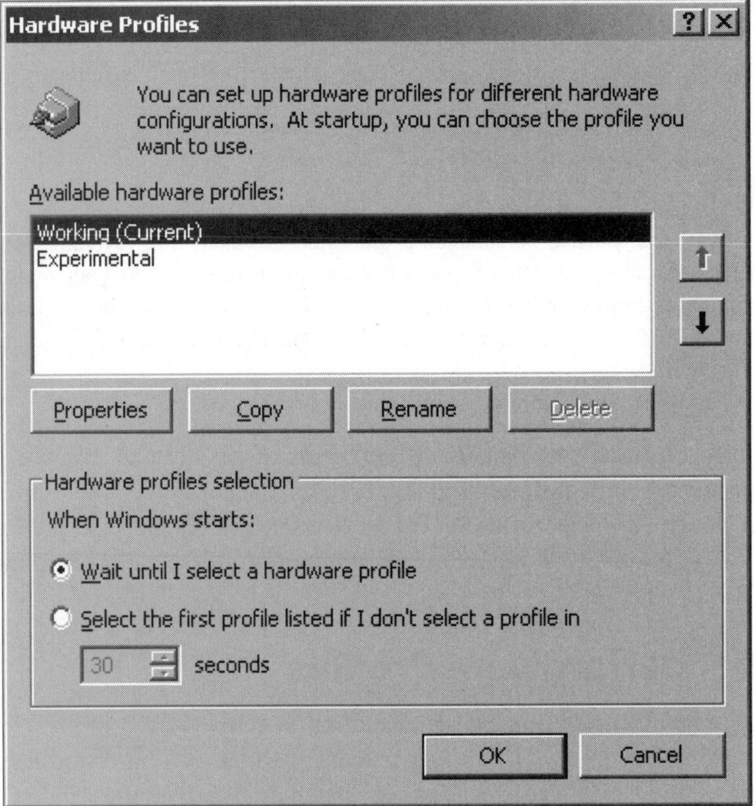

Fig. 11.1. Before installing a new device that isn't listed in the HCL, create additional hardware profile

3. Check if the hardware profiles are usable. Try to start the operating system using each of them.

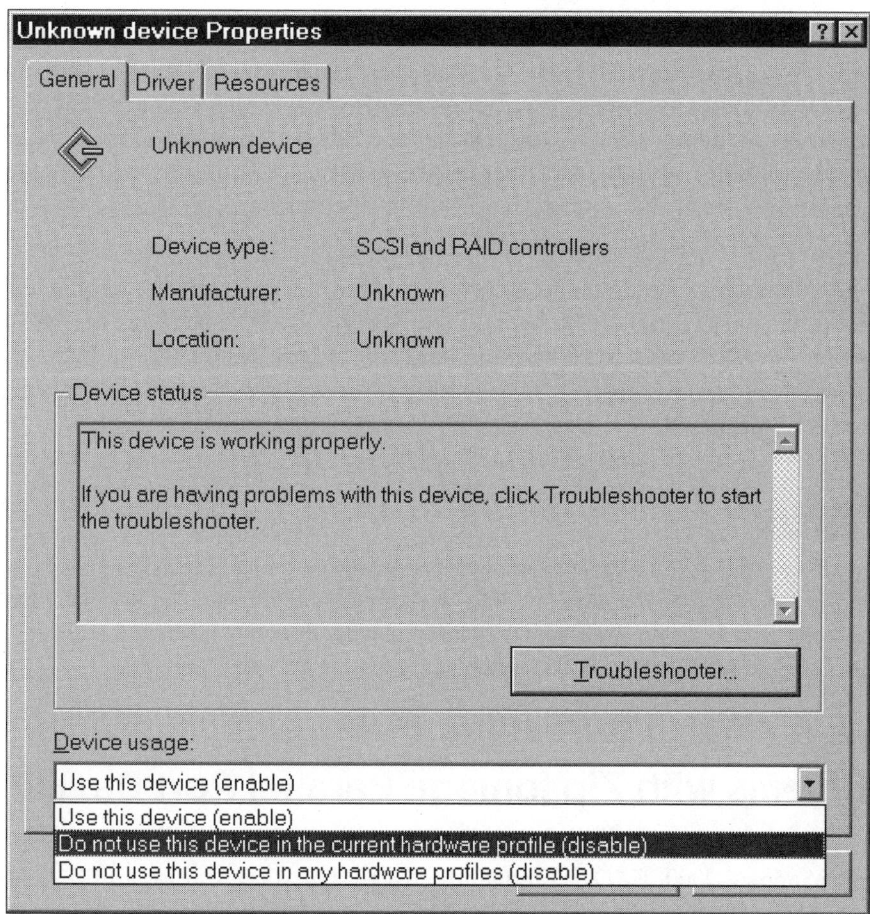

Fig. 11.2. Despite the fact that the Device Manager states that **This device is working properly**, a newly installed device will cause problems. Disable it in the current hardware profile

4. Start the computer using the Working profile, and proceed with installing the new device and its drivers using the Hardware Wizard. If the system prompts you to reboot the computer, don't reboot the system immediately. Start the Device Manager, find the newly installed device in the list and select the **Properties** command from the context menu. You'll see the **General** tab of the properties window for this device. If the newly installed device is incompatible, you'll immediately see that "something is wrong" (despite the phrase "This device is working properly" displayed in the **Device status** field, as shown in Fig. 11.2). For example, this device may be marked as an Unknown device,

which means that the device is really unknown to the system. In short, this device really may cause problems (in our case, you'll probably get the blue screen after the reboot). To avoid possible problems, disable this device in the current hardware profile by selecting the **Do not use this device in the current hardware profile (disable)** option from the **Device usage** list. Thus, the problem device will be disabled in the current hardware profile, and will remain enabled in the experimental hardware profile.

5. Now reboot the system, and select the experimental hardware profile (where the problem device is enabled). Did you see the BSOD? Nothing horrible happened, because you have a working hardware profile where the problem device is disabled. In most cases, you'll be able to boot the system using the working hardware profile.

NOTE

I recommend that you always have a working hardware profile (which contains no errors and enables no problem devices). This type of profile often provides an easier method of recovering a system with configuration problems than the Advanced startup menu, displayed during Windows 2000 startup after pressing the <F8> key.

Problems with Zip Iomega Parallel Port Device

This is a problem encountered by many users; and because of this, it's present in many Windows 2000 FAQs (Frequently Asked Questions). Zip Iomega parallel port devices often cause boot problems (blue screen), despite the fact that they're listed in the Windows 2000 HCL. If you've also encountered this problem, then you've probably installed the device incorrectly. Notice that Zip Iomega drivers written for Windows NT 4.0 and Windows 95/98 (these drivers are supplied on the companion CD) are incompatible with Windows 2000. If you need to install the Zip Iomega parallel port device and use it under Windows 2000, then you'll need Microsoft-supplied drivers for this device.

To install Zip Iomega parallel port device under Windows 2000, proceed as follows:

1. Switch your device to the parallel port.
2. Start Windows 2000, launch the System applet in Control Panel, navigate to the **Hardware** tab and click the **Device Manager** button.

3. Expand the Ports node in the hardware tree, select the port to which the new device is connected, and select the **Properties** command from the context menu. The properties window for the port will open. Navigate to the **Port Settings** tab (Fig. 11.3).

4. Set the **Enable legacy Plug and Play detection** checkbox.

5. Reboot the system. After the reboot, the Zip Iomega device will be detected and installed automatically.

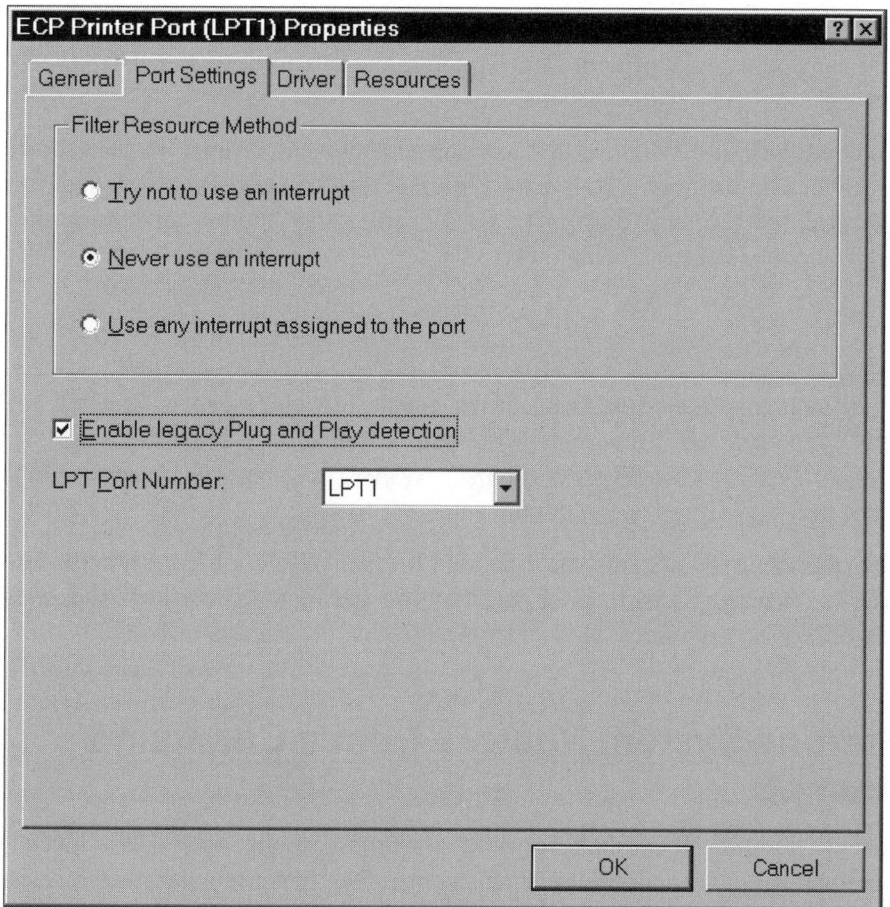

Fig. 11.3. To install the Zip Iomega parallel port device, set the **Enable legacy Plug and Play detection** on the **Port Settings** tab of the properties window for the port to which the device is connected

NOTE

If you install the Zip Iomega parallel port device using the method described above, the device will work correctly. Don't attempt to install the Iomega Zip Tools software, however, because these utilities aren't Windows 2000-compatible. An attempt to install these tools will cause problems.

How Can I See the Horrible Blue Screen of Death?

Have you ever seen the Blue Screen of Death? If you haven't, most people will consider you a lucky person. What... you're curious to see what it is? Well, here you are!

Windows 2000 and Windows XP has one undocumented function that allows you to generate an artificial STOP error ("Blue Screen of Death") and manually create a crash dump (Memory.dmp). The STOP screen that appears after using this feature will contain the following message:

```
*** STOP: 0x000000E2 (0x00000000,0x00000000,0x00000000,0x00000000)
The end-user manually generated the crashdump.
```

By default, this feature is disabled. To enable it, you'll need to edit the registry and reboot the computer. Open the `HKEY_LOCAL_MACHINE\SYSTEM\CurrentControlSet\Services\i8042prt\Parameters` registry key, add the `REG_DWORD CrashOnCtrlScroll` value and set it to 1.

After rebooting the system, you'll be able to manually "crash" the system. To view the Blue Screen of Death, press and hold on the right <Ctrl> key, and press the <Scroll Lock> key twice.

Starting System Restore from a Command Prompt

System Restore is certainly one of the most useful tools introduced with Windows XP (experienced users must remember that a similar feature exists in Windows ME). However, what can you do, if you are unable to start your Windows XP-based computer normally or in the Safe Mode? Is the tool quite useless for such cases? Well, not quite.

If your computer is unable to start normally or in the Safe mode, try the following tip to start System Restore from the command prompt.

To start the System Restore tool when you are unable to start your Windows XP-based computer normally or in Safe mode, temporarily change the Windows shell from Explorer.exe to Progman.exe:

1. Start your computer to Safe Mode with the Command Prompt.

NOTE

You must log on as the administrator or a user that has administrator rights.

2. At the command prompt, type `regedit`, and then press <Enter>.
3. View the following registry key:

   `HKEY_LOCAL_MACHINE\SOFTWARE\Microsoft\WindowsNT\CurrentVersion\Winlogon`

4. In the right pane, modify the `Shell` value entry by changing its value from Explorer.exe to Progman.exe, then click **OK** and close Regedit.exe.
5. At the command prompt, type `shutdown -r`, and then press <Enter> to restart your computer.
6. Log on as the administrator or a user with administrator rights.
7. When Program Manager starts, click **Run** on the **File** menu, type `%SystemRoot%\system32\restore\rstrui.exe`, and then press <Enter>.
8. Follow the instructions on the screen to begin restoring your computer to a previous, functional state.

NOTE

Most users wonder whether or not System Restore restores passwords. Because System Restore only rolls back the local machine state, it will restore the passwords that are cached in the local system registry. For example, program passwords such as Hotmail Messenger or Yahoo Messenger will be restored. Notice, however, that actual passwords for such programs reside on the respective Web server, and System Restore will only restore the password remembered by the program. Domain passwords are also restored (notice, however, that part of the information related to joining domains is stored in Active Directory, and this information is not rolled back by System Restore).

On the other hand, System Restore will not roll back Windows XP passwords and hints. This is by design. It is intended to prevent confusion as well as those situations when you lock out your computer because the restore point included old passwords that you do not remember. By the same reason, System Restore will not restore the passwords and hints for Internet Explorer and Content Advisor.

How to Re-Create Missing ASR Floppy Disk

Well, you have tried all troubleshooting steps but nothing happens, and, finally, you have decided to run the Automated System Recovery (ASR) process. And, most unfortunately, when you decided to do so, you discover that your ASR diskette is missing. Does it mean that everything is lost? No, it doesn't, since if your media storing ASR backup is usable, you can re-create the missing ASR floppy disk.

Perhaps you have wondered what the ASR disk contains (and it isn't difficult just to look and find out that the Asr.sif and Asrpnp.sif files contained on the ASR diskette are ASCII files that can be viewed or edited with any text editor, such as Notepad.exe). What's even better is that these files can be extracted from the ASR backup set and then copied to a floppy disk that can be used for an ASR procedure.

Therefore, to recreate a missing ASR diskette, do the following:

1. Format a 1.44 megabyte (MB) floppy disk and insert the disk into the floppy disk drive of the computer.
2. In **System Tools**, start the Backup program. When the **Backup or Restore Wizard** screen is displayed, click **Next**.
3. Click **Restore Files and Settings**, and then click **Next**.
4. In the **What to Restore** dialog box, select the media that contain the ASR backup. Ensure that the media are inserted.
5. Expand the **Automated System Recovery Backup Set** that corresponds to the ASR floppy disk that you want to create.
6. Expand the second instance of the drive letter that contains the system files. Expand the *Windows_folder*/Repair folder.
7. Click the following files from this repair folder: Asr.sif, Asrpnp.sif, and Setup.log (Fig. 11.4), and then click **Next**.
8. At the **Completing Backup or Restore Wizard** screen, click **Advanced**.

9. At the **Where to Restore** screen, set the **Restore Files to:** dialog box to **Single Folder**, and then set the **Folder Name** dialog box to the root of your floppy drive, for example, "A:\".

10. Click **Next**. The other options in this wizard are not mandatory and do not affect the transfer of files to the floppy disk. When the wizard is finished, the files are copied to the location that you had previously specified. The ASR floppy disk is ready for use in the event of an ASR restore operation.

NOTE

The Asr.sif and Asrpnp.sif files must reside on the root of the floppy disk drive to be used during ASR restore operation.

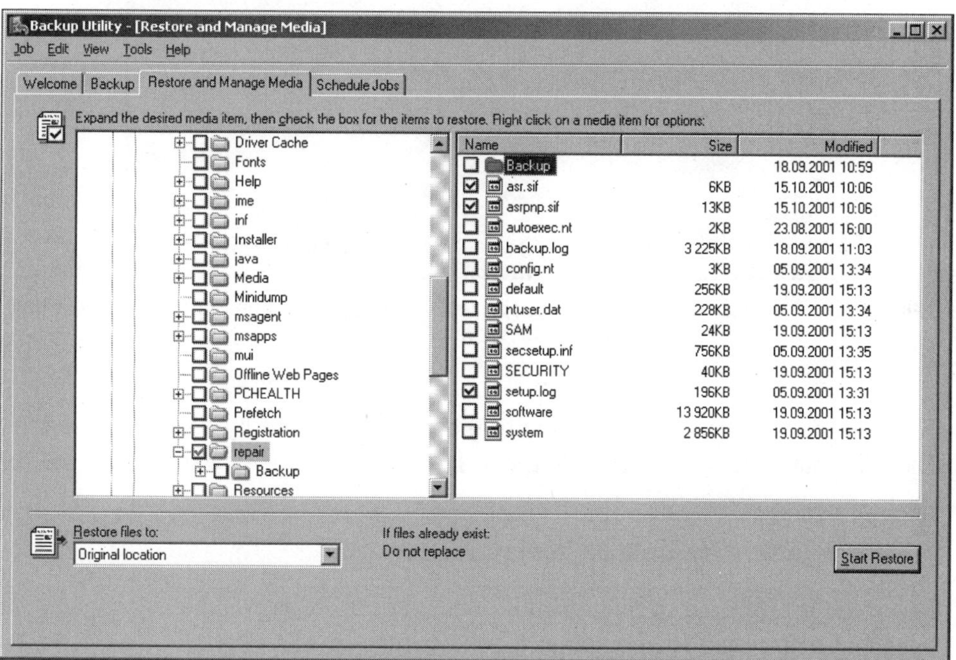

Fig. 11.4. Re-creating the missing ASR floppy disk

Troubleshooting Shutdown Problems

Sometimes, when you want to shut down or restart Windows XP, you may see a dialog similar to the one shown in Fig. 11.5. Even worse, this may happen persistently, thus preventing you from shutting down correctly. The source of this problem lies in the fact that when Windows XP shuts down, each running process is given 20 seconds to perform cleanup work by default. If a process does not respond within this timeout period, Windows XP displays this dialog.

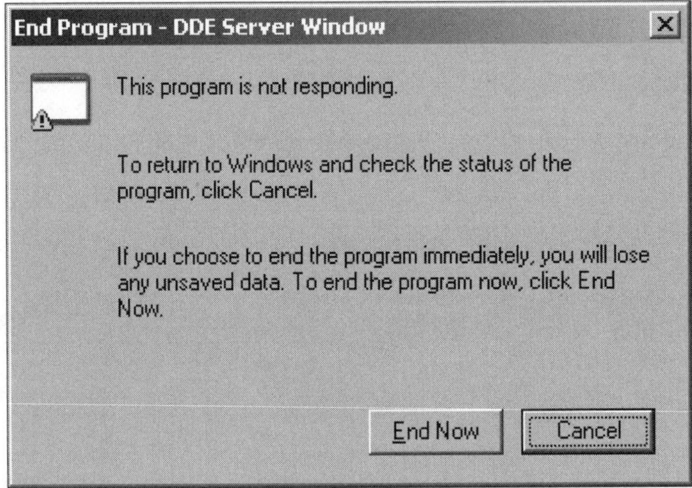

Fig. 11.5. This process doesn't respond within the default time-out, thus preventing Windows XP from shutting down

To solve this problem, you can modify the default timeout by editing the registry. The time-out value is specified by the `WaitToKillAppTimeout` value under the following registry key:

```
HKEY_CURRENT_USER\Control Panel\Desktop
```

This value is expressed in milliseconds. You can use Registry Editor to modify this value and then restart the computer for the change to take effect.

NOTE

In general, it is not recommended that you increase the shutdown time, because, in case of power failure, your Uninterruptible Power Supply (UPS) may not be able to provide backup power for the computer long enough to allow all the processes, as well as the operating system, to shut down properly.

Configuring Windows NT/2000/XP to Clear the Paging File at Shutdown

Some third-party programs may temporarily store unencrypted (plain-text) passwords or other sensitive information in memory. Since Windows XP is based on the Windows NT/2000 kernel, this information may be present in the paging file, thus presenting a potential danger to the system security. Therefore, users who really care for security may wish to clear the Windows NT/2000/XP paging file (Pagefile.sys) during shutdown, so that no unsecured data is contained in the paging file when the shutdown process is complete.

NOTE

This tip is applicable to all versions of Windows NT/2000/XP, starting with Windows NT 3.51. It's important to keep in mind that clearing the paging file is not a substitute for a computer's physical security. Still, it helps to secure your data when Windows NT/2000/XP is not running.

To clear the paging file at shutdown, proceed as follows:

1. If you are working with Windows XP, start Regedit.exe. If you are working with Windows NT/2000, start Regedt32.exe.
2. Open the following registry key:

```
HKEY_LOCAL_MACHINE\SYSTEM\CurrentControlSet\Control\Session Manager\
Memory Management
```

3. Find the `ClearPageFileAtShutdown` value (`REG_DWORD` data type) and set its value to 1. If this value doesn't exist, create it.

NOTE

This change does not take effect until you restart the computer.

How to Unlock a Windows XP Workstation

In Windows XP, you can lock and unlock a workstation either manually (Fig. 11.6) or by means of a program (for example, by using a screen saver). For example, you can lock your workstation at the office, and then connect to it from other location and continue working with your documents. When you return to your workplace, you can unlock your workstation.

When a user logs on to a computer, the Winlogon Service stores a hash of the user's password for unlock attempts made in the future. When the user attempts to unlock the workstation, this stored copy of the password is verified. If the password entered at the unlock dialog request and stored hash match, the workstation is unlocked. If the password entered does not match the stored hash, the workstation attempts to logon (authenticate the password). If the logon process succeeds, the local hash is updated with the new password. If the logon process is unsuccessful, the unlock process will also be unsuccessful.

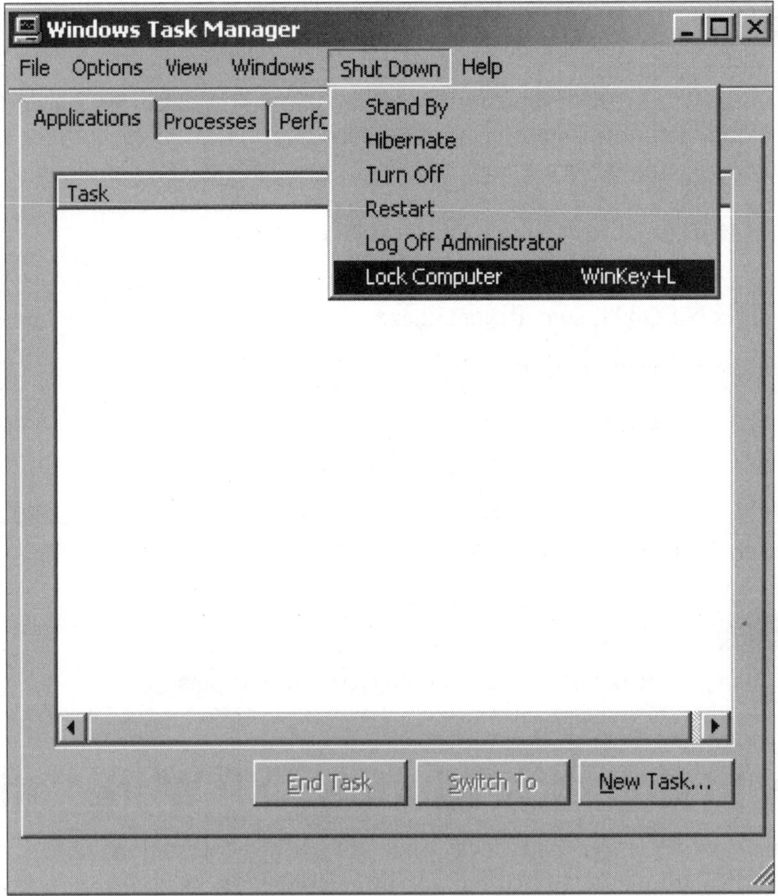

Fig. 11.6. Locking a workstation

NOTE

This only happens when you have Fast User Switching disabled. When you join a Windows XP Professional computer to a domain, the Welcome Screen logon (and Fast User Switching) is disabled.

The unlocking process described above was designed in order to limit network traffic generated by the workstation. However, if you need to specify more stringent security, you can edit the following registry setting: `ForceUnlockLogon` (`REG_DWORD` data type) under the following registry key:

```
HKEY_LOCAL_MACHINE\Software\Microsoft\WindowsNT\CurrentVersion\
Winlogon
```

If this value is set to 0 (the default value), the system doesn't force authentication; if it is set to 1, online authentication is required to unlock the workstation, which can force a validation at the domain controller for the user who attempts to unlock the computer.

Other Problems

Certainly, startup and shutdown problems are the most important ones. As a result, we discussed them first. However, in the process of doing your everyday work using Windows 2000/XP, you may encounter many other problems, some of which may be solved only by editing the registry.

Enabling Debug Logging for User Profiles and System Policy

If you experience problems with user profiles or group policy processing, the debug logging will prove helpful for troubleshooting purposes. In Windows NT 4.0, this required the user to have a debug build of the Userenv.dll file. In Windows 2000 and Windows XP, this functionality is built into the operating system. However, it is not enabled by default. If you need to troubleshoot user profiles and system policy processing, you can enable it by editing the registry as follows:

1. Start Registry Editor and open the following registry key:

   ```
   HKEY_LOCAL_MACHINE\Software\Microsoft\WindowsNT\CurrentVersion\
   Winlogon
   ```

2. Add the `REG_DWORD` registry value named `UserEnvDebugLevel` (or simply modify the value if it already exists). Set the value to `10002 (Hex)`.

3. Restart the computer. The log file is written to the *%SystemRoot%*\Debug\UserMode\Userenv.log file.

Configuring the Backup Utility

If you back up your system on a regular basis, you've already noticed that the Backup utility supplied with Windows 2000/XP excludes certain files from the backup and recovery processes. To view the list of these files start the Backup program, then select the **Options** command from the **Tools** menu and go to the **Exclude Files** tab (Fig. 11.7).

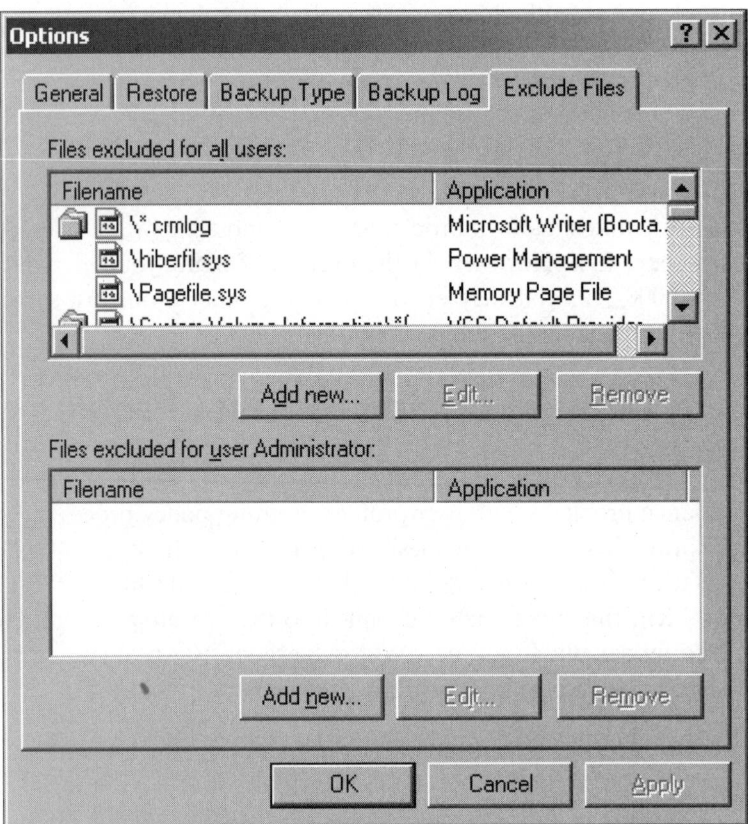

Fig. 11.7. The **Exclude Files** tab of the **Options** window of the Backup built-in utility

By default, Windows 2000/XP supports the list of files and folders excluded from the backup and recovery processes preformed using Backup (Ntbackup.exe) and other backup software compatible with Windows 2000 or Windows XP.

Under normal conditions, these files need to be excluded from the backup and recovery procedures. However, there may be some situations when the system administrator or advanced Windows 2000/XP user needs to include these files into the backup copy.

The files excluded from the backup and recovery processes are listed in the registry under the following registry key: `HKLM\SYSTEM\CurrentControlSet\Control\BackupRestore\FilesNotToBackup`. The content of this key is shown in Fig. 11.8.

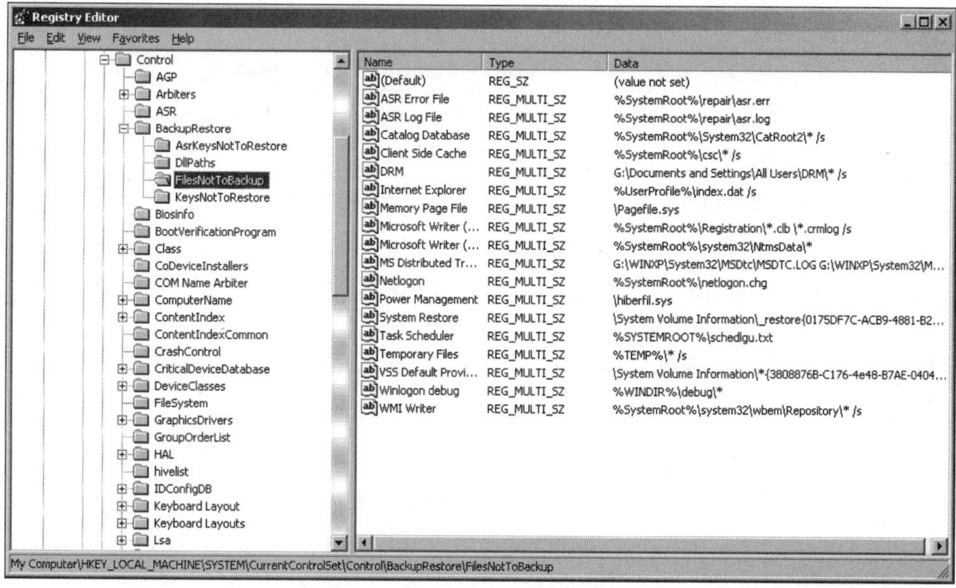

Fig. 11.8. The `HKLM\SYSTEM\CurrentControlSet\Control\BackupRestore\FilesNotToBackup` registry key

Of course, the **Exclude Files** tab of the **Options** window in the Backup program has buttons such as **Add new**, **Edit**, and **Remove**. These command buttons allow you to edit the list of files excluded from backup and recovery processes. However, all the changes entered here will be put in force only in relation to the user who performed this modification (they'll be written into the registry under `HKEY_CURRENT_USER`). Thus, if you need to edit the list of files excluded from backup and recovery procedures for the whole system, you'll have to edit the registry manually.

Default settings listed under the `FilesNotToBackup` key (they're all `REG_MULTI_SZ` values) are listed in Table 11.3.

Table 11.3. The List of Default Settings Under the *FilesNotToBackup* Key

Setting	Data
ASR error file*	*%SystemRoot%\repair*asr.err
ASR log file*	*%SystemRoot%\repair*asr.log
Digital Rights Management (DRM) folder*	*%SystemDrive%\Documents and Settings\All Users*DRM * */s*
Catalog database*	*%SystemRoot%\System32\CatRoot2\ * /s*
Client Side Cache	*%SystemRoot%*\csc* /s
ComPlus	*%SystemRoot%*\Registration*.crmlog /s
Internet Explorer	*%UserProfile%*\index.dat /s
Memory Page File	\Pagefile.sys
Microsoft Writer (Bootable state)*	*%SystemRoot%*\Registration\ **.clb* \ **.crmlog /s*
Microsoft Writer (Service state)*	*%SystemRoot%*\system32\NtmsData\ *
MS Distributed Transaction	*%SystemRoot%*\System32\DTCLog\MSDTC.LOG
Netlogon*	*%SystemRoot%*\netlogon.chg
NtFrs	*%SystemRoot%*\ntfrs\jet* /s *%SystemRoot%*\debug\NtFrs* *%SystemRoot%*\sysvol\domain \DO_NOT_REMOVE_NtFrs_PreInstall_Directory* /s *%SystemRoot%*\sysvol\domain \NtFrs_PreExisting___See_EventLog* /s *%SystemRoot%*\sysvol\staging\domain\NTFRS_*
Power Management	\hiberfil.sys
VSS Default Provider	\System Volume Information*{3808876B-C176-4e48-B7AE-04046E6CC752} /s
Temporary Files	*%TEMP%** /s

* New to Windows XP

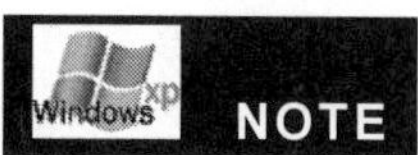

Notice that the HKLM\SYSTEM\CurrentControlSet\Control\BackupRestore registry key in Windows XP also contains a new subkey, HKEY_LOCAL_MACHINE\SYSTEM\CurrentControlSet\Control\BackupRestore\AsrKeysNotToRestore, which contains a list of keys not to be restored by the ASR process (Fig. 11.9). It points to the database of critical devices that should not be edited, since these critical devices need to be re-enumerated by Windows XP Setup during ASR process.

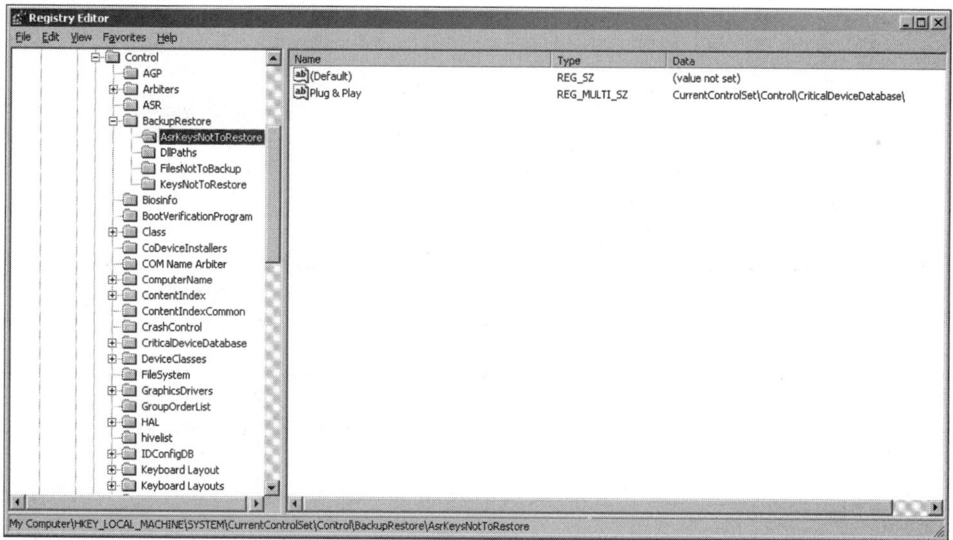

Fig. 11.9. The contents of the HKEY_LOCAL_MACHINE\SYSTEM\CurrentControlSet\Control\BackupRestore\AsrKeysNotToRestore registry key (new in Windows XP)

The situation is even worse for the registry keys, because some registry keys are also excluded from the backup procedures by default. These keys aren't listed on the **Exclude Files** tab of the **Options** window; consequently, you can't edit this list using the user interface. This list is stored in the registry under HKLM\SYSTEM\CurrentControlSet\Control\BackupRestore\KeysNotToRestore (Fig. 11.10).

The list of default settings present under this key is shown in Table 11.4.

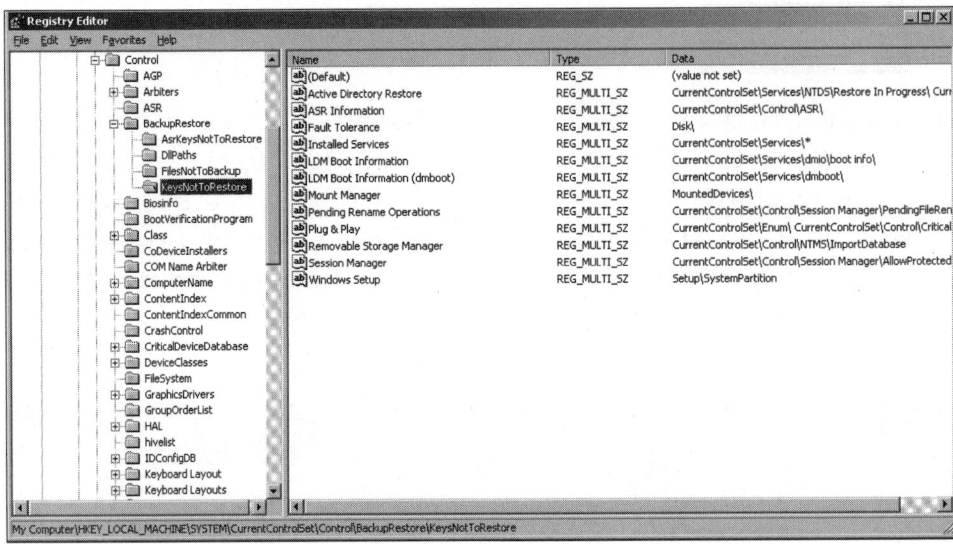

Fig. 11.10. The contents of the `HKLM\SYSTEM\CurrentControlSet\Control\BackupRestore\KeysNotToRestore registry` key

Table 11.4. Default Settings Stored under the *HKLM\SYSTEM\Current ControlSet\Control\BackupRestore\KeysNotToRestore* Registry Key

Setting	Value
Active Directory Restore	CurrentControlSet\Services\NTDS\Restore In Progress \CurrentControlSet\Services\NTDS\Parameters \New Database GUID
ASR Information*	CurrentControlSet\Control\ASR\
Fault Tolerance	Disk\
Installed Services	CurrentControlSet\Services*
LDM Boot Information	CurrentControlSet\Services\dmio\boot info\
LDM Boot Information (dmboot)*	CurrentControlSet\Services\dmboot\
Mount Manager	MountedDevices\
Pending Rename Operations	CurrentControlSet\Control\Session Manager\ PendingFileRenameOperations
Plug and Play	CurrentControlSet\Enum\CurrentControlSet \Control\CriticalDeviceDatabase\

continues

Table 11.4 Continued

Setting	Value
Removable Storage Manager*	CurrentControlSet\Control\NTMS\ImportDatabase
Session Manager	CurrentControlSet\Control\Session
Windows Setup	Setup\SystemPartition

* New in Windows XP.

Removing Invalid Items from the List Displayed by the Add/Remove Programs Wizard

The Add/Remove Programs applet in Control Panel is intended for adding, removing, or modifying the applications installed in your Windows 2000/XP system. In Windows 2000/XP, this wizard has significantly improved and has a nice user interface (Fig. 11.11).

However, despite all these improvements, there may be some problems with the wizard. For example, if one of your applications wasn't removed correctly (and completely), the reference to the application continues to appear in the **Currently installed programs** list. Any attempt to use the Add/Remove Programs wizard for removing the application (by clicking the **Change/Remove**) results in a series of system messages. These messages inform you that some files necessary for the correct removal of the application weren't found, and the removal procedure can't be completed. The nonexistent application remains in the list.

How can you solve this problem? To remove a nonexistent application from the **Currently installed programs** list, proceed as follows:

1. Start Regedit.exe and open the `HKEY_LOCAL_MACHINE\SOFTWARE\Microsoft\Windows\CurrentVersion\Uninstall` key (Fig. 11.12).
2. Within this key, find the subkey created by the application that you want to remove from the list. If the name of that key isn't evident, browse all the keys and view the `DisplayName` value, which specifies the strings displayed by the Add/Remove Programs wizard in the list of installed applications.

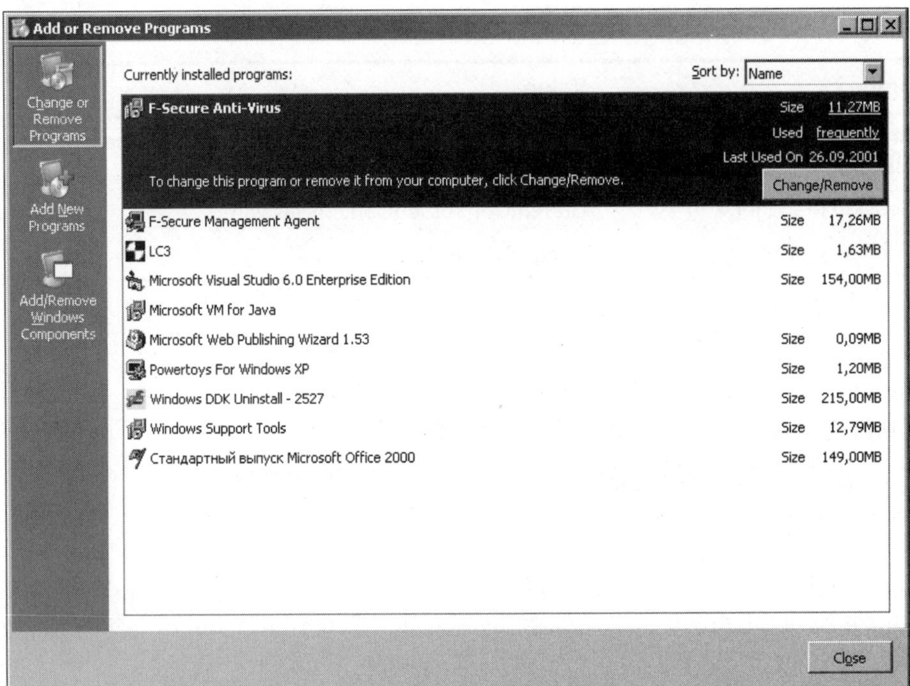

Fig. 11.11. The **Add or Remove Programs** window

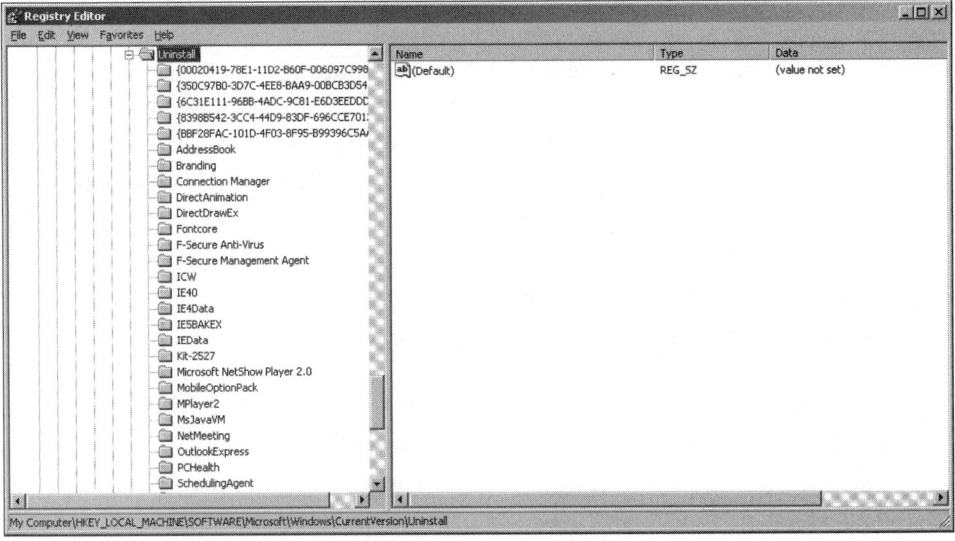

Fig. 11.12. The `HKEY_LOCAL_MACHINE\SOFTWARE\Microsoft\Windows\CurrentVersion\Uninstall` registry key

3. When you find the key whose `DisplayName` value specifies the name of the application that you want to delete from the list, delete this key with all its contents. Warning! Never try to delete the whole `Uninstall` key!
4. Close the registry editor. Then verify that the Add/Remove Programs wizard no longer displays the incorrectly deleted application.

NOTE

If you proceed according to this recommendation, you'll delete only the reference to the string displayed by the Add/Remove Programs wizard. However, it's possible that some of the files installed by the incorrectly deleted application will still remain in your system. To remove the application completely, you'll need to delete all its files and registry entries used by the program. You can do this operation manually only if you're an advanced user (if you do this, don't forget to backup the registry before proceeding any further).

Configuring the Disk Quota Event Logging

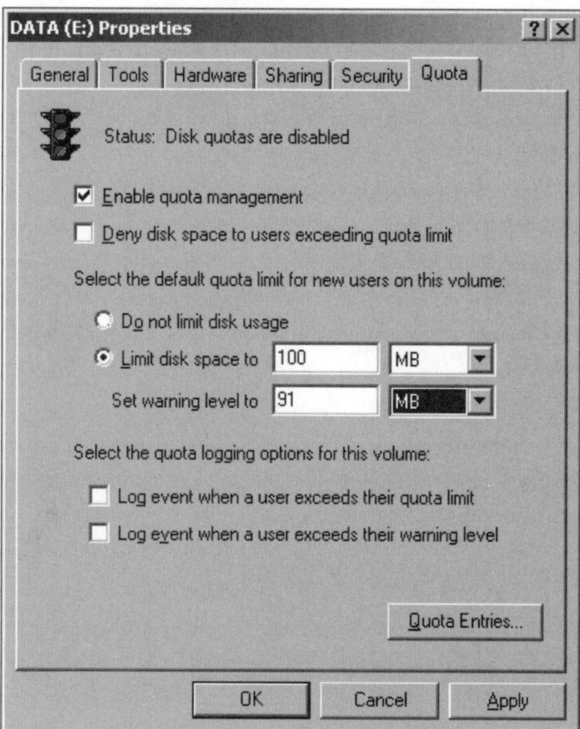

Fig. 11.13. The **Quota** tab of the NTFS drive properties window

Most advanced users and system administrators have noticed the new and useful Disk Quota capability, introduced with Windows 2000/XP. Disk Quota events are written to the event log (if enabled) using the logging option in **Quota** properties for a drive using the NTFS file system (Fig. 11.13).

By default, Disk Quota event logging occurs asynchronously (once per hour). If you need to configure the system to log Disk Quota events immediately when a user exceeds one of the threshold values, you have to edit the registry. Start the registry editor, open the `HKEY_LOCAL_MACHINE\System\CurrentControlSet\Control\FileSystem` key and create the `REG_DWORD` value named `NtfsQuotaNotifyRate`, which, by default, isn't present in the registry. Specify the required frequency of the Disk Quota event logging (specify the value in seconds).

Summary

In this chapter, we discussed methods of solving some common Windows 2000/XP problems using the registry. In practice, of course, there are many more problems like these. You'll find many methods of using the registry to find solutions. I wish you good luck on this difficult, but very interesting road.

Chapter 12

Advanced Customization and Troubleshooting Tips

Just the place for a Snark! I have said it twice:
That alone should encourage the crew.
Just the place for a Snark! I have said it thrice:
What I tell you three times is true.

Lewis Carrol
The Hunting of the Snark

Now, as we have discussed the most common problems, the time has come to consider more advanced customization and troubleshooting topics. You have probably already encountered some of the tips provided here, and perhaps even in the previous chapters of this book. However, here we will cover these topics in more detail, and, after all, "what I tell you three times is true".

Interface Customizations

First, I would like to describe some useful UI customizations, most of which can't be done by the GUI tools and administrative utilities.

Registry Values for Configuring Start Menu in Windows XP

In *Chapter 1* we briefly discussed the methods of customizing the taskbar and Start menu in Windows XP by means of the standard Graphical User Interface (GUI). We have also noted that for most users, especially beginners, this method of customization is preferable. However, for advanced users there are lots of capabilities allowing one to customize Windows XP user interface by using Group Policy editor (Gpedit.msc) or by editing the registry directly. Let us cover these settings in more detail.

The most convenient way to edit the taskbar and **Start** menu features is provided by the Group Policy editor. To start editing these policies, proceed as follows:

1. Click **Start**, click **Run**, type **mmc**, and then click **OK**.
2. From the **File** menu, select the **Add/Remove Snap-in** command, go to the **Standalone** tab, and click **Add**.

3. From the **Available Standalone Snap-ins** list, select the **Group Policy** option and then click the **Add** button. When the **Select Group Policy object** window opens, select the **Local Computer** option to edit the local Group Policy object, or click **Browse** to find the Group Policy object that you want.

4. Click **Finish**, then **Close**, then **OK**. The Group Policy snap-in opens the Group Policy object for editing. Expand the console tree in the left pane of this window as follows: **User Configuration | Administrative Templates | Start Menu and Taskbar** (Fig. 12.1).

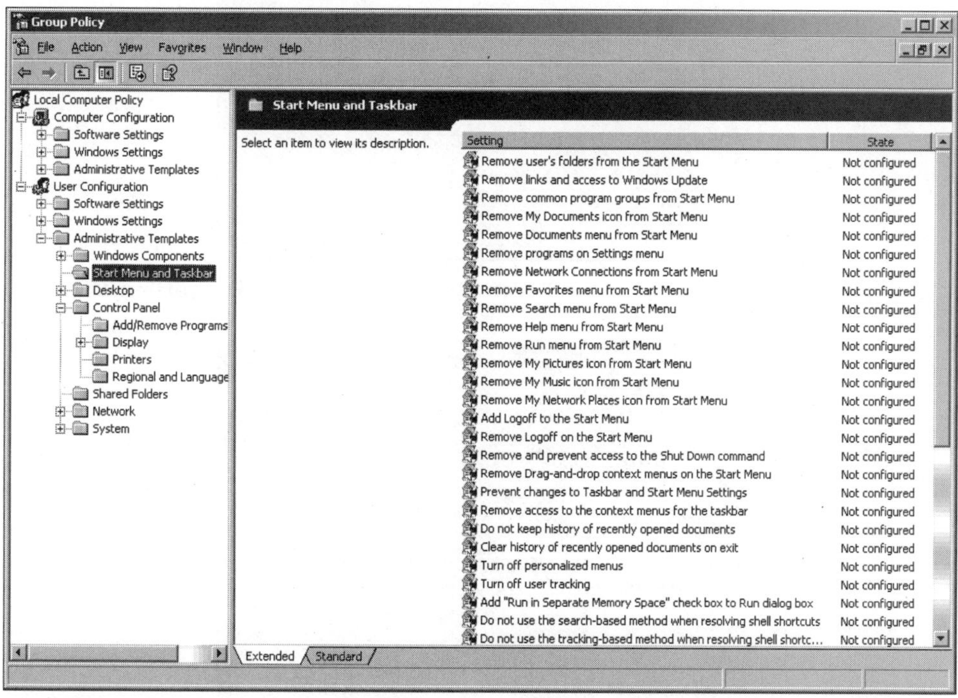

Fig. 12.1. Editing **Start** menu and taskbar policies using Group Policy editor

Let us consider the utilization of these policies on the example of the **Force classic Start Menu Properties** policy.

1. Go to the right pane of the Group Policy window and double-click the **Force classic Start Menu** item in the list of available policies. The **Force classic Start Menu Properties** window will open (Fig. 12.2). To view the explanation of the policy settings, click the **Explain** tab (Fig. 12.3).

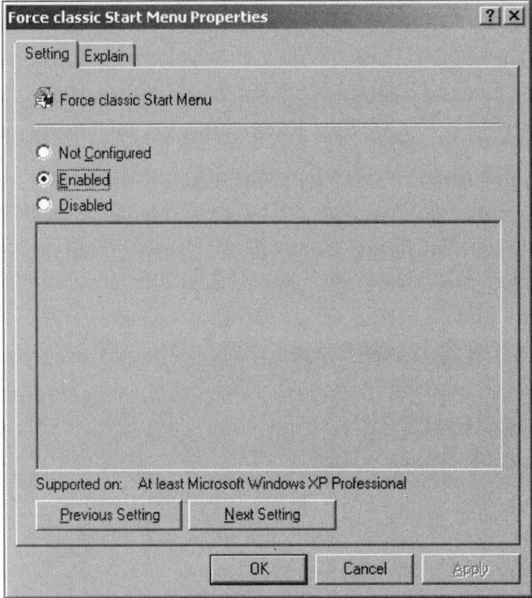

Fig. 12.2. The **Setting** tab of the **Force classic Start Menu Properties** window

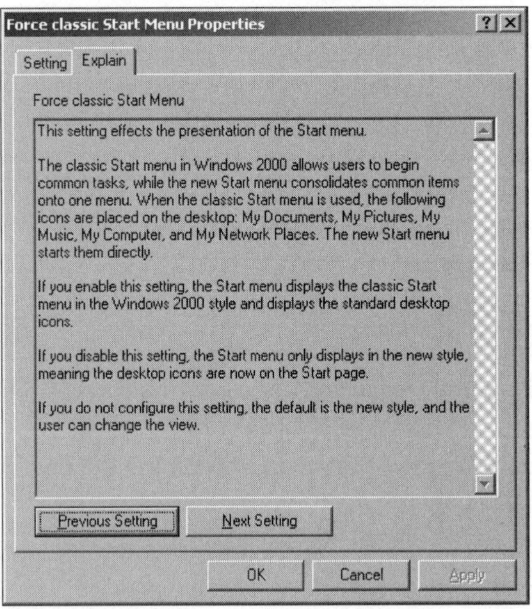

Fig. 12.3. The **Explain** tab of the policy properties window explains the effect of applying the currently selected policy

2. To set the selected policy, set the **Enabled** radio button and click **Apply**.

3. Now, to view the effect of the application of this policy, open the **Taskbar and Start Menu Properties** window and go to the **Start Menu** tab. Notice that the **Start menu** radio button, which is present by default, has become unavailable, and the user is now forced to use the classic Windows NT/2000-style **Start** menu (Fig. 12.4).

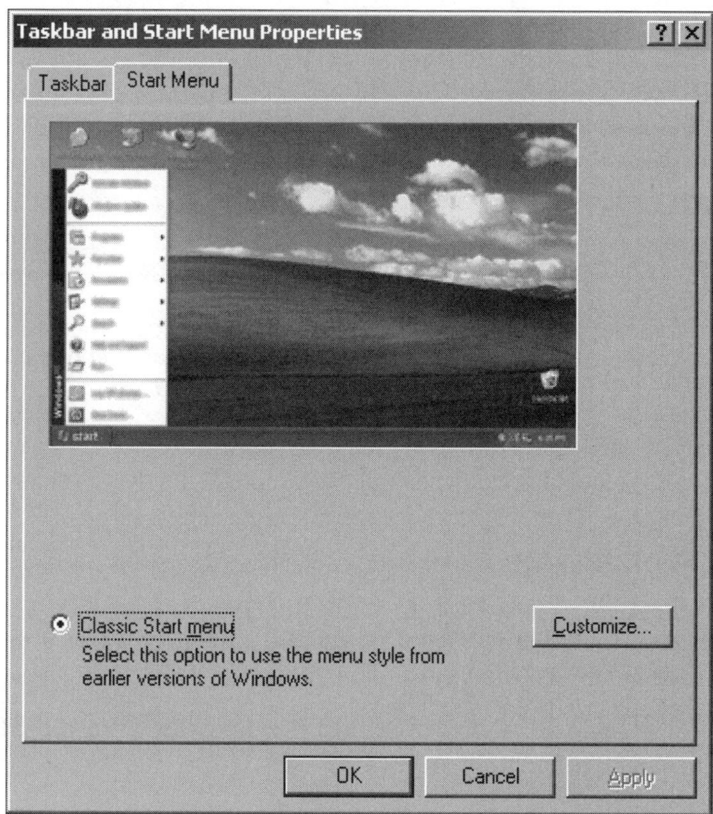

Fig. 12.4. The effect of applying the **Force classic Start Menu** policy

You can certainly achieve the same result by editing the registry directly. For example, by enabling the **Force classic Start Menu** policy you create the `NoSimpleStartMenu` registry value (`REG_DWORD` data type) under the `HKEY_CURRENT_USER\Software\Microsoft\Windows\CurrentVersion\Policies\Explorer` registry key (Fig. 12.5).

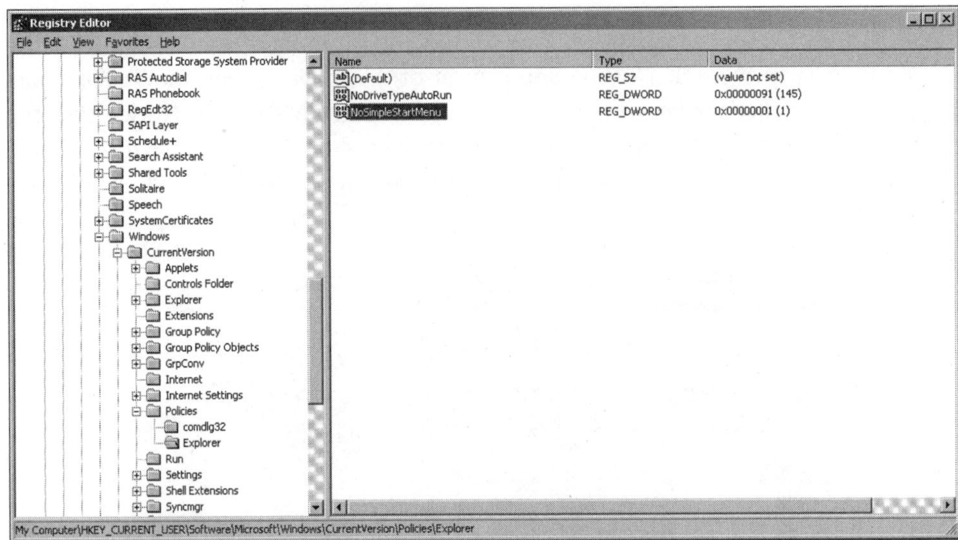

Fig. 12.5. The `HKEY_CURRENT_USER\Software\Microsoft\Windows\CurrentVersion\Policies\Explorer` registry key reflects the effect of applying the **Force classic Start Menu** policy

Other registry values that you can create to customize the taskbar and Start menu are listed below. Except when specially noted, all these values are of the `REG_DWORD` data type. They reside under the following registry key:

```
HKEY_CURRENT_USER\Software\Microsoft\Windows\CurrentVersion\Policies\
Explorer
```

If the value is set to 1, the restriction is enabled, when the value is set to 0, the setting is disabled.

- `NoStartMenuPinnedList`—removes pinned programs list from the **Start** menu, along with the Internet and E-mail checkboxes.
- `NoStartMenuMFUprogramsList`—removes the frequently used programs list from the **Start** menu.
- `NoStartMenuMorePrograms`—removes the **More Programs** option from the **Start** menu.
- `NoCommonGroups`—removes common program groups from the Start menu (these are the items in the All Users profile in the **More Programs** list).
- `GreyMSIAds`—displays partially installed programs in gray on the **Start** menu.

- `NoWindowsUpdate`—disables and removes links to Windows Update. Also locks access to the **windowsupdate.Microsoft.com** site.
- `DisableMyPicturesDirChange`—prevents the user from changing the path to his My Pictures folder.
- `DisableMyMusicDirChange`—prevents the user from changing the path to his My Music folder.
- `DisableFavoritesDirChange`—prohibits the user to change the path to his Favorites folder.
- `NoStartMenuMyMusic`, `NoSMMyPictures`, `NoFavoritesMenu`, and `NoRecentDocsMenu`—removes all user shell folders (except My Documents) from the **Start** menu. Also removes appropriate checkboxes from the Start menu customization dialog.
- `NoSMMyDocs`—removes My Documents folder from the **Start** menu along with appropriate checkbox from the **Start** menu customization dialog.
- `DisablePersonalDirChange`—prevents the user from changing the path to his My Documents folder.
- `MaxRecentDocs`—specifies the maximum number of shortcuts to recently used documents displayed in the Recent Documents submenu.
- `ClearRecentDocsOnExit`—clears the history list when the user logs off.
- `NoRecentDocsMenu`—removes the Recent Documents folder from the **Start** menu.
- `NoFavoritesMenu`—removes the **Favorites** menu from the **Start** menu, and removes an appropriate checkbox from the **Start** menu customization dialog.
- `NoNetworkConnections`—removes the **Network Connections** item from the **Start** menu, along with the corresponding checkbox which is normally available in the **Start** menu customization dialog.
- `NoStartMenuNetworkPlaces`—removes the **Network Places** item from the **Start** menu and appropriate checkbox from the **Start** menu customization dialog.
- `NoRecentDocsNetHood`—prohibits the adding of remote shared folders to the Network Places whenever the user opens a document in the shared folder.
- `NoSMHelp`—removes the **Help** item from the **Start** menu (notice, however, that this will not prevent Help files from running).
- `NoFind`—removes the **Search** command from the **Start** menu and disables the appropriate option in the **Start** menu customization dialog.

- `NoRun`—removes the **Run** command from the **Start** menu and disables the appropriate checkbox in the **Start** menu customization dialog. Also disables the ability to run programs from Task Manager or by pressing <Winkey> + <R>.
- `MemCheckBoxInRunDlg`—adds the **Run in Separate memory Space** checkbox to the **Run** dialog, which allows 16-bit programs to run in a separate VDM (Virtual DOS Machine).
- `NoSetTaskbar`—prevents any changes from being made to the Taskbar and **Start** menu settings and removes the **Taskbar and Start Menu** item from Control Panel and from the **Start** menu.
- `NoInstrumentation`—prevents the system from remembering the programs, paths and documents used.
- `NoUserNameInStartMenu`—removes user name from the **Start** menu.
- `NoResolveSearch`—prevents the system from searching the target drive to resolve a shortcut.
- `NoResolveTrack`—prevents the system from using NTFS tracking features when resolving shell shortcuts.
- `ForceStartMenuLogoff`—prevents users from removing the **Logoff** option from the **Start** menu.
- `StartmenuLogoff`—disables the **Logoff** option in the **Start** menu and prevents users from adding it.
- `NoClose`—removes the **Turn Off Computer** option from the **Start** menu and prevents users from shutting down the system using the standard shutdown UI.
- `NoChangeStartMenu`—disables drag-and-drop modifications of the **Start** menu (other customization methods remain available, if they weren't explicitly disabled).
- `HKCU\Software\Microsoft\Windows\CurrentVersion\Policies\NonEnum\{20D04FE0-3AEA-1069-A2D8-08002B30309D}`–removes **My Computer** item from the **Start** menu and disables the corresponding checkbox in the Start menu customization dialog.

NOTE

If the values listed above are created under `HKEY_CURRENT_USER`, they will be applicable only to the currently logged on user. If you want them to apply to all new users, create them under the `HKEY_USERS\.DEFAULT\Software\Microsoft\Windows\CurrentVersion\Policies\Explorer` registry key.

Changing the Behavior of Taskbar Grouping

By default, when you enable the **Group similar taskbar buttons** option at the **Taskbar** tab of the **Taskbar and Start Menu Properties** window, items are grouped only when the taskbar buttons begin to get too small, and then the item that you opened first, is grouped first. Take note of the fact, however, that Windows XP user interface only allows you to enable or disable the taskbar grouping feature, but doesn't provide you with the ability to change its behavior.

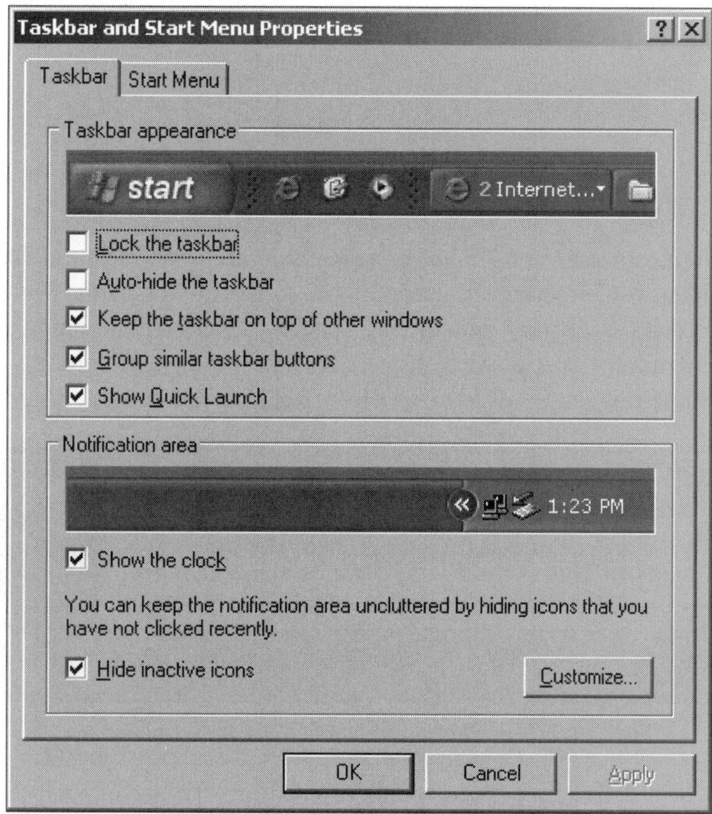

Fig. 12.6. The **Taskbar** tab of the **Taskbar and Start Menu Properties** dialog

Therefore, registry editing is the most appropriate way to change the default behavior of the taskbar buttons grouping feature. To customize it according to your requirements, create the `TaskbarGroupSize` value (`REG_DWORD` data type) under the following registry key:

```
HKEY_CURRENT_USER\Software\Microsoft\Windows\CurrentVersion\
Explorer\Advanced
```

The taskbar grouping behavior depends on the values you assign to the `TaskbarGroupSize` registry value entry. These values are as follows:

- 0—(default) groups by age (oldest group first)
- 1—groups by size (largest group first)
- 2—groups any group of size 2 or more
- 3—groups any group of size 3 or more

Log off and then back on for this change to take effect.

Disabling Notification Area Balloon Tips

Actually, Notification Area balloon tips (Fig. 12.7) are a nice feature, especially for beginners. However, experienced users may become tired of them. For example, if one of your disks is running out of free space, you certainly wouldn't like to be persistently reminded of this fact. If you are like me, you'll certainly agree that sometimes these tips simply distract you from your current work.

Fig. 12.7. An example of Notification Area balloon tip

Therefore, you'll definitely wish to disable the feature. To accomplish this, proceed as follows:

1. Start Regedit.exe, and expand the following key:

```
HKEY_CURRENT_USER\Software\Microsoft\Windows\CurrentVersion\
Explorer\Advanced
```

2. Create a new `REG_DWORD` value and name it `EnableBalloonTips`. Set this value to 0.
3. Quit Registry Editor, then log off and then log back on.

NOTE

These steps disable all Notification Area balloon tips for the current user. However, there is no way to disable balloon tips for specific program only.

Preventing a Program from Being Displayed in the Most Frequently Used Programs List

Fig. 12.8. Windows XP Simple **Start** menu

If you like Windows XP Simple **Start** menu feature, you have undoubtedly noticed that it maintains a list of the most frequently used programs (Fig. 12.8). Now suppose that you want to continue using this feature, but don't want some specific programs to appear in that list. What can you do about it? Of course, you can right-click the required shortcut and select the **Remove from This List** command from the context menu. However, this will not prevent the program from appearing in that list if you use it some time later. You can also configure the **Start** menu to specify the number of shortcuts in the list of most frequently used programs (if you don't want the list of most frequently used programs to be displayed, set the value in the **Number of programs on the Start menu** field to 0) and clear this list if desired by clicking the **Clear List** button (Fig. 12.9).

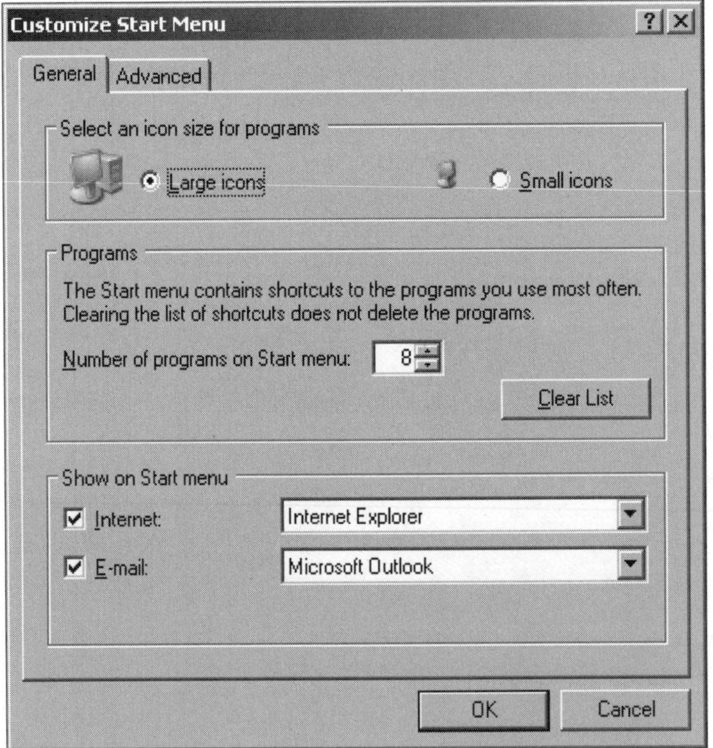

Fig. 12.9. The **General** tab of the **Customize Start Menu** window

This, however, doesn't solve the problem, since you only need to prevent some specific application (Regedit.exe, for example) from appearing in the list. At the same time, you don't want to disable this feature altogether.

This task can't be accomplished using the GUI tools. However, if you edit the registry, you can easily achieve the desired result. To do so, follow these steps:

1. Start Registry Editor (Regedit.exe).
2. Add an empty string value named `NoStartPage` to the following registry key, where *Program name.exe* is the name of the executable file that is used to start the program:

   `HKEY_CLASSES_ROOT\Applications\`*`Program name.exe`*
3. Quit Registry Editor, and then restart the computer.

The application will be removed from the list of frequently used programs and will never appear in that list again.

Disabling Mail Notification Display on the Windows XP Welcome Screen

The Welcome Screen is displayed by default on Windows XP Personal Edition and Windows XP Professional-based computers that are not members of a domain. Under your name on the Welcome screen, there is a hyperlink that indicates the number of unread e-mail messages (Fig. 12.10), which, if you click it, reveals which account the messages are from, and how many each e-mail provider contains.

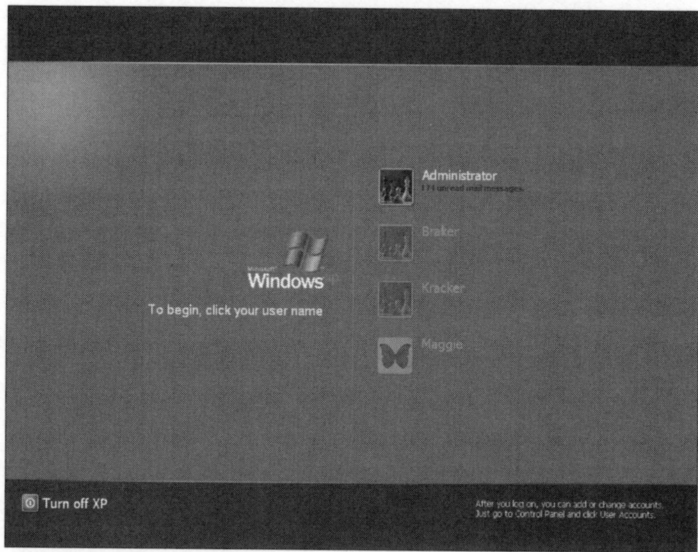

Fig. 12.10. By default, Welcome screen displays a hyperlink under a user name, indicating the number of unread e-mail messages

NOTE

This e-mail hyperlink is only displayed if the e-mail client that supports this feature is running on your computer. Currently unread e-mail notification is supported by Outlook Express and Windows Messenger. If you use other mail clients, this notification will not appear.

This feature can't be disabled using GUI tools, and Welcome Screen can't be reconfigured to populate the unread message count from a particular e-mail account.

Once again, to work around this behavior, you'll need to edit the registry.

If you want to disable the unread e-mail notification altogether, proceed as follows:

1. Start Regedit.exe, and expand the following registry key: `HKEY_CURRENT_USER\Software\Microsoft\Windows\CurrentVersion\UnreadMail` (Fig. 12.11)
2. Right-click the `UnreadMail` subkey and select the **Permissions** command from the right-click menu.
3. Click the System account, and then click to clear the **Full Control** and **Special Permissions** check boxes for **Allow** permissions. The System account should have **Read** permissions only (Fig. 12.12).
4. Click **OK** and quit Registry Editor.

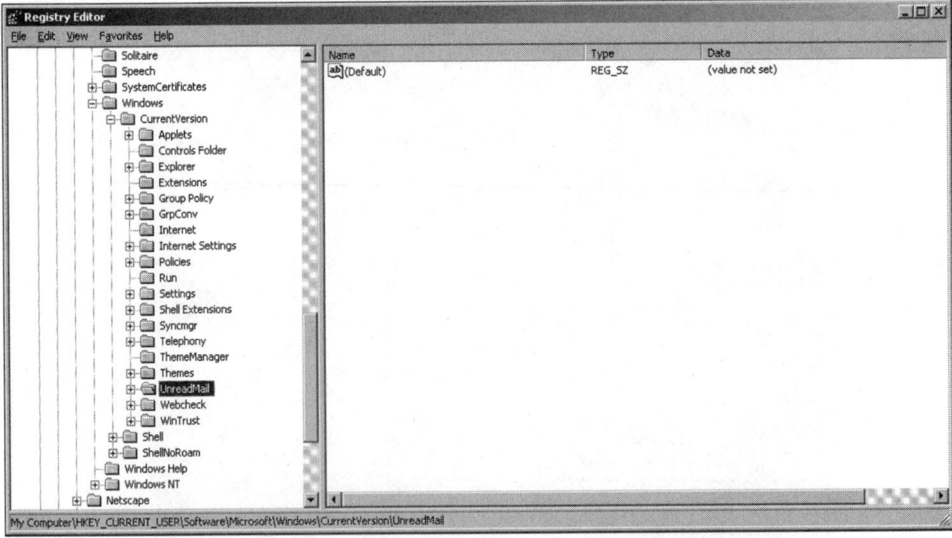

Fig. 12.11. The contents of the `HKEY_CURRENT_USER\Software\Microsoft\Windows\CurrentVersion\UnreadMail` registry key

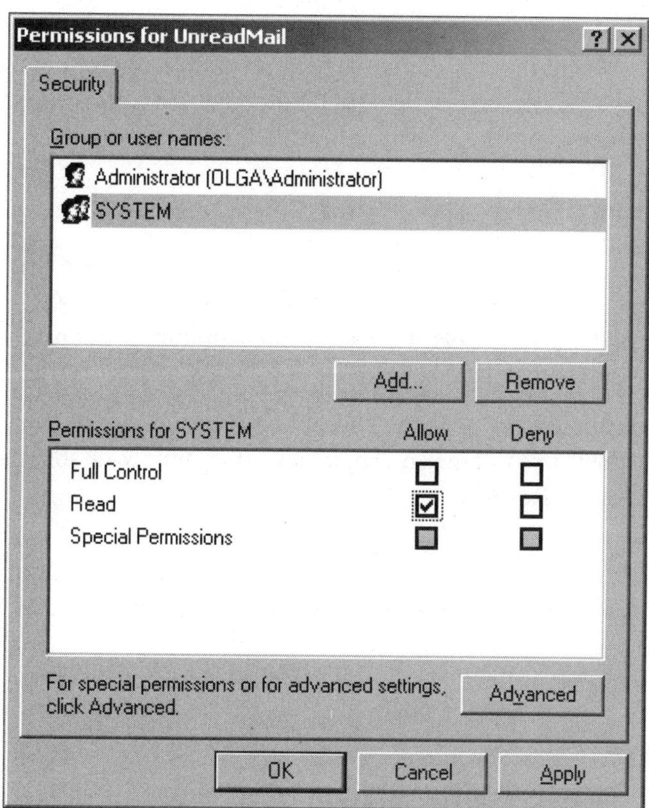

Fig. 12.12. To block the unread e-mail notification at the Welcome screen, provide the read-only permissions for the System account on the `UnreadMail` registry key

Now the System account will be prevented from updating Welcome Screen with any e-mail information, since it will be unable to modify the `UnreadMail` registry key.

If you have several e-mail accounts, and want to prevent only one of them from updating Welcome screen, expand the `UnreadMail` registry subkey. You'll notice that it contains nested subkeys for each of your e-mail accounts.

Select the subkey corresponding to the account that you want to prevent from updating Welcome Screen, and set the System permissions to that key to read-only.

Troubleshooting Aids

If you are interested, you'll find plenty of registry-editing tips and tricks, mainly intended to customize the Windows XP User Interface. Unfortunately, it's impossible to describe them all, and even the books specially dedicated to this topic usually show only the top of the iceberg. However, there are some registry-editing techniques that can be used as troubleshooting aids. In this section, I'll describe some which have proved to be the most helpful.

Customizing System Restore

Let us return once again to the System Restore feature, which we briefly discussed in *Chapter 2.* It is one of the most useful features of Windows XP, but, unfortunately, some users tend to disable it, since in their opinion, it consumes too much free disk space (no less than 200 MB).

If you are an administrator, and don't want the users to disable System Restore, you can prevent them from doing so. To achieve this, simply disable the GUI tools for configuring System Restore.

NOTE

To perform these tasks, log on as Administrator or user with administrative privileges.

There are two alternative methods allowing you to perform this task. Let us consider them both.

Using Use Group Policy Editor

To prevent users from disabling or configuring System Restore, proceed as follows:

1. Start Group Policy Editor and expand the console tree as follows: **Computer Configuration | Administrative Templates | System | System Restore** (Fig. 12.13).

1. Double-click **Turn off System Restore**, and then on the **Setting** tab, select **Disable.** After you apply this policy, System Restore will be turned on and enforced.

2. Double-click **Turn off Configuration**, and then on the **Setting** tab, select **Enable**. For more information about what these settings do, click the **Explain** tab on the **Properties** dialog box.

3. Click **Apply**, and then click **OK**.

NOTE

These settings are only read at boot time, therefore it is necessary to reboot the system.

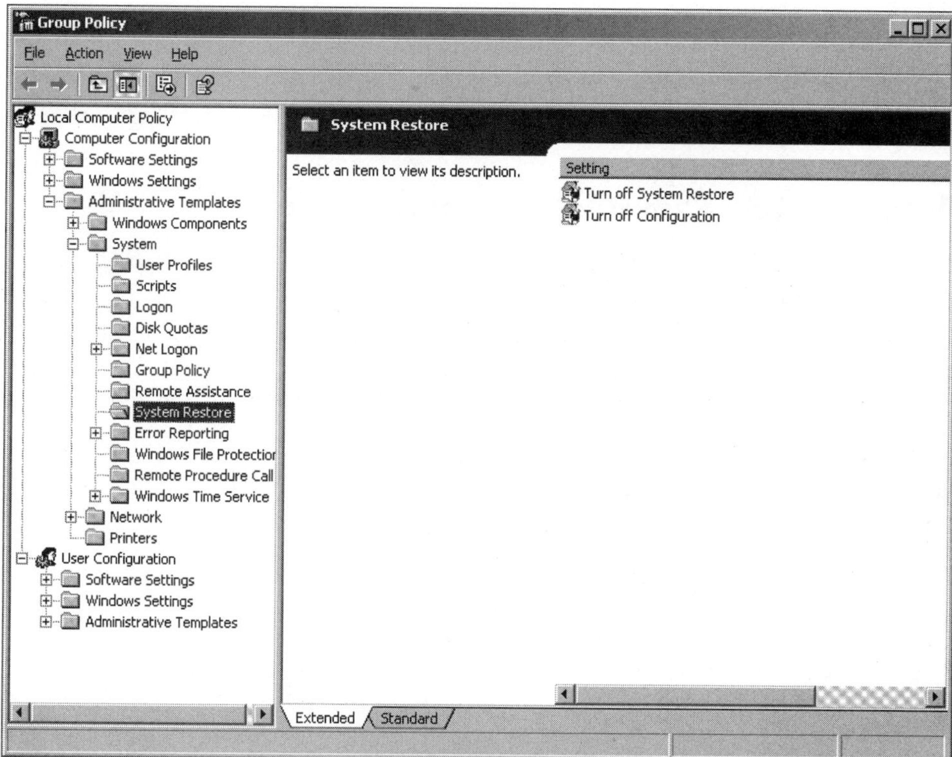

Fig. 12.13. Configuring System Restore using Group Policy Editor

If users try to access System Restore Configuration, the **System Properties** dialog box is present, but the **System Restore** tab is not.

Using Registry Editor to Disable System Restore

The same task can be performed by direct registry editing. To use Registry Editor for disabling System Restore Configuration UI, proceed as follows:

1. Start Regedit.exe and expand the following key:

   `HKEY_LOCAL_MACHINE\SOFTWARE\Policies\Microsoft\Windows NT`

2. Under `HKEY_LOCAL_MACHINE\SOFTWARE\Policies\Microsoft\Windows NT`, create a new nested key, named `SystemRestore`.

3. Within this key, create a new REG_DWORD value named DisableConfig, and set this value to 1.

4. Close Regedit.exe and reboot the system.

More about System Restore Configuration

As an administrator, you can modify many values related to System Restore by editing the registry directly. This is especially important, if you disable the System Restore Configuration UI, as was described in the previous two sections. Keep in mind, however, that you must do it with care and caution, since you may be unable to reverse the changes that you have introduced by editing the registry directly.

Windows XP registry has three keys that relate to the System Restore feature. These keys are listed below:

- HKEY_LOCAL_MACHINE\System\CurrentControlSet\Services\Sr
- HKEY_LOCAL_MACHINE\System\CurrentControlSet\Services\Srservice
- HKEY_LOCAL_MACHINE\Software\Microsoft\WindowsNT\CurrentVersion\SystemRestore

NOTE

The first two keys are related to the System Restore filter and System Restore service. It is not recommended that one modify these keys, since this may cause the Windows XP operating system to become unstable.

The contents of the third System Restore registry key are shown in Fig. 12.14. Here you can edit some REG_DWORD values. Note, however, that this key also contains several values that you should not edit.

The list of values that you can use to configure System Restore is provided below. These values can be edited without risk of damage to the operating system.

- CompressionBurst—as was outlined in *Chapter 2*, on NTFS drives System restore compresses the archived data when the computer is idle. This value (in seconds) sets the idle time compression interval. The System Restore service can compress data for the amount of time that is specified in this value, and then stop. Then, at the next idle time, the computer can repeat the process.

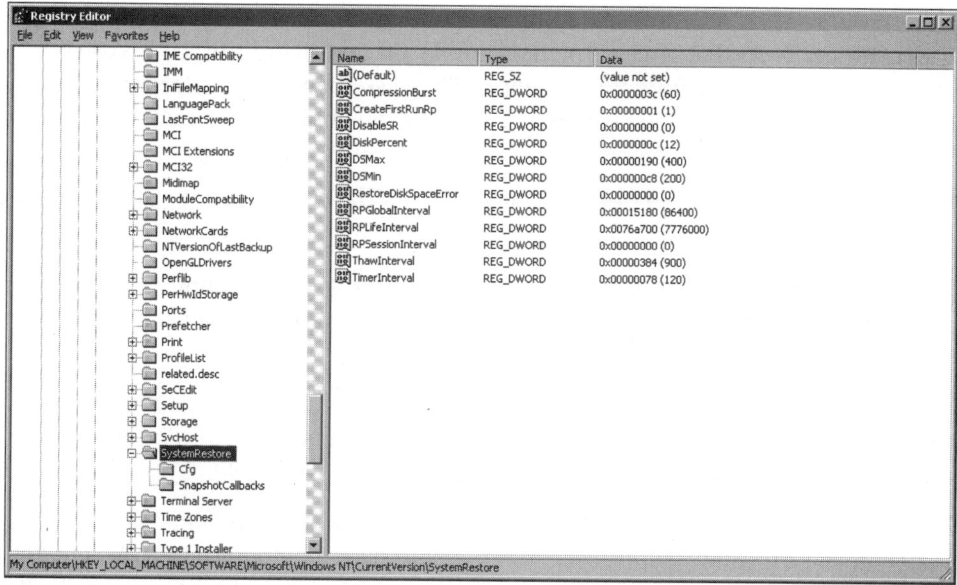

Fig. 12.14. The contents of the `HKEY_LOCAL_MACHINE\Software\Microsoft\WindowsNT\CurrentVersion\SystemRestore` registry key

- `DiskPercent`—this value relates to the percentage of disk space that System Restore uses for its data store. The default value is 12 percent. The data store size is always calculated as "`max(12 percent, DSMax)`" regardless of the size of the hard disk. The maximum (max) size is what is specified in `DSMax`. For hard disk sizes that are less than 4 gigabytes (GB) in size, 12 percent is less than 400 megabytes (MB), so `max(12 percent, DSMax)` equals 400 MB. For hard disk sizes that are greater than 4 GB, 12 percent is greater than 400 MB, so `max(12 percent, DSMax)` equals 12 percent. This data store size is not a reserved disk space, and the data store size is used only on demand.
- `DSMax`—this value specifies the maximum size for the System Restore data store. The default size of the data store is 400 MB. The data store size is always calculated as `max(12 percent, DSMax)` regardless of the size of the hard disk. The maximum (max) size is what is specified in `DSMax`. For hard disk sizes that are less than 4 GB, 12 percent is less than 400 MB, so `max(12 percent, DSMax)` equals 400 MB. For hard disk sizes that are greater than 4 GB, 12 percent is greater than 400 MB, so `max(12 percent, DSMax)` equals 12 percent. This data store size is not a reserved disk space, and the data store size is used only on demand.

- DSMin—this value relates to the minimum amount of free disk space that System Restore needs so that it can function during the installation process. Also, this value relates to the minimum amount of free disk space that is needed for System Restore to reactivate and to resume the creation of restore points after System Restore has been disabled because of low disk space.
- RestoreStatus—this value specifies if the last restore operation failed (0), succeeded (1), or had been interrupted (2).
- RPGlobalInterval—this value specifies, in seconds, the amount of time that System Restore waits before it creates the automatic computer check points for elapsed time. The default value is 24 hours.
- RPLifeInterval—this value specifies, in seconds, the restore points Time to Live (TTL). When a restore point reaches this time and it is still on the system, it gets deleted. The default value is (7776000), which will be 90 days.
- RPSessionInterval—this value specifies, in seconds, the amount of time that System Restore waits before it creates the automatic computer check points for session time (the amount of time that the computer has been on). The default value is zero (0), which means that this feature is turned off.
- ThawInterval—this value specifies, in seconds, the amount of time that System Restore waits before it activates itself from a disabled state (after the conditions for this process to occur have been met). If you start the System Restore user interface, System Restore is activated immediately.

NOTE

All the other values that you find under this key should not be modified under any circumstances, since this may lead to the system malfunction. Pay special attention to this caution, since Microsoft provides quite a reasonable explanation about why you should not modify these values directly. For example, the DisableSR value, as its name implies, turns System Restore on or off. However, you should never turn the System Restore off in the registry, because if you do, the existing restore points will not be removed. If you modify the CreateFirstRunRp value, you can place your system into an unrecoverable situation.

Enabling Windows Installer Logging

To help diagnose several Windows Installer issues, Windows XP provides several logging services that can be activated via the registry. After the entries have been added and enabled, you can retry the problem installation and Windows Installer will track the progress. Log files have the standard LOG filename extension. They are stored in your Temp folder under random names starting with `Msi` letters.

To enable Windows Installer logging, start Registry Editor, and create a new `REG_SZ` value entry named `Logging` under the `HKEY_LOCAL_MACHINE\Software\Policies\Microsoft\Windows\Installer` registry key. Set it to value that could contain the characters form the list below ("voicewarmup", for example).

The letters in the value field can be in any order. Each letter turns on a different logging mode. Each letter's actual function is as follows for MSI version 1.1:

- `i`—Status messages
- `w`—Non-fatal warnings
- `e`—All error messages
- `a`—Start up of actions
- `r`—Action-specific records
- `u`—User requests
- `c`—Initial UI parameters
- `m`—Out-of-memory or fatal exit information
- `o`—Out-of-disk-space messages
- `p`—Terminal properties
- `v`—Verbose output
- `+`—Append to existing file
- `!`—Flush each line to the log
- `*`—Wildcard, log all information except for the v option. To include the v option, specify "`/l*v`"

NOTE

This should be used only for troubleshooting purposes and should not be left on because it will have adverse effects on system performance and disk space. Each time you use the Add/Remove Programs tool in Control Panel, a new Msi*.log file is created.

Resetting TCP/IP Settings in Windows XP

If you carefully view the list of networking components for a network interface in Windows XP, you'll notice a strange fact—the **Uninstall** button is disabled when Internet Protocol (TCP/IP) is selected (Fig. 12.15). According to the explanation provided by Microsoft, this is because the TCP/IP stack is considered a core component of the operating system; therefore, it is not possible to uninstall it in Windows XP (Windows .NET is expected to behave the same way).

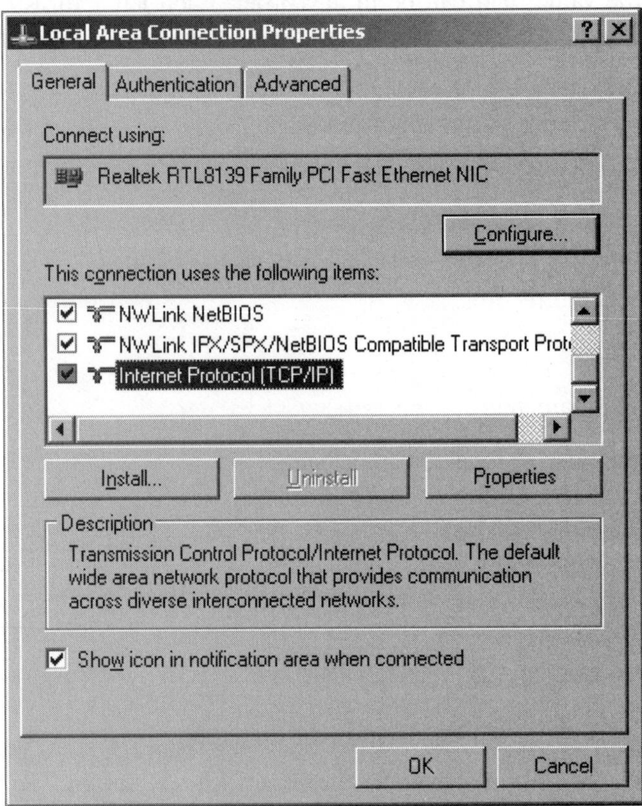

Fig. 12.15. In Windows XP, the **Uninstall** button is disabled when you select TC/IP protocol in the **Local Area Connection Properties** window

However, what should you do, if you want to reset the TCP/IP stack by returning it to its original state (as it was when the operating system was installed)? Obviously, you can't remove it and reinstall it again (as was the case in the previous versions of Windows NT/2000). However, there is a convenient workaround provided by the `netsh` (NetShell) utility, which provides a command-line interface for configuring and monitoring Windows XP networking.

In Windows XP, `netsh` utility provides a `reset` command, which rewrites registry keys related to TCP/IP. Consequently, you will get the same result will be as you would have had you removed the TCP/IP stack and then reinstalled it again.

To reset TCP/IP settings in the registry, go to the command line (Start | Run, type `cmd` and press <Enter>), then issue the following command:

```
netsh int ip reset [log_file_name]
```

where *log_file_name* is the name of the LOG file where the action taken will be recorded. If you don't specify the full pathname to the LOG file, it will be created in the current directory.

The command will reset TCP/IP settings stored under the following registry keys:

```
HKLM\SYSTEM\CurrentControlSet\Services\Tcpip\Parameters\

HKLM\SYSTEM\CurrentControlSet\Services\DHCP\Parameters\
```

NOTE

If the log file already exists, the new log will be appended to the end of existing file. Also notice that the contents of the actual log file will depend on the system configuration. There may be situations when no actions will be logged. Usually, this happens if the TCP/IP registry settings have not been changed since original Windows XP installation.

Enabling Remote Assistance in Windows XP

When discussing troubleshooting problems, one musn't forget that Windows XP now includes a nice feature—Remote Assistance. It provides a convenient way for an administrator to connect to the user's computer and to show him or her how to eliminate the problem. After establishing the connections, the administrator can view the user's screen and even (with the user's permission) use his mouse and keyboard.

This feature is installed and enabled by default. However, if someone has disabled it, you can re-enable Remote Assistance using one of the following two methods.

Enabling Remote Assistance in Control Panel

1. Start the System applet in Control Panel and go to the **Remote** tab (Fig. 12.16).
2. Verify that the **Allow Remote Assistance invitations to be sent from this computer** checkbox is selected.
3. Click **Advanced** to set the amount of time that you want to enable access to your computer. The **Remote Assistance Settings** window will open (Fig. 12.17).
4. If you want the user who connects to take control of your computer, click to select the **Allow this computer to be controlled remotely** check box.
5. Click **OK**.

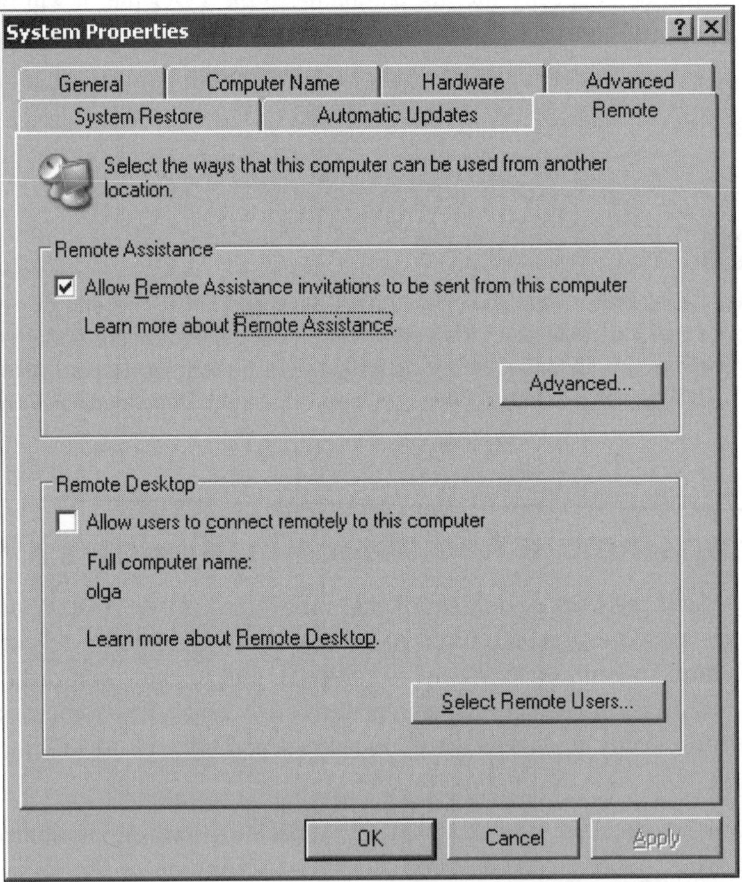

Fig. 12.16. The **Remote** tab of the **System Properties** window

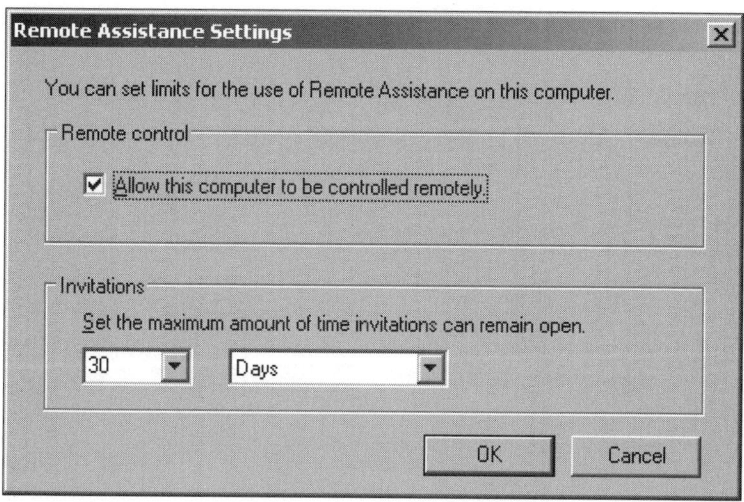

Fig. 12.17. The **Remote Assistance Settings** window

NOTE

To use Remote Assistance, both you and your assistant must use compatible operating systems (Windows XP or later) and Windows Messenger or a MAPI-compliant e-mail account (Microsoft Outlook or Outlook Express). Furthermore, both of you need to be connected to the Internet.

Enabling Remote Assistance in the Registry

To enable Remote Assistance in the registry, proceed as follows:

1. Start Regedit.exe and locate the following key:

```
HKEY_LOCAL_MACHINE\SYSTEM\CurrentControlSet\Control\Terminal Server
```

2. Under this key, locate the `fAllowToGetHelp` value (Fig. 12.18). If this value does not exist, create a new `REG_DWORD` value and name it `fAllowToGetHelp`.
3. Set this value to `1` to enable connections. The value of `0` disables the feature.
4. Click **OK** and quit Registry Editor. Remote Assistance is enabled immediately; there is no need to restart the computer.

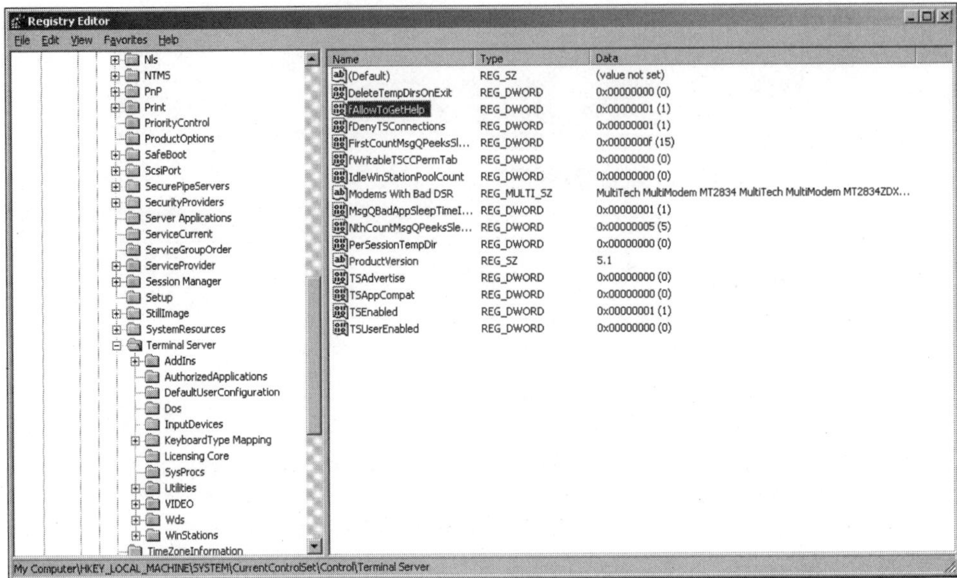

Fig. 12.18. Enabling the Remote Assistance feature in the registry

Configuring a Windows XP Computer to Receive Remote Assistance Offers

After enabling the Remote Assistance feature, it is necessary to configure the Windows XP-based computer to receive Remote Assistance offers. Before you start configuring the computer of the novice user to accept Remote Assistance offers, make sure that the following requirements are met:

- The Group Policy on the computer of the novice user must be configured to enable Remote Assistance offers.
- The computers of the novice and expert users must be members of the same domain, or members of trusted domains.
- Both computers must have Windows XP installed (or a newer operating system).

To configure the Offer Remote Assistance policy setting, proceed as follows:

1. Start the Microsoft Management Console (MMC) Group Policy snap-in and locate the **Offer Remote Assistance** policy in the **Local Computer Policy | Computer Configuration | Administrative Templates | System | Remote Assistance** folder (Fig. 12.19).

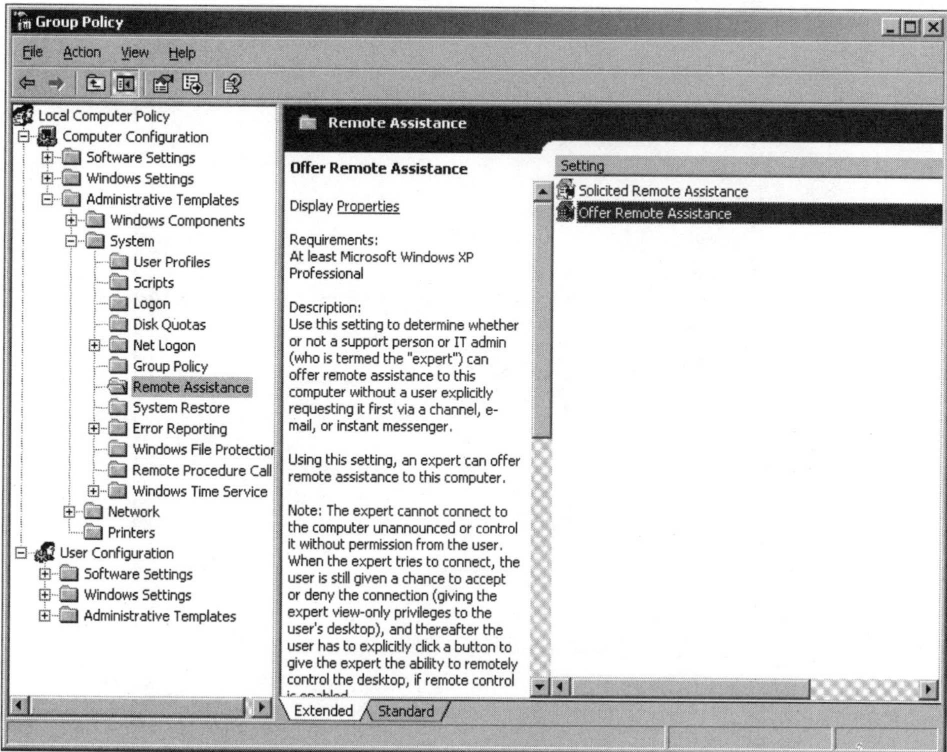

Fig. 12.19. Configuring the system policy to enable Windows XP computer to receive Remote Assistance offers

2. Double-click the **Offer Remote Assistance** policy.
3. On the **Offer Remote Assistance Properties** dialog box (Fig. 12.20), click **Enable**.
4. Next, select one of the options that specify, whether or not the expert users can:
   - View the computer of the novice user
   - View and control the computer of the novice user

NOTE

The setting that you select applies to the entire group that is listed. The **Offer Remote Assistance** policy setting does not provide a mechanism to enable one group of users to have the ability to view the computer of the novice user and a second group of users to have the ability to view and control the computer of the novice user. There can be only one group.

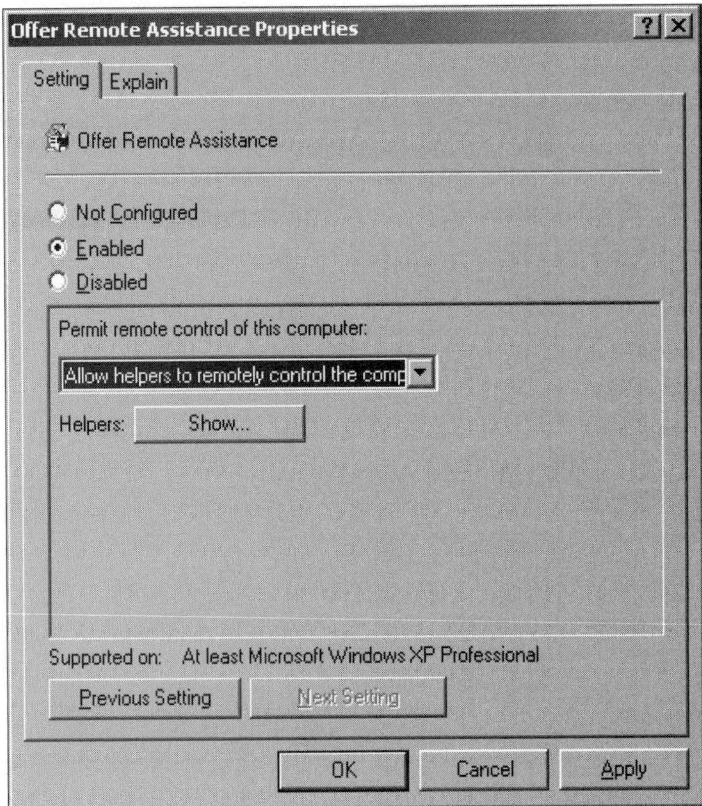

Fig. 12.20. The **Offer Remote Assistance Properties** dialog

5. Click **Show**. The **Show Contents** dialog box is displayed.
6. Click **Add** to add the Domain Users and Domain User Groups.
7. Click **OK**, and then click **OK** to close the **Show Contents** dialog box and the **Offer Remote Assistance Properties** dialog box.
8. Quit the MMC Group Policy snap-in.

These policies will be effective immediately. You do not have to restart the computer.

NOTE

Populate the properties of the **Offer Remote Assistance** Group Policy with care and caution, since you are unable to verify if domain accounts that have been entered are really valid and recommended as experts'. Carefully test the policy before you start applying it in your organization. Also notice that the Offer Remote Assistance policy is not available in Microsoft Windows XP Home Edition.

Troubleshooting Service Startup Problems

Sometimes, you may encounter a situation in which a service can't start because of a logon failure. If this happens, the system might display error messages, and when you restart the system next time, the following error messages may be logged in the system event log:

```
Source: Service Control Manager
Event ID: 7000
Description:
The %service% service failed to start due to the following error:
The service did not start due to a logon failure.
```

No information in the **Data** field will be available.

```
Source: Service Control Manager
Event ID: 7013
Description:
Logon attempt with current password failed with the following error:
Logon failure: unknown user name or bad password.
```

No information in the **Data** field will be available (Fig. 12.21).

When you attempt to manually start the service, the following error message might be displayed:

```
Microsoft Management Console
Could not start the %service% service on Local Computer
Error 1069: The service did not start due to a logon Failure.
```

This behavior can occur for any of the following reasons:

- The password on the account the service is configured to use to log on to has been changed
- The password data in the registry is damaged
- The right to log on as a service is revoked for the specified user account

To resolve these issues, you can configure the service to use the built-in system account, change the password for the specified user account to match the current password for that user, or restore the user's right to log on as a service.

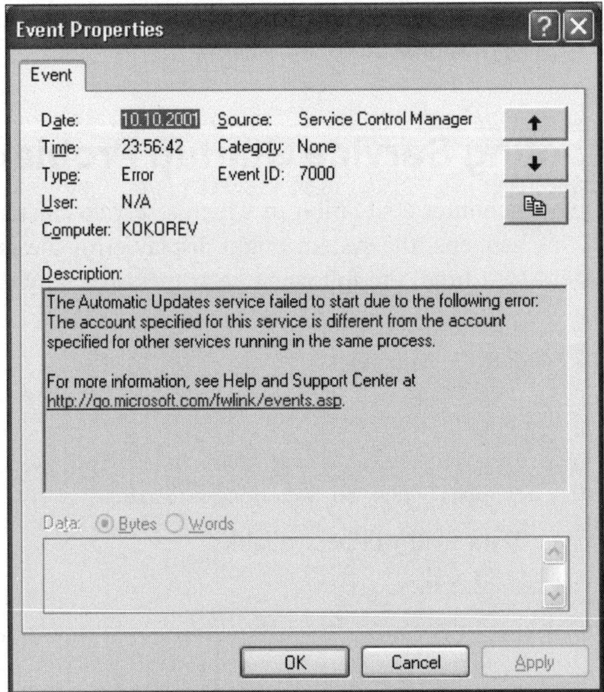

Fig. 12.21. The **Event Properties** window displaying the error message on the service startup failure due to logon failure

If the right to log on as a service is revoked for the specified user account, restore the right. The procedure is somewhat different for domain controllers and member servers/client workstation.

If the problem takes place at the controller of an Active Directory domain, proceed as follows:

1. Start the Active Directory Users and Computers Microsoft Management Console (MMC) snap-in.
2. Right-click the Organizational Unit (OU) in which the user right to log on as a service was granted. By default, this is in the Domain Controllers OU.
3. Right-click the container, and then click **Properties**.
4. On the **Group Policy** tab, click **Default Domain Controllers Policy**, and then click **Edit**. This starts Group Policy Manager.

5. Expand the **Computer Configuration object** by clicking the plus sign (+) next to the policy object. Under the **Computer Configuration object**, expand **Windows Settings**, and then expand **Security Settings**.
6. Expand **Local Policies**, and then click **User Rights Assignment**.
7. In the right pane, right-click **Log on as a service**, and then click **Security**.
8. Add the user to the policy, and then click **OK**.
9. Quit Group Policy Manager, close **Group Policy properties**, and then close the Active Directory Users and Computers MMC snap-in.

If the problem arises at the member server or a standalone computer, perform the following steps:

1. Start the Local Security Settings MMC snap-in.
2. Expand **Local Policies**, and then click **User Rights Assignment** (Fig. 12.22)
3. In the right pane, right-click **Log on as a service**, and then click **Properties**. The **Log on as service Properties** window will open (Fig. 12.23)
4. Add the user to the policy, and then click **OK**.

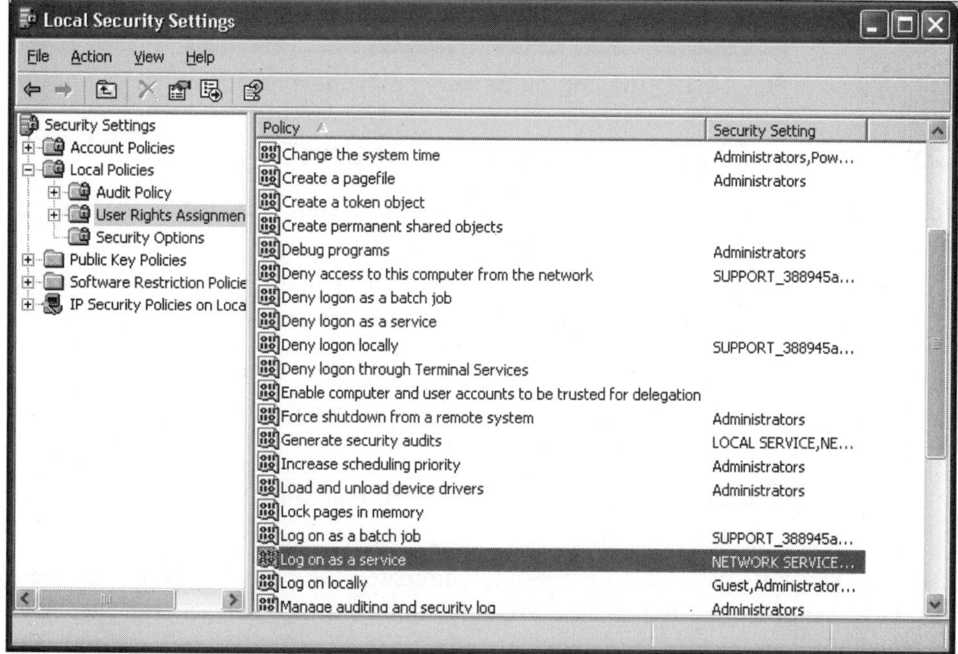

Fig. 12.22. Restoring the right for the user account to log on as service

Fig. 12.23. The **Log on as service Properties** dialog

Configuring Service Logon Information

To configure the password for the specified user account to match the current password for that user, employ the following steps:

1. Start the Administrative Tools applet in Control Panel, then double-click the **Services** icon.
2. Right-click the appropriate service, and then click **Properties**.
3. The service properties window will open. Go to the **Log On tab** (Fig. 12.24), change the password, and then click **Apply**.
4. Go to the **General** tab (Fig. 12.25), and click the **Start** button to restart the service.

If the service starts, you have successfully eliminated the problem. However, there may be situations when the service wouldn't start with the user account you have specified. In such a case, you may reconfigure the service to start up with the built-in system account.

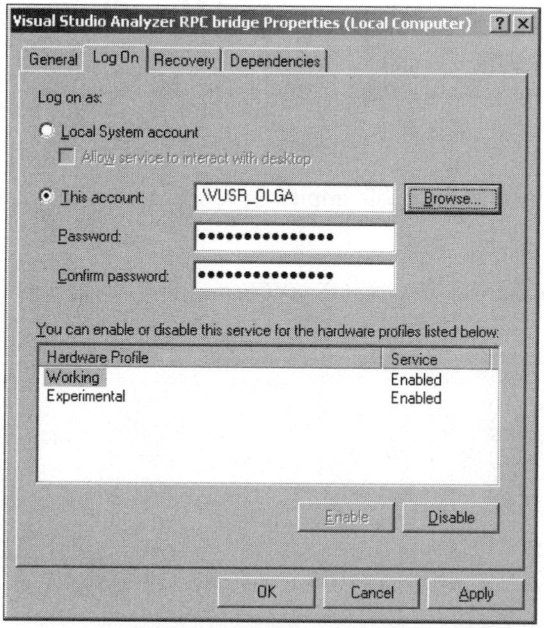

Fig. 12.24. The **Log On** tab of the service properties window

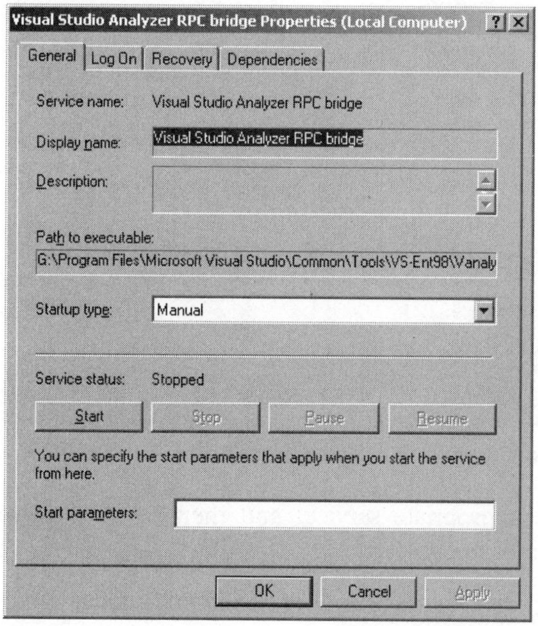

Fig. 12.25. The **General** tab of the service properties window

Configuring the Service to Start Up with the Built-in System Account

To configure the service to start up with the built-in system account, perform the following steps:

1. Start the Administrative Tools applet in Control Panel, then double-click the **Services** icon.

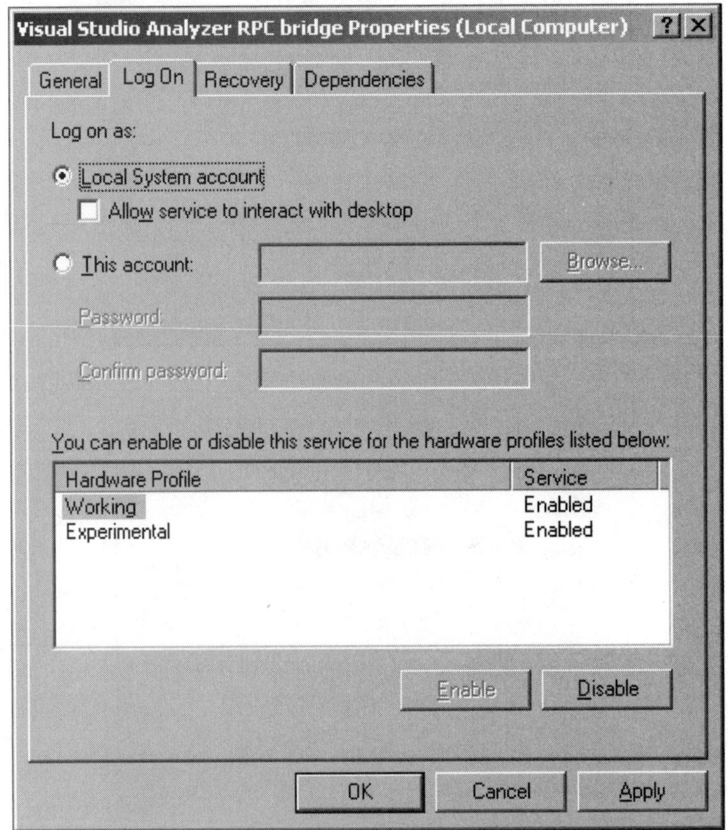

Fig. 12.26. Configuring the service to start up with the Local System account

2. Right-click the appropriate service, and then select the **Properties** command from the right-click menu.
3. Go to the **Log On** tab, set the **Local System Account** radio button, and then click **Apply**. If the service needs to interact with the desktop, set the **Allow**

service to interact with desktop checkbox. Task Scheduler is an example of the built-in system service that requires interaction with the desktop. Some third-party services (for example, F-Secure Authentication agent) also need to interact with the desktop. However, most services don't need this feature, and typically you may leave this checkbox unselected.

4. Go to the **General** tab and click the **Start** button to restart the service.

Using Registry Editor to Troubleshoot Service Startup Problems

If you are able to start the Services tool, you can use the procedures described above to troubleshoot service startup problems. Sometimes, however, there may be situations when you are unable to use the Services administrative tool. For example, the computer may hang when you start this tool, and the following message is displayed:

```
The RPC Server is unavailable
```

It is logical to suppose then, that the problem has been caused by the Remote Procedure Call (RPC) service startup failure due to a logon failure with that service or a dependency service. Some services have dependency services that do not start until their dependency services start first. For example, the Alerter service depends on the Workstation service (Fig. 12.27). To view the dependencies for a specific service, right-click the required service, select the **Properties** command from the context menu, and go to the **Dependencies** tab. As you can see, the dependencies list for the RPC service is quite long (Fig. 12.28).

This, of course, prevents you from starting the Services tool and using the safe method of configuring services. If this situation occurs, proceed as follows to work around the problem:

1. Start Registry Editor and locate the `ObjectName` value under the `HKEY_LOCAL_MACHINE\SYSTEM\CurrentControlSet\Services\`*`ServiceName`* registry key.
2. Modify that value entry by setting its value to `localsystem` (Fig. 12.29), then click OK and quit Registry Editor.
3. Attempt to restart the service. You may need to restart the computer for some services to restart properly.

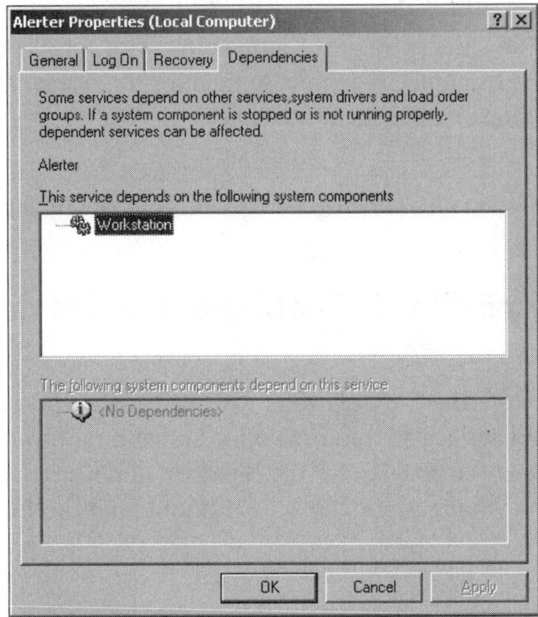

Fig. 12.27. The Alerter service depends on the Workstation service

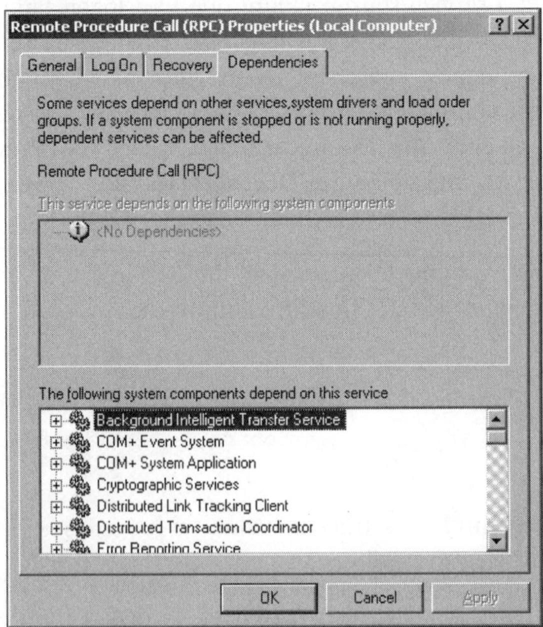

Fig. 12.28. The dependencies list for RPC service is quite long

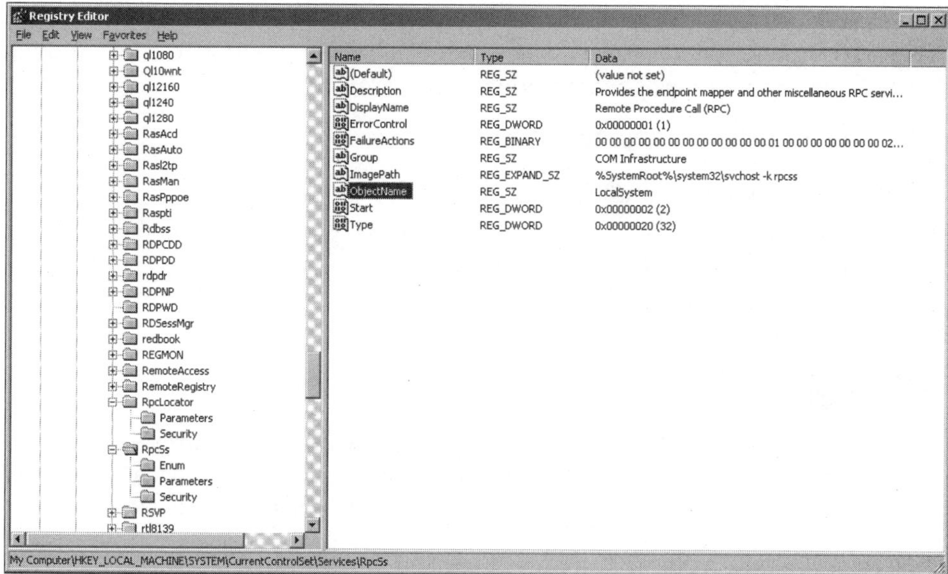

Fig. 12.29. The `ObjectName` value under `HKEY_LOCAL_MACHINE\SYSTEM\CurrentControlSet\Services\`*`ServiceName`*

If you cannot start the Registry Editor, you can modify the service account information by performing a parallel installation of the operating system.

Disabling a Service or Driver that Prevents Windows NT/2000/XP from Booting

If you have managed to detect the service or device driver that prevents your Windows NT/2000/XP from booting, and you have installed a parallel copy of the operating system, which is bootable, you can try to eliminate the problem using the following procedures:

1. Boot into a parallel copy of the system, and start Regedit.exe (Windows XP) or Regedt32.exe (Windows NT/2000).
2. Go to the `HKEY_LOCAL_MACHINE` root key
3. Use the **Load Hive** command to open the following registry file in the original Windows NT/2000/XP installation:

   %SystemRoot%\System32\Config\System

   When prompted to assign a name for the hive to be loaded, assign it a name other than System (for example, System1).

4. Go to the `HKEY_LOCAL_MACHINE\SYSTEM1\Select` registry key and note the value for `Current:REG_DWORD` (this selects which `ControlSet00x` to load when booting and is the one that needs modification):
5. Perform the following steps to disable a service:
   - Go to the following registry key:
     `HKEY_LOCAL_MACHINE\TEST\ControlSet00x\Services \`<*Name of suspected service*>, where *x* is the value of `Current:REG_DWORD`
   - Change the value of `Start:REG_DWORD`: to 0x4.

NOTE

As was outlined in *Chapter 6* where we discussed service startup options, other valid startup options for the service include 0x2 (Automatic), 0x3 (Manual), and 0x4 (Disabled). Thus, by setting the `Start` value to 0x4 you disable the suspected service.

To disable a device driver, proceed as follows:

   - Go to the `HKEY_LOCAL_MACHINE\SYSTEM1\ControlSet00x\Services\`<*Name of suspect Driver*> where x is the value of `Current:REG_DWORD`
   - Change the value of `Start:REG_DWORD`: to 0x4.

NOTE

As was shown in *Chapter 6*, other valid startup options for device drivers include 0x0 (Boot), 0x1 (System), 0x2 (Automatic), 0x3 (Manual), and 0x4 (Disabled).

6. After you have introduced all required modifications, unload the SYSTEM1 hive, quit Registry Editor and try to reboot the original versions of Windows NT/2000/XP.

Summary

In this chapter we have briefly considered some advanced customization and troubleshooting topics, which, as I hope, will help you to get the most out of your Windows XP operating system (and troubleshoot it, if necessary). Notice that all the tricks described here can be performed using the built-in tools of the operating system. However, there are also lots of valuable third-party tools and utilities, which can prove to be really useful for your everyday work with Windows NT/2000/XP. These will be discussed in the next chapter.

Chapter 13

Third-Party Registry Utilities

> Shall I refuse my dinner because I do not fully understand the process of digestion?
>
> *Oliver Heaviside*

Each new version of the Microsoft operating systems, including Windows XP, provides many new configuration or administrative utilities. Each of these tools offers new and more convenient methods of editing the registry than built-in registry editors (Regedt32.exe or Regedit.exe). Despite this fact, some registry tricks (for example, most of those presented in the previous chapter) can't be performed without editing the registry directly. Microsoft is including more and more advanced methods of editing the registry, and most of them are implemented as Control Panel applets of new administrative utilities and wizards. However, third-party developers aren't asleep on the job, either.

If you're an experienced Internet user, you'll find lots of useful and handy freeware utilities to help you maintain and troubleshoot your registry.

In this chapter, I'll provide a small list of Windows NT/2000/XP registry utilities, which I personally consider to be the most helpful.

Windows XP PowerToys

Ever since the release of Windows 95, Microsoft has supplied a set of PowerToys for each of the major releases of the Windows operating systems. PowerToys are small applications enhancing operating system functionality in several ways, enabling users to boost productivity, configure the system UI in various ways, and generally, to expand the OS capabilities. Since the first release, PowerToys has become a favorite of most users, and they really deserve this popularity. No wonder that users began asking whether or not there will be PowerToys for Windows XP when this OS was still under construction. And, of course, Microsoft didn't disappoint them. Now, with the release of Windows XP, Microsoft is already working on the PowerToys for Windows XP, which is expected to become available for free downloading on October 25, 2001.

At the moment of this writing, a beta version was available for downloading from Microsoft's Windows beta site, and this brief review was written based on that particular version.

NOTE

Experienced users may find various pre-release versions of the Windows XP PowerToys on the Internet. However, I don't recommend that you test or use any other version of these, except for the one downloaded from Microsoft's public Web site. And, in any case, don't test the pre-release versions of the PowerToys on your production machines.

Let us consider the most useful Windows XP PowerToys in more detail, just to provide you with an idea about what they are, what to expect, and what you'll really need.

Bulk Resize for Photos

This toy enhances the built-in Windows XP capabilities of working with images. It allows you to resize a picture or group of pictures, without changing the originals.

To use Bulk Resize for Photos, select any image, or group of images, right-click, and select the **Resize Pictures** command from the popup menu (Fig. 13.1). The **Resize Pictures** dialog will appear (Fig. 13.2), which provides you with quite a large set of options. For example, you can resize the images to 640x480 (small), 800x600 (medium), 1024x768 (large) or even 240x320 (palm-sized, for Windows CE-based Pocket PC devices). When you resize the images, new versions are created with slightly different filenames. However, you also have an option to resize original images without creating copies.

You will certainly notice that this PowerToy functions in a manner which is somewhat similar to the **Send Pictures via E-mail** built-in Windows XP functionality (Fig. 13.3). However, it provides more control over resizing options and allows you to resize multiple images at a time. Just compare the screenshots shown in Figs 13.2 and 13.3 to feel the difference!

This PowerToy is certainly useful and recommended for installation.

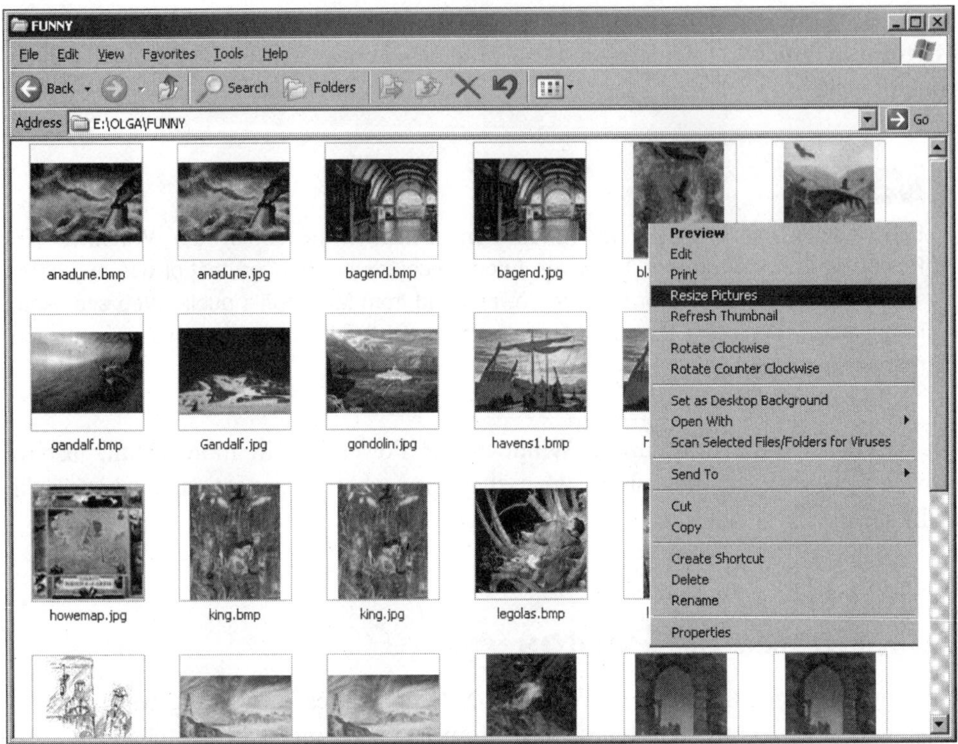

Fig. 13.1. Notice the **Resize Pictures** command in the right-click menu

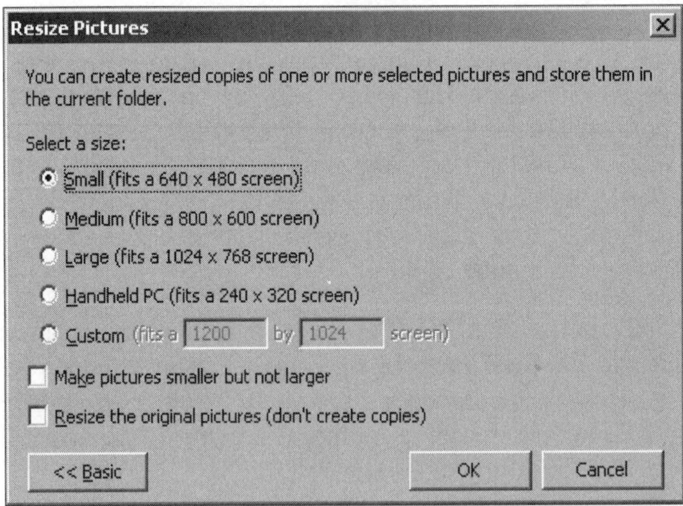

Fig. 13.2. The **Resize Pictures** dialog

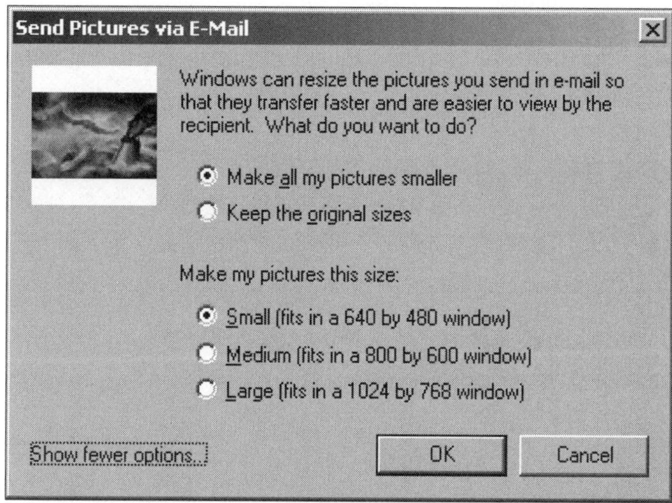

Fig. 13.3. Windows XP provides built-in Send Pictures via E-Mail functionality, but it provides fewer options that Bulk Resize PowerToy

Faster User Switcher

This toy is a Windows XP-specific shell enhancement exploiting Fast User Switching technology implemented in Windows XP. It is intended to make Fast User Switching even faster, because it allows you to bypass the Welcome screen.

Notice that you can't use this Toy if Fast User Switching is disabled. To test Fast User Switcher, make sure that Fast User Switching is enabled and two or more users are logged on simultaneously. After that, press and hold down the Windows Key and repeatedly press <Q> to scroll the list of available users. When you see the user name that you need, release both keys, and the system will switch to that user.

Open Command Window Here

Open Command Window Here is one of the most valuable PowerToys, allowing you to easily drop to command prompt from any Windows Explorer folder. After it is installed, the **Open Command Window Here** menu item will be available in the right-click menu in any Windows Explorer folder (Fig. 13.4). Just right-click a folder, choose **Open Command Window Here**, and you'll open a command prompt session (with the selected folder as the default directory). Additionally, if you right-click a folder icon in a Windows Explorer window, you'll also have the **Open Command Window Here** command available in the resulting menu.

If you like to work at a command prompt, this toy is a must-have.

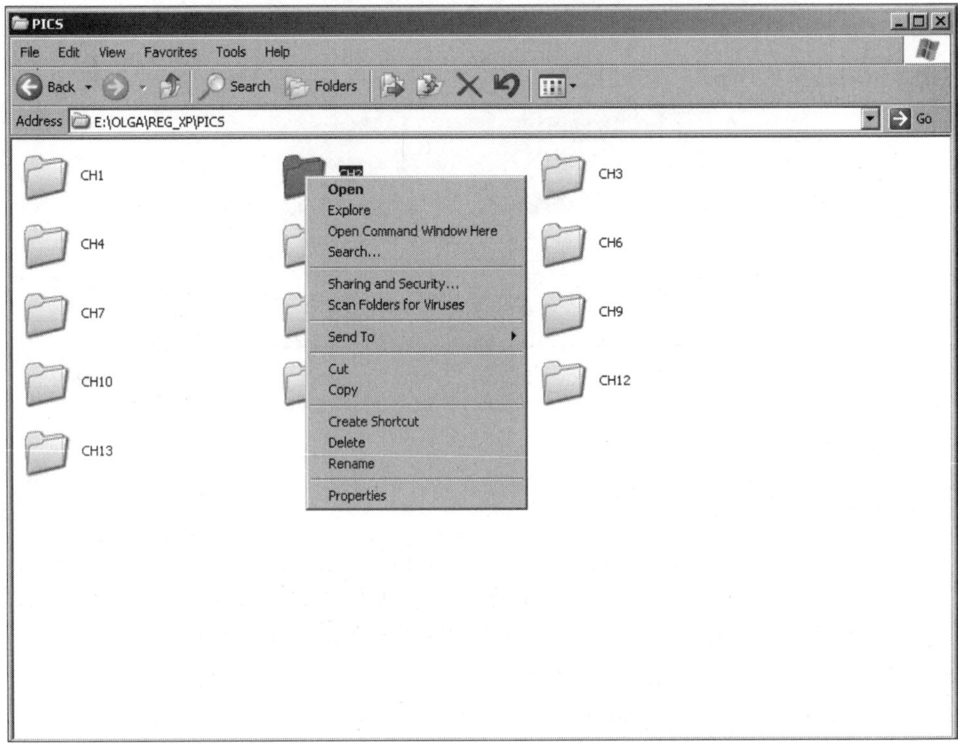

Fig. 13.4. The Open Command Window Here PowerToy adds the **Open Command Window Here** command to the right-click menu in My Computer and Windows Explorer

Shell Audio Player

Shell Audio Player just offers another way to play music in Windows XP. The Shell Audio Player is a Taskbar toolbar that allows you to play MP3 and WMA files and playlists. You enable it by right-clicking the Taskbar and choosing the Audio Player command from the **Toolbars** menu. What this will give you is a new toolbar, with **Play**, **Previous**, **Next**, and **Playlist Editor** buttons (Fig. 13.5). Keep in mind that you might have to unlock the Taskbar and resize the toolbar to view all the buttons.

Fig. 13.5. The Audio Player toolbar provides just another way to play music in Windows XP

The Shell Audio Player is a good idea, however, in my opinion, its implementation needs to be improved. I suppose that in future releases of PowerToys this player will provide more advanced functionality.

The PowerToy Calculator

The PowerToy Calculator immediately reminded me of my school years, when I dreamed about an advanced scientific graphing calculator (Fig. 13.6). For those who study math, it will be a handy tool.

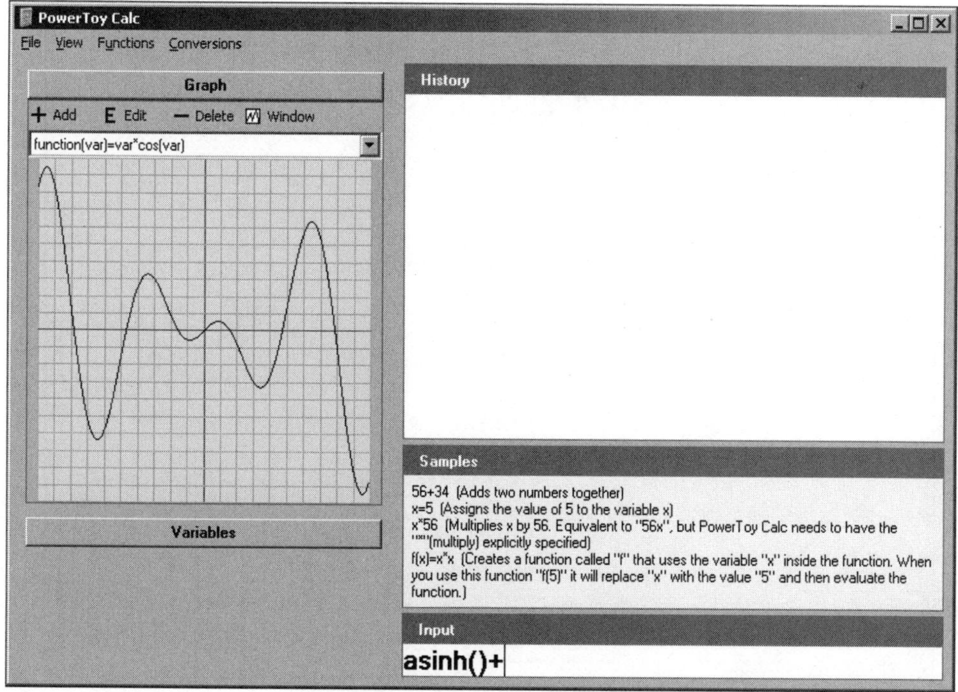

Fig. 13.6. The PowerToy Calculator

Tweak UI for Windows XP

The Windows XP version of Tweak UI is the most valuable of all PowerToys included in the current release. It provides a safe and convenient way of customizing various system settings, which are not available in the default Windows XP user interface. Normally, to produce the same result without Tweak UI, you'll need to edit the system registry. As was already mentioned in *Chapter 1*, this tool provides alternative methods of editing the Registry, which usually is safer than doing so via Regedit.exe.

In contrast to all the previous releases of Tweak UI, which were implemented as Control Panel applets, Tweak UI for Windows XP (Fig. 13.7) is a standalone executable file. You can place this EXE file in any folder and start it from there, since it doesn't need to be installed prior to use. Tweak UI for Windows XP displays a hierarchical tree of available options in the left pane. After you select an option in the left pane, the right pane will display configuration settings available for selection (Fig. 13.8).

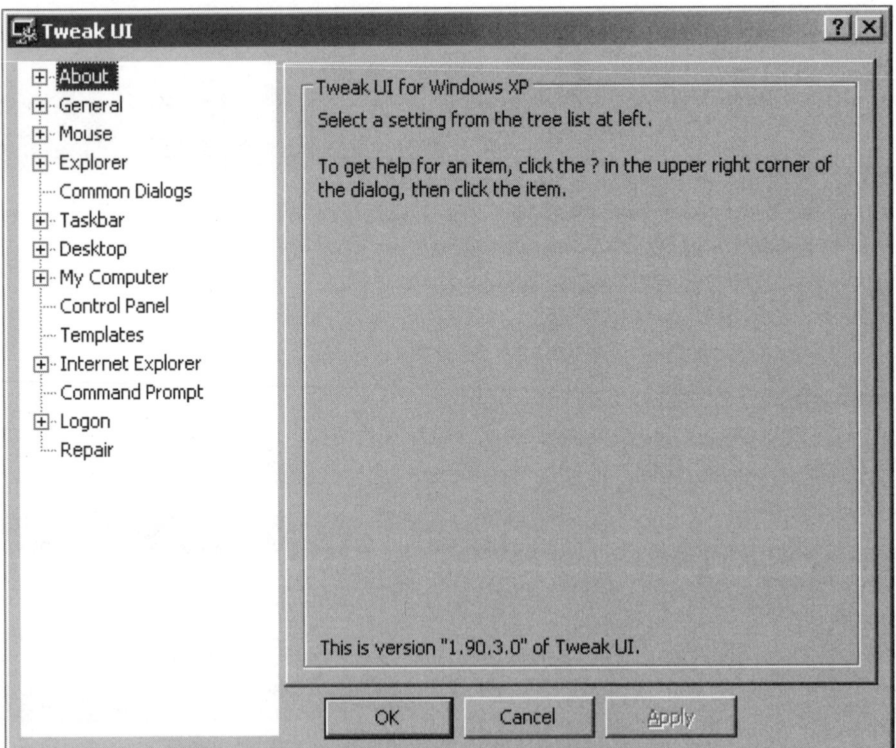

Fig. 13.7. Tweak UI for Windows XP

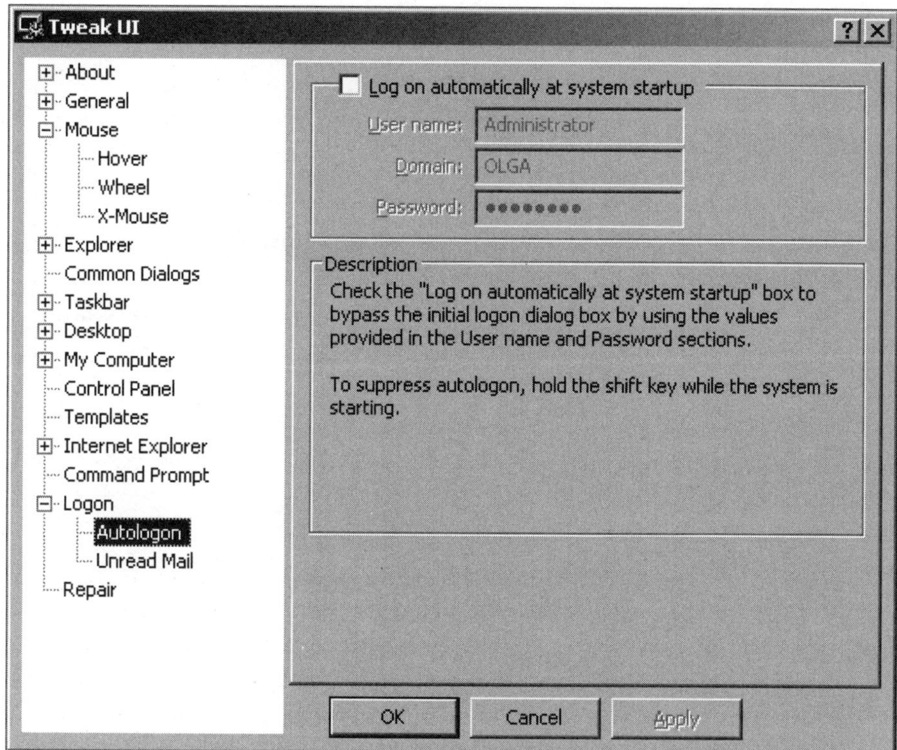

Fig. 13.8. After you select an option in the left pane of the **Tweak UI** window, the right pane will display a set of available configuration settings

NOTE

Before you install Windows XP PowerToys and start playing with this version of TweakUI, make sure that you have deleted any older copies of TweakUI.

This tool is a must for all users who want to customize Windows XP according to his or her requirements and to get the most out of the system. The new Tweak UI enables you to do practically any kind of customization, including quite a few difficult tasks, such as configuring various UI visual effects, error beeps, cursor shadow, etc.; and configuring the taskbar, shell folders and the CD Burning cache. In my opinion, one of the best features provided by this tool is its capability to perform some basic repairing tasks (Fig. 13.9).

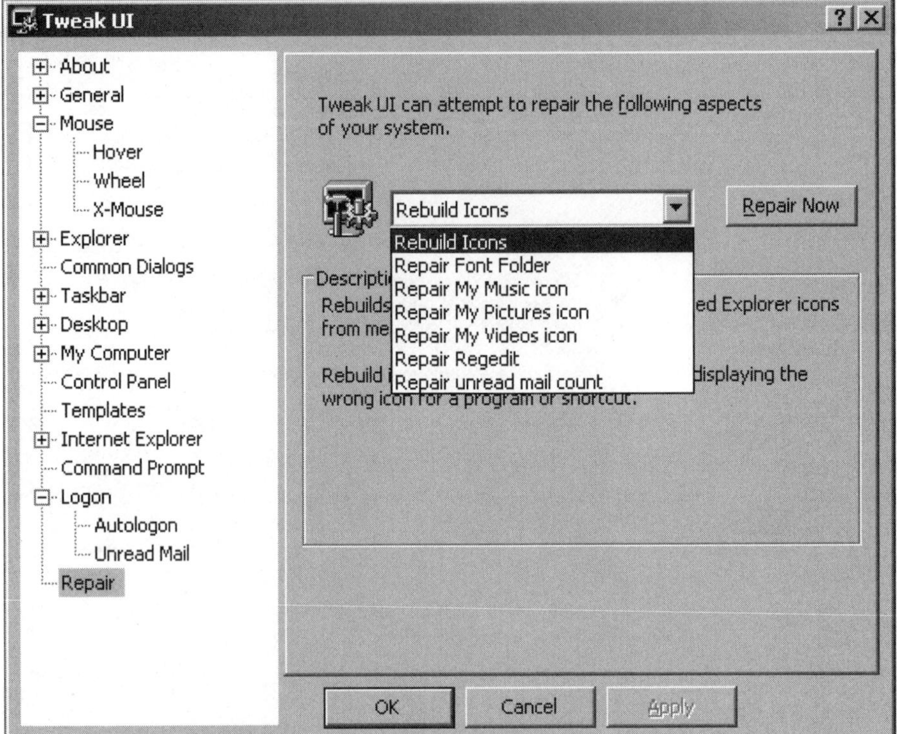

Fig. 13.9. Tweak UI provides a set of repairing options

Even this alone makes the tool extremely useful and highly recommended to most users. To conclude the discussion of PowerToys for Windows XP, I'd say that it is up to you to decide whether you need it or not. Furthermore, in this chapter, we didn't cover all of the Toys included in this collection. Rather, I tried to draw your attention to the tools that I personally considered to be useful and convenient. If you like the new Windows XP user interface, you'll probably like many other Toys not covered here.

RegMaid Utility—Cleaning Your Registry

RegMaid is a utility developed by Microsoft and intended to help you track down and cleanup problematic OLE entries in the Registry database. RegMaid is quite easy to use, and at the same time, it provides the user with as much information on the problem registry entries as possible (Fig. 13. 10). This information can then be used to make decisions about the entries you want to delete and which you want to repair.

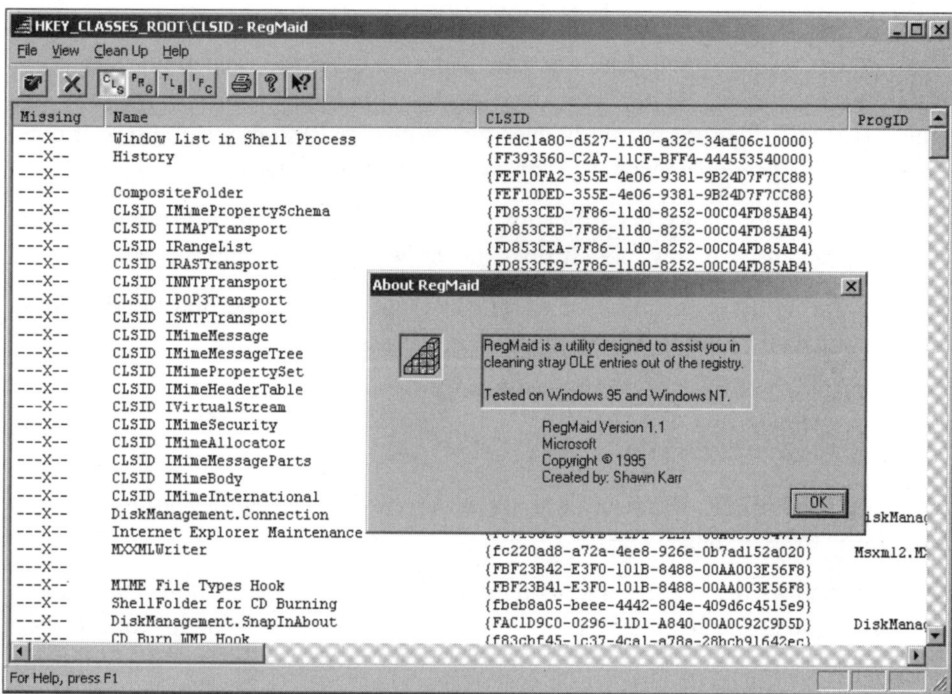

Fig. 13.10. The RegMaid utility main window

Information on the OLE components is stored in the registry under `HKEY_CLASSES_ROOT` registry key, where you typically find subsections such as `CLSID`, `TypeLib`, `Interface`, and `ProgId`.

The RegMaid utility considers `CLSID` entries problematic if they contain a handler or server entry for a file that can't be found. There are several ways in which this situation may occur. A few of the most common include: deleting the file, moving the file or a broken network path.

`ProgId` entries will be considered broken when the associated `CLSID` cannot be found in `HKEY_CLASSES_ROOT\CLSID`. As a result, deleting `CLSID` entries will cause related `ProgId` entries to be listed.

`TypeLib` entries are considered broken when the associated file cannot be found.

`Interface` entries are considered broken when the `TypeLib` entry cannot be matched to one in `HKEY_CLASSES_ROOT\TypeLib`. Consequently, deleting `TypeLib` entries will allow RegMaid to identify the associated problem.

RegMaid provides information about the entries believed to be problematic in a form of the report, where the user can make multiple row selections. Once selections have been made, the user can then delete them from the registry. Although RegMaid does not currently have an **Archive** or **Restore** capabilities, it does provide a printed report mechanism for each of the four views.

Windows 9*x* and Windows NT officially support this utility, but I also tested it on Windows 2000 and Windows XP. It does indeed work, and is rather useful.

This freeware utility is essential for advanced users, and can be downloaded from the Microsoft Download Center (**http://www.microsoft.com**).

Regmon—Registry Monitoring

Developed by Mark Russinovich and Bryce Cogswell, this registry utility, among all others, is truly brilliant.

Regmon monitors the registry and displays all information concerning the system-wide registry access. This unique tool is implemented as a combination of a device driver and GUI, and it's certainly a must for anyone who studies Windows NT/2000/XP internals or troubleshoots problems caused by an inconsistent registry (Fig. 13.11).

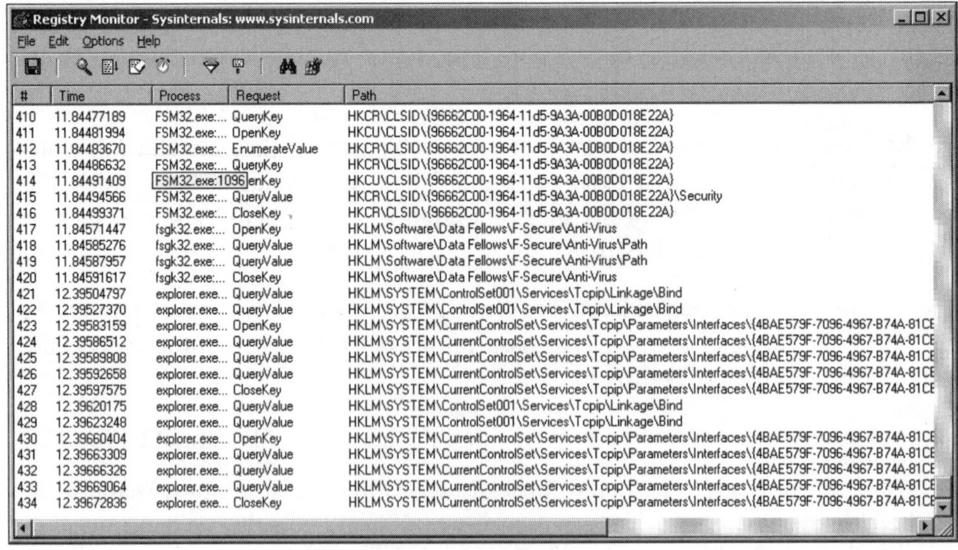

Fig. 13.11. Regmon at work

The Regmon utility supports process filtering, allows you to save its output in the ASCII file and even monitors boot-time registry activity.

The authors not only provide it as a freeware, but also supply technical information on the details of implementation and even provide the source code.

Supported operating systems: Windows 95/98, Windows NT 4.0, and Windows 2000. It also works fine with Windows XP.

Download from: **http://www.sysinternals.com**.

NTFSDOS Professional

This is another popular utility from Mark Russinovich and Bryce Cogswell. Although NTFSDOS isn't a registry-editing tool, it deserves mention here because it's a valuable tool for quick recovery of the missing or corrupt files needed to load Windows NT/2000 (these files, of course, include registry hives). NTFSDOS Professional is a small utility, and can be started from system disks.

NTFSDOS Professional also contains the NTFSCHK tool for checking NTFS disks under DOS. It will allow you to check the hard disk and perform recovery, if boot problems are caused by corruption of the NTFS disk structures.

Download the trial version of NTFSDOS Professional from **http://www.sysinternals.com**.

Note that although NTFSDOS Professional isn't a freeware, the authors do provide a freeware utility of this type—NTFSDOS (which is provided with the source code).

RegSafe Professional from Imaginelan

If you edit the registry on a regular basis, perhaps you are not satisfied with the standard functionality provided by built-in registry-editing tools, supplied with Windows NT/2000/XP. If so, then RegSafe Professional from Imaginelan is just for you!

RegSafe Professional Edition 2.0 is a suite of tools designed to provide Network Administrators, IS/IT professionals, and Power Users with the ability to perform advanced Registry management on 32-bit Windows PCs. RegSafe provides comprehensive Registry editing and management capabilities not found in other professional level Registry editing tools, all from within a protected environment (Fig. 13.12).

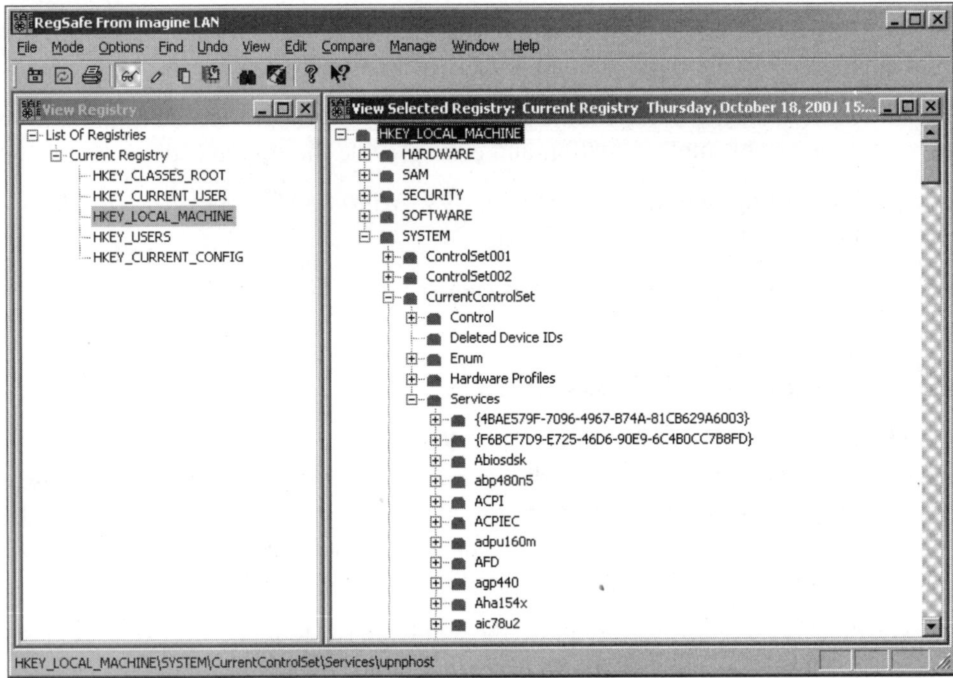

Fig. 13.12. RegSafe is a powerful registry editor with extended functionality

The most attractive features of RegSafe are listed below:

- *Protected Environment.* RegSafe automatically saves a copy of the Registry *before* you introduce any modifications. In *Chapter 3*, where we discussed new functionality of the Regedit.exe utility supplied with Windows XP, I pointed out that despite all its advantages, the new Regedit version lacks the Read-Only mode (which, as you remember, was present in Regedt32.exe). Well, RegSafe has this useful function, which is particularly appropriate for beginners who have only just begun to study the registry structure. Furthermore, in contrast to standard registry-editing tools (Regedit.exe and Regedt32.exe), it has Undo functionality, which is available when editing the registry. Unlike other Registry editing tools, if you make a mistake while editing with RegSafe, you won't trash your system. Even if you mistakenly delete something from your registry, the first thing RegSafe does is to take a registry snapshot, and then prompts you to confirm the operation (Fig. 13.13). If you realize later that you have made an error, you can easily undo it (Fig. 13.14) Really great!
- *Registry Comparison.* RegSafe goes far beyond simple Registry Editing. Consider, for example, its powerful Comparison features. Compare Current or

Snapshot Registries, compare keys/values within the same Registry, compare access control lists (ACL) on Windows NT/2000/XP systems. It's fantastic!

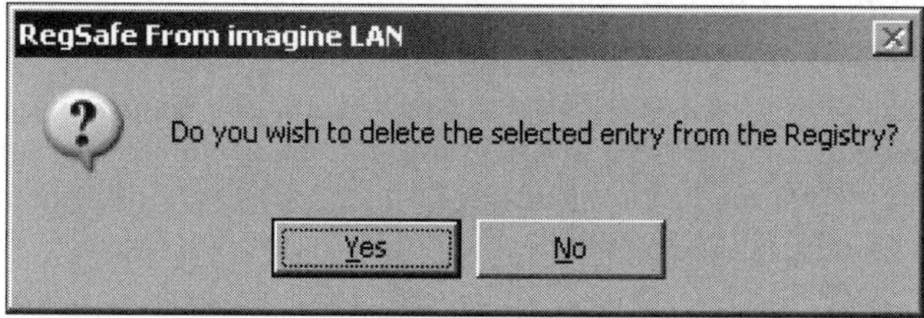

Fig. 13.13. RegSafe prompts the user to confirm deletion of registry entries

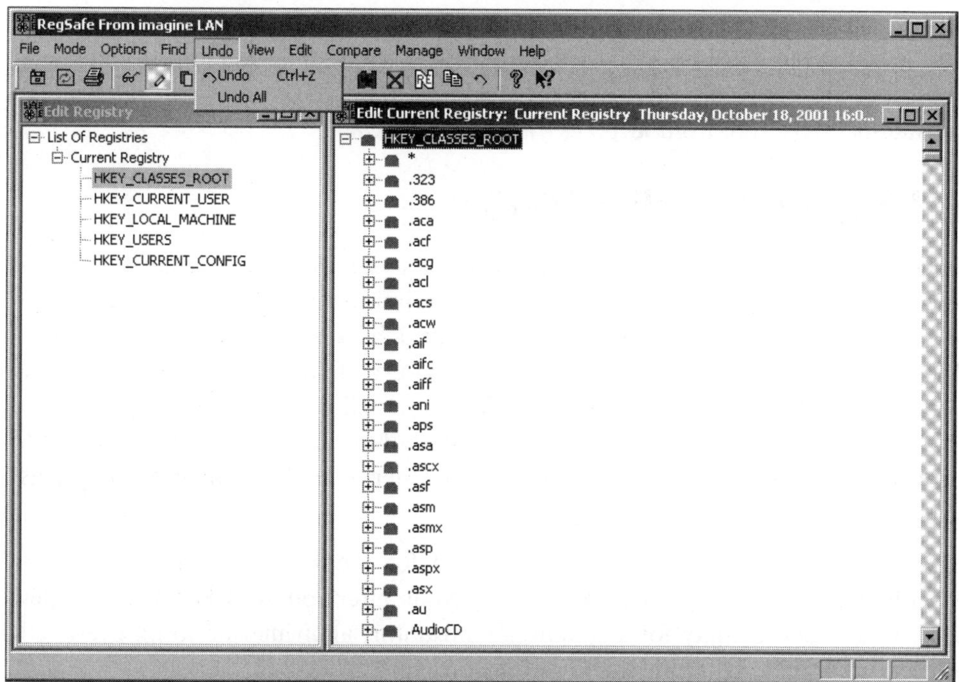

Fig. 13.14. Great! It has Undo functionality

- *Powerful export features.* Administrators and other advanced users will appreciate RegSafe's export feature, which allows portions of a Registry or Registry comparison results tree to be exported to a REG file (Regedit4 format).
- *Partial or full registry restoration.* If an unwanted change to the Registry was made, or a problem with the Registry is detected, RegSafe can

perform a *partial* or *full* restoration of a Registry snapshot to the current ("live") Registry.

- *Registry restoration for non-booting systems.* Well, I am a big fan of restoring unbootable systems (it just became my favorite hobby). If you are like me, you'll appreciate the capabilities provided by RegSafe in this field. The developers of this magnificent program have implemented the so-called Command Prompt SOS technology, which helps to restore the registry on all existing Windows versions (yes, really on all of them, including Windows 9*x*, ME, NT/2000/XP systems with FAT, FAT32, and NTFS-formatted drives). In addition, RegSafe provides Recovery Console restoration on Windows 2000/XP.

All this makes this tool a registry editor of choice for anyone, from beginners to experts. Furthermore, the "Editor Only" version of RegSafe is FREE (despite the fact that its functionality is limited in comparison to the fully-functional retail versions, it is still the most powerful registry-editing tool I have ever seen). Download this indispensable tool from **http://www.imaginelan.com**.

ERD Commander 2000

Since the release of Windows 2000, Microsoft has significantly enhanced and improved the built-in system reliability tools. In Windows XP, these tools have been improved one step further. However, if your job is to support and maintain Windows installations, including emergency recovery of damaged systems, you may wonder why Microsoft didn't include such functionality as booting DOS disks to recover damaged Windows 2000/XP installations. After all, Recovery Console is a great tool, but still, it is somewhat limited. Furthermore, there may be situations when you'll have difficulties starting it.

If you are missing the ease of booting ERD for recovering damaged Windows NT/2000/XP installations, I'd like to turn your attention to ERD Commander 2000. It is an ideal utility for a system administrator, allowing one to fix nearly all problems that prevent Windows NT/2000 from booting.

NOTE

The current version of this powerful tool is intended for use with Windows NT/2000. Windows XP is not fully supported. However, in some situations ERD Commander 2000 will prove helpful even with Windows XP. An example of such a situation is one in which you only need to replace damaged system files by their valid backup copies, or simply copy several files from the system that doesn't boot. If you encounter such a situation, don't hesitate to use ERD Commander 2000. It will help.

To install ERD Commander 2000, you'll need the distribution files of this program (visit the **http://www.sysinternals.com/ntw2k/freeware/erdcommander2k.shtml** to download the Read-Only version for free or order the Read-Write fully functional version, the Windows 2000 distribution CD and, optionally, five 3.5-inch diskettes). The ERD Commander 2000 Setup program will prompt you to select the installation type (Fig. 13.15). You'll have the option to create boot diskettes, a bootable CD-ROM image or to install ERD Commander 2000 on your hard disk (in this case, ERD Commander 2000 will be added as an alternate Boot.ini startup option).

NOTE

You can install ERD Commander 2000 even when running Windows XP. Notice, however, that in this situation you must do so on the basis of Windows NT/2000 distribution files. When Setup prompts you (Fig. 13.16), insert your Windows NT/2000 distribution CD or specify an alternate location for the installation files. Don't create ERD Commander 2000 boot media based on the Windows XP distribution files—the Setup program will run OK, but the result will be practically useless.

After you complete ERD Commander 2000 installation, you'll be able to boot into a command-line from a set of 3.5" floppy disks, from a CD-ROM, or directly from the hard disk. ERD Commander 2000 allows users to perform practically all recovery-related operations by accessing and modifying files on NTFS and FAT disk volumes. ERD Commander 2000's environment mirrors the standard NT/2000 console-mode environment, so users familiar with the commands of these operating systems can intuitively work with this tool.

When you boot a damaged system using ERD Commander 2000 boot floppies or bootable CD, you'll be provided access to all drives and devices available in the downed Windows NT/2000/XP system, including removable drives.

NOTE

Since ERD Commander 2000 is not intended for resolving disk corruption problems, only drives that are consistent enough to be recognized by Windows NT/2000 file systems will be accessible with *ERD Commander.*

Administrators can then remove or replace corrupted drivers, update system files, correct security mistakes that prevent the OS from booting, make recoveries from improperly installed Service Packs or other updates, and many more.

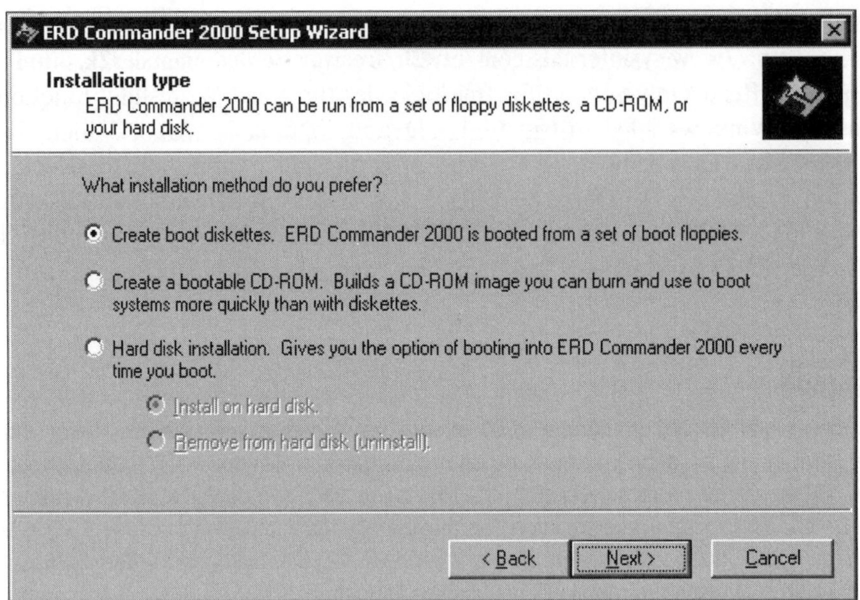

Fig. 13.15. ERD Commander 2000 Setup Wizard prompts you to select installation method

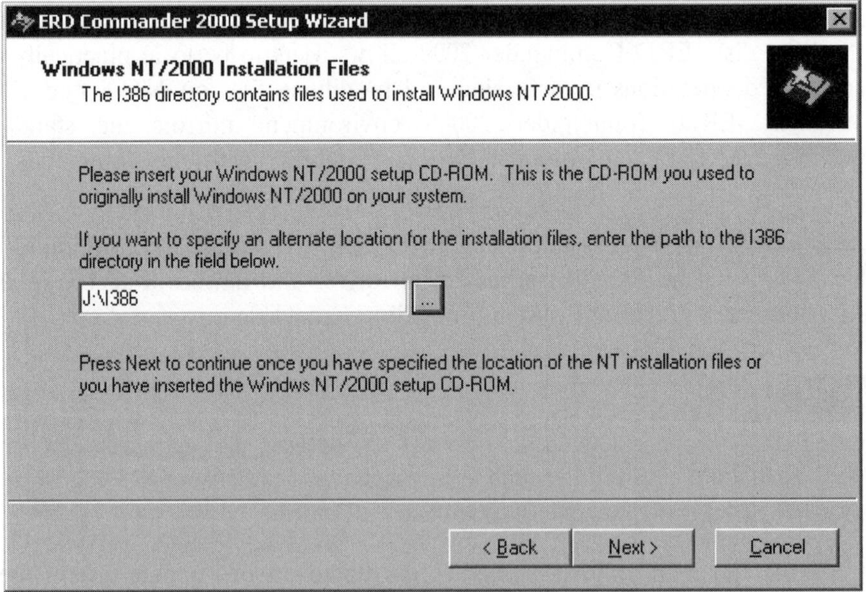

Fig. 13.16. Next, ERD Commander 2000 Setup Wizard prompts you to insert your Windows NT/2000 distribution CD or specify an alternate location for the installation files

ERD Commander 2000 works fine on NT 4.0 and Windows 2000. As was already mentioned, this utility is not intended for Windows XP. However, some tasks, such as replacing corrupted files or copying important data from the dead system can be accomplished successfully using, for example, ERD Commander 2000's boot floppies.

The current version of ERD Commander 2000 includes the following convenient features:

- Built-in registry editor
- Built-in file editor
- Options of the hard drive, CD-ROM, or floppy disks installation
- Batch-file support
- Command and output logging
- Emergency Repair Disk images for Windows 2000

Summary

I only listed the registry utilities that I tested myself, and can recommend to my readers. You may wish to test other utilities of this class, some of which you can find visiting the links provided in *Appendix 1— "Internet resources"*.

Chapter 14

Automating Registry Management with WSH

R is for Rocket.

Ray Bradbury

When it comes to software development and distributing the applications to end-users, the Registry Editor is only suitable for testing purposes. Setup programs, REG files, and INF files provide more capabilities for convenient and safe registry modification. Furthermore, if you are going to automate Windows and introduce registry modifications at the speed of a rocket, you'll certainly appreciate the script usage.

In *Chapter 10* we already touched the problem and even provided a small code excerpt, which illustrated the usage of WSH. Introduced with Windows 2000, WSH is capable of creating simple, but flexible and powerful scripts to automate network administration. Because WSH is language-independent, you're free to select any scripting language you prefer: Visual Basic Scripting Edition (VBScript), JScript, or Perl. WSH also supports COM, allowing you to enjoy the advantages of new technologies such as Windows Management Instrumentation (WMI).

Now, the time has come to consider this topic in more detail. Of course, it is impossible to provide a detailed description of WSH, WMI, or scripting languages, such as VBScript or Jscript, within a single chapter (after all, each of these topics deserves a separate book, and quite a comprehensive one, since I encountered volumes of JScript and Perl that comprised more than 1500 pages). Therefore, if you want a detailed language reference, simply buy one of those books at your local bookstore.

However, we will consider the registry-related topics, and, in particular, the `RegRead`, `RegWrite`, and `RegDelete` methods provided by WSH. We will also consider their practical usage and provide several simple, but useful scripts.

Basic Information on Microsoft Windows Script Host

Microsoft Windows Script Host (WSH) is a language-independent scripting host for Windows Script-compatible scripting engines. It brings simple, powerful, and flexible scripting to the Windows 32-bit platform, allowing you to run scripts from both the Windows desktop and the command prompt.

Windows Script Host is ideal for non-interactive scripting needs such as logon scripting, administrative scripting, and machine automation.

The Benefits of Windows Script Host

Windows Script Host offers the following benefits:

- Two ways to run scripts, WScript.exe and CScript.exe. WScript.exe provides a Windows-based properties page for setting script properties; CScript.exe provides command-line switches for setting script properties.
- Support for multiple files. You can call multiple scripting engines and perform multiple jobs from a single Windows Script (WSF) file.
- Low memory requirements.
- Mapping of script extensions to programmatic identifiers (ProgIDs). When you start a script from the Windows desktop or the command prompt, the script host reads and passes the specified script file contents to the registered script engine. Instead of using the `HTML SCRIPT` tag to identify the script, the host uses file extensions; for example, *VBS* for Microsoft Visual Basic® Scripting Edition (VBScript) files, and *JS* for Microsoft JScript® files. The use of extensions means you no longer need to be familiar with the ProgID for a given script engine. Windows Script Host handles this for you by maintaining a mapping of script extensions to ProgIDs, launching the appropriate engine for a given script.

Windows XP includes the latest version of Windows Script Host—version 5.6.0 (Fig. 14.1). Versions of Windows Script Host implemented by Microsoft operating systems are listed in Table 14.1.

Table 14.1. WSH Versions Implemented by Microsoft Operating Systems

Host Application	1.0	2.0	5.1	5.6
Microsoft Windows 98	x			
Microsoft Windows ME			x	
Microsoft Windows NT 4 Option Pack	x			
Microsoft Windows 2000		x		
Microsoft Windows XP				x

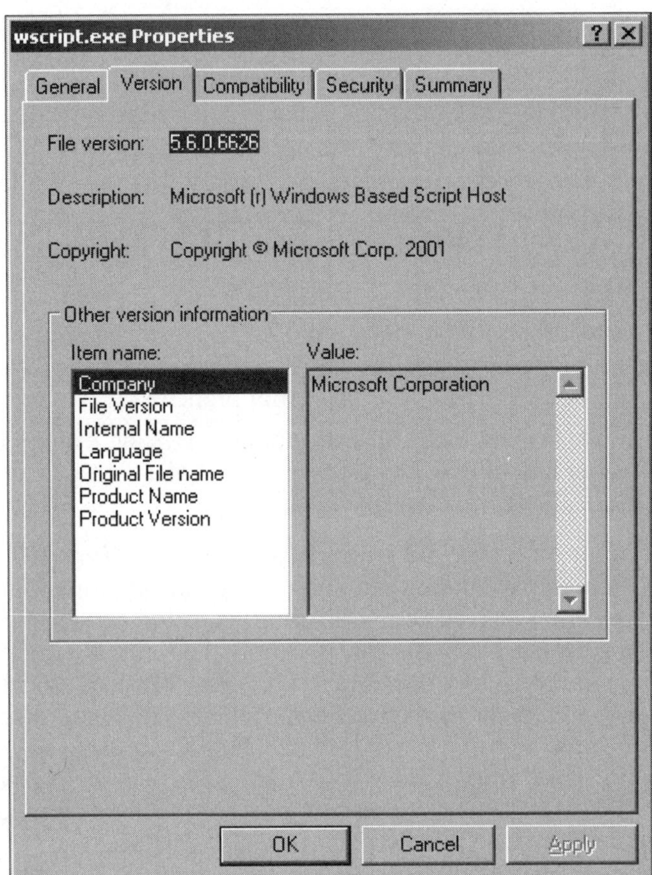

Fig. 14.1. Windows XP includes the latest version of Windows Script Host—version 5.6.0

In comparison to previous versions, this one provides the following enhancements in functionality.

- *Argument handling has been improved*—handling and documenting command line arguments is simpler. The process of integrating your scripts with other command line scripts has been simplified, and it is easier to create scripts that can supply the user with help information. Refer to the following table for information on the WSH language features that connect you to this new functionality.
- *You can run scripts remotely*—you can load scripts onto several remote computer systems, and start them all running simultaneously. While a remote script is running, you can check on its progress, and after it has finished, you can ensure

that it ran correctly, or find out what caused it to terminate prematurely. There is a new dispatch object used to create remote WSH objects—the `Controller` object. In addition, there is a new object that represents an instance of a running script—the `Remote WSH` object.

- *When you start new processes, you can treat them as objects*—you determine the status of spawned processes, and access their standard I/O streams.
- *You can access the current working directory*—you can determine/modify the active process' current working directory.
- *Security issues unique to scripts have been addressed*—Windows Script Host, a powerful a flexible tool for automating Windows, can at the same time be dangerous if used improperly or with malicious intentions. Windows Script Host 5.6, included with Windows XP, implements a new security model, which enables users to verify the authenticity of a script before running it. Script developers can sign their scripts to prevent unauthorized modifications. Administrators can enforce strict policies that determine which users have privileges to run scripts locally or remotely.

NOTE

Windows provides a standard mechanism for signing code via signcode.exe. Unfortunately, signcode.exe doesn't ship with Windows, but rather with the Windows SDK. The most useful and interesting article on this important topic can be downloaded from **http://msdn.microsoft.com/library/default.asp?url=/library/en-us/dnclinic/html/scripting10082001.asp**

Windows Script Host Object Model

As everything in modern Microsoft operating systems, WSH is object-oriented. The Windows Script Host object model consists of 14 objects. The root object is the `WScript` object.

The Windows Script Host object model provides a logical, systematic way to perform many administrative tasks. The set of COM interfaces it provides can be placed into two main categories:

- *Script Execution and Troubleshooting.* This set of interfaces allows scripts to perform basic manipulation of the Windows Script Host, output messages to the screen, and perform basic COM functions such as `CreateObject` and `GetObject`.

- *Helper Functions.* Helper functions are properties and methods for performing actions such as mapping network drives, connecting to printers, retrieving and modifying environment variables, and manipulating registry keys. Administrators can also use the Windows Script Host helper functions to create simple logon scripts.

NOTE

For purposes of accessing the registry, the most important object is `WshShell`, which will be discussed in the next section.

WshShell Object

Provides access to the native Windows shell. The `WshShell` object is a child object of the `WScript` object—you must use the `WScript` method `CreateScript` to create a `WshShell` object (i.e., `WScript.CreateObject("WScript.Shell")`). You create a `WshShell` object whenever you want to run a program locally, manipulate the contents of the registry, create a shortcut, or access a system folder. The `WshShell` object provides the `Environment` collection. This collection allows you to handle environmental variables (such as `WINDIR`, `PATH`, or `PROMPT`).

RegRead Method

The `RegRead` method returns the value of a key or value name from the registry. This method uses the following syntax:

```
Object.RegRead(strName)
```

where:

`Object`—`WshShell` object

`strName`—string value indicating the key or value-name whose value you want

The `RegRead` method can return the values of the following data types: `REG_SZ`, `REG_DWORD`, `REG_BINARY`, `REG_EXPAND_SZ`, and `REG_MULTI_SZ`.

You can specify a key name by ending *`strName`* with a final backslash. Do not include a final backslash to specify a value name. A value entry has three parts: its name, its data type, and its value. When you specify a key name (as opposed to a value name), `RegRead` returns the default value. To read a key's default value, specify the name of the key itself. Fully qualified key names and value names begin with a root key. You must use abbreviated versions of root key names with the `RegRead` method. The five possible root keys are listed in Table 14.2.

Table 14.2. Abbreviations for the Registry Root Key Names

Root Key Name	Abbreviation
HKEY_CURRENT_USER	HKCU
HKEY_LOCAL_MACHINE	HKLM
HKEY_CLASSES_ROOT	HKCR
HKEY_USERS	HKEY_USERS
HKEY_CURRENT_CONFIG	HKEY_CURRENT_CONFIG

RegWrite Method

The `RegWrite` Method creates a new key, adds another value to an existing key (and assigns it a value), or changes the value of an existing value name. This method uses the following syntax:

```
Object.RegWrite(strName, anyValue [,strType])
```

where:

Object—`WshShell` object

strName—string value indicating the key name, value name, or value you want to create, add, or change

anyValue—the name of the new key you want to create, the name of the value you want to add to an existing key, or the new value you want to assign to an existing value name

strType—optional. String value indicating the value's data type

Specify a key name by ending *strName* with a final backslash. Do not include a final backslash to specify a value name. The `RegWrite` method automatically converts the parameter *anyValue* to either a string or an integer. The value of *strType* determines its data type (either a string or an integer). The options for *strType* are listed in Table 14.3.

Table 14.3. Acceptable Values of the strType Argument for the RegWrite Method

Converted to	*strType*
string	`REG_SZ`
string	`REG_EXPAND_SZ`
integer	`REG_DWORD`
string	`REG_BINARY`

NOTE

The `REG_MULTI_SZ` type is not supported for the `RegWrite` method.

Fully qualified key names and value names are prefixed with a root key. You must use abbreviated versions of root key names (if one exists) with the `RegWrite` method. Abbreviated names of the registry root keys used by the `RegWrite` method are the same as those for the `RegRead` method.

RegDelete Method

The `RegDelete` method is used to delete a registry key or one of its values from the registry. This method uses the following syntax:

`Object``.`**`RegDelete`**`(`*`strName`*`)`

where:

`Object`—`WshShell` object

`strName`—string value indicating the name of the registry key or key value you want to delete

Specify a key-name by ending *`strName`* with a final backslash; leave it off to specify a value name. Fully qualified key names and value names are prefixed with a root key. You must use abbreviated versions of root key names (if one exists) with the `RegDelete` method. There are five possible root keys you can use; they are the same as for the `RegRead` and `RegWrite` methods.

JScript Example

A simple example written in JavaScript (JScript in Microsoft's implementation), illustrating the usage of these methods is provided in Listing 1. This code creates a registry key `HKEY_CURRENT_USER\Software\MyCoolSoftware`, sets its `Default` value (`REG_BINARY` data type) to 1, then creates just another `REG_SZ` value entry under this key and assigns it the "This is a test!" string value.

Listing 14.1. JScript Example Illustrating Registry Access

```
   // The simplest example illustrating registry access using JScript
   // Use this module at your own risk

// Setting variables


var vbOKCancel = 1;
var vbInformation = 64;
var vbCancel = 2;
var result;


// Creating wshShell object


var WshShell = WScript.CreateObject("WScript.Shell");

{

// prompting the user

   result = WshShell.Popup("Do you want to create a new registry setting?",
                           0,
                           "Registry Access using JScript",
                           vbOKCancel + vbInformation);
   if (result != vbCancel)
   {

    WshShell.RegWrite ("HKCU\\Software\\MyCoolSoftware\\", 1, "REG_BINARY");
    WshShell.RegWrite ("HKCU\\Software\\MyCoolSoftware\\MySuperProgram",
                       "This is a test!", "REG_SZ");
```

```
    var bKey =    WshShell.RegRead ("HKCU\\Software\\MyCoolSoftware\\");
    WScript.Echo   (WshShell.RegRead   ("HKCU\\Software\\MyCoolSoftware\\
    MySuperProgram"));
    }

//prompting the user

result = WshShell.Popup("Do you want to delete newly created settings?",
                        0,
                        "Registry Access using JScript",
                        vbOKCancel + vbInformation);
    if (result != vbCancel)
    {
    WshShell.RegDelete
("HKCU\\Software\\MyCoolSoftware\\MySuperProgram");
    WshShell.RegDelete ("HKCU\\Software\\MyCoolSoftware\\");
    }
}
```

To test this script, enter the code provided in this listing using any text editor (for example, Notepad.exe), and save the file with the JS filename extension. If you double-click this file WSH server will start and execute the script. Notice that this script prompts the user to confirm adding new registry entries (Fig. 14.2), displays the contents of the newly created registry entry (Fig. 14.3) and then asks the user if the newly created registry key and value entry contained within it should be deleted (Fig. 14.4).

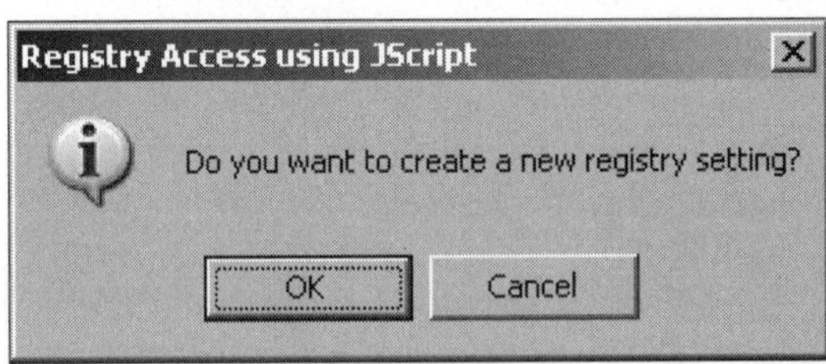

Fig. 14.2. The dialog prompting the user to confirm creating of a new registry setting

Fig. 14.3. Displaying the contents of the newly created registry entry

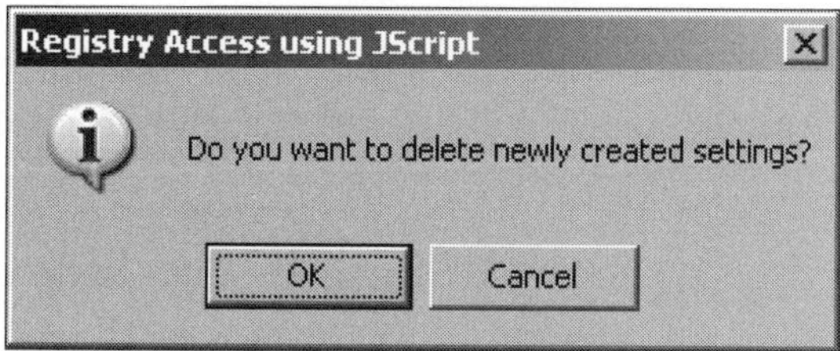

Fig. 14.4. The dialog prompting the user to confirm deletion of the newly created registry setting(s)

These dialog boxes allow the user to check modifications introduced to the registry at each step, using, for example, Registry Editor (Fig. 14.5).

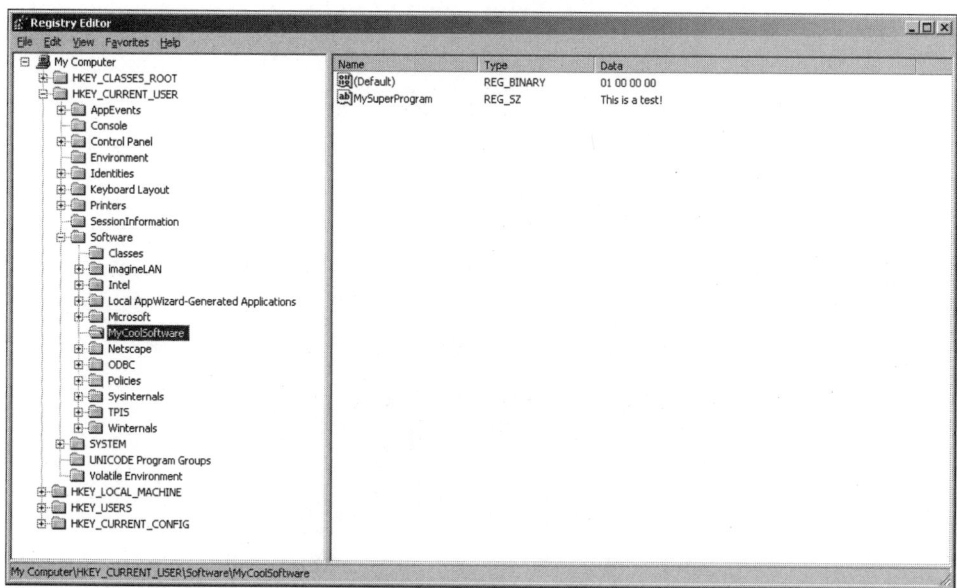

Fig. 14.5. You can use Registry Editor to check modifications introduced to the registry at each step of the script

VBScript Examples

If you prefer VBScript, you can also use the above-described methods for accessing the registry (notice the difference in the syntax of JScript and VBScript).

Enabling and Disabling Changes to the Start Menu

A small example is provided below, developed using VBScript, which, in contrast to the previous one, does something useful—it enables or disables changes to the **Start** Menu.

In the previous chapter, we discussed the values that control the **Start** menu. One such value is the `NoChangeStartMenu` under `HKEY_CURRENT_USER\SOFTWARE\Microsoft\Windows\CurrentVersion\Policies\Explorer`. When this value is set to 1, one cannot make changes, and when this value is set to 0, changes are allowed. Our small VBScript example reads the `NoChangeStartMenu` value from the registry, displays the **Start** menu status, and prompts the user if he wants to enable (Fig. 14.6) or disable (Fig. 14.7) changes to the **Start** menu.

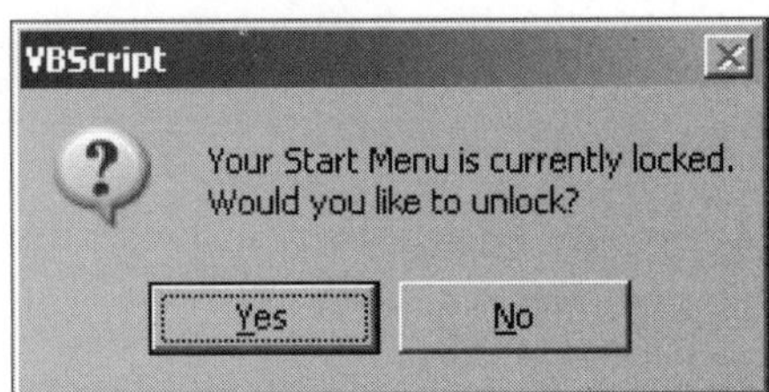

Fig. 14.6. Prompt for the user to unlock **Start** menu

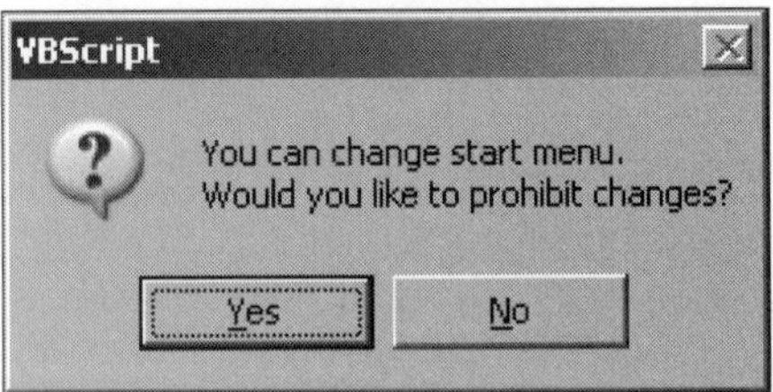

Fig. 14.7. Prompt for the user to lock **Start** menu

The source code for this example is provided in Listing 14.2.

Listing 14.2. Source Code for the VBScript Example that Enables or Disables Changes to the Start Menu

```
' Code for enabling and disabling Start menu changes

Option Explicit

Dim WSHShell, RegKey, NoChangeStartMenu, Result

Set WSHShell = CreateObject("WScript.Shell")

RegKey =
"HKCU\Software\Microsoft\Windows\CurrentVersion\Policies\Explorer\"

NoChangeStartMenu = WSHShell.RegRead (regkey & "NoChangeStartMenu")

If NoChangeStartMenu = 1 Then 'Changes in Start Menu are prohibited

   Result = MsgBox("Your Start Menu is currently locked." & _
        vbNewLine & "Would you like to unlock?", 36)

   If Result = 6 Then 'clicked yes
      WSHShell.RegWrite regkey & "NoChangeStartMenu", 0
   End If

Else 'Start Menu can be changed

   Result = MsgBox("You can change start menu." & _
        vbNewLine & "Would you like to prohibit changes?", 36)

   If Result = 6 Then 'clicked yes
      WSHShell.RegWrite regkey & "NoChangeStartMenu", 1
   End If

End If

' End code
```

Enabling and Disabling System Restore

The example presented in this section illustrates how you can use Windows Management Instrumentation to automate your work with the System Restore feature.

Before we proceed any further, let us provide a brief description of WMI scripting capabilities utilization. WMI scripting is a library of automation interfaces. COM-compliant scripting languages use these automation interfaces to access WMI infrastructure. All WMI automation objects, methods and properties are implemented by the Wbemdisp.dll file.

NOTE

To run WMI, you must have administrator privileges.

To access WMI through WMI scripting library, you need to perform three basic steps, which are common to most WMI scripts:

1. Connect to the Windows Management service.
2. Retrieve instances of WMI managed objects.
3. Call a method or access a managed object's property.

NOTE

To learn more about powerful WMI scripting capabilities, see the Microsoft Windows 2000 Professional Resource Kit or Microsoft Windows 2000 Server Resource Kit, where you can find more than 50 WMI-based scripts, enabling you to manage everything on the target computer, from boot configuration to user accounts.

The example in Listing 14.3 automates the task of enabling or disabling System Restore on the specified drive. When it is begun, this code creates `WshShell` object, then requests user input, prompting the user if it is required to enable or disable System Restore (Fig. 14. 8). To proceed further, the user must enter an appropriate text string (`enable` or `disable`) into the text field at the bottom of this dialog and click **OK**.

Next, the script prompts the user to specify the drive, on which it is necessary to take the specified action (Fig. 14.9). Specify the drive using the following format: `<drive_letter>:\`, for example, `C:\`.

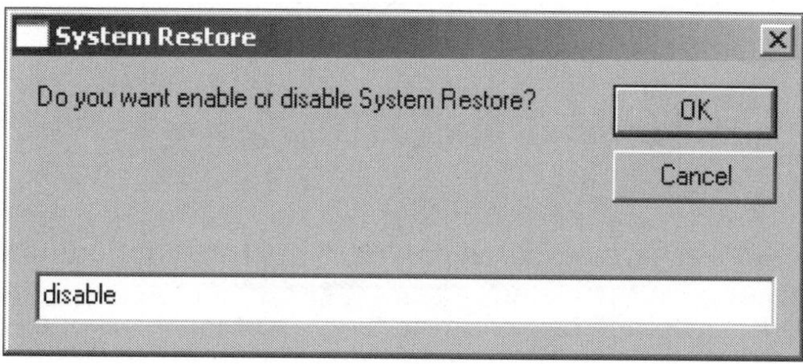

Fig. 14.8. Dialog box prompting the user to specify whether System Restore must be enabled or disabled

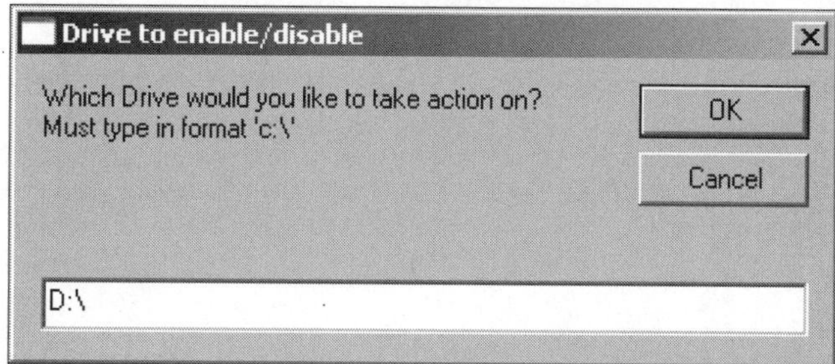

Fig. 14.9. Dialog box prompting the user to specify the drive on which the specified action must be taken

The script runs and performs the specified action on the specified drive. After it is done, it displays a message box, informing the user of the result (Fig. 14.10). To make sure that the specified action was performed successfully, start the System applet in the Control Panel, go to the **System Restore** tab, and check if System Restore is actually turned off for the specified drive (Fig. 14.11).

Now let us consider the code that implements this series of actions (Listing 14.3).

As was already mentioned, to use WMI scripting the code must connect to the Windows Management service, retrieve instances of the WMI-managed objects, and then call a method or access a managed object's property. In the example presented below, we connect to WMI using the WMI's moniker named `winmgmts` and `SystemRestore` class.

NOTE

A moniker is a standard COM mechanism for binding to a COM object. Detailed information on the WMI moniker syntax can be found at the following address: **http://msdn.microsoft.com/library/psdk/wmisdk/scintro_6tpv.htm**.

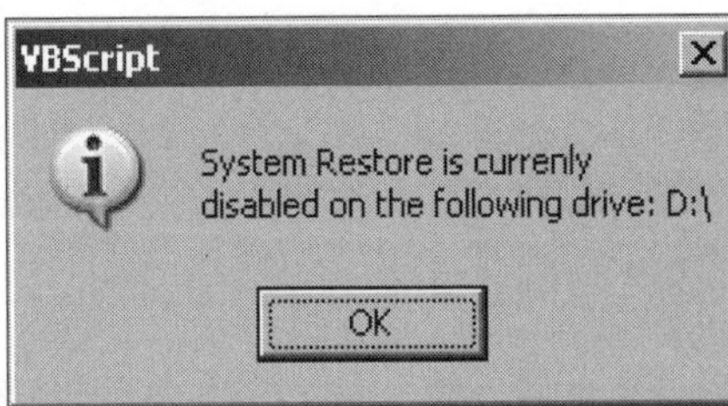

Fig. 14.10. The message box informing the user of the result of the operation

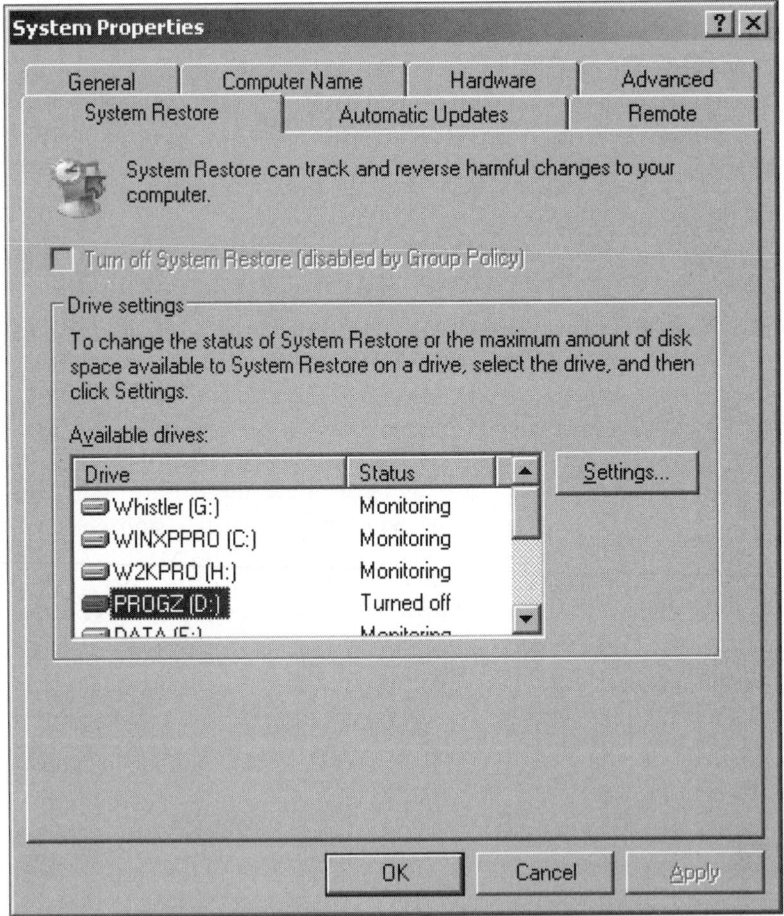

Fig. 14.11. Use the System Restore UI to check if System Restore is actually turned off for the drive you have specified when running the script

Listing 14.3. VBScript Code for Enabling/Disabling System Restore on the Specified Drive

```
' Begin code for enabling or disabling System Restore
Option Explicit


Dim WSHShell, onoff, drive, SRP, eSRP, Result


'Creating WSHShell object
Set WSHShell = CreateObject("WScript.Shell")
'Requesting user input
onoff = inputbox ("Do you want to enable or disable System Restore?",
"System Restore")
Drive = inputbox ("Which Drive would you like to take action on? Must
type in format 'c:\'", "Drive to enable/disable")
'using WMI moniker and SystemRestore class to access WMI
set SRP = GetObject("winmgmts:\\.\root\default:SystemRestore")
If onoff = "enable"  then
eSRP = SRP.enable(drive)
Result = MsgBox("System Restore is currenly" & _
        vbNewLine & "enabled on the following drive: " &  Drive, 64)
end if
If onoff = "disable" then
eSRP = SRP.disable(drive)
Result = MsgBox("System Restore is currenly" & _
        vbNewLine & "disabled on the following drive: " &  Drive, 64)
end if


' End code
```

Creating Restore Point Automatically

What else can we do with WMI and System Restore? Well, let us try to create a restore point automatically. Now, since we have already created several scripts, this is an easy task. Let us decide what our script must do. First, it must ask the user whether he or she wants to create a new restore point (Fig. 14.12).

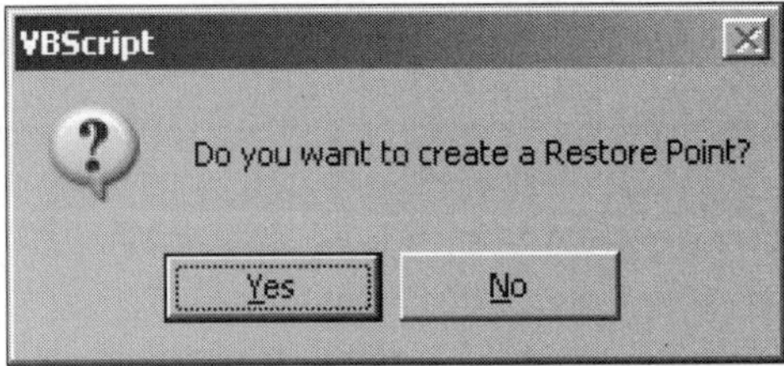

Fig. 14.12. Dialog prompting the user to create a restore point

Next, if the user clicks **Yes**, we must provide the user with the capability to enter the resource point description (Fig. 14.13).

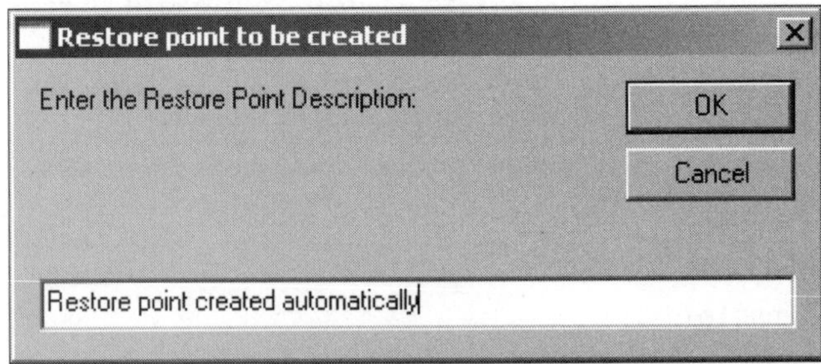

Fig. 14.13. The dialog prompting the user to provide a description for the restore point to be created

After the user provides a restore point description, we use WMI moniker and SystemRestore class to access WMI, and then create a new restore point using the description provided by the user. A very simple code performing these tasks is provided in Listing 14.4.

Listing 14.4. Automatic Creation of the Restore Point

```
Option Explicit

Dim WSHShell, SRP, CSRP, description, Result

Set WSHShell = CreateObject("WScript.Shell")

Result = MsgBox("Do you want to create a Restore Point?", 36)

     If Result = 6 Then 'clicked yes
     description = inputbox ("Enter the Restore Point Description:",
"Restore point to be created")
```

```
        'use WMI moniker and SystemRestore class
         set SRP = getobject("winmgmts:\\.\root\default:Systemrestore")

         CSRP = SRP.createrestorepoint (description, 0, 100)

      end if

    ' End code
```

After running this script, start System Restore and check if the restore point was actually created. The screenshot shown in Fig. 14.14 shows four test restore points, which I created automatically in the process of testing this script.

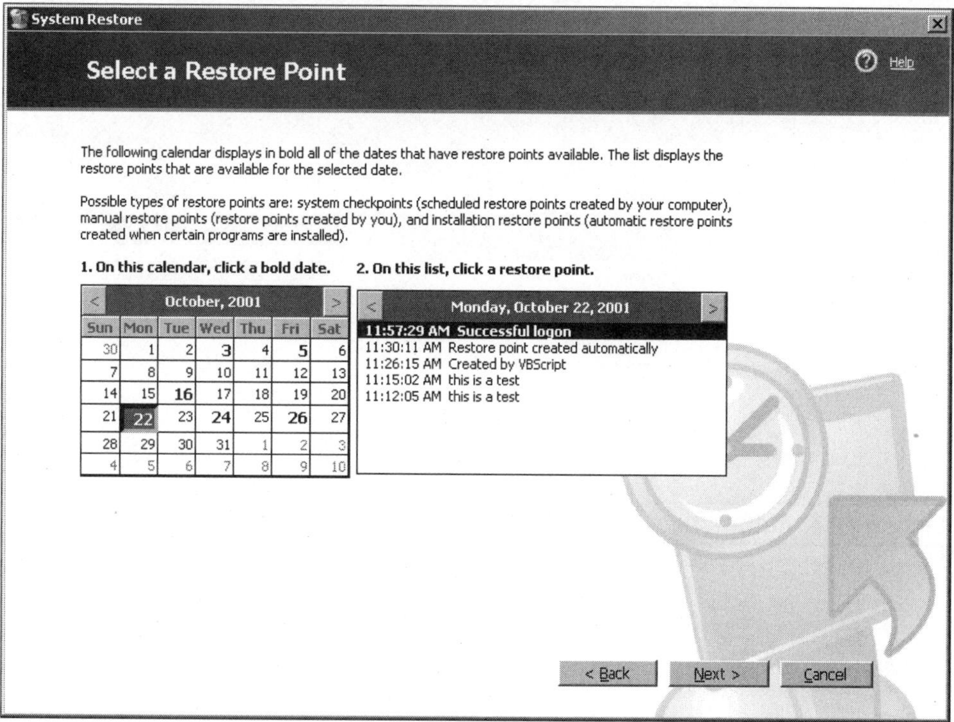

Fig. 14.14. The System Restore window displaying automatically created restore points

Now, after carefully testing the script and making sure that it works, let us consider what practical use we can make of it. For example, wouldn't it be nice, if after each successful logon, the users (especially those who experiment with the registry) were prompted to create a restore point? As you remember, Windows XP is successfully loaded only after at least one user logs onto the system, and at that point the Clone control set is copied to the **LastKnownGood** configuration. Well, in my opinion, it makes sense if you also create a restore point at that time, just to be on the safe side. This small script can serve this purpose if you assign it as a logon script.

To do so, just copy the script file to the *%SystemRoot%*\System32\GroupPolicy\User\Scripts\Logon directory, then start the Group Policy editor, and expand the console tree as shown in Fig. 14.15 (**User Configuration | Windows Settings | Scripts**). Double-click the **Logon** policy to open the **Logon Properties** window (Fig. 14.16), click the **Add** button and add our script to the list of logon scripts for the local computer.

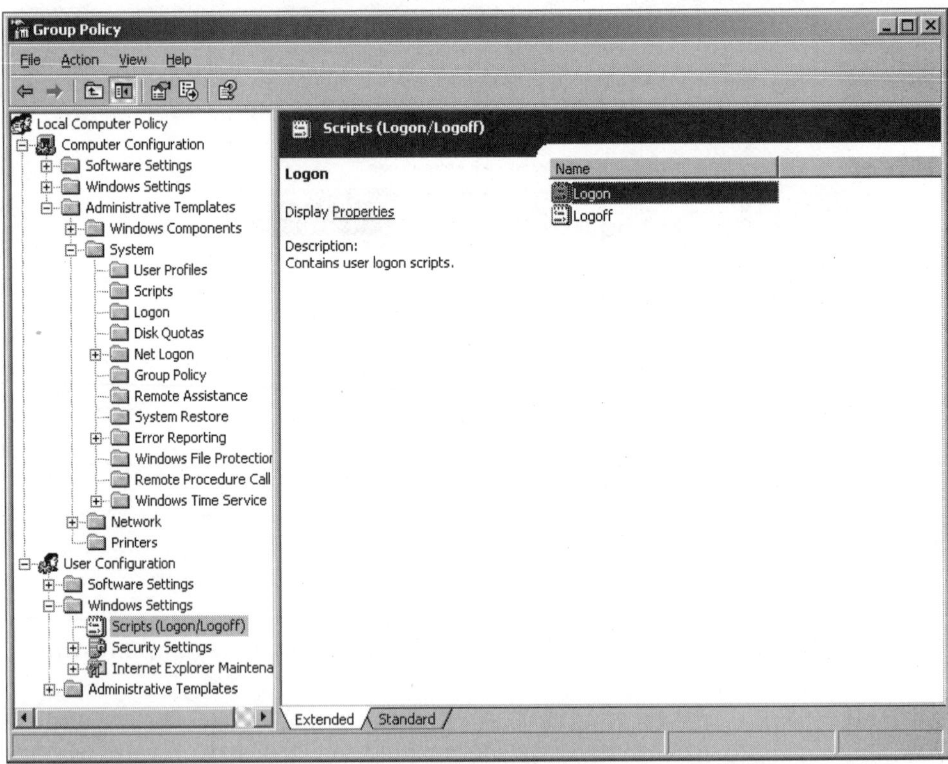

Fig. 14.15. The **Group Policy** window

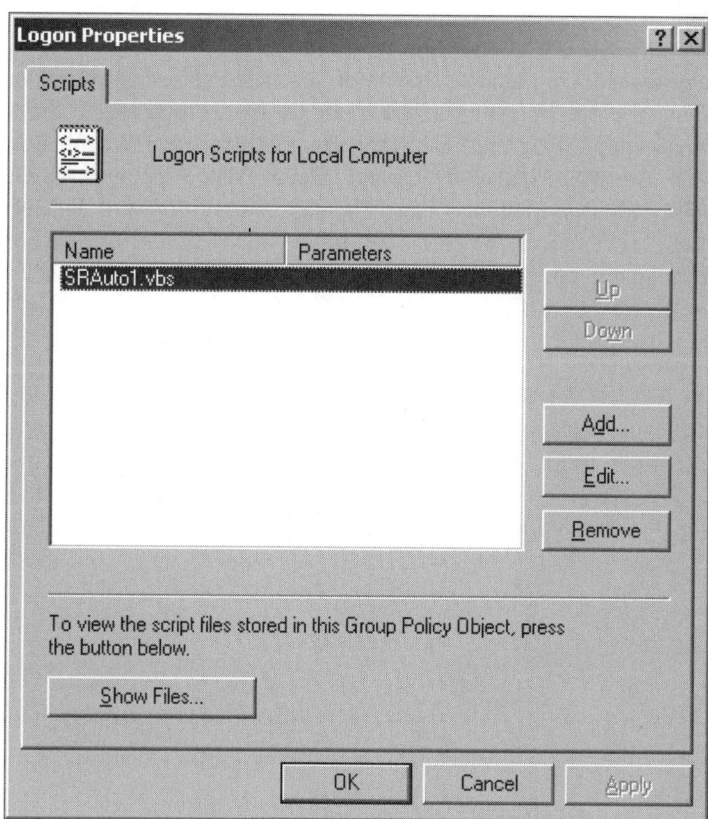

Fig. 14.16. The **Logon Properties** window

Now, each time the user logs onto the local computer, he or she will be prompted to create a restore point.

Summary

Thus, we have created several scripts, starting with the simplest example that can be used for demonstration purposes only, and proceeding further to create a small but useful one. The strongest point of WSH is its simplicity and the ease with which it can be used. Of course, there are certain limitations (for example, the `RegRead`, `RegWrite`, and `RegDelete` methods discussed earlier in this chapter provide no direct way of checking if the registry keys or values which you are going to create, delete, or modify already exist). For this purpose, you'll need to write a special application using any of the development environments available to you (such as Visual Basic, Visual C++, or Delphi).

NOTE

The topic of registry programming is one of the most interesting but rather difficult. To those of you who are interested in the topic, I'd like to recommend the following two books: "Windows NT Registry Guide" by Weiying Chen and Wayne Berry (Addison-Wesley Pub. Co., ISBN 0201694735) and "Visual Basic Programmer's Guide to Windows Registry" by Don Kiely and Zane Thomas (Marbry Software, Incorporated, ISBN 1890422266). As I already emphasized, nearly each chapter of this book deserves to be enhanced and developed into a separate volume. This topic, however, is the first candidate!

On the other hand, a Windows script is simply a text file that you can create with any text editor you feel comfortable with—just be sure to save your script file with a WSH-compatible script extensions (JS, VBS, or WSF). At the same time, the capabilities of WSH are rather powerful, and if you master it, you'll certainly be able to provide a quick and efficient solution within a matter of minutes.

Appendix 1

Internet Resources

Since operating systems are constantly changing to newer versions and various Service Packs are being released, practically every book has one common drawback—once it has been written, changes can only be made in the new edition (revised and corrected). While writing this book, I faced some difficult conditions—with respect to beta versions and Release Candidates of the Windows XP Professional and Home Edition operating systems. I tried to carefully test all the tips and recommendations provided in the book, but...

The best source of information on Windows NT/2000/XP is the Internet. A list of the most informative and reliable links is provided below.

- **http://www.wugnet.com**

The site of the Windows Users Group Network (WUGNET), which contains lots of information on the Microsoft Windows, including Windows 9*x*/ME and Windows NT/2000/XP. On this site, you can find technical support information on the various aspects of Windows operating systems, Internet, e-mail, shareware, hardware, games, software development, help authoring, multimedia, many Microsoft products, and many more.

- **http://www.winsupersite.com/faq/**

A comprehensive set of resources and late-breaking news on the newest releases of Windows operating systems, including Windows XP, Windows.NET Server ("Whistler Server") and even Windows "Longhorn" – the next Windows interim release that is due in late 2002. You'll find news, FAQs, Tech Showcases, and much more. Interested in Windows 2000 or Windows ME FAQs instead? No problem, you'll find it under "Retired FAQs". This site is supported by Windows expert Paul Thurrott, the author of many bestsellers (including the new one: "Teach Yourself Windows 2000 Server").

This site is recommended for all advanced Windows users who work with Windows 2000/XP. The author concentrates on the new Windows functionality and illustrates how to use most features with practical examples.

❐ **http://www.ntfaq.com**

Windows NT FAQ site provides a large collection of FAQs that covers all Windows NT/2000 topics, including backup and recovery, Active Directory, registry, security, Windows Script Host, and much more. Windows XP FAQ and Windows 2000/XP tips and tricks free e-mail newsletter have recently been added. You can also download compiled versions of FAQ in one of the following standard formats: HTML, HTML Help, or Windows Help. An excellent resource for those who need to find answers to their questions.

❐ **http://www.winplanet.com/winplanet/**

This site contains a variety of Windows-related news, reviews, tips, tutorials, downloads, and a free weekly Windows newletter.

❐ **http://www.jsiinc.com/reghack.htm**

Provides quite a large amount of various Windows NT/2000 registry tips, tricks, and hacks. If you are looking for such things, this is the place for you. It is constantly updated, and hacks arrive daily. No book can compare to it!

❐ **http://www.windowsitlibrary.com/**

As its name implies, this is the Windows IT professional's free online technical reference library. An excellent resource that covers nearly all Windows NT/2000 topics.

❐ **http://www.swynk.com/**

SWYNK.COM is the single largest independent resource for Microsoft .NET Enterprise™ and Windows Server technologies. On this site, you'll find the very latest information on Windows XP/2000/NT, SQL, SMS, and Exchange Servers. It provides lots of Windows NT/2000/XP-related resources, including technical articles, Web-based discussion boards, and Windows scripts.

❐ **http://www.osr.com**

This is a site for true professionals! The OSR Open Systems Resources, Inc. has devoted this entire site to Windows NT/2000/XP customized software development, including development of file systems and device drivers. You can subscribe to it in the NT Insider magazine here (free of charge). If you're an NT-programmer, or plan to become one, this site's for you.

❐ **http://www.sysinternals.com**

The Systems Internals site is supported by Mark Russinovich and Bryce Cogswell. These names speak for themselves. Besides the Regmon and NTFSDOS utilities mentioned in *Chapter 13*, you'll find lots of handy utilities here for Windows 9*x* and Windows NT/2000 (most with the source code) and valuable technical information. This is my favorite site.

- **http://www.registrysecrets.com/**

This site focuses solely on the Windows NT registry. If you're an experienced Windows NT user, then you're probably familiar with the book "1001 Secrets for Windows NT Registry" by Tim Daniels (in my humble opinion, it's the same as a translator's dictionary for the administrator). You can always find reliable and up-to-date information concerning Windows NT registry at this site.

- **http://www.winreg.com/**

This is another site dealing exclusively with the registry. You'll find information concerning Windows 95/98 and Windows NT registries, texts for beginners, FAQ, lots of utilities, and much more. When I was checking each link in this listing of Internet resources, I visited this site, and it was "under construction" but with the promise to become available very soon.

- **http://www.microsoft.com/hwdev/**

If you're going to gain a proper understanding of all Windows NT/2000/XP working principles, then this is the most reliable source of information for you to read. The Windows Driver and Hardware Development site provides tools, information, and services for driver developers and hardware designers who create products that work with the Microsoft Windows family of operating systems. The site is constantly being updated with tons of late-breaking news, including Windows XP news, OnNow design news, Device and Driver news, and provides valuable downloads, such as specifications, white papers, and, finally, the newest versions of Windows DDK. I can't personally state that the DDK documentation is light reading (especially when you're reading it for the first time). However, there's no other way to become a professional.

- **http://www.microsoft.com/**

This site is certainly well known to everyone, and it remains among the most reliable and informative sources of information concerning all Microsoft products, including, of course, Windows XP. Search the Knowledge Base, and perhaps you'll find the answers to your questions. As concerns the registry, go to the Microsoft Downloads Center (**http://www.microsoft.com/downloads/search.asp**), select the operating system you are working with, and search using the **Registry** keyword.

You'll find quite a log of registry patches and various registry tools and utilities (some of them are supplied with the source code).

- **http://msdn.microsoft.com/msdnmag**

MSDN Journal is the most interesting resource for those who want to gain knowledge of Windows NT/2000/XP internals. You'll find articles written by Matt Pietrek, Jeffrey Richter, and other popular authors. Now it also includes the Microsoft Systems Journal. The latest (November 2001) issue provides quite a lot of interesting information on Windows XP, so don't miss it.

- **http://www.win2000mag.com/**

Windows 2000 Magazine is intended for Windows NT/2000/XP professionals. Subscribers have unlimited access to all published materials and archives for the last 5 years, but even guest access will give you lots of valuable information.

- **http://www.labmice.net/**

Lots of information on Windows 2000, and much more! Visit it, and you won't be disappointed. This portal contains tons of useful links related to all aspects of running Windows 2000. Contains quite a large collection of useful resources on the registry, security, scripting (resource centers, online tutorials, code examples, and much more).

- **http://www.windrivers.com/**

On this site, you can find latest driver updates for Windows NT 4.0/Windows 2000/ Windows XP (a list of drivers is quite impressive). In addition, it offers a large amount of valuable technical support information, tips, tricks, and texts for beginners.

- **http://www.aelita.net/**

Lots of technical information and Windows NT/2000 utilities, including ERDisk for Windows NT/2000 (or simply ERDisk) and ERDisk for Active Directory, which deliver automated backup and fast, remotely managed recovery of your Windows NT/2000 enterprise systems' configuration and Active Directory. They bridge the gap between native disaster recovery tools, which have limited functionality, and full network backups, which can take hours to retrieve and restore. These utilities are not shareware, but you can download trial versions.

- **http://www.radium.ncsc.mil/tpep/library/rainbow/**

This is the "Rainbow Series". In my modest opinion, it doesn't require any comments.

❒ **http://www.microsoft.com/security/default.asp**

Microsoft Security Advisor is recommended for anyone who really cares about the security of their Windows NT/2000/XP systems. Contains tons of security-related information for IT professionals, software developers, and consumers.

❒ **http://www.ntsecurity.com/default.htm**

This is a security-related site containing lots of reviews, documents, advisories and much more. For example, here you can download trial versions for Windows NT/2000 administration utilities such as SecureIIS, which stopped CodeRed and Nimda before these worms became widely known. Also provides a lot of useful links to other security-related sites, so don't forget to bookmark it.

❒ **http://www.@stake.com**

@stake has assembled the best minds in digital security, including the L0pht Heavy Industries group, to help you understand and mitigate security risks. The LC3 (the latest version of the award-winning password auditing and recovery application, L0phtCrack), mentioned in *Chapter 9*, can be downloaded from **http://www.@stake.com/research/lc3/index.html**. You can also download L0phtCrack 1.5, an unsupported command-line version for researchers (not intended for production password auditing). If you want dictionary files, don't forget to download them from **http://packetstormsecurity.org/Crackers/wordlists/indexsize.shtml**.

❒ **http://www.iss.net**

This site is not specific to Windows NT/2000/XP. However, it offers tons of valuable security information (don't forget to visit security library at **http://xforce.iss.net/security_library/**). Evaluation versions of security tools are also available for download (they are quite large, so don't forget to free up at least 120 MB of disk space).

Summary

The list provided here doesn't include all the Internet resources dedicated to Windows NT/2000/XP. If you're interested in this topic, you'll find many more useful resources there. As for me, I've provided the ones that I personally like the best, and at the time of this writing there were no dead links in this list.

Appendix 2

Bibliography

A single book can't provide an answer to every question. Often, even an encyclopedia can't provide all the necessary information (and this book certainly isn't an encyclopedia). In this appendix, I provide a list of books that may help you find the answers to your questions.

1. *Tim Daniels.* "1001 secrets for Windows NT Registry". NEWS/Four-Hundred Books, 1998, ISBN 1882419685

2. *Paul Robichaux, Robert Denn.* "Managing the Windows 2000 Registry". O'Reilly & Associates, Incorporated, 2000, ISBN 1565929438

3. *Nathan Wallace, Anthony Sequeira.* "Windows 2000 Registry Little Black Book", 2nd edition. Coriolis Group, 2001, ISBN 1576108821

4. *Kathy Ivens.* "Admin911: Windows 2000 Registry". McGraw-Hill Professional, 2000, ISBN 0072129468

5. *Jerry Honeykutt.* "Microsoft Windows 2000 Registry Handbook". Macmillan USA Publishing, 2000, ISBN 0789716747

6. *Kathy Ivens.* "Optimizing the Windows Registry". IDG Books Worldwide, 1998, ISBN 076453159X

7. *Paul J. Sanna.* "Windows 2000 Registry". Prentice Hall PTR, 2000, ISBN 0130300640

8. *Weiying Chen, Wayne Berry.* "Windows NT Registry Guide". Addison-Wesley Pub., 1997, ISBN 0201694735

9. *Don Kiely, Zane Thomas.* "Visual Basic Programmer's Guide to Windows Registry". Marbry Software, Incorporated, 1998, ISBN 1890422266

Glossary

A

Access Control List (ACL)—the part of the security descriptor that lists access rights to the specified object. Access control lists contains Access Control Entries (ACE).

Access Control Entry (ACE)—an ACE is an individual entry in an ACL. An ACE contains a SID and describes the access rights that a particular user or group of users has to a system resource. The set of all ACEs on the object are used to determine whether an access request to the object is granted.

ACPI (Advanced Configuration and Power Interface)—an abstract interface that defines a power management and configuration mechanism for hardware and operating systems. Part of the industry-wide OnNow Initiative, ACPI is defined in the industry-sponsored ACPI Specification.

APIPA—Windows 2000/XP feature providing automatic configuration of IP-addresses (Automatic Private IP Addressing or APIPA).

APM (Advanced Power Management)—a legacy power management scheme based on the approach to BIOS implementation used in Windows 95.

Auditing—a tracing activity of the system users by logging events of the specified types in the system Security log. Registry activity can also be audited.

Automated System Recovery (ASR)—the new emergency recovery system that replaced the ERD functionality. Automated System Recovery (ASR) is a two-part recovery system that allows you to restore Windows XP operating system states by using files saved to tape media, and hard disk configuration information saved to a floppy disk.

B

Big Endian Format—a method of representing the value when the highest bit ("big end") appears first.

Blue Screen of Death (BSOD)—a STOP error or kernel-mode error. The state when Windows NT/2000 can't correct the hardware problem, inconsistent data, or other errors. The system stops to prevent further corruption of data.

Boot partition—the partition used for starting up the operating system. Both primary (active) partitions and logical drives on extended partitions can be used as boot partitions.

Boot.ini—the file necessary to boot Windows NT/2000/XP. Contains options that allow you to select the operating system and its boot options.

C

Class GUID—the Globally Unique Class Identifier (GUID) that identifies the class.

Co-installer—a Win32 DLL that assists in device installation on Windows 2000/XP systems. Coinstallers are called "helpers" by the Device Installer or filters for Class Installers.

D

Device Tree—the device tree contains information about the devices present on the system. The OS builds this tree when the machine boots, using information from drivers and other components, and updates the tree as devices are added or removed.

Devnode—a devnode is an internal structure that represents a device on the system. There's a devnode for each device on the machine and the devnodes are organized into a hierarchical device tree. The PnP Manager creates a devnode for a device when the device is configured. On Windows 2000/XP, a devnode contains the device stack (the device objects for the device's drivers) and information about the device such as whether the device has been started and which drivers have registered for notification on the device.

E

Enumerator—an *enumerator* is a component that discovers PnP devices based on a PnP hardware standard. In Windows 2000, the tasks of an enumerator are carried out by a PnP bus driver in partnership with the PnP Manager. A device is typically enumerated by its parent bus driver, such as PCI or PCMCIA. Some devices are enumerated by a bus filter driver, such as ACPI.

ERD (Emergency Repair Disk)—the disk used for emergency recovery of the damaged Windows NT/2000 systems. In Windows XP, systems ERD functionality has been replaced by ASR (Automated System Recovery).

Executive—the set of kernel-mode components providing the basis of the Windows NT/Windows 2000 operating systems.

G

GUID—the Globally Unique Identifier, which represents a unique 128-bit value.

H

HAL (Hardware Abstraction Layer)—executive components that provide support for the Kernel, I/O Manager, kernel-mode debuggers, and low-level device drivers.

HCL (Hardware Compatibility List)—the list of hardware devices compatible with Windows NT/2000. The devices listed in HCL were tested for compatibility by Microsoft.

Hardware ID—a vendor-defined string used by the PnP Manager to find an INF file match for a device.

Hardware profiles—a set of instructions used to describe specific computer equipment for the operating system. These instructions are used to specify to the operating system which drivers it should load during boot process.

Hardware Recognizer—each time Windows NT/2000/XP starts, the hardware recognizer creates a list of the devices it's detected and stores it in the registry. On Intel-based computers, hardware detection is performed by the hardware recognizer (Ntdetect.com) and Windows NT/2000/XP kernel (Ntoskrnl.exe)

Hive—the registry is subdivided into components, called hives for their resemblance to the cellular structure of a beehive. The Registry hive is a discrete body of keys, subkeys, and values rooted at the top level of the registry hierarchy. The main difference between registry hives and other groups of registry keys is that hives are constant registry components. Hives aren't created dynamically when the system boots, and they aren't deleted when someone shuts the system down.

K

Kernel—the kernel is the portion of the operating system that manages and controls access to hardware resources. It performs thread scheduling and dispatching, interrupt and exception handling, and multiprocessor synchronization.

Kernel mode—the processor access mode in which the operating system and privileged programs run. Windows NT/2000/XP kernel is the Ntoskrnl.exe.

L

Little Endian Format—when using the little-endian format, the lowest bit ("little end") appears first when representing the value.

Legacy drivers—the drivers that don't provide PnP support. Windows 2000 supports legacy Windows NT drivers, but these drivers don't support new Plug and Play and power management functionality.

N

Nonpaged pool—a based region for which all processes share a set of PTEs. The Memory Manager guarantees that a nonpaged pool is resident in physical memory at all times; therefore, this region can be accessed from any process's address space without causing a page fault. However, a nonpaged pool is a limited system resource.

O

OnNow—a computer industry initiative to make computers more power-efficient, reducing startup time and adding the ability to shut off idle devices.

P

Paged pool—a based region that can be paged in and out of a process's working set. Each process has its own set of PTEs that map paged pool into its address space.

POST (Power-on Self-Test)—the POST routine is a set of tests intended to verify if the hardware functions correctly. If there are problems related to computer hardware or BIOS settings, POST will emit a series of beeps. POSTs are controlled by your computer's BIOS and may differ from machine to machine. Because of this, I recommend that you always have at hand the documentation supplied with your computer.

PDO—Physical Device Object. A device object created by a bus driver. A PDO represents the underlying bus driver in the stack of PnP drivers for a device. The PDO is at the bottom of the device stack of drivers for a device.

Power Policy—the set of rules that determine how and when a system or device changes power state.

Plug and Play (PnP)—Plug and Play is the set of specifications developed by Microsoft, Intel, Compaq, and other vendors. It represents a combination of the general approach to designing PCs and a set of specifications describing hardware architecture. All Plug and Play components are intended for the same general purpose: to provide automatic functioning of the PC, peripheral devices, and their drivers with minimum intervention from the user. Users who work with a system that meets all Plug and Play requirements don't need to worry if the newly installed device will cause hardware conflict with another device.

PnP Manager—the PnP Manager has two parts: the kernel-mode PnP Manager and the user-mode PnP Manager. The kernel-mode PnP Manager interacts with OS components and drivers to configure, manage, and maintain devices. The user-mode PnP Manager interacts with user-mode setup components, such as Class Installers, to configure and install devices. The user-mode PnP Manager also interacts with applications; for example, to register an application for notification of device changes and to notify the application when a device event occurs.

Power Manager—the Power Manager is a new Windows 2000 component, which is responsible for managing power usage for the system.

R

Recovery Console—a Windows 2000/XP administrative tool with a command-line interface that provides additional options for emergency recovery of the damaged systems.

S

SAM—Security Account Manager. An integral subsystem that maintains a database of information on user accounts, including passwords, any account groups a given user belongs to, the access rights each user is allowed and any special privileges a given user has.

SID—Security identifier. A value, unique across time and space, that identifies a process in the Security system. SIDs can either identify an individual process, usually containing a user's logon identifier or a group of processes.

System partition—an active partition that contains the files needed to initialize and start the operating system.

System State data—the whole set of system configuration files. This set is slightly different for Windows 2000/XP Professional and server platforms. The System State Data set defined in Windows 2000/XP Professional includes the following files:

- The registry
- COM+ classes registration database
- Boot files, which are necessary to boot the system

The System State Data set for Windows 2000 Server operating systems includes all the same components included in the System State Data set for Windows 2000 Professional, plus the following data:

- The Certificate Services database, if the server is a certificate server
- The Active Directory database and the \SYSVOL directory, if the server is a domain controller
- All information required to restore the cluster, if the server runs the cluster service. This information includes the registry checkpoints and quorum resource log, containing information on the cluster database.

U

User mode—the non-privileged processor mode in which the application code, including protected subsystem code, executes. User-mode applications can't gain access to system data except by calling subsystem-supplied functions, which, in turn, call system services.

V

Volume snapshots—a technology that provides a copy of the original volume at the instant a snapshot is made. Volume snapshots allow users or applications to continue working while a backup occurs. A snapshot of the volume is made at the time a backup is initiated. Data are then backed up from the snapshot rather than from the original volume. The original volume continues to change as the process continues, but the snapshot of the volume remains constant. This is helpful if users need access to files while a backup is taking place, since it significantly reduces the time required to accomplish the backup job. Additionally, the backup application can back up files that are kept open. In previous versions of Backup, including the one supplied with Windows 2000, files open at the time of the backup were skipped.

W

WDM (Windows Driver Model)—a common set of services designed to allow driver writers for certain classes of devices to construct drivers with binary compatibility between the Microsoft® Windows® 98 and Windows 2000 operating systems. (This binary compatibility is only possible on Intel Architecture-compatible processors.)

WHQL (Windows Hardware Quality Lab)—a Microsoft group whose purpose is to ensure hardware functionality across the Windows Family of Operating Systems.

Index

S

T

U

V

W

Z

Windows .NET Domains & Active Directory

A. Tchekmarev

The book is intended for system administrators who have general knowledge of Windows 2000 or Windows XP/.NET. It opens with basic information vitally important for understanding the Active Directory™ service architecture, as well as for the proper use of this service and many system utilities: the fundamentals of LDAP protocol, Active Directory and DNS interoperation, and Active Directory concepts. The book proceeds with the issues that are the most difficult when deploying Windows .NET domains, including upgrading from Windows NT 4.0 and Windows 2000 domains; planning Active Directory; installing Active Directory and adding domain clients; and monitoring and tuning Active Directory. It describes methods of performing common administrative tasks, as well as how to use various instruments for this purpose: administrative snap-ins, system tools, and scripts. Some of these tasks are: creating directory objects; publishing network resources; searching the directory for various object types; delegating administration; audit; managing user environment; triggering replication; and backing up and restoring Active Directory.

This book focuses on troubleshooting problems that occur *after* deploying Windows .NET domains (i.e. while maintaining Active Directory), as well as system tools that should be used for solving such problems. (Many tools from the *Windows Support Tools* and *Windows Resource Kit* packs are covered.) These topics are highly valuable for administrators, but relatively rarely discussed in computer books. The general characteristics given for system tools help administrators to easily choose the proper instrument for a specific task. The most useful tools' commands are discussed in examples. The following tasks are covered, among many others: verifying domain controllers, directory partitions, and group policy objects; exporting and importing Active Directory objects; reconstructing domains and forests; managing domain trusts; and tuning security.

The last chapters cover the *Active Directory Service Interfaces* (ADSI), a flexible and powerful instrument for performing various administrative tasks. The chosen narration style helps the non-programmer to learn the main ADSI concepts and to begin to write his/her own scripts. These chapters contain annotated listings of ready-to-use scripts that illustrate programming principles or methods of solving specific administrative tasks. These principles and tasks vary, ranging from simple ones, such as creating users, to complex ones, such as extending the Active Directory schema or managing security descriptors for directories, files, and other system objects.

The book contains a reference on registry keys related to Active Directory, as well as Active Directory objects and attributes that have no user interface, but can be valuable for administrators. The list of frequently asked questions ("How to...?"), placed at the end of the book, helps a reader quickly locate answers to specific tasks. The book also contains a glossary and index.

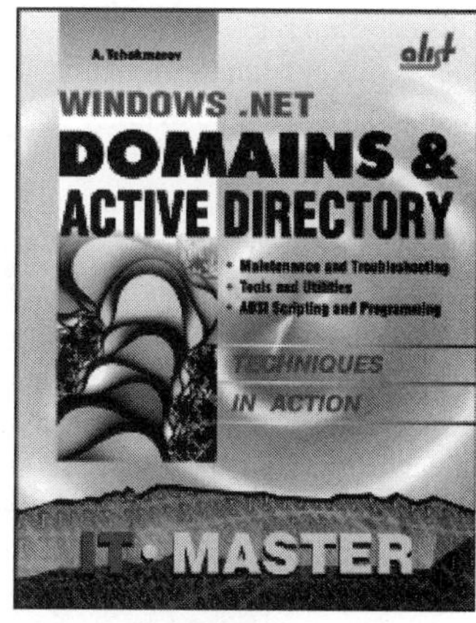

ISBN: 1-931769-00-1

PRICE: $39.95

PUB DATE: August 2002

PAGES: 560pp

SOFTCOVER: 7.375 x 9.25

PC Overclocking, Optimization, & Tuning, the second edition

V. Rudometov, E. Rudometov

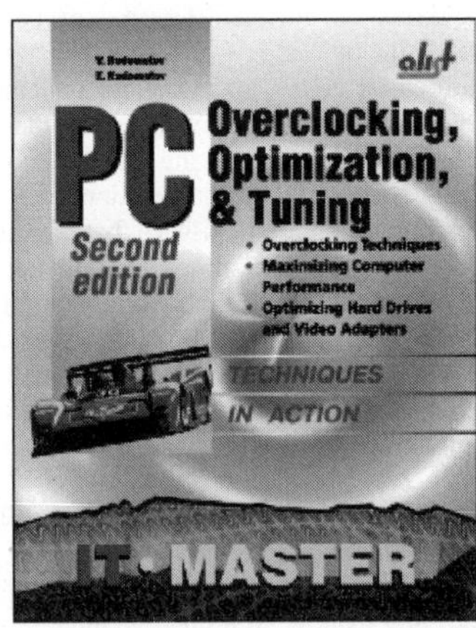

This one-stop reference guide contains various recommendations and advice for tuning, optimizing and overclocking almost all computer elements to achieve maximum computer performance. It offers the most detailed information on overclocking processors, memory, hard drives, and video adapters, allowing for a significant increase in performance for all types of computers, including both current and earlier models. Many different problems that one may face in the overclocking procedure are analyzed and solved in this book. This book also pays special attention to to the problem of cooling a computer when it has been overclocked. There are many computer test results for different overclocked systems that give a clear idea of what one can and should gain from overclocking. The book also covers several other topics concerning computer performance optimization, including: selecting various BIOS Setup settings, and optimizing hard drives and video adapters. There is also a very clear description of the compression technique given, which provides an increase in hard drives' information capacity. The information on hardware monitoring will help to control the computer's operation, which is useful for both normal and overclocked modes. In additon, the book also provides descriptions of several programs that are very helpful in tuning and testing computer elements, thus allowing one to achieve maximum performance. Where necessary, the writers have given descriptions of major computer elements like processors, hard drives, memory, motherboards, and chipsets. Furthermore, this book covers various aspects of creating and administrating computer networks in different operating systems. Moreover, it contains a comprehensive list of Web addresses that can help advanced users in searching for the most up-to-date information concerning PC overclocking.

Key features: description of several third-party testing programs for diagnostic and fine-tuning assistance; selecting various BIOS Setup settings; optimizing hard drives and video adaptors; troubleshooting the most common problems that occur while using a computer in overclocking modes.

ISBN: 1-931769-05-2
PRICE: $39.95
PUB DATE: April 2002
PAGES: 496pp
SOFTCOVER: 7.375 x 9.25

Creating Your Web Site with ColdFusion

R. Akhayan

Focusing on Web design, this book opens up the possibilities of working with comprehensive, high-performance, and easily expandable Macromedia ColdFusion platforms for creating dynamic Web sites and building large-scale e-commerce systems. Each chapter deals with a particular area of ColdFusion theory. Most chapters also include practice with the ColdFusion Markup Language (CFML) tags and functions used in that area in order to give the user a fuller understanding. The book covers the basic steps of installing and setting up the software, necessary skills for ColdFusion beginners, and the stages of planning web applications, including setting goals, defining business rules, developing a database, and designing the project. The basics of the CFML language are covered, as well as are managing applications using configuring files, working with data using SQL syntax, building diagrams, managing files, organizing a search engine for the site, and planning and generating statistical pages. You'll also find a description of how to use: the CFSCRIPT language; the mail server; COM, CORBA, and EJB objects; WML pages for developing WAP applications; Web Distributed Data Exchange; servlets; and JavaServer Pages. The book is oriented towards novices who have had a little experience using HTML and JavaScript, users specializing in Web technology, and professional Web developers who are acquainted with other such tools, but want to widen their horizons by learning the basics of yet another Web application development tool — ColdFusion.

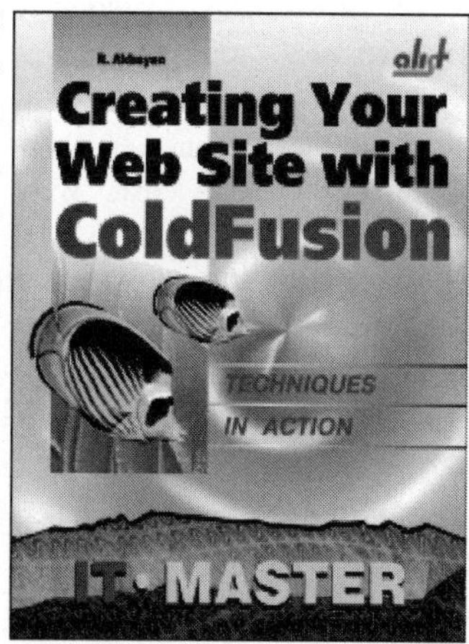

ISBN: 1-931769-03-6
PRICE: $34.95
PUB DATE: February 2002
PAGES: 400pp
SOFTCOVER: 7.375 x 9.25

Key Features

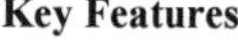

- Explains the principles of building Web applications
- Shows you how to develop your own Web site
- Includes theoretical lessons on using CFML
- Teaches you how to create your own database
- Goes through actual project development using ColdFusion
- Contains reference material for the CFML language

Creating Your Web Site with PHP

O. Koterov

This is an excellent, easy-to-understand tutorial for those Web designers who want to improve their skills using modern effective tools. — it looks at web programming technology, using the most recent version of the PHP language to write useful Web scripts, create Web pages, and design your own Web site in its entirety. Basic information accompanies simple examples in PHP and C, with an extensive amount of commentary on each one. This book also provides instructions on installing and setting up an Apache web server on a Windows platform. Also, there are many practical examples, illustrated by various samples of programs and library functions that ease the burden on the web developer. This instructional volume on the PHP language contains extensive information, which can quickly turn a novice who knows, say, at least one algorithmic language, into a web programmer. It covers the basics of the HTTP and CGI protocols, how to develop lengthy scripts in PHP, the syntax of the language and working with simple functions, object-oriented programming in PHP using interface ideology, manipulations with strings and arrays, creating a database, and much more. This book is intended both for those who are acquainted only with the basics of web programming and for more experienced programmers who want to become more familiar with PHP in its latest version. It is, above all, for anyone who, in a minimal amount of time, would like to begin professional programming on the web.

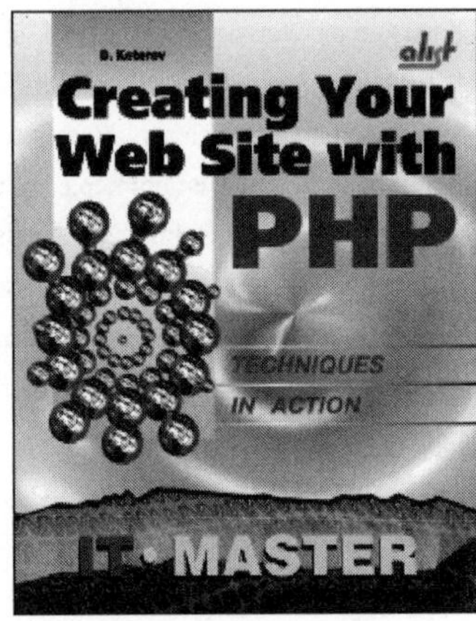

ISBN: 1-931769-04-4
PRICE: $34.95
PUB DATE: January 2002
PAGES: 500pp
SOFTCOVER: 7.375 x 9.25

Key Features

- CGI (Common Gateway Interface)
- PHP capabilities and syntax
- Choosing tools for developing web programs
- Configuring the Apache web server when developing a site
- Working with MySQL databases and the SQL language